Successful CATALOGS

Successful CATALOGS

by STEVE WARSAW

RETAIL REPORTING CORPORATION, NEW YORK

Copyright © 1989 by Retail Reporting Corporation

All rights reserved. No part of this book may be reproduced
in any form, by mimeograph or any other means,
without permission in writing from the publisher.

Retail Reporting Corporation
101 Fifth Avenue
New York, NY 10003

Distributors to the trade in the United States and Canada:
Van Nostrand Reinhold
115 Fifth Avenue
New York, NY 10003

Distributed outside of the United States and Canada:
Hearst Books International
105 Madison Avenue
New York, NY 10016

Library of Congress Cataloging in Publication Data:
Main Entry under the title: Successful Catalogs

Printed and Bound in Hong Kong
ISBN 0-934590-30-3

Designed by Bernard Schleifer

CONTENTS

ABOUT THE AWARDS

ACA AWARDS

Founded in 1986, the American Catalog Awards, sponsored by "Catalog Age" Magazine, honor the best catalogs in 26 consumer and 11 business-to-business categories.

Each catalog is evaluated for "its effectiveness as a marketing tool in relation to the company's customer profile and marketing objectives, as [they are] stated on the American Catalog Awards entry form." In other words: the company puts down, in black on white, what they intended to accomplish and then submits samples to the ACA of the catalog they produced to achieve their goal.

After an initial screening process, the finalists are carefully examined by a panel of 21 judges that reads like a list of direct marketing "Who's Who". As one would expect, the group includes both merchandising and design experts: key decision makers for successful mailorder programs—professionals accustomed to looking critically at every aspect of a catalog as part of their daily schedule.

Each catalog is assessed on design, production, copy, merchandising and customer service. Of particular note is the fact that the panel does not feel compelled to fill the award list in any category. Their rationale is simple: given the high quality of all entries, those chosen to receive the top awards should "clearly reflect this across-the-board level of excellence". One look at the winners discussed herein will show catalogs that exemplify these standards.

ECHO AWARDS

Since 1917, the Direct Marketing Association (DMA, originally, the Direct Mail/ Marketing Association) has served as the trade association of the direct response industry. Shortly after its founding, the association began honoring the best among the year's campaigns and catalogs. In 1979, the name "ECHO" was conferred upon the awards.

Sometimes referred to as the "Academy Awards of Direct Marketing", the Echos have much in common with the Oscars. They are conferred by one's peers in the industry—by those who are in the business and know what differentiates "good" from "great."

Overlaying all Echo awards is a statement of "Immediate Objective". Was this program designed to: 1). Produce orders? 2). Acquire viable leads and inquiries? or 3). Generate store traffic? This establishes a level playing field for all entrants, no matter how big or small. First, consumer catalog apples are compared to other apples (not business-to-business multimedia oranges). Secondly, the success of a campaign is judged in part against a yardstick established by the company itself. Thus, an Echo Award represents not only excellence as determined by the industry, but also by that unflinching critic, the bottom line.

A word about the judges themselves: each year, they are chosen from among the best in every aspect of direct response, from copy to design, and from production to marketing. Clearly, a "sizzle-only" campaign would not make through the first round.

The judging process is both long and conscientious. In the first round, the entry portfolios—over 1,600 in 1988—are regionally divided among four cities, and examined by at least three judges per entry. A portfolio that makes it to the second round will be evaluated by five different judges. The third round involves yet another five judges, and only then does the entry qualify for the final round of five more judges. Each winning entry, then, will have been seen by at least 18 judges during the evaluation process (a total of as many as 450 judges take part in the entire program). Clearly, a catalog or campaign that achieves a winning consensus among so many professionals richly deserves its ultimate award.

PIA AWARDS

The finest quality print work . . . outstanding graphic design . . . these are the standards promoted by the Printing Industries of America [PIA] Graphic Arts Awards Competition, the most prestigious, international event of its kind in the graphic arts industry.

Chosen from over 6,700 entries, the winners exemplify a successful combination of printing excellence and graphic design. The competition's judges are all professionals drawn from the fields of printing, design, advertising, graphic communications and marketing.

INTRODUCTION

Catalogs Catalogs Catalogs. Mailboxes groan, coffee tables overflow and refuse companies are delighted with the compact tonnage. The world seems awash with catalogs. Why? Because they work. They get the job done in a cost effective manner. If this was not true, you can rest assured the media bucks would fly elsewhere.

Some say there's a catalog glut. "Not true", say the catalog merchants, "the problem is a shortage of customers". Example: less than 1.9% (around 4,500,000) of our population qualify as "well to do, upscale, active mailorder buyers" in the Horchow/ Tiffany image. Relatively the same statistics apply across other market segments. List rentals and swaps being what they are; if your home or office is identified as a dyed-in-the-wool mailorder buyer, you *will* receive a whole lot of catalogs. It's a case of too many merchants chasing too few customers thereby causing catalog inflation.

You're about to see examples of some of the best catalogs in the business. Many of these publications have won prestigious awards. Some have been chosen just because they did what they set out to do, and darned well. Others are featured because they serve as excellent examples of a genre or because they exemplify a special technique or marketing focus.

First a note, to all those deserving catalog publishers who are not aboard this edition of "Successful Catalogs", please forgive us. We know that you, of all people, will understand our space limitations.

Catalogs have different products to sell and different audiences to address; thus, they cannot all be judged by the same criteria. At the beginning of each chapter, you'll find a short introduction to a discrete group of catalogs. We hope in these introductory remarks to give you a synoptic picture of their target markets and the critical merchandising factors surrounding each group. As you'll see, these elements may vary widely, even within a given subject area; ergo, their presentations can be quite different.

Some markets and products lend themselves to catalog presentations that are absolute works of art. Other categories necessitate a far more pragmatic approach. Museum-quality catalogs require of the reader that he or she have a certain degree of sophistication, cultural background and imagination. If the reader lacks these qualities, the designer's subtleties and mood implications do not elucidate; instead, they obfuscate. Down-to-earth catalogs, long on exposition and graphically realistic, are the workhorses of the trade. They communicate. They sell. They get the job done.

Realistically, most catalog programs aim at a creative target somewhere between these two extremes. And while some catalog concepts may lean in *avant* directions such as *haut couture* or *Star Wars*, others simply present the merchandise, the facts and the pitch. In either case, designers are faced with three universal challenges:

1. *Abiding by the proven rules of catalog selling and corporate image projection;*

2. *while at the same time, getting as much product and information as possible on a page;*
3. *and still make the whole thing attractive and interesting to the reader.*

Constantly evolving direct response techniques guide all the creative functions from layout, typeface and copy through art style and background treatment. And they all have but one objective: to involve the reader, and to steer that reader along the path leading to a consummated sale.

Are these rules inviolate? Absolutely not! After all, what are rules for, if not to be challenged. The top performing "control" of today is just another target for tomorrow's marketing team. And cataloging, like OTC retailing, is a fluid marketplace. But, violate these rules at your peril! And only with the full knowledge that you're treading on the tail of a snake that can give your ego an awfully expensive bite.

Your bulging postboxes give witness to the fact that catalogs are not extinct. Some have even said, "The catalog industry is alive and well."

Most sensible folks wouldn't dream of owning a hat store just because they wear hats. Opening a store is not a project that anyone should undertake lightly. There's site selection, leasing, fixtures, recruiting & training, advertising, and a myriad of other things one must deal with in order to open a store. Most entrepreneurs are aware of these factors; ergo: there aren't a whole lot of hat stores.

Start-up catalog programs have their own set of challenges. And, they can be far more complex than those faced by the store owner. For instance, before mailing Le Catalog des Chapeaux, our hat-wearing friend has to deal with these facts:

1. *Merchandise commitments must be made 'way in advance—sometimes a year or more. On top of that, both backup orders and remainder merchandising have to be planned for and the concepts sold to vendors.*
2. *A very sophisticated, computer-based Customer Service module is absolutely essential.*
3. *Statistical analysis and list regression knowledge has to be available to reduce cost per order (very few mail order companies can afford buckshot mailings these days).*
4. *Designing and engineering the physical components of a cost-effective catalog program require considerable experience in all phases of graphic production.*
5. *And, one can have a whole career in the fields of database maintenance and manipulation, sophisticated list rental procedures and list management economics.*
6. *Not to mention the need for the same or greater merchant-buying skills as those of a retail store owner.*

These are not qualities easily found in the offices of a typical OTC retail operation.

The bottom line is, quite simply, a catalog program—aside from its value as a research tool, a traffic-building vehicle, and a PR platform—is a very complex mechanism used to move products and services from seller to buyer, just like a store. The foregoing notwithstanding, there are substantive differences between over-the-counter (OTC) retail store selling and catalog programs.

- *Catalogs can have national reach, while store trading areas are usually less than 30 miles from each door.*
- *Catalogs with narrowly defined product emphasis should be able to carry a much deeper line and have more product knowledge than a multi-line store.*
- *Catalogs are very powerful marketing tools, especially when increased market penetration is the objective. For example: with about 70% of our viable female population in the workplace, most of today's shoppers spend less time in fewer stores. They will come to your store or buy by phone or mail if, and only if, you can convince them that your offerings are worth their time—the right catalog can do that job.*

As you look at and read about the catalogs on these pages, you'll note that most of the best known names and most appealing presentations are what and where they are because they are experts in their field.

The entrepreneurs behind these programs have bought it, sold it, fixed it and used it for years—and that product knowledge bursts forth as a shining light in their catalogs.

A few major store chains, Saks Fifth Avenue, Bloomingdale's and Neiman-Marcus for example, publish and mail two discrete kinds of catalogs: mailorder catalogs and catalogs designed to encourage store traffic. Other stores design their catalogs to serve the dual functions of order generation and traffic building. In either case, these well-known merchants use their areas of greatest expertise as promotional leverage points.

All manufacturers and merchants with winning catalog programs have discovered a few basic rules that keep them ahead of the pack:

- *Unless there's a good reason to do otherwise, focus each catalog effort on a specific market.*
- *Stay in touch with your customers—the more frequently, the better.*
- *Don't attempt to be all things to all people.*
- *Use your computer and modern printing and addressing technology. Break down your customer and prospect files into their smallest possible, economically viable segments. Then, offer each of those segments only the items they are most likely to buy.*
- *Do everything possible to avoid out-of-stock situations.*
- *Test, re-test and test again before making any major moves.*

- *Back your products with unconditional guarantees.*
- *Make sure Customer Service is everyone's top priority.*

Given the proper attitude on the part of top management, mail order programs and the invisible database systems that support them provide the ideal basis for a return to the essentials of good retailing.

If we analyze our sales slips (via computer), we find we know a great deal about our customers. Much more than we ever learned from their credit card application. We know their buying habits. We can see if they have (or buy for) children, and come very close to knowing the age of those kids. We can track their preferences for a given designer, an historical period or their predilection for a certain color palette.

Then, we can really get serious and massage our database against a national demographic database, a TRW credit and buying pattern database, and a couple of warranty and mail order buyers lists. By now, we have enough information to come up with everything there is to know about our customer except the date of her next appointment with her hairdresser.

Armed with all these facts, we can tailor our mailings to individual customers, who will be grateful for the information. We can offer each man or woman a range of items to fit their life-style, their age-level and their personal taste.

Catalog reputations are made (and lost) based on the three legs of a mailorder merchant's philosophical tripod: Quality, Service and Merchandise Selection. (Note that price is *not* the major consideration.) We've discussed service and merchandise selection (or positioning); a word now about quality.

From a pragmatic point of view, poor quality means returned merchandise, which can cost a purveyor the profit from the next 10-12 sales of the same item. Even more importantly, it can mean the loss of the offended customer—forever.

Good Quality is just that—good. It does not offend. Most likely, it will not be returned. But does not engender confidence. After all, what have you (the seller) done but accept your customer's money in return for an adequate product. To enhance old customers and build your reputation with newcomers, only Great Quality or The Best will do.

Qualitative expressions are relative, of course. You may advertise ''The best $50 SLR camera on the market'', but if you can add ''and the only $50 SLR with these features *and* a 3-year unlimited warranty'', then it will be perceived as The Best. Or, if you offer a $500 cashmere pullover as an item of Great Quality, then be sure that it is tailored by old world craftsmen of cloth from Ilorini.

There's a basic fact of mailorder life, well known to the publishers featured here: ''Our main objective is to build a solid customer base, not to make an immediate sale''. Stated another way, ''Attrition is a dirty word!'' You'll recognize this attitude in every successful catalog. Watch for the signs. They're not always self-evident, but they're always there.

I
RETAIL CATALOGS

"Retailing is a fast-moving, ever-changing game."
Yes, but. . . .

Fashions and merchandise change—almost overnight in some categories. And POS, UPC and EDI have wrought massive changes in accounting, purchasing, inventory control and internal distribution methodologies. Despite all this, many retail managements are downright sluggish when it comes to changing their catalogs and direct mail efforts. Matter of fact, a well-rounded direct response program is a rare bird indeed in the OTC (Over-The-Counter) retail environment.

On the leading edge of the retail direct marketing community are familiar names such as Saks Fifth Avenue, Brooks Brothers and Neiman-Marcus. These famous stores are in the process of building mega-million dollar mailorder sales programs. Their names are so familiar partially *because* of their mailorder programs. And, their mailorder programs are succeeding, partially *because* their names are so familiar. It's sort of like compound interest. Public relations efforts, media exposure, fine customer service, great merchandise, attractive stores and interesting catalogs are the investment. The dividends accrue exponentially because *all* of those efforts (investments) have a positive effect on *both* OTC and mailorder sales.

"But almost all large OTC retailers are mailing catalogs to their existing customers," you say, "What's the difference between what they are doing and the dual purpose, mailorder/traffic-building catalog programs at the more marketing oriented stores?" There are dramatic differences between the two. Let's look at a comparison.

Anatomy of a Traditional Department Store Traffic-Building Catalog Program

1. *In most cases, 4 to 8 catalogs are mailed per year. The merchandise displayed may promote items or categories, but everything shown will be available at all stores in the chain.*
2. *Catalogs are sent to all active charge account customers plus occasional distribution to unsegmented, compiled local resident lists. Newspaper inserts (FSI's) are scheduled for important holidays or vendor-furnished material.*
3. *Most catalogs are event or vendor driven, e.g. Christmas, Mothers Day, back-to-school, winter white sale, Estee Lauder-furnished mailers, etc..*
4. *Phone and mail orders are considered a nuisance. The focus is on store traffic, not customer service. Order-taking is treated as a function of the accounting department, or is passed to sales assistants behind the counters.*
5. *Catalog copy is short, frilly, trendy and traffic oriented. Photography, art and layout are designed to convey fashion statements, shopping excitement, mood and store image.*

Anatomy of a Dual Purpose (Direct Response Cum Traffic Building) Catalog Program

1. *Anywhere from 8 to 40 or more catalogs. Catalogs may carry merchandise that is not available in any of the stores.*
2. *Most catalogs are targeted to segments of the house list identified as containing potential customers for the merchandise featured in each book. Only the big, seasonal, general merchandise catalogs get general distribution. Newspaper insertions are limited to selected groups of subscribers. Frequently, mailings are sent to non-subscriber areas to achieve complete coverage without duplication.*
   Rental of outside lists can be national in scope, but very selective as to demographics and buying habits. Only lists of identified mailorder buyers are rented outside of store market areas.
3. *The majority of catalogs are directed to customer interests, as opposed to being event or vendor driven. Vendor contributions are welcome, but space and position allocations are made entirely by store marketing executives. Major seasonal and holiday events still have great impact, but specialty catalogs increase overall volume and flatten seasonal peaks and valleys.*
4. *Telephones and mailorder desks are staffed by well-trained, dedicated customer service representatives. Phone and mail orders are promoted heavily in the catalogs.*
   Cross-selling and up-selling functions are programmed into the database and appear on the screen at each customer service workstation.
   Outbound telemarketing may be used to inform regular customers of sales events in merchandise categories appropriate to their interests.
5. *Catalog copy is long, expository, and composed so as to move the reader through the STOP, LEARN, WANT, NEED, ORDER sequence. It should anticipate customers' questions and provide all the answers. But the overall presentation must lean heavily upon photography and illustration for detail and ambience.*
   Photography clearly delineates all product features, colors and textures—sometimes at the expense of vitality and mood. Layouts must include provision for close-up demonstration, headlines, subheads, callouts, keys, phone bugs and long copy.

You may well ask, "If the synergisms of a mailorder cum traffic building catalog program are so obvious, why aren't more retailers getting into the act?" Clearly, there are major decisions that must be made before an OTC retailer can seriously consider moving into mailorder.

1. *The first is a question of commitment: Is this going to be a full-fledged direct response effort, or just a minor adjunct to the main (OTC) business? On-the-side mailorder businesses do not usually work* unless *there is a business plan that sets specific performance milestones. When those milestones are reached, they should quickly trigger a stronger push towards full-scale mailorder. Halfhearted efforts usually do more harm than good. Mailorder customers are very intolerant of poor fulfillment or uncivil, unintelligent customer service communicators. Stores that treat customers poorly when they buy by mail or phone risk alienating that customer permanently.*

2. *The question of merchandise allocation is paramount. Will the mailorder catalog have its own dedicated merchandise? Will it, in effect, be treated as a separate store?*

3. *How will buyers' open-to-buy (and their careers) be affected? What responsibility will they have for mailorder overstocks and out of stock situations?*

4. *Will a whole new fulfillment facility have to be created to pick and pack individual orders? These days, mailorder customers are accustomed to 24-to 48-hour turnarounds. Returned merchandise will average between 10% and 20% in the RTW categories. Extensive refurbishing and customer communications modules are required to deal with these returns and exchanges.*

5. *Who will call the shots when it comes to merchandising the catalogs? Mailorder customers may not be interested in many of the trendy, high velocity OTC items. Conversely, a fair number of mailorder best-sellers may turn out to be poor traffic builders.*

6. *And the two biggest questions:*
   (a). Where is the OTC retailer going to find the talent and experience needed to implement a direct response marketing program? (b). Will those individuals be given the authority, staff, time and budget to make it all work?

(POTENTIAL) BUYERS BEWARE!

A store may mail 4 or 44 catalogs per year, but before every catalog goes into production, there are pagination meetings. These are akin to rites of passage through which all store buyers must pass. Sometimes these sessions are completed in a single day. Larger catalogs may take a week or more to merchandise. To outsiders, the whole process of merchandising and creating a catalog must seem a wild and crazy thing, suitable for serialization on daytime TV. In fact, it is an impressive exercise in human psychodynamics and merchandising know-how.

The scene: a large, spartan, well-lighted, room with long tables, folding chairs, ashtrays, shelves and racks. On one side of the table sit: General Merchandise Managers (GMM's), fashion coordinator(s), ad department folk and senior store executives. Before this awe-inspiring panel flows a steady stream of buyers and merchandise managers. Their job is to sell the merchandise they have selected for the upcoming catalog to these stern-faced judges.

Questions resolved during pagination sessions are:

• *Final Yes/No decisions (is the item in or out?)*

• *What quantitative and financial commitments should be made for each item? And will the vendor make a contribution?*
• *How much space should be allocated to each item?*
• *Where should it be positioned in the book?*
• *What manner of creative presentation will do the best selling job.*

For an item to earn a place in any catalog, it must meet a demanding series of criteria. First, just as in buying for OTC purposes, image, quality, timeliness and vendor considerations are of primary importance. On top of those basics, catalog programs have an additional set of item-specific questions that must be answered:

• *How well will it photograph?*
• *Can a reasonably small amount of copy explain the product?*
• *Will the vendor back us up if the item is a runaway success? And, will he accept returns if it bombs?*
• *Does it fit in with the overall theme of this particular catalog?*
• *Will samples be available* in the right color and size *when we need them for photography?*

DATABASE MARKETING IS MORE THAN JUST A MADISON AVENUE BUZZWORD

The cost of producing and mailing catalogs has risen dramatically in the last few years—far more than has the CPI. These cost escalations were recently exacerbated by a huge 25% increase in Third Class postage fees and a 20% year-to-year increase in paper cost. Short of cutting down the weight of their catalogs, the two best defenses mailers have against runaway cost increases are: (1). sophisticated internal database manipulation and (2). high-tech, statistics-based list regression techniques.

Modern computers and EDP staffs have the capability to track the purchasing patterns of individual customers. Based upon this information, each household is then sent only those catalogs which address the resident's interests—catalogs merchandised and designed to push individual ''buy buttons''.

ELECTRONICS AND THE NCA CHASE

Customer attrition is a major marketing department problem. 20% or more upscale U.S. families move every year. Traditionally, newspapers, magazines, electronic media, telemarketing campaigns and publicity have been frontline NCA (New Customer Acquisition) weapons. Surprisingly, catalog mailings sometimes outperform all of the older NCA methods on a Cost Per Customer (CPC) basis. But, CPC is only one factor in the equation. Another consideration has to do with the value of a new customer over time.

We know that, to be successful, OTC store advertising has to generate store traffic and item sales—now. But modern age marketing mavins take a much longer view. They are far more interested in the value of a customer over 3, 5, or 10 years. All communications media (and various combinations thereof) are constantly being tracked to determine their efficacy as NCA vehicles; including their effect on long term buying patterns as well as immediate sales.

FROM ELECTRONICS TO THE PRINTED PAGE

Customized catalogs and inkjet printing are two of the mechanical extensions of database marketing that permit stores and direct marketers to zero in on individual customers. Computer-driven equipment in modern printing plants is capable of delivering catalogs and order forms that are custom-collated and individually addressed. This is accomplished by combining the base catalog with a variable selection of "swing pages". As a result, each personalized catalog contains products known to be of interest to specific persons on the mailing list. In modern printing plants, with presses running at more than 35,000 impressions per hour, this feat is performed "in-line".

Computer-driven inkjet printing on both the outside back cover of the catalog and on the order form offers a number of advantages over the old Cheshire label format. Converts to the cause of inkjet printing cite a number of reasons for using this modern addressing technology:

1. Labels can, and do, fall off catalogs, particularly when glossy stocks and ink are involved. Inkjet is permanent.
2. Source codes printed on the order form generate a wealth of marketing information. When peel-off labels are used instead of ink-jetting, only about 60% of this valuable information is captured.
3. Today's inkjet printing is much more attractive than the old glued-on paper label.
4. Personalized messages can be added to the label area on either the order form or the cover. For instance, "Mrs. Jones, you might be interested in the Calvin Klein suits on pages 12, 13 and 14. A matching scarf by Kenzo is featured on page 28."
5. And, perhaps most important of all, customer service is improved. Fulfillment, customer service communications and order tracking are greatly enhanced when legible, accurate information is available from an inkjet printed order form.

WHO IS GOING TO DO ALL THIS WORK?

The physical construction of a catalog may be managed in a number of different ways. Some stores have a large, extremely talented, full-time advertising staff. Art directors and copywriters may work on both retail ads and the more creative aspects of catalog production. At these stores, a separate Direct Mail Division is usually responsible for such things as production scheduling, separations, printing and mailing. Here, the store is, in fact, acting as a prime contractor or house agency, farming out only such things as photography, art and typography.

An alternative at the other end of the spectrum are the specialized catalog agencies used by hundreds of stores. These very sophisticated organizations can manage a catalog project from the point at which the merchandise and mailing lists are chosen to the time the book arrives on the customer's doorstep. (You'll find more about these catalog agencies in the final chapter of this book.)

WHAT'S RIGHT FOR ME?

So there we have it, retail catalogs really come in *three* forms: pure traffic-building, pure mailorder and programs that are a combination of the two. Appearances aside, these catalogs vary

Store buyers are subject to tremendous pressures. They must know their customers' preferences for specific items. They make judgments as to acceptable price points. They have to predict—within a narrow range—how many SKU's (sizes and colors) will move for each style chosen. They are prepared to fight with vendors for price, margin, delivery and advertising allowance.

On top of all that, they have to second guess macro fashion trends, predict the direction of the economy and prophesy the weather—all for a point in time six or eight months in the future.

Having coped with all those details, the beleaguered buyer must then convince his or her GMM, most of the senior store executives, the Fashion Coordinator and the Direct Mail Manager and his staff that her judgment is perfect. She has to stand up in front of that crowd and convince them that her items will justify the position and space allocation she has asked for in the upcoming catalog.

And another thing: she has to demonstrate to all and sundry that the item will photograph well, be good grist for the copywriters' mill, and that she can get the proper sample for photography from the vendor in a timely manner. In addition to all of the above, the item must be: a hot traffic-builder, represent well the merchandising philosophy of the store, generate enough mail and telephone response to vindicate her judgment and, at the very least, pay for its advertising space.

The job is a hot-seat inside a pressure cooker. It leads to sleepless nights, short fingernails and a fragmented love-life. But it is also exhilarating, contemporary and the shortest way to the top in the retail business. To be a really good buyer, you need to be fashion-aware, indefatigable, a good psychologist, have a hard-bargaining mean streak in your gut, be a team player, love merchandise and carry a first class ouija board.

widely as to frequency, distribution and operational sophistication. At some stores, ill-conceived false starts have discouraged entry into true mailorder. Other stores have prospered in the mailorder business by virtue of a well thought-out business plan and greater understanding of the structure and methodology of a direct response operation.

The scope and direction of a catalog plan is really a management call. We know that (in most cases) the market is there. The next step is to evaluate the available talent and their knowledge of the industry. If everyone in the store has an undiluted OTC background, then until that changes, traffic-building catalogs are the safer way to go. On the other hand, if substantive mailorder experience is available, either in-house or through a consultant, then direct response should prove to be a fruitful enterprise.

Lately, your mail boxes have been full of retail catalogs. Some lean heavily towards mailorder, others are pure traffic-builders, and a fair number fall somewhere in between. We've selected only a few from each group to illustrate the differences in approach. Using these catalogs as examples, you'll be able to evaluate the stores in your own area and decide for yourself which direction they are taking.

FAMOUS RETAIL CATALOGS

We've selected a group of representative catalogs to illustrate different approaches by different stores to a single objective: traffic-building. You'll note how regional life-styles and customer demographics affect some of these presentations. And clearly, their methods, their messages and their styles are far apart. But the aim is the same: to reinforce image and create immediate excitement.

Catalog agencies prepared some of these books, others were produced in-house. Some stores produce the majority of their catalogs, and hire agencies to handle the overflow. Others choose to contract out all of their publications. As management changes are made, and the size and scope of advertising departments ebb and flow, the in-house versus outside agency production balance tends to change.

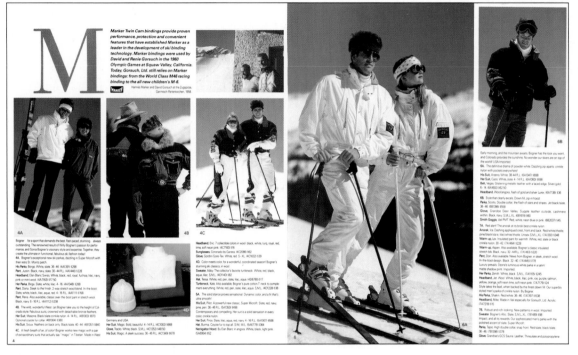

GORSUCH CATALOG—Vail, Colorado Winter 1987/88
Pluzynski/Associates, *Agency*

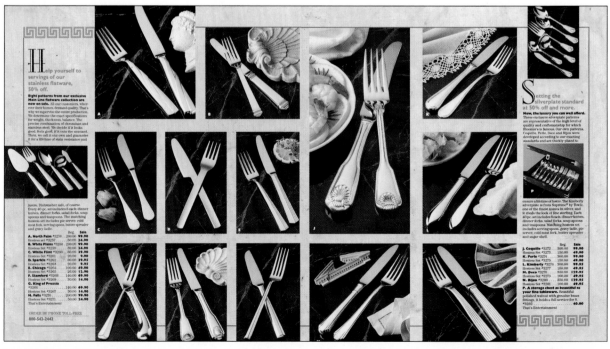

BLOOMINGDALE'S—Living Quarters Fall '87
Mediterranean Odyssey
Pluzynski/Associates, *Agency*

In either case, the considerable funds required for catalog production and distribution come from two primary sources. In the first instance, vendors can sometimes be persuaded to come up with coop advertising dollars. But the amount of their participation is not a constant. It will go up or down according to two prime considerations: the reputation of the store, and the volume the vendor is doing with the store. The second source of funds is the store itself; but here again, there's more than one spigot from whence flows the financial fuel. There are departmental budgets, item-related budgets, and institutional advertising budgets.

What's more, at mailorder-oriented stores, the catalogs are expected to be self-funding by virtue of mail and telephone sales. Other merchants insist that the catalogs be fully funded by vendor dollars. Most retailers find themselves doing a constant balancing act among all of the above.

We've labeled these illustrations by store name and date, to give you a feel for the stores and the images they've chosen to project. The merchandise in some instances is almost identical. The presentations are decidedly not.

A&S—Spirit, Spring '86

A&S—Spirit, Spring '86, Filofax, Fall '86
Doris Shaw, Executive Vice President, *Marketing and Communications*
Anthony Veziras and Joseph Yewdell, *General Merchandise Managers*
Diane Wren, *Merchandising Vice President*
Nicole Shomer, *Catalog Director*
Richard Martino, *Creative Director/Art Director*
Andrew Kay, *Copy Chief*
Martino & Company, *Agency*
William Garrett and Jessie Gerstein, *Photographers*
Spencer Press, *Printer, Spirit, Spring '86*
Alden Press, *Printer, Filofax, Fall '86*
Offset Separations, *Color Separators*

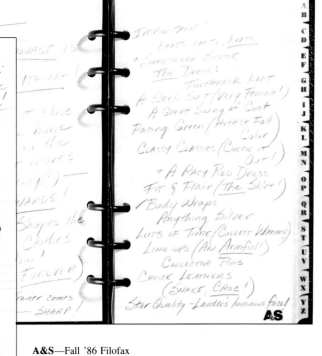

A&S—Fall '86 Filofax

In a fabulous facsimile of a leatherbound, tabbed notebook, A&S has keynoted their fall digest-catalog with two pages of inspired handwritten jottings; as if actual copywriter's meeting notes were stripped into the catalog. Thereafter, every spread has at least one handwritten, pertinent comment, concluding, on the inside back cover, with "Tel. # 1-800-824-6881 (ask for details)". Obviously, at A&S style *and* service equal sales.

HESS'S—Fall '87
Fred Bentelspacher, *Director of Sales
  Promotion and Public Relations*
Ed Klova, *Creative Director*
Allied Graphic Arts, *Agency*

Luxurious leathers to have and to hold

JORDAN MARSH—This is Christmas! 1987
Robert Gottlieb, *Senior Vice President, Marketing*
Jill Stahl, *Catalog Director*
Joel Benjamin, *Vice President, Creative Director*
Ront Arcovio, *Art Director*
Georgeanne Eyler, *Copy Chief (1987)*
Laurie Cacace, *Copy Chief (1988)*
Allied Graphic Arts, *Agency*

SILK COMPLEMENTS SUEDE   SOFT SUITING

MAY D&F—Holiday 1987
Pluzynski/Associates, *Agency*

B. ALTMAN & CO.

One of New York's fine old stores is having its face (and floors) lifted. The venerable B. Altman & Co. has just opened its fabulous new 2nd floor to paeans from the trade press and a laudable amount of business from customers. Remodeling work is already underway on other floors, and we can look forward to a continued evolutionary process as Altman's goes "continental" on a grand scale.

Altman's new management team, headed by President Jack Schultz is also in the process of redirecting the emphasis of their catalog operations. We recently had a talk with Vice President Phil Blanco, Altman's Director of Marketing, and he was kind enough to give us an overview of their new catalog program.

During the latter years of management by the Altman Foundation, the catalog program was gradually moving in the direction of a full-fledged mailorder operation, a la Bloomingdale's by Mail and Saks Fifth Avenue's Folio Collection. George Hanley (then Vice President of Marketing) had, over a period of years, built up all of the support mechanisms necessary for a profitable mailorder division. His efforts had resulted in: high velocity fulfillment, a powerful marketing-oriented database structure, improved customer service facilities and a heightened awareness among the store's buyers of the vicissitudes of mailorder merchandising.

New management means a new, and/or different perspective and, as Phil Blanco pointed out, for at least the next few years, all of Altman's financial and management resources will be devoted to restructuring their OTC retail operations. The major thrust of Altman's new catalog operations will be to back the OTC plan to the hilt. That means mailorder will have to take a back seat in favor of traffic-building catalogs.

Phil Blanco is well aware that the unusually broad merchandise base of the Altman's stores would provide a perfect platform from which to launch a renewed direct response effort. But it appears that, for now at least, mailorder will have to wait until the new management's primary objectives for the store are achieved.

Does this mean that catalogs are going to take a back seat? Emphatically, no! For instance, last year B. Altman & Co. mailed 12 catalogs. 1989 will see at least 18. Is the old "shotgun" media

and mailing list approach coming back? Again, the answer is: not by a long shot. Catalogs will be increasingly directed towards specific groups of customers. These cells or segments of Altman's customer file consist of individuals who have been identified as buyers of merchandise associated with the categories represented in each targeted catalog.

It follows, then, that Altman's catalogs will be more category based than item based. They will be aimed *towards* a particular group of individuals, as opposed to *at* everybody. Altman's is famous for its traditionally-minded customer base. The new thrust will include those same valued, card-carrying Altman's conservatives, but will reach out to include their children, as well.

Winter White Sale (1988-89)
Philip Blanco, *Director of Marketing*
Agency: *In-house*

Fashion will play a substantive role in Altman's future, but they will be fashions of quality, not the short-lived, trendy quirk-of-the-month variety. The sophisticated international traveler will be very much at home in the new Altman's. And, wonder of wonders, the all but forgotten Personal Shopping Service will be alive and well in most of the stores.

As the new catalogs are published, we can look forward to more contemporary fashions and accessories. But we will still see

Altman's fabulous tabletop, cookware and home furnishings departments well represented as usual.

Altman's is a true high-end, full-line department store, and Mr. Shultz and his team have given no indication that they are about to abandon that enviable position, either in the stores or in print. These pages from recent Altman's catalogs show the beginnings of the new look and the changing merchandise emphasis. We will be avidly following the Altman's story as it evolves towards an even more targeted catalog marketing program.

B. ALTMAN & CO.—Holiday Surprise (1988)

Special purchases and savings of 25% to 30%

Fall '88

Folk Art Christmas 1988

Heartwarmers

Favorites

BROOKS BROTHERS

In these days of disco-inspired fashions, DRAM chips and hard disks, deadly decibel levels and endemic decadence—there is a retreat from it all. There is, still, a sanctum, an understated, traditional respite from intrusive high-tech. This "place" is really a state of mind called Brooks Brothers. Its nexus is to be found at 44th Street and Madison Avenue in (of all the unlikely places to find peace and quiet) Manhattan.

Both the store and BB's catalogs deliver the same clear message. Brooks Brothers sells Quality, Tradition, Good Taste. The "Brooks Look" is not for conspicuous dressers. Instead, Brooks believes, their customer must be enhanced by the apparel, not the reverse. One also feels secure and confident in the knowledge that one's leaders and peers will be aware of your good judgment in choosing Brooks as your tailor.

As a result of this philosophy, and as befits a clothier whose doors first opened in the year 1818, no trendy, high velocity, forward-fashion look is to be found either in these catalog pages or in any of the 50 Brooks Brothers stores.

In 1976 Brooks opened a Women's Department. And why not! Women compete in the same business arena as do men. The dress codes are much the same. And, though there's precious little evidence to be found in many other establishments, women do understand and appreciate the quality and service offered by Brooks Brothers.

Brooks Brothers publishes dedicated Women's catalogs for the Spring and Fall seasons. Styles are directly to the point for the career woman at work and at home. Again, simplicity, good taste and understated elegance are the keynotes.

BROOKS BROTHERS
George Hanley, *Senior Vice President, Marketing and Sales Promotion*
Mildred Schlesinger, *Advertising Director*
David J. Sharp, *Copywriter*
Carleen Cusick, *Circulation Manager*
Pam Napolitano, *Assistant to the Advertising Director*

CONSIDER YOUR COMFORT

A. New Spring colors and a new relaxed fit for our popular bold striped shirts. Cut and sewn in our own USA workrooms of fine imported cotton gingham in purple or jade on white. Sizes 4 to 16. (123Y) $40
B. Our exclusive cross-over collar shirt of soft imported pinpoint cotton oxford has a pleat front and faggoting on the collar. Pink or white. Made in the USA for us in sizes 4 to 16. (102Y) $52
C. Crisp tailored pajamas of imported cotton broadcloth are her favorites. Made in the USA exclusively for us with coat style top, long leg elastic waist bottoms. In white with bright pink piping or blue with white. Sizes small, medium or large. (003Y) $37
D. Our plush cotton terry velours robe makes an ideal wrap after bath or shower. In white, pink or light blue. Imported in sizes small, medium or large. (056Y) $74

E. We think you will enjoy the honeycomb texture of our new cotton crew neck sweater. You will also appreciate the range of attractive colors it comes in: pink, white, yellow, black, mint green or sand. Knitted in the USA in small, medium or large. (200W) $48
F. For those who prefer a shorter skirt length, we offer this casual of bleached blue cotton denim. It comes unlined with slash pockets, white buttons on the back vent and zipper closing. Made in the USA in sizes 4 to 16. (182V) $40

To Place Credit Card Orders
CALL TOLL FREE
1-800-247-1000
In N.J. Call Toll Free
1-800-272-1035
See order blank
for exact hours.
FOR ALL OTHER INQUIRIES
during business hours
Eastern time, call our
toll-free numbers
1-800-654-6595
and in NJ 1-800-221-5823.

20

21

Heraldry in Silk
A. We think you will enjoy the distinction...and elegance...of our exclusive heraldic design silk scarves. 36" square in black or red. (246Z) $60

A Floral in Rich Challis
B. Purple-plum blooms on classic black for our exclusive new challis dress. Made for us in the USA of a fluid rayon-wool blend. With covered placket, drop waist, self belt and pleated skirt. Sizes 4 to 14. (219V) $210

The Brooks Woman Loves Plaid
C. Here is the coat dress you will reach for again and again for its easy fit and distinctive good looks. The fine imported wool in black and deep red has a neckline that invites pearls, a set-in waist and a pleated skirt that moves with you. A very special new Autumn dress. Made in the USA in 4 to 14. (222V) $268

Simplicity in Navy
D. Here, classic style combines with classic material for this exclusive new dress. Our navy wool gabardine gives day-into-evening perfection. With easy-on button front and easy-to-enhance jewel neck; plus a self hip belt. 4 to 16. USA made. (221V) $238

A Bouquet in Silk
E. These 36" square silk scarves feature our exclusive floral in red or black. (243Z) $60

To Place Credit Card Orders
CALL TOLL FREE
1-800-274-1815
See order blank for exact hours.

10

11

Photographs taken in studios and on location are used almost exclusively in women's catalogs to illustrate both on-and off-figure merchandise. This is unlike the traditional artwork style oft-times employed for mens' and boys' figures. Photography seems a wise choice for the ladies. Fabrications, movement of the garments and fashion details are infinitely more variable in women's clothing than in men's. Photography can deal with these elements far more effectively than a drawing. It's also important to remember that women mailorder shoppers are more accustomed to ordering from photographs of merchandise rather than from catalogs that use artwork renditions.

A pervasive yet simple statement prevails in the BB catalogs, "Our customers—conservative, well appointed gentlemen and ladies all—will be dressed for this season as shown herein. These items may be purchased only at Brooks Brothers."

The contemporary designer labels that sprout prolifically at other stores are not to be seen at Brooks. The only label in evidence is the Golden Fleece logo that Brooks has adapted from the 15th Century crest of Philip the Good, Duke of Burgundy.

A great percentage of the items sold at Brooks are manufactured in their own factories, all of them located in the United States. A few merchandise lines are produced under contract by other manufacturers who have worked with Brooks over a period of years. Middlemen, and their considerable cost in dollars and quality-control, are virtually eliminated.

A tight rein on the manufacturing process and an *evolutionary* approach to fashion make the "Brooks" wardrobe a prerequisite for members of the more traditional Establishment. It also gives real dimension to the meaning of the term "investment clothing".

In spite of an obvious adherence to the fashion version of the "old school tie", Brooks Brothers has a remarkable history of apparel innovation. Ready-made suits, button-down shirts, Shetland sweaters, foulard ties, camels-hair Polo coats and even the ubiquitous Dacron/cotton wash-and-wear shirt were all introduced by Brooks. The latter, believe it or not, 35 years ago.

Brooks Brothers FALL 1988

Give me the boy . . . .

Though surprisingly little space is given to the Boys category in these catalogs, the merchandise selection covers all the essentials. Presumably, younger fry are expected to come into the store to purchase, since proper fit can be such a variable feast during the sprouting years.

"The Brooks Man" gets his start at an early age (at size "Boys 8"). And what a thrill it is to go shopping with Dad, to actually wear the same clothes he wears—well, almost the same.

Teen years bring a greater variety of offerings from Brooks, and just in time. Prep school can be just as tough as Wall Street when it comes to peer group approbation. A young man fitted out with shirts, ties, sweaters, plus blazer, slacks and a trench coat from Brooks Brothers has a definite edge in that competitive circuit.

FOR BOYS

When they launched their advertising and direct mail catalog program from such bedrock foundations, George Hanley, Brooks Brothers' Senior Vice President of Marketing and Sales Promotion, and Mildred Schlesinger, Advertising Director, did the obvious. They spoke to Brooks' customers in their own language, and they avoided the clutter of many look-alike catalogs. The Brooks Look is a unique 7″ X 10-⅞″, 4-color presentation. The covers and inside artwork are quickly recognizable. Where photographs are used, the lighting and styling are clean and simple. Merchandise details and color alternatives are clearly stated.

Extraordinary care is exercised in the area of color control. Ektachrome assemblies are prepared with great attention to the color of each item. If necessary, actual fabric swatches are sent to the separation house to verify a color. When a Brooks customer receives his or her Brooks package in the mail, the last thing s/he wants is an off-color surprise.

Shoppers who buy by mail and phone tend (statistically) to be conservative in their fashion choices. Brooks Brothers' head copywriter, David Sharp, is in a unique position to take advantage of this happy fact. If a button is moved from season to season, a lapel made ⅛th inch wider or perhaps a color shade deepened, that's news! And, in the catalog, Brooks' customers are not only told all the basic facts about the change, they are frequently favored with information about *why* the change was made.

Brooks does not inundate their customers with catalogs. Unlike many stores who mail 24 or more catalogs each year, Brooks customers receive only 6. The implication is that BB's customers have more important things to do than to wade through a pile of irrelevant catalog pages. After all, why should one ever need to add more than a few very choice items to one's wardrobe each season?

Haberdashery and accessories are an important element of the Brooks Look. Pegged pants and Gucci belts will simply not do!

As is the case with most good fashion, the little touches make the difference. The right hat, the correct portfolio, the appropriate bow tie or silk square establish the wearer as a member of the cognoscenti—in this case, the Establishment.

There is an implicit statement in BB's carefully chosen selection of accoutrement: "Why go elsewhere for accessories? You cannot possibly go wrong if you let us help you with your choice."

A. A Brooks Brothers favorite, our 3-button "346" hopsack blazer. It is tailored in the USA exclusively for us, using porous weave polyester-and-worsted. With patch pockets and "346" brass buttons in slate blue, navy, bottle green or tan. Sizes 38 to 46, 48 regular; 38 to 43 short, 39 to 46, 48 long; 42 to 46, 48 extra long; 39 to 46, 48 medium long for men 5'10" to 6'. (057M) **$205**

B. Cool, colorful 2-button cotton India Madras sport coat, tailored in the USA in sizes 38 to 48 regular, 38 to 42 short; 40 to 46 long; 42 to 44, 46 extra long. (137K) **$175**

C. Our classic 3-button seersucker sport coat, made in the USA exclusively for us of imported washable cotton. With patch pockets in grey-and-white or blue-and-white. Sizes as B. (058K) **$175**

D. This season, we offer a new shade of blue for our 2-button sport coat of imported cotton chambray. Tailored in the USA exclusively for us. Sizes as B. (138K) **$170**

E. We developed imported polyester-and-worsted Brooks-Aire to be so light in weight, it barely weighs a pound. Yet it is highly wrinkle resistant. Tailored in the USA on our exclusive 2-button model in a tan ticweave with red windowpane overplaid. Sizes 38 to 46 regular; 38 to 42 short; 40 to 46, 48 long; 38 to 44, 46 extra long; 40 to 44, 46 medium long proportioned for men 5'10" to 6'. (134K) **$250**

F. Double-pleated brown "346" trousers of imported tropical weight worsted. Made in the USA with a fuller leg and pre-attached suspender buttons. Even sizes 32 to 42 regular, 32 to 38 short, 34 to 42 long; 33, 35, 37 regular. (123K) **$85**

G. Our lightest weight navy blazer is tailored in our own USA workrooms, using Brooks-Blend worsted-and-polyester for a fine hand and wrinkle control. This 3-button model comes with patch pockets and Golden Fleece buttons. Sizes as A. (060M) **$315**

H. Own Make trousers of a superb imported Superfine worsted noted for its light weight and superior hand. From our USA workrooms in tan, medium or oxford grey. Sizes as F. (065K) **$135**

WARM WEATHER SPORT COATS AND BLAZERS

J. New sport trousers, made in the USA of imported polyester-and-cotton designed to be very lightweight and comfortable. Navy-red-green plaid. Sizes as F. (112J) **$58**

CALL TOLL FREE
1-800-247-1000
To Place Credit Card Orders
In N.J. Call Toll Free 1-800-272-1035
See order blank for exact hours.

5

When Henry Sands Brooks first opened the door of his new store 170 years ago, his clientele were sailors and waterfront workers. His merchandise ran heavily towards foul weather gear and sweaters. What a start for the store that has since become the custodian of the Eastern Establishment's standards of attire.

Today, Brooks Brothers is perhaps best known for their business suits, blazers and slacks. Not long ago, many of the more "standard fabrics" suit jackets and pants were stacked high but separately on tables in the store. One could be fitted to perfection with a size 44 jacket and size 28 trousers (when young and athletic) or size 44 jacket and 44 trousers (as time took its toll).

To this day, a Brooks Brothers suit can still be assembled from disparate sizes—on an open stock basis, if you will. The stacked tables have given way to racks, but this extraordinary accommodation is still available.

Head To Toe

A. Our exclusive Brooks Traveller is designed for executives on the go. Made in England for us, it features a lightweight, water repellent tan cotton gabardine shell with warm navy wool blend zip-in liner. Plus, an inside zippered passport pocket. Even sizes 36 to 46 regular, 36 to 42 short, 40 to 46 long and extra long. (052N) **$385***

B. Poplin rain hat of a water repellent polyester-and-cotton. In tan with navy-red grosgrain band. Made in the USA in sizes 6⅞ to 7⅜. (007D) **$18**

Distinctive fur felt hats from Canada with a soft velours finish, braid band. Sizes 6⅞ to 7⅜.
C. Green Tyrolean. (062D) **$82**
D. Camel color. (063D) **$72**

E. Our black nylon umbrella has a solid brass duck's head handle. (178C) **$28**

F. Shoe trees of aromatic unfinished cedar will absorb moisture while maintaining proper shoe shape. With spring attachment. Small, medium, large or extra large. (109H) **$20.50** per pair

G. Varnished pinewood shoe shine kit with polish and brushes for brown and black shoes. (103H) **$35**

H. Classic all-leather casual slip-on with handsewn moccasin front. Brown or black. Sizes 9-13A, 8-13B, 7-13C, 7-13D, 7-11E (no 12½). (006H) **$72**

J. Our exclusive tassel slip-on is of supple calfskin with welt construction, leather heels and soles. Black, brown or oxblood. Sizes 9-13A, 8-13B, 7-13C, 7-12D, 7-11E (no 12½). (001H) **$170**

All our hose is machine washable and, except where noted, come in one size that fits all.

K. Hand-tied cable half hose of soft, warm cashmere with nylon for durability. In khaki, red, yellow, grey, navy, green or black. Made in the USA of imported yarns. (104D) **$19**

L. Exclusive 5 x 3 rib Golden Fleece hose, made for us in England of Merino wool with nylon reinforced heel and toe. In grey, black or navy. Sizes 10½ to 13 (over-the-calf hose also in size 14).
Over-the-calf. (001D) **$13.50**
Half hose. (002D) **$12.50**
Anklet. (003D) **$10.50**

M. Luxurious cashmere-and-nylon hose with our exclusive intarsia Argyll panels on grounds of navy, grey, khaki or black. Made in the USA of imported yarns.
Over-the-calf. (155D) **$25**
Anklet. (156D) **$20**

N. Shrinkage treated sport hose of 82% lambswool, with 18% nylon for extra wear. Red-ivory, navy-green, ivory-navy or grey-red. Made in the USA. (154D) **$12**

P. Solid cashmere hose with nylon for support. Navy, grey, yellow, black or khaki. Made in the USA of imported yarns.
Extra long anklet. (113D) **$15**
Over-the-calf. (114D) **$19**

*Price slightly higher from Denver west.

34   35

23

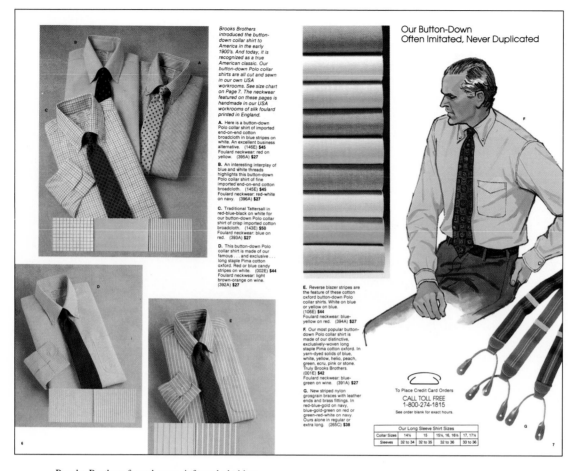

Brooks Brothers introduced the button-down collar shirt to America in the early 1900's. And today, it is recognized as a true American classic. Our button-down Polo collar shirts are all cut and sewn in our own USA workrooms. See size chart on Page 7. The neckwear featured on these pages is handmade in our USA workrooms of silk foulard printed in England.

A. Here is a button-down Polo collar shirt of imported end-on-end cotton broadcloth in blue stripes on white. An excellent business alternative. (146E) **$45** Foulard neckwear: red on yellow. (395A) **$27**

B. An interesting interplay of blue and white threads highlights this button-down Polo collar shirt of fine imported end-on-end cotton broadcloth. (145E) **$45** Foulard neckwear: red-white on navy. (396A) **$27**

C. Traditional Tattersall in red-blue-black on white for our button-down Polo collar shirt of crisp imported cotton broadcloth. (143E) **$50** Foulard neckwear: blue on red. (393A) **$27**

D. This button-down Polo collar shirt is made of our famous . . . and exclusive . . . long staple Pima cotton oxford. Red or blue candy stripes on white. (002E) **$44** Foulard neckwear: light brown-orange on wine. (392A) **$27**

E. Reverse blazer stripes are the feature of these cotton oxford button-down Polo collar shirts. White on blue or yellow on blue. (106E) **$44** Foulard neckwear: blue-yellow on red. (394A) **$27**

F. Our most popular button-down Polo collar shirt is made of our distinctive, exclusively-woven long staple Pima cotton oxford. In yarn-dyed solids of blue, white, yellow, helio, peach, green, ecru, pink or stone. Truly Brooks Brothers. (001E) **$42** Foulard neckwear: blue-green on wine. (391A) **$27**

G. New striped nylon grosgrain braces with leather ends and brass fittings. In red-blue-gold on navy, blue-gold-green on red or green-red-white on navy. Ours alone in regular or extra long. (265C) **$38**

Our Button-Down
Often Imitated, Never Duplicated

To Place Credit Card Orders
CALL TOLL FREE
1-800-274-1815
See order blank for exact hours.

Our Long Sleeve Shirt Sizes				
Collar Sizes	14½	15	15½, 16, 16½	17, 17½
Sleeves	32 to 34	32 to 35	32 to 36	33 to 36

Brooks Brothers formal wear, informal clothing, nightwear and ties are world-famous, but their shirtings must be known throughout the universe.

First among the foremost are Brooks roll collar button-down oxfords. Brought to these shores from England's polo fields by John Brooks in the year 1900, this buttoned-up button-down style is still the top seller in the department.

Imitators have tried for years to match the soft collar roll featured on the Brooks shirts—so far, without success. It is said that numerous laundering only improve the look. As a testimony to the shirts' innate ruggedness, the Kennedys are said to have created the "Hyannis" look by playing touch football and sailing while wearing ancient, but still presentable, Brooks Brothers button-down shirts and chinos.

The customer files in the Brooks archives are a contribution to the history of our times. The names of statesmen, royalty, generals, presidents and social pacesetters fill these vaults.

The Duke of Windsor, Presidents Theodore and Franklin Roosevelt, Presidents Wilson, Hoover, Kennedy, Nixon and Ford, F. Scott Fitzgerald, Generals Grant, Sherman, Hooker and Sheridan, Cary Grant, Fred Astaire, Rudolph Valentino, Clark Gable, John O'Hara, Andy Warhol, J.P. Morgan, various Astors, Vanderbilts and Rockefellers were and are all valued customers.

Today, men and women of equally great stature are being dressed by Brooks Brothers. They are treated to the same attention to personal life-style and preference as were those legendary customers. But, with the understanding, as always, that their requests will be tempered by the dictates of proper Brooks Brothers respect for tradition.

Via mailings totaling 12 million plus catalogs every year, the Brooks Brothers interpretation of traditional good taste is now reaching an audience covering the entire North American continent. In addition, 22 new stores in Japan are spreading the word in Asia.

In a world full of punk, funk and junk, it's nice to think that perhaps the old ways may yet become the new wave.

BULLOCK & JONES

Bullock & Jones and their advertising agency, Humbert Clark, richly deserve the praise and awards that have been heaped upon them for the B&J catalog. Both the merchandising and the presentation are imaginative, professional and tasteful. But, catalogs are not designed to win awards. At least, that's not what the client usually has in mind. His prime objective is to move merchandise. Here too, B&J's outstanding catalog is fulfilling its function—in spades, and in one of the toughest markets there is.

Here is a single-store California-based retailer doing a sales job that should be the envy of all its peers. They are successfully selling high priced casual and everyday clothing to an affluent male customer—by mail.

These affluent male, mailorder clothing buyers are hard to find and even more difficult to convince. If one accepts the DMA's estimate that 35% of US citizens now shop regularly by mail, and that 75% of these shoppers are women; then the remaining 8%-9% must be divided up amongst male hobbyists, children and teenagers, etc. The implication is clear. There are not a whole lot of well-to-do men out there ordering $500 blazers from a catalog.

Once flushed, these rare birds require more than the usual blandishments before they can be convinced to buy. The merchant's reputation and status amongst his (the buyer's) peers must be top drawer. Proffered attire should reek of quality construction and contemporary design, but generally eschew the avant-garde. Very definitely, our prospective peacock needs to be sure that the treatment he receives at the hands of the purveyor will be sensitive, concerned, helpful and courteous.

Bullock & Jones opened their doors 136 years ago; an upstart by Saville Row standards, but in San Francisco, a conservative establishment occupying landmark premises. Their philosophy:

From the day in 1853 when Frank D. Bullock and John Luther Jones first opened their doors in San Francisco, Bullock & Jones' purpose and priority have been in clear focus: To offer discerning customers the very finest in men's apparel.

Clothing chosen for its superb quality, timeless style, and superlative materials and manufacture.

These words are not merely puffery from a copywriter's pen. The clothing offered by Bullock & Jones is of the highest quality. As a result, folks in the Bay Area know and respect Bullock & Jones. They're familiar with the stock, the standards and the fine service offered by this 136 year old institution.

But, in New Haven, Bullock & Jones might be confused with California's Bullocks Department Store (if there is even a glimmer of recognition). How, then, can this three-story, single-store merchant presume to mail to, and receive orders from, all 50 States of the Union? How can they translate a local reputation into a national franchise? Enter the B&J catalog. It's all up to this little 4.75 ounce bundle of printed pages to:

1. *find and reach a precise but tiny market segment,*
2. *establish and maintain an aura of prestige,*
3. *present garments and accessories in an attractive manner to a discerning, but generally skeptical customer.*

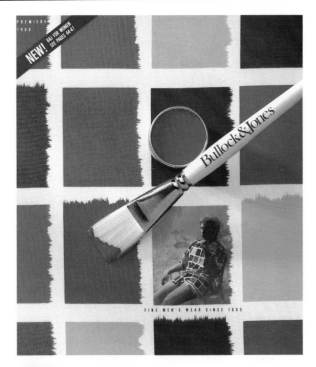

BULLOCK & JONES—Premiere 1988
Sidney Goodwill, *President*
Susan Wilde, *Merchandiser*
Eric Goodwill, *Catalog Director*
Humbert-Clark [San Francisco], *Agency*
Jerry Humbert, *Creative Director*
Maureen Pond, *Art Director*
Mary Bush, *Copy Chief*
Henry Janowsky, *Production Manager*
John Carlson, Judy Houston, Ronnie Poon and
    David Martinez, *Photographers*
Graphic Arts Center [Portland, OR], *Printer, on
    70# Sonoma Gloss for cover and 60# Sonoma
    Gloss for text*
Graphic Arts Center, *Color Separator*

Quite a mission statement!

The ACA judges at "Catalog Age" are a tough group. They are not easily swayed, nor are they prone to extravagant praise. Nevertheless, they have obviously been very impressed with the catalogs of Bullock & Jones. For the third successive year, B&J has been judged tops in their category. Here are a few quotes from ACA judges, describing some of the outstanding characteristics of this year's winner:

The Bullock & Jones Premiere 1988 catalog's deceptively simple presentation of classic clothing for men, judges unanimously concur, richly deserves the Gold Award in the Apparel Over $100 category.

What distinguishes this catalog is Bullock & Jones' superb off-figure display of quality men's clothing, which never allows itself to fall prey to a passing fashion whim. Men know that they can trust Bullock & Jones to help them select a traditional wardrobe that will hold up to the test of time.

This book's clean layout, sharp photography, strong organization and thorough merchandising set it well apart

a. Our Dotted Birdseye Tie gives tradition a new twist. Finest quality English silk is woven with bright dots on dark birdseye patterned grounds to create a tie of uncommon elegance and unusual appeal. Wine or blue. Made in England. R1618 $50

b. 'Caprice' Silk Blazer. Surprisingly versatile, in cranberry or blue. Natural shoulder, center vent. Fully lined. Tailored in U.S.A. of imported twill-weave silk. 39 to 46 Regular (except 45); 42 to 48 Long (except 45 and 47). R3703 $325

e. Bold Stripe Shirts. Made in U.S.A. of fine cotton broadcloth. Wine, navy, green, pink, or light blue stripes on white. 15 (32-34); 15½ and 16 (32-36); 16½ and 17 (33-36); 17½ (34-36). R2032 $55

f. English Knit Tie. 2¾" wide, with velvet keeper, satin neckband. Wool/alpaca/mohair, in green, royal, dusty rose, yellow or wine. R1636 $20

g. The 16-Color Cotton Argyle. A one-of-a-kind sleeveless slipover, sure to set off your sportswear basics. Purest knit wizardry, with 16 different colored diamonds hand-intarsia-knitted into the front. Hand-looped neck. Imported, in S,M,L,XL sizes. R2440 $85

h. Facile® Suede Shirt Jacket. As soft, supple, and luxurious as natural suede, but it won't waterspot, stiffen, or wrinkle. And it's washable. Now in four colors—blue, pink, tan, and red. Made in America. Polyester/polyurethane. R2752. Sizes S,M,L,XL Regular $295; XXL Regular and L, XL Long $355

Extra-ordinary. That's what we strive for, never leaving well-enough alone. So we can continue to offer you innovative patterns, new colors, more sizes – and the finest natural and manmade fibers.

c. The Jumbo Glen Plaid Shirt takes a new stance on a classic pattern. Button-down collar, long sleeves. Blue with raspberry overcheck. Made in America of fine cotton broadcloth. Sizes S,M,L,XL. R2352 $55

d. The 'Raleigh' Slip-on by Bally. Swiss-crafted of ultra-soft Cervo nappa calfskin, with horse bit trim, leather sole, and rubber heel. Brown or black. Narrow width: 8-12,13; medium: 6½-12,13; wide: 7-11,12,13. R7796 $170

Order Toll-Free
800/227-3050
Within California
800/858-5868

14

15

PREMIER 1988 CATALOG
Bullock & Jones has mastered the art of off-figure fashion photography. Layout, lighting and superb styling impart a lifelike sense of movement to every item on the page.

from the relatively few successful menswear catalogs. "It's one of the best displays of off-figure clothing I've seen in a long time."

High-quality paper, exceptional color reproduction, superior photo styling and abundant white space characterize the Bullock & Jones catalog. The off-figure presentation for which the company is noted also encompasses all the principles of good eyeflow. Notice how the tie draped in the upper left corner [on page 14] draws the eye to the blazers, shirt and shoes sold on that page, and how the ties fanned out next to the striped shirts [on page 15] pull readers through the spread to the sweater and jackets on the right-hand page.

This isn't like walking into a department store. There's no reason why all the sportcoats and all the slacks have to be grouped together. The scattered presentation gives readers a much better feel for the way different items complement each other.

. . . and, because no models are featured, the emphasis is where it should be—on the clothes. It also means the catalog can include a lot of products per page without looking crowded.

Subtle touches used throughout the book—leaving collar buttons open on woven sports shirts, and buttoning all of them on dress shirts (shown with ties) — add credibility to the products. "The way the clothing is arranged indicates a very conscious thought all the way through . . . my compliments to the photo stylist."

As the ACA judges point out, Bullock & Jones has eschewed models. That immediately causes a trade-off. On-figure photostyling is easier. Off-figure styling of shirts, coats and slacks is an abstruse and abstract art, with few expert practitioners. Fortunately, B&J has access to the best.

Another consideration: if models were used in this catalog, their direct cost would require an increase in sales of approximately 25%. Is that expectation realistic? The full story paints an even darker picture. Our 25% figure does not include a number of additional hidden costs. Where there are models, there are also: casting department salaries and expenses, makeup people, hair stylists, food and entertainment, travel expenses, and innumerable diet Cokes and bottles of Perrier. We should probably be looking for at least a *thirty to thirty-five percent sales increase* to cover all the costs associated with the use of models. A substantial undertaking, to say the least.

In designing the Bullock & Jones catalog, Humbert Clark Agency has wisely leaned towards high-key photography. This almost shadowless photographic style obviates many styling problems.

- *Wrinkles and hard folds tend to disappear.*
- *The well-filled shadows give a light, clean feel to the merchandise.*
- *Colors are captured with great accuracy and relate well to each other.*
- *Silhouetted items do not plug-up as they would if dramatic lighting were used.*

a. Italian Terry Lined Kimono. An extraordinary robe of many colors and all-around comfort. Cotton plisse stripes, lined in cozy natural cotton terry. Made in Italy. One size. R1722 $210

b. Our 'Paint Box' Sport Shirt. Random squares of fresh paint color make this unique print art to wear! Made in America of pure cotton. Short sleeves. Sizes S,M,L,XL. R2351 $49

At Bullock & Jones, we select sportswear with three criteria in mind: Performance. Comfort. Style and distinction. Why settle for anything less?

●

e. The Mutli Tattersall Shirt breezes through warm weather, yet always looks crisp. Made in America of cotton and polyester. Short sleeve. Sizes S,M,L,XL. R2375 $39

c. Royal Thames Crew Shirt is authentically "yar", with boat neck and Royal Thames Yacht Club crest. Made in Italy of finest mercerized cotton. Sizes S,M,L,XL. R2394 $49

d. Batiste Windowpane Shirt. Cool and comfortable even in the warmest climates. Made in America of lightweight cotton batiste. Short sleeves. Blue or white. Sizes S,M,L,XL. R2354 $55

f. Our Colorful Sailing Jacket is pure cotton aviator cloth, tightly woven to resist wind and water. Cotton mesh and nylon taffeta lining. Zip fly front, dolman sleeves with elastic snap cuffs. Zip pockets. Shirt style collar. Imported, in S,M,L,XL sizes. R2749 $85

g. Linen and Cotton Walking Shorts are trim and comfortable when temperatures climb. Fully lined. Tailored in U.S.A. Red, white, khaki or navy. Sizes 32 to 42. R2840 $60

h. Pure Pima Cotton Knit Shirt. Luxuriously soft, but remarkably sturdy. Pre-shrunk Peruvian cotton, with mother of pearl buttons and banded sleeves. Light blue, maize, navy, pink, white, red, and black. Imported. Sizes S,M,L,XL. R2316 $37.50

j. Our 'Yacht' Deck Shoe by Bally is clearly destined for shore duty as well. Lace front leather uppers with non-skid rubber sole. Swiss-made in navy or white. Medium width: 6½–12,13. R7724 $160

Order Toll-Free
800/227-3050
Within California
800/858-5868

21

a. Terry Beach Jacket. All you need over your swim trunks for lunch at the pool. Zip front, two pockets, short sleeves, and elasticized waistband. Made in U.S.A. of white cotton and polyester knit terry. Sizes S,M,L,XL. R2802 $48

b. Terry-lined Stripe Kimono, so welcome after swim or shower. Brilliant stripes on crisp white cotton broadcloth, with absorbent white cotton terry lining. Made in U.S.A. One size. R1721 $75

c. Pure Cotton Sweat Separates. Active classics in preshrunk, breathable cotton. Smooth knit outside, absorbent French terry inside. Imported, in M,L,XL. Sweatshirt with drop shoulder, in yellow, jade, grey, black, pink, or royal. R2805 $55. Sweat pants with elastic and drawstring waist, elastic cuffs, two on-seam pockets, in royal, grey, or black. R2806 $55 Henley pullover with single button neck. Black, royal or grey. R2807 $55

Enjoy life's little extras. The things that make active and leisure hours easier and more fun, like a terry-lined robe, the crispest white shorts, a night shirt from Savile Row.

●

d. The Sea Island Knit Shirt. Luxuriously soft cotton with crisp white woven collar. Made in England, in red, blue, natural, or green. Short sleeves. Sizes S,M,L,XL. R2398 $60

e. Our Short Sleeve Batiste Shirt combines absolute comfort with ease of care. Made in America of lightweight cotton and polyester. Full cut, with one pocket. Royal, yellow, white, or red. Sizes S,M,L,XL. R2393 $35

f. White Pinpoint Walk Shorts. Pleated front, fully lined. Made in U.S.A. of pure cotton pinpoint oxford cloth. Sizes 32 to 42. R2824 $55

g. Striped Shorty Pajamas by Derek Rose of Savile Row. In fine, lightweight cotton. Short sleeve top. Knee length, elasticized waist bottoms. Made in England, in blue, yellow, red, or green. M,L,XL. R1801 $55

h. Patchwork Stripe Night Shirt by Derek Rose of Savile Row. Exclusively B&J, boldly striped in four colors. Made in England of fine, lightweight cotton. Sizes S,M,L,XL. R1802 $49

Order Toll-Free
800/227-3050
Within California
800/858-5868

36

37

We're talking California here! Every item on these pages might have been illustrated differently, had they been in an Ivy League catalog. Brooks Brothers and B. Altman & Co. carry very similar lines, but their customers are used to more color-saturated, dramatic presentations.

Premiere 1987

a. Our Cotton and Linen Shirt has the smart details that set it apart from others. Two pleated pockets, military-style epaulets and short sleeves. Made in U.S.A. of imported fabric. Red, royal, black, light blue, white or peach. S,M,L,XL. L2377 $55

b. 'Alex' by Bally of Switzerland. You couldn't find a more comfortable after-work shoe. Crafted of Ultima suede and soft llama calf so it's light as a feather. With rubber sole and heel. Grey, denim blue and tan as shown, dark brown or off-white. Medium width: 6-12,13. L7735 $125

c-e. Crisp Linen and Cotton Check Shirts. None are more apropos for spring and summer. Cool and breezy, with short sleeves and a pocket, they're ideal mates for slacks and shorts. Made in America of imported fabric, in sizes S,M,L,XL.
c. Ecru checks with subtle overcheck. L2325 $65
d. Bold navy and white block plaid. L2326 $65
e. Shades of blue on white. L2327 $65

f. The 'Nairobi' Jacket. It may be a jungle out there, but you'll face it comfortably in this update of the big game hunter's favorite. It's equipped with four button flap pockets, epaulets, belt and button cuffs. Durable 100% cotton twill, imported. S,M,L,XL. L2713 $90

You are welcome to charge it. Use your VISA, MasterCard, American Express or Diners/Carte Blanche.

The sporty windcheater jacket, reversible for double versatility

g. Pure Pima Interlock Shirt. Its superior softness is evident with your first touch. Of pre-shrunk Peruvian cotton, with mother of pearl buttons and banded sleeves. In ten glorious colors: pink, navy, sky blue, red, ecru, royal blue, white, peach, black and maize. Imported. S,M,L,XL. L2316 $36

h. The Reversible Windcheater Jacket gives you two jackets in one. With rib knit cuffs and waistband. Made in U.S.A., in red reversing to navy polyester/cotton. Sizes 38 to 46 Regular, 42 to 46 Long. L2701 $95

j. Our Pleated Linen Slacks are the essence of ease when the weather warms. Handsomely textured and light in weight, with pleated front, belt loops and straight legs. Tailored in U.S.A. of 100% linen. Taupe, off white or black, in 32 to 42. L2598 $75

k. 'Devon,' Our Cabled Cotton Crewneck comes from England where a substantial summer sweater is imperative. Yet it feels so good, you'll wear it on into fall. Drop shoulder style, in yellow or natural, 38 to 48. L2441 $80

Just because everything is shown off-figure does *not* mean that everything looks the same. Here we have a series of pages to illustrate the point. Hangers, store dummies, inserts and some very unusual silhouette treatments allow every spread to have a life of its own.

Swatching is always a problem for catalogers. When garments come in a number of colors, a difficult choice has to be made. Either: 1). show little patches (fabric swatches), or 2). show the garment itself. Stamp-size swatches save space and allow one to use macro-photographic techniques to

show texture and detail. On the other hand, full-figure shots are far more representative of real-life effect and color. During thirty years of split-run tests for our clients, the full-figure approach has out-pulled the postage stamp alternative in almost every instance.

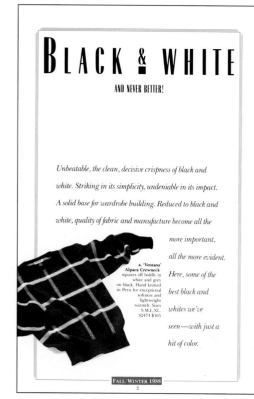

BLACK & WHITE

AND NEVER BETTER!

Unbeatable, the clean, decisive crispness of black and white. Striking in its simplicity, undeniable in its impact. A solid base for wardrobe building. Reduced to black and white, quality of fabric and manufacture become all the more important, all the more evident. Here, some of the best black and whites we've seen—with just a hit of color.

a. 'Ventana' Alpaca Crewneck squares off boldly in white and grey on black. Hand knitted in Peru for exceptional softness and lightweight warmth. Sizes S,M,L,XL. S2474 $165

Fall/Winter 1988

b. Our Silk Twill Shirt makes its mark in graphic plaid. Imported silk tailored in America with a smooth concealed placket and soft collar. Slightly oversized for an easy fit. Sizes S,M,L,XL. S2359 $145

c. The Paisley Sport Shirt shows its colors in imported red cotton twill, patterned allover with a smaller, spaced paisley. One pocket. Made in U.S.A. with long sleeves. Sizes S,M,L,XL. S2345 $65

d. Our Glen Plaid Sport Coat, quintessentially black and white, scaled up for extra impact. Woven in England of super lambswool with the luxurious hand of cashmere. Tailored in America with center vent, full lining. 38 to 46 Regular, 40 to 46 Long. S2725 $395

e. Pleated Worsted Slacks promise all day neatness in wrinkle resistant English wool. Tailored in U.S.A. with belt loops, straight legs. Charcoal, as shown, or black, grey, or blue. 32 to 42 Regular. S5856 $125

f. Caiman Crocodile Belt. The ultimate accessory, a cherished gift. Crafted in Italy with leather lining, solid brass buckle. Black or brown. 32 to 44 sizes. S124 $175 See page 10 for Richfield shoes.

Fall and Winter 1988

Bullock & Jones has a consistent story to tell. Their job is to "*offer discerning customers the very finest in men's apparel*". This theme is repeated in all

B&J media. But sometimes there's an important fashion statement to be made. On those occasions, the message rings out loud and clear, as illustrated in this impressive spread.

Autumn '88

a. Our 'Treviso' Jacquard Crewneck is knitted in Italy of wool with the softness of cashmere and a comfortable mid-weight. The striking navy jacquard pattern has the look of foulard, in deep rich tones. Sizes S,M,L,XL. S2403 $135

b. Our Pleated Whipcord Slacks promise lasting good looks with fewer wrinkles. Tailored in U.S.A. with double forward pleats, on-seam pockets, belt loops, and braces buttons. Charcoal, grey, or dark brown wool. 32 to 42 Regular. S3833 $145

c. The Cashmere Polo Shirt. Luxury sportswear from one of Scotland's premier knitters. Full fashioned, with long sleeves. Lightweight, single-ply cashmere in ruby, teal, or natural. Sizes S,M,L,XL. S2402 $295

d. Herringbone English Hose by Pantherella. Knitted of extra-fine merino wool. Over-the-calf length in acorn, navy, wine, or black. Regular fits 10½ to 11½, Large fits 12 and 13. S1403 $20

e. Our Wool Lined Trench Coat by Rodex of London. Tailored with all the traditional details in water-repellant polyester/cotton with a warm wool blend button-in liner. British tan or black. Imported. 38 to 46 Regular, 38 to 42 Short, 40 to 46 Long. S3905 $495

f. Our Mini Check Sport Shirt is a handsome patchwork in navy, red, and green. Made in America in soft cotton with a button-down collar. Sizes S,M,L,XL,XXL. S2553 $75

g. The Eight Color Repp Tie, handmade in England. A marvel of versatility, ideal for travel, since there's little it won't complement. Woven silk. S1653 $50

h. The Cashmere Sleeveless Slipover adds luxury, warmth, and color. Knitted in Scotland of single-ply cashmere. Wine, grey, green, natural or navy. Sizes 38 to 48. S2412 $155

j. The Ultimate Penny Loafer by Alden. Handmade in U.S.A. of fine imported aniline calfskin. Fully leather lined, with leather sole and leather and rubber heel. Black, walnut brown, or, not shown, brown, burgundy. AA width: 9 to 12,13; A width: 8½ to 12,13; B width: 8 to 12,13; C width: 6½ to 12,13; D and E widths: 6 to 12,13. S7102 $170

k. Enamel Blazer Buttons from Italy mark the ubiquitous blazer as yours alone. Enamel on brass with a burnished antique look, in shield or duck designs. Set of four large and six small buttons. S0723 $65

l. Hickey Freeman's 'Diamond Head' Blazer, an all-season favorite in wrinkle resistant 80% wool/20% mohair hopsack. Hand tailored in U.S.A. with soft shoulder, center vent, and flap pockets. Fully lined. French blue, burgundy, black, or bottle green. Not shown, navy. 40 to 48 Regular, 38 to 42 Short, 42 to 48 Long. S3701 $575

Order Toll-Free
800/227-3050
Within California
800/858-5868

4   B&J AUTUMN 1988
5

Similar merchandise? Yes. But the layouts are quite different. In every case, eye movement is controlled and smooth. No shocks or jolts, just a comfortable flow. These pages would present a challenge to any art director, but the Humbert Clark Agency team seems to take this sort of dare in stride.

a. Our Honey Lambsuede Blazer is such understated luxury. Tailored in America with center vent, flap pockets. S3754 38 to 46 Regular; 38 to 42 Short $465; 40 to 46 Long $495

b. Plaid Viyella® Sport Shirt in bold black and white. Washable cotton and wool is woven in England for superior comfort and warmth. Made in U.S.A. Sizes M,L,XL. S2348 $110

c. Our Paisley Viyella® Sport Shirt is a marvelous blend of cotton and wool, woven in England for exceptional richness of color. Wine or blue. Made in U.S.A. Sizes M,L,XL. S2358 $110

d. 'Verona' Cashwool Crewneck is made in Italy of pure wool with the softness of cashmere. Neat burgundy and grey basketweave pattern with solid burgundy ribbing. Sizes S,M,L,XL. S2400 $165

e. The Silk Sport Shirt. A sophisticated casual, with mother-of-pearl buttons. Made in U.S.A. of imported silk. Wine, white, green, or black. Sizes M,L,XL. S2304 $95

f. The Original Tassel Moccasin from Alden Shoe Company. Handmade in America from premium imported calfskin, fully leather lined. Leather sole with leather/rubber heel. Black or burgundy. AA width: 8 to 12,13; A width: 8½; to 12,13; B width: 8 to 12,13; C width: 6½; to 12,13; D and E widths: 6 to 12,13; EE and EEE widths: 6 to 12. S7101 $170

g. Our Cashmere Glen Plaid Sport Coat distinguishes itself—and you—in traditional black and white with a red overplaid. Tailored in America with soft shoulders, center vent, two buttons. 38 to 46 Regular; 38 to 41 Short; 40 to 48 Long. S3756 $650

h. Snap Tab Collar Shirt. Always neat, in fine cotton broadcloth. Made in America, in white, pink, blue, helio. Sizes 14½ (32-33); 15 (32-35); 15½ and 16 (32-36); 16½ and 17 (33-36). S2006 $48

j. The Repp Stripe Tie will be a handsome basic in your tie wardrobe. Handmade in America, lined to the tip. Pure woven silk in black or black with wine. S1657 $35

k. Our Cashmere Blazer is unparalleled in looks and luxury. Tailored in U.S.A. with soft shoulder, center vent. Black, grey, burgundy, natural, as shown, or navy. 38 to 46 Regular; 38 to 42 Short; 40 to 46 Long. S3751 $595

l. Running Clocks Hose by Pantherella. A discreet yet novel allover neat pattern in featherweight merino wool with nylon for shape retention. Over-the-calf in navy, brown, or grey. Made in England. Regular fits 10½ to 11½, Large fits 12 and 13. S1416 $20

m. Cashmere Mock Turtleneck. A classic whose popularity is once again on the rise. Full fashioned in Scotland of lightweight single-ply cashmere. Natural, blue, cream, wine, grey, black. Sizes S,M,L,XL. S2458 $235

B&J for women
pages 43-47

BULLOCK & JONES FOR WOMEN

a. Our Facile® Sweatshirt is as soft and supple as suede, but it won't waterspot, stiffen, or wrinkle. Ideal for travel in washable polyester/polyurethane. Green, cream, or red. Made in U.S.A. Sizes S,M,L. S4038 $285

c. 'Barbara' Cashmere Cardigan is slightly shorter with a fitted waistband. Goldtone nugget buttons. Knitted in Scotland of finest two-ply yarns. Ruby, ivory, or teal. Sizes S,M,L. S4030 $325

d. The 'Beverly' Cashmere Skirt coordinates with the cashmere cardigan or tunic. Easy-fitting, 24" length in luxurious two-ply cashmere knitted in Scotland. Ruby, ivory, or teal. Sizes S,M,L. S4031 $265

e. The Cashmere Tunic. Purest luxury to pair with everything. Knitted in Scotland of two-ply cashmere. Slightly oversized, in teal, ruby, or ivory. Sizes S,M,L. S4029 $325

b. 'Abbey' Stack Heel Pump by Bally. The walking pump par excellence, in soft, flexible kidskin with kidskin lining. Leather sole and rubber heel. Black, cognac, red, or dark green in Slim 7 to 11; Narrow 6 to 11; Medium 4 to 11; C width 5 to 10. S7910 $165

f. The Aquascutum Trenchcoat. A new classic with concealed button front, gently padded shoulders, swing back and deep yoke. Easy-cut to wear comfortably over suits. British tan water repellant cotton/polyester with signature check lining. Imported for sizes 4 to 16. S4035 $395

g. Ghurka Spectator Bag. The perfect size, in black grained Khyber calf with saddle leather trim. Resists water spotting. Made in U.S.A. S6002 $275

h. Wide Contour Belt by Ghurka. Rich black and tan waxhide leather, with solid brass fittings. Made in U.S.A. 3" width. Sizes S,M,L. S6003 $70

j. Aquascutum Umbrella in the signature club check with belt border. Wooden stick and handle. Imported, in nylon. S4037 $110

k. Aquascutum Silk Scarf. Lavish 31½" square of imported silk, patterned with the signature club check and belt border. S4036 $75

l. Our Navy Knit Top is the perfect foil for accessories. Nicely oversized for an easy fit, with drop shoulders, one pocket. Flat knit wool imported from Italy for sizes 6 to 12. S4027 $245

m. The Navy Knit Shirt has a wide ribbed waistband for flattering comfort. Made in Italy in flat knit, wool. 24" length. Sizes 6 to 12. S4028 $145

Somehow, Bullock & Jones seems to have had access to some sophisticated split-run research—or else, they're as intuitive as hell. On these "Bullock & Jones for Women" pages, we suddenly see apparel shown on models.

The story: Off-figure works for virtually all menswear. It does *not* do a good selling job for some women's fashions. Dresses, skirts, coats and lingerie come in hundreds of fabrications, each with its own hand and movement. Still life photography cannot catch those nuances. Proportions and lengths are impossible to depict except on a live model or a full-scale mannequin. Bullock & Jones has opted for a mixed bag of photo-techniques in their women's section, and they've steered exactly the correct course. On-figure where necessary, off-figure when it works. Humbert Clark Agency is to be congratulated for choosing this client. They make a great team and a great catalog.

Bounce strobe, location shooting and umbrella-shaped lights keep on-figure photography from being too much of a technical trauma for the fashion photographer. Still-life photographers sometimes have a different story to tell, especially when the layout calls for dark, dramatic, moody lighting. Dramatic lighting looks masculine. It creates an aura of strength and mystery. But it also dramatically increases the odds that the merchandise will look rumpled instead of relaxed.

Leanna Clark and Jerry Humbert had many years of general advertising agency experience under their belts when they started their new agency 14 years ago. Today, they serve a client base that includes such famous names as Macy's, Gumps, Gardener's Eden and many others. They have broad experience in all kinds of lighting and illustration techniques; and they know how to use lighting to create an ambience. Wrinkles aside, why then did the Humbert Clark staff settle on this particular photographic convention for Bullock & Jones? Because, high-key is right for the California look. It's right for the colorful merchandise. It works with their very creative use of white space as a design element. And, it permits the reader's eye to move freely from element to element, both on the page and across the spread.

With such excellent manufacturing resources and fine catalog programs in hand, B&J's owners must be tempted to open more stores. Experience has shown that properly sited new stores can rely on the existing mailorder buyers to provide a start-up customer base. And, there are shoppers who simply will not buy through the mail. For these customers, catalogs function as if they were solely traffic-building publications. One can only assume, in B&J's case, that the industry-wide problem of finding, training and retaining good sales help is the roadblock. Recruiting sales associates capable of maintaining Bullock & Jones' high standards presents an almost insurmountable obstacle. Too bad! All the other synergistic elements are in place. Ah, but then, timing is everything.

CASWELL-MASSEY

Caswell-Massey is America's oldest firm of chemists and perfumers—older, in fact, than the United States itself. Founded in 1752 by Dr. William Hunter, a physician from Edinburgh, Scotland, Caswell-Massey can boast of 237 years of uninterrupted service to the rich, the famous and local communities.

No longer a single-door chemist and apothecary shop, today's Caswell-Massey's approximately 30 stores are oases for the self-indulgent. C-M is *the* prestigious purveyor of premium proprietary and imported personal care and fragrance products on this continent.

Caswell-Massey moved from Newport, Rhode Island, to the Island of Manhattan in 1860, the year before the start of the Civil War. These days, pills, potions and live leeches will have to be found elsewhere, since the metamorphosed and expanded Caswell-Massey offers apothecary services only in their Lexington Avenue store. No longer an exclusive sanctum for the carriage trade, the mahogany wood, mirrored interiors of the stores have become a respite from the crass commercial world for an ever-broadening group of customers.

Eighty percent of the fragrance and personal care items sold in C-M stores today have been created by Caswell-Massey proprietors, past and present. The Taylor family, owners of this historical firm since 1936, have created more than their share of the recipes and formulae for C-M products seen on the store shelves and in the catalogs.

THE FINEST IN FRAGRANCE & PERSONAL CARE SINCE 1752
CASWELL-MASSEY

Christmas 1987

CASWELL-MASSEY—Christmas 1987
Adam Taylor, *President*
Patricia Doescher McElroy, *Marketing Manager*
Joshua Taylor, *Creative Director*
Kiyoshi Kanai, *Designer*
Adam Taylor and Patricia McElroy, *Merchandisers*
Helen Cronin, *Copywriter*
George Pete and Gabrielle Keller, *Photographers*
Patricia McElroy, *Production Manager*
Perlmuter Printing [Brecksville, OH], *Printer, on 60# Spider Web Gloss for cover and 45# Spider Web Gloss for text*
Flower City [Rochester, NY], *Color Separator*

After 118 years of practice, they finally got it right. Caswell-Massey first opened their doors in Newport, Rhode Island, in 1752. This photograph, taken on the Fourth of July, 1870, illustrates a side of Newport society rarely seen in today's Chamber of Commerce publicity releases. Upstairs, "Bowling, Pool & Billiards". Downstairs, Caswell-Massey and Company, Dispensing Chemists—an ideal juxtaposition in the event of aching muscles, bruises and contusions.

Caswell-Massey's new store at 1121 Broadway opened in 1882 at a time when there were real, live clerks behind every retail counter.

Four members of the Taylor family currently serve on the Board of Directors at Caswell-Massey. They are: Ralph Taylor, eighty-five years young, and his youthful brother Milton (a mere 81). Milton's two sons, Adam and Josh, represent the younger generation.

It is not unusual to have fastidious patrons ask Caswell-Massey to formulate scents that are exclusively theirs. Mr. Ralph Taylor is especially happy to oblige, if he can meet with the customer; or if he can be provided with an extensive portrait of that individual's life-style and personal preferences. John Berendt wrote an article about one of these special orders for "Cosmopolitan" Magazine. He tells the story of a conversation with Ralph Taylor. The subject was a recent special order from a customer who knew exactly how to play this luxurious game.

"A gentleman has just written to ask us to make him an exclusive fragrance, and to incorporate it in an entire personal line of toiletries: cologne, shaving lotion, after-shave, skin cream, bath oil, soap, talc, and shampoo. They will all have the same unique fragrance that will come to be identified only with him.

He tells us he is forty-two but looks younger, that he's six feet tall and weighs one hundred seventy pounds. He dislikes large parties and organized activities, is not athletic, has two daughters, and dresses conservatively. He likes ballet, symphonies, opera, and rare books, but not colonial architecture. He also tells us which of his wife's perfumes he likes best and how he responds to each of the Caswell-Massey fragrances. He likes our Jockey Club but not our Aura of Patchouli. And he doesn't want a lemony scent; he feels lemon is ubiquitous these days."

Mr. Taylor is clearly delighted with this man and with the challenge he's providing [says Mr. Berendt, who continues quoting Mr. Taylor].

"I intend to tell him that we will be happy to accommodate him. The way we normally proceed with this kind of request is to make up five basic scents. After a five-week trial period, he chooses one of them. Then I send him five variations on the one he's selected, and after another trial period, he makes a final decision.

"Our fee for developing the fragrance is two thousand dollars, a one-time charge, payable in advance. After that, we charge the normal price for whatever product he orders. The only items that he'll have to order in quantity are soaps and talcs. If he wants soap, for instance, he will have to order sixty gross at a time."

Which means that, at $3.50 and three weeks per bar, including development charges, the man would receive a bill of $32,240 and enough soap to last 498 years!

While celebrities still make up the most visible segment of Caswell-Massey's trade, reason and common sense on the part of management have broadened the C-M's customer base without in any way sacrificing quality standards. New stores in new states and cities bring their unique line of personal care products to a highly receptive, younger audience. Overseas, both Harrods and Liberty of London carry the Caswell-Massey line. To extend their marketing reach even farther, Caswell mails four catalogs per year—over one million in all—to a select audience, many of whom have never set foot in a C-M store.

Caswell-Massey has taken advantage of the synergism between store and catalog to build a solid and much broader market serving people of good taste, regardless of income. For some of us, $3.50 for a bar of soap might seem extravagant, but for others, a different logic prevails. Is it not sensible, for instance, to invest that small sum in the delights promised by the catalog copy for Caswell-Massey India Soap?

Caswell-Massey's roots in early American history do not prevent them from moving swiftly and confidently into the future. In the past few years, Caswell-Massey has increasingly used four-color photography to illustrate their products. They've managed this segue (from artwork to photography) just as gracefully as they have all the other changes in their catalog format.

Today, most of us are accustomed to seeing photographs used in catalogs. Our eyes are trained to react to realistic photographic images, as opposed to interpretive artwork. Caswell-Massey is keeping pace with the times, and moving towards the use of more photography. This change indicates to their customers that, although the company is steeped in tradition, they are keeping up with the technological advances in their industry. The message is reinforced by a letter from company President Adam Taylor in this very catalog:

> Dear Readers,
>
> The future is an endless universe of technological wizardry, while the past is a deep reservoir of wisdom and charm.
>
> Which should be considered more valuable?
>
> At Caswell-Massey, we believe the ultimate value is found in a combination of the two: A dauntless exploration of the frontiers of possibility, informed by the voice of experience.

A Sampling of Beautiful Soaps

ENJOY a variety of fragrant essences and extracts with our elegant Soap Sampler collections. Since each makes a distinctive and impressive gift, you may wish to order several.

Garden Soap Sampler
Our garden soaps contain beneficial levels of natural ingredients for specialized complexion aid: Buttermilk is nourishing and soothing; Oatmeal calms and soothes sensitive skin; Avocado & Honey, rich in Vitamin A, is conducive to healthy skin; Strawberry Cold Cream is mild and moisturizing; Almond Meal & Witch Hazel is deep-cleansing and refining; Cucumber & Glycerine is a delightful skin softener. Six 3.25 oz. bars, one each of six types $17.00
00446 Garden Soap Sampler

Orchard Soap Samplers
The sprightly lather of our colorful orchard soaps releases the delicious bouquet of sun-ripe fruit. We offer two different assortments of six 3.25 oz. soaps, color-matched to their fruit fragrances $17.00
00617 SAMPLER No. 1 (Black Currant, Green Apple, Lemon, Pomegranate, Raspberry, and Mandarin)
00637 SAMPLER No. 2 (All-new Plum, Apricot and Pear, plus Black Currant, Pomegranate, and Raspberry)

Floral Soap Samplers
Our floral soaps are triple-milled for lasting luxury, with twice the aromatic essence found in most scented soaps. We offer two different assortments of six delightful 3.25 oz. soaps . . $17.00
00426 SAMPLER No. 1 (Damask Rose, Gardenia, Jasmin de Grasse, Blue Hyacinth, Purple Lilac, and Fougère/Fern)
00427 SAMPLER No. 2 (Lily of the Valley, Red Carnation, Sandalwood, English Lavender, Narcissus, and Mimosa)

India Soap Sampler
Romance fills the air when our most exotic scented soaps are brought to lather, releasing the enticing aroma of Patchouli, the fascinating aura of Musk, and the mysterious scent of Ginseng. Six 3.25 oz. bars, two in each fragrance. $17.00
00634 India Soap Sampler

To order, call • (212) 620-0900

Herbal Soap Sampler
The natural extracts of our herbal soaps allow you to enjoy the mystic properties of legendary herbs: Angelica, a richly aromatic inhalation; Calendula, a classic balm; Comfrey, nature's healer; Eucalyptus, which works with steam to help relieve congestion; Peppermint, a cooling sensation; and Chamomile, for natural, healthy radiance. Six 3.25 oz. bars, one of each herbal essence $17.00
00627 Herbal Soap Sampler

Glycerine Soap Sampler
Our glycerine soaps are without equal for softening, conditioning and protecting the moisture balance of the skin. Each jewel-tone translucent soap is suffused with the fragrance of exotic flowers: Acacia Honey, Tea Rose, Freesia, Wisteria, Hibiscus, and Ylang-Ylang. Six 3 oz. bars, one in each fragrance $17.00
00446 Glycerine Soap Sampler

Treasures of India

A QUEST for rare essences and spices impelled the early explorers to sail the seven seas. When DaGama dropped anchor off Calicut in 1498, India's splendor was revealed to the world. . . .

Caswell-Massey India Soap
Romance fills the air when our exotic scented soaps are brought to lather. To complement their intriguing aromas, we commissioned a triptych of the ceremonies of Indian betrothal: Enticing Patchouli perfumes the scene of the courtship; fascinating Musk permeates the scene of the bride's grooming ritual; and mysterious Ginseng censes the scene of the nuptial procession. Box of three 3.25 oz. bars, made in U.S.A., choice of scent. $8.50
00630 Ginseng
00632 Musk
00631 Patchouli

India Soap Sampler
00634 Six 3.25 oz. bars, two in each fragrance. $17.00

Sandalwood Soap
A favorite from our floral collection, the warm spicy aroma of India's prized Bangalore Sandalwood is equally suited to men and women. Box of three 3.25 oz. bars, made in U.S.A. $8.50
00412 Sandalwood Soap

Sandalwood Paste
The hypnotic blend of Bangalore sandalwood and amber extract in a powerful, alluring paste. Used very sparingly on the pulse points, allowing the rich fragrance to mellow for thirty minutes, it creates a veil of lasting aroma. Glass pot, ½ oz., imported from India $5.50
53000 Sandalwood Paste

Sandalwood Fan
Sandalwood is so valuable that every tree is owned and controlled by the government of India. Our intricately carved fan is handcrafted in India of pure sandalwood, for a lifetime of fragrant breezes. (Thirty-five years ago, an Indian businessman presented the owner of Caswell-Massey with a business card printed on sandalwood. It remains as fragrant today as it was then.). . $12.50
82000 Sandalwood Fan

To order, call • (212) 620-0900

Romance fills the air when our exotic scented soaps are brought to lather. To complement their intriguing aromas, we commissioned a triptych of the ceremonies of Indian betrothal: Enticing Patchouli perfumes the scene of the courtship; fascinating Musk permeates the scene of the bride's grooming ritual; and mysterious Ginseng censes the scene of the nuptial procession.

Copy such as this permits a certain logic: a $5.00 cocktail only lasts ten minutes. But we can indulge in all the romance and gratification of India Soap for up to three weeks, and it's only $3.50. Incredible! How can they do it?

Much of the copious publicity surrounding Caswell-Massey is attributable to their extraordinary predilection for the past. Where else would one find at retail such venerable relics as beeswax earplugs, goose-quill toothpicks, lavender smelling salts, bear grease, paste-on beauty marks, snuff, and a plethora of potpourri? For generations, the almond and cucumber soaps have been best sellers. And, traditionally-minded male shoppers can still buy straight razors, mustache scissors, boar-bristle toothbrushes and badger-bristle shaving brushes.

Mahogany shelves and medleys of potpourri do indeed evoke images of the past. One can almost imagine horse and carriage arriving at the doors of the Caswell-Massey emporium and gerontological gargoyles being gracefully guided to a seat at the mirrored counter, where. . . POP! Puncture that dream sequence. 'Tain't so.

These days the stores prosper and proliferate; and the crowd gets younger. Caswell-Massey is not due for a dose of Geritol yet, nor are there any indications that they ever will be. Some of the "soft" rationales for C-M's marketing success are:

- *Young, affluent, sophisticates are "into" personal care products based on natural formulae. And that is precisely in line with the C-M manifesto.*
- *The nation-wide intellectual movement away from built-in obsolescence and poorly manufactured designer-labeled goods provides another lift for the quality oriented Caswell-Massey philosophy. The Taylor family has always had a deep commitment to product integrity. That sense of dedication remains to this day. The Taylors and the newer top echelon at C-M consistently search the world to find the best ingredients, the rarest essences, the most skilled craftsmen.*
- *Life has become incredibly complex. Technology reigns. We seem to move from one crescendo to another, not once in a lifetime or a year, but now, once in almost every day. The products of Caswell-Massey promise escape from this buffeting. They suggest that peace is possible, if only for a few moments.*
- *If the scent of a delicious, self-indulgent bath lingers on your skin—or is replenished with a matching cologne—or is reinforced by the faint reminder of the potpourri in your dresser drawer—then, subliminal memories of those images and tranquillity are there, all day, to soften the edges of your stress-packed, realtime situations.*

In addition to these subjective permutations, there are some very down-to-earth merchandising and marketing actions that have been fashioned by the C-M marketing group in recent years. Catalog programs are on a steep ascent. And the rate of new store openings is hardly indicative of a somnolent corporation.

Packaging is, and always has been, a key factor in the marketing of personal care and cosmetic items. In the world of mass marketing, it is not at all unusual for a bottle to be more costly than the contents within. The container is the only visual and tactile communications link the manufacturer has with his customer every day—at a time when they are feeling most sensuous, and when their receptors are most sensitive.

Caswell-Massey's packaging is also a tremendous asset to their catalog program. A plain bottle, box or tube has little to say about its contents. No matter how creatively a photographer might use the tools of his trade—lighting, diffusion, props, exposure, dimension, styling—he cannot, to purloin a phrase, make a silk purse from a sow's ear.

The photographer's objective is to capture the essence and function of his subject on film. He has to find the element or elements that make an item unique—and desirable. His job is made much easier when the packaging helps to tell the story.

Expansion has become a way of life at Caswell-Massey. As of 1989, Caswell has thirty doors spread over 18 states. As to the future, we understand that plans are afoot to accelerate the rate of new store openings over the next few years. As we mentioned earlier, Caswell-Massey mailed one million catalogs in 1988. This direct marketing effort will continue to expand in step with new store openings. These catalogs, in addition to driving store

Caswell-Massey's publications are one of those rare catalog birds that we look forward to seeing every season. They're always fresh and new. The artwork and typography are lively and entertaining, yet packed with information. Caswell's 236-year history is never forgotten, but never belabored. In almost every case, one is made aware of the antecedents of the product and why Caswell-Massey chose to offer that particular item to their customers. The consistent copy theme is: "We created and/or discovered this for you, because we care about you."

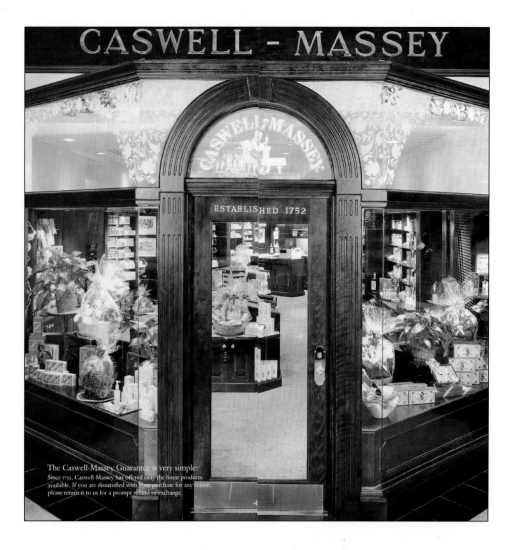

Caswell-Massey is making vigorous inroads into the retail community. To emphasize this direction, a 2-page spread on pages 48-49 of this catalog shows a large photograph of the front of a typical new Caswell-Massey emporium. On the same spread, an unequivocal copy block reiterates Caswell-Massey's uncomplicated and all-inclusive guarantee. The message is clear: Inside these doors is someone you can trust.

traffic, are directly responsible for more than 15% of Caswell-Massey's gross sales—more than four times the dollar volume of the average C-M store.

The Plan: stores where concentrations of customers are dense enough to maintain store traffic, catalogs to reach individuals no matter where they may be, and where the two market segments overlap, the catalog performs the dual function of building both store traffic and mailorder sales.

Caswell-Massey has a difficult marketing job. A goodly percentage of their customers are diplomats, socialites, celebrities and others in our society who live contemporary, on-the-go life-styles. Another group of customers are traditionalists, some of whom have been C-M customers for more than fifty years. The common denominator that Caswell shares with these customers is the certitude that they all deserve to be pampered.

COACH LEATHERWARE

There are many roads to success in the retail/mailorder world, but few have attempted the precision and style of the refined and understated Coach Leatherware catalogs. Coach manufactures a line of classic, high-quality men's and women's leathergoods. True, the products are not unique, but the presentation is. It has to do with style. This is a tightly run ship in every sense of the word: well organized, squeaky-clean, no extraneous fluff, firm hand on the tiller, controlled. Coach Leatherware is now a division of Sara Lee, and the hand at Coach's steady helm is that of President Lew Frankfurt.

The digest-sized Coach catalogs are masterpieces of calculated understatement. Laced throughout with photos and stories of Coach craftsmen at work, these gems have only two messages:

1. *"We produce only the finest leathergoods available"*.
2. *"Every item is perfectly capable of selling itself"*.

Design and photography are absolutely pure. Minimal props, no slashed type and no discounted prices. Each item of merchandise is allowed to make its own statement without embellishment.

The books have been produced for the last five years by Pluzynski/Associates in Manhattan. Ed Pluzynski and his team are, of course, delighted with the positive results these years have shown. He credits Lew Frankfurt with providing the driving force to constantly test and refine Coach's presentations and marketing.

A catalogue of classic Coach® bags, belts, wallets, briefcases and other accessories made out of natural leather and solid brass.

Holiday 1987

COACH LEATHERWARE—Holiday 1987
Lew Frankfurt, *President*
Lorilea Boulden, *Catalog Director*
Pluzynski/Associates, *Agency*
Jim Alexander, *Consultant*
John Schwarz, *Designer*
Donald Penny, *Photographer*
Arandell-Schmidt [Menomonee Falls, WI], *Printer, on 65# Hopper Coachweave for cover and 60# Sterling Web Dull for text*
Color Control [Redmond, WA], *Color Separator*

Makers of fine leathergoods for men and women.
Winter 1988

We note, with interest, what appears to be a test of a new cover design for Coach. Traditionally, their covers have been a handsome and very distinctive embossed design. However, the cover of their Winter 1988 catalog is a 4-color photograph, sans embossing. This break with tradition will certainly get the attention of old customers. There is no question that this is a new catalog, and consumers will assume that the merchandise has been refreshed. Happily, the Coach Leatherware identity is still loud and clear, with the original logo at the top of the page, and a strong rendition of the famous Coach Tag dead center where it cannot be missed.

One of the many steps that goes into the making of a Coach bag or briefcase is the assignment of an individual registration number. The machine shown here brands the number onto the item's inside pocket.

The number is unique to that particular Coach bag or briefcase, and can prove to be quite helpful should your bag ever need repair.

A registration card can be found in every Coach bag or briefcase. By completing the card and returning it to us, you are identified as a Coach consumer and are assured of a continued subscription to future Coach catalogues as well as information on new Coach items and colors.

All Coach products can be ordered directly from our factory and are sent to you free of any shipping or handling charges. To order call toll-free, day or night: (800) 223-8647

Nº9755 Pocket Purse $104

A member of the Coach collection that is favored by consumers in our retail stores. Women appreciate the fact that it offers as much room as our Basic Bag and has three pockets to keep things organized. There's a full-length outside pocket for quick access, another under the flap and a drop pocket inside. Comes with a 44″ detachable strap. A shorter (36″) strap can be substituted upon request. Dimensions: 9½″ x 5¾″ x 2″

Available in all ten Coach Colors shown on page two. Pictured in Red.

9

Every Coach product is stamped with a unique registration number. Registration cards are furnished for customers to fill in and send to Coach. This can be useful if repairs are ever needed. And incidentally, when you return your registration card, it assures your place on the Coach mailing list.

Coach Lightweights are introduced on these pages with their own distinctive color palette. These elegant styles are made of full-grain, natural Glove Tanned Cowhide, an usually soft and supple leather. A tight detail photo illustrates the fine stitching and seam binding that are the hallmarks of this line.

A Few Words About Coach® Lightweights

Taupe
Saddle
Buckskin
Bone
Khaki
Honey
Cocoa
Wine
Blue
Red
Black

These Coach Tags represent the eleven Coach Lightweights Colors now in production for our Coach Lightweights Collection featured on pages 28 through 39 in this catalogue. Because the natural color tones of our leather are difficult to reproduce in print, this chart is intended only as a guide.

Since its recent introduction, our Coach Lightweights Collection has been warmly embraced by our consumers.

Classically styled, Coach Lightweights are made of full-grain, natural Glove Tanned Cowhide—carefully prepared in a special process that renders it soft, supple, and long wearing.

These unstructured bags are meant to be worn often for work and leisure. The pouch-like shapes are designed to take full advantage of the leather's light, soft, supple qualities and include the details you have come to expect from Coach—solid brass hardware, outside seam bindings and handy inside pockets.

Coach Lightweights are available in a wide range of colors—from deep rich earth tones to several lighter shades. This palette of eleven distinctive colors complements the new silhouettes and also gives you a broad range of options—appropriate for every climate and every season.

Nº4040 Swinger $106

A bag with easy elegance and classic styling. Complements both casual and business attire and goes easily from daytime to evenings out. This crescent shape holds quite a lot while still offering a slender silhouette. Solid brass zipper closure, inside pocket, and a 38″ detachable shoulder strap with solid brass nautical hardware. Dimensions: 12″ x 8¼″ x 3½″

Black, Blue, Bone, Cocoa, Red, Saddle, Taupe, Wine shown on page 28. Pictured in Black.

Fine stitching and outside seam binding are details found on Coach Lightweights.

Nº 7215 Squeeze Keycase in British Tan, $18, shown on page 40.

28

29

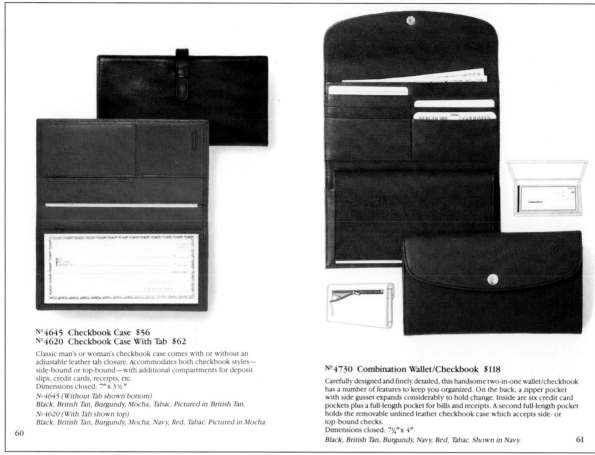

N⁰ 4645 Checkbook Case $56
N⁰ 4620 Checkbook Case With Tab $62

Classic man's or woman's checkbook case comes with or without an
adjustable leather tab closure. Accommodates both checkbook styles—
side-bound or top-bound—with additional compartments for deposit
slips, credit cards, receipts, etc.
Dimensions closed: 7″x 3½″
N⁰ 4645 (Without Tab shown bottom)
Black, British Tan, Burgundy, Mocha, Tabac. Pictured in British Tan.
N⁰ 4620 (With Tab shown top)
Black, British Tan, Burgundy, Mocha, Navy, Red, Tabac. Pictured in Mocha.

60

N⁰ 4730 Combination Wallet/Checkbook $118

Carefully designed and finely detailed, this handsome two-in-one wallet/checkbook
has a number of features to keep you organized. On the back, a zipper pocket
with side gusset expands considerably to hold change. Inside are six credit card
pockets plus a full-length pocket for bills and receipts. A second full-length pocket
holds the removable unlined leather checkbook case which accepts side- or
top-bound checks.
Dimensions closed: 7¼″ x 4″
Black, British Tan, Burgundy, Navy, Red, Tabac. Shown in Navy.

61

Where appropriate, pen-and-ink drawings are used
to highlight product features not shown in the
photos. On other pages, a second photograph serves
the same purpose.

Coach's utter simplicity of design is illustrated by
this spread. The copy is explicit, informative and
concise, yet it conveys a sense of warmth and
informality. The type face scans well, but is not
obtrusive. There is more than one kind of craftsman
on the Coach Team. The catalog is crafted as well as
the products it sells. The ACA Gold Award is well
deserved.

N⁰ 5190 Envelope Portfolio $176

Women are finding the softer, less structured appearance of this
legal-size brief ideal for much more than business. Spacious enough
for a day's worth of work yet trim enough to function beautifully as a
purse or a tote. There's plenty of room for newspapers, files or even
your shoes. The envelope flap has no closure so it adjusts smoothly
to cover the bag's contents. An inside zipper pocket keeps keys,
coins and wallet handy and secure. The mid-length straps are long
enough to wear over the shoulder. Dimensions: 16½″x 11″x 3½″
*Black, British Tan, Burgundy, Flannel Grey, Mocha, Navy, Putty, Red,
Tabac shown on page two. Pictured in Putty.*

N⁰ 5180 Metropolitan Brief Bag $222

This handsome, legal-size case is a favorite choice among men and women
who shop our Coach stores. They find its size perfect for business needs, and
its features ideal for travel or commuting. It has a roomy interior, a full-length
outside back pocket for newspapers and often-used files, a gussetted pocket
under the flap for bulky items, and an inside drop pocket for small items. The
shoulder strap detaches, and the solid brass buckles tuck away neatly inside.
Dimensions: 16″x 11″x 2½″
*Black, British Tan, Burgundy, Flannel Grey, Mocha, Navy, Tabac shown on
page two. Pictured in Black.*

44

45

CRATE & BARREL

The following letter was published on the first page of a special Crate and Barrel catalog. President Gordon Segal celebrated C & B's 25th year in business with a statement of principle. The following excerpts exemplify an attitude that all upscale life-style storekeepers, both large and small, would do well to consider carefully.

Twenty Five Years Of Crate and Barrel Gifts

Our stores now stretch from the East coast to the California coast. Our catalogues now reach nearly 4 million people. Our buyers now travel to corners of the world we wouldn't have even imagined 25 years ago.

But in spirit our company still remains "small".

We're still entrepreneurial. We still realize it's our customers, not our products or our store fixtures, that are the most important part of the Crate and Barrel.

We still believe they want gifts that are truly unique. But, we still believe they'll always need basic items for the home that are not only beautifully designed, but affordably priced.

We still believe they have rapidly changing life-styles and that a store should be as prepared to equip a home office one year as it was a gourmet cook's kitchen a few years before.

We still believe they have a vast array of shopping choices and that a store's responsibility is to make those choices easier by only offering what it considers to be the very best in a category, whether it's dinnerware that will last for generations or a tin of English toffee that may only last through Christmas Day.

We still believe customers will always want something that seems to have almost disappeared today — service— and the friendly, knowledgeable, imaginative sales staff that supplies it.

And we still believe one more thing. We still believe that after 25 years, a store should be as excited about the future as the day it opened.

CRATE & BARREL—Crate and Barrel Gifts
Gordon Segal, *President*
Carla Swirsky, *Catalog Director*
Herb Krug & Associates, *Consultant*
Tom Shortlidge and Ron Villani, *Designers*
Meg Pradelt, *Copywriter*
Laurie Rubin, *Photographer*
Foote & Davies, *Printer, on 80# Mesa for cover and text*
Graphic Arts Studio [Barrington, IL], *Color Separator*

25 years, 20 stores and many millions of catalogs later, Mr. Segal is still running the Crate and Barrel business with the same enthusiasm and philosophy as when he started. He has identified some of the keys to his success from which all may profit:

- *Insist upon exemplary Customer Service.*
- *Train buyers to project sensitivity and react swiftly to their (largely contemporary) customers' wants and needs.*
- *Select unique products from all over the world, and purchase directly, not through distributors.*
- *Assist customers by offering the best in each merchandise category.*
- *Be constantly aware of macro marketing trends.*

If you are blessed with a Crate and Barrel store in your neighborhood, you may have experienced these principles in action. You may also have noticed the excitement generated by the ever-changing displays and frequently refreshed merchandise.

Those of us who are fortunate enough to be on the Crate and Barrel mailing list feel the same way about the catalogs. The books present items that are the newest, the most unusual and yet, one is made to feel, the most practical to be had anywhere. As one American Catalog Awards judge noted: ''The format has, basically, remained the same, but the catalog always looks fresh because the merchandise always looks fresh.''

The gourmet/tabletop industry has had a number of difficult years in recent history. A number of independent stores and store chains have gone under or been merged out of existence. Through all this turmoil, Crate and Barrel continues to grow and be successful. Gordon Segal's years of management successes and consideration for his employees have provided a firm foundation for growth.

Exhibiting an equal sensitivity to his customers' desires, new lines such as storage, furniture, linens, lighting and luggage have been added to Crate and Barrel's merchandise mix. But one thing will not change: Mr. Segel's consumer-oriented mindset.

The production of the Crate & Barrel catalog shows a caring attitude. Type is easily read, well keyed, and the four-color reproduction is precise. Mixed paper stocks of good quality lend enough bulk to this 40-page catalog to give it the hand of a larger book. And, while one might argue for an order form printed on offset stock, this is, after all, a retail (not mailorder) catalog.

On the creative side: utterly simple layouts permit the merchandise to make its own statements. Ample use of white space keeps the reader's eye fresh and permits the use of captions to help relate copy to art. While all these elements are very well done, special accolades are reserved for the photographer/stylist/director team responsible for the photographs. Technically, the photos reflect a great *simpatico* for the

merchandise. Lighting, camera angles and densities change as items change in reaction to the individuality of each product.

Two additional creative assets help to make these photos stand out from the mundane. The first is an almost subliminally whimsical attitude towards the placement of the photographic subjects.

A. The color of these flared vases is rich and sophisticated, yet soothing and easy to live with. It has an ability to blend into virtually any room setting or become a striking focal point. Handblown in America exclusively for Crate and Barrel, these elegant vases come in floor and table sizes. 7½"H x 5¾"D. #4257. $23.95 ($3.00). 12¼"H x 8"D. #4258. $36.95 ($3.75). Blue glass marbles support floral arrangements. Approximately 250 marbles. #4259. $5.95 ($2.75).

B. Add drama, elegance and beauty to any occasion with these spectacular 10¾" tall flute champagnes. Their distinctive combination of clear and colored glass is achieved by blowing the bowl from cobalt glass cased in clear crystal, then pulling the stem from the clear glass only. Set of four 7 oz. champagnes. #4266. $27.95 ($2.50).

C. The beauty of this handblown optic vase lies not only in the alternating panels of clear and luster glass, but also in the revival of a glass-making technique that is traditional in Czechoslovakia but rarely seen here. A Crate and Barrel exclusive, this 8"H vase is especially lovely when light plays off the bands of luster cranberry, amber, violet and blue. #4265. $21.95 ($2.25).

D. The delicate swirl of color on these crystal clear balls will hold the same fascination for you today as the colored balls of your childhood. And at half the price of 1984, there's something nostalgic about the cost too.

Handblown in the famed Swedish glass factory of Kosta Boda, the set of six includes 2 each in red, green and blue swirls. #4267. Reg. $60.00. Special selling, $29.95 ($2.50).

E. Used together or separately, our exclusive new cobalt pitcher and ever-popular Crescent barware present a distinctive alternative for serving cocktails or any beverage. The classic all-purpose pitcher is handblown, has an ice lip and generous 2-quart capacity. #4260. $19.95 ($2.50). The beautifully simple handblown barware has cut and polished rims. Set of six 14 oz. highballs. #4261. $23.95 ($2.50). Set of six 10 oz. double old fashioneds. #4262. $23.95 ($2.50).

F. Combining color, form and function, this simple glass bowl becomes so much more than a well-priced piece of handblown glass. Its simple, classic form works in any environment and allows it to function as a centerpiece or serving bowl. 10" diameter. #4263. $19.95 ($2.50). New this year, 5¼" individual bowls add to the versatility of the larger bowl. Set of six. #4264. $29.95 ($3.00).

G. These lovely handblown oval glass ornaments have a delicate luster finish to add shimmer and sparkle to your tree. Approximately 3½" long. Set of six. #4268. $14.95 ($2.50).

Phone Orders: For your convenience, you can shop by phone 24 hours a day. To place your order, call Toll Free 1-800-323-5461.

B. Blue Flute Champagnes.

C. Ribbon Vase.

D. Kosta Line Ornaments.

E. Cobalt Pitcher and Crescent Barware.

F. Cobalt Bowl.

G. Luster Ornaments.

A. Flared Cobalt Vases and Marbles.

A. This new stoneware dinnerware has the look of natural terracotta, but is actually durable, dishwasher safe stoneware. With a glossy white glaze, it's generously sized and reasonably priced. 20-piece starter set includes 4 each of dinner plate, salad plate, soup, cup and saucer. #5221. $79.95 ($7.00). 5-piece completer set. #5222. $39.95 ($4.00).

B. This oven-safe covered casserole can be used for baking and serving. Natural terracotta outside, it is glazed inside. 7½"x4½"H. #1244. $14.95 ($2.50).

C. For serving hot dips, this 3-piece set has a glazed 1 quart terracotta bowl, warming stand and candle. #1246. $16.95 ($2.50). Set of 10 replacement candles. #5205. $3.50 ($.75).

D. Our beechwood mug rack is an attractive way to keep 8 mugs handy. #1236. $9.95 ($2.25). Set of six 10 oz. stoneware mugs are dishwasher and microwave safe. #5223. $17.95 ($2.50).

E. This beechwood, slice and serve crumb catcher has a removable slat top and a serrated bread knife. 16"x8½". #1249. $15.95 ($2.25).

F. Our maple handled knives have riveted, full-tang blades made of high carbon and stainless steel. Our 7-piece set includes a 3½" utility, 5" boner, 6" utility/trimmer, 9" slicer, 8" chef's knife, 10" sharpening steel, in a solid maple block. #1247. Reg. $122.00. Special selling, $89.95 ($3.50).

A. Sienna Dinnerware.

B. Terracotta Casserole.

C. Hot Dip Server.

D. Mug Tree and Sienna Mugs.

E. Crumb Catcher.

I. Knife Block Set.

G. Classic Pitcher.

J. Fajitas Server and Accessories.

H. Canisters with Scoops and Spice Jars.

F. Oak Canister Set.

K. Chip/Dip and Salsa Set.

G. The superior quality of the porcelain used in this creamy white 3 qt. pitcher helps to retain the temperatures of beverages served in it. The classic design is American-made by Hall China. #1243. $17.95 ($2.25).

H. These gleaming white, airtight ceramic canisters have convenient wooden scoops. Savings of 40% off regular prices. 35 oz. jar. #1237. $19.95 ($1.75). 56 oz. jar. #1238. $21.95 ($1.75). 70 oz. jar. #1239. $23.95 ($1.75). Airtight 3 oz. spice jars. 6 white ceramic jars. #1241. $19.95 ($2.00). 6 glass jars. #1242. $19.95 ($2.00).

I. These solid oak canisters have plastic liners and snug fitting lids. 4-pc. set. #1248. Special selling, $69.95 ($4.00).

J. Our exclusive new fajitas server combines a handled, oval cast iron skillet and a thick wood board to protect your table. Set of skillet and board. #1250. $14.95 ($2.25). Seasonings and condiments for making fajitas. 11½ oz. jar of marinade, a 4¾ oz. bottle of seasonings, an 11½ oz. bottle of medium hot, fresh salsa and a cookbook. #1251. $19.95 ($2.25).

K. Serve chips and dips in this one-piece terracotta server. Glazed inside, it is dishwasher safe. 10"D. #1245. $16.95 ($2.50). To complete the party, add our Tex-Mex set. Includes 1 jar each of chili con queso, mild salsa and extra hot green salsa. Set of 3. #1283. $14.95 ($2.25).

A. Produced by the world famous Villeroy and Boch factory and available in America only at Crate and Barrel, this elegant porcelain glazed dinnerware is a rich, dramatic red subtly edged in black. The 20-piece starter set includes 4 each of 10½" dinner plate, 8½" salad plate, soup/cereal bowl, cup and saucer. #5212. Open stock, $188.00. Special selling, $99.00 ($5.50). 8" serving bowl. #5213. $18.95 ($2.00). Sugar and creamer. #5214. $22.95 ($2.00). 12½" round platter. #5215. $22.95 ($2.00).

B. These stoneware pieces from Bennington Potters are microwave, oven and dishwasher safe. All have soft white interiors and matte black exteriors. Set of four oval bakers. #1217. Reg. $24.00. Special selling, $19.95 ($2.75). New, 12 oz. soup bowls. Set of four. #1218. Reg. $24.00. Special selling, $19.95 ($2.75). Set of four 12 oz. mugs. #1219. Reg. $20.00. Special selling, $16.95 ($2.75).

C. Calphalon's® new stir-fry pan has a unique shape, almost like a flat-bottomed wok. Coupled with Calphalon's® superior conductivity, easy-clean surface and stay-cool handle, it answers today's need to eat well with little time and effort. Recipes included 10½"D. #1216. $43.95 ($2.50).

D. This new Krups espresso has a unique heating system that delivers consistently hot water and steam to make rich espresso and foam several cups of cappuccino. This stainless

A. Granada 20-Piece Starter Set Accessories.

B. Bennington Mugs, Bakers and Soups.

C. Calphalon Stir-Fry Pan.　　D. Krups Espresso Novo.

E. Mugs and Tray Set.　　F. 35-Bottle Wine Rack.

G. Jumbo and Demi Cups and Saucers.　　H. Electric Wok.

and black electric espresso also has a removable 28 oz. water tank with water level indicator, removable drip tray, one- and two-cup stainless coffee baskets and a stainless frothing pitcher. #1220. Reg. $275.00. Special selling, $225.00 ($6.00).

E. Our exclusive high fired Italian ceramic mugs have a grey, faux granite glaze with a snappy red rim. Microwave and dishwasher safe. Set of four 15 oz. mugs. #5216. $32.95 ($2.50). To complement the mugs, lacquered gallery trays in white with black speckles and red rim. 16¾"x 11¼"x 1½" and 19"x 12¼"x 1¾". Set of two. #2201. $29.95 ($3.00).

F. Made in France, this professional style black iron wine rack provides secure, properly angled storage for 35 bottles of wine. A compact 27"x 20"x 10"D. #2202. $26.95 ($3.75).

G. The rich black and vibrant red glazes of these high fired Italian ceramics are lead-free. Cups hold 22 oz. Set of two jumbos. #5217. $14.95 ($2.50). Set of four 3 oz. espresso cups and saucers. #5218. $18.95 ($2.50).

H. With all the versatility of a Chinese wok and the added convenience of its own electric heat source, this new electric wok becomes an indispensable asset. Made of die-cast aluminum, it is thermostatically controlled and has a non-stick surface. Included with the 6½ qt., 14" wok are a steaming rack, wooden spatula and spoon and recipe book. #1215. $69.95 ($3.00).

17

A. Set a dramatic holiday table or dine colorfully all year with our exclusive, deep red German ceramic dinnerware. Dishwasher and microwave safe. 20-piece starter set includes 4 each of dinner plate, salad plate, soup/cereal, cup and saucer. #5219. $89.95 ($7.00). 5-piece completer set. #5220. $49.95 ($4.00).

B. This outfitted picnic hamper has everything in it but the food. Equipped for 4, it contains melamine dinner plates, acrylic wine glasses, plastic flatware, a 54"x54" red and white cotton tablecloth and napkins, two 4-cup food boxes, covered salt and pepper shakers, cutting board and spreader, combination knife/cork-screw/cap lifter and 4 candleholders with candles. 30-piece set is our exclusive. #2251. $74.95 ($5.25).

Phone Orders: For your convenience, you can shop by phone 24 hours a day. To place your order, call Toll Free 1-800-323-5461. If number is busy call Toll Free 1-800-228-5000. Illinois residents call 1-800-942-8791.

A. Redstone Dinnerware.

B. Outfitted Picnic Hamper.

C. Beechwood Cooler/Ice Bucket.　　D. Placemats and Napkins.

E. Beechwood Bowl.　　F. Lazy Susan.

G. Wood Chip Trees.　　H. Electric Candle Lights.

I. Maple Wine Rack.　　J. Straw Reindeer.

C. This simply styled, staved beechwood cooler is large enough to cool a bottle of wine or keep a party going for hours. 11½"Hx8"D. #2256. $29.95 ($2.50).

D. These imported, all-cotton, 13"x 18" placemats and easy-care 19"x 19" napkins make a wonderful gift. Set of 8 red mats. #3216. $22.95 ($2.00). Set of 8 check mats. #3217. $22.95 ($2.00). Set of 8 red napkins. USA. #3218. $15.95 ($1.75).

E. This divided bowl can be filled with nuts, crudités, candy for holiday entertaining. 8½"D. #1284. $13.95 ($2.25).

F. Created of 1¾" thick beechwood, our lazy susan is a generous 14" diameter, rotates smoothly. #1282. $14.95 ($2.50).

G. These handcrafted natural pine trees are handcrafted in Germany. Set includes one each of a 4",5",6",7" and 8" tree. #4252. $18.95 ($2.00).

H. Recreate a European tradition by lighting a window each night during the Christmas season. Made in Sweden. Holds 5 white electric candles. UL approved, it is 12"H, 14"W. #4253. Special selling, $24.95 ($2.75). Set of 3 spare bulbs. #4254. $3.50 ($.75).

I. This maple wine rack can assume any desired configuration. Up to 40 bottle capacity. #2255. $59.95 ($5.25).

J. These handcrafted straw reindeer have a graceful simplicity. Handmade in Spain. Approximately 14"H. Set of 2, as shown. #2254. $59.95 ($3.00).

21

In the more obvious cases of whimsey, dinnerware is stacked in an improbable state of imbalance, counterweighted by an out-of-context piece of flatware or stemware. Elsewhere, one has to look carefully for more subtle evidence of droll humor. Example: woodenware sets, more or less straight, except that one piece has been knocked over, spilling its contents (in a carefully contrived pattern) over the tablecloth. As you look at these photos, observe how the homeowner seems to have left the room for only a minute—unaware that a leprechaun lurked, ready to tweak things just a wee bit askew. All these little touches add a lilt to each page, hint at fun to come, and keep the reader entranced.

The second paean of praise is for the photo stylist and/or director for their choice of props.

A. For a home office, this 50"x23½"x29"H oak desk can be used as is, or equipped with our slide-out keyboard drawer and monitor bridge. Easy to assemble. Oak desk. #2207. $225.00 ($32.00). Keyboard drawer. #2208. $49.95 ($5.00). Monitor bridge. #2209. $44.95 ($4.00). The scaled-down classic Stendig calendar, in warm taupe and red. 18"x24". #2203. $11.95 ($2.50).

B. Our exclusive 3-piece solid oak top table set has an 18"x40"x16½"H coffee table and a pair of 18"x18"x15"H cocktail tables underneath it. Easy to assemble. #2205. $135.00 ($9.00).

C. This solid oak wine and glass rack holds 20 bottles, plus up to 12 glasses. 36" high, with a 14"x19" top, it doubles as a bar. #2211. $99.00 ($9.00).

D. This 3-shelf, rolling oak cart is designed to be used almost anywhere in the home. 24"Hx 19¾"Wx14⅝"D. #2210. $64.95 ($8.00).

E. Simplify entertaining with this 5-piece set. The solid oak cart stores 4 tray tables and expands from 12"x24"x35¼"H to 28"x24" with its leaves up. Cart with 4 tray tables. #2212. $199.00 ($13.00). Set of four oak tray tables on a stationary storage rack. #2213. $99.95 ($10.00).

F. American made for Crate and Barrel, this solid oak cart has 27½"x 20" shelves, and its gliding middle shelf holds top or front loading VCRs. #2214. $135.00 ($13.00).

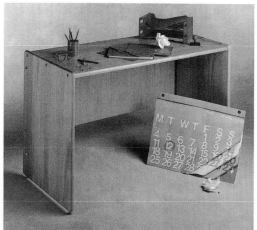

A. Oak Desk and Calendar.

C. Oak Wine Rack.

D. Oak Multipurpose Cart.

B. Coffee Table Set.

E. Oak Entertainment Set.

F. Oak TV/VCR Cart.

Beautiful though an item may be, the highest and best use of the product is not always self-evident. Enter the stylist to set things right. She knows that heavy-handed, cluttered accessorizing can kill a product and confuse the customer. At the other extreme, a total absence of props may leave too much of the expository burden on copy (which, in this book, is minimal). The Crate and Barrel creatives have, in almost every instance, hit just the right balance. Minimal though the props may be, there's at least a hint of purpose in almost every photograph, a little welcome guidance for the customer. Another example of how much Crate and Barrel cares.

HAMMACHER SCHLEMMER

No doubt by now you've decided catalog programs are a serious, complex business. Quite right—for management and investors. But there's the other side. From the reader's point of view, catalogs are a form of entertainment, a source of information, an indicator of trends and database of prices, new products and new ideas. Catalogs are fun! It's fun reading about your hobby or about new products that relate directly to your business. It's fun going through an incentive catalog, picking out the award you have just won. Boat owners can warm their hearts, if not their hauled-out yachts, with the glow of a Spring catalog from "Boat US".

High on our list of entertaining, fun catalogs is Hammacher Schlemmer's gee-gaw loaded, male oriented compilation of absolute nonessentials.

The first page in the history of Hammacher Schlemmer was written on New York's Bowery in 1848. Starting as a hardware store, Hammacher later become known as the place to buy Hard to Find Tools. As the years went by, swages, sawbummers, plumb bobs and pin punches were replaced by esoteria such as piano repair tools and replacement parts for pianos (HS was the largest source in the East), automotive accessories for the new horseless carriage, and fancy commode pulls.

In the year 1881, Hammacher Schlemmer published their first catalog. Since then, they have published at least one catalog every year—for 107 years—making theirs one of the oldest catalog programs in the United States. Early Hammacher catalogs were not exactly mere bulletins or flyers. They were full-fledged books that bulked to a thousand and more pages by the early 1900s.

Time passed, wars were fought and won, and the New York social set migrated northward. In 1926, Hammacher Schlemmer made the move uptown—in fact, and in merchandising philosophy. Customers of the new store at 147 East 57th Street were greeted by doormen in tophats and tailcoats, and a sales staff dressed in dark suits, starched collars and ties.

The modish uptown HS customer had plenty of disposable income and a penchant for the unusual. In response to the whims of their new carriage trade franchise, Hammacher Schlemmer became 'Purveyors of the Unique'. Gone were the last vestiges of the original hardware heritage. In its place came a flood of the newest, the most unusual, and in some cases, the most delightfully impractical items ever offered to the public.

Some of the most unusual items of bygone days are with us now as virtually indispensable household appliances. A list of Hammacher's "firsts" would have to include: The first Pop-up Toaster (1930), Electric Dry Shaver (1934), Automatic Steam Iron (1948), Electric Toothbrush (1955), the Microwave Oven and the Telephone Answering Machine (1968), Mr. Coffee (1973), Cordless Telephone (1975), and the Cuisinarts' Food Processor in 1976. One could hardly imagine then that these esoteric, sometimes one-of-a-kind devices—to be found only on Hammacher's shelves—would become ubiquitous, tonnage commodities discounted today in every shopping mall across our Nation.

At Hammacher Schlemmer, innovation is still the rule. Recent catalogs have featured: Three-person Submarines at a bargain $22,500, a space-age, $30,000, Wind-Propelled Land Cruiser, an Orthopedic Pet Bed, an electronic Deer Repeller for your auto, an

HAMMACHER SCHLEMMER
John R. MacArthur, *Chairman*
Richard Tinberg, *President*
Tom Yocky, *Director of Marketing*
James Summers, *Creative Director*

Fun catalogs are serious business at Hammacher Schlemmer. Though there are three stores (Beverly Hills, Chicago and New York), the catalogs bring in 75% of gross receipts. To accomplish this kind of mailorder sales volume, Hammacher mails over twenty million catalogs every year. Their two million active customers can receive up to ten catalogs per year, depending upon their buying habits and annual purchase amounts.

Electric Clam & Oyster Knife, a Motorized Dispensing Spice Rack, a Talking Computer Bridge Player, and an Electronic Cat Door that opens for your cat only.

Not all Hammacher's items are new. Many of the best sellers are held over. Two Hammacher Schlemmer classics that come to mind are the English Heated Towel Stand (if you've ever used one of these, you'll understand why), and a really rugged little Hand-held Vacuum—manufactured and sold continuously in the Hammacher Schlemmer catalog since 1937.

A typical bit of Hammacher product history:

One night in 1967, a gentleman from Indiana inverted a saucepan over a small electric motor in an attempt to assuage his wife's debilitating bout of sleeplessness. He thereby invented "white sound" and the first of the now omnipresent soothing sound machines for insomniacs. The original machine, and many of the more advanced versions, have been introduced and sold exclusively by Hammacher Schlemmer.

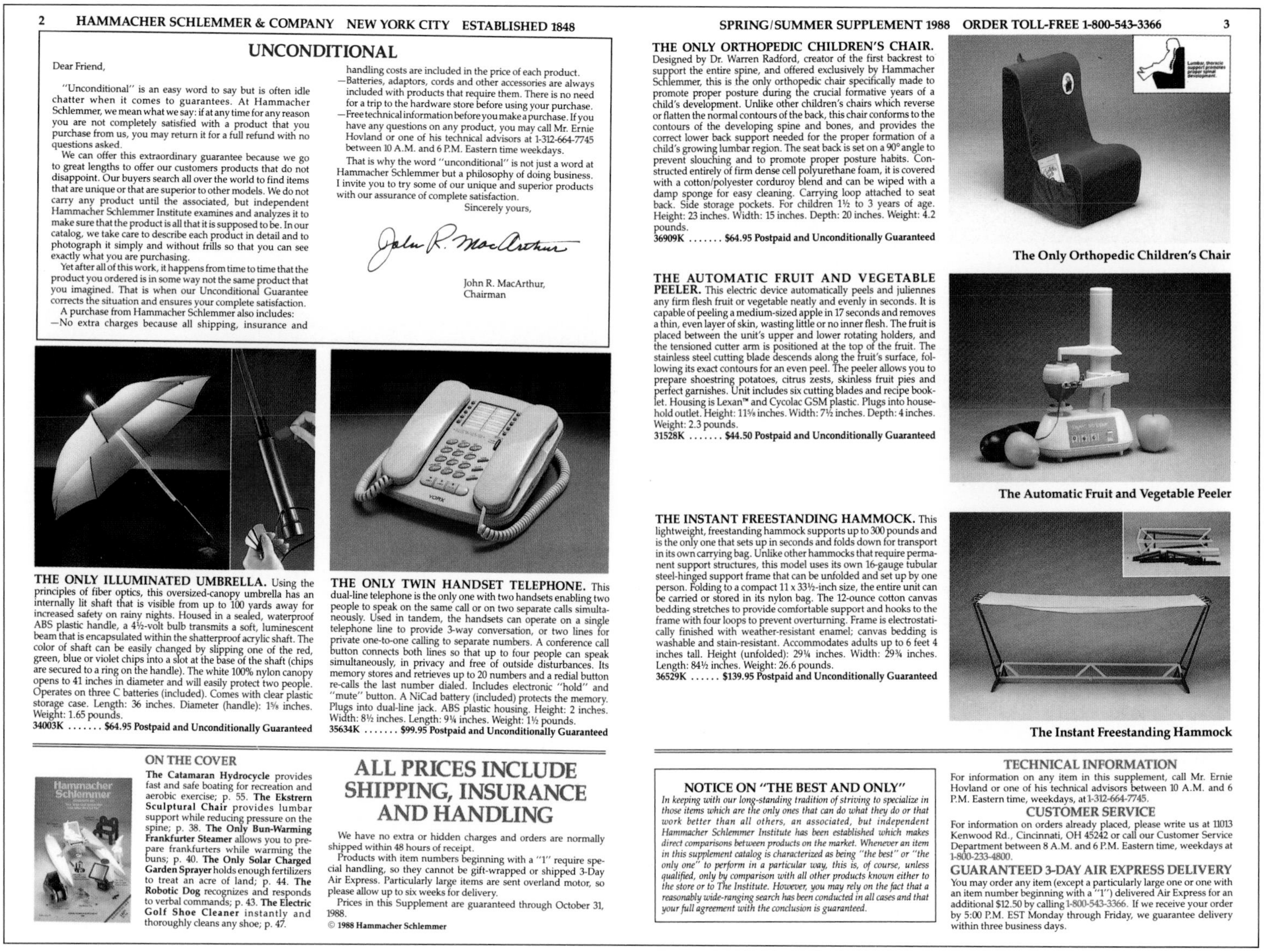

2 HAMMACHER SCHLEMMER & COMPANY NEW YORK CITY ESTABLISHED 1848

UNCONDITIONAL

Dear Friend,

"Unconditional" is an easy word to say but is often idle chatter when it comes to guarantees. At Hammacher Schlemmer, we mean what we say: if at any time for any reason you are not completely satisfied with a product that you purchase from us, you may return it for a full refund with no questions asked.

We can offer this extraordinary guarantee because we go to great lengths to offer our customers products that do not disappoint. Our buyers search all over the world to find items that are unique or that are superior to other models. We do not carry any product until the associated, but independent Hammacher Schlemmer Institute examines and analyzes it to make sure that the product is all that it is supposed to be. In our catalog, we take care to describe each product in detail and to photograph it simply and without frills so that you can see exactly what you are purchasing.

Yet after all of this work, it happens from time to time that the product you ordered is in some way not the same product that you imagined. That is when our Unconditional Guarantee corrects the situation and ensures your complete satisfaction.

A purchase from Hammacher Schlemmer also includes:

—No extra charges because all shipping, insurance and handling costs are included in the price of each product.

—Batteries, adaptors, cords and other accessories are always included with products that require them. There is no need for a trip to the hardware store before using your purchase.

—Free technical information before you make a purchase. If you have any questions on any product, you may call Mr. Ernie Hovland or one of his technical advisors at 1-312-664-7745 between 10 A.M. and 6 P.M. Eastern time weekdays.

That is why the word "unconditional" is not just a word at Hammacher Schlemmer but a philosophy of doing business. I invite you to try some of our unique and superior products with our assurance of complete satisfaction.

Sincerely yours,

John R. MacArthur

John R. MacArthur,
Chairman

THE ONLY ILLUMINATED UMBRELLA. Using the principles of fiber optics, this oversized-canopy umbrella has an internally lit shaft that is visible from up to 100 yards away for increased safety on rainy nights. Housed in a sealed, waterproof ABS plastic handle, a 4½-volt bulb transmits a soft, luminescent beam that is encapsulated within the shatterproof acrylic shaft. The color of shaft can be easily changed by slipping one of the red, green, blue or violet chips into a slot at the base of the shaft (chips are secured to a ring on the handle). The white 100% nylon canopy opens to 41 inches in diameter and will easily protect two people. Operates on three C batteries (included). Comes with clear plastic storage case. Length: 36 inches. Diameter (handle): 1⅝ inches. Weight: 1.65 pounds.
34003K .... $64.95 Postpaid and Unconditionally Guaranteed

THE ONLY TWIN HANDSET TELEPHONE. This dual-line telephone is the only one with two handsets enabling two people to speak on the same call or on two separate calls simultaneously. Used in tandem, the handsets can operate on a single telephone line to provide 3-way conversation, or two lines for private one-to-one calling to separate numbers. A conference call button connects both lines so that up to four people can speak simultaneously, in privacy and free of outside disturbances. Its memory stores and retrieves up to 20 numbers and a redial button re-calls the last number dialed. Includes electronic "hold" and "mute" button. A NiCad battery (included) protects the memory. Plugs into dual-line jack. ABS plastic housing. Height: 2 inches. Width: 8½ inches. Length: 9¼ inches. Weight: 1½ pounds.
35634K .... $99.95 Postpaid and Unconditionally Guaranteed

ON THE COVER

The Catamaran Hydrocycle provides fast and safe boating for recreation and aerobic exercise; p. 55. **The Ekstrern Sculptural Chair** provides lumbar support while reducing pressure on the spine; p. 38. **The Only Bun-Warming Frankfurter Steamer** allows you to prepare frankfurters while warming the buns; p. 40. **The Only Solar Charged Garden Sprayer** holds enough fertilizers to treat an acre of land; p. 44. **The Robotic Dog** recognizes and responds to verbal commands; p. 43. **The Electric Golf Shoe Cleaner** instantly and thoroughly cleans any shoe; p. 47.

ALL PRICES INCLUDE SHIPPING, INSURANCE AND HANDLING

We have no extra or hidden charges and orders are normally shipped within 48 hours of receipt.

Products with item numbers beginning with a "1" require special handling, so they cannot be gift-wrapped or shipped 3-Day Air Express. Particularly large items are sent overland motor, so please allow up to six weeks for delivery.

Prices in this Supplement are guaranteed through October 31, 1988.

© 1988 Hammacher Schlemmer

SPRING/SUMMER SUPPLEMENT 1988 ORDER TOLL-FREE 1-800-543-3366 3

THE ONLY ORTHOPEDIC CHILDREN'S CHAIR. Designed by Dr. Warren Radford, creator of the first backrest to support the entire spine, and offered exclusively by Hammacher Schlemmer, this is the only orthopedic chair specifically made to promote proper posture during the crucial formative years of a child's development. Unlike other children's chairs which reverse or flatten the normal contours of the back, this chair conforms to the contours of the developing spine and bones, and provides the correct lower back support needed for the proper formation of a child's growing lumbar region. The seat back is set on a 90° angle to prevent slouching and to promote proper posture habits. Constructed entirely of firm dense cell polyurethane foam, it is covered with a cotton/polyester corduroy blend and can be wiped with a damp sponge for easy cleaning. Carrying loop attached to seat back. Side storage pockets. For children 1½ to 3 years of age. Height: 23 inches. Width: 15 inches. Depth: 20 inches. Weight: 4.2 pounds.
36909K .... $64.95 Postpaid and Unconditionally Guaranteed

The Only Orthopedic Children's Chair

THE AUTOMATIC FRUIT AND VEGETABLE PEELER. This electric device automatically peels and juliennes any firm flesh fruit or vegetable neatly and evenly in seconds. It is capable of peeling a medium-sized apple in 17 seconds and removes a thin, even layer of skin, wasting little or no inner flesh. The fruit is placed between the unit's upper and lower rotating holders, and the tensioned cutter arm is positioned at the top of the fruit. The stainless steel cutting blade descends along the fruit's surface, following its exact contours for an even peel. The peeler allows you to prepare shoestring potatoes, citrus zests, skinless fruit pies and perfect garnishes. Unit includes six cutting blades and recipe booklet. Housing is Lexan™ and Cycolac GSM plastic. Plugs into household outlet. Height: 11⅝ inches. Width: 7½ inches. Depth: 4 inches. Weight: 2.3 pounds.
31528K .... $44.50 Postpaid and Unconditionally Guaranteed

The Automatic Fruit and Vegetable Peeler

THE INSTANT FREESTANDING HAMMOCK. This lightweight, freestanding hammock supports up to 300 pounds and is the only one that sets up in seconds and folds down for transport in its own carrying bag. Unlike other hammocks that require permanent support structures, this model uses its own 16-gauge tubular steel-hinged support frame that can be unfolded and set up by one person. Folding to a compact 11 x 33½-inch size, the entire unit can be carried or stored in its nylon bag. The 12-ounce cotton canvas bedding stretches to provide comfortable support and hooks to the frame with four loops to prevent overturning. Frame is electrostatically finished with weather-resistant enamel; canvas bedding is washable and stain-resistant. Accommodates adults up to 6 feet 4 inches tall. Height (unfolded): 29¼ inches. Width: 29¾ inches. Length: 84½ inches. Weight: 26.6 pounds.
36529K ...... $139.95 Postpaid and Unconditionally Guaranteed

The Instant Freestanding Hammock

NOTICE ON "THE BEST AND ONLY"

In keeping with our long-standing tradition of striving to specialize in those items which are the only ones that can do what they do or that work better than all others, an associated, but independent Hammacher Schlemmer Institute has been established which makes direct comparisons between products on the market. Whenever an item in this supplement catalog is characterized as being "the best" or "the only one" to perform in a particular way, this is, of course, unless qualified, only by comparison with all other products known either to the store or to The Institute. However, you may rely on the fact that a reasonably wide-ranging search has been conducted in all cases and that your full agreement with the conclusion is guaranteed.

TECHNICAL INFORMATION

For information on any item in this supplement, call Mr. Ernie Hovland or one of his technical advisors between 10 A.M. and 6 P.M. Eastern time, weekdays, at 1-312-664-7745.

CUSTOMER SERVICE

For information on orders already placed, please write us at 11013 Kenwood Rd., Cincinnati, OH 45242 or call our Customer Service Department between 8 A.M. and 6 P.M. Eastern time, weekdays at 1-800-233-4800.

GUARANTEED 3-DAY AIR EXPRESS DELIVERY

You may order any item (except a particularly large one or one with an item number beginning with a "1") delivered Air Express for an additional $12.50 by calling 1-800-543-3366. If we receive your order by 5:00 P.M. EST Monday through Friday, we guarantee delivery within three business days.

Chairman John R. MacArthur makes a number of key statements in his "UNCONDITIONAL" letter on the inside front cover. He makes the point that their guarantee is of the "no questions asked" variety, but he takes the commitment much further. MacArthur describes the independent Hammacher Schlemmer Institute's product checks, and goes on to convey two important sales messages: 1). Batteries are included (where required) to save his customers from having to go to the local hardware store to buy same *before* using their new toy, and 2). All handling and shipping charges are included in the price of each product.

On this opening spread, a number of other messages are delivered:

- *A brief description and reference page numbers are given for items shown on the front cover.*
- *Customer Service and Technical Information telephone numbers are listed.*
- *Air Express Delivery is offered at a flat rate of $12.50.*
- *A more detailed description of the Hammacher Schlemmer Institute is given, along with a discussion of the meaning of their labels "The Best" or "The Only One".*

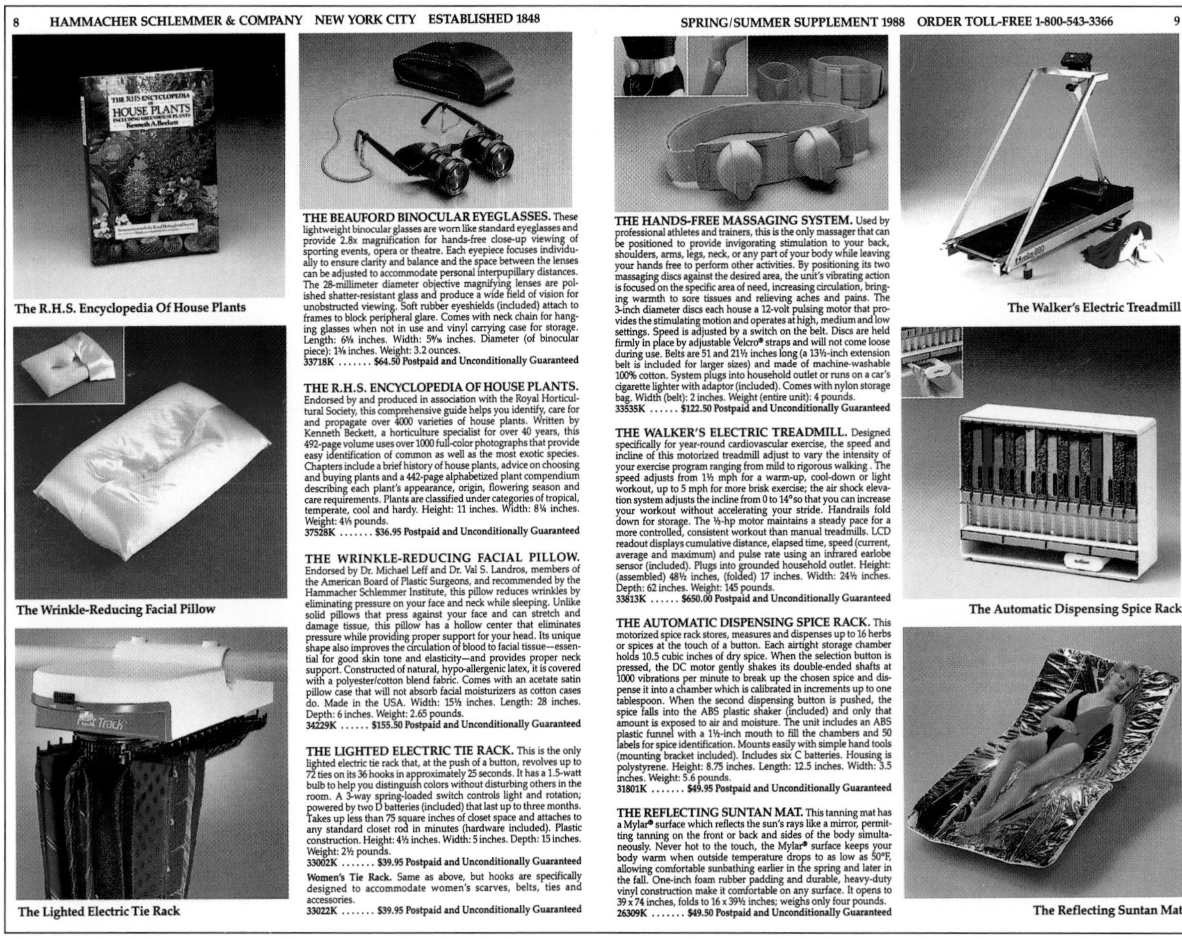

8 HAMMACHER SCHLEMMER & COMPANY NEW YORK CITY ESTABLISHED 1848

The R.H.S. Encyclopedia Of House Plants

The Wrinkle-Reducing Facial Pillow

The Lighted Electric Tie Rack

THE BEAUFORD BINOCULAR EYEGLASSES. These lightweight binocular glasses are worn like standard eyeglasses and provide 2.8x magnification for hands-free close-up viewing of sporting events, opera or theatre. Each eyepiece focuses individually to ensure clarity and balance and the space between the lenses can be adjusted to accommodate personal interpupillary distances. The 28-millimeter diameter objective magnifying lenses are polished shatter-resistant glass and produce a wide field of vision for unobstructed viewing. Soft rubber eyeshields (included) attach to frames to block peripheral glare. Comes with neck chain for hanging glasses when not in use and vinyl carrying case for storage. Length: 6⅝ inches. Width: 5 9/16 inches. Diameter (of binocular piece): 1⅜ inches. Weight: 3.2 ounces.
33718K .... $64.50 Postpaid and Unconditionally Guaranteed

THE R.H.S. ENCYCLOPEDIA OF HOUSE PLANTS. Endorsed by and produced in association with the Royal Horticultural Society, this comprehensive guide helps you identify, care for and propagate over 4000 varieties of house plants. Written by Kenneth Beckett, a horticulture specialist for over 40 years, this 492-page volume uses over 1000 full-color photographs that provide easy identification of common as well as the most exotic species. Chapters include a brief history of house plants, advice on choosing and buying plants and a 442-page alphabetized plant compendium describing each plant's appearance, origin, flowering season and care requirements. Plants are classified under categories of tropical, temperate, cool and hardy. Height: 11 inches. Width: 8¼ inches. Weight: 4⅕ pounds.
37528K .... $36.95 Postpaid and Unconditionally Guaranteed

THE WRINKLE-REDUCING FACIAL PILLOW. Endorsed by Dr. Michael Leff and Dr. Val S. Landros, members of the American Board of Plastic Surgeons, and recommended by the Hammacher Schlemmer Institute, this pillow reduces wrinkles by eliminating pressure on your face and neck while sleeping. Unlike solid pillows that press against your face and can stretch and damage tissue, this pillow has a hollow center that eliminates pressure while providing proper support for your head. Its unique shape also improves the circulation of blood to facial tissue—essential for good skin tone and elasticity—and provides proper neck support. Constructed of natural, hypo-allergenic latex, it is covered with a polyester/cotton blend fabric. Comes with an acetate satin pillow case that will not absorb facial moisturizers as cotton cases do. Made in the USA. Width: 15½ inches. Length: 28 inches. Depth: 6 inches. Weight: 2.65 pounds.
34229K ...... $155.50 Postpaid and Unconditionally Guaranteed

THE LIGHTED ELECTRIC TIE RACK. This is the only lighted electric tie rack that, at the push of a button, revolves up to 72 ties on its 36 hooks in approximately 25 seconds. It has a 1.5-watt bulb to help you distinguish colors without disturbing others in the room. A 3-way spring-loaded switch controls light and rotation; powered by two D batteries (included) that last up to three months. Takes up less than 75 square inches of closet space and attaches to any standard closet rod in minutes (hardware included). Plastic construction. Height: 4½ inches. Width: 5 inches. Depth: 15 inches. Weight: 2½ pounds.
33002K .... $39.95 Postpaid and Unconditionally Guaranteed

Women's Tie Rack. Same as above, but hooks are specifically designed to accommodate women's scarves, belts, ties and accessories.
33022K .... $39.95 Postpaid and Unconditionally Guaranteed

SPRING/SUMMER SUPPLEMENT 1988 ORDER TOLL-FREE 1-800-543-3366 9

THE HANDS-FREE MASSAGING SYSTEM. Used by professional athletes and trainers, this is the only massager that can be positioned to provide invigorating stimulation to your back, shoulders, arms, legs, neck, or any part of your body while leaving your hands free to perform other activities. By positioning its two massaging discs against the desired area, the unit's vibrating action is focused on the specific area of need, increasing circulation, bringing warmth to sore tissues and relieving aches and pains. The 3-inch diameter discs each house a 12-volt pulsing motor that provides the stimulating motion and operates at high, medium and low settings. Speed is adjusted by a switch on the belt. Discs are held firmly in place by adjustable Velcro® straps and will not come loose during use. Belts are 51 and 21½ inches long (a 13½-inch extension belt is included for larger sizes) and made of machine-washable 100% cotton. System plugs into household outlet or runs on a car's cigarette lighter with adaptor (included). Comes with nylon storage bag. Width (belt): 2 inches. Weight (entire unit): 4 pounds.
33535K ...... $122.50 Postpaid and Unconditionally Guaranteed

THE WALKER'S ELECTRIC TREADMILL. Designed specifically for year-round cardiovascular exercise, the speed and incline of this motorized treadmill adjust to vary the intensity of your exercise program ranging from mild to rigorous walking . The speed adjusts from 1½ mph for a warm-up, cool-down or light workout, up to 5 mph for more brisk exercise; the air shock elevation system adjusts the incline from 0 to 14° so that you can increase your workout without accelerating your stride. Handrails fold down for storage. The ½-hp motor maintains a steady pace for a more controlled, consistent workout than manual treadmills. LCD readout displays cumulative distance, elapsed time, speed (current, average and maximum) and pulse rate using an infrared earlobe sensor (included). Plugs into grounded household outlet. Height: (assembled) 48½ inches, (folded) 17 inches. Width: 24½ inches. Depth: 62 inches. Weight: 145 pounds.
33813K ...... $650.00 Postpaid and Unconditionally Guaranteed

THE AUTOMATIC DISPENSING SPICE RACK. This motorized spice rack stores, measures and dispenses up to 16 herbs or spices at the touch of a button. Each airtight storage chamber holds 10.5 cubic inches of dry spice. When the selection button is pressed, the DC motor gently shakes its double-ended shafts at 1000 vibrations per minute to break up the chosen spice and dispense it into a chamber which is calibrated in increments up to one tablespoon. When the second dispensing button is pushed, the spice falls into the ABS plastic shaker (included) and only that amount is exposed to air and moisture. The unit includes an ABS plastic funnel with a 1½-inch mouth to fill the chambers and 50 labels for spice identification. Mounts easily with simple hand tools (mounting bracket included). Includes six C batteries. Housing is polystyrene. Height: 8.75 inches. Length: 12.5 inches. Width: 3.5 inches. Weight: 5.6 pounds.
31801K .... $49.95 Postpaid and Unconditionally Guaranteed

THE REFLECTING SUNTAN MAT. This tanning mat has a Mylar® surface which reflects the sun's rays like a mirror, permitting tanning on the front or back and sides of the body simultaneously. Never hot to the touch, the Mylar® surface keeps your body warm when outside temperature drops to as low as 50°F, allowing comfortable sunbathing earlier in the spring and later in the fall. One-inch foam rubber padding and durable, heavy-duty vinyl construction make it comfortable on any surface. It opens to 39 x 74 inches, folds to 16 x 39½ inches; weighs only four pounds.
26309K .... $49.50 Postpaid and Unconditionally Guaranteed

The Walker's Electric Treadmill

The Automatic Dispensing Spice Rack

The Reflecting Suntan Mat

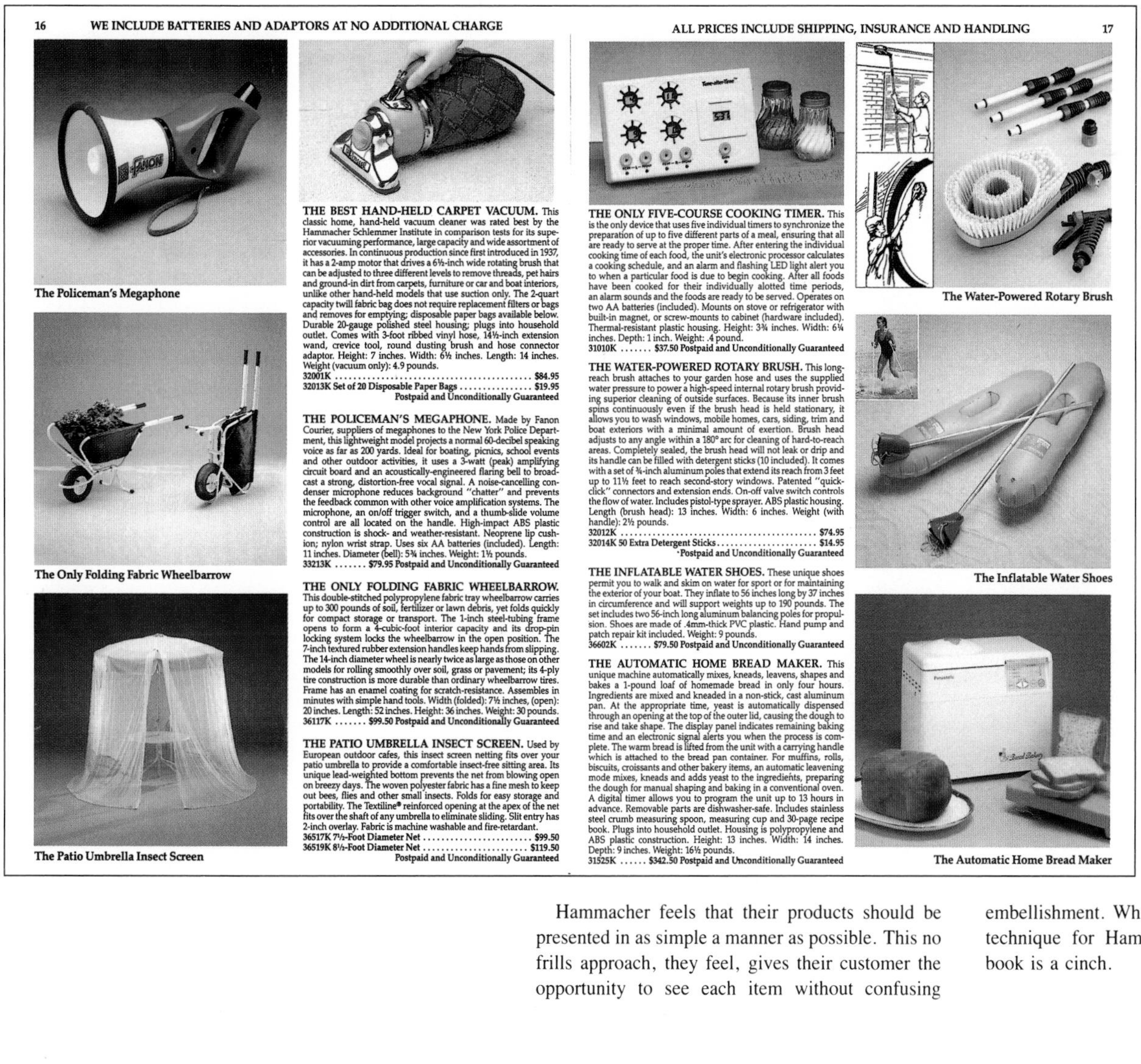

16 WE INCLUDE BATTERIES AND ADAPTORS AT NO ADDITIONAL CHARGE

The Policeman's Megaphone

The Only Folding Fabric Wheelbarrow

The Patio Umbrella Insect Screen

THE BEST HAND-HELD CARPET VACUUM. This classic home, hand-held vacuum cleaner was rated best by the Hammacher Schlemmer Institute in comparison tests for its superior vacuuming performance, large capacity and wide assortment of accessories. In continuous production since first introduced in 1937, it has a 2-amp motor that drives a 6½-inch wide rotating brush that can be adjusted to three different levels to remove threads, pet hairs and ground-in dirt from carpets, furniture or car and boat interiors, unlike other hand-held models that use suction only. The 2-quart capacity twill fabric bag does not require replacement filters or bags and removes for emptying; disposable paper bags available below. Durable 20-gauge polished steel housing; plugs into household outlet. Comes with 3-foot ribbed vinyl hose, 14½-inch extension wand, crevice tool, round dusting brush and hose connector adaptor. Height: 7 inches. Width: 6½ inches. Length: 14 inches. Weight (vacuum only): 4.9 pounds.
32001K $84.95
32013K Set of 20 Disposable Paper Bags $19.95
Postpaid and Unconditionally Guaranteed

THE POLICEMAN'S MEGAPHONE. Made by Fanon Courier, suppliers of megaphones to the New York Police Department, this lightweight model projects a normal 60-decibel speaking voice as far as 200 yards. Ideal for boating, picnics, school events and other outdoor activities, it uses a 3-watt (peak) amplifying circuit board and an acoustically-engineered flaring bell to broadcast a strong, distortion-free vocal signal. A noise-cancelling condenser microphone reduces background "chatter" and prevents the feedback common with other voice amplification systems. The microphone, an on/off trigger switch, and a thumb-slide volume control are all located on the handle. High-impact ABS plastic construction is shock- and weather-resistant. Neoprene lip cushion; nylon wrist strap. Uses six AA batteries (included). Length: 11 inches. Diameter (bell): 5¾ inches. Weight: 1½ pounds.
33213K .... $79.95 Postpaid and Unconditionally Guaranteed

THE ONLY FOLDING FABRIC WHEELBARROW. This double-stitched polypropylene fabric tray wheelbarrow carries up to 300 pounds of soil, fertilizer or lawn debris, yet folds quickly for compact storage or transport. The 1-inch steel-tubing frame opens to form a 4-cubic-foot interior capacity and its drop-pin locking system locks the wheelbarrow in the open position. The 7-inch textured rubber extension handles keep hands from slipping. The 14-inch diameter wheel is nearly twice as large as those on other models for rolling smoothly over soil, grass or pavement; its 4-ply tire construction is more durable than ordinary wheelbarrow tires. Frame has an enamel coating for scratch-resistance. Assembles in minutes with simple hand tools. Width (folded): 7½ inches, (open): 20 inches. Length: 52 inches. Height: 36 inches. Weight: 30 pounds.
36117K .... $99.50 Postpaid and Unconditionally Guaranteed

THE PATIO UMBRELLA INSECT SCREEN. Used by European outdoor cafes, this insect screen netting fits over your patio umbrella to provide a comfortable insect-free sitting area. Its unique lead-weighted bottom prevents the net from blowing open on breezy days. The woven polyester fabric has a fine mesh to keep out bees, flies and other small insects. Folds for easy storage and portability. The Textiline® reinforced opening at the apex of the net fits over the shaft of any umbrella to eliminate sliding. Slit entry has 2-inch overlay. Fabric is machine washable and fire-retardant.
36517K 7½-Foot Diameter Net $99.50
36519K 8½-Foot Diameter Net $119.50
Postpaid and Unconditionally Guaranteed

ALL PRICES INCLUDE SHIPPING, INSURANCE AND HANDLING 17

THE ONLY FIVE-COURSE COOKING TIMER. This is the only device that uses five individual timers to synchronize the preparation of up to five different parts of a meal, ensuring that all are ready to serve at the proper time. After entering the individual cooking time of each food, the unit's electronic processor calculates a cooking schedule, and an alarm and flashing LED light alert you to when a particular food is due to begin cooking. After all foods have been cooked for their individually alotted time periods, an alarm sounds and the foods are ready to be served. Operates on two AA batteries (included). Mounts on stove or refrigerator with built-in magnet, or screw-mounts to cabinet (hardware included). Thermal-resistant plastic housing. Height: 3¾ inches. Width: 6¼ inches. Depth: 1 inch. Weight: .4 pound.
31010K .... $37.50 Postpaid and Unconditionally Guaranteed

THE WATER-POWERED ROTARY BRUSH. This long-reach brush attaches to your garden hose and uses the supplied water pressure to power a high-speed internal rotary brush providing superior cleaning of outside surfaces. Because its inner brush spins continuously even if the brush head is held stationary, it allows you to wash windows, mobile homes, cars, siding, trim and boat exteriors with a minimal amount of exertion. Brush head adjusts to any angle within a 180° arc for cleaning of hard-to-reach areas. Completely sealed, the brush head will not leak or drip and its handle can be filled with detergent sticks (10 included). It comes with a set of ¾-inch aluminum poles that extend its reach from 3 feet up to 11½ feet to reach second-story windows. Patented "quick-click" connectors and extension ends. On-off valve switch controls the flow of water. Includes pistol-type sprayer. ABS plastic housing. Length (brush head): 13 inches. Width: 6 inches. Weight (with handle): 2½ pounds.
32012K $74.95
32014K 50 Extra Detergent Sticks $14.95
·Postpaid and Unconditionally Guaranteed

THE INFLATABLE WATER SHOES. These unique shoes permit you to walk and skim on water for sport or for maintaining the exterior of your boat. They inflate to 56 inches long by 37 inches in circumference and will support weights up to 190 pounds. The set includes two 56-inch long aluminum balancing poles for propulsion. Shoes are made of .4mm-thick PVC plastic. Hand pump and patch repair kit included. Weight: 9 pounds.
36602K .... $79.50 Postpaid and Unconditionally Guaranteed

THE AUTOMATIC HOME BREAD MAKER. This unique machine automatically mixes, kneads, leavens, shapes and bakes a 1-pound loaf of homemade bread in only four hours. Ingredients are mixed and kneaded in a non-stick, cast aluminum pan. At the appropriate time, yeast is automatically dispensed through an opening at the top of the outer lid, causing the dough to rise and take shape. The display panel indicates remaining baking time and an electronic signal alerts you when the process is complete. The warm bread is lifted from the unit with a carrying handle which is attached to the bread pan container. For muffins, rolls, biscuits, croissants and other bakery items, an automatic leavening mode mixes, kneads and adds yeast to the ingredients, preparing the dough for manual shaping and baking in a conventional oven. A digital timer allows you to program the unit up to 13 hours in advance. Removable parts are dishwasher-safe. Includes stainless steel crumb measuring spoon, measuring cup and 30-page recipe book. Plugs into household outlet. Housing is polypropylene and ABS plastic construction. Height: 13 inches. Width: 14 inches. Depth: 9 inches. Weight: 16½ pounds.
31525K ...... $342.50 Postpaid and Unconditionally Guaranteed

The Water-Powered Rotary Brush

The Inflatable Water Shoes

The Automatic Home Bread Maker

Hammacher feels that their products should be presented in as simple a manner as possible. This no frills approach, they feel, gives their customer the opportunity to see each item without confusing embellishment. What's more, there's a plus in this technique for Hammacher: pickup from book to book is a cinch.

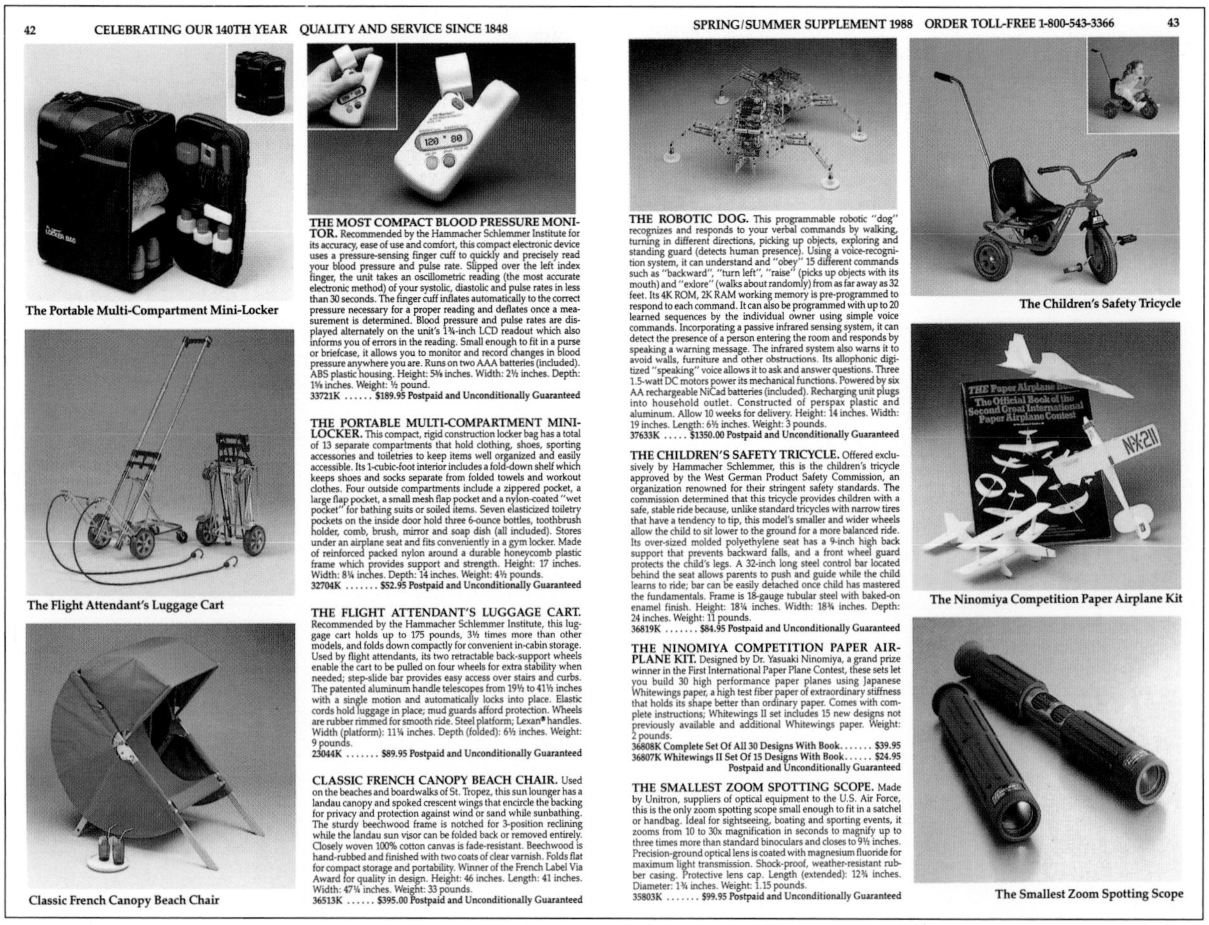

THE MOST COMPACT BLOOD PRESSURE MONITOR. Recommended by the Hammacher Schlemmer Institute for its accuracy, ease of use and comfort, this compact electronic device uses a pressure-sensing finger cuff to quickly and precisely read your blood pressure and pulse rate. Slipped over the left index finger, the unit takes an oscillometric reading (the most accurate electronic method) of your systolic, diastolic and pulse rates in less than 30 seconds. The finger cuff inflates automatically to the correct pressure necessary for a proper reading and deflates once a measurement is determined. Blood pressure and pulse rates are displayed alternately on the unit's 1¾-inch LCD readout which also informs you of errors in the reading. Small enough to fit in a purse or briefcase, it allows you to monitor and record changes in blood pressure anywhere you are. Runs on two AAA batteries (included). ABS plastic housing. Height: 5⅜ inches. Width: 2½ inches. Depth: 1⅝ inches. Weight: ½ pound.
33721K ...... $189.95 Postpaid and Unconditionally Guaranteed

The Portable Multi-Compartment Mini-Locker

THE PORTABLE MULTI-COMPARTMENT MINI-LOCKER. This compact, rigid construction locker bag has a total of 13 separate compartments that hold clothing, shoes, sporting accessories and toiletries to keep items well organized and easily accessible. Its 1-cubic-foot interior includes a fold-down shelf which keeps shoes and socks separate from folded towels and workout clothes. Four outside compartments include a zippered pocket, a large flap pocket, a small mesh flap pocket and a nylon-coated "wet pocket" for bathing suits or soiled items. Seven elasticized toiletry pockets on the inside door hold three 6-ounce bottles, toothbrush holder, comb, brush, mirror and soap dish (all included). Stores under an airplane seat and fits conveniently in a gym locker. Made of reinforced packed nylon around a durable honeycomb plastic frame which provides support and strength. Height: 17 inches. Width: 8¼ inches. Depth: 14 inches. Weight: 4½ pounds.
32704K .... $52.95 Postpaid and Unconditionally Guaranteed

The Flight Attendant's Luggage Cart

THE FLIGHT ATTENDANT'S LUGGAGE CART. Recommended by the Hammacher Schlemmer Institute, this luggage cart holds up to 175 pounds, 3½ times more than other models, and folds down compactly for convenient in-cabin storage. Used by flight attendants, its two retractable back-support wheels enable the cart to be pulled on four wheels for extra stability when needed; step-slide bar provides easy access over stairs and curbs. The patented aluminum handle telescopes from 19½ to 41½ inches with a single motion and automatically locks into place. Elastic cords hold luggage in place; mud guards afford protection. Wheels are rubber rimmed for smooth ride. Steel platform; Lexan® handles. Width (platform): 11¼ inches. Depth (folded): 6½ inches. Weight: 9 pounds.
23044K .... $89.95 Postpaid and Unconditionally Guaranteed

CLASSIC FRENCH CANOPY BEACH CHAIR. Used on the beaches and boardwalks of St. Tropez, this sun lounger has a landau canopy and spoked crescent wings that encircle the backing for privacy and protection against wind or sand while sunbathing. The sturdy beechwood frame is notched for 3-position reclining while the landau sun visor can be folded back or removed entirely. Closely woven 100% cotton canvas is fade-resistant. Beechwood is hand-rubbed and finished with two coats of clear varnish. Folds flat for compact storage and portability. Winner of the French Label Via Award for quality in design. Height: 46 inches. Length: 41 inches. Width: 47¼ inches. Weight: 33 pounds.
36513K ...... $395.00 Postpaid and Unconditionally Guaranteed

Classic French Canopy Beach Chair

THE ROBOTIC DOG. This programmable robotic "dog" recognizes and responds to your verbal commands by walking, turning in different directions, picking up objects, exploring and standing guard (detects human presence). Using a voice-recognition system, it can understand and "obey" 15 different commands such as "backward", "turn left", "raise" (picks up objects with its mouth) and "exlore" (walks about randomly) from as far away as 32 feet. Its 4K ROM, 2K RAM working memory is pre-programmed to respond to each command. It can also be programmed with up to 20 learned sequences by the individual owner using simple voice commands. Incorporating a passive infrared sensing system, it can detect the presence of a person entering the room and responds by speaking a warning message. The infrared system also warns it to avoid walls, furniture and other obstructions. Its allophonic digitized "speaking" voice allows it to ask and answer questions. Three 1.5-watt DC motors power its mechanical functions. Powered by six AA rechargeable NiCad batteries (included). Recharging unit plugs into household outlet. Constructed of perspax plastic and aluminum. Allow 10 weeks for delivery. Height: 14 inches. Width: 19 inches. Length: 6½ inches. Weight: 3 pounds.
37633K ..... $1350.00 Postpaid and Unconditionally Guaranteed

The Children's Safety Tricycle

THE CHILDREN'S SAFETY TRICYCLE. Offered exclusively by Hammacher Schlemmer, this is the children's tricycle approved by the West German Product Safety Commission, an organization renowned for their stringent safety standards. The commission determined that this tricycle provides children with a safe, stable ride because, unlike standard tricycles with narrow tires that have a tendency to tip, this model's smaller and wider wheels allow the child to sit lower to the ground for a more balanced ride. Its over-sized molded polyethylene seat has a 9-inch high back support that prevents backward falls, and a front wheel guard protects the child's legs. A 32-inch long steel control bar located behind the seat allows parents to push and guide while the child learns to ride; bar can be easily detached once child has mastered the fundamentals. Frame is 18-gauge tubular steel with baked-on enamel finish. Height: 18¼ inches. Width: 18¾ inches. Depth: 24 inches. Weight: 11 pounds.
36819K .... $84.95 Postpaid and Unconditionally Guaranteed

The Ninomiya Competition Paper Airplane Kit

THE NINOMIYA COMPETITION PAPER AIRPLANE KIT. Designed by Dr. Yasuaki Ninomiya, a grand prize winner in the First International Paper Plane Contest, these sets let you build 30 high performance paper planes using Japanese Whitewings paper, a high test fiber paper of extraordinary stiffness that holds its shape better than ordinary paper. Comes with complete instructions; Whitewings II set includes 15 new designs not previously available and additional Whitewings paper. Weight: 2 pounds.
36808K Complete Set Of All 30 Designs With Book....... $39.95
36807K Whitewings II Set Of 15 Designs With Book...... $24.95
Postpaid and Unconditionally Guaranteed

THE SMALLEST ZOOM SPOTTING SCOPE. Made by Unitron, suppliers of optical equipment to the U.S. Air Force, this is the only zoom spotting scope small enough to fit in a satchel or handbag. Ideal for sightseeing, boating and sporting events, it zooms from 10 to 30x magnification in seconds to magnify up to three times more than standard binoculars and closes to 9½ inches. Precision-ground optical lens is coated with magnesium fluoride for maximum light transmission. Shock-proof, weather-resistant rubber casing. Protective lens cap. Length (extended): 12¾ inches. Diameter: 1¾ inches. Weight: 1.15 pounds.
35803K .... $99.95 Postpaid and Unconditionally Guaranteed

The Smallest Zoom Spotting Scope

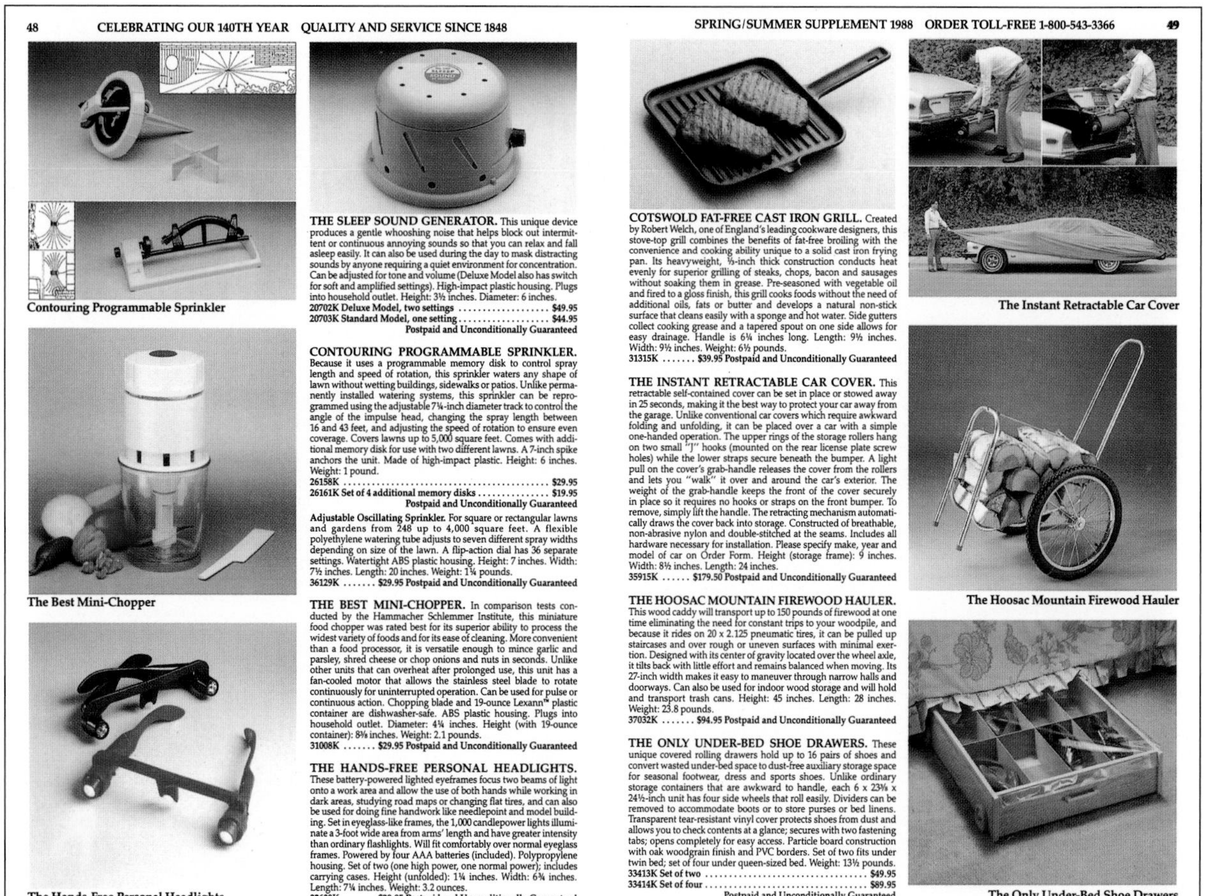

Contouring Programmable Sprinkler

THE SLEEP SOUND GENERATOR. This unique device produces a gentle whooshing noise that helps block out intermittent or continuous annoying sounds so that you can relax and fall asleep easily. It can also be used during the day to mask distracting sounds by anyone requiring a quiet environment for concentration. Can be adjusted for tone and volume (Deluxe Model also has switch for soft and amplified settings). High-impact plastic housing. Plugs into household outlet. Height: 3½ inches. Diameter: 6 inches.
20702K Deluxe Model, two settings $49.95
20703K Standard Model, one setting.................... $44.95
Postpaid and Unconditionally Guaranteed

CONTOURING PROGRAMMABLE SPRINKLER. Because it uses a programmable memory disk to control spray length and speed of rotation, this sprinkler waters any shape of lawn without wetting buildings, sidewalks or patios. Unlike permanently installed watering systems, this sprinkler can be reprogrammed using the adjustable 7¼-inch diameter track to control the angle of the impulse head, changing the spray length between 16 and 43 feet, and adjusting the speed of rotation to ensure even coverage. Covers lawns up to 5,000 square feet. Comes with additional memory disk for use with two different lawns. A 7-inch spike anchors the unit. Made of high-impact plastic. Height: 6 inches. Weight: 1 pound.
26158K $29.95
26161K Set of 4 additional memory disks $19.95
Postpaid and Unconditionally Guaranteed

Adjustable Oscillating Sprinkler. For square or rectangular lawns and gardens from 248 up to 4,000 square feet. A flexible polyethylene watering tube adjusts to seven different spray widths depending on size of the lawn. A flip-action dial has 36 separate settings. Watertight ABS plastic housing. Height: 7 inches. Width: 7½ inches. Length: 20 inches. Weight: 1¼ pounds.
36129K .... $29.95 Postpaid and Unconditionally Guaranteed

The Best Mini-Chopper

THE BEST MINI-CHOPPER. In comparison tests conducted by the Hammacher Schlemmer Institute, this miniature food chopper was rated best for its superior ability to process the widest variety of foods and for its ease of cleaning. More convenient than a food processor, it is versatile enough to mince garlic and parsley, shred cheese or chop onions and nuts in seconds. Unlike other units that can overheat after prolonged use, this unit has a fan-cooled motor that allows the stainless steel blade to rotate continuously for uninterrupted operation. Can be used for pulse or continuous action. Chopping blade and 19-ounce Lexann™ plastic container are dishwasher-safe. ABS plastic housing. Plugs into household outlet. Diameter: 4¼ inches. Height (with 19-ounce container): 8⅜ inches. Weight: 2.1 pounds.
31008K .... $29.95 Postpaid and Unconditionally Guaranteed

THE HANDS-FREE PERSONAL HEADLIGHTS. These battery-powered lighted eyeframes focus two beams of light onto a work area and allow the use of both hands while working in dark areas, studying road maps or changing flat tires, and can also be used for doing fine handwork like needlepoint and model building. Set in eyeglass-like frames, the 1,000 candlepower lights illuminate a 3-foot wide area from arms' length and have greater intensity than ordinary flashlights. Will fit comfortably over normal eyeglass frames. Powered by four AAA batteries (included). Polypropylene housing. Set of two (one high power, one normal power); includes carrying cases. Height (unfolded): 1¼ inches. Width: 6¾ inches. Length: 7¼ inches. Weight: 3.2 ounces.
32638K .... $29.95 Postpaid and Unconditionally Guaranteed

The Hands-Free Personal Headlights

COTSWOLD FAT-FREE CAST IRON GRILL. Created by Robert Welch, one of England's leading cookware designers, this stove-top grill combines the benefits of fat-free broiling with the convenience and cooking ability unique to a solid cast iron frying pan. Its heavyweight, ⅓-inch thick construction conducts heat evenly for superior grilling of steaks, chops, bacon and sausages without soaking them in grease. Pre-seasoned with vegetable oil and fired to a gloss finish, this grill cooks foods without the need of additional oils, fats or butter and develops a natural non-stick surface that cleans easily with a sponge and hot water. Side gutters collect cooking grease and a tapered spout on one side allows for easy drainage. Handle is 6¼ inches long. Length: 9½ inches. Width: 9½ inches. Weight: 6½ pounds.
31315K .... $39.95 Postpaid and Unconditionally Guaranteed

The Instant Retractable Car Cover

THE INSTANT RETRACTABLE CAR COVER. This retractable self-contained cover can be set in place or stowed away in 25 seconds, making it the best way to protect your car away from the garage. Unlike conventional car covers which require awkward folding and unfolding, it can be placed over a car with a simple one-handed operation. The upper rings of the storage rollers hang on two small "J" hooks (mounted on the rear license plate screw holes) while the lower straps secure beneath the bumper. A light pull on the cover's grab-handle releases the cover from the rollers and lets you "walk" it over and around the car's exterior. The weight of the grab-handle keeps the front of the cover securely in place so it requires no hooks or straps on the front bumper. To remove, simply lift the handle. The retracting mechanism automatically draws the cover back into storage. Constructed of breathable, non-abrasive nylon and double-stitched at the seams. Includes all hardware necessary for installation. Please specify make, year and model of car on Order Form. Height (storage frame): 9 inches. Width: 8½ inches. Length: 24 inches.
35915K ...... $179.50 Postpaid and Unconditionally Guaranteed

THE HOOSAC MOUNTAIN FIREWOOD HAULER. This wood caddy will transport up to 150 pounds of firewood at one time eliminating the need for constant trips to your woodpile, and because it rides on 20 x 2.125 pneumatic tires, it can be pulled up staircases and over rough or uneven surfaces with minimal exertion. Designed with its center of gravity located over the wheel axle, it tilts back with little effort and remains balanced when moving. Its 27-inch width makes it easy to maneuver through narrow halls and doorways. Can also be used for indoor wood storage and will hold and transport trash cans. Height: 45 inches. Length: 28 inches. Weight: 23.8 pounds.
37032K .... $94.95 Postpaid and Unconditionally Guaranteed

The Hoosac Mountain Firewood Hauler

THE ONLY UNDER-BED SHOE DRAWERS. These unique covered rolling drawers hold up to 16 pairs of shoes and convert wasted under-bed space to dust-free auxiliary storage space for seasonal footwear, dress and sports shoes. Unlike ordinary storage containers that are awkward to handle, each 6 x 23⅜ x 24½-inch unit has four side wheels that roll easily. Dividers can be removed to accommodate boots or to store purses or bed linens. Transparent tear-resistant vinyl cover protects shoes from dust and allows you to check contents at a glance; secures with two fastening tabs; opens completely for easy access. Particle board construction with oak woodgrain finish and PVC borders. Set of two fits under twin bed; set of four under queen-sized bed. Weight: 13½ pounds.
33413K Set of two $49.95
33414K Set of four $89.95
Postpaid and Unconditionally Guaranteed

The Only Under-Bed Shoe Drawers

Excellent, long copy, clean photography and emphasis on product performance (as opposed to creative superlatives) have been the hallmark of all Hammacher's catalogs. It's a browse book. A catalog that becomes a friend during those all-too-brief quiet moments. The products are fun, but on the other hand, one has the sense that Hammacher is quite serious about maintaining their standards.

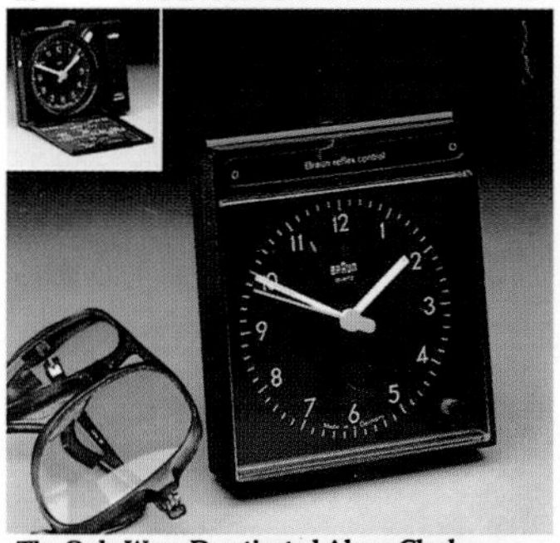

The Only Wave-Deactivated Alarm Clock

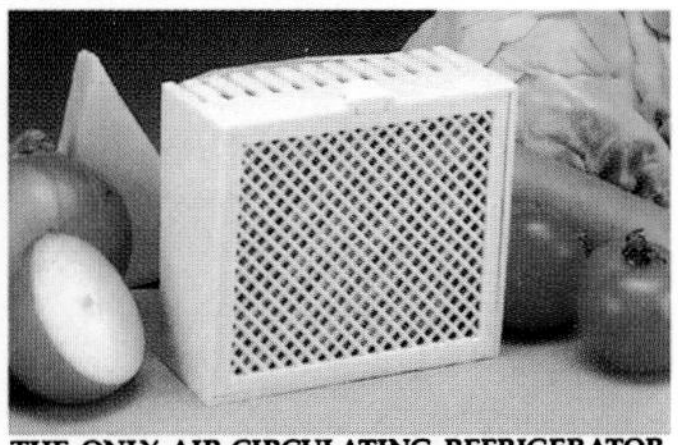

THE ONLY AIR-CIRCULATING REFRIGERATOR FRESHENER. This cordless electric air freshener circulates and filters the air inside your refrigerator to eliminate odors and reduce moisture to keep food fresher longer. The unit's motorized fan is controlled by a light sensing, photoconductive cell that is activated each time the refrigerator door is opened. The fan runs for 15 seconds, drawing stale air through a highly porous carbon filter with over 30,000 square meters of surface area to remove odors. Unlike baking soda which only neutralizes odors and quickly decomposes, this unit's chemically treated carbon filter eliminates mold-producing moisture without needing replacement for up to one year. Operates on four AA batteries (included). An LED light indicates when battery replacement is required. Height: 3½ inches. Width: 4 inches. Diameter: 3½ inches. Weight: .7 pound.
30609K Set of Two $29.95
Postpaid and Unconditionally Guaranteed

THE ONLY WAVE-DEACTIVATED ALARM CLOCK. This is the only clock incorporating an alarm system that can be turned off instantly with a simple wave of the hand. Using an infrared sensing system, it detects the heat emitted by the body as it passes within 24 inches of the clock face to temporarily shut off the alarm. Operating like the "snooze" button found on other alarm clocks, this unit's alarm repeats every four minutes until the "off" bar is pressed. The clock face emits a constant light while the "snooze" is operating. Quartz crystal movement. Analog hands are luminescent. ABS plastic housing. Operates on two AA batteries (included). Height: 3⅞ inches. Length: 3½ inches. Depth: 2 inches. Weight: 4.2 ounces.
35713K .... $39.95 Postpaid and Unconditionally Guaranteed

Voice-Deactivated Travel Alarm. Similar to above, but uses a condenser microphone to turn off the alarm at the sound of your voice or clap of your hands. High-impact Makralon™ housing has a built-in penlight and folding cover with a timetable of the world. Uses one AA battery (included). Width: 2⅝ inches. Length: 3⅜ inches. Depth: ⅞ inch. Weight: ¼ pound.
35714K .... $39.95 Postpaid and Unconditionally Guaranteed

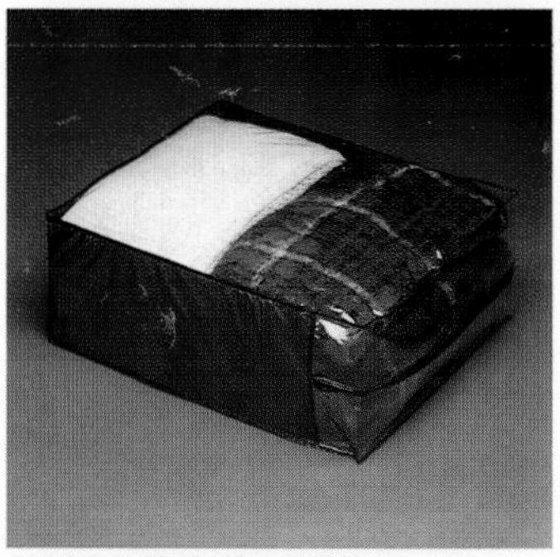

The Largest Blanket Storage Bag

THE LARGEST BLANKET STORAGE BAG. Offered exclusively by Hammacher Schlemmer, this oversized storage bag is 48% larger than other storage bags and is twice as thick to provide superior protection for your large blankets and quilts. Its 3.62-cubic-foot capacity allows you to store two queen-size blankets or one king-size quilt. This pliable 8-guage transparent vinyl bag protects blankets from moisture, dust, odors, mildew and insects without cracking and splitting. The bag's bottom is reinforced with moisture-resistant nylon; edges are strengthened with vinyl piping. Double zipper uses nylon glides to prevent contents from snagging. Height: 27 inches. Width: 21 inches. Length: 11 inches. Weight: .55 pound.
32113K .... $34.95 Postpaid and Unconditionally Guaranteed

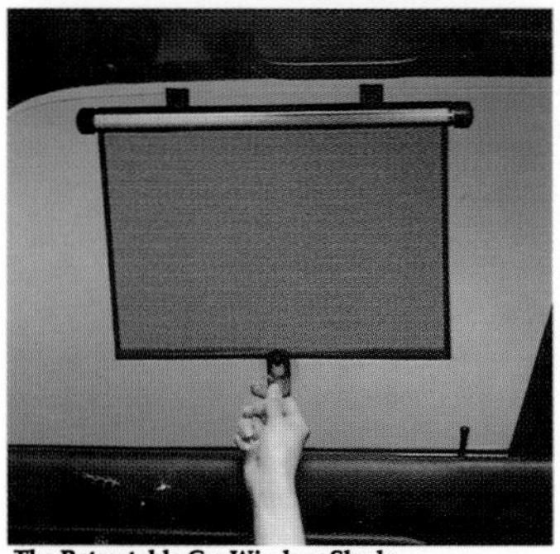

The Retractable Car Window Shade

THE RETRACTABLE CAR WINDOW SHADE. This unique roll-up window shade effectively blocks sunlight from passengers' eyes yet lets you see through it to ensure peripheral vision by eliminating glare from side windows. The 20 x 16-inch perforated vinyl shade has a reflective exterior that prevents sunlight from entering, and because it reflects the sun's rays, it helps keep the vehicle's interior temperature cool while driving. The spring-loaded roller tube attaches in seconds using either the built-in brackets that fit over the top of the window or two vinyl suction cups. The shade rolls up automatically to 1½ x 16 inches for storage. Set includes two shades. Weight: 15 ounces.
35909K .... $24.95 Postpaid and Unconditionally Guaranteed

INDEX

For credit card orders call **TOLL-FREE** 24 hours a day 7 days a week **1-800-543-3366**

Hammacher Schlemmer
ESTABLISHED 1848

For credit card orders call **TOLL-FREE** 24 hours a day 7 days a week **1-800-543-3366**

1 ORDERED BY: If information is incorrect, please print correct information.

Phone ( ) ______ ☐ Day ☐ Night

2 SHIP TO: (If different from "ORDERED BY")
☐ Mr. ☐ Mrs. ☐ Ms. First Name Middle Initial Last Name
Street/Box No./Apt. No. Route
City State Zip
Ship To Day Time Phone ( ) ______
Gift Message (if desired) ______

3	PAGE NO.	ITEM NO.	QTY.	SIZE	COLOR	MONOGRAMMING FIRST INITIAL	MIDDLE INITIAL	LAST INITIAL	DESCRIPTION	GIFT WRAP $3.50	AMOUNT
1											
2											
3											
4											
5											
6											
7											

4 PAYMENT METHOD

Check or Money Orders: AMOUNT ENCLOSED $ ______
☐ MasterCard ☐ VISA ☐ Diners Club ☐ Carte Blanche ☐ American Express
Card Account Number:
Month Year
Card Expiration Date Required Customer Signature
Card Issuing Bank Name: ______

ITEM TOTAL ▶
Applicable Sales Tax For Shipments to NY, IL, OH and CA. ▶
Regular POSTAGE & HANDLING FREE in continental United States ▶ INCLUDED
Optional 3-DAY AIR DELIVERY (see reverse side) ▶
SHIPPING for destinations outside continental U.S. (see reverse side) ▶
TOTAL ▶

POSTPAID AND UNCONDITIONALLY GUARANTEED

When a catalog is as interesting as this one, the tendency is to go through it more than once before ordering. But what happens when it's time to pick up the phone or fill in the order form?

What bleeping page was that bleeping widget on?!?! The thoughtful folks at Hammacher have thought of that one, too. A delightfully detailed index is positioned right where the order form is stitched into the book. It's also the first place an experienced mailorder shopper would look to find the 800 number. Though you can't see it, there's a great copy Headline on the back of the BRE, where it cannot be missed. It reads "Why our guarantee is like a FREE TRIAL". I suspect — nay I promise— that line will be seen elsewhere 'ere long.

NEIMAN-MARCUS

The story of Neiman-Marcus is not just a story about catalogs full of His & Her Aircraft, Camels and Health Farms. Nor is it a treatise on real estate, Texas Oilionaires, expensive merchandise or even the Marcus family.

The Neiman-Marcus story is a yarn about an attitude.

Neiman's customers are affronted by the effete, but will pay heavily for quality and style. They expect their favorite salesperson to give guidance, not guff. They expect Neiman's to be their arbiter of good taste—Southwestern style. NM's upscale customer relies upon the store to keep her wardrobe completely up to date. She must be wearing the best quality and the most stylish, or advanced fashions, at home, or when she is visiting Paris, New York, London or Rome.

But now there's a new challenge for Neiman-Marcus, the invasion from the East. The Southwest is absorbing more and more renegades, radicals and retirees from the East. The retail community is changing inexorably to keep pace with this growing demographic segment. Newer, smaller specialty stores and boutiques flourish. Mailorder merchants are increasing their market share. Meanwhile, many old line department stores—some of them directed from Central Offices 1000-1500 miles away—are in danger of becoming part of the background tapestry.

The struggle against compromise and homogeneity has become increasingly more difficult for the Neiman-Marcuses of the world.

Neiman's catalog department and the public relations campaign supporting the catalog operation have been a most effective pair of weapons against the bland, me-too, vendor-coop driven, copycat merchandise statements of some other stores.

Specialty store retailing in particular, I soon learned, consisted of a mass of minutiae, and you made and kept your customers by your ability to remember small details, such as anniversary dates or birthdays; a promise to get a certain evening bag in time for a special occasion; an assurance that a purchase wouldn't be billed until the following month; a promise that the dress bought for a girlfriend would be billed to the Mr., not the Mrs., account. . . .

In the preceding quote from *Minding The Store*, Stanley Marcus was speaking of a mindset appropriate to specialty stores. On examination, however, is this not also an important item for the agenda of a mailorder merchant? As a matter of fact, Neiman-Marcus and other successful mailorder and mailorder-cum-OTC retailers have picked up the ball that other stores have dropped. Mr. Marcus's "management of minutiae" has now become part of a function called "customer service", but the principles are exactly the same.

Mailorder programs, and the invisible databased systems that support them, provide the ideal basis for a return to these essentials of good retailing. Management of minutiae is what computers do best.

Neiman-Marcus knows their various customer sectors intimately. They can design mailings to suit the preferences of individual customers. They can offer each man or woman (or segment of their customer list) a selection of items most suited to their life-style, their age level and their personal taste.

In the retail store, a wide range of merchandise must be carried in order to serve a broad base of customers. But the catalog—

NEIMAN-MARCUS—Christmas 1987 Catalog
Tom Raney, *Executive Vice President, Sales Promotion*
Ann Barrington, *Catalog Director*
Edward Nunns, *Designer*
Pat Morgan, *Merchandiser*
Patricia West Stehr, *Copywriter*
David McCabe, *Fashion Photography*
Greg Booth & Associates, *Still Photography*
Dan Rizzie, *Cover Art*
Case-Hoyt [Rochester, NY], *Printer, on 80# Mead Web for cover and 60# Somerset Gloss for text*
Color Control, Inc. [Redmond, WA], *Color Separator*

Tom Raney and his creative crew at Neiman-Marcus have done it again. They've created another prize winner, and another world class example of how a catalog should flow.

aimed directly to the customer's interests—will get customers into the store or on the telephone order line. From there on, it's up to the combined efforts of the buyer/display/sales team. And, those are three areas of Neiman-Marcus's greatest strength.

Neiman-Marcus has mastered the art of customer entertainment and inspiration. Stories abound of their promotions and store-wide events. They have, in addition, been a leader in creating new formats for their direct mail programs. By tailoring these formats to suit the merchandise as well as the market, these books have inspired NM's customers to buy.

A wide variety of catalog shapes and sizes have been designed and mailed with great success. Sizes have ranged from 5-½″ X 11″ tall verticals to 10″ X 13″ tabloids.

In one very successful series, a number of 3-⅔″ X 8-½″ loose leaves were inserted in a heavy, double-pocket folder. The folder, in turn, was inserted into an outer envelope along with a smaller BRE (business reply envelope). On one side of each leaf was a

Every merchandise classification is treated to a look all its own. Every spread has logic and purpose. The reader is left with a sense that the Neiman-Marcus staff has worked diligently on behalf of their customers—as indeed they have, for a full year.

4-color photograph. On the obverse side was an order form. Advertising copy might appear either side of the sheet. A Neiman's customer could choose any number of items to order simply by selecting the pertinent insert, filling in the order form (size, colors, personalization, etc.), and placing them in the BRE.

Loose leaf formats are especially valuable to retailers. Contents of these mailings can be varied to conform to specific market segments or store locations. At one time, these packages had to be manually collated and inserted by workers sitting at long tables. The project was tedious, slow and expensive. Today, computer-based bindery operations are capable of getting the same collating and inserting job done with automatic, in-line equipment.

One spread tells of a day when you can become a part of the Ringling Bros. and Barnum & Bailey Circus troupe for a day — $5000.00 (including 25 free tickets for friends). Then, without drawing a deep breath, we jump to a section of gifts for $25 and under. A yacht charter for only $29,000 per week (plus expenses, of course) seems completely at ease surrounded by precious jewels and children's dolls.

THE GREATEST SHOW ON EARTH®

HIS OR HERS

ONCE IN A **LIFETIME**

We know there's still a secret child inside you—one that wanted to run away with the circus the first time you heard the call of a calliope, saw a sparkling lady fly through the air, laughed 'til you couldn't get your breath when the clowns came tumbling out, thought there was no scent as wondrous as hot roasted peanuts. That's no dust mote in your eye—it's a magic spangle that's always been with you to remind you of the past enchantment. So come out! Run away, run away for one special day, with the most famous circus of them all, Ringling Bros. and Barnum & Bailey!

It'll be a day you'll never forget, because you'll be part of this extraordinary family. You'll experience the spotlight and the backstage excitement. Your day will be tailored especially for you... man or woman. Just imagine what might be waiting for you—perhaps hiding all this time in your dreams. Would you like to ride in the dazzling opening parade? Join the merry mayhem of the clowns in the pre-performance walkabout acts? Have clowning lessons, elephant riding lessons, low-wire walking lessons? Perhaps you've always wanted to be a ringmaster? Meet the animal trainers? Your personal representative of the circus staff, the ringmaster, and two clowns are your hosts to create a day to make your dreams come true.

Extra specials: prior to the circus you'll be outfitted for costumes—clown, ringmaster, showgirl. You'll also be fitted for an official satin tour jacket and the official Circus Worker's coverall—those are presents to take home. You'll also take home photographs of your special day.

With your reservation, you'll also receive 25 complimentary tickets to the performance—so your friends and family can see you in the ring! And... you must be over 10 years old.

Here's how it works. Call 1-800-NEIMANS (1-800-634-6267) for the circus schedule, and make your reservation early, as only 10 are available. Only one reservation available per town, so you may want to choose an alternate location.

Phone lines for reservations will open at 10:00 a.m. Central Time, November 10th, 1987.

And now, Ladies and Gentlemen, the options for your day at the circus.

54A. For a couple, 7,500.00.
54B. For one, 5,000.00.

Prices do not include transportation. Again, call 1-800-NEIMANS (1-800-634-6267) for your day with RINGLING BROS. and BARNUM & BAILEY!

SAMPLE N-M's CREATIVE GIFT IDEAS: A SELECTION FOR ONLY

TWENTY FIVE DOLLARS

AND UNDER

A glass jar, topped with an openwork lid of pewter in a dogwood-cluster design, is filled with potpourri. Open top lets the fragrance drift into the air. 3 x 3". From Cosmetics.

20A. Potpourri jar, 12.00 (2.50).

A patchwork cosmetic case in subtle shades, mock-crocodile texture. This zippered case was made by Sharif exclusively for Neiman-Marcus. 9 x 5". From Cosmetics.

20D. Cosmetic case, 20.00 (2.50).

Grooming kit in faux ostrich. Inside: nail file, 2 cuticle scissors, tweezer, and cuticle pusher; 6 makeup brushes and a mirror. 6 x 4¼". An N-M exclusive. Cosmetics.

20E. Manicure/makeup kit, 25.00 (2.50).

Thirty pairs of one-size knee high hose, each individually packed, and stashed in a drum-shaped clear box. You'll find advanced colors from mint to shocking pink; classic colors from white to black. An N-M exclusive, from Casual Legwear.

20B. Leg Lines hose, 25.00 (2.50).

A replica of an oblong tortoise shell box holds a collection of 5 makeup brushes with brown wooden handles; a good selection of the most-needed items. The set is an N-M exclusive. The box measures 8¾ x 2". Cosmetics.

20C. Makeup brushes in box, 20.00 (2.50).

An N-M Epicure Shop tradition, and a special Texas treat: Texas Chewy Pecan Pralines, each individually wrapped for freshness. They're a melange of buttery caramel, loaded with giant Texas pecan halves. From Epicure.

21A. Pralines, 2 lb. box, 18.00 (2.50).

N-M's own soft brown plush Teddy bear, made exclusively for us by Gund, comes dressed with its own bright red N-M signature sweatshirt. This huggable Teddy measures 12½" tall. From Toys.

21B. N-M Teddy, 25.00 (2.50).

A multiple gift: A 5¼" square black satin box with beaded top is packed with eau de toilette samplers: 4ml "must" de Cartier," 7ml "First" by Van Cleef & Arpels, 5ml "La Nuit de Rabanne," and 4ml "Balahé" by Léonard. N-M exclusive. Cosmetics.

21C. Fragrance sampler in a reusable box, 25.00 (2.50).

Compact and handy, our exclusive comb and mirror in a case. Comb and mirror frame are tortoise-colored, snap-close case is brown. Closed, measures 4 x 3½". From Small Leather Goods.

21D. N-M comb/mirror set, 8.00 (2.50).

If you know someone who can't get enough chocolate—here's the perfect tongue-in-cheek gift. Six tubes of flavored toothpaste: Chocolate Mint, Chocolate Orange, and Chocolate Nut. 1 oz. tubes. N-M exclusive. Cosmetics.

21E. Chocolate toothpaste, 12.00 (2.50).

And for those who would choose chocolate over the finest vintage wine: the champagne bottle, packed with edible corks of chocolate with hazelnut fillings. Made by Godiva. 14 ounces. Epicure.

21F. Champagne corks, 25.00 (2.50).

FENDI – creative, innovative, high style from the sisters Fendi, imported from Italy.

Designed especially for N-M, a natural skin on skin Golden sable coat with a luxuriantly proportioned collar. Fur origin: Canada.

60A. Golden sable coat, 125,000.00.

The elegant drapery of Fendi's natural skin on skin Golden sable "butterfly" poncho, with a one-button closing. Fur origin: Canada.

60B. Golden sable poncho, 85,000.00.

A petal poncho of stenciled, dyed, embossed muskrat is worn here with a fringed, charcoal cashmere shawl trimmed in natural muskrat and squirrel fur rosettes. Also in black, camel, or navy. Not shown, stenciled, dyed, embossed muskrat petal scarf to match. Fur origins: muskrat, from U.S.A.; squirrel, from Canada.

60C. Muskrat poncho, 9,500.00.
60D. Cashmere shawl, 3,995.00.
60E. Muskrat petal scarf, 995.00.

Fendi accessories of white cotton and polyurethane signature canvas trimmed with Scotch-colored calf leather.

60F. Tall bucket bag, 295.00 (6.50).
60G. Shoulder bag, 250.00 (6.50).
60H. Pouch accordion bag, 95.00 (4.50).
60J. Half flap, rectangle bag, 175.00 (6.50).
60K. Checkbook/registry, 30.00 (3.50).
60L. Keyholder/coinpurse, 40.00 (4.50).
60M. Continental wallet, 150.00 (5.50).
60N. Flapover eyeglass case, 50.00 (4.50).

Our in-house master craftsman and designer Jerry Sorbara creates a coat with cut away front. Made of cat lynx bellies with brightener added. Fur origin: U.S.A.

61A. Cat lynx coat, 89,500.00.

By Jerry Sorbara, a batwing-sleeve jacket of natural ranch and natural Blue Iris mink, geometrically arranged. Fur: U.S.A.

61B. Batwing jacket, 11,500.00.

Bisang – classic, superb, luxe – trademarks of André and Lisa Bisang designs, exclusively for Neiman-Marcus. From the collections, a full-length man's coat in brûlée dyed, skin on skin velvet mink. Her coat is a collarless, Mondrian blue-dyed skin on skin velvet mink. Fur origin: Denmark.

61C. His coat, 19,500.00.
61D. Her coat, 19,500.00.

Sensible luxury: warm gloves knit of cashmere and wool blend, with handsewn palms of cabretta leather. In natural color; one size fits all. Imports, made with imported and domestic yarn. Man's Store.

88A. Leather-palm gloves, 38.00 (3.50).

Our exclusive mohair and nylon sweater, constructed with a deep crossover V neck in a Fair Isle-style pattern. Colors as shown, sizes S,M,L,XL. An Import. Red turtleneck not included. From Man's Store.

88B. V-neck pullover, 75.00 (4.50).

Ralph Lauren nightwear: long sleeved red cotton knit nightshirt, and blue cotton denim robe with red cowboy print lining. Made in the U.S. from imported fabrics. Both, P,S,M,L. From Sleepwear. The Australian sleeping roll is merino sheepskin with cowhide straps. From Mail Order only.

88C. Robe, 190.00 (6.50).
88D. Nightshirt, 95.00 (4.50).
88E. Sleeping roll, 610.00 (6.50).

Mid-weight, pure lambswool plaid throws woven in Scotland. Choose hunter green background or navy. They measure 48 x 72; fringed on both ends. Fine Linens.

88F. Lambswool throws, each 90.00 (4.50).

A FARSIGHTED
VIEW
FOR THE **N-M MAN**

Here, it's rugged wear from Ralph Lauren. Left figure: long jean jacket in stonewashed 14 oz. cotton denim with plaid wool lining. From the U.S. Sizes S-XL. Marled black pullover sweater with shawl collar. Wool/silk/linen; rag handknit import. S-XL. Brushed cotton plaid shirt with button-down collar. Red/white/blue. Imported. Sizes S-XL. Indigo cotton denim jeans with zipper fly. From the U.S. Available in sizes 30-34-36-38.

Right figure: down-filled expedition jacket of imported cotton parachute cloth in cream; collared in natural coyote fur from the U.S. Sizes S-XL. Heavyweight red cotton knit crewneck sweater is all-import, sizes S-XL. Two-pocket blue plaid workshirt in brushed cotton, pre-washed for softness. An import; sizes S-XL. Fuller cut black brushed cotton chino pant with buckle detail and dress extension at waist. From the U.S. 30-34-36-38. From the Man's Store.

89A. Long jean jacket, 150.00 (5.50).
89B. Black sweater, 197.50 (6.50).
89C. Tri-color plaid shirt, 65.00 (4.50).
89D. Indigo denim jeans, 49.50 (3.50).
89E. Fur-trimmed jacket, 595.00 (6.50).
89F. Red crewneck sweater, 62.50 (4.50).
89G. Blue plaid workshirt, 52.50 (4.50).
89H. Black chino pants, 62.50 (4.50).

Customers are invited to stroll through this book, savoring the beautiful location shots in Scotland, where furs are shown as all furs should be worn—in a castle—and the men lounge on craggy rocks o'er the moor in their Ralph Lauren parachute cloth parkas. This is a catalog to study, not bash through in an hour.

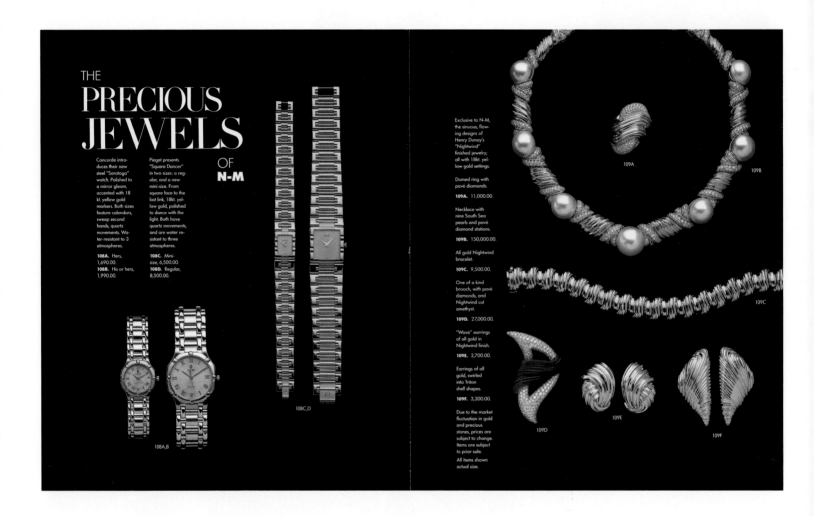

THE
PRECIOUS JEWELS
OF
N-M

Concorde introduces their new steel "Saratoga" watch. Polished to a mirror gleam, accented with 18 kt. yellow gold markers. Both sizes feature calendars, sweep second hands, quartz movements. Water-resistant to 3 atmospheres.

108A. Hers, 1,690.00.
108B. His or hers, 1,990.00.

Piaget presents "Square Dancer" in two sizes: a regular, and a new mini-size. From square face to the last link, 18kt. yellow gold, polished to dance with the light. Both have quartz movements, and are water resistant to three atmospheres.

108C. Mini-size, 6,500.00.
108D. Regular, 8,500.00.

108A,B

108C,D

Exclusive to N-M, the sinuous, flowing designs of Henry Dunay's "Nightwind" finished jewelry; all with 18kt. yellow gold settings.

Domed ring with pavé diamonds.
109A. 11,000.00.

Necklace with nine South Sea pearls and pavé diamond stations.
109B. 150,000.00.

All gold Nightwind bracelet.
109C. 9,500.00.

One of a kind brooch, with pavé diamonds, and Nightwind cut amethyst.
109D. 27,000.00.

"Wave" earrings of all gold in Nightwind finish.
109E. 2,700.00.

Earrings of all gold, swirled into Triton shell shapes.
109F. 3,300.00.

Due to the market fluctuation in gold and precious stones, prices are subject to change. Items are subject to prior sale.
All items shown actual size.

109A   109B   109C   109D   109E   109F

And the time spent will be well rewarded. Shoppers will find all that's needed for every name on their list. Art students might well use this book as the basis for a dissertation. Merchants old and new cannot fail to derive inspiration from this one-of-a-kind display of only the best.

This is a mailorder book and a retail catalog, but most of all, it is the centerpiece for the public relations banquet Neiman-Marcus has been serving to their customers for generations.

Stanley Marcus summed up the essence of specialty retailing in a short phrase that has equal application to all well-conceived catalog programs:

There is never a good sale for Neiman-Marcus unless it's a good buy for the customer.

The new catalog lives up to the tradition of excellence set by the Marcus family many years ago, yet it is as contemporary as tomorrow. A delicately balanced combination, and one that is not easily realized. Somehow these folks from Dallas seem to get better all the time!

POTTERY BARN

When the DMA bestows an ECHO Award upon a catalog, the honor reflects more than praise for a pretty book. Performance and the ability to live up to, or exceed, planned sales objectives is the judges' primary yardstick.

Pottery Barn just happens to have done both.

The formal portfolio information that accompanied the Pottery Barn Autumn 1987 catalog submission to the DMA judges included the following:

Program Objectives: (A) Introduce Pottery Barn catalog as profitable mail order sales vehicle that could reach $25 million sales within 3 years, and be profitable in its initial mailing, (B) Reposition stores of 40 year old company to increase sales, and revitalize image to contemporary customer.

Major Benefits (Products): Well designed, affordable home furnishings and accessories appealing to customers' personal style.

Program Strategy: Develop a high style catalog of excellent production quality with emphasis on home categories overlooked by other stores. Utilize Williams-Sonoma expertise in list selection and store promotion.

RESULTS: Catalog produced sales in excess of plan ($885,000) and profit contribution of 10%. Large list universes tested for rapid rollout; store sales increased 28% during Fall promotion period and 72% during Spring promotion period.

It would seem that Williams-Sonoma's Pottery Barn Division has a good leg up on their "25-million in 3 years" objective. Certainly the production quality is top drawer. Well planned, well lit and creatively styled photography is backed up with first class separations. Presswork, ink and paper all indicate a craftsman's care and an open purse. On-press color control is smooth with no jumps or unevenness, and register is tightly maintained in spite of some difficult knockouts and delicate reverse-type serifs.

AUTUMN 1987

POTTERY BARN—Autumn 1987
Elspeth Martin, *Catalog Manager*
James West, *Sales and Circulation Director*
Hidell-Andres, *Designer*
Danna Walters Lyman, *Merchandiser*
Greg Booth & Associates, *Photographer*
Kate Matracia, *Production Manager*
Katherine Schermerhorn and Audrey Baer Johnson, *Catalog Production*
Bobby Knight Studio, *Mechanical Art*
Foote & Davies [Atlanta, GA], *Printer, on 100# Javelin for cover and 50# Northcote for text*
Color Control [Seattle, WA], *Color Separator*

Pottery Barn has merchandised an eclectic book, running the gamut from high-tech kitchen electronics to Corinthian pedestals and plaster cherubs. The glue holding this seemingly disparate amalgam together is a headline/spread layout technique that gives order to the mix.

The front cover sets the autumnal mood with merchandise from a spread headed "AUTUMN BRUNCH" plus props (actually more merchandise from other pages).

COLORS OF ITALY

A PASTA BOWLS
Here is a set of pasta bowls with a refreshingly different look. We worked directly with Hall China to create the unusual turquoise and orchid glazes that enhance colors of pasta. Each piece is fired at extremely high temperatures to create a lustrous, chip-resistant porcelain that stands up to the heat of both ovens and microwaves, and is dishwasher safe.
Orchid Pasta Bowls, 7½" diam.
Set of four #02-299131 $30.00
Turquoise Serving Bowl, 12" diam.
#02-299123 $18.00

B PASTA SERVERS
These pasta servers are made in Sweden of natural unfinished beechwood. Use them as salad servers too. 11" long. **The pair**
#02-285510 $7.50

CLASSIC COOKWARE
Our pure white Chantal™ cookware is attractive, practical and designed for years of use. Crafted of heavy gauge steel, each pan is coated with multiple layers of high-fired enamel for a durable finish that stands up to high temperatures. This set features tempered glass lids and black enameled bottoms that absorb heat rapidly. Best of all, it's easy to clean and is even dishwasher safe. Includes 1½ and 3 qt. saucepans with lids, 5½ qt. open kettle with steaming basket, and 9½" skillet with a lid that also fits the kettle.
Four-piece set
#02-285908
Open Stock Value $310.00
Special Price $260.00*

Special Bonus!
With the purchase of the 4-piece Chantal™ cookware set you will receive a **free** 9 qt. stockpot and lid (retail value $100.00).*
*Sorry no gift wrap available.

C CAPPUCCINO AND ESPRESSO CUPS
Cappuccino and espresso were never more daring! These vibrant stoneware cups and saucers were created by a San Francisco designer inspired by the Italian flair for color. He perfected a spectacular two-tone glazing technique which allows the pastel hues to merge perfectly at the rim of each cup. We chose the same color combinations (shown at right) for both the cappuccino and espresso cups and saucers. **Sets of four**
Cappuccino Cups and Saucers
#02-299156 $40.00
Espresso Cups and Saucers
#02-299149 $32.00

To order by phone, call 415-421-3400

Espresso is made by forcing steam and water through coffee grounds, extracting a strong, richly flavored brew. Traditionally, dark roasted coffee beans are used, either French Roast or Italian Espresso.

Cappuccino is a combination of espresso and steamed milk. Pour the foamy milk over the espresso. Vary the proportions to your taste.

Caffe Latte is a combination of equal portions of espresso and steamed milk. A hint for caffe latte and cappuccino: after steaming your milk in a narrow pitcher, let it stand for 1 minute, then pour the hot milk over your coffee and spoon the foam on top. Caffe latte and cappuccino may be sprinkled with cinnamon, cocoa or sugar.

G ESPRESSO MAKER
Now you can make authentic espresso and cappuccino at home with this professional-quality Italian pump machine. The Italians have been designing machines to speed up or "express" their coffee making for almost a century. By forcing hot water and steam under pressure through rich, dark coffee grounds, they have learned to extract the very essence of the bean in the fastest, most flavorful way. The state-of-the-art machine brews up to six cups with the *crema* of authentic espresso; and it also steams milk for frothy cappuccino or caffe latte. 9½" x 4½" x 11½" high.
#02-292045 Regularly $175.00
Special Price $149.00

H ESPRESSO SPOONS
In Italy, no espresso drink is complete without one of these miniature spoons. Just 4¼" long, they are the perfect size for the meditative stirring of a morning espresso or cappuccino. 18/8 stainless steel.
Set of six #02-297606 $12.00

D CIOCCOLOTTI DIPPING COOKIES
Divinely addictive dipping cookies are a Tuscan tradition that dates back to the 13th century. When dipped in hot coffee and chocolate drinks, their twice-baked crispness melts to a wonderful blend of bittersweet chocolate and crunchy almond slices. Cioccolotti are now created in the USA from a family recipe that has been handed down through the generations. A recipe is included for *cioccolotti affogato,* a cookie and ice cream dessert. 8 oz.
#02-296897 $7.00

E CAFFE LATTE GLASSES
From French bistros to Italian coffee bars, these traditional 12 oz. glasses have warmed the hearts and hands of Europeans for generations. The durable tempered glass can handle a hot caffe latte as well as a cold glass of milk or soda; the beveled design is easy to hold. And the price is beautifully inexpensive! **Set of six** #02-299503 $12.00

F DINER SHAKERS
From truck stops to trendy restaurants, these classic chrome and glass shakers have served American diners for decades. So why not adapt this dependable design to shake cinnamon and cocoa onto your morning cappuccino? Combined with our faithful sugar shaker, they will infuse your coffee service with nostalgic style. Still made in the USA.
Set of three #02-297978 $8.00

16   17

In a very logical admixture, the spread titled "COLORS OF ITALY" combines precise definitions of Italian coffees with a melange of merchandise appropriate to the category. Even the white enamel cookware in the lower left corner calls to mind the casas of many old Italian friends—until the $260 price tag reminds us that Pottery Barn is definitely uptown Italian.

"STYLE ELEMENTS" headlines a spread of decorative doo-dads, including the ubiquitous Corinthian Pedestal. Classic Cherubs mix with 1950s aluminum bowls and a Minnesota Indian birch bark basket to redefine the word eclectic. Not unaware of this potential misadventure in immiscibility, the copywriter in his subhead quotes a line from Michael Graves in "Metropolitan Home": "I like to create a tension between elements, a dialogue, if you will. . .".

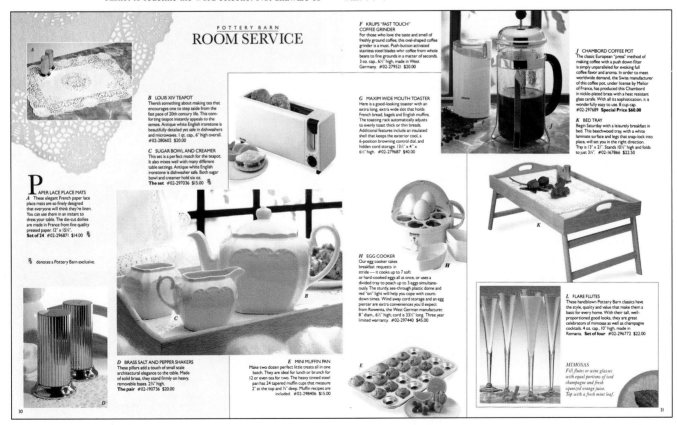

"ROOM SERVICE" provides a delightful excuse for a spread of self-indulgent *ante meridiem* prerequisites. "Your choice madam, coffee from the Chambord Coffee Pot or a spot of tea poured from the Louis XIV teapot. Muffins, English or blueberry? And of course you'll have a Mimosa from a Flared Flute to top it all off."

This spread typifies the clean presentation and carefully controlled manner in which the reader's eye is moved throughout this catalog. Copy pops (although my personal prejudice favors serif typefaces), and relates easily to the photographs. The splendid photography loses not a whit of product detail, even in the high-key shots.

Throughout, the copy is top-drawer professional. Long where necessary and short where embellishment of the photograph would be redundant. Historical information and recipes dot the pages to lend authority by providing information.

Seven of the thirty-six pages of this catalog seem to test the upper limits of the Lillian Vernon giftshop genre of catalog merchandise. ''CHRISTMAS HEARTH'', ''NATURAL ARRANGEMENTS'' and ''BY CANDLELIGHT'' are the headlines. Whatever degree of mailorder success these categories may achieve, store traffic cannot help but be positively affected.

In the opinion of both the DMA and ACA judges, the Pottery Barn catalog rightly deserves the accolades it has received. We concur. The production is rich, the corporate image it projects is outstanding and the 1987 Autumn book did a profitable $1.26 per copy in mail order sales alone. Couple that figure with its powerful performance as a traffic-builder, and you have a winner, by any standard.

SAKS FIFTH AVENUE

Rarely does one see a catalog program as beautifully sculptured as is the "folio" program at Saks Fifth Avenue. It is a sophisticated process, masterfully tailored to the taste of a sophisticated audience.

In 1975-76, SFA inaugurated the "folio" program and published 4 catalogs. In 1987, a total of 44 "folio" catalogs were produced and mailed. A thundering 11-fold increase!

Saks "folio" catalogs have three missions to accomplish:

1. *Presentation of merchandise to facilitate mail and telephone ordering.*
2. *Drive retail traffic into the Saks stores.*
3. *Finally, "folio" must, at all times, project and enhance the quintessential Saks Fifth Avenue image.*

Price points cover a wide range. Presentation mirrors seasonality. And a rich mix of merchandise reflects the diverse activities and life-styles of the upscale Saks Fifth Avenue customer.

Saks Fifth Avenue now operates 45 stores in 18 States. While most of these stores are in 5 States (California, Florida, New York, Texas and Illinois), other stores are in major cities across our nation. From a merchandising point of view, the dissimilar nature of these various marketplaces presents quite a challenge.

Items that are wildly successful in Beverly Hills may die in New York City. Certainly, timing for the swimsuit category will differ from region to region. A visit to some of the SFA stores across the US reveals that merchandise varies from region to region. As you might expect, the individual SFA stores generally stock merchandise that is correct for their market at the appropriate time of year. Regionalized "folio" catalogs are equally sensitive to geographically variable customer taste and seasonal timing.

As a substrate of regional selection within their customer file, Saks' sophisticated computers track individual buying habits. Specialized catalogs are then mailed only to those customers who are targeted as viable prospects for the featured merchandise.

In seemingly inverse proportion, as the number of catalogs has grown larger, more and more of the creative and production work has moved in-house. Today, only photography, separations and printing are "outside" purchases.

SFA's executives feel that the investment in a large advertising staff is worthwhile because: 1). there are shorter lines of communication between department heads and buyers, the advertising department and senior management, 2). direct production responsibility equals better quality control, 3). it makes for greater continuity of the Saks image.

At Saks, staff writers are trained to use lengthy copy when necessary, for: the exposition of a fashion statement, explanation of a designer's point of view, the communication of Saks Fifth Avenue's forecast of exciting new trends to watch (or simply) a complex product description. Just as frequently, the copy is short, leaving it to the merchandise and the mood — as established by the graphic presentation—to generate excitement and desire.

Working with carefully chosen outside creative resources, Saks' advertising staff positions each issue of "folio" and every category of merchandise quite precisely. Objectives are:

"REAL CLOTHES"—slightly oversize 8-⅜" X 10-⅞" format. This catalog cover is printed on a distinctive khaki-colored Carnival Groove paperstock.

Another award winning "folio" catalog! "Real Clothes" was selected for the prestigious 1987 Silver Echo Award by the Direct Marketing Association.

- *To present a look that is correct for the target age group and market segment.*
- *To demonstrate the lightplay, fabrication and movement of the featured garment.*
- *To see, as if through a jeweler's loupe, all the color and facets of a keepsake diamond, or to convey the smell and feel of a fine leather accessory.*

Always one to take advantage of modern print production capabilities, Saks now inserts four-color order forms in most of their high-run "folios". Incremental cost for four-color is minuscule, given the fixed costs of paper, press time and distribution at these quantities. The pluses are: better store image, the ability to tell a merchandise-related color story, and (let's not forget this factor) increased sales.

Fashion photo sessions usually generate dozens of shots that never get printed. At Saks, these outtakes are not wasted. In a video studio right in SFA's own advertising department, these stills become lively and exciting videotape promotions. In one version, the tapes are shown to customers on the retail floor (POP). With different voice-over, the tape becomes a training film for the sales staff. In yet another incarnation, the tapes go outside the store for promotional and recruiting purposes.

Model selection (casting) plays a significant role in the presentation of the Saks Fifth Avenue image and merchandise. Not only do the clothes fit the models, the models fit the clothes. The extraordinary care taken by Saks in their choice of models is demonstrated in all these examples of "folio". Even—or especially—in the children's books. The kids look real in the clothes. In a few cases, they even seem to have slightly outgrown them. Just like the real thing.

As we look closely at the "folio" catalogs on these pages, watch carefully for the subtle shifts in creative techniques as merchandise and seasons change—although the classic Saks "folio" look is never compromised.

The private label line of "REAL CLOTHES" would seem to be right on target for Saks, given their customer franchise in this market segment. Definitely young and just as definitely quality con-scious, the "REAL CLOTHES" type of customer—young men and women—is in the market for versatility, value and vitality.

In this "REAL CLOTHES" catalog, the mer-chandise emphasis is on easy weekend sportswear, accessories and ensembles for this important young group of customers.

"SPRING/SUMMER and AUTUMN folios"—full size format.

Where the SFA "folio" catalog program all began in 1975. Here are the store-wide men's and women's macro-fashion statements for the new season. Layouts and photographs are simple and uncluttered. Each garment is presented in a straightforward manner that clearly highlights style, color and fabrication. Accessory suggestions are made where appropriate. Fashion statements are precise and bold, with no more than three items shown on any one page.

Silk springs.
The belted jumpsuit with a sleek modern and the pure luxuriance of washed silk. By Carole Little, in black, rose, or lilac. Imported for sizes 4 to 14. (74-262) $154. (3.15) Contemporary Sportswear, D/722.

Opposite page:
Walk softly.
Designed by Fiamma Ferragamo... the sleekly contoured flat of anaconda grained leather with leather-light black micro soles. White, beige, black, or camel. Imported from Italy for full and half sizes 7 to 10AAA, 6½ to 10AA, 5½ to 10B. (74-259) $95. (3.00) Designer Shoes, D/423.

Classic elegance.
From the Gucci Lino Collection... a subtle accompaniment. The mid-size camera bag, of vinyl coated canvas with rich, full-grained callskin trim and adjustable shoulder strap. 10½" x 7" x 3", imported from Italy in white or black. Available in select SFA stores and through Folio. (74-260) $215. (3.10) Gucci Collections, D/220.

With a twist!
Our exclusive woven leather belt with an asymmetrical goldtone buckle. 2¼" in brown. Imported from Italy for sizes S,M,L. (74-260) $100. (2.85) Belts, D/88.

59

New outerwear.
The pure silk shell fashioned into an easy jacket. For all weather wear, water repellent, too. With zippered front, a stand-up collar, and drawstring waist. Inside, it's lightly plumped with soft polyester fiberfill. Plum or bronze. Imported for sizes S,M,L. (61-629) $170. (1.79) Better Coats, D/182.

Active-oriented.
The fun and spirit of soft comfort can be found here, with David Brown's acrylic sweatshirt dress. The swingy shape looks great alone, or with a favorite belt that you may add. In periwinkle, or red. Made in U.S.A. for sizes XS,S,M,L. (61-277) $50. (3.10) Loungewear, D/46.

Trompe l' oeil.
To fool the eye... the cream cotton crewneck sweater patterned with one multi-colored floral scarf that wraps around. Ours exclusively, imported for sizes S,M,L. (61-350) $102. (3.45) Contemporary Sweaters, D/717.

One easy piece.
Style that really accompanies you everywhere. Here, a soft wool jersey jumpsuit from Carole Little. With deep sleeves, a belted waist, slightly tapered leg. Made in America. Misses sizes 4 to 14 in plum, black, or wintergreen. (61-278) $158. (3.45) Contemporary Sportswear, D/722.

65

folio
SAKS FIFTH AVENUE
AUTUMN 1988

"GIFTS AND OTHER GOOD THINGS"—full size format.

Twice each year Saks Fifth Avenue publishes an out-and-out gift catalog. Mailings are timed so that personalized items can be easily delivered in time for Graduation and Christmas.

"GIFTS AND OTHER GOOD THINGS FROM SAKS" has its roots in a little 4″ X 5″ catalog called "MONOGRAM". First published in 1976, it was a runaway winner from the start. Back then, every "MONOGRAM" item had to be a personalized product. Not so today.

In this incarnation, the Saks gift "folio" features moderately priced gifts, jewelry, lingerie, domestics and stationery—with or without names or initials.

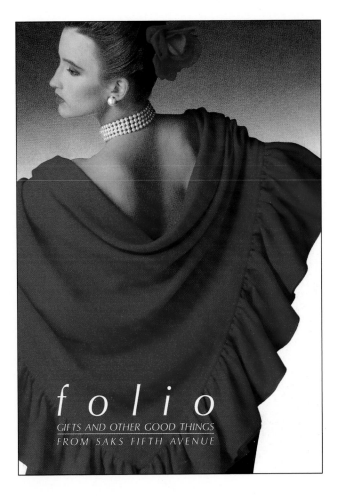

folio
GIFTS AND OTHER GOOD THINGS
FROM SAKS FIFTH AVENUE

"THE WORKS"—full size format.

More than 70% of Saks female customers hold down full-time jobs. For many, shopping—even at Saks—is no longer a recreational pursuit.

Directed to the needs of these well-heeled career women, "THE WORKS" features palettes, colors and items that work together. Outfits are featured (as opposed to items). Prices appear to be very much in line with the thoughtful, relatively conservative nature of this customer group.

"The Works" game plan: separates that work together, contrapuntal and coordinated color palettes, accessories with flair and function, all packaged under "The Works" (private) label.

SAKS FIFTH AVENUE
THE WORKS

"THE MEN'S STORE folio"—full size format.

The Saks Man has a special look. The "Saks Men's Store folio" reflects his taste and gives fashion advice, plus style and accessory direction to their male customers.

Presenting a well-rounded cross-section of the menswear area, this "folio" features clothing and accessories ranging from formal to casual. There are Regional Editions for various sections of the country, plus an edition exclusively for Saks' New York customers.

Dramatic lighting in the Bachrach mode portrays the senior executive look where business suits and formal outfits are presented. Casual poses and backgrounds lighten the mood for informal separates. Yet, careful casting and lighting retain the quiet, aloof attitude of the Saks customer—even at play.

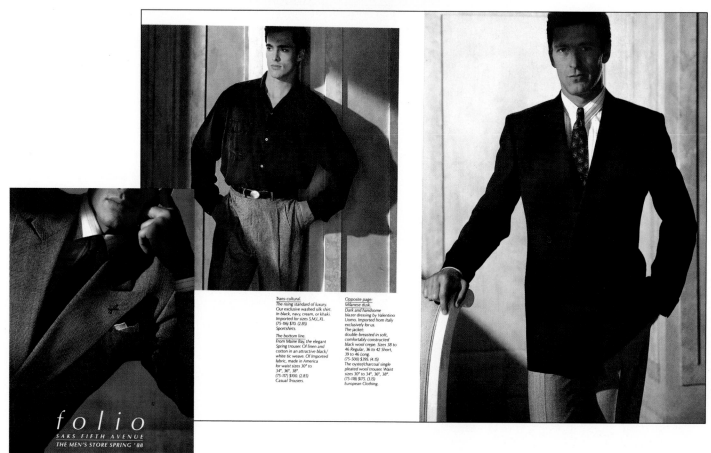

St. John Spring '88 Collection

f o l i o

BRUNO MAGLI

AT SAKS FIFTH AVENUE

"SINGLE SOURCE" CATALOGS—usually digest format.

When a special event or promotion warrants, a dedicated mini-folio, featuring the work of just one design house, is mailed. Recent participants in these solo promotions were: FERRAGAMO shoes, ST. JOHN's knitwear collection and the BRUNO MA-GLI line of imported Italian shoes.

"K.I.D.S folio"—full size format. Sizes 4-20, mailed twice each year.

Saks Fifth Avenue pays attention to their kids, a lot! The Children's category has always been one of Saks' strong points. A broad line of merchandise is represented, fitting just about all occasions for these age groups.

In the real world, children are not always exuberant, bouncy and smiling. They go to school, fix their sister's hair and teach their little brother how to throw a ball. And, they spend many pensive minutes and hours working hard at the difficult process of growing up.

"K.I.D.S. folio" captures these moods and moments. The children are believable, the situations real and the clothing seems just right for each setting. What more can a catalog do to "sell the merch"?

''SAKS CHRISTMAS GIFT BOOK''—10-5/8" X 7-5/8" oblong book in 1988.

The definitive Saks Fifth Avenue collection of gift suggestions. With, most thoughtful from the hurried, harried Christmas shopper's point of view, an index on the opening spread. No camels-for-two here. Just a collection of rare, and in some cases exclusive, items in excellent taste, presented with utter simplicity.

With the rest of the world screaming ''Christmas!'', it is hardly necessary for Saks to belabor the season. Instead, the SFA ''Christmas folio'' murmurs discretely that it is, indeed, the Holiday Season. ''Come shop with us, have fun, and it is quite unlikely that you'll be mauled (or malled) in the process''.

Lucky the man or woman whose gift is selected from these pages. And, whether you're a five-figure gift giver or in the ''twenty-five dollar and under'' group, you'll be delighted with choices Saks presents for your Christmas delectation.

SPECIAL CATEGORY ''folios''—all formats.

Delicacy in flight. L'Air du Temps by Nina Ricci. Exquisitely timeless...a fragrant lure of gardenia, jasmine, carnation, and spice bouquets. The sensuality, reflected in Lalique's lovely double dove flacon.
Lalique Crystal Double Dove Flacon, 1 oz. (9A) $175. (2.85)
Lalique Crystal Double Dove Flacon, ½ oz. (9B) $100. (2.85)
Eau de Toilette, 2.5 oz. (9C) $31. (2.85)

9

''PULSE POINTS''—Award winning catalog. Perfume compendium, personal care and cosmetics. Beautifully staged photography. Mailed once each year in time for Christmas gift giving.

folio
SAKS FIFTH AVENUE
DIRECTIONS 1988

''DIRECTIONS''—oblong digest format. Presents shoes from various Saks shoe departments and designers at a wide range of price points.

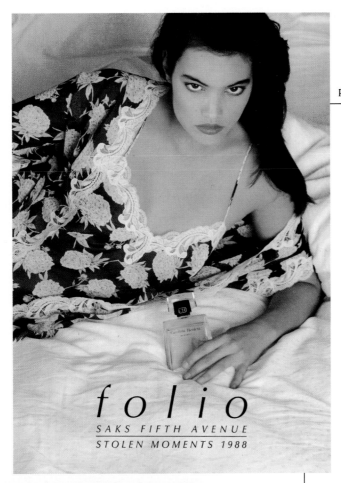

folio

SAKS FIFTH AVENUE

STOLEN MOMENTS 1988

"STOLEN MOMENTS"—Lingerie, sleepwear, personal care and cosmetics for women.

A revelation of leg!
Our exclusive lace control top pantyhose with ultra sheer legs. In white or black nylon. Made in America for sizes P(4'10" to 5'3"), M(5'4" to 5'10"), T(5'6" and over). (82-127) 12.50 (2.85) Hosiery, D/12.

folio

SOME ENCHANTED EVENING

SAKS FIFTH AVENUE

"SAKS SPECIAL OCCASION DRESSING"— Very Special Occasion misses dresses and accessories. Photography usually done in fabulous locations. In this case, Maximes in New York, and a real New Orleans Plantation.

Soft suiting in a breath of peach silk satin back crepe. From L. Perez, imported for sizes 6 to 16 (75-115) 460. (4.35) Fifth Avenue Dresses, D/526.

SHARPER IMAGE

If you're a member of a young, active, mailorder buying household, odds are that The Sharper Image seems like an old friend. (Actually, SI has only been mailing catalogs for 10 years.) Sharper Image's striking graphics, intensely informative copy and always-fresh merchandise created a new standard, right from its very first issue. Today, Sharper Image is surrounded by would-be imitators, but the ranks of the me-too catalogs are thinning rapidly as they discover there's more to running a HiTech consumer mailorder business than publishing good looking catalogs.

Richard Thalheimer's catalog of toys for grown-ups has become a benchmark against which all catalogs in this field are measured. But, there's much more to his story than just a pretty book.

The first direct response test for SI was a series of ads run in "Runner's World" Magazine. Richard is an avid runner; ergo, a runner's watch was his first mailorder item. As usual, Instant Fame turns out to be anything but an instant process. Sharper Image's "out of town tryouts" were a series of ever-expanding, yet relatively inexpensive, non-catalog, direct response efforts.

The use of print media and the number of items advertised expanded gradually until the premier catalog issue in 1979. By that time, art and copy formats and a basic merchandising theme were all coalescing into sharp focus. Since those early years, Sharper Image has increased its product lines exponentially. From a nucleus offering of small, ultra-modern electronic gadgets, the line has grown to include everything from exercise machines to jewelry, and from birdfeeders to electronic chess sets.

Then came the stores. The first in 1981. Then there were four (1984), another 10 by 1985. And today, there are 62 stores in the United States and three more in Japan. In a complete turnabout, 1988 OTC retail accounted for over 75% of all sales. By contrast, in 1984, mailorder generated 90% of SI's income.

In the past, most companies that have split their sales between mailorder and OTC retail have found it desirable to set up two discrete marketing and merchandising departments: one for the catalog program and another to merchandise and promote retail store operations. The fundamental economic and operating philosophies of the two very different sales channels are usually immiscible. The above notwithstanding, it is certainly more efficient if both operations are able to share vendors, G&A functions and warehouse facilities.

It will be interesting to watch as Sharper Image makes its mailorder/OTC transition. We can only hope that the great

Captain your own summer cruise boat.

THE SHARPER IMAGE—Jewelry and Gemstones 1988
Agency: *In-house*

—May 1987
Agency: *In-house*

Foote & Davies [Lincoln, NE], *Printer, on 80# Champion Panaprint for cover and 45# Mead Northcote 'RMP' for text*
Atlanta Color Concepts [Atlanta, GA], *Color Separator*

catalogs and intriguing merchandise keep showing up in our mailbox every month or so. After all, if Thalheimer isn't around to copy from, where are all the me-tooers going to get their ideas?

The judging panel of the Direct Marketing Association (numbering up to 450 members) awarded the Gold Echo to Sharper Image for their Jewelry and Gemstones catalog. Small wonder! This little beauty produced $545,000 in sales with an average order of $378. A stunning performance for any consumer mailorder effort.

Sharper Image's impeccable reputation for quality

and service was most assuredly a causative factor for this success. But the $20 appraisal offer described on the back cover must also have made a major contribution. In the highly unlikely event that every single customer of this catalog would take advantage of the offer, the cost to SI would have been a trifling 5% of sales. A small price, indeed, to pay for this kind of high margin, high ticket sales activity.

"Jewelry and Gemstones" has all the hallmarks one
has come to expect from Sharper Image:

- *Creative marketing (the appraisal offer and
  the Frequent Buyers program).*
- *Compelling layouts and expert photography.*
- *Exactly the right amount of copy for each
  item, well written, legible, and easy to find.*
- *Expensive (top ticket $10,000, but many of
  the lovely baubles are priced under $1,000).*
- *And finally, faultless reproduction of some
  very difficult subjects.*

Another Sharper Image catalog, another Gold Award. This time from the American Catalog Awards judges. These pages (and the underlying sales figures) are the reasons for ACA's accolades. Careful study will reward the reader with chapter and verse on how to design and execute a successful catalog. All of the important selling elements we've discussed in other chapters are assembled on these pages from the Sharper Image May issue.

The graphic Master Class illustrated on these SI pages needs no further exposition from us. But a word of caution is in order: this treatment works for Sharper Image—for their market, their products and their way of doing business. A plethora of out-and-out knock-offs have tried—and failed. In some other instances, art directors have recognized the

merits of SI's designs, and have attempted to use exactly the same format, but for different products sold to different markets. They too have failed.

The lessons we should expect to learn from a study of these pages cannot be instilled at the copy machine. Rather, absolute product knowledge and intimate understanding of your customer's psyche—in the hands of a well-trained, direct response oriented creative staff—are the bricks and the mortar from which great catalogs are constructed.

Looking at these pages with the aforementioned thoughts in mind, what do we see? We see many of the basic mailorder rules in practice. Callouts, long copy, crisp illustrations, frequent reference to 800 numbers and special offers, easy-reader layouts and type, and much more.

We also sense the impact of an authority: there is no doubt about the fact that this presentation is being made by an expert in his field. Throughout the book there flows a sense of dedication to customer service (which, incidentally, is backed up by courteous store personnel and by a knowledgeable and equally well-trained telephone staff).

This is grist that any creative staff can work with to come up with their own package. The end result may not, and probably should not, look a bit like the Sharper Image catalog, but the pre-writing, pre-layout cognitive process may well derive its inspiration from Richard Thalheimer's baby. If this should happen in your shop, drop Richard a line to let him know. He'll be thrilled that someone finally got the message.

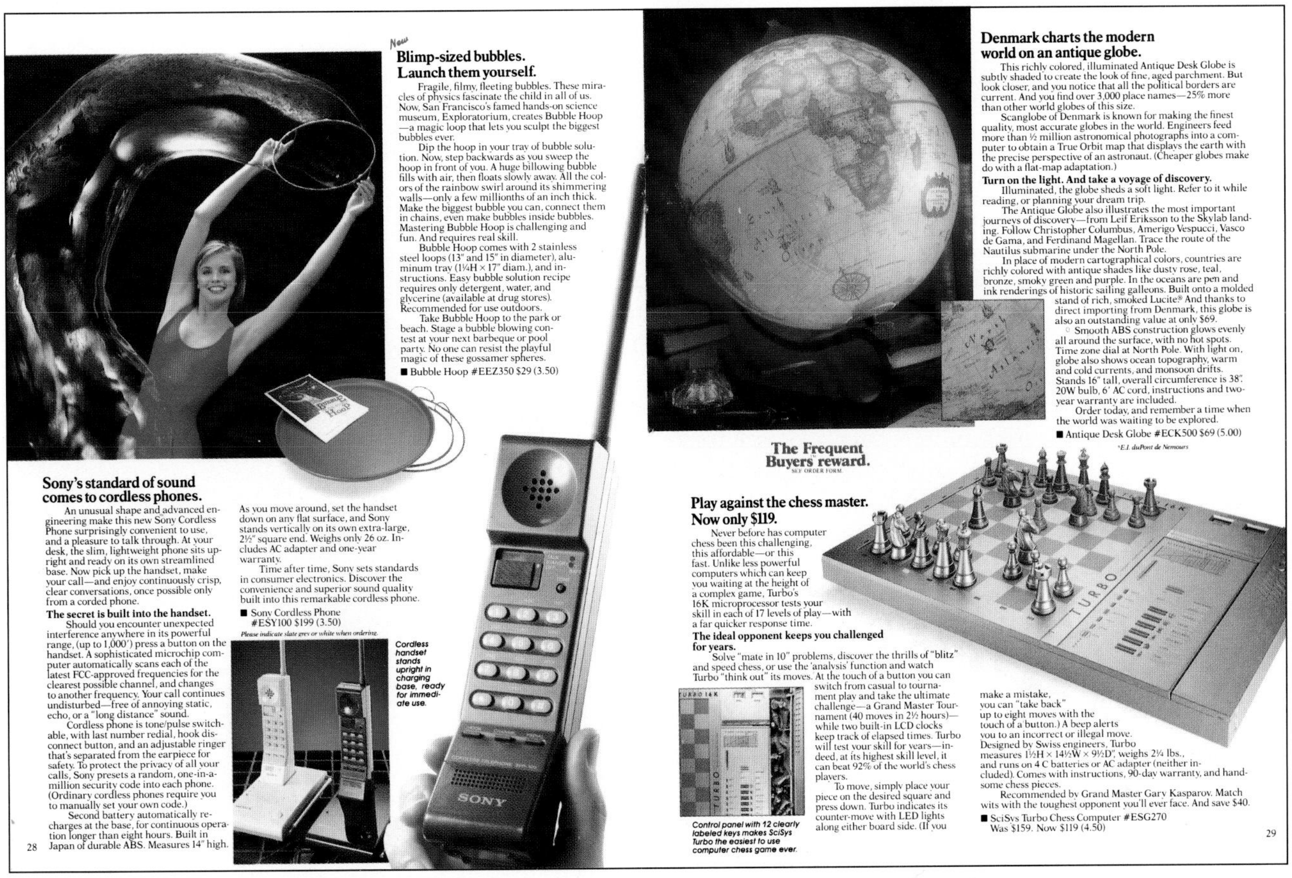

New

Blimp-sized bubbles. Launch them yourself.

Fragile, filmy, fleeting bubbles. These miracles of physics fascinate the child in all of us. Now, San Francisco's famed hands-on science museum, Exploratorium, creates Bubble Hoop—a magic loop that lets you sculpt the biggest bubbles ever.

Dip the hoop in your tray of bubble solution. Now, step backwards as you sweep the hoop in front of you. A huge billowing bubble fills with air, then floats slowly away. All the colors of the rainbow swirl around its shimmering walls—only a few millionths of an inch thick. Make the biggest bubble you can, connect them in chains, even make bubbles inside bubbles. Mastering Bubble Hoop is challenging and fun. And requires real skill.

Bubble Hoop comes with 2 stainless steel loops (13" and 15" in diameter), aluminum tray (1¼H × 17" diam.), and instructions. Easy bubble solution recipe requires only detergent, water, and glycerine (available at drug stores). Recommended for use outdoors.

Take Bubble Hoop to the park or beach. Stage a bubble blowing contest at your next barbeque or pool party. No one can resist the playful magic of these gossamer spheres.

■ Bubble Hoop #EEZ350 $29 (3.50)

Sony's standard of sound comes to cordless phones.

An unusual shape and advanced engineering make this new Sony Cordless Phone surprisingly convenient to use, and a pleasure to talk through. At your desk, the slim, lightweight phone sits upright and ready on its own streamlined base. Now pick up the handset, make your call—and enjoy continuously crisp, clear conversations, once possible only from a corded phone.

The secret is built into the handset.

Should you encounter unexpected interference anywhere in its powerful range, (up to 1,000') press a button on the handset. A sophisticated microchip computer automatically scans each of the latest FCC-approved frequencies for the clearest possible channel, and changes to another frequency. Your call continues undisturbed—free of annoying static, echo, or a "long distance" sound.

Cordless phone is tone/pulse switchable, with last number redial, hook disconnect button, and an adjustable ringer that's separated from the earpiece for safety. To protect the privacy of all your calls, Sony presets a random, one-in-a-million security code into each phone. (Ordinary cordless phones require you to manually set your own code.)

Second battery automatically recharges at the base, for continuous operation longer than eight hours. Built in Japan of durable ABS. Measures 14" high. As you move around, set the handset down on any flat surface, and Sony stands vertically on its own extra-large, 2½" square end. Weighs only 26 oz. Includes AC adapter and one-year warranty.

Time after time, Sony sets standards in consumer electronics. Discover the convenience and superior sound quality built into this remarkable cordless phone.

■ Sony Cordless Phone #ESY100 $199 (3.50)

Please indicate slate grey or white when ordering.

Cordless handset stands upright in charging base, ready for immediate use.

28

Denmark charts the modern world on an antique globe.

This richly colored, illuminated Antique Desk Globe is subtly shaded to create the look of fine, aged parchment. But look closer, and you notice that all the political borders are current. And you find over 3,000 place names—25% more than other world globes of this size.

Scanglobe of Denmark is known for making the finest quality, most accurate globes in the world. Engineers feed more than ½ million astronomical photographs into a computer to obtain a True Orbit map that displays the earth with the precise perspective of an astronaut. (Cheaper globes make do with a flat-map adaptation.)

Turn on the light. And take a voyage of discovery.

Illuminated, the globe sheds a soft light. Refer to it while reading, or planning your dream trip.

The Antique Globe also illustrates the most important journeys of discovery—from Leif Eriksson to the Skylab landing. Follow Christopher Columbus, Amerigo Vespucci, Vasco de Gama, and Ferdinand Magellan. Trace the route of the Nautilus submarine under the North Pole.

In place of modern cartographical colors, countries are richly colored with antique shades like dusty rose, teal, bronze, smoky green and purple. In the oceans are pen and ink renderings of historic sailing galleons. Built onto a molded stand of rich, smoked Lucite® And thanks to direct importing from Denmark, this globe is also an outstanding value at only $69.

Smooth ABS construction glows evenly all around the surface, with no hot spots. Time zone dial at North Pole. With light on, globe also shows ocean topography, warm and cold currents, and monsoon drifts. Stands 16" tall, overall circumference is 38". 20W bulb, 6' AC cord, instructions and two-year warranty are included.

Order today, and remember a time when the world was waiting to be explored.

■ Antique Desk Globe #ECK500 $69 (5.00)

*E.I. duPont de Nemours

The Frequent Buyers reward.
SEE ORDER FORM

Play against the chess master. Now only $119.

Never before has computer chess been this challenging, this affordable—or this fast. Unlike less powerful computers which can keep you waiting at the height of a complex game, Turbo's 16K microprocessor tests your skill in each of 17 levels of play—with a far quicker response time.

The ideal opponent keeps you challenged for years.

Solve "mate in 10" problems, discover the thrills of "blitz" and speed chess, or use the 'analysis' function and watch Turbo "think out" its moves. At the touch of a button you can switch from casual to tournament play and take the ultimate challenge—a Grand Master Tournament (40 moves in 2½ hours)—while two built-in LCD clocks keep track of elapsed times. Turbo will test your skill for years—indeed, at its highest skill level, it can beat 92% of the world's chess players.

To move, simply place your piece on the desired square and press down. Turbo indicates its counter-move with LED lights along either board side. (If you make a mistake, you can "take back" up to eight moves with the touch of a button.) A beep alerts you to an incorrect or illegal move. Designed by Swiss engineers, Turbo measures 1½H × 14½W × 9½D", weighs 2¼ lbs., and runs on 4 C batteries or AC adapter (neither included). Comes with instructions, 90-day warranty, and handsome chess pieces.

Recommended by Grand Master Gary Kasparov. Match wits with the toughest opponent you'll ever face. And save $40.

■ SciSys Turbo Chess Computer #ESG270 Was $159. Now $119 (4.50)

Control panel with 12 clearly labeled keys makes SciSys Turbo the easiest to use computer chess game ever.

29

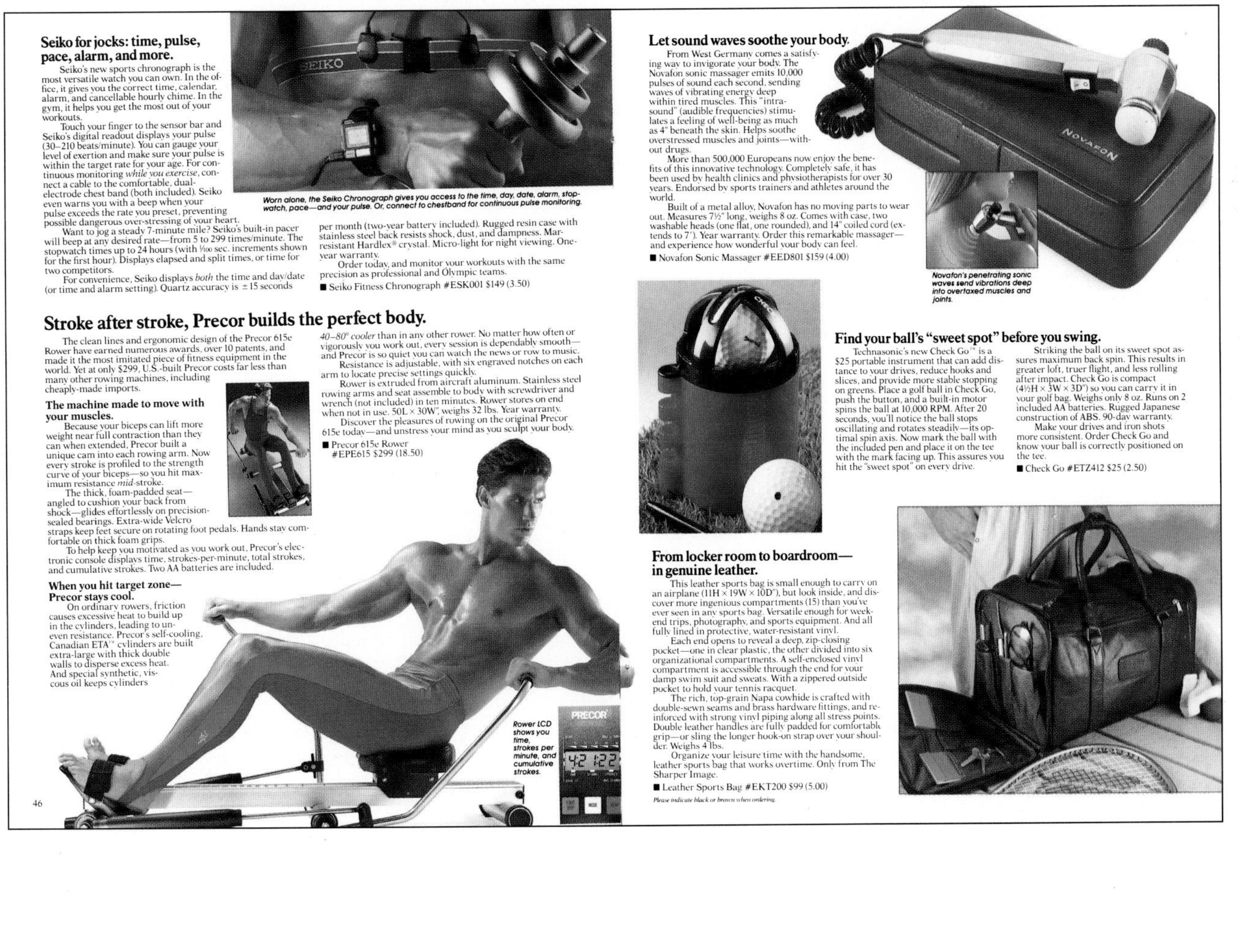

Seiko for jocks: time, pulse, pace, alarm, and more.

Seiko's new sports chronograph is the most versatile watch you can own. In the office, it gives you the correct time, calendar, alarm, and cancellable hourly chime. In the gym, it helps you get the most out of your workouts.

Touch your finger to the sensor bar and Seiko's digital readout displays your pulse (30–210 beats/minute). You can gauge your level of exertion and make sure your pulse is within the target rate for your age. For continuous monitoring *while you exercise*, connect a cable to the comfortable, dual-electrode chest band (both included). Seiko even warns you with a beep when your pulse exceeds the rate you preset, preventing possible dangerous over-stressing of your heart.

Want to jog a steady 7-minute mile? Seiko's built-in pacer will beep at any desired rate—from 5 to 299 times/minute. The stopwatch times up to 24 hours (with 1/100 sec. increments shown for the first hour). Displays elapsed and split times, or time for two competitors.

For convenience, Seiko displays *both* the time and day/date (or time and alarm setting). Quartz accuracy is ±15 seconds per month (two-year battery included). Rugged resin case with stainless steel back resists shock, dust, and dampness. Mar-resistant Hardlex® crystal. Micro-light for night viewing. One-year warranty.

Order today, and monitor your workouts with the same precision as professional and Olympic teams.

■ Seiko Fitness Chronograph #ESK001 $149 (3.50)

Worn alone, the Seiko Chronograph gives you access to the time, day, date, alarm, stop-watch, pace—and your pulse. Or, connect to chestband for continuous pulse monitoring.

Stroke after stroke, Precor builds the perfect body.

The clean lines and ergonomic design of the Precor 615e Rower have earned numerous awards, over 10 patents, and made it the most imitated piece of fitness equipment in the world. Yet at only $299, U.S.-built Precor costs far less than many other rowing machines, including cheaply-made imports.

The machine made to move with your muscles.

Because your biceps can lift more weight near full contraction than they can when extended, Precor built a unique cam into each rowing arm. Now every stroke is profiled to the strength curve of your biceps—so you hit maximum resistance *mid*-stroke.

The thick, foam-padded seat—angled to cushion your back from shock—glides effortlessly on precision-sealed bearings. Extra-wide Velcro straps keep feet secure on rotating foot pedals. Hands stay comfortable on thick foam grips.

To help keep you motivated as you work out, Precor's electronic console displays time, strokes-per-minute, total strokes, and cumulative strokes. Two AA batteries are included.

When you hit target zone—Precor stays cool.

On ordinary rowers, friction causes excessive heat to build up in the cylinders, leading to uneven resistance. Precor's self-cooling, Canadian ETA™ cylinders are built extra-large with thick double walls to disperse excess heat. And special synthetic, viscous oil keeps cylinders *40–80° cooler* than in any other rower. No matter how often or vigorously you work out, every session is dependably smooth—and Precor is so quiet you can watch the news or row to music.

Resistance is adjustable, with six engraved notches on each arm to locate precise settings quickly.

Rower is extruded from aircraft aluminum. Stainless steel rowing arms and seat assemble to body with screwdriver and wrench (not included) in ten minutes. Rower stores on end when not in use. 50L × 30W", weighs 32 lbs. Year warranty.

Discover the pleasures of rowing on the original Precor 615e today—and unstress your mind as you sculpt your body.

■ Precor 615e Rower #EPE615 $299 (18.50)

Rower LCD shows you time, strokes per minute, and cumulative strokes.

46

Let sound waves soothe your body.

From West Germany comes a satisfying way to invigorate your body. The Novafon sonic massager emits 10,000 pulses of sound each second, sending waves of vibrating energy deep within tired muscles. This "intrasound" (audible frequencies) stimulates a feeling of well-being as much as 4" beneath the skin. Helps soothe overstressed muscles and joints—without drugs.

More than 500,000 Europeans now enjoy the benefits of this innovative technology. Completely safe, it has been used by health clinics and physiotherapists for over 30 years. Endorsed by sports trainers and athletes around the world.

Built of a metal alloy, Novafon has no moving parts to wear out. Measures 7½" long, weighs 8 oz. Comes with case, two washable heads (one flat, one rounded), and 14" coiled cord (extends to 7'). Year warranty. Order this remarkable massager—and experience how wonderful your body can feel.

■ Novafon Sonic Massager #EED801 $159 (4.00)

Novafon's penetrating sonic waves send vibrations deep into overtaxed muscles and joints.

Find your ball's "sweet spot" before you swing.

Technasonic's new Check Go™ is a $25 portable instrument that can add distance to your drives, reduce hooks and slices, and provide more stable stopping on greens. Place a golf ball in Check Go, push the button, and a built-in motor spins the ball at 10,000 RPM. After 20 seconds, you'll notice the ball stops oscillating and rotates steadily—its optimal spin axis. Now mark the ball with the included pen and place it on the tee with the mark facing up. This assures you hit the "sweet spot" on every drive.

Striking the ball on its sweet spot assures maximum back spin. This results in greater loft, truer flight, and less rolling after impact. Check Go is compact (4½H × 3W × 3D") so you can carry it in your golf bag. Weighs only 8 oz. Runs on 2 included AA batteries. Rugged Japanese construction of ABS. 90-day warranty.

Make your drives and iron shots more consistent. Order Check Go and know your ball is correctly positioned on the tee.

■ Check Go #ETZ412 $25 (2.50)

From locker room to boardroom—in genuine leather.

This leather sports bag is small enough to carry on an airplane (11H × 19W × 10D"), but look inside, and discover more ingenious compartments (15) than you've ever seen in any sports bag. Versatile enough for weekend trips, photography, and sports equipment. And all fully lined in protective, water-resistant vinyl.

Each end opens to reveal a deep, zip-closing pocket—one in clear plastic, the other divided into six organizational compartments. A self-enclosed vinyl compartment is accessible through the end for your damp swim suit and sweats. With a zippered outside pocket to hold your tennis racquet.

The rich, top-grain Napa cowhide is crafted with double-sewn seams and brass hardware fittings, and reinforced with strong vinyl piping along all stress points. Double leather handles are fully padded for comfortable grip—or sling the longer hook-on strap over your shoulder. Weighs 4 lbs.

Organize your leisure time with the handsome, leather sports bag that works overtime. Only from The Sharper Image.

■ Leather Sports Bag #EKT200 $99 (5.00)

Please indicate black or brown when ordering.

TIFFANY & CO.

One word—"Tiffany"—projects a whole series of cinemascopic images: quality, expensive, *arbiter elegantiarum*, diamonds/gems/silver/tabletop/stationery/gifts and more. Where did all those mental wide-screen impressions come from? TV commercials? No. Radio sponsorship? No. Full page newspaper ads? No (in spite of the fact that wider coverage might be justified by the number of Tiffany doors: four overseas and nine in the United States).

Instead, Tiffany's media choices reflect an attitude that differs from the mass media, paid-for, saturation approach common to a number of other stores. True, tasteful, understated Tiffany ads do appear with some regularity in a select group of magazines and newspapers. And yes, a similar demographic customer profile is targeted by Tiffany's very attractive catalogs, mailed 4 times each year. But the powerhouse that really promotes the Tiffany Image is the multifaceted Public Relations Program in all its glorious manifestations.

- *"Breakfast at Tiffany's", the Tiffany Diamond, and "The Diamonds of Tiffany" (a traveling collection on exhibit from coast to coast).*
- *There's a constant barrage of press releases, backed up by a fact-packed press kit full of human interest anecdotes; as well as a fascinating chronology of Tiffany milestones.*
- *Celebrity customers buy (and sometimes sell) diamonds and other "named" jewelry items; as famous in some circles as are their owners. Sporting awards were created in Tiffany's workshop for the Belmont Cup, the Super Bowl and the NBA. Tiffany has been winning international awards for its silver pieces since 1867, when they became the first American company to be so honored. Even the Great Seal of the United States was redesigned by Tiffany in 1885 to correct some errors in the original.*

These occasions and hundreds of others are recorded by Tiffany's PR staff, and disseminated in a carefully monitored flow of lively communications to the media. They, in turn, reciprocate by running the stories because editors know their readers will want to hear more about the world renowned Tiffany & Co. And the self-renewing circle of fame is once more refreshed.

Easy enough to do, you might say, if your name is Tiffany, and you've got 150 years of history on your side. Right! That does make the job easier for the present PR Staff, but Charles Lewis Tiffany was doing the same thing from the day he first opened his "Stationery & Fancy Goods" shop on New York's West Side. It took imagination to sell four inch slices of the first transatlantic telephone cable. It took imagination and a lot of intestinal fortitude to buy more than a third of the French Crown Jewels when King Louis Phillipe was overthrown: a magnificent collection of almost 680 carats, which included the famous Diamond Girdle of Marie Antoinette and Empress Eugenie's Great Diamond Necklace.

To state that Tiffany has manufactured PR since Day One may be a slight exaggeration. Perhaps one might rather say that they

SPRING SELECTIONS
1988

TIFFANY & CO.

TIFFANY & CO.—Selections
Suzanne McMillan, *Group Vice President, Marketing*
Susan Korb Jomo, *Director of Advertising and Publications*
Kevin O'Halloran, *Vice President of Direct Mail*
Cheryl Lewin, *Art Director*
Lewin Design Associates, *Agency*
Brad Bealmear and Josh Haskin, *Photographers*
Case-Hoyt [Rochester, NY], *Printer*

The now-famous robin's egg hue has marked the covers of Tiffany catalogs since the very first issue in 1845. And since the beginning, it has been an integral part of Tiffany's public image. Originally titled "Catalogue of Useful and Fancy Articles", this book has been published continuously since 1877, making it one of the longest lived catalogs in the world.

have not missed many occasions over the years for favorable mention in the press. Before the jewels and silver and celebrities, Charles Tiffany was selling items such as head ornaments, horse and dog whips, moccasins and 17 preparations for the hair—and getting famous. His first mailorder catalog, published in 1845 (more than 25 years before "Monkey" Ward got into the act), added watches, clocks, silverware, umbrellas, Chinese bric-a-brac and bronzes. Still no celebrities, but the PR mill was alive and well.

There's not a retailer, a manufacturer or a distributor alive who does not have a story to tell. Put that story in the hands of a PR professional, and there is the beginning of a Public Relations program. Nurture and feed the program, and there will arise a reputation and an image. From these will eventually spring a positive predisposition to buy the sponsor's products and services.

Exclusive By Design

A. From the Tiffany's Classics Collection™ men's quartz strap watch in fourteen karat gold, with date and sweep second hand, $1,050.
B. Cuff links of black onyx and fourteen karat gold, $495.
C. "Black Shoulder" note cards engraved on white stock, 12 x 12", twelve cards, $40.
D. "Bow" ear-clips of diamonds set in platinum, $9,650.
E. "Fallen Leaf" pin in matte and polished eighteen karat gold, $725.
F. From Tiffany's collection of one-of-a-kind estate jewelry, emerald and diamond ring set in platinum, circa 1920, $38,500. Subject to prior sale.
G. Choker of black onyx with pavé diamond accent and eighteen karat gold clasp, $1,600.
H. From Tiffany's collection of one-of-a-kind estate jewelry, bar pin with sapphires and diamonds set in platinum, circa 1900, $2,250.
J. "Rose" box in hand-painted Battersea enamel, designed by Sybil Connolly, $140.
K. "Bee" pin in eighteen karat gold with pavé diamonds and ruby "eyes," $1,200.
L. H-link bracelet in fourteen karat gold, $750.
M. Tiffany's Back to Glamour® bow ear-clips in eighteen karat gold with rubies, $1,525.
N. *Tiffany's 150 Years*, by John Loring, Design Director of Tiffany & Co., with an introduction by Louis Auchincloss. This new book celebrates Tiffany's legendary history, $50.

Cover: "Foulard" powder case by Jean Schlumberger in eighteen karat gold, $14,850.

Relying on the merchandise itself and the cultured and discriminating taste of their readers, words are kept to an absolute minimum. Because of Tiffany's reputation, photographs alone suffice to tell the story. Collections by Jean Schlumberger, Elsa Peretti and Paloma Picasso are identified in headlines, but the balance of the items are generic Tiffany: produced in their own workshops or manufactured to their uncompromisingly strict specifications.

Paloma Picasso Designs

A. "X" pin in sterling silver, $275.
B. "X" ear-clips in sterling silver, $175. In eighteen karat gold, $750.
C. "Scribble" pin in sterling silver, $195.
D. "Love and Kisses" pin in sterling silver, $185.
E. "X" bracelet in sterling silver, $325.
F. "Hearts" necklace of black onyx and hematite with an eighteen karat gold double ring clasp, $650.
G. "Oak Leaf" brooch in eighteen karat gold, $1,175.
H. Eighteen karat gold strap watch with quartz movement, $4,600.
J. "Scribble" earrings in eighteen karat gold for pierced ears, $350.
K. "Scribble" pin in eighteen karat gold, $575.
L. "Love and Kisses" pin in eighteen karat gold, $375.
M. "X" earrings in eighteen karat gold for pierced ears, $300.
N. "Love and Kisses" ring in eighteen karat gold, $550.
O. "Dove" brooch in sterling silver, $350.
Designs copyrighted by Paloma Picasso

To place an order or ask about an item in the catalogue, please call **800-526-0649** *between 8:00 and 7:00 EST on weekdays; 9:30 and 5:30 EST on Saturdays.*

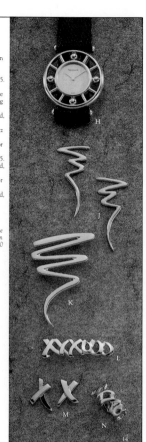

Natural Adornments

Emeralds and diamonds in eighteen karat gold.
A. Earrings for pierced ears, $2,750.
B. Ring, $5,000.
C. Pendant on a 16" chain, $1,725.
D. "Feather" pendant in eighteen karat gold with pavé diamonds, only at Tiffany, $785.
E. Diamond bracelet in eighteen karat gold, $6,700.
F. "Pansies" in eighteen karat gold with diamonds for pierced ears, only at Tiffany, $750.
Amethysts in eighteen karat gold:
G. Earrings for pierced ears, $300.
H. Ring with diamonds, $1,275.
J. Pendant with diamonds, $875.
K. Bar pin of garnet, citrine, peridot, tourmaline, aquamarine and amethyst in eighteen karat gold, $925.
L. "Fallen Leaf" pin in matte and polished eighteen karat gold, only at Tiffany, $725.
M. Cultured pearl choker with diamonds in eighteen karat gold, only at Tiffany, $5,100.
N. Ear-clips of cultured pearls and diamonds in eighteen karat gold, only at Tiffany, $3,450.
O. "Leaves" ear-clips of diamonds set in platinum, exclusively at Tiffany, $7,300.
P. "Ribbon Leaf" ear-clips in matte and polished eighteen karat gold, only at Tiffany, $975.
Q. "Ribbon Leaf" pin in matte and polished eighteen karat gold, only at Tiffany, $850.
R. From the Tiffany Classics Collection™, diamond and fourteen karat gold quartz bracelet watch, $2,650.
S. Diamond ring in eighteen karat gold, $1,350.
T. Diamond ring in eighteen karat gold, $4,800.
U. "Tiffany Tulip" cachepot in hand-painted Italian earthenware, 8½" diameter, $140.

Without sacrificing an iota of image, Tiffany successfully mails more than 10 million catalogs each year. Clearly, all these households are not in the market for six-figure cocktail rings. Yes, Tiffany & Co. has a well deserved reputation for offering their well-heeled customers some of the most costly baubles known to the civilized world. But if one ''shops'' these Tiffany catalogs, there's a real surprise. The majority of items are priced very competitively.

There's the genius. Sell the most of the best and forget the rest. Be sure the world knows you're the leader. Be the one to set the standards. And then protect your reputation by treating the customer fairly.

II
BUSINESS-
TO-BUSINESS

The very name of this Chapter is misleading. There just didn't seem to be any better handle to hang on this heterogeneous collection of catalogs. Perhaps "Non-Consumer" would serve better?

The term "Business-to-Business" (BTB) implies a commonality of markets and products that does not exist in the real world. For every one of the 1,050 SIC codes (or each of the 5,000 telephone company yellow page headings), there is a discrete marketplace. And in each marketplace there are different buy-buttons to be pushed.

Given: that buyers are people—in all industries. That they will react to the same stimuli at work as at home. That most of the tried and true rules of Direct Response Marketing obtain in the business world.

However: Financial executives react to a different set of triggers and verbiage than do their engineering associates. The semantics of the MIS department are as Sanskrit to the Human Resources Director. Each trade, each product line, each service-vendor and each Department of the Government has its own vernacular and sensibilities.

Ergo: there is quite clearly no single presentation methodology that will suffice for the entire, so-called Business to Business market.

To reach a broad market and sell a number of items, the traditional and relatively inexpensive catalog usually turns out to be ideal BTB communications vehicle. At the other extreme, the most cost effective vehicle might be the super-expensive sequential promotion.

A sequential (staggered) series of promotion packages can be a formidable attention-getter. The contents of any one package in the set might include anything from a major league baseball to a letter, or one piece of an unidentified assembly kit (subsequent mailings deliver the rest of the kit). In most cases, these high-priced, super-targeted packages consist of a series of two, three or more highly creative direct response packages. It's not at all unusual for these promotions to reach only a couple of hundred, or perhaps as few as 50 recipients.

Costly, sequential promotional packages work: 1). If the product or service being sold carries a substantial price tag. 2). And/or if the length of the potential relationship is to be a long enough to justify the promotional cost. 3). If you're sure the follow-up will be timely and well planned. 4). And, if the recipient carries enough clout in the target organization to be able to make a buying decision—sans committee.

At the other extreme of BTB marketing are firms such as vendors of expendable supplies. These companies may have to reach dozens and even hundreds of buyers and prospects at all departmental levels within a client-company. Even worse: as you can imagine, this broad spectrum of buyers has been considerably fragmented and expanded with the advent of the ubiquitous desktop computer. Catalogs and low cost per unit promotional mailings serve these markets best.

The consumer direct response industry is on a fast track. But in spite of all the hullabaloo, these highly-touted gains are as naught compared to the rate of growth of BTB advertisers. Reason? A simple matter of return on investment, and the astronomical increases in the cost of a sales call.

Today, it costs more than $250 to plunk one salesman down in a face-to-face meeting with a prospect or customer. Note, I did not say, "get the order", only a meeting. Another industrial sales statistic: on average, it takes five sales calls to make a sale; ergo, $250 X 5 = $1,250—to make one sale one time!

Every facet of a business-to-business advertising campaign has to be focused upon reducing these sales costs. Catalogs can and do play a major role in accomplishing this end result. But they cannot do the job alone. Direct mail, telemarketing, ads in trade publications, and yes, even the in-person sales calls are all viable campaign components.

If, before a salesman arrives, his customer is well versed in the product, and/or if he has invited a sales call, then the sales call will be doubly effective. Better yet, if the customer might be inclined to make a reasonable percentage of his purchases by mail or phone—then almost any cost of promotion can be justified by the diminished requirement for face-to-face selling.

Big mailers in the BTB arena have another serious problem. The name of the game is names, and valid names are hard to come by. People move from job to job. They are transferred within their company. They move from city to city. They resign, resurface, retire and expire. One business list compiler states that his company makes 12 million phone calls every year in an attempt to verify names and titles. Even that heroic effort is not enough. Recent experience has shown that some compiled lists can be as much as 3 and 4 years out of date.

Where compiled lists do not work, prospecting for new

customers can be very difficult. The solution many of the most sophisticated BTB mailers are exploring is based upon enhancements of their own databases. The techniques that work best are: phone verifications, more frequent list-cleaning mailings, improved input from the salesforce and state-of-the-art data management techniques.

In most of our BTB examples, the catalogs were conceived as key parts of a multimedia marketing system. That they have done their job well is demonstrated by the sales figures they've helped to produce. They are all very different in style and content (or both), although some are head-to-head competitors.

We've tried to give you some feel for the markets and the thought process behind each of these books. In some cases, the catalogs are deceptively simple in appearance. But more often than not, a closer look reveals a highly sophisticated, thoroughly reasoned direction and presentation. These companies are all winners. They've done their homework, and now we have a chance to look over their shoulders.

AT&T

The breakup of American Telephone & Telegraph has many of their old customers befuddled—very. We have seen dear old Ma Bell replaced with a bunch of RBOC's (Regional Bell Operating Companies), Sprint, MCI and AT&T Communications long-line services, and a plethora of network communications vendors including AT&T's own Network Services, along with Tellabs, SCI Atlanta and others. The question of who can legally sell what (as decreed by the Court of Judge Greene) is, to many of us, a very gray area. RBOC's and AT&T can *transmit* information, but neither AT&T or the RBOC's are allowed to *generate* information content. RBOC's may not manufacture "customer premises equipment", but where does firmware end and equipment begin?

You might well wonder what all this has to do with AT&T's business-to-business (BTB) catalogs. The answer is, it points out the dire need for a positive corporate image, crystal clear customer communications, and correct market positioning—in the face of relentless competition and customer confusion. Here, catalogs can help.

On their toes? Yes! Competitive? Yes! On the cutting edge of technology? And how! But, they are quite certain that a hot-shot, highly promotional image is not for Ma Bell. AT&T must constantly reinforce the proposition that they're in this game for the long haul. That's the edge they started out with. It's the security blanket that makes them the source of choice for major corporations and start-ups alike.

Working with their direct marketing agency, Ogilvy & Mather Direct, they initiated their catalog program with the following mission statement:

> *Provide an easy and convenient way for customers to purchase enhancement and peripheral products and services.*
> *Reinforce customer's initial system purchase decision.*
> *Generate revenue in an efficient manner.*
> *Allow the sales force to concentrate on selling systems, rather than add-ons.*
> *Demonstrate AT&T's position as the leader in telecommunications equipment.*

Four of these mission statements are fairly standard objectives. Most BTB catalog programs have similar goals in mind when putting together a book. But look at the last one. "Demonstrate AT&T's position as the leader in telecommunications equipment." That's a lot to ask of a catalog!

AT&T's advertising agency, Ogilvy & Mather Direct, spearheaded by President Jerry Pickholz and Senior Vice President Pamela M. Reese, represents one of the most powerful direct marketing engines in the world. Working closely with their client's marketing strategists, O&M's direct marketing team forged a modern catalog classic. It fulfills all of the prerequisites of the mission statement, using words and pictures aimed precisely at the level of their customers' communication skills.

Pluzynski/Associates, Inc. was chosen by Ogilvy & Mather to manage the studio and printing functions for this project. Pluzynski is well-known as a top quality production resource in the field of upscale catalogs and sales promotion material. These combined

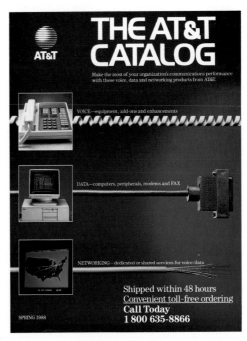

AT&T—Spring 1988
Ogilvy & Mather Direct, *Agency*
Pluzynski/Associates, *Creative Services*

talents successfully concluded all five modules of the mission with clarity, vitality and great good taste.

This is a catalog for electronic professionals, written and designed by advertising professionals. As witness, this copy excerpt:

> ". . .your 7406D Voice Terminal and an asynchronous data terminal can be used to communicate at speeds up to 19.2Kbps with computers connected to your System 75 or 85. The 7406D Data Stand provides the necessary RS-232C Interface, supporting simultaneous transmission of voice and asynchronous data signals to 1 digital port. . . ."

In spite of the necessity for such technically explicit copy, the AT&T catalog is designed for humans. The O&M/AT&T copy/edit team has transliterated what might have been absolute high-tech gobbledygook into interesting, well-written prose, aimed at readers in the communications industry. The creative artists then added excellent layouts, fine photography and super-legible typeface. Result: a catalog that is right on target.

This book creates a positive image of authority and solidity without being fusty or proselytizing. It treats products that are on the cutting edge of communications and data processing technology as if they had been around for decades. One gets the impression that the AT&T folks are very comfortable with all this high tech. And that is exactly the right position statement for AT&T to make. Brenda Lewis, President of Transactions Marketing, a specialist in creating marketing strategies for communications industry products and services, had this to say about AT&T:

No other firm knows as much about the state-of-the-art analog/digital conversion that has been and is now taking place. Not a single competing outfit has had anywhere nearly the networking experience. And when it comes to gaining access to the senior management of the largest corporations in the US, who would you bet on to get in the door first?

AT&T's catalog has introduced one futuristic element that we're sure to see in other catalogs, and soon. Appearing prominently on the order form and back cover is the line: "It's easy to order direct from AT&T, By *FAX*, mail or phone!" All a customer needs to do is fill out the order form, poke it in a FAX machine (or scan it) and push the button. It's quick, it's convenient and it generates error-free hardcopy.

This high-tech business catalog manages to be user-friendly.

800 numbers are prominently and frequently displayed. Graphic elements do their job—they elucidate. Complex networking concepts are diagrammed and described with utmost clarity, but without the slightest hint of talking down to an obviously sophisticated audience.

Perhaps one of the reasons we feel so "at home" with AT&T's catalog is its physical appearance. The best of direct marketing's tools-of-the-trade are here—just as they are in the better consumer catalogs. There are callouts, captions, oft-repeated phone and customer service bugs, headlines and subheads, and "NEW" where it's needed. There's even the familiar friendly message on the inside front cover.

This catalog confirms once again: tried and true direct response devices always produce results. It matters not if the product be truffles or telephones. The proof: in spite of sales expectations that were very optimistic, the AT&T catalog revenue exceeded projections by 300%! 'Nuff said?

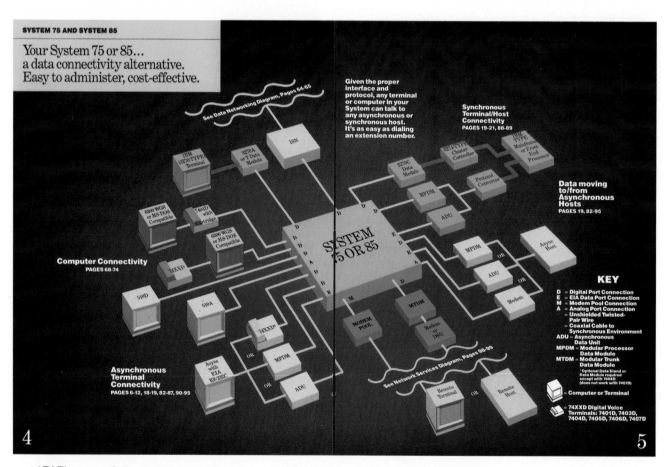

AT&T's agency, Ogilvy & Mather, has designed a cover that almost forces the reader to open the catalog. The entire graphic thrust is an invitation to move on to the inside. Once there, pages 4-5 establish the overriding theme of this catalog: connected systems. The headline touches the three major concerns of communications and MIS executives: Connectivity, Easy Administration, Cost-effectiveness.

Early buyers of voice and data communications systems often found themselves with equipment that

was not truly a system and software that required the constant attention of programmers. These installations were capable of performing to specification, but the costs in administrative time and real dollars made them extravagant in terms of value received.

The new generation of communications buyers demands high performance and easy access connectivity across a number of protocols and operating systems. AT&T addresses these systems integration and networking requirements throughout this catalog.

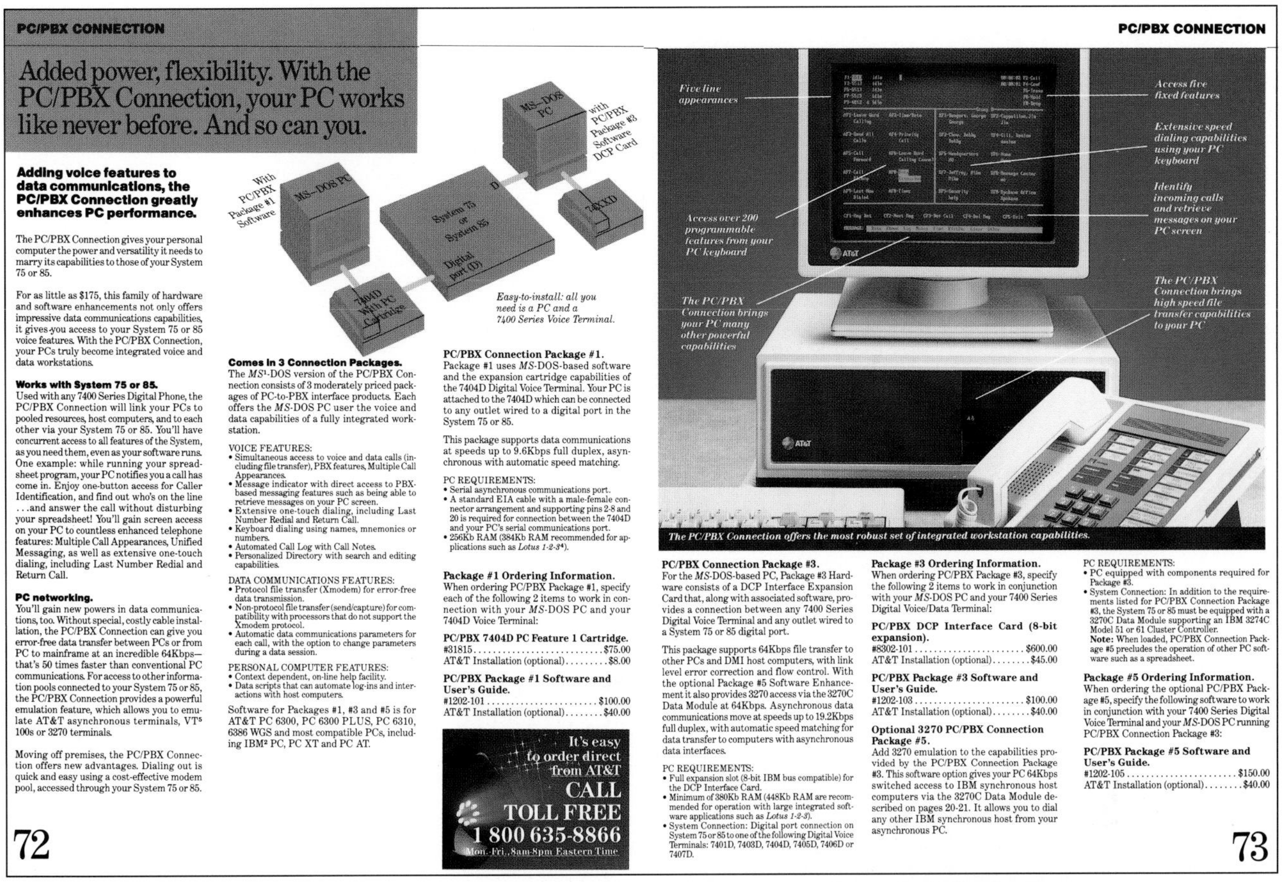

PC/PBX CONNECTION

Added power, flexibility. With the PC/PBX Connection, your PC works like never before. And so can you.

Adding voice features to data communications, the PC/PBX Connection greatly enhances PC performance.

The PC/PBX Connection gives your personal computer the power and versatility it needs to marry its capabilities to those of your System 75 or 85.

For as little as $175, this family of hardware and software enhancements not only offers impressive data communications capabilities, it gives you access to your System 75 or 85 voice features. With the PC/PBX Connection, your PCs truly become integrated voice and data workstations.

Works with System 75 or 85. Used with any 7400 Series Digital Phone, the PC/PBX Connection will link your PCs to pooled resources, host computers, and to each other via your System 75 or 85. You'll have concurrent access to all features of the System, as you need them, even as your software runs. One example: while running your spreadsheet program, your PC notifies you a call has come in. Enjoy one-button access for Caller Identification, and find out who's on the line ...and answer the call without disturbing your spreadsheet! You'll gain screen access on your PC to countless enhanced telephone features: Multiple Call Appearances, Unified Messaging, as well as extensive one-touch dialing, including Last Number Redial and Return Call.

PC networking. You'll gain new powers in data communications, too. Without special, costly cable installation, the PC/PBX Connection can give you error-free data transfer between PCs or from PC to mainframe at an incredible 64Kbps—that's 50 times faster than conventional PC communications. For access to other information pools connected to your System 75 or 85, the PC/PBX Connection provides a powerful emulation feature, which allows you to emulate AT&T asynchronous terminals, VT[5] 100s or 3270 terminals.

Moving off premises, the PC/PBX Connection offers new advantages. Dialing out is quick and easy using a cost-effective modem pool, accessed through your System 75 or 85.

With PC/PBX Package #1 Software
MS-DOS PC
7404D With PC Cartridge
System 75 or System 85
Digital port (D)
MS-DOS PC
with PC/PBX Package #3 Software & DCP Card
74XXD

Easy-to-install: all you need is a PC and a 7400 Series Voice Terminal.

Comes in 3 Connection Packages. The MS^1-DOS version of the PC/PBX Connection consists of 3 moderately priced packages of PC-to-PBX interface products. Each offers the MS-DOS PC user the voice and data capabilities of a fully integrated workstation.

VOICE FEATURES:
- Simultaneous access to voice and data calls (including file transfer), PBX features, Multiple Call Appearances.
- Message indicator with direct access to PBX-based messaging features such as being able to retrieve messages on your PC screen.
- Extensive one-touch dialing, including Last Number Redial and Return Call.
- Keyboard dialing using names, mnemonics or numbers.
- Automated Call Log with Call Notes.
- Personalized Directory with search and editing capabilities.

DATA COMMUNICATIONS FEATURES:
- Protocol file transfer (Xmodem) for error-free data transmission.
- Non-protocol file transfer (send/capture) for compatibility with processors that do not support the Xmodem protocol.
- Automatic data communications parameters for each call, with the option to change parameters during a data session.

PERSONAL COMPUTER FEATURES:
- Context dependent, on-line help facility.
- Data scripts that can automate log-ins and interactions with host computers.

Software for Packages #1, #3 and #5 is for AT&T PC 6300, PC 6300 PLUS, PC 6310, 6386 WGS and most compatible PCs, including IBM[2] PC, PC XT and PC AT.

PC/PBX Connection Package #1. Package #1 uses MS-DOS-based software and the expansion cartridge capabilities of the 7404D Digital Voice Terminal. Your PC is attached to the 7404D which can be connected to any outlet wired to a digital port in the System 75 or 85.

This package supports data communications at speeds up to 9.6Kbps full duplex, asynchronous with automatic speed matching.

PC REQUIREMENTS:
- Serial asynchronous communications port.
- A standard EIA cable with a male-female connector arrangement and supporting pins 2-8 and 20 is required for connection between the 7404D and your PC's serial communications port.
- 256Kb RAM (384Kb RAM recommended for applications such as Lotus 1-2-3[4]).

Package #1 Ordering Information. When ordering PC/PBX Package #1, specify each of the following 2 items to work in connection with your MS-DOS PC and your 7404D Voice Terminal:

PC/PBX 7404D PC Feature 1 Cartridge.
#31815 .... $75.00
AT&T Installation (optional) $8.00

PC/PBX Package #1 Software and User's Guide.
#1202-101 .... $100.00
AT&T Installation (optional) $40.00

It's easy to order direct from AT&T CALL TOLL FREE 1 800 635-8866 Mon.-Fri., 8am-8pm Eastern Time

72

PC/PBX CONNECTION

Five line appearances
Access five fixed features
Extensive speed dialing capabilities using your PC keyboard
Identify incoming calls and retrieve messages on your PC screen
Access over 200 programmable features from your PC keyboard
The PC/PBX Connection brings high speed file transfer capabilities to your PC
The PC/PBX Connection brings your PC many other powerful capabilities

The PC/PBX Connection offers the most robust set of integrated workstation capabilities.

PC/PBX Connection Package #3. For the MS-DOS-based PC, Package #3 Hardware consists of a DCP Interface Expansion Card that, along with associated software, provides a connection between any 7400 Series Digital Voice Terminal and any outlet wired to a System 75 or 85 digital port.

This package supports 64Kbps file transfer to other PCs and DMI host computers, with link level error correction and flow control. With the optional Package #5 Software Enhancement it also provides 3270 access via the 3270C Data Module at 64Kbps. Asynchronous data communications move at speeds up to 19.2Kbps full duplex, with automatic speed matching for data transfer to computers with asynchronous data interfaces.

PC REQUIREMENTS:
- Full expansion slot (8-bit IBM bus compatible) for the DCP Interface Card.
- Minimum of 380Kb RAM (448Kb RAM are recommended for operation with large integrated software applications such as Lotus 1-2-3).
- System Connection: Digital port connection on System 75 or 85 to one of the following Digital Voice Terminals: 7401D, 7403D, 7404D, 7405D, 7406D or 7407D.

Package #3 Ordering Information. When ordering PC/PBX Package #3, specify the following 2 items to work in conjunction with your MS-DOS PC and your 7400 Series Digital Voice/Data Terminal:

PC/PBX DCP Interface Card (8-bit expansion).
#8302-101 .... $600.00
AT&T Installation (optional) $45.00

PC/PBX Package #3 Software and User's Guide.
#1202-103 .... $100.00
AT&T Installation (optional) $40.00

Optional 3270 PC/PBX Connection Package #5. Add 3270 emulation to the capabilities provided by the PC/PBX Connection Package #3. This software option gives your PC 64Kbps switched access to IBM synchronous host computers via the 3270C Data Module described on pages 20-21. It allows you to dial any other IBM synchronous host from your asynchronous PC.

PC REQUIREMENTS:
- PC equipped with components required for Package #3.
- System Connection: In addition to the requirements listed for PC/PBX Connection Package #3, the System 75 or 85 must be equipped with a 3270C Data Module supporting an IBM 3274C Model 51 or 61 Cluster Controller.

Note: When loaded, PC/PBX Connection Package #5 precludes the operation of other PC software such as a spreadsheet.

Package #5 Ordering Information. When ordering the optional PC/PBX Package #5, specify the following software to work in conjunction with your 7400 Series Digital Voice Terminal and your MS-DOS PC running PC/PBX Connection Package #3:

PC/PBX Package #5 Software and User's Guide.
#1202-105 .... $150.00
AT&T Installation (optional) $40.00

73

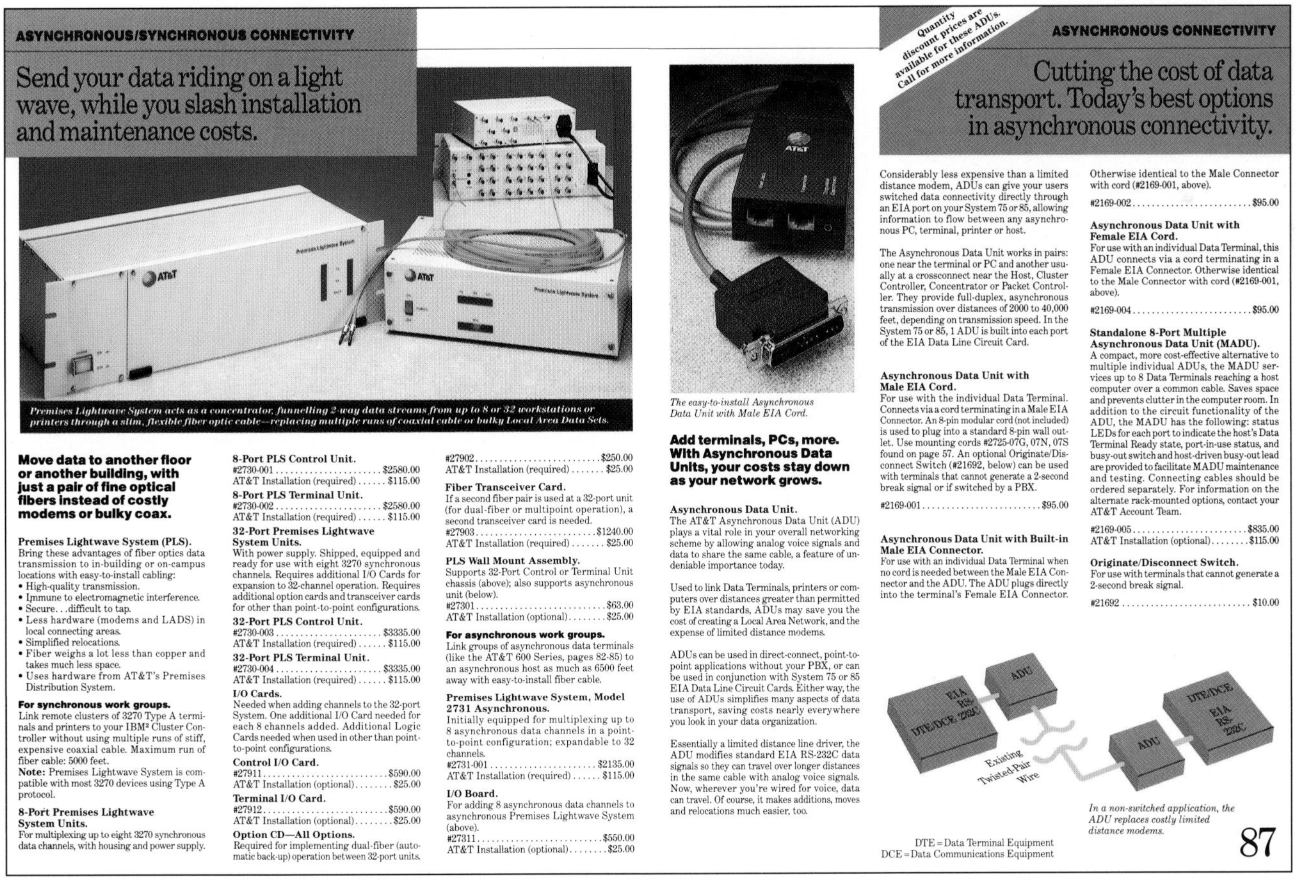

ASYNCHRONOUS/SYNCHRONOUS CONNECTIVITY

Send your data riding on a light wave, while you slash installation and maintenance costs.

Premises Lightwave System acts as a concentrator, funnelling 2-way data streams from up to 8 or 32 workstations or printers through a slim, flexible fiber optic cable—replacing multiple runs of coaxial cable or bulky Local Area Data Sets.

Move data to another floor or another building, with just a pair of fine optical fibers instead of costly modems or bulky coax.

Premises Lightwave System (PLS). Bring these advantages of fiber optics data transmission to in-building or on-campus locations with easy-to-install cabling:
- High-quality transmission.
- Immune to electromagnetic interference.
- Secure...difficult to tap.
- Less hardware (modems and LADS) in local connecting areas.
- Simplified relocations.
- Fiber weighs a lot less than copper and takes much less space.
- Uses hardware from AT&T's Premises Distribution System.

For synchronous work groups. Link remote clusters of 3270 Type A terminals and printers to your IBM[2] Cluster Controller without using multiple runs of stiff, expensive coaxial cable. Maximum run of fiber cable: 5000 feet.

Note: Premises Lightwave System is compatible with most 3270 devices using Type A protocol.

8-Port Premises Lightwave System Units. For multiplexing up to eight 3270 synchronous data channels, with housing and power supply.

8-Port PLS Control Unit.
#2730-001 .... $2580.00
AT&T Installation (required) $115.00

8-Port PLS Terminal Unit.
#2730-002 .... $2580.00
AT&T Installation (required) $115.00

32-Port Premises Lightwave System Units. With power supply. Shipped, equipped and ready for use with eight 3270 synchronous channels. Requires additional I/O Cards for expansion to 32-channel operation. Requires additional option cards and transceiver cards for other than point-to-point configurations.

32-Port PLS Control Unit.
#2730-003 .... $3335.00
AT&T Installation (required) $115.00

32-Port PLS Terminal Unit.
#2730-004 .... $3335.00
AT&T Installation (required) $115.00

I/O Cards. Needed when adding channels to the 32-port System. One additional I/O Card needed for each 8 channels added. Additional Logic Cards needed when used in other than point-to-point configurations.

Control I/O Card.
#27911 .... $590.00
AT&T Installation (optional) $25.00

Terminal I/O Card.
#27912 .... $590.00
AT&T Installation (optional) $25.00

Option CD—All Options. Required for implementing dual-fiber (automatic back-up) operation between 32-port units.
#27902 .... $250.00
AT&T Installation (required) $25.00

Fiber Transceiver Card. If a second fiber pair is used at a 32-port unit (for dual-fiber or multipoint operation), a second transceiver card is needed.
#27903 .... $1240.00
AT&T Installation (required) $25.00

PLS Wall Mount Assembly. Supports 32-Port Control or Terminal Unit chassis (above); also supports asynchronous unit (below).
#27301 .... $63.00
AT&T Installation (optional) $25.00

For asynchronous work groups. Link groups of asynchronous data terminals (like the AT&T 600 Series, pages 82-85) to an asynchronous host as much as 6500 feet away with easy-to-install fiber cable.

Premises Lightwave System, Model 2731 Asynchronous. Initially equipped for multiplexing up to 8 asynchronous data channels in a point-to-point configuration; expandable to 32 channels.
#2731-001 .... $2135.00
AT&T Installation (required) $115.00

I/O Board. For adding 8 asynchronous data channels to asynchronous Premises Lightwave System (above).
#27311 .... $550.00
AT&T Installation (optional) $25.00

The easy-to-install Asynchronous Data Unit with Male EIA Cord.

Add terminals, PCs, more. With Asynchronous Data Units, your costs stay down as your network grows.

Asynchronous Data Unit. The AT&T Asynchronous Data Unit (ADU) plays a vital role in your overall networking scheme by allowing analog voice signals and data to share the same cable, a feature of undeniable importance today.

Used to link Data Terminals, printers or computers over distances greater than permitted by EIA standards, ADUs may save you the cost of creating a Local Area Network, and the expense of limited distance modems.

ADUs can be used in direct-connect, point-to-point applications without your PBX, or can be used in conjunction with System 75 or 85 EIA Data Line Circuit Cards. Either way, the use of ADUs simplifies many aspects of data transport, saving costs nearly everywhere you look in your data organization.

Essentially a limited distance line driver, the ADU modifies standard EIA RS-232C data signals so they can travel over longer distances in the same cable with analog voice signals. Now, wherever you're wired for voice, data can travel. Of course, it makes additions, moves and relocations much easier, too.

ASYNCHRONOUS CONNECTIVITY

Quantity discount prices are available for these ADUs. Call for more information.

Cutting the cost of data transport. Today's best options in asynchronous connectivity.

Considerably less expensive than a limited distance modem, ADUs can give your users switched data connectivity directly through an EIA port on your System 75 or 85, allowing information to flow between any asynchronous PC, terminal, printer or host.

The Asynchronous Data Unit works in pairs: one near the terminal or PC and another usually at a crossconnect near the Host, Cluster Controller, Concentrator or Packet Controller. They provide full-duplex, asynchronous transmission over distances of 2000 to 40,000 feet, depending on transmission speed. In the System 75 or 85, 1 ADU is built into each port of the EIA Data Line Circuit Card.

Asynchronous Data Unit with Male EIA Cord. For use with the individual Data Terminal. Connects via a cord terminating in a Male EIA Connector. An 8-pin modular cord (not included) is used to plug into a standard 8-pin wall outlet. Use mounting cords #2725-07G, 07N, 07S found on page 57. An optional Originate/Disconnect Switch (#21692, below) can be used with terminals that cannot generate a 2-second break signal or if switched by a PBX.
#2169-001 .... $95.00

Asynchronous Data Unit with Built-in Male EIA Connector. For use with an individual Data Terminal when no cord is needed between the Male EIA Connector and the ADU. The ADU plugs directly into the terminal's Female EIA Connector.

EIA RS-232C DTE/DCE
ADU
Existing Twisted-Pair Wire
ADU
DTE/DCE EIA RS-232C

DTE = Data Terminal Equipment
DCE = Data Communications Equipment

In a non-switched application, the ADU replaces costly limited distance modems.

Otherwise identical to the Male Connector with cord (#2169-001, above).
#2169-002 .... $95.00

Asynchronous Data Unit with Female EIA Cord. For use with an individual Data Terminal, this ADU connects via a cord terminating in a Female EIA Connector. Otherwise identical to the Male Connector with cord (#2169-001, above).
#2169-004 .... $95.00

Standalone 8-Port Multiple Asynchronous Data Unit (MADU). A compact, more cost-effective alternative to multiple individual ADUs, the MADU services up to 8 Data Terminals reaching a host computer over a common cable. Saves space and prevents clutter in the computer room. In addition to the circuit functionality of the ADU, the MADU has the following: status LEDs for each port to indicate the host's Data Terminal Ready state, port-in-use status, and busy-out switch and host-driven busy-out lead are provided to facilitate MADU maintenance and testing. Connecting cables should be ordered separately. For information on the alternate rack-mounted options, contact your AT&T Account Team.
#2169-005 .... $835.00
AT&T Installation (optional) $115.00

Originate/Disconnect Switch. For use with terminals that cannot generate a 2-second break signal.
#21692 .... $10.00

87

Copy is king in the high-tech catalogs, but type changes, callouts, diagrams and captions all serve to direct reader attention to major sales features. Here: ''Voice and PC data communications are channeled though PBX or optical cable at costs as low as $175 per terminal.'' Note the repeated references to cost cutting and economy in most headlines.

AT&T makes frequent use of tables to assist its customers in selecting exactly the right system for their organization. Six systems for smaller companies are described in the table on page 29. The most important capabilities and features of each system are highlighted in the table. An interesting touch: across the top of this table, there is a page reference to help customers locate detailed information about each product.

On page 48, the customer who already owns a Dimension PBX system is assured that his system can be upgraded. This discussion with its accompanying table is followed by three pages describing the circuit boards and packs that are available. In addition, page 51 is devoted to a group of Code Carrier Diagrams to assist the customer in identifying the slots in his system that can accommodate upgrade circuit packs.

SYSTEM 75 AND SYSTEM 85

The 7406D Digital Voice Terminal: our affordable answer to your growing voice and data needs.

AT&T's 7406D Digital Voice Terminal delivers digital technology at an affordable price.

With its digital technology and multi-line convenience, the 7406D Voice Terminal is a cost-effective achiever!

7406D Digital Voice Terminal.
This Digital Voice Terminal brings you updated telephone features and data communications capabilities. The 7406D allows you to take greater advantage of your AT&T System 75, System 85 and MERLIN II features for optimum productivity and efficiency in all your office communications. It's designed to keep up with your growing communications needs.

Up to 5 line appearances.
Ideal for the person who frequently uses the phone, the 22-button 7406D features multi-line capability, allowing you to handle multiple incoming and outgoing calls quickly and efficiently. If a second call comes in while you're on the phone, you can quickly note what line appearance it's on, and put the first call on Hold with professional ease. The 7406D has 11 programmable buttons that can be programmed for System features such as Send All Calls or Leave Word Calling. With a shift feature on 7 of these buttons, 18 features and/or Speed Dial numbers can be supported. Five other buttons can be used for line appearances. A Personalized Ringing feature lets you distinguish your own incoming calls from your neighbor's, even when you're down the hall.

Modular data connectivity.
Because the 7406D is a digital phone, it facilitates data connections through your System 75, System 85 or MERLIN II System, becoming the phone for the future as well as the present. Add the 703A Data Service Unit (7406D Data Stand), for example, and it becomes a vital link in your data network, supporting asynchronous connectivity at speeds up to 19.2Kbps.

A built-in one-way loudspeaker is ideal for group listening or initiating calls hands-free, an important timesaving feature. Press the Speaker button before dialing, and when the second party answers, pick up the phone to talk.

The 7406D can be mounted vertically on walls or other surfaces to save desk space. A two-way Speakerphone or Headset can be added to your 7406D.

It's easy to order direct from AT&T CALL TOLL FREE 1 800 635-8866 Mon.-Fri., 8am-8pm Eastern Time

Specifications:
• Dimensions: 8½"W, 8½"D, 4½"H.
• System Connection: Connects to the AT&T System 75, System 85 or MERLIN II System using a standard digital port connection.
• Requires no external power source if used in standalone configuration.

Note: Cannot plug in Headset Adapter and external Speakerphone at the same time. For wall mounting, order Wall Mounting Kit (#31821A, below).

#3183-BDTA (Black) $360.00
#3183-CLRA (Misty Cream) $360.00
AT&T Installation (optional) $75.00

Note: If your System 75 or System 85 Administration Software does not support the 7406D, administer it as a 7405D.

Wall Mounting Kit for 7406D.
#31821A $18.00
AT&T Installation (optional) $37.50

Add a Display, and the 7406D Voice Terminal becomes a more powerful communications tool.

7406D Digital Voice Terminal with Display.
It's everything the 7406D is, and more. With the addition of the 48-character Liquid Crystal Display (LCD), the 7406D Voice Terminal becomes an all-in-one messaging vehicle, allowing you to take greater advantage of the convenient messaging features in your System 75 and 85. Messages are easy to access, calls easier to return. By putting a greater amount of information at your fingertips, the 7406D with Display contributes to a smoother flow of communications between you and everyone you work with.

Display for message retrieval.
The 48-character Display continues to function whether you're on the phone, or not.

When you've been out of the office, your Message Waiting Light will let you know a message is waiting. If your System 75 or 85 is equipped with the necessary messaging software, you can flash through your messages, and scan a caller's ID, even as you talk! Every message remains in the System 75 or 85 mailbox until you choose to have it deleted. In this, and many other ways, the 7406D with Display helps you manage your time and your calls—with optimum efficiency.

Note: If your System 75 or System 85 Administration Software does not support the 7406D with Display, administer it as a 7405D.

All other features and capabilities of the 7406D are found on this Display version. If wall mount is desired, order Wall Mounting Kit (#31820A, below).

#3182-LCDA (Black) $550.00
#3182-CLRA (Misty Cream) $550.00
AT&T Installation (optional) $75.00

Wall Mounting Kit for 7406D with Display.
#31820A (Black) $20.00
#31820A + M (Misty Cream) $20.00
AT&T Installation (optional) $48.00

7406D Data Stand.
With this optional adjunct, your 7406D Voice Terminal and an asynchronous data terminal can be used to communicate at speeds up to 19.2Kbps with computers connected to your System 75 or 85. The 7406D Data Stand provides the necessary RS-232C Interface, supporting simultaneous transmission of voice and asynchronous data signals to 1 digital port in your System 75, System 85 or MERLIN II System. With your 7406D (without Display), an asynchronous terminal connected to the 7406D Data Stand allows you to access messaging features within your System. Requires almost no additional desk space. It cannot be used with a wall-mounted set.

Use the 7406D Data Stand to establish RS-232C data connectivity.

Data Stand Prerequisites:
• 7406D Voice Terminal or 7406D with Display.
• Single Digital Adjunct Power Arrangement (#31757A) or Multiple Digital Adjunct Power Arrangement (#31758A), found on page 16. The Multiple Arrangement is required if either a Speakerphone or Headset is used in addition to the Data Stand.

Note: If your System 75 or System 85 Administration Software does not support the 7406D Data Stand, administer it as a 7405D with DTDM.

#31824A $380.00
AT&T Installation (recommended) .. $75.00

7406D Designation Forms.
A package of 25 additional forms to re-label your 7406D Voice Terminal.
#31823A (Black) $25.00
#31823A + M (Misty Cream) $25.00

For additional accessories for the 7406D, see pages 16-17 and 57.

Image labels: *Message Waiting Light* · *A built-in one-way loudspeaker* · *Selectable ring button* · *5 Feature buttons with two LEDs* · *7 programmable feature buttons with shift, for up to 14 functions* · *5 Line appearance/feature buttons with red "in use" and green "call status".*

The 7406D Voice Terminal with its easy-to-read 48-character message Display.

9

Item-oriented pages in the AT&T catalog are sometimes loaded with copy, especially when the items themselves have little graphic appeal. Given good-looking products, the Ogilvy & Mather team was able to create graphically powerful spreads to work as a counterpoint to the more technical pages. The overall effect is a lively, interesting book that delivers a wealth of information.

Good salesmen ask for the order many times during a sales call. Professionals in the direct response business do the same. A very high percentage of all the spreads in this catalog carry the AT&T telephone-ordering bug. It is not done because they are the telephone company. It's done because it is the correct and profitable thing for any mailorder merchant to do.

Selling product on the back cover is another sign of the mailorder professional. The OBC is one of the most valuable positions in any catalog. Why donate it all to the USPS, babies and pussycats?

Catalog #: 2CS

The 7407D: Doing more for you than any other AT&T Voice Terminal.
If you require MORE in a Voice Terminal, this is the one for you. It has more line appearances and more programmable feature buttons than any other AT&T Voice Terminal, plus a display panel that eclipses all other AT&T units.

A real timesaver!
Improving your performance is what these features do best. For an upper-level executive or for busy support staff, this unit has the capabilities and visual assistance to speed incoming and outgoing calls, show System features in use, and give easy and rapid access to extensive and frequent messages. And its two-way speakerphone leaves hands free to work while you are talking. Turn to pages 6-7 for all the details.

It's Easy to Order Direct from AT&T CALL TOLL FREE 1 800 635-8866 Mon.-Fri., 8am-8pm Eastern Time

American Transtech
P.O. Box 45038
Jacksonville, FL 32232-9974

Forwarding and Address Correction Requested

BULK RATE U.S. POSTAGE PAID AT&T

© AT&T 1988. All rights reserved. Printed in USA.

PM-1963

CAPRI ARCHITECTURAL

There is only one category of catalogs large enough to be measured in lineal yards of shelf space. You're right, it's building supplies. The entire shelf of Sweets Catalogs (really a compendium of manufacturer and distributor catalogs) now measures five and a third *yards*. This mind-boggling collection is broken down into ten discrete building trade and engineering sections. The "General Building" set alone consists of 19 separate books, each measuring 4-inches across the spine.

To make any one catalog stand out in that kind of a crowd is not easy. And to compound the challenge, the readers of the Sweets catalogs are talented, creative architects and builders. They know good design from bad, and they have a very high regard for quality, product knowledge and support.

Capri Architectural is positioned right across most segments of the 600,000-firm building trades fray. Their lighting products and systems are found in residential, commercial, restaurant and hospitality installations from coast to coast. Great distribution, but fierce competition.

Capri engaged the firm of John Caldwell Design, and asked them to undertake the challenge of creating a breakthrough catalog concept. And quite a challenge it was! For starters, their new catalog began life with a problem. Commercial lighting fixtures are dull. In most instances they are recessed into ceilings and walls, and can't be seen at all. Obviously, this is another case where the righteous route is to sell the sizzle, not the steak.

To further complicate the issue, Capri's potential customers are a mixed bag, ranging from rank tyros to top-level lighting engineers. We got in touch with John Caldwell, and he was gracious enough to send us some-behind-the-scenes comments on their pre-production thought process.

CAPRI ARCHITECTURAL
Larry Collins, *Advertising Manager*
    [Capri Lighting]
John Caldwell Design, *Design Office*
John Caldwell, *Art Director*
Carl Muller, *Designer*
Larry Collins, John Caldwell and
    Elizabeth Quick, *Copywriters*
Joe Carlson Studio, *Photography*
George Rice & Sons [Los Angeles],
    Printer, on Quintessence stock for cover and text
George Rice & Sons, *Color Separator*

The Capri Architectural catalog was created to not only show the company's products in the most attractive light, but also to explain the proper selection and uses of lighting. It was decided in our first brainstorming sessions, that many people did not understand the appropriate light sources and their uses. So we decided to add a strong educational slant to the book. In other words, tell people what the appropriate light source and appropriate product would be in any given situation. We believe that this catalog has received the awards that it has because of this educational component as well as its graphic appearance. The illustrations and charts were designed to help clarify lighting output and uses.

The challenge of the book was to deal with the needs of interior designers and/or small contractors with very little technical knowledge of lighting, as well as lighting and electrical engineers who needed extensive technical data. To satisfy both groups and still keep the attractiveness and drama of lighting alive was our biggest challenge.

Educational content, engineering data and sizzle: marry these three elements, add a dash of product presentation/demonstration/exposition and come up with a catalog. A tall order! Let's see how Caldwell Design handled this one.

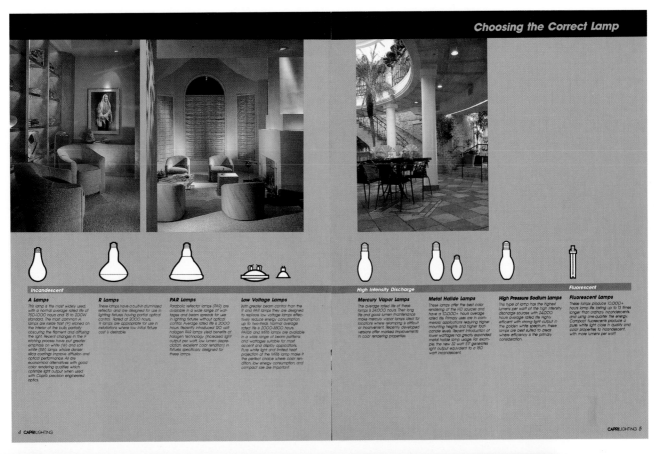

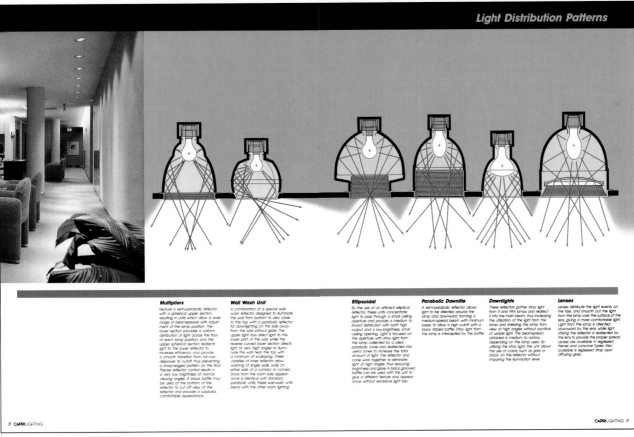

Sizzle, and a lot of it. But the educational component is here on every page. While answering the questions:

- *What is lighting all about?*
- *What should my light sources do?*
- *What kind of lamps are right for my job?*

Capri has also managed to infuse their presentation with a unique cachet signifying discrimination and substance.

Muted, dull-finish overall tints contrast with varnished 4-color photographs. Uncluttered, unpeopled room sets appeal to architects and designers. The copy on each spread is adequate to the purpose; but, for the more technically inclined, additional pages are included in an all type-and-graph format.

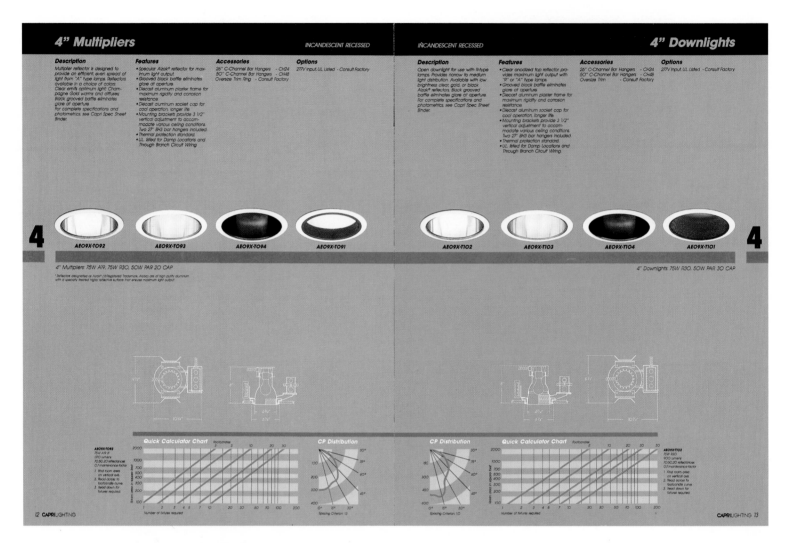

We are twelve pages into the catalog before the first selling spread is found. Even here, delicate reverse line-drawings describe more than just installation specifications. They indicate actual construction of the recessed lights, and the tables below yield fixture distribution and footcandle (power) information.

The implication is clear: if Capri lighting is good enough for these fabulous situations, it must be good enough for me.

Product Matrix

The products in Capri's Architectural Lighting Catalog have been arranged in order of nominal trim diameter to aid in planning a coordinated appearance of the finished ceiling. Listed below the trim diameters are the pages on which the various types of lighting fixtures will be found. For an explanation of the techniques of lighting application for these products see pages 6-9 of the catalog.

Incandescent	4"	5"	6"	8"	10"
Multipliers	12		14	19	
Wall Washers			15	20	
Ellipsoidals			16	21	24
Open Downlights	13		17	22	
Lensed Downlights					25
Adjustable Downlights			18	23	26
Retractable Downlights					26
Recessed Squares			27		
Surface Cylinders-Round	28	28			
Surface Cylinders-Square	29	29			

H.I.D.	6"	8"	10"	12"
Multipliers	32	36	41	46
Wall Washers	33	37, 38	42	
Ellipsoidals	34	39	43	
Parabolics				44
Open Downlights	35	40		
Lensed Downlights			45	47

Low Voltage	4"	6"
Downlights	50	52, 54
Adjustable	51	53, 54, 55
Retractable		55

Fluorescent	8"	10"
Downlights	58	59

Value Group	6"
Incandescent Downlights	60, 61
H.I.D. Downlights	62
Fluorescent Downlights	63

Credits

Graphic Design: John Coldwell Design. Studio Photography: © Joe Carlson Studio 1986. Location Photography: Cover - Interior Design: 2GF Partnership, Portland, OR. Photo: © Dick Busher 1985. Inside front cover - US Bancorp. Page 1 - Mack residence. Interior Design: Mojo/Sturner. Photo: © Mark Ross, Pages 2, 3 - Photos: © Joe Carlson Studio 1986. Page 3 - United Jersey Bank. Interior Design: Keller/Williams. Photo: © Mark Ross 1986. Page 4 - Interior Design: Charlotte Jensen & Associates.

Lighting Consultant: Michael K. Souter. Lighting Design. Photos: Mary E. Nichols. Page 5 - Hamlet Gardens. Interior Design: Saul Goldin. Photo: © Gil Edelstein 1986. Pages 8, 10 - United Jersey Bank. Interior Design: Keller/Williams. Photo: © Mark Ross 1986. Page 30 - Photo: © Gil Edelstein 1986. Page 57 - Photo: © Mark Ross 1986. Photometry: Lighting Research Laboratory, Orange, CA. General Electric. Lithography: George Rice & Sons.

Design Policy

Capri Lighting reserves the right to make any changes in the design and construction of the products listed in this catalog which may be required by law or by the rules of any regulatory body. Products are union made by International Brotherhood of Electrical Workers (IBEW).

Index

CAPRILIGHTING

6430 E. Slauson Ave, Los Angeles, California 90040 (213) 726-1800 • Telex 69-8688

© Capri Lighting 1986 All Rights Reserved International Copyright Secured Printed in USA 5OM ALO2   ⊕ THOMAS

An unusually well thought-out reference graces the inside back cover. In a soft-spoken way, this table guides the reader to the catalog page where fixtures of a given size are shown. Since the function of fixtures varies, while the rim diameter must remain a constant, this convenient resource leads the designer directly to the pages of his immediate interest.

The dominant feature of the outside back cover is an index sorted by part number. (A standard index-by-category is on page 1.) This has become an indispensable element of business-to-business catalogs, particularly in these days of computer-assisted design (CAD).

CAD programs can plug the right light fixture (or steel beam, for that matter) where it belongs, predicated upon the architect's design and pre-formatted illumination or structural formulae. Hardcopy printouts, a by-product of the CAD-generated blueprint, usually suggest three or more sources from an approved-vendor list for any given fixture.

At this point, the architect or builder may want to refer to a manufacturer's catalog for detailed product information before making a firm specification. Ideally, the CAD program or his own familiarity with the line will lead the designer to do a direct part-number lookup. If your index and his program (or memory) are both up to date, this system is the fastest way to get your company written into his set of specifications. And that's what BTB catalogs are all about.

Capri Architectural's catalog deserves to be successful. They've touched all the right bases, from design and flow to very buttoned-up cross-references. It's a masterful job of presentation in a thoughtful, user-friendly package. And, it works!

DUN & BRADSTREET

Not to put too fine a point on it, to the average citizen, lists of lists are somewhat less than exciting. However, to a media director, a list of mailing lists can be an inspiration. In this case, the lists we are referring to are business mailing lists. The example we're using is Dun & Bradstreet's Catalog of U.S. Businesses and Executives.

Art directors and copywriters can rely on creative rap sessions with other AD's, account execs and writers for some of their ideas. But the lonely media buying executive rarely has the opportunity to kick ideas around with knowledgeable peers. Instead, his choice of advertising vehicles is most frequently influenced by media reps, client preferences, research reports, barcar conversations, extensive reading of trade publications or all of the above.

Outside influences notwithstanding, final media decisions are usually made in a quiet office with the door closed and pencil and paper (or computer) at hand. With client, product and market in mind, our forlorn media director must sort out all the possible alternatives and come up with winning choices.

In this lonely situation, mental triggers help. A well laid out catalog of lists can substitute for the rap session as an idea generator; especially if it is cross-indexed by at least alpha and industry (SIC) to stimulate the creative process. Once preliminary choices have been made, potential list selections can be ranked and typed into a wordprocessor. Turn on the printer, run a sort program, and out pops a synoptic list of lists rated according to their probability of success.

Back when our media director friend closed his office door, he made an important decision. He decided which catalog of lists to use as his research tool. Dun & Bradstreet is not without competition. List rental is as profitable a profession as the world's oldest. You own it, you sell it, and you still own it. There are a plethora of business list compilers out there flogging their wares. And for most, catalogs are their primary sales tool.

Our media friend is going to select one catalog to work with. When he goes to his bookshelf, the list of lists he'll pick up is the one that feels good to him. He wants to be inspired, not confused. He needs information, not obfuscation. He'll go to the catalog that is pleasant to read, and where his areas of interest are easily found.

When the time comes to buy, chances are he'll cut his purchase order in favor of his favorite catalog.

D&B handles all of these prerequisites well, and much more. Every word, every service and every product offered in the catalog is sensitive to the needs of their clientele. In addition to basic list rentals, D&B offers customized databases which can be installed on your own computer. Marketing maps and analysis services are available. D&B even offers a management tool used to track field operations and sales leads. When a company offers consultative services, you get the impression they are real professionals. And one assumes professionals would certainly not deliver sloppy, out-of-date lists (the bane of the business).

Dun's list catalog won DMA's Echo Bronze Award in 1988. With all the pretty picture books to be found in the catalog world, this must have come as a surprise to many. It might have been less of a shock if the catalog's financial performance had been published.

In its first eight months, this seemingly staid compendium delivered an astounding 1600% return on investment. To explain

DUN & BRADSTREET—Catalog of U.S. Businesses and Executives
Burmeister & Dominus Direct Marketing, *Agency*
Dale Burmeister, *Copywriter*
Hausman Productions, *Design*
Newtype [Clifton, NJ], *Typography*
KMI Production Services, Inc., *Printing and Mailing*
DunsMatch, *Data Processing*

performance like that, a buzzword from the desktop computer vernacular comes to mind: user-friendly. D&B was obviously the catalog of choice in many a media buyer's mind!

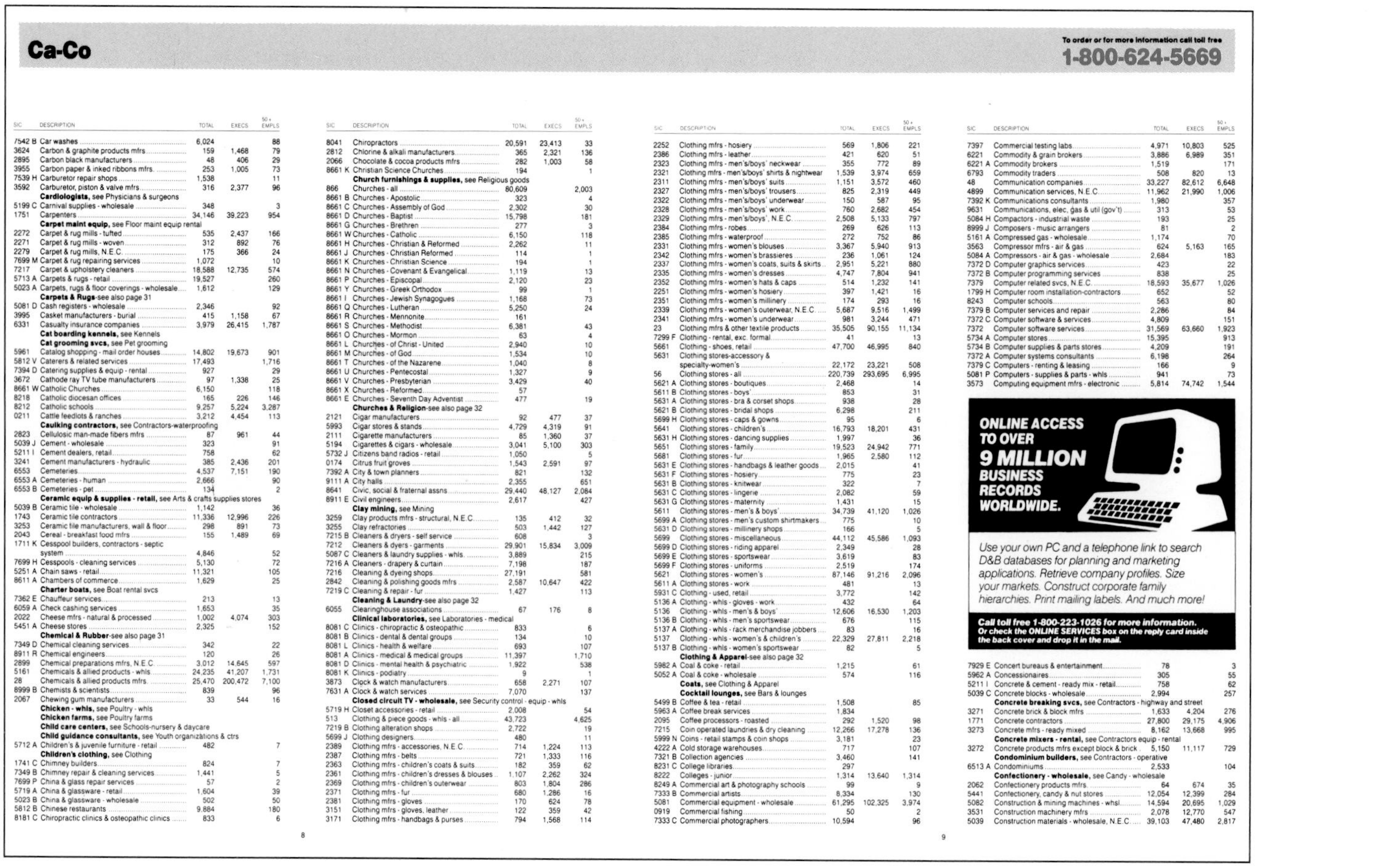

Ca-Co

SIC	DESCRIPTION	TOTAL	EXECS	50+ EMPLS
7542 B	Car washes	6,024		
3624	Carbon & graphite products mfrs.	159	1,468	79
2895	Carbon black manufacturers	48	406	29
3955	Carbon paper & inked ribbons mfrs.	253	1,005	73
7539 H	Carburetor repair shops	1,538		11
3592	Carburetor, piston & valve mfrs.	316	2,377	96
	Cardiologists, see Physicians & surgeons			
5199 C	Carnival supplies - wholesale	348		3
1751	Carpenters	34,146	39,223	954
	Carpet maint equip, see Floor maint equip rental			
2272	Carpet & rug mills - tufted	535	2,437	166
2271	Carpet & rug mills - woven	312	892	76
2279	Carpet & rug mills, N.E.C.	175	366	24
7699 M	Carpet & rug repairing services	1,072		10
7217	Carpet & upholstery cleaners	18,588	12,735	554
5713 A	Carpets & rugs - retail	19,527		260
5023 A	Carpets, rugs & floor coverings - wholesale	1,612		129
	Carpets & Rugs see also page 31			
5081 D	Cash registers - wholesale	2,346		92
3995	Casket manufacturers - burial	415	1,158	67
6331	Casualty insurance companies	3,979	26,415	1,787
	Cat boarding kennels, see Kennels			
	Cat grooming svcs, see Pet grooming			
5961	Catalog shopping - mail order houses	14,802	19,673	901
5812 V	Caterers & related services	17,493		1,716
7394 C	Catering supplies & equip - rental	927		29
3672	Cathode ray TV tube manufacturers	97	1,338	25
8661 W	Catholic Churches	6,150		118
8218	Catholic diocesan offices	165	226	146
8211	Catholic schools	9,257	5,224	3,287
0211	Cattle feedlots & ranches	3,212	4,454	113
	Caulking contractors, see Contractors-waterproofing			
2823	Cellulosic man-made fibers mfrs	87	961	44
5039 J	Cement - wholesale	323		91
5211 I	Cement dealers, retail	758		62
3241	Cement manufacturers - hydraulic	385	2,436	201
6553	Cemeteries	4,537	7,151	190
6553 A	Cemeteries - human	2,666		90
6553 B	Cemeteries - pet	34		2
	Ceramic equip & supplies - retail, see Arts & crafts supplies stores			
5039 B	Ceramic tile - wholesale	1,142		36
1743	Ceramic tile man-made fibers	11,336	12,996	226
3253	Ceramic tile manufacturers, wall & floor	298	891	73
2043	Cereal - breakfast food mfrs	155	1,489	69
1711 K	Cesspool builders, contractors - septic system	4,846		52
7699 H	Cesspools - cleaning services	5,130		72
5251 A	Chain saws - retail	1,321		105
8611 A	Chambers of commerce	4,589		25
	Charter boats, see Boat rental svcs			
7362 E	Chauffeur services	213		13
6059 A	Check cashing services	1,653		35
2022	Cheese mfrs - natural & processed	1,002	4,074	303
5451 A	Cheese stores	2,325		152
	Chemical & Rubber see also page 31			
7349 D	Chemical cleaning services	342		22
8911 R	Chemical engineers	120		26
2899	Chemical preparations mfrs, N.E.C.	3,012	14,645	597
5161	Chemicals & allied products - whls	24,235	41,207	1,731
28	Chemicals & allied products mfrs	25,470	200,472	7,100
8999 B	Chemists & scientists	839		96
2067	Chewing gum manufacturers	33	544	16
	Chicken - whls, see Poultry whls			
	Chicken farms, see Poultry farms			
	Child care centers, see Schools-nursery & daycare			
	Child guidance consultants, see Youth organizations & ctrs			
5712 A	Children's & juvenile furniture - retail	482		7
	Children's clothing, see Clothing			
1741 C	Chimney builders	824		7
7349 B	Chimney repair & cleaning services	1,441		5
7699 P	China & glass repair services	57		2
5719 A	China & glassware - retail	1,604		39
5023 B	China & glassware - wholesale	502		50
5812 B	Chinese restaurants	9,884		180
8181 C	Chiropractic clinics & osteopathic clinics	833		6

SIC	DESCRIPTION	TOTAL	EXECS	50+ EMPLS
8041	Chiropractors	20,591	23,413	33
2812	Chlorine & alkali manufacturers	365	2,321	136
2066	Chocolate & cocoa products mfrs	282	1,003	58
8661 N	Christian Science Churches	194		1
	Church furnishings & supplies, see Religious goods			
866	Churches - all	80,609		2,003
8661 B	Churches - Apostolic	323		4
8661 S	Churches - Assembly of God	2,302		30
8661 G	Churches - Baptist	15,798		181
8661 C	Churches - Brethren	277		3
8661 W	Churches - Catholic	6,150		118
8661 I	Churches - Christian & Reformed	2,262		11
8661 J	Churches - Christian Reformed	114		1
8661 K	Churches - Christian Science	194		1
8661 T	Churches - Covenant & Evangelical	1,119		13
8661 F	Churches - Episcopal	2,310		23
8661 P	Churches - Greek Orthodox	99		1
8661 U	Churches - Jewish Synagogues	1,168		73
8661 Q	Churches - Lutheran	5,250		24
8661 R	Churches - Mennonite	161		
8661 E	Churches - Methodist	6,381		43
8661 L	Churches - Mormon	63		4
8661 M	Churches - of Christ - United	2,940		10
8661 M	Churches - of God	1,534		10
8661 V	Churches - of the Nazarene	1,040		8
8661 X	Churches - Pentecostal	1,327		9
8661 O	Churches - Presbyterian	3,429		40
8661 X	Churches - Reformed	327		
8661 C	Churches - Seventh Day Adventist	477		19
	Churches & Religion see also page 32			
2121	Cigar manufacturers	92	477	37
5993	Cigar stores & stands	4,729	4,319	91
2111	Cigarette manufacturers	85	1,360	37
5194	Cigarettes & cigars - wholesale	3,041	5,100	303
5732 J	Citizens band radios - retail	1,050		5
0174	Citrus fruit groves	1,543	2,591	97
7392 A	City & town planners	821		132
9111 A	City halls	2,355		651
8641	Civic, social & fraternal assns	29,440	48,127	2,084
8911 E	Civil engineers	2,617		427
	Clay mining, see Mining			
3259	Clay products mfrs - structural, N.E.C.	135	412	32
3255	Clay refractories	503	1,442	127
7215 B	Cleaners & dyers - self service	608		3
7212	Cleaners & dyers - garments	29,901	15,834	3,009
5087 C	Cleaners & laundry supplies - whls	3,888		215
7216 A	Cleaners - drapery & curtain	7,198		187
7216	Cleaning & dyeing shops	27,191		581
2842	Cleaning & polishing goods mfrs	1,268	10,647	422
7219 C	Cleaning & repair - fur	1,427		113
	Cleaning & Laundry see also page 32			
6055	Clearinghouse associations	67	176	8
	Clinical laboratories, see Laboratories - medical			
8081 C	Clinics - chiropractic & osteopathic	833		6
8081 B	Clinics - dental & dental groups	134		10
8081 A	Clinics - health & welfare	693		107
8081 A	Clinics - medical & medical groups	11,397		1,710
8081 A	Clinics - mental health & psychiatric	1,922		538
8081 A	Clinics - podiatry	9		1
3873	Clock & watch manufacturers	658	2,271	107
7631 A	Clock & watch services	7,070		137
	Closed circuit TV - wholesale, see Security control - equip - whls			
5719 H	Closet accessories - retail	2,008		54
513	Clothing - piece goods - whls - all	43,723		4,625
7219 B	Clothing alteration shops	2,722		19
5699 J	Clothing designers	480		11
2389	Clothing mfrs - accessories, N.E.C.	714	1,224	113
2387	Clothing mfrs - belts	721	1,333	116
2363	Clothing mfrs - children's coats & suits	182	359	62
2361	Clothing mfrs - children's dresses & blouses	1,107	2,262	324
2369	Clothing mfrs - children's outerwear	803	1,804	286
2371	Clothing mfrs - fur	680	1,286	16
2385	Clothing mfrs - gloves - leather	170	624	78
3151	Clothing mfrs - gloves, leather	122	359	42
3171	Clothing mfrs - handbags & purses	794	1,568	114

SIC	DESCRIPTION	TOTAL	EXECS	50+ EMPLS
2252	Clothing mfrs - hosiery	569	1,806	221
2386	Clothing mfrs - leather	421	820	51
2323	Clothing mfrs - men's/boys' neckwear	355	772	89
2311	Clothing mfrs - men's/boys' shirts & nightwear	1,539	3,974	659
2311	Clothing mfrs - men's/boys' suits	1,151	3,572	460
2327	Clothing mfrs - men's/boys' trousers	825	2,319	449
2322	Clothing mfrs - men's/boys' underwear	150	587	95
2328	Clothing mfrs - men's/boys' work	760	2,682	454
2329	Clothing mfrs - men's/boys', N.E.C.	2,508	5,133	797
2384	Clothing mfrs - robes	269	626	113
2385	Clothing mfrs - waterproof	272	750	86
2331	Clothing mfrs - women's blouses	3,367	5,940	913
2342	Clothing mfrs - women's brassieres	238	1,061	124
2337	Clothing mfrs - women's coats, suits & skirts	2,951	5,221	880
2335	Clothing mfrs - women's dresses	4,747	7,804	941
2352	Clothing mfrs - women's hats & caps	514	1,232	141
2251	Clothing mfrs - women's hosiery	397	1,421	16
2351	Clothing mfrs - women's millinery	174	293	16
2339	Clothing mfrs - women's outerwear, N.E.C.	6,681	9,516	1,499
2341	Clothing mfrs - women's underwear	981	3,244	471
23	Clothing mfrs & other textile products	35,505	90,155	11,134
7299 F	Clothing - rental, exc. formal	41		13
5661	Clothing - shoes, retail	47,700	46,995	840
5631	Clothing stores-accessory & specialty-women's	22,172	23,221	508
56	Clothing stores - all	220,739	293,695	6,995
5621 A	Clothing stores - boutiques	2,468		14
5611 B	Clothing stores - boys	863		31
5631 A	Clothing stores - bra & corset shops	938		28
5621 B	Clothing stores - bridal shops	6,298		211
5699 H	Clothing stores - caps & gowns	95		6
5641	Clothing stores - children's	16,793	18,201	431
5631 H	Clothing stores - dancing supplies	1,997		36
5631 C	Clothing stores - family	19,523	24,942	771
5681	Clothing stores - furriers	1,965	2,580	112
5631 E	Clothing stores - handbags & leather goods	2,015		41
5631 B	Clothing stores - hosiery	775		23
5631 G	Clothing stores - knitwear	322		7
5631 D	Clothing stores - lingerie	2,082		59
5631 G	Clothing stores - maternity	1,431		15
5611	Clothing stores - men's & boys'	34,739	41,120	1,026
5611	Clothing stores - men's custom shirtmakers	775		10
5631 D	Clothing stores - millinery shops	166		1
5699	Clothing stores - miscellaneous	44,112	45,586	1,093
5699 D	Clothing stores - riding apparel	2,349		28
5631 B	Clothing stores - sportswear	481		13
5699	Clothing stores - uniforms	2,519		174
5611	Clothing stores - women's	87,146	91,216	2,096
5611	Clothing stores - used, retail	3,772		142
5136 A	Clothing - whls - gloves - work	432		64
5136	Clothing - whls - men's & boys'	12,606	16,530	1,203
5136 B	Clothing - whls - men's sportswear	676		115
5137 A	Clothing - whls - men's custom jobbers	83		16
5137	Clothing - whls - women's & children's	22,329	27,811	2,218
5137	Clothing - whls - women's sportswear	82		5
	Clothing & Apparel see also page 32			
5962 A	Coal & coke - retail	1,215		61
5052 A	Coal & coke - wholesale	574		116
	Coats, see Clothing & Apparel			
	Cocktail lounges, see Bars & lounges			
5499 B	Coffee & tea - retail	1,508		85
5963 A	Coffee break services	1,834		291
2095	Coffee processors - roasted	292	1,520	98
7215	Coin operated laundries & dry cleaning	12,266	17,278	136
5999 N	Coins - retail stamps & coin shops	3,181		23
4222 A	Cold storage warehouses	717		107
7321 B	Collection agencies	3,460		141
8231 C	College libraries	297		
8222	Colleges - junior	1,314	13,640	1,314
8249 A	Commercial art & photography schools	99		9
7333 B	Commercial artists	8,334		130
5081	Commercial equipment - wholesale	61,295	102,325	3,974
0919	Commercial fishing	50		2
7333 C	Commercial photographers	10,594		96

SIC	DESCRIPTION	TOTAL	EXECS	50+ EMPLS
7397	Commercial testing labs	4,971	10,803	525
6221	Commodity & grain brokers	3,886	6,989	351
6221 A	Commodity brokers	1,519		171
6793	Commodity traders	508	820	13
48	Communication companies	33,227	82,612	6,648
4899	Communication services, N.E.C.	11,962	21,990	1,006
7392 A	Communications consultants	1,980		357
9631	Communications - elec, gas & util (gov't)	313		53
5084 H	Compactors - industrial waste	193		25
8999 J	Composers - music arrangers	81		2
5084 A	Compressed gas - wholesale	1,174		70
3563	Compressor mfrs - air & gas	924	5,163	165
5084 A	Compressors - air & gas - wholesale	2,684		183
7372 D	Computer graphics services	423		22
7372 B	Computer programming services	838		25
7379	Computer related svcs, N.E.C.	18,593	35,677	1,026
1799 H	Computer room installation-contractors	652		52
8243	Computer schools	563		80
7379 B	Computer services and repair	2,286		84
7372	Computer software & services	4,809		151
7372	Computer software services	31,569	63,660	1,923
5734 A	Computer stores	15,395		913
5081 P	Computers - supplies & parts - whls	941		73
3573	Computing equipment mfrs - electronic	5,814	74,742	1,544

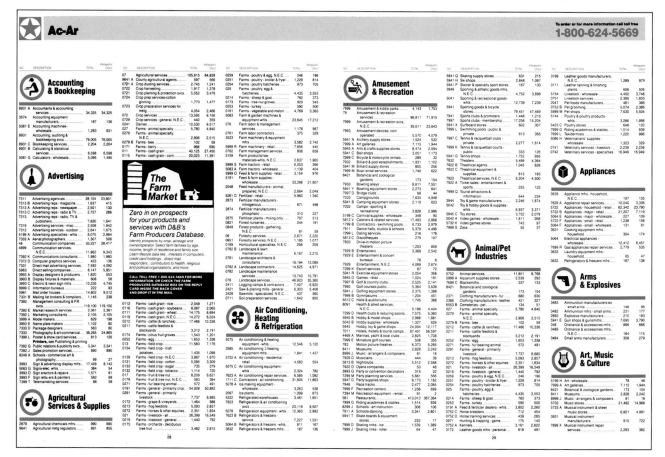
SIC	DESCRIPTION	TOTAL	EXECS	50+ EMPLS
7929 E	Concert bureaus & entertainment	78		3
5962 A	Concessionaires	305		55
5211 I	Concrete & cement - ready mix - retail	758		62
5039 C	Concrete blocks - wholesale	2,994		257
	Concrete breaking svcs, see Contractors - highway and street			
3271	Concrete brick & block mfrs	1,633	4,204	239
1771	Concrete contractors	27,800	29,175	4,906
3273	Concrete mfrs - ready mixed	8,162	13,668	995
	Concrete mixers - rental, see Contractors equip - rental			
3272	Concrete products mfrs except block & brick	5,150	11,117	729
	Condominium builders, see Contractors - operative			
6513 A	Condominiums	2,533		104
	Confectionery - wholesale, see Candy			
2062	Confectionery products mfrs	64	674	35
5441	Confectionery, candy & nut stores	1,254	12,399	284
5082	Construction & mining machines - whsl	14,594	20,695	1,029
3531	Construction machinery mfrs	2,078	12,770	547
5039	Construction materials - wholesale, N.E.C.	39,103	47,480	2,817

Ac-Ar

Accounting & Bookkeeping

SIC	DESCRIPTION	TOTAL	PRIMARY ONLY
8931 A	Accountants & accounting services	34,325	34,325
3574	Accounting equipment manufacturers	187	136
5081 C	Accounting machines - wholesale	1,283	631
8931	Accounting, auditing & bookkeeping svcs	76,005	76,005
8931 C	Bookkeeping services	2,204	2,204
8931 B	Calculating & statistical services	6,598	6,598
5081 D	Calculators - wholesale	5,095	1,495

Advertising

SIC	DESCRIPTION	TOTAL	PRIMARY ONLY
7311	Advertising agencies	28,104	23,801
7313 B	Advertising reps - magazine	2,501	814
7313 A	Advertising reps - newspaper	2,727	286
7313 C	Advertising reps - radio & TV	2,727	286
7313	Advertising reps - radio, TV & publishers	7,820	1,641
7319	Advertising services - misc	2,508	1,942
7312	Advertising services - outdoor	2,674	1,439
7319 A	Advertising specialties - whls	6,075	2,984
7333 A	Aerial photographers	1,307	506
48	Communication companies	33,227	28,417
7390 A	Communications consultants	11,962	9,343
7372 D	Computer graphics services	423	136
7331	Direct mail advertising services	7,592	4,092
5963	Direct selling companies	8,147	5,851
3993 A	Display designers & producers	1,820	553
3993 B	Display fixtures & materials	608	58
3641 E	Electric & neon sign mfrs	10,235	4,745
8999 C	Information bureaus	222	93
5961	Mail order houses	14,802	9,512
7331 B	Mailing list brokers & compilers	1,145	238
7392	Management consulting & P.R. svcs	119,100	119,100
7392 E	Market research services	2,361	2,361
7392 L	Marketing consultants	2,105	2,105
3993 A	Model makers	1,039	518
3999 A	Name plate makers	1,102	80
7333 D	Package designers	542	80
7333	Photography & art-commercial	36,265	24,865
7399 L	Poster & show card services	813	126
	Printers, see Publishing & printing		
7392 G	Public relations & publicity svcs	3,341	3,341
7392 J	Sales promotion services	890	890
8249 A	Schools - commercial art & photography		
3993	Sign & advertising display mfrs	17,409	8,142
5063 G	Sign-elec. whls	423	91
3993 D	Sign erectors & repairs	1,571	81
3993 F	Sign letts-ers & painters	582	69
7399 T	Telemarketing services	88	58

Agricultural Services & Supplies

SIC	DESCRIPTION	TOTAL	PRIMARY ONLY
2879	Agricultural chemicals mfrs	990	690
9641	Agricultural mktg regulators	891	855
07	Agricultural services	105,615	84,828
9641 A	County agricultural agents	597	566
0721 A	Crop dusting services	2,745	1,241
0722	Crop harvesting	1,917	1,378
0721	Crop planting & protection svcs.	5,552	3,476
0724	Crop prep services-cotton ginning	1,773	1,477
0723	Crop preparation services for mktg	4,054	2,466
07	Crop services - general, N.E.C.	13,595	9,156
0724	Crop services - general, N.E.C.	440	359
0241	Dairies	10,530	9,517
0279	Farms - animal specialty	1,768	1,594
011	Farms - animal specialty, N.E.C.	2,906	2,515
0279 B	Farms - bee	102	59
0171	Farms - berry	966	690
011	Farms - cash grain	40,125	27,450
0115	Farms - cash grain - corn	20,023	11,391

SIC	DESCRIPTION	TOTAL	PRIMARY ONLY
0112	Farms - cash grain - rice	2,049	1,271
0116	Farms - cash grain - soybeans	8,087	2,065
0111	Farms - cash grain - wheat	14,175	6,694
0119	Farms - cash grain, N.E.C.	14,272	6,024
0212	Farms - cattle (& ranches)	17,466	10,336
0211	Farms - cattle feedlots & stockyards	3,212	2,191
0174	Farms - citrus fruit groves	1,543	1,201
0252	Farms - egg	1,653	1,338
013	Farms - field crop - Irish potatoes	11,583	7,176
0134	Farms - field crop - Irish potatoes	1,435	1,098
0139	Farms - field crop - N.E.C.	3,687	1,670
0131	Farms - field crop - cotton	3,095	3,309
0132	Farms - field crop - tobacco	735	379
0132	Farms - field crop - tobacco	1,114	720
0179	Farms - fruit & tree nut	8,209	6,621
0271	Farms - fur-bearing animal	567	359
0191	Farms - general - primary crop	54,928	50,862
0291	Farms - general - primary		
0172	Farms - grape & vineyards	1,464	988
0213	Farms - hog feedlots	5,093	2,857
0214	Farms - horses & other equines	2,351	1,834
021	Farms - livestock - general	1,440	792
0175	Farms - orchards - deciduous tree fruit	3,482	2,815

Air Conditioning, Heating & Refrigeration

SIC	DESCRIPTION	TOTAL	PRIMARY ONLY
5075	Air conditioning & heating equipment - whls	12,546	5,120
3585	Air conditioning & heating equipment mfrs	1,841	1,437
5075 C	Air conditioning - residential - retail	4,583	554
2097	Ice packing	1,099	873
5078	Refrigerated warehouses	7,737	5,685
7623	Refrigeration & air conditioning svcs	23,119	9,507
3585	Refrigeration equipment - whls	12,363	2,983
7623 B	Refrigeration equipment - service	7,227	1,531
5064 B	Refrigerators & freezers mfrs	187	136
3632	Refrigerators & freezers mfrs	187	136

Amusement & Recreation

SIC	DESCRIPTION	TOTAL	PRIMARY ONLY
7996	Amusement & kiddie parks	4,143	1,753
79	Amusement & recreation services	96,811	71,915
7999	Amusement & recreation svcs, N.E.C.	39,611	23,643
7993	Amusement devices, coin operated	5,570	4,079
5941 A	Archery supply stores	1,524	532
7999 A	Art galleries	7,115	1,944
5945 A	Arts & crafts supplies stores	8,474	2,594
5941 C	Bait shops	3,051	1,173
7999 D	Bicycle & motorcycle rentals	249	69
7932	Billiard & pool establishments	1,931	1,102
5941 M	Billiard supply stores	805	256
7999 M	Boat rental services	1,740	622
8421	Botanical and zoological gardens	813	193
7933	Bowling alleys	8,611	7,551
5941 Y	Bowling equipment stores	2,273	641
7992 T	Bridge clubs	68	44
7033	Campgrounds	7,835	4,948
5941 B	Camping equipment stores	2,110	623
7032	Camps - sporting & recreational	3,826	2,986
5199 C	Carnival supplies - wholesale	348	90
5812 V	Caterers & related services	17,493	2,868
1799 B	Contractors - swimming pools	6,733	2,979
7911	Dance halls, studios & schools	4,718	1,945
7299 L	Dating services	216	178
5813 C	Discotheques	279	107
7833	Drive-in motion picture theaters	1,203	859
7929 B	Entertainers	3,369	2,542
7929 E	Entertainment & concert bureaus	78	8
7929	Entertainment, N.E.C.	4,069	2,674
7299 K	Escort services	90	9
5941 R	Exercise equipment stores	2,054	366
5945 D	Games - retail	1,024	191
7997 B	Golf & country clubs	2,525	2,141
7992	Golf courses-public	5,364	3,639
5941 D	Golf equipment stores	2,315	969
7999 B	Gymnasiums	1,204	451
6512 C	Halls & auditoriums	1,745	368
8411	Health & allied services, N.E.C.		
7299 D	Health clubs & reducing salons	5,186	4,404
5945 B	Hobby & model shops	2,988	1,681
5042 B	Hobby supplies - wholesale	1,327	629
5945	Hobby, toy & game shops	7,407	6,920
7011	Hotels, motels & tourist courts	67,401	60,549
4469 A	Marinas, yacht & boat clubs	2,825	1,708
7999 K	Miniature golf courses	508	265
783	Motion picture theaters	6,373	5,265
8411	Museums	2,828	2,242
8999 J	Music - arrangers & composers	81	18
7929 D	Musicians	508	385
7929 A	Nightclubs	5,512	2,568
7922 D	Opera companies	68	60
3993 G	Party or convention decorators	1,182	190
5947 D	Party supply stores	6,681	160
7999 E	Race tracks	2,457	469
7948	Race tracks		
7996 F	Recreation centers	1,232	694
7394 M	Recreation equipment - rental	918	379
581	Restaurants	413,013	367,364
7999 H	Riding academies & stables	1,514	929
8299 I	Schools - art instruction	306	106
8411	Schools-dancing	3,341	2,801
7623	Horse training services	858	290
5941 T	Skate board & equipment stores	233	170
7999 J	Skating rinks - ice	1,539	1,130
7999 J	Skating rinks - roller	64	47
5941 Q	Skating supply stores	631	215
5941 H	Ski shops	2,848	1,067
5941 E	Soccer & specialty sport stores	167	133
3949	Sporting & athletic goods mfrs, N.E.C.	4,752	3,898
5041	Sporting & recreational goods - whls	514	154
5941	Sporting goods & bicycle stores	79,451	47,469
5941	Sports clubs & promoters	1,448	1,216
7997	Sports clubs - membership	15,204	415
5941 X	Surfboard stores	602	307
7999	Swimming pools - public & private	913	356
7997 C	Tennis & racquetball clubs - private	2,277	1,614
7999 K	Tennis & racquetball courts - public	333	126
5941 G	Tennis shops	1,752	695
7832	Theaters	5,499	4,364
7922 B	Theatrical equipment & supplies	1,045	626
7922	Theatrical equipment & supplies mfrs, N.E.C.	6,204	4,500
7922 A	Ticket sales - entertainment & sports	125	
7999 Q	Tourist attractions & information	644	234
3944	Toy & game manufacturers	1,633	824
5042	Toy & hobby goods & supplies - whls	6,937	3,371
5064 E	Video games - retail	3,752	2,079
5732 K	Video games stores	1,811	266
5732 K	Video games - wholesale	743	97
7999 S	Zoos	55	37

Animal/Pet Industries

SIC	DESCRIPTION	TOTAL	PRIMARY ONLY
0752	Animal services	11,851	8,768
5999 A	Aquarium supplies stores	2,539	292
5154 A	Blacksmiths	681	168
8421 A	Botanical and zoological gardens	173	154
2371	Clothing manufacturers - fur	680	630
2386	Clothing manufacturers - leather	421	327
6553 B	Cemeteries - pet	34	51
0279	Farms - animal specialty	5,780	4,840
011	Farms - animal specialty, N.E.C.		
0279 B	Farms - bee	102	59
0211	Farms - cattle feedlots & stockyards	3,212	2,191
0252	Farms - egg	1,653	1,338
0291	Farms - general - primarily livestock	7,737	6,685
0213	Farms - hog feedlots	5,093	2,857
0214	Farms - horses & other equines	2,351	1,834
021	Farms - livestock - all	28,990	16,549
0219	Farms - livestock - general	2,004	1,440
0251	Farms - poultry - broiler & fryer	1,229	814
0252	Farms - poultry hatcheries	1,707	1,158
0254	Farms - poultry, N.E.C.	973	705
0754	Horse training services		
0971	Hunting & trapping - game	175	140
3172	Leather goods mfrs - personal	818	491
3199	Leather goods manufacturers, N.E.C.		
3111	Leather tanning & finishing plants	606	506
5154	Livestock - wholesale	4,450	3,748
0751	Livestock services	2,389	1,633
2047	Pet foods manufacturers	461	366
0752 D	Pet grooming	5,074	2,386
5999 M	Pet shops	7,650	5,504
0254	Poultry & poultry products - wholesale	3,286	1,996
5144	Poultry & poultry products - wholesale		
0752 A	Poultry stores	648	120
7699 L	Taxidermists	1,220	996
5086 H	Veterinarians' supplies - wholesale	1,323	329
0742	Veterinary services - livestock	2,239	2,229
0742	Veterinary services - specialties	16,949	16,949

Appliances

SIC	DESCRIPTION	TOTAL	PRIMARY ONLY
3639	Appliance mfrs - household	197	135
7629 A	Appliance repair services	10,040	3,336
5722 A	Appliances - household - retail	62,342	23,797
5722 B	Appliances - major - retail	21,207	7,119
5722 C	Appliances - major - wholesale	227	109
5064	Appliances - small - wholesale	1,238	158
5722 D	Appliances - small - wholesale	91	81
3631	Cooking equipment mfrs - household	304	174
5064	Electrical appliances - wholesale	12,412	6,451
7699 R	Gas appliance repair services	2,779	535
3633	Laundry equipment mfrs - household	65	47
3632	Refrigerators & freezers mfrs	187	136

Arms & Explosives

SIC	DESCRIPTION	TOTAL	PRIMARY ONLY
3483	Ammunition manufacturers-ex small arms	146	95
3482	Ammunition mfrs - small arms	231	177
2892	Explosive manufacturers	210	183
5941 E	Gun shops & gunsmiths	7,695	3,790
3484	Ordnance & accessories mfrs	666	666
	Ordnance & accessories mfrs, N.E.C.	164	115
3484	Small arms manufacturers	358	279

Art, Music & Culture

SIC	DESCRIPTION	TOTAL	PRIMARY ONLY
5199 H	Art - wholesale	78	46
7999 A	Art galleries	7,115	1,944
8421	Botanical & zoological gardens	2,828	2,242
8411	Museums	2,828	2,242
5733	Music stores	21,492	14,966
8999 J	Music - arrangers & composers	81	18
5736	Musical instrument & sheet music stores	6,821	4,193
3931	Musical instrument manufacturers	910	722
7699 X	Musical instrument repair services	2,293	382

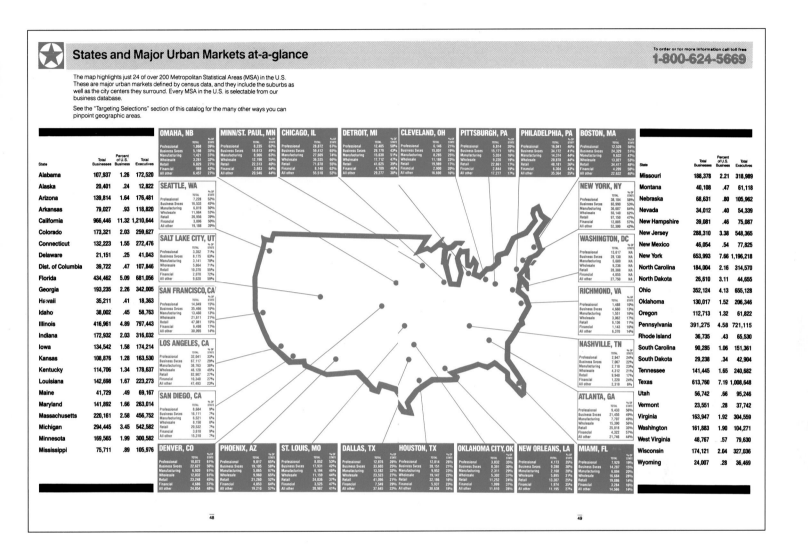

States and Major Urban Markets at-a-glance

The map highlights just 24 of over 200 Metropolitan Statistical Areas (MSA) in the U.S. These are major urban markets defined by census data, and they include the suburbs as well as the city centers they surround. Every MSA in the U.S. is selectable from our business database.

See the "Targeting Selections" section of this catalog for the many other ways you can pinpoint geographic areas.

State	Total Businesses	Percent of U.S. Business	Total Executives
Alabama	107,937	1.26	172,520
Alaska	20,401	.24	12,822
Arizona	139,814	1.64	176,481
Arkansas	79,027	.93	118,820
California	966,446	11.32	1,210,644
Colorado	173,321	2.03	259,627
Connecticut	132,223	1.55	272,476
Delaware	21,151	.25	41,043
Dist. of Columbia	39,722	.47	107,846
Florida	434,462	5.09	681,056
Georgia	193,235	2.26	342,005
Hawaii	35,211	.41	18,363
Idaho	38,002	.45	58,763
Illinois	416,961	4.89	797,443
Indiana	172,932	2.03	316,032
Iowa	134,542	1.58	174,214
Kansas	108,876	1.28	163,530
Kentucky	114,706	1.34	178,637
Louisiana	142,698	1.67	223,273
Maine	41,729	.49	69,167
Maryland	141,892	1.66	263,014
Massachusetts	220,161	2.58	456,752
Michigan	294,445	3.45	542,582
Minnesota	169,565	1.99	300,582
Mississippi	75,711	.89	105,976

State	Total Businesses	Percent of U.S. Business	Total Executives
Missouri	188,378	2.21	318,989
Montana	40,108	.47	61,118
Nebraska	68,631	.80	105,962
Nevada	34,012	.40	54,339
New Hampshire	39,081	.46	75,087
New Jersey	288,310	3.38	548,365
New Mexico	46,054	.54	77,825
New York	653,993	7.66	1,196,218
North Carolina	184,004	2.16	314,570
North Dakota	26,610	.31	44,655
Ohio	352,124	4.13	655,128
Oklahoma	130,017	1.52	206,346
Oregon	112,713	1.32	61,822
Pennsylvania	391,275	4.58	721,115
Rhode Island	36,735	.43	65,530
South Carolina	90,285	1.06	151,361
South Dakota	29,238	.34	42,904
Tennessee	141,445	1.65	240,682
Texas	613,760	7.19	1,008,648
Utah	56,742	.66	95,246
Vermont	23,551	.28	37,742
Virginia	163,947	1.92	304,559
Washington	161,883	1.90	104,271
West Virginia	48,767	.57	79,630
Wisconsin	174,121	2.04	327,036
Wyoming	24,007	.28	36,469

OMAHA, NB

	TOTAL	% OF STATE
Professional	1,868	39%
Business Svces	5,198	35%
Manufacturing	1,421	37%
Wholesale	3,261	32%
Retail	6,829	27%
Financial	969	42%
All other	6,457	27%

SEATTLE, WA

	TOTAL	% OF STATE
Professional	7,228	52%
Business Svces	16,533	45%
Manufacturing	6,819	50%
Wholesale	11,984	53%
Retail	20,956	39%
Financial	3,896	50%
All other	19,188	39%

SALT LAKE CITY, UT

	TOTAL	% OF STATE
Professional	3,352	71%
Business Svces	8,175	63%
Manufacturing	3,141	70%
Wholesale	5,864	71%
Retail	10,370	55%
Financial	2,070	72%
All other	9,628	59%

SAN FRANCISCO, CA

	TOTAL	% OF STATE
Professional	14,949	15%
Business Svces	35,466	16%
Manufacturing	13,468	13%
Wholesale	21,611	21%
Retail	47,081	15%
Financial	6,498	17%
All other	30,095	14%

LOS ANGELES, CA

	TOTAL	% OF STATE
Professional	32,641	33%
Business Svces	67,117	29%
Manufacturing	38,763	38%
Wholesale	46,129	45%
Retail	82,907	27%
Financial	10,340	27%
All other	47,493	23%

SAN DIEGO, CA

	TOTAL	% OF STATE
Professional	8,684	9%
Business Svces	15,111	7%
Manufacturing	6,521	6%
Wholesale	8,150	8%
Retail	20,532	7%
Financial	3,818	9%
All other	15,310	7%

MINN/ST. PAUL, MN

	TOTAL	% OF STATE
Professional	8,235	62%
Business Svces	18,613	49%
Manufacturing	8,906	63%
Wholesale	12,196	59%
Retail	22,513	49%
Financial	3,683	64%
All other	20,546	44%

CHICAGO, IL

	TOTAL	% OF STATE
Professional	28,872	67%
Business Svces	59,412	65%
Manufacturing	27,609	74%
Wholesale	36,535	66%
Retail	71,678	55%
Financial	8,140	62%
All other	55,518	52%

DETROIT, MI

	TOTAL	% OF STATE
Professional	12,405	50%
Business Svces	29,179	43%
Manufacturing	15,830	51%
Wholesale	17,712	47%
Retail	41,625	39%
Financial	4,709	46%
All other	29,277	38%

CLEVELAND, OH

	TOTAL	% OF STATE
Professional	6,145	21%
Business Svces	15,801	19%
Manufacturing	8,285	25%
Wholesale	11,198	23%
Retail	22,861	17%
Financial	2,900	20%
All other	16,690	16%

PITTSBURGH, PA

	TOTAL	% OF STATE
Professional	6,814	20%
Business Svces	15,171	18%
Manufacturing	5,024	16%
Wholesale	9,229	19%
Retail	19,989	17%
Financial	2,844	19%
All other	17,277	17%

PHILADELPHIA, PA

	TOTAL	% OF STATE
Professional	16,641	46%
Business Svces	34,172	41%
Manufacturing	14,374	44%
Wholesale	20,878	44%
Retail	48,181	36%
Financial	6,364	43%
All other	35,364	43%

BOSTON, MA

	TOTAL	% OF STATE
Professional	12,526	58%
Business Svces	24,329	51%
Manufacturing	9,632	47%
Wholesale	13,027	53%
Retail	34,417	48%
Financial	4,209	58%
All other	22,532	46%

NEW YORK, NY

	TOTAL	% OF STATE
Professional	38,184	58%
Business Svces	65,990	53%
Manufacturing	36,607	64%
Wholesale	55,140	62%
Retail	97,150	47%
Financial	12,885	57%
All other	52,306	42%

WASHINGTON, DC

	TOTAL	% OF STATE
Professional	13,617	NA
Business Svces	28,130	NA
Manufacturing	5,689	NA
Wholesale	9,236	NA
Retail	28,388	NA
Financial	4,855	NA
All other	27,750	NA

RICHMOND, VA

	TOTAL	% OF STATE
Professional	1,488	10%
Business Svces	4,660	13%
Manufacturing	1,551	16%
Wholesale	3,062	11%
Retail	6,136	11%
Financial	1,143	16%
All other	6,370	14%

NASHVILLE, TN

	TOTAL	% OF STATE
Professional	2,947	24%
Business Svces	7,067	22%
Manufacturing	2,718	23%
Wholesale	4,312	21%
Retail	9,940	17%
Financial	1,229	24%
All other	2,319	6%

ATLANTA, GA

	TOTAL	% OF STATE
Professional	8,433	56%
Business Svces	21,455	49%
Manufacturing	7,707	49%
Wholesale	15,390	56%
Retail	25,018	35%
Financial	4,322	57%
All other	21,746	44%

DENVER, CO

	TOTAL	% OF STATE
Professional	10,872	61%
Business Svces	22,627	58%
Manufacturing	6,920	61%
Wholesale	12,832	61%
Retail	23,248	45%
Financial	4,686	61%
All other	24,854	48%

PHOENIX, AZ

	TOTAL	% OF STATE
Professional	9,017	65%
Business Svces	19,105	58%
Manufacturing	5,865	67%
Wholesale	9,960	65%
Retail	21,260	52%
Financial	4,853	64%
All other	19,210	57%

ST. LOUIS, MO

	TOTAL	% OF STATE
Professional	8,052	53%
Business Svces	17,931	42%
Manufacturing	6,194	46%
Wholesale	11,159	44%
Retail	24,836	37%
Financial	3,525	47%
All other	20,987	41%

DALLAS, TX

	TOTAL	% OF STATE
Professional	12,876	26%
Business Svces	33,683	25%
Manufacturing	13,582	32%
Wholesale	23,523	27%
Retail	41,096	21%
Financial	7,549	29%
All other	37,645	22%

HOUSTON, TX

	TOTAL	% OF STATE
Professional	12,814	26%
Business Svces	28,151	21%
Manufacturing	9,852	23%
Wholesale	19,147	22%
Retail	32,186	16%
Financial	5,937	23%
All other	38,638	18%

OKLAHOMA CITY, OK

	TOTAL	% OF STATE
Professional	3,832	35%
Business Svces	8,391	30%
Manufacturing	2,311	29%
Wholesale	5,302	31%
Retail	11,252	24%
Financial	1,999	37%
All other	11,810	28%

NEW ORLEANS, LA

	TOTAL	% OF STATE
Professional	4,173	35%
Business Svces	9,280	30%
Manufacturing	2,168	28%
Wholesale	5,895	31%
Retail	13,307	25%
Financial	1,974	35%
All other	11,195	27%

MIAMI, FL

	TOTAL	% OF STATE
Professional	7,929	19%
Business Svces	14,287	15%
Manufacturing	6,084	20%
Wholesale	16,684	28%
Retail	19,886	14%
Financial	3,284	18%
All other	14,566	14%

48   49

HEWLETT PACKARD

Hewlett Packard's award-winning catalog successfully bridges the gap between the highly promotional catalogs of the typical office supply dealer and the up-scale, image-conscious PR vehicles produced by some high visibility corporations.

In bestowing the Silver Award to Hewlett Packard, the ACA judges clearly felt that the company has successfully created a format that is "clean, easy to follow and well suited for [its] built-in audience".

The cover photomontage is a melange of Hewlett Packard hardware, Hewlett Packard software, a pretty lady, a handsome man, and the north side of a southbound pair of Levi's jeans. Cover copy is strong and promotional. "COMPUTER USERS CATALOG Summer 1987" tells us what it is. "CALL HP DIRECT—Fast, easy ordering—800-538-8787—We ship within 24 hours" tells the reader this is a direct response catalog, and you will get fast action on your order (a not inconsiderable consideration these days).

Reversed in white out of a red corner panel is the loud whisper, pssssst, "Disc prices reduced". Switch to yellow-on-red for "SAVE UP TO 31% on quantity purchases of 3.5″ and 5.25″ discs"; back to the KO type for "DETAILS ON PAGE 59." About those jeans: they're explained by, "HP computers monitor sales of Levi's jeans throughout the world. SEE INSIDE COVER FOR DETAILS." And yes, they drew a mixed reaction from the ACA jury.

HEWLETT PACKARD—Computer Users Catalog Summer 1987
Kathy Roslund, *Catalog Director*
Crane Auvil & Associates, *Designer*
Toni Robinson, *Copywriter*
Light Design, Sollecito Photography and Jeff Hicks & Associates, *Photographers*
Scott Anderson, *Marketing Communications Manager*
Banta Company [Menasha, WI], *Printer, on 7PT Warrenflo Gloss for cover and 40# Catalog Supreme for text*
Solzer & Hall [San Francisco], *Color Separator*

The inside front covers 1 & 2 are devoted to customer concerns. Pictures of the General Manager, Telemarketing Manager, Distribution Manager and Marketing Manager are shown with a signed message from each. In each of the messages, except that of the general manager, the normal worries of a direct response customer—retail or business to business—are addressed.

The General Manager has chosen to deliver a negative sell, ". . . but if your PC has unexplained dropouts, memory loss or other intermittent problems, you'd better check your cables. If HP made them. . . " and so on, to make the point that the other guy's stuff is no good.

Another negative sales presentation is uncorked with a vengeance at the beginning of the disc and tape products section. How's this for scare tactics?

"A customer shipped his HP 82901 disc drive back to us for repair. The repair cost is going to be $460. plus lost time and data. All caused by the non HP flexible disc the customer used. Even though it was a 'name brand' disc, it wasn't manufactured to HP specifications for our disc drives."

IBM got in hot water with that sort of coercive selling not too very long ago. They have since abandoned the practice. Even then, their negative pitch was only made by salesmen, not in print. Some purchasers may wimp out, play it safe and buy the HP discs. But it's a good bet that a larger number of potential customers are offended by threats of that sort.

Trust and long-term, mutually profitable associations are what direct response is all about, not adversarial relationships. If the price/performance/

value facts are there, one does not need coercion. If the product cannot deliver the promise, then change the product, change the price or get out of the kitchen. Far more powerful, we think, would be an increased use of customer testimonials, which the ACA judges noted, are scattered throughout the catalog and are "very effective in reinforcing customer confidence". The above notwithstanding, the HP catalog is really a fine piece of work. It is very well organized, easy to find one's way around in and very powerfully merchandised.

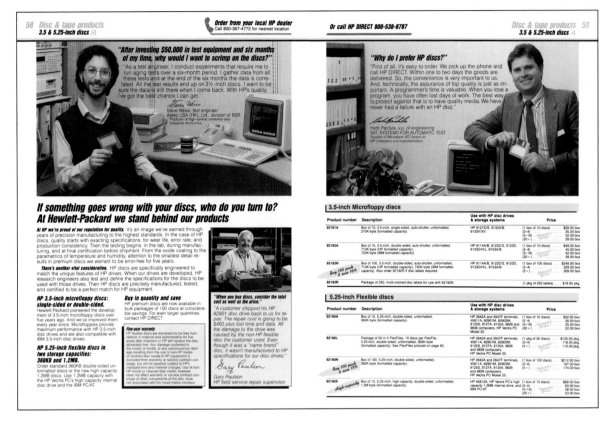

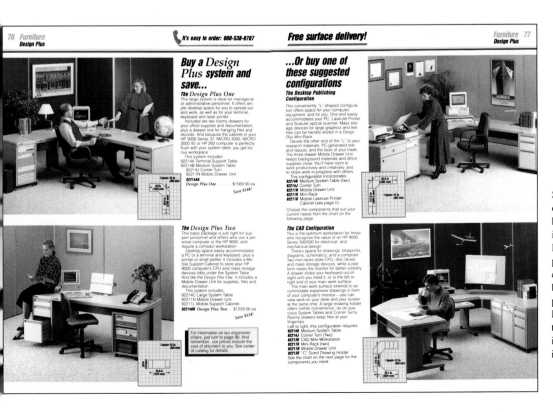

Special kudos to the copywriters for another piece of outstanding work! Hewlett Packard's copy leans heavily towards customer benefits. What a refreshing change from the run-of-the-mill business catalog! Virtually every copy block leads off with a positive approach, leading to the solution of a customer problem. And, better yet, other serious buy-buttons such as "wants" and "needs" are pushed by these very professional copy persons. Product exposition is not lacking, far from it. But the nuts and bolts are where they should be, following (not before) the "hey, stop and look at this item" and the "here's what it can do for you".

There are nine sections in the catalog, each devoted to a merchandise category. The sections are logically sequenced and well presented.

In addition to the eminently coherent pagination of the main body of the catalog, there is a very thoughtful and explicit 11-page index in the center of the book. For the normal human-type reader, the first half of the index is done alphabetically. There are the typical subheads and individual product listings we are all accustomed to. For the Hewlett Packard power-user professionals, there's another index sorted only by part numbers.

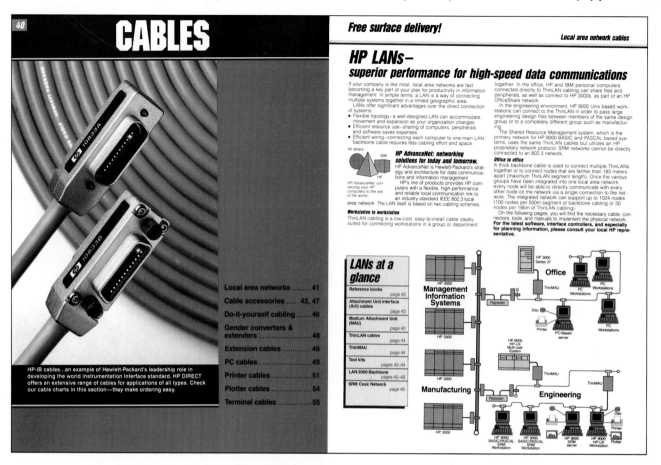

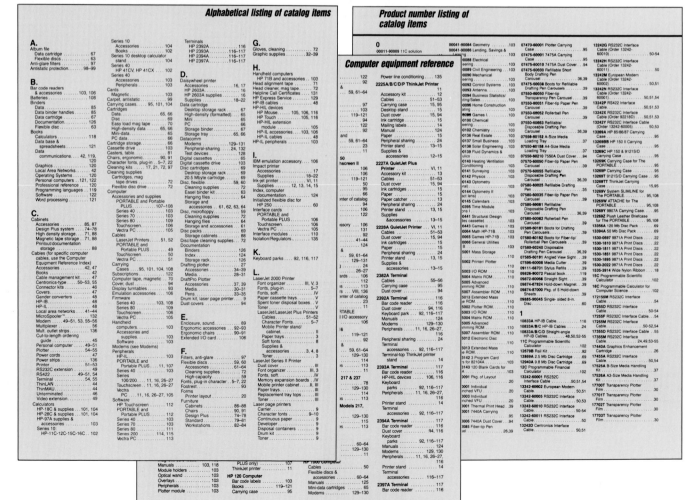

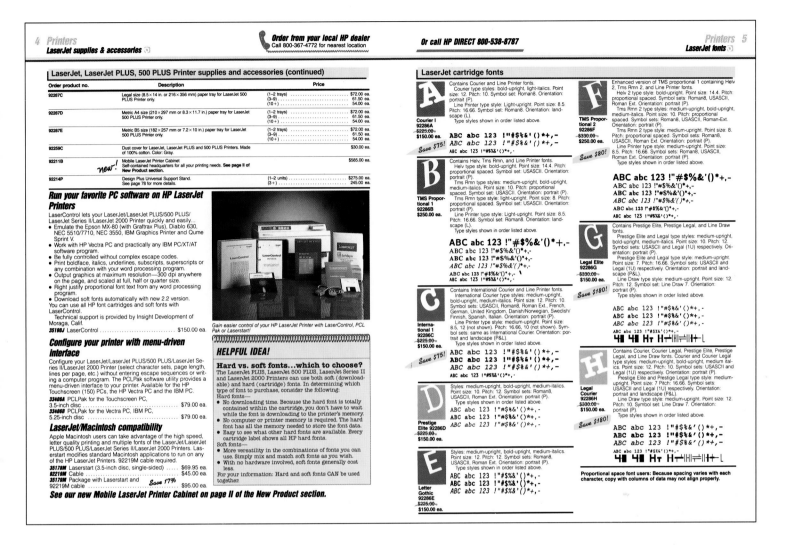

Where pages are really loaded with items and SKU's, typeset rules, color bars and background tints are employed with good taste and excellent effect to relieve the clutter. Unfortunately, the designers of the HP catalog felt it necessary to use sans serif type. And in some cases, sans serif light! In all probability, the art directors must have felt that on such heavily populated pages, a typeface with serifs would load the pages with too much color-weight. They may be correct, 'though many would disagree.

Since this is a perfect bound book, there is another alternative. At very little extra expense, black and white or two color pages could have been added and bound in as needed to relieve the space crunch. These extra pages might consist of nothing more than line art and type. By opening up some additional white space for serif type, they would have made the entire catalog more legible. Money well spent, indeed.

Denny Hatch, publisher of ''Who's Mailing What!'', a real insiders' newsletter for the professional direct response community, approvingly quotes Vrest Orten's 1977 landmark article on type design, ''Why Johnny Can't Read'':

William Caslon first came out with a complete specimen sheet of his magnificent English type in 1734. At the same time, other similar typefaces were being designed: Baskerville, Bell, Janson, and Garamond, to mention a few. All these performed the two proper functions of a typeface: 1) to make the printed page easy, agreeable, and pleasant to read; 2) to create, by the harmonious relationship of type, a comfortable, inviting page of printing — all without the reader's knowing why! These classic types achieve that purpose because of their perfect proportions between thin and heavy lines, thin and heavy curves, and the height and width of each letter. The letters fit together in such a way that the reader is never conscious of each letter, but only of word and sentence.

Sans serif type does just the opposite. Each letter stands alone and yells for attention. Each letter is the same width in all its parts; there are no contrasts. A page of sans serif type is like a landscape with two hundred hills in the distance, all exactly the same shape, size and height. The words for both are monotonous *and* unnatural. *[''Who's Mailing What!'', 8/85, p. 9]*

INMAC

What does it take to grow a business from a standing start to sales of 223 million dollars per year in a mere 13 years? A great deal of good ol' country luck, you say? Darned right! But Jim Willenborg and Ken Eldred, founding partners of Inmac (a direct marketer of computer supplies and aftermarket products) have an abundance of more useful answers.

Here's what Jim and Ken had to work with as Inmac was about to be launched back in 1975:

An ill-served group of computer users and owners—*left dangling in the wind by older office supply firms and computer dealers*. The imagination to see an unfulfilled need, *and visualize the fulfillment thereof*. A specialized marketing niche—*in this case, computer equipment, furniture, supplies and accessories*. Ability to learn—*about computer users' needs and the techniques of direct marketing*. Hard work*: the partners wrote catalog copy from 7 to 9 every morning (and then they went to work)*. Righteous attitudes *about: ethics, customer service, management skills and leadership*. Initial Investment*: $5,000.00 (total assets year-end 1987: $68,541,000.00)!* Commitment *and the mental toughness to roll the dice for high stakes*. A schedule *that called for the first 9,000, 20-page, black & white catalogs to be in the mail by early Spring, 1976*.

During the first 7 years, Inmac sales took off like a rocket. They roared aloft, and attained an enviable rate of 50 million dollars per year by 1983. Since then, the pace hasn't slowed one bit. There's been another 450% increase in the past 5 years! And, what's even more impressive: 50% of Inmac's total sales are generated overseas. Who said Americans can't compete with the rest of the world?

Today, Inmac boasts 27 stocking offices in the US, Canada and 6 overseas countries. Additional countries are being added at the rate of approximately one every year. Sales are compounding at 35% per year, and net income rose 26% in fiscal 1988.

Unlike any other manufacturing segment in the world, computer and communications technologies are evolving so swiftly that so-called durables have become de facto disposables. Equipment that was built to last for decades is discarded in a matter of a few months or years. On top of that, normal business cycles can, and have, savaged the computer industry. The bust in 1985 is a good example. Yet, there's little evidence of any long-term reduction in demand for the kind of products sold in this catalog.

How could a young upstart company carve a 223 million dollar chunk out of their competition's market share; and accumulate 450,000 customers along the way—in only 13 years? As you might expect, there's no single answer to that question. Marketing weapons take many forms, some tangible, some ephemeral. In Inmac's case, one can identify a few of each.

Big Gun #1, The Catalog.

An in-house operation from start to finish. A goodly-sized creative and production staff. A photo studio in the plant. Hands-on participation by Inmac's top executives. Over 24 million catalogs, offering 2,700 items, mailed to a house list of more than 2 million names.

The Power Plant.

A database driven by a proprietary software package called INMAIL. Analysis and segmentation are the name of the game in mail order, and Inmac has the winning equipment, systems, software and personnel to come out on top.

A Plethora of Customers In A Booming Industry.

Over 30 million computers are currently installed in US businesses and homes. These systems range from PC's to parallel processors. The average PC is replaced about every three years. Larger black boxes last only a little longer. All these new installations require connectors, peripherals and system modifications. It seems Wall Street doesn't have an exclusive on churning!

Flexible Manufacturing Capacity.

Perpetual change is implicit in a rapidly evolving technology. Imagine this headache: "Last year we needed 2 million widgets, this year we only need 20 thousand." Or this one: "Japantech just came out with a new PC, faster than a mini, and it only costs fifty dollars. They'll sell 5 million a month, but it uses player piano rolls instead of diskettes."

An exaggeration? Not by much. Crazy as it may sound, that's just about where the computer industry is today. Old fashioned, stick-in-the-mud, bureaucratic suppliers just can't cut it on this playing field. The field is level enough, but look out, the rules have been changed.

Inmac's answer to these frenetic waves of change? Stay on top of all designs and quality standards. Own some plants and buy private label items from other sources. Have a real dedication to product quality, and back this up with solid guarantees. *More than 90% of products sold by Inmac carry the Inmac name.*

Super Customer Service.

(You've heard us emphasize this factor over and over.) Better than 90% of Inmac's orders are out the door within 24 hours.

There are two absolutely essential ingredients required to make that level of performance possible: *anticipation* and *investment*.

Inmac knows what their customers are going to need—even before the customers do. They plan manufacturing, sourcing and delivery systems far in advance, so as to have items on hand to fulfill these anticipated orders. This ability to anticipate is partially a product of their in-house database. Inmac's computers track orders and inventory to come up with sales and velocity reports. Then, sophisticated forecasting tools massage those numbers against externally generated data. Result: solid extrapolations of how many of which will be needed when.

Anticipation also requires research. Inmac keeps track of virtually all new product developments in the computer world. But that's just part of the story. They also track the expansion and contraction of their *customers'* SIC's and product lines. And, of course, they keep close watch on their direct competition. Put all these data in a pot, stir in a little intuition, and you have a recipe for Anticipation a la Inmac.

The Intangibles.

Inmac is a no-nonsense, lean company. There's a lot of competition out there. Price and service are what Inmac's customers want, and bureaucratic behemoths have a problem with both of those requirements.

Most computer users are not hackers (computer buffs). They are people who use computers in the everyday course of doing business. They are doctors, architects, accountants, automobile designers, pilots, brokers and store owners. They come from every persuasion and profession. Only a rare few speak computerese fluently.

MIS directors are not created by cookie-cutters either. Mainframe mentality is still endemic. (You may remember those guys who always said, ''It can't be done. . .'', or more frequently, ''Yeeees, maybe, but it might take about 24 months. . . .'') Other Management Information Services directors cut their teeth on Apple II's, application programs and Star Wars. For the latter group, LAN's, lasers and ''C'' Compilers are a piece of cake. To further complicate matters, the management structures of MIS departments come in all kinds of flavors. Some, as you might expect, report to Accounting. In other companies, they come under the direction of Purchasing, General Administration, Marketing, Sales and even the Engineering department.

If you square all the audience variables extant in these two customer segments (customer interests and MIS management methods), you begin to get an idea of the complexity of the problem. The Inmac catalog team have to communicate comprehensibly to all of the above.

Inmac started out by (admittedly) borrowing from the ''Norm Thompson'' catalog's approach to copywriting. Essentially, it is laid-back, amusing, informative and well organized. Charts and graphs are employed freely—where they serve a useful purpose. Illustrations that elucidate functions and relationships abound. Insert photos and close-up shots dig into details, demonstrate operating techniques, explain product features and clarify copy points.

In all major product areas, and when new products are being introduced, Inmac takes the time and space to engage their readers in a lively (if one-sided) discussion. As an example: diskettes are hardly the glamour-pusses of the computer world. They're little flat, floppy things with holes in the middle, come in three sizes, and store data.

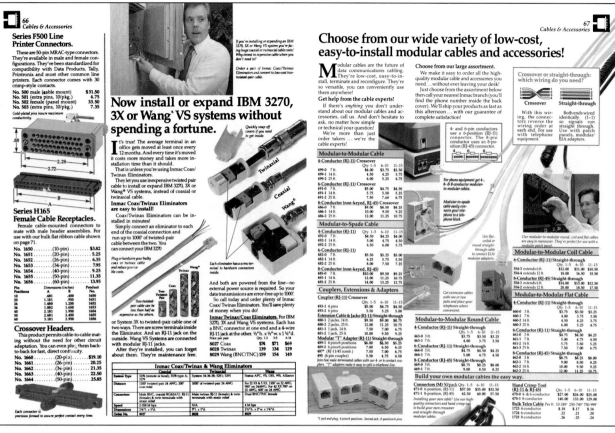

"Not by a long shot", say Inmac's writers, "That's only a tenth of the story. Here's how *we* describe our Inmac Plus diskettes": [emphasis added]

. . . then a good thing got even better. In 1983, we began to test every disk for 100% read/write accuracy at a 60% clipping level—twice as high as most systems require. So you could use them in less-than-perfect drives—and still enjoy perfect performance every time.

And we're still the only company to give each disk its very own registration number. It helps us keep a watchful eye on how well every Inmac Plus disk performs—in our facility and in yours.

That was yesterday's Inmac Plus disk. Now say hello to today's.

New First Time Certification Yields a New Level of Security.

In addition to our clipping level tests, every Inmac Plus disk you now order is 'first time certified.' Which is computereze for saying we enter data on each disk, read it back and read it again. If a single error shows up—that disk is scrapped.

It's a test only Inmac Plus, and disks from IBM and Wang must pass. It's also an extremely accurate way to tell how well a disk will perform—before our customers entrust their data to it.

Inmac's copy then goes on to describe the benefits of their flip-top easel case and their easily erasable labels. It finishes with a bang—a prominent display of the Inmac lifetime diskette guarantee bug. Look at the great job this copy has done by: delivering the facts, answering objections, and stroking the emotions and insecurities of a variegated audience. Terrific copywriting style! Relaxed, conversational, "You" oriented (not "me" or "it"). Tells the story well and clobbers the competition.

Professional salesmen welcome "sales objections" when they are sitting across the desk from a recalcitrant customer. These objections are recognized as a form of selling opportunities. The most common selling opportunity Other-Company disk salesmen, such as Inmac, run into is a version—stated or implied—of:

The salesman who sold us our IBM (or HP, or Wang, or XYZ) computer told us we have to use his diskettes. Otherwise, the guarantee on the computer might not be any good.

Implication: better buy the brand he's flogging (and CYA).

Like all good salespeople, Inmac's writers meet this "opportunity" head-on, and deal with it before the customer has a chance to verbalize (and thereby lock-in) his concerns. Referring to Inmac's 'first time certified' test, they slip in this banana peel for Mr. Brandname Salesman to step on: "It's a test only Inmac Plus, and *disks from IBM and Wang* must pass."

Checkmate!

In addition to a massive line of equipment, Inmac does sell computer-related commodities such as paper, printer ribbons, pens, and plotter film. But that's not necessarily where the ROI action is. Every item has to earn its keep. If sales are poor, it's out. If sales are OK, it will likely be repeated in a future catalog, and be given more, less or the same amount of space, depending upon its degree of success. If, on the other hand, sales are fantastic, Katie bar the door! More space, more frequency, and possibly a plug on the cover.

Inmac issues a new catalog each month. Paginations change, but in a recent book, the breakdown by merchandise category looked something like this:

The plot thickens when you examine these figures carefully. Workstation Furniture, as a discrete chapter, leads in total square inches. In addition, furniture and related items are scattered throughout other chapters in the Inmac catalog. This is especially true in the chapters devoted to ''Workspace Maximizers'' and ''Productivity Boosters''.

Thus, it might be fair to say that over 20% of Inmac's pages, in the June, 1988 issue, were devoted to Furniture and Accessories, in the broader sense of the word. An interesting product mix for a so-called computer catalog.

What is even more astonishing is that 90% of this furniture will be on its way to you within 24 hours after it's ordered! Imagine trying to get that kind of schedule accommodation at your local office furniture store.

Lest you dash off to start a competing catalog, be aware that Inmac is not alone in the field. Serious and effective competition comes from both U.S. and international computer supply firms. On top of that, new companies keep surfacing, and older office supply companies are increasing the amount of sales support allocated to computer-related products.

Then there's another major consideration for potential competitors: Inmac ships 85% of their orders on the day they are received. 90% are fulfilled within 24 hours. This kind of performance doesn't come easily or cheaply. The inventory investment to support this level of customer service at all 27 Inmac locations is more than 25-million dollars.

Inmac seems to have put it all together. Exemplary management, great service, the funds to do the job and a pacesetting catalog program. Theirs is a field for quick-footed heavy hitters with a diverse range of marketing and management skills. Faint of heart or shallow-pockets need not apply.

NATIONAL GEOGRAPHIC EDUCATIONAL SERVICES

We've become accustomed to using the word "catalog" (or catalogue) when describing a magazine-like publication full of items for sale. This usage stretches the definition considerably. In the original nounal context, a catalog was an alphabetical list of the contents of a library. At best, these catalogs might contain some brief notes concerning the names or subjects listed.

The *Random House Dictionary of the English Language* suggests a far better title for what we have been calling catalogs: "*catalogues raisonnes*": *A catalog with notes or commentary on the items listed; a classified, descriptive catalog.*

The National Geographic Educational Services (NGES) quite deservedly won the 1988 DMA Echo Silver Award for their *catalogue raisonne*. In a field where most catalogs in their field revert back to the original definition, National Geographic has come up with a stunning example of fine organization and presentation.

NGES's market consists of the 14,800 public libraries and approximately 90,000 kindergarten through 12th grade schools in the United States. National Geographic's staff produces and sells multimedia teaching aids such as: audio and AV cassettes, computer courseware, films, sound filmstrips, books, kits, globes, atlases and maps.

AV's, books and computerware are all exciting and stimulating products. But it's quite something else to design an attractive presentation selling four, six or even 23 of these items from a single catalog page. NGES has solved this dilemma by drawing on the seasoned creative professionals of the "National Geographic" Magazine's editorial and production staff.

Masterful typography, superb layouts and intelligent selection of pickup photographs all combine to enliven what might otherwise have been a dull cataloging of teachers' aids. From the sensitive opening spread to the extremely informative index, every page of this *catalogue* presents a thought-provoking, inspiring message to teachers and librarians. What's more, you come away with the feeling that with these study tools, learning (and teaching) can be fun.

NATIONAL GEOGRAPHIC—1988 Film and Video Catalog

Cletis G. Pride, *Vice President, Promotion and Educational Services*

Wendy C. Rogers, *Assistant Director, Educational Services*

Carl W. Harmon, *Assistant Manager, Educational Services*

F. William Rath, *Executive Art Director*

Joan Anderson, *Creative Director*

Richard Fletcher, *Designer*

Mary J. Lindsay, *Art Director*

James V. Bullard, *Copy Editor*

M. Elizabeth Murphy, *Copywriter*

Anne Barker, *Production Manager*

Robert L. Feige, *Assistant Director, Production*

What's New for 1988?

■ **Science**

Choose from 16 new science films and videos—for every grade level! Introduce K-3 students to the natural world with *Animals that Live in the City, Backyard Birds, How Animals Get Their Food, Where Animals Live, Animals A to Z, Mammals and Their Young,* and *Animal Guessing Games.* Children in grades 4-6 will be intrigued by *Color: Light Fantastic* and *The Great Cover-Up: Animal Camouflage.* For grades 7-12, there's *The Living Ocean.* These students will also learn about basic anatomy with *Our Immune System* and *The Human Body Series: Circulatory and Respiratory Systems, Digestive System, Nervous System, Reproductive Systems, Muscular and Skeletal Systems.*

■ **Social Studies**

Two new social studies films and videos expand the world for students: *1917: Revolution in Russia* for grades 9-12 and *China: Sichuan Province* for grades 7-12.

■ **New Low Prices**

Now you can save when you order 25 or more video copies of a single title. The Society will manufacture VHS or Beta for $40 a copy. If you'd like a mix of titles, you may order 100 videos of various titles for $50 a copy. Each video comes in a durable case with Teacher's Guide and Synopsis label.

You can save on all National Geographic films and videos with our volume-discount policy. Video duplication rights are also available for a modest fee (see page 41).

■ **Previews**

All titles may be previewed in 16mm film. Titles released since 1984 may also be previewed in video (see page 41).

Science
■ Grades K-3

The World of Pets Series

A valuable introduction to the behavior, anatomy, health needs, and care of popular pets. Students will discover a wealth of fascinating facts about animals. *Teacher's Guide included with each film.*

Dogs

A family shops for a puppy at a pet store, but after reading about dogs, buys one from a breeder. The children begin to learn the needs of their puppy and to understand its body language. Dramatic footage shows dogs that herd sheep, help police and blind people, and perform tricks.
For grades K-3. © 1985
No. 51050   16-minute color video $172
No. 05689   16-minute color film $280

Fish

The purchase of several goldfish signals the beginning of a learning adventure for your students and the students in the film. Closeup photography introduces the basic anatomy of a fish. Slow-motion photography reveals the fish's means of locomotion.

In the classroom, the children carry out an experiment designed to discover whether goldfish can discriminate colors. Classroom work with Siamese fighting fish introduces an unusual instance of behavior. *For grades K-3.* © 1985 Winner: Silver Award, Houston International Film Festival
No. 51073   16-minute color video $172
No. 05690   16-minute color film $280

Cats

A family observes the behavior and development of newborn kittens. Close attention is paid to the cat's sensory anatomy and to the meaning of its play.

Another family adopts a cat and begins to care for and love its new pet. The children learn why the cat has been neutered.
For grades K-3. © 1985
No. 51031   16-minute color video $172
No. 05688   16-minute color film $280

SAVE 10% when you purchase the complete series.
No. 51250 Discounted video series $464.40
No. 05691 Discounted film series $756.00

Engaging films and videos explore the animal world.

Animal Guessing Games

Students have fun learning about some of their favorite animals. Sharpen observation skills with closeup looks at animal features. Match mothers and babies and guess who lives where. *For grades K-3.* © 1988
NEW Available March
No. 51322   15-minute color video $79.95
No. 50438   15-minute color film $280.00

Mammals and Their Young

Here is a look at a great variety of mammals and the diverse environments they inhabit. Nurtured by their mothers and taught to varying degrees, mammals survive and develop in different ways. *For grades K-3.* © 1988
NEW Available March
No. 51321   15-minute color video $79.95
No. 50434   15-minute color film $280.00

Animals A to Z

Youngsters see some of their favorite, familiar animals and meet some new, exotic ones as they travel through this animal alphabet. From anteaters to zebras, the ABC's were never quite so much fun. *For grades K-3.* © 1988
NEW Available March
No. 51320   15-minute color video $79.95
No. 50430   15-minute color film $280.00

Where Animals Live

Students will see how familiar and exotic animals have adapted to their environments. A rain forest, a desert, a swamp, and the Arctic are just a few of the diverse habitats this film surveys. *For grades K-3.* © 1988
NEW Available March
No. 51319   15-minute color video $79.95
No. 50424   15-minute color film $280.00

How Animals Get Their Food

A review of animal diets. Many animals—from caterpillars to proboscis monkeys, rely totally on plants for their food. Lions, spiders, and other animal eaters have developed elaborate methods of capturing their prey. Some animals eat almost anything, while others specialize in one food source. Hummingbirds have developed amazing adaptations to exploit their particular food. *For grades K-3.* © 1988
NEW Available March
No. 51318   15-minute color video $79.95
No. 50420   15-minute color film $280.00

Save 10% with series purchase.
No. 51335 Discounted video series $359.75
No. 50442 Discounted film series $1,260.00

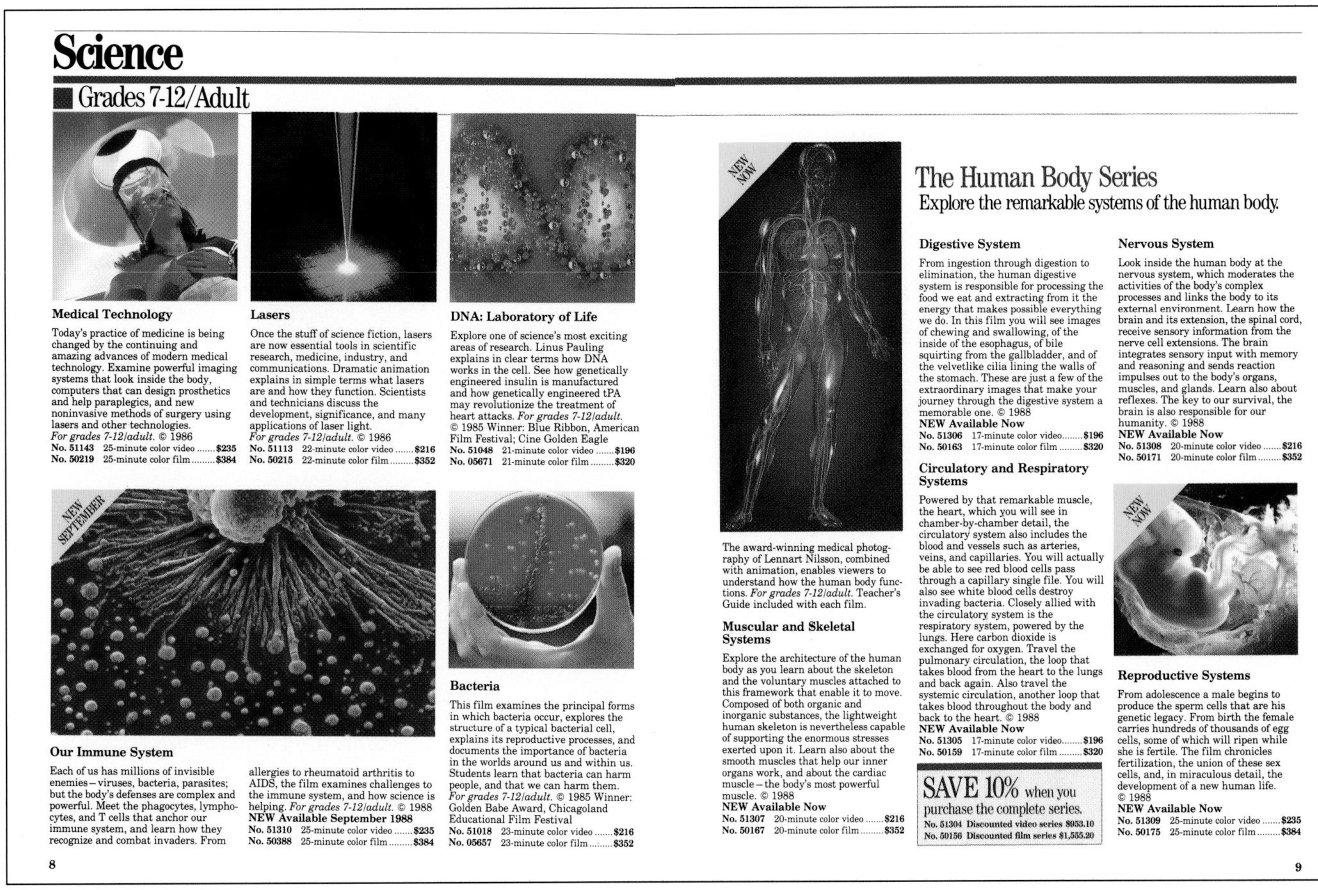

Science

Grades 7-12/Adult

Medical Technology

Today's practice of medicine is being changed by the continuing and amazing advances of modern medical technology. Examine powerful imaging systems that look inside the body, computers that can design prosthetics and help paraplegics, and new noninvasive methods of surgery using lasers and other technologies.
For grades 7-12/adult. © 1986
No. 51143 25-minute color video **$235**
No. 50219 25-minute color film **$384**

Lasers

Once the stuff of science fiction, lasers are now essential tools in scientific research, medicine, industry, and communications. Dramatic animation explains in simple terms what lasers are and how they function. Scientists and technicians discuss the development, significance, and many applications of laser light.
For grades 7-12/adult. © 1986
No. 51113 22-minute color video **$216**
No. 50215 22-minute color film **$352**

DNA: Laboratory of Life

Explore one of science's most exciting areas of research. Linus Pauling explains in clear terms how DNA works in the cell. See how genetically engineered insulin is manufactured and how genetically engineered tPA may revolutionize the treatment of heart attacks. *For grades 7-12/adult.* © 1985 Winner: Blue Ribbon, American Film Festival; Cine Golden Eagle
No. 51048 21-minute color video **$196**
No. 05671 21-minute color film **$320**

NEW SEPTEMBER

Our Immune System

Each of us has millions of invisible enemies—viruses, bacteria, parasites; but the body's defenses are complex and powerful. Meet the phagocytes, lymphocytes, and T cells that anchor our immune system, and learn how they recognize and combat invaders. From allergies to rheumatoid arthritis to AIDS, the film examines challenges to the immune system, and how science is helping. *For grades 7-12/adult.* © 1988
NEW Available September 1988
No. 51310 25-minute color video **$235**
No. 50388 25-minute color film **$384**

Bacteria

This film examines the principal forms in which bacteria occur, explores the structure of a typical bacterial cell, explains its reproductive processes, and documents the importance of bacteria in the worlds around us and within us. Students learn that bacteria can harm people, and that we can harm them. *For grades 7-12/adult.* © 1985 Winner: Golden Babe Award, Chicagoland Educational Film Festival
No. 51018 23-minute color video **$216**
No. 05657 23-minute color film **$352**

8

NEW NOW

The Human Body Series

Explore the remarkable systems of the human body.

The award-winning medical photography of Lennart Nilsson, combined with animation, enables viewers to understand how the human body functions. *For grades 7-12/adult.* Teacher's Guide included with each film.

Muscular and Skeletal Systems

Explore the architecture of the human body as you learn about the skeleton and the voluntary muscles attached to this framework that enable it to move. Composed of both organic and inorganic substances, the lightweight human skeleton is nevertheless capable of supporting the enormous stresses exerted upon it. Learn also about the smooth muscles that help our inner organs work, and about the cardiac muscle—the body's most powerful muscle. © 1988
NEW Available Now
No. 51307 20-minute color video **$216**
No. 50167 20-minute color film **$352**

Digestive System

From ingestion through digestion to elimination, the human digestive system is responsible for processing the food we eat and extracting from it the energy that makes possible everything we do. In this film you will see images of chewing and swallowing, of the inside of the esophagus, of bile squirting from the gallbladder, and of the velvetlike cilia lining the walls of the stomach. These are just a few of the extraordinary images that make your journey through the digestive system a memorable one. © 1988
NEW Available Now
No. 51306 17-minute color video **$196**
No. 50163 17-minute color film **$320**

Circulatory and Respiratory Systems

Powered by that remarkable muscle, the heart, which you will see in chamber-by-chamber detail, the circulatory system also includes the blood and vessels such as arteries, veins, and capillaries. You will actually be able to see red blood cells pass through a capillary single file. You will also see white blood cells destroy invading bacteria. Closely allied with the circulatory system is the respiratory system, powered by the lungs. Here carbon dioxide is exchanged for oxygen. Travel the pulmonary circulation, the loop that takes blood from the heart to the lungs and back again. Also travel the systemic circulation, another loop that takes blood throughout the body and back to the heart. © 1988
NEW Available Now
No. 51305 17-minute color video **$196**
No. 50159 17-minute color film **$320**

SAVE 10% when you purchase the complete series.
No. 51304 Discounted video series $953.10
No. 50156 Discounted film series $1,555.20

Nervous System

Look inside the human body at the nervous system, which moderates the activities of the body's complex processes and links the body to its external environment. Learn how the brain and its extension, the spinal cord, receive sensory information from the nerve cell extensions. The brain integrates sensory input with memory and reasoning and sends reaction impulses out to the body's organs, muscles, and glands. Learn also about reflexes. The key to our survival, the brain is also responsible for our humanity. © 1988
NEW Available Now
No. 51308 20-minute color video **$216**
No. 50171 20-minute color film **$352**

NEW NOW

Reproductive Systems

From adolescence a male begins to produce the sperm cells that are his genetic legacy. From birth the female carries hundreds of thousands of egg cells, some of which will ripen while she is fertile. The film chronicles fertilization, the union of these sex cells, and, in miraculous detail, the development of a new human life. © 1988
NEW Available Now
No. 51309 25-minute color video **$235**
No. 50175 25-minute color film **$384**

9

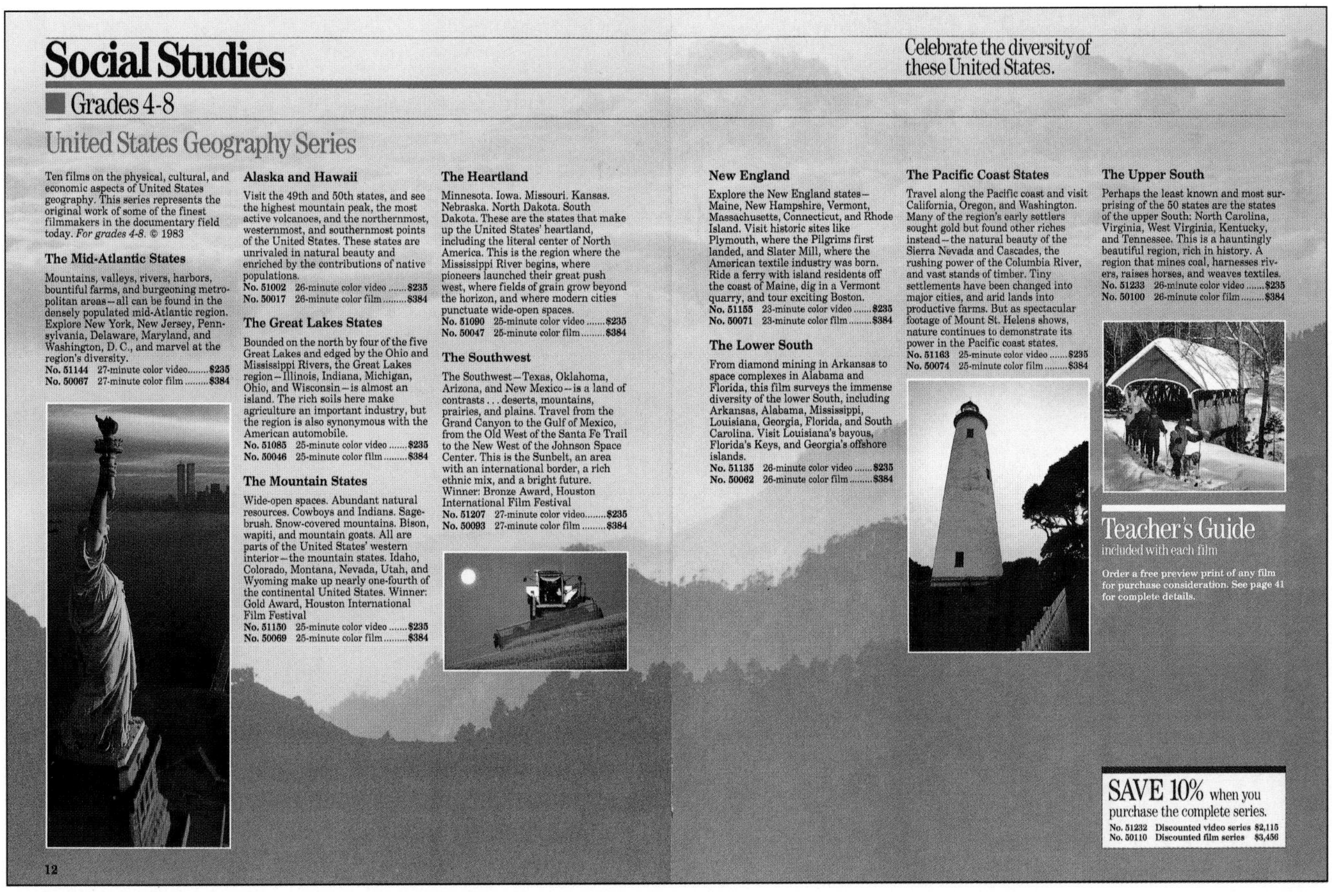

Social Studies

Celebrate the diversity of these United States.

Grades 4-8

United States Geography Series

Ten films on the physical, cultural, and economic aspects of United States geography. This series represents the original work of some of the finest filmmakers in the documentary field today. *For grades 4-8.* © 1983

The Mid-Atlantic States

Mountains, valleys, rivers, harbors, bountiful farms, and burgeoning metropolitan areas—all can be found in the densely populated mid-Atlantic region. Explore New York, New Jersey, Pennsylvania, Delaware, Maryland, and Washington, D. C., and marvel at the region's diversity.
No. 51144 27-minute color video........ **$235**
No. 50067 27-minute color film **$384**

Alaska and Hawaii

Visit the 49th and 50th states, and see the highest mountain peak, the most active volcanoes, and the northernmost, westernmost, and southernmost points of the United States. These states are unrivaled in natural beauty and enriched by the contributions of native populations.
No. 51002 26-minute color video **$235**
No. 50017 26-minute color film **$384**

The Great Lakes States

Bounded on the north by four of the five Great Lakes and edged by the Ohio and Mississippi Rivers, the Great Lakes region—Illinois, Indiana, Michigan, Ohio, and Wisconsin—is almost an island. The rich soils here make agriculture an important industry, but the region is also synonymous with the American automobile.
No. 51085 25-minute color video **$235**
No. 50046 25-minute color film **$384**

The Mountain States

Wide-open spaces. Abundant natural resources. Cowboys and Indians. Sagebrush. Snow-covered mountains. Bison, wapiti, and mountain goats. All are parts of the United States' western interior—the mountain states. Idaho, Colorado, Montana, Nevada, Utah, and Wyoming make up nearly one-fourth of the continental United States. Winner: Gold Award, Houston International Film Festival
No. 51150 25-minute color video **$235**
No. 50069 25-minute color film **$384**

The Heartland

Minnesota. Iowa. Missouri. Kansas. Nebraska. North Dakota. South Dakota. These are the states that make up the United States' heartland, including the literal center of North America. This is the region where the Mississippi River begins, where pioneers launched their great push west, where fields of grain grow beyond the horizon, and where modern cities punctuate wide-open spaces.
No. 51090 25-minute color video **$235**
No. 50047 25-minute color film **$384**

The Southwest

The Southwest—Texas, Oklahoma, Arizona, and New Mexico—is a land of contrasts . . . deserts, mountains, prairies, and plains. Travel from the Grand Canyon to the Gulf of Mexico, from the Old West of the Santa Fe Trail to the New West of the Johnson Space Center. This is the Sunbelt, an area with an international border, a rich ethnic mix, and a bright future. Winner: Bronze Award, Houston International Film Festival
No. 51207 27-minute color video........ **$235**
No. 50093 27-minute color film **$384**

New England

Explore the New England states—Maine, New Hampshire, Vermont, Massachusetts, Connecticut, and Rhode Island. Visit historic sites like Plymouth, where the Pilgrims first landed, and Slater Mill, where the American textile industry was born. Ride a ferry with island residents off the coast of Maine, dig in a Vermont quarry, and tour exciting Boston.
No. 51155 23-minute color video **$235**
No. 50071 23-minute color film **$384**

The Lower South

From diamond mining in Arkansas to space complexes in Alabama and Florida, this film surveys the immense diversity of the lower South, including Arkansas, Alabama, Mississippi, Louisiana, Georgia, Florida, and South Carolina. Visit Louisiana's bayous, Florida's Keys, and Georgia's offshore islands.
No. 51135 26-minute color video **$235**
No. 50062 26-minute color film **$384**

The Pacific Coast States

Travel along the Pacific coast and visit California, Oregon, and Washington. Many of the region's early settlers sought gold but found other riches instead—the natural beauty of the Sierra Nevada and Cascades, the rushing power of the Columbia River, and vast stands of timber. Tiny settlements have been changed into major cities, and arid lands into productive farms. But as spectacular footage of Mount St. Helens shows, nature continues to demonstrate its power in the Pacific coast states.
No. 51163 25-minute color video **$235**
No. 50074 25-minute color film **$384**

The Upper South

Perhaps the least known and most surprising of the 50 states are the states of the upper South: North Carolina, Virginia, West Virginia, Kentucky, and Tennessee. This is a hauntingly beautiful region, rich in history. A region that mines coal, harnesses rivers, raises horses, and weaves textiles.
No. 51233 26-minute color video **$235**
No. 50100 26-minute color film **$384**

Teacher's Guide included with each film

Order a free preview print of any film for purchase consideration. See page 41 for complete details.

SAVE 10% when you purchase the complete series.
No. 51232 Discounted video series $2,115
No. 50110 Discounted film series $3,456

12

Specially Priced Titles

Selected films and videos now available at 30% and 60% discounts.

Here's the perfect opportunity to build your film or video library. For grades K-12/adult, you'll find proven classroom winners in science, social studies, literature—some in French and Spanish.

These sparkling films and videos have each been discounted. You will also want to take advantage of our volume discount offer. See page 41.

All films and videos come with a Teacher's Guide (except TV Specials). We will send you VHS videos unless you specify Beta or U-Matic. Free previews are available. See page 41 for full ordering information.

■ Science

Grades K-6

Mammals

Mammals are probably the most familiar animals on Earth. Young students will learn that they themselves are mammals. Using both common and uncommon examples, the film identifies those characteristics that set mammals apart and helps sharpen students' classifying skills.
Youngsters will learn that even whales and bats are mammals, that about one-half of all mammals are rodents, and that household pets may be relatives of large, wild mammals. They will also observe mother mammals caring for their young.
For grades K-4. © 1979 Winner: Chris Bronze Plaque, Columbus Film Festival; Learning AV Award.
No. 51137   12-minute color video **$59.95**
No. 50063   12-minute color film **$150.50**

Look at Zoos

Youngsters will discover the ways in which scientists study animals in zoos and the ways in which zoo veterinarians work to keep the animals healthy. They'll find that zoos are increasingly performing another important function, that of preserving species in danger of extinction in the wild.
For grades K-6. © 1978
No. 51132   12-minute color video **$59.95**
No. 50060   12-minute color film **$136.50**

Chimpanzees

Students will observe the behavior of chimpanzees, the animals closest to man. The chimpanzees at Tanzania's Gombe National Park gather and eat food, make sleeping nests, and play with other members of their family. Students will also observe mother chimpanzees caring for their young.
For grades 3-6. © 1978 Winner: Learning AV Award; AMTEC Award of Merit
No. 51035   12-minute color video **$59.95**
No. 50244   12-minute color film **$136.50**

Portrait of a Whale

The right whale is one of the largest and rarest of the great whales. Students will see whales flippering, lobtailing, and breaching, probably all forms of communication. They will discover that the largest animal on Earth is also extremely gentle.
For grades K-6. © 1976 Winner: AMTEC Award of Merit
No. 51178   12-minute color video **$59.95**
No. 50307   12-minute color film **$136.50**
No. 51258   Video unit in French **$59.95**
No. 50348   Film unit in French **$136.50**

Birds

A survey of birds around the world sets the stage for students to learn what a bird is, how many species exist, what their calls sound like, where they live, how they get food, and how some of them attract mates.
A fascinating sequence records an American Indian dance in which the dancers' costumes and movements are based on the appearance and motions of a hawk. *For grades 2-6.* © 1978
No. 51024   12-minute color video **$59.95**
No. 50237   12-minute color film **$136.50**

The Cat's Meow

Here is a cat-and-mouse story that stars several playful mice, an inquisitive house cat, and a venturous alley cat. The stages—an ordinary household and an alley. The age-old rivalry between cat and mouse is shown as both a serious struggle for survival and a comic standoff between two lively opponents.
For grades K-6. © 1977
No. 51032   10-minute color video **$59.95**
No. 50242   10-minute color film **$136.50**
No. 51257   Video unit in French **$59.95**
No. 50347   Film unit in French **$136.50**

**Order Toll Free
1-800-368-2728**
Weekdays, 8:00 a.m. to 4:00 p.m. Eastern time.
In Maryland, call 1-301-921-1330.

Animal Babies

This film introduces your students to a variety of familiar and exotic animals and their offspring. Students will see many animal babies and be able to compare such things as size, number of babies born at a time, habitat, and parental care. Youngsters will observe young fish, reptiles, amphibians, birds, and mammals. *For grades 2-6.* © 1981 Winner: Certificate of Excellence, Audubon International Environmental Film Festival
No. 51007   15-minute color video **$59.95**
No. 50019   15-minute color film **$150.50**

Learning About Reptiles

Alligators and crocodiles, turtles and tortoises, lizards and snakes—all these creatures are reptiles. These scaled, cold-blooded animals are examples of adaptations to environments ranging from a desert to the ocean.
Students will learn that baby reptiles look almost exactly like their parents and take care of themselves from birth. *For grades 2-6.* © 1979
No. 51119   12-minute color video **$59.95**
No. 50055   12-minute color film **$150.50**

What Energy Means

With a little help from his older sister, a young student learns about the various forms of energy, from chemical energy to light energy. He also discovers that one form of energy can be converted to another; the difference between fuel and energy; and the need to conserve fuels. *For grades 2-6.* © 1982 Winner: Gold Award, Houston International Film Festival
No. 51242   15-minute color video **$59.95**
No. 50105   15-minute color film **$150.50**

Dinosaurs: Puzzles from the Past

Join two students as they explore the world of dinosaurs. Colorful animation introduces the vast variety of dinosaurs, both meat-eaters and plant-eaters. Visit a site in Canada where actual excavations of dinosaur fossils are taking place. A scientist shows how fossils are combined to form recognizable structures. In a museum in Ottawa, reconstructed dinosaurs dwarf visitors as they did inhabitants of the world they ruled for millions of years. *For grades K-6.* © 1981
No. 51046   20-minute color video **$69.95**
No. 50031   20-minute color film **$198.50**

Tadpoles and Frogs

Students follow the miraculous transformation of tadpole into frog. First they observe the tiny frog eggs as they hatch into transparent tadpoles. The story proceeds in diary fashion, using a young student's drawings to chronicle the changes as the tadpoles begin to swim, grow, develop hindlimbs and forelimbs, and finally emerge as frogs. *For grades K-6.* © 1979
No. 51218   12-minute color video **$59.95**
No. 50097   12-minute color film **$150.50**

18   19

Index

37

III
INCENTIVE CATALOGS

Alfred Fuller, founder of the Fuller Brush company, made this statement repeatedly in talks with his executive team:

Making brushes is the easiest part of our business. The most important things we must concentrate on every day are recruiting, training and retention.

Employee attrition is one the most expensive, time-consuming, nonproductive headaches in any company. In some direct selling and insurance companies, it can run to over 100% per year. But if hiring, training and motivating are done properly, the firing (almost) never has to happen.

What, then, is the missing link? Why all this employee churning? It seems to stem from a well-known fact: most of us employ only 15% or less of our brain's capability. It follows, then, we all have the potential to improve our productivity by quantum leaps. Problem: how do we accomplish this elusive objective? If only we could learn faster, remember more, concentrate harder, develop good study habits, apply rational thought, etc., etc.—we could get a heck of a lot more done.

Mental and physical disabilities aside, the solution to increased productivity lies in individual motivation. We need incentives.

Formal incentive and award programs have been around since the very early 1900s, but the majority of us have little understanding of how they work. We know they exist. We see them in action almost every day, but the underlying concepts and machinations are anything but obvious. Why do certain groups of consumers react better to travel incentives than to toasters and card tables? Why is one item better than another for awards catalogs? What criteria are used to measure a motivation program's effectiveness?

Once upon a time, the business incentive industry was fairly straightforward. Rewards were offered to employees in the form of a catalog chock full of highly desirable products for the home. All these goodies could be "purchased" with award points. The points were earned by achieving a set of predetermined corporate goals. Incentive salesmen, many of whom were behavioral psychologists, worked with their clients to maximize the effect of what today would be considered relatively plain vanilla, precanned programs.

The first major break with tradition came when large-scale incentive travel was introduced in the 1950s. By the mid-60s, travel packages were producing 50% of business incentive dollar volume. Travel has a lot going for it as an award device. It's cost effective for the client, and it's profitable for the incentive companies. But above all, the associated group dynamics make travel an award most recipients enjoy to the full.

At about the same time travel awards were on the rise, another seminal change was taking place in the Incentive Industry. It became apparent that larger groups of employees and customers should be encompassed within the structure of motivational programs. Clearly, a salesforce is only as good as the rest of the team, therefore, management's goals had to be communicated up and down the line. Then, once everyone was on the same wavelength, appropriate motivational tools had to be created for every level within the client organization.

Above a certain income (usually an individual's comfort level), personal motivation requires something other than a bigger paycheck. The employer has to reach deeper into the employee's psyche to attain results. He has to find the hooks within each individual that will make him want to strive for more.

One of the most compelling hooks is peer group approbation. "What will the neighbors think when they see this new 200-inch TV?" "How will my fellow workers react to me after I've won the trip to The Peoples Republic of China?"

Family involvement is another hook, a real grabber. A beautifully produced 12" X 13" catalog is sent to the employee's home. And right there, in glowing color, is the refrigerator, the fur coat, the dining room suite or the travel package of his wife's dreams. The children are in a Fantasy Land castle full of computer games, camping gear, trips to Disneyland and five-foot Pandas. Now, Dad had better produce! The whole family is focused upon the program.

All the players in the marketing game are aware that the average sales force has one basic problem: typically, 20% of a firm's salesmen produce 80% of all orders. As is the case with most sales predicaments, this problem can be converted into a tremendous opportunity. Why an opportunity? Because fully 80% of the sales force is operating far below their potential. Yet, these underachievers have the same academic and physical capabilities as their more successful brethren. All management has to do is crank up a reasonable percentage of this bunch and get them into high gear. Good-bye competition, hello happy stockholders!

Enter the incentive/motivation program, and some fundamental parameters:

1. *Let's establish and prioritize our company's marketing objectives. Then, define a time-frame within which we can reasonably expect to accomplish those objectives.*
2. *Now we'll take a close look at the individuals in each group of employees who will be invited to participate. What makes them tick? Who are their idols, their associates? What is their family structure and what are their families' dreams.*
3. *How much can we afford to spend on this incentive package? What is the range of immediate financial consequences one might expect as the result of this program? What will the long-term effect be? And, what do we do for an encore, lest there be a letdown?*

Incentive programs are one of management's strongest building blocks. And, the incentive catalog is frequently the bedrock upon which the program's foundation is based. The award catalog may be filled with TV's, toasters and mink coats. In another incarnation, it may offer exotic travel destinations and cruise packages. In either case, it fulfills the functions of a primary hardcopy communications medium, a variable feast of award carrots, and a long-lived reminder and prod.

In many cases, the incentive catalog does not start life as a single-client catalog, for two very good reasons: 1). catalogs are expensive to produce, and 2). there is an even greater cost, i.e. inventory to back up the catalog. On the other hand, different clients have different staffs, they are in different parts of the country, and their incentive budgets can be very different.

Given these two antithetical forces, what does one do? For sure, no single catalog will suit all clients.

Typically, an incentive catalog will consist of a core of more or less universal items (the master catalog), surrounded by a number of swing pages or customized printed signatures. In addition, pagination can be re-sequenced, and one-of-a-kind covers and fly-leaves are created for each client. The result: customized catalogs tailored to fit the demographics, regional bias, psychographics and corporate objectives of each sponsoring company.

In another incarnation, the premium/award master catalog may be broken down by items and price points. These price/category lines are then put into a series of smaller catalogs called "plateau books". The first level plateau book may contain items worth approximately $25.00; level two, $50.00 items; with subsequent levels reaching $500.00 or more. The appropriate plateau book is then delivered to the individual who has sold (or purchased) a predetermined amount of goods or services.

There are a number of other methods for customizing catalogs to suit various clients. As you will see, S&H Motivation has a three-level catalog program that virtually eliminates duplication of merchandise from one group of employees to another. Regardless of the mechanics, the objective is universal: present the products that pull the participants' triggers.

The catalog is only one facet of a total incentive package, albeit an important one. The first step is always a careful analysis of a client's business and his objectives. This research phase leads to an outline of the program plan. In turn, the outline highlights all the diverse elements that will be brought into play during execution of the program.

In this volume, we are primarily interested in catalogs and what they can accomplish. But consider: the incentive catalog has to speak in the tongue of the reader. Travel catalogs that feature shots of hairless hardbodies are wrong for Midwestern family folks. Audiophiles are everywhere, but camping equipment is a low traffic item on the streets of Manhattan.

But catalogs are just another form of communication. The very *raison d'etre* of Motivational or Performance companies is founded upon their ability to communicate more clearly than most of us. The art of trans-disciplinary communication is a hard-won skill. Computer programers have to understand the whole situation before they can start to write a program aimed at generating

solutions instead of facts. In a similar vein, salesmen—who are emotionally quite different from programmers—need understandable information PLUS a healthy serving of motivation to get them cranked up. Unfortunately, in some organizations the term "intra-corporate communications" is an oxymoron.

Glaring gaps in corporate communications might be blamed on any number of factors such as: varying academic qualifications, personal conceits or the corporate hierarchical structure. They can certainly be censured for chronically disparate language. To get past these disparities and arrive at consensus and inspiration, there must first be understanding. And understanding must, in some cases, be preceded by *transliteration*. Following the process of transliteration, recognizable words become meaningful phrases, phrases become thoughts, and thoughts engender cognitive and emotional response. Only then do we achieve meaningful communications!

When firms such as Business Incentives set out to solve these communications gaps, they first take a hard look at the needs of their clients. Then, they apply all their communication and motivational skills to serve these needs. Here is a sample of the type of "Need List" BI might identify for a particular client:

New Product Introductions
Cost Containment
Change of Product Mix
Training
Expanded Distribution
Quality Enhancement
Retraining a Sales Force
Efficient Data Management
Improved Management of Assets
Improved Cash Flow
Achieving Sales Forecasts
Expense Management
Promotional Emphasis on Product line

Once all hands agree upon the *needs*, the program shifts into high gear. *Needs* inspire objectives, and objectives point to solutions. Next, a pivotal component, the catalog, takes shape. Then introduction, instruction and inspiration click into place at all levels. Result: Performance.

On the following pages, we'll take a look at three firms in the corporate incentive industry, and one packager of consumer incentive programs. Competing in the corporate world are: Business Incentives, Inc. of Minneapolis, Minnesota, the Carlson Marketing Group (also out of Minneapolis) and Chicago's S&H Motivation, Inc. An exciting glimpse into the future of the consumer incentive industry is illustrated in a story about the new electronic media from the Sperry & Hutchinson Company of Green Stamps fame. A close look at these companies will provide an insight into the incentive business as it is practiced today.

BUSINESS INCENTIVES, INC.

Business Incentives, Inc. (BI) is a fine example of a pure, business-oriented incentive company. They are not involved in trading stamps, cents-off coupons or any other mass consumer incentives or premiums. The majority of BI's programs are directed toward the executives, sales forces and dealer organizations of Fortune 100 firms, including some of the Top 10. For each of their clients, the 700-member BI staff prepares customized programs that include (among many other components) catalogs, brochures, letters and promotional products utilizing just about every ink-on-paper medium known to man.

Twice each year, 282 new catalog pages are merchandised and produced—564 pages in all. From this bank of master pages, custom catalogs are collated for each BI client. In addition, every incentive program has its own individualized covers and insert pages. The finished books—usually consisting of 48, 112 or 160 pages—are the heart of the motivational program.

Modern executives have recognized that employee motivation is a complex specialty, far beyond the ken of most of today's specialist-managers. Vice President, Larry Schoenecker, eldest son of BI founder and CEO, Guy Schoenecker, describes a contemporary incentive program in these words:

IT IS A PERFORMANCE CONTINUUM:
To get people to do what you want them to do—to cause change—is a highly orchestrated, ongoing process. We believe this process is never static. It's a continuum, a moving target that must be addressed on a consistent basis.

Before creating a new Performance Program, a company like Business Incentives digs down to the very core of their client's motives.

Are the objectives short-term or long? Shall we opt for volume? Or for profit? Or for a combination of both? Can we sacrifice tomorrow's growth for today's sales? Do we want to retain staff or let the weaker members self-destruct?

Then, the research team gathers every tiny bit of information available about the staff members to whom the incentive program is directed—the men and women who are going to earn these awards.

What is their financial comfort level? What are their hobbies, sports interests, recreations? Are they psychologically secure individuals, or is constant reinforcement necessary? What are their family situations, and will it help to involve the wife and kids in the program?

Once all the pieces have been assembled, the incentive plan is introduced to employees with a Bang, not a memo. The format for the introduction is a formal, and sometimes very theatrical, meeting. The script, design and production of the meeting is conceived as an integral part of the overall program. Everything is orchestrated so as to create the desired effect; to push the right motivational buttons. These events have evolved far beyond the old-fashioned pep talks given by the president or the sales manager. They've metamorphosed into an art-form called Business Theater.

Travel Album

Awards Album

BUSINESS INCENTIVES INC.
Guy Schoenecker, *CEO*
Larry Schoenecker, *Vice President*
Agency: *In-house*

In an unusual and dramatic presentation, Business Incentives (BI) combines travel awards with a 104-page, perfect bound merchandise catalog, all in one hardcover leatherette folder. The effect is overwhelming. This format keeps the whole program in front of the participant in a protected, long-lived package.

The Business Incentives, Inc. catalogs shown on these pages fall into two groups, product catalogs and travel catalogs. Since the mid-1970s, travel packages have represented about one-half of all executive and sales force incentive awards. BI has reacted to this demand, as have others in their industry, with travel packages and programs to meet virtually any taste.

A generic offering created by Business Incentives is the *A La Carte* Awards program. The graphic centerpiece of the *A La Carte* program is a handsome hardbound folder encompassing not one, but two separate catalogs. A travel catalog is presented on the inside front cover, an Awards Album featuring 104 pages of very upscale products is on the right.

Participants in the Awards program earn *A La Carte* Cheques. These Cheques are good at all Hyatt Hotels, Club Med, on virtually all the world's commercial airlines, and aboard Cunard and Norwegian Caribbean Lines cruise ships. They will buy you any number of complete holiday packages to Mexico, Hawaii, Japan, Europe and the Caribbean. Special sports packages include skiing, hunting, sailing, tennis, golf and fishing. And of course, *A La Carte* Cheques can be used to buy the products featured in the BI Incentives Awards Album.

The *A La Carte* presentation has won Printing Industries of America's top award for catalogs in 1988. What's more, if there were an award for the best "Comprehensive Incentive Awards Program", Business Incentives' *A La Carte* package would have to be at, or very near the top.

At this very moment, motivational mavins throughout the industry are undertaking a new, and even more wondrous, award-point tracking methods. Gone are the sticky stamps and labored bookkeeping of yesteryear. Even the Cheques, checks and passbooks are an endangered species. Soon, most incentive awards point tracking will be in the form of computer-to-computer communications. Right now, client-generated sales reports are automatically converted into award credits by computers in BI's offices.

H O L I D A Y S

SUNNY

skies are status quo in Mexico and the Caribbean. And A la carte Cheques can take you to all the hot spots.

A la carte Holidays include 10 Caribbean island adventures. From Aruba to Barbados to St. Croix, the Caribbean is filled with spectacular beaches and luxury hotels. Each Holiday introduces you to a very special island.

The Caribbean isn't the only place to escape winter. There's also plenty of sunshine South of the Border. A la carte Holidays serves up 5 Mexican Fiestas. Some are to familiar places — like Acapulco and Cancun. Others, to locations like Ixtapa-Zihuatanejo, give you a chance to explore the newest names on the Mexican resort scene.

The Travel Album Indicator provides descriptions, and pricing that will help you find your place in the sun.

The resorts of Mexico and the Caribbean are among the best in the world. You can expect fine dining, fascinating sightseeing and sports activities to suit every style and taste.

Resort

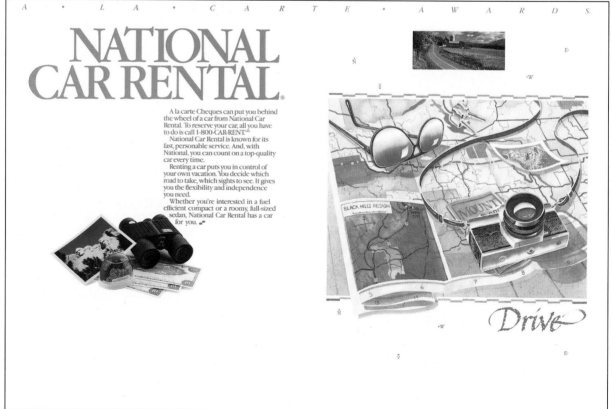

A • L A • C A R T E • A W A R D S.

NATIONAL CAR RENTAL.

A la carte Cheques can put you behind the wheel of a car from National Car Rental. To reserve your car, all you have to do is call 1-800-CAR-RENT.

National Car Rental is known for its fast, personable service. And, with National, you can count on a top-quality car every time.

Renting a car puts you in control of your own vacation. You decide which road to take, which sights to see. It gives you the flexibility and independence you need.

Whether you're interested in a fuel efficient compact or a roomy, full-sized sedan, National Car Rental has a car for you.

Drive

There's a message on these pages. It goes something like this:

There's absolutely no doubt, travel is fun! Do it your way or come along on one of our tours. The folks here at BI love these vacation spots, and we want to share them all with you.

Your preferred destination may be the Club Med or Stockholm. You can rent a car or take a cruise. But it's yours. You've earned the A la carte Awards to do with as you will.

The other half of the *A la carte* Awards folder hits home with a truly unique incentive catalog. It has words. Real copywriter's honest to goodness selling words. Why with just a few tweaks, this book could become a mailorder catalog.

The analogy is meant as a compliment. Mailorder is not an easy sell. After all, the printed page is the whole store. Any catalog that succeeds in that arena has to be good, and when it comes to selling, my hat's off to the BI catalog.

Business Incentives has chosen to show fewer items per page. But every product has double im-

pact. There's plenty of good copy, and the layouts call for large and vibrant photographs. This is not a static book. The items have a life of their own, even when they are shown without models. Where models do grace the photographs, they are obviously enjoying who they are and what they're doing.

Designing and coordinating an exquisite table is an art . . . every piece, every pattern should reflect a graciousness and beauty that bids everyone welcome. Each element you select today will be treasured tomorrow for the memories it holds, the joys it reflects, the loves and lives it has shared. The sparkle of crystal, the gleam of silver and the lustre of china glowing in soft candlelight set the tone for years of memorable meals. These elegant table appointments can now be yours. Whether you start anew or expand what you have, this selection includes world famous names in crystal, silverware and china. Just consult your Awards Album indicator for the many listings of the patterns available.

A 33-6105-00 Reed and Barton sterling silver flatware in elegant "18th Century" fluted pattern. 4-piece place setting. 33-6104-00 (not shown) Kirk Stieff sterling silver 4-piece place setting, intricate "Old Maryland Engraved" pattern.

B 33-8849-†† Traditional Nottingham English lace tablecloth updated for today's busy hostess in an easy care 70% polyester/30% cotton blend. Beige. Specify size: 54" x 70", 70" x 90", 70" x 108".

C Sparkling Waterford crystal stemware in graceful "Sheila" pattern. Brilliantly hand cut by master artisans in Ireland. 33-6102-00 Wine, each. 33-6103-00 Flute champagne, each.

D 33-6101-00 World-renowned Lenox china in baroque "Autumn" pattern . . . blue scrolls and colorful bouquets accented with 24K gold borders. 5-piece place setting.

E 33-8621-00 After-dinner coffee in the living room is such a pleasant way to finish a meal. This serving cart is easily mobile and classically styled by Butler with carved legs and lower shelf. 4-way matched veneer top has a burl border and brass-plated gallery rails at each end. Choice veneers on selected hardwoods are finished in a hazel brown. 31½"W x 20½"D x 29¾"H.

F 33-7018-00 Candles displayed in silver add so much romance and warmth to an evening. French gadroon borders decorate this pair of silverplate candlesticks from Sheffield Silversmiths. Octagonal bases and turned columns complete the look. Pair. 9" tall.

G 33-8848-00 This cheerful arrangement of blooming silk flowers will dazzle your table with its beauty. An artist's colorful palette of blossoms, perfectly presented in a cut glass bowl. 24"W x 15"H.

H 33-5501-00 Your guests will feel like royalty being served from this magnificent coffee set by Oneida Silversmiths. The "Baronet" pattern is ornate in the stately English tradition, yet refined as only 18th century design can be. The heavy silverplate set includes a 48-oz. coffee pot, covered sugar, creamer and 12" round tray.

J 33-8847-00 This "Rittenhouse Square" china cabinet traces its design to the 18th century Philadelphia-Chippendale school of cabinetmaking. Henredon displays its carving virtuosity with an arched and pierced broken pediment characteristic of this period. The upper doors enclose 2 glass shelves with plate grooves and interior lights. A bronze mirrored back panel reflects the beauty of your display. The lower doors open to a silver storage drawer and adjustable shelf. Finest mahogany veneers on maple solids. 42"W x 16½"D x 85"H.

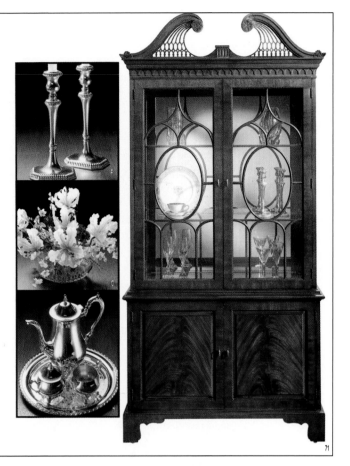

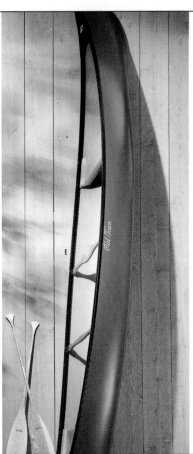

A 33-9940-†† Coast Guard regulations require a flotation garment for all water sports, fishing and boating. This Stearns sports vest has zipper front and four handy Velcro-close pockets. Made with tough oxford nylon outershell and lining. Adjustable sides for fit, comfort and freedom of movement. Tan. Specify size: S/M or L/XL.

B Hand-sewn "Yellowstone" hiker from H.H. Brown offers all the comfort of a moccasin plus the security of 5-eye laces. Features a Gore-Tex® bootie and an exclusive cushioned arch support footbed. Ranger outsole and nylon quarters for lightness and comfort. Tan Whaler color. 33-8107-†† Men's shoe. Specify size: M 7-11. 33-8108-†† Ladies' shoe. Specify size: M 6-9.

C 33-0114-†† Deerskin gloves for men are a cool weather necessity. These are unlined for greater agility and fit, with stitch detailing on the back. Deep tan color. Specify size: M-L-XL.

D 33-8941-00 This very versatile "Hot Stuff" LP gas cooker from Char-Broil will let you grill a burger, deep fry fish, boil shrimp or steam clams all in one compact unit with 154 sq. in. cooking area. Includes 3-gallon aluminum pot with lid, chromed steel fry basket, grill adapter kit, hose and regulator. LP tank not included.

E 33-8956-00 When you cut ties to civilization for extended periods, you put new meaning in cargo capacity. This XL Tripper multi-purpose canoe from Old Town boasts 1700 lbs. capacity . . . yet it paddles easily and turns quickly. Constructed of extremely durable Oltonar/Royalex® with a shallow-V hull and deep-V entry. Also features roto-molded decks/seats; vinyl gunwales with aluminum inserts. Handles outboards up to 8 hp for big water use. Dark green. 20'L x 41"W x 16½"D.

F Both men and women will appreciate the warmth and versatility of this sweater and vest combo from Tundra Knitwear. The zip-front twill vest boasts warm sherpa lining and a soft knit back. The crew neck pullover sweater is knitted in an original pattern from unspun, virgin Scandinavian wool. Mostly grey. Specify unisex size: S-M-L-XL. 33-0290-†† Vest. 33-0291-†† Sweater.

G 33-0212-00 Surround yourself in down when the wind is up and the mercury low. The Browning Alaskan parka for men is fully down insulated except for 8" of water-resistant polyester fill around the hem . . . this poly barrier keeps moisture from "wicking" up the hem and reaching the down. Feature-packed with genuine coyote-trimmed hood, heavy 2-way zipper, Velcro neck closure. Front cargo pockets. Tan. Specify size: S-M-ML-L-XL.

H To meet the demand for luggage that can handle all modes of travel, Boyt took the materials used in their top-of-the-line gun cases and created these Boundary Lake bags which are designed to take rough treatment. Made of heavy, water-repellent cotton canvas . . . then reinforced with leather and solid copper rivets, each bag has plenty of space and a 2" wide web shoulder strap. 33-4519-00 Shell bag. 15"x11"x3½". 33-4520-00 Small duffle. 18"x12"x12". 33-4521-00 Medium duffle. 26"x12"x12".

CARLSON MARKETING GROUP

When advice is offered, it is usually wise to consider the source. When the advice is being sold as something that will improve your business, the caveat is redoubled. And when the advisors are positioned so as to be directly in touch with a goodly percent of your employees, one tends to become ve-e-e-ry careful, indeed.

The Carlson Marketing Group and their E. F. MacDonald Division sell corporate performance; which means they sell advice and the systems and products to make the advice work. The question then must arise, "Is Carlson's advice any good?" Well, let's consider the source. Who are they? They are the second largest firm in the Incentive Industry with 29 office locations in the United States. They also serve 20 countries in Europe, the Orient and Canada. "Good for them," you might say, "But what can they do for me? What's their track record?"

Therein lies a remarkable success story. Carlson Marketing is a division of The Carlson Companies. According to "Forbes" Magazine, Carlson is the 17th largest privately-held corporation in the nation. If compared to publicly-held companies, Carlson would rank in the top 125 on the "Fortune 500" list. With 127 different profit centers, the list is too long for these pages, but many of you will recognize some of the holdings of the Carlson Hospitality Group, including: Radisson Hotels, Colony Resorts, Country Inns, TGI Friday's and Country Kitchen Restaurants.

"Curt" Carlson founded the Carlson Companies in 1938. The original business was the Gold Bond Trading Stamps Company, a head-to-head competitor of S&H Green Stamps, Blue Chip and a few regional consumer-oriented incentive companies. Today, The Carlson Companies encompass 75 corporations with more than 50,000 employees, generating annual revenues of 4-billion dollars. Advice from a group of super-achievers with this kind of track record is certainly worth listening to.

In addition to the Hospitality Division, The Carlson Companies are firmly established in a number of other business categories. These include hotel and restaurant design, diversified real estate investments and travel. But marketing and incentive programs are still the mainstay of the company.

In 1964, the Performance Incentive Company (PIC) came into being as a division of the Carlson Companies. In 1981, Carlson acquired the well-known E. F. MacDonald Co., a heavyweight in the motivation and incentive industries. Shortly thereafter, The Carlson Marketing Group was formed to position PIC and MacDonald under the same corporate umbrella. With this move, Carlson became the second largest company in the rapidly changing performance/incentive industry. As you might expect, their list of clients reads like a "Who's Who" of the Fortune 500.

CARLSON MARKETING GROUP
Curtis L. Carlson, *Chairman and CEO, Carlson Companies*
Edwin C. Gage, *President, Carlson Companies*
Robert L. Voyles, *Vice President, Marketing Services*

Richard Sullivan, *Vice President/ Regional Manager*
Michael Blandford, *Account Executive*
Karen Donati, *Account Representative*
William J. Raser, *Marketing Director*
JoAnne Ferris, *Marketing Specialist*
Ralph Winn, *Senior Art Director*
Philip V. Kobbe, *Executive Art Director*
Chuck Carlson, *Creative Supervisor*
Scott Wiehoff, *Production Manager*

Today, merchandise and travel awards are still powerful incentives, but the planning and delivery systems surrounding the actual awards have become complex, highly sophisticated programs. This page from the Carlson Marketing Group brochure illustrates the depth of corporate involvement typical of a modern day motivational program. Of particular interest are the 8 discrete functions of the "Learning Systems" adjunct, which, in turn, is only one of the 11 primary operational functions of a modern motivational program.

Every Product and Service to Meet Your Needs

PLANNING
- Market Research
- Rules Structure
- Awards Planning
- Administrative Design
- Promotional Planning
- Learning Systems
- Recognition Systems
- Meeting Design
- Productivity/Cost Containment Planning
- Global Marketing

COMMUNICATION
- **Print and Dimensional Promotion**
  Copywriting
  Graphic Design
  Communication Campaigns
  Direct Mail
  Sales Promotion
  Collateral Materials

- **Administration and Data Base Management**
  Performance Measurement
  Progress Reports
  List Management
  Voice-Response Computer
  Executive Inquiry

- **Corporate Meetings and Trade Shows**
  Multi-image AV
  Video
  Set Design
  Scripting
  Live Talent
  Business Theatre
  Guest Speakers
  Coaching

LEARNING SYSTEMS
- Custom Learning Programs
- Customer Service
- Wellness Programs
- Instrumentation
- Certification
- Consultants Network
- Seminar Services
  Workshops and Seminars
- Consulting Services
  Organizational Intervention
  Long-Term Growth Programs

AWARDS
- **Merchandise**
  Deluxe/Intermediate Catalogs
  Gallery Awards
  Specialty Catalogs
  Special Merchandise Selection
  Promotional Merchandise
  Pick-A-Gift Albums

- **Travel**
  Full-Service Incentive Travel
  Meetings Travel
  Group Travel (Associations/Conventions)
  Individual Incentive Travel
  V.I.P. Checks®

- **Group and Individual Incentive Travel Packages**
  Classic Collection
  Exhibit of American Collectibles
  Museum of International Treasures

- **Recognition**
  Custom Designs
  Original Creations
  Traditional Awards
  Awards for Sales, Safety, Merit, Length of Service, Productivity

- **Fulfillment**
  Warehousing and Distribution
  Order Processing
  Customer Service
  Guaranteed Satisfaction

Today's merchandise and travel awards are designed to reflect credit on the lofty goals of the incentive program, the corporate image *and* the awardees. The majors in the motivational field—Maritz, Carlson, S&H and Business Incentives—have all (to a greater or lesser degree) settled into a pattern of choosing top name merchandise for their executive catalogs. If you browse through Carlson's E. F. MacDonald catalog, for instance, you'll come upon the same brands and items you'd expect to find in a fine department store. We did just that, and here is just a small sample of the famous names we found:

Stemware: Baccarat Crystal

Tabletop: Lenox, Royal Doulton, Gorham, Orrefors, Mikasa, Reed & Barton, Wedgwood, Waterford, Noritake, Corning

Furniture: Henredon, Hancock & Moore, Stiffel

Linens: Fieldcrest, Springmaid

Ladies Ready-to-Wear & Accessories: Mary McFadden, Cartier Fragrances, Christian Dior, Must de Cartier, Stanley Blacker

Mens Ready-to-Wear & Accessories: Hickey-Freeman, Seiko, Longines, Tissot, Pulsar, Hathaway, Ralph Lauren, Hart Schaffner & Marx, Christian Dior

Mens Shoes: Freeman, Johnson & Murphy

Cameras & Electronics: Zenith, Canon, Toshiba, Mitsubishi, Nikon, Minolta, Vivitar, Bausch & Lomb, RCA, Sony, Magnavox, JVC, Teak-tech, Yamaha, Kenwood, Pansonic, Technics, Marantz

Office Furniture & Electronics: Panasonic, Apple Macintosh, Hancock & Moore, AT&T Computers

Major Appliances: GE, Jenn-air, Tappan, Whirlpool, Litton, Magic Chef

Lawn & Garden: Black & Decker, Lawn Boy, Toro, John Deere

Tools: Skil, Stanley, Nicholson, Lufkin, Shopcraft Shopsmith

Fishing Tackle: Daiwa, Shakespeare, Abu-Garcia

Hunting Equipment: Winchester, Browning, Remington

Golf: Hogan, Titleist, MacGregor, Spalding, Dunlop, Foot-Joy Shoes, Hathaway/Jack Nicklaus

A 51-1368W GRADUATED BEAD NECKLACE. Striking 30" graduated bead necklace. Bead sizes range from 8mm to 22mm. Specify silver tone or gold tone.

B 51-1367W BUTTON STYLE EARRINGS. Gleaming earrings have 14K gold filled posts. For pierced ears only. Specify silver tone or gold tone.

C 55-1397W SILK BLOUSE. 100% silk crepe de Chine. Features diamond print and a detachable tie. (Belt not included). Specify: white, pink, blue; plus even size 8-18.

D 55-1425W BREIER OF AMSTERDAM LEATHER SKIRT. Fine soft leather in an A-line style. Perfect with blouses, shirts or sweaters. Features side button closure. (Belt not included). Specify black or medium brown; plus even size 6-16.

E 55-1429W BREIER OF AMSTERDAM SUEDE TOP. Fine lambsuede features. Satin lined. Perfect with your favorite pants or skirt. (Belt not included). Specify lilac or sapphire blue; plus even size 6-16.

F 55-1430W BREIER OF AMSTERDAM SUEDE SKIRT. Fine lambsuede, satin lined. Features elastic waist. If skirt and top are to match, order at same time. (Belt not included). Specify lilac or sapphire blue; plus even size 6-16.

G 55-1403W BUCKS COUNTY CASHMERE TURTLENECK PULLOVER. 100% cashmere so soft to the touch. Features set-in sleeves. Specify: grey, scarlet, beige heather, sky blue, white, black or navy; plus even size 34-40.

H 55-1428W BREIER OF AMSTERDAM SUEDE JACKET. Fine lambsuede. An outstanding jacket with pants. Features a perforated detail and a zip front. Specify red or camel; plus even size 6-16.

J 55-1426W BREIER OF AMSTERDAM LEATHER JACKET. Fine luxuriously soft leather in a classic belted hip length model. Perfect with pants or skirt. Specify red or dark brown; plus even size 6-16.

K 55-1427W BREIER OF AMSTERDAM SUEDE BLAZER. Fine lambsuede. Features a detachable belt. The cut is ever so smart and contemporary. Specify red or camel; plus even size 6-16.

L 55-1243W KAMEN CASHMERE COAT. 100% cashmere provides warmth without bulk or weight. Features self-tie belt. Specify beige or black; plus even size 6-16.

M 55-1391W BURBERRY TRENCH COAT. Poly/cotton shell. Liner is all wool plaid zip-out. This is the classic trench that all other coat manufacturers emulate. British tan. Specify even size 6-14 petite (42½" length); 6-16 regular (46" length).

N 55-918W GATES LADIES' GLOVES. Soft cashmere lined leather dress gloves. Specify color: red, black, brown or navy; plus size: small, medium, large or extra large.

P 50-916W COACH® LEATHER HANDBAG. The Coach bag that started the look. Constructed of full grain, natural glove tanned cowhide. Solid brass zipper, detachable shoulder strap. W-11", H-7", D-1½". Specify: red, black, putty, navy and tabac.

R 50-917W COACH® LEATHER HANDBAG. Classically styled pouch that holds a lot but does not look it. Inside zipper compartment. Constructed of full grain, natural glove tanned cowhide. Solid brass hardware. W-9¾", H-8", D-3¼". Specify: black, British tan, navy, burgundy or tabac.

See last page for warranty information.

62   63

A 54-2198W SILK FOULARD TIE. 100% silk processed so that most liquids will run off, leaving no stain. Specify: red, yellow, grey or camel.

B 54-2215W CHRISTIAN DIOR COTTON SHIRT. 100% cotton. Specify white or blue; plus neck and sleeve size. 14½-16 neck, 32 sleeve; 14½-17½ neck, 33-34 sleeve; 15-17½ neck, 35 sleeve.

C 50-924W GATES MEN'S GLOVES. Soft cashmere lined leather dress gloves. Specify brown or black; plus size: small, medium, large or extra-large.

MEN'S DRESS HOSIERY. Fits sizes 10-13 and is available in black, navy or brown. Packed one color per box.
D 54-1599W WOOL BLEND HOSIERY. 65% wool/35% nylon, in over-the-calf length. Three pairs per box. Specify color.
• 54-2202W WOOL BLEND HOSIERY. 65% wool/35% nylon. Crew length. Three pairs per box. Specify color.
• 54-981W NYLON HOSIERY. 100% nylon, static free. Over-the-calf length. Six pairs per box. Specify color.
• 54-2216W NYLON HOSIERY. 100% nylon, static free. Crew length. Six pairs per box. Specify color.
• 54-2143W ORLON® HOSIERY. 65% Orlon®, 30% nylon, 5% spandex in leg for stay-up neatness. Treated with built-in deodorant. Crew length. Four pairs per box. Also available in oxford color. Specify color.
• 54-2218W COTTON HOSIERY. 96% cotton/4% Lycra®. Over-the-calf length. Three pairs per box. Specify color.
• 54-2217W COTTON HOSIERY. 96% cotton/4% Lycra®. Crew length. Three pairs per box. Specify color.

E 54-2214W CHAPS SUIT BY RALPH LAUREN. 100% worsted wool. Medium weight for year-round comfort. Features soft shoulders, two button front with center vent. Grey tick weave. Specify size: 38-44, 46 regular; 38, 40, 42 short; 40-44, 46 long.
HATHAWAY DURABLE PRESS SHIRT. Cotton/polyester blend. Solid colors available in blue, white or ecru; stripes available in navy or burgundy. Sizes 14½-16 neck, 32 sleeve; 14½-17½ neck, 33 & 34 sleeve; 15-17½ neck, 35 sleeve. Short sleeves also available.
F 54-1998W HATHAWAY POPLIN SHIRT. Specify solid color, neck and sleeve length.
G 54-1715W HATHAWAY STRIPED SHIRT. Specify color of stripe, neck and sleeve length.
H 54-2151W BURBERRY TRENCH COAT. Poly/cotton shell. Plaid wool zip-out liner. Cotton plaid self liner. British tan. Specify even size 38-48 regular; 38-42 short; 40-46 long.
J 54-2035W B.W. HARRIS TOPCOAT. 100% wool with satin lining in the new longer proportion. Specify camel or navy; plus even size: 36-46 regular; 40-46 long.
K 54-2034W CHAPS SUIT BY RALPH LAUREN. Fine wool/polyester blend. Nine-month weight. Features soft shoulders, two button front with center vent. Specify: steel blue, navy or grey pin stripe, or solid steel blue, grey, navy or tan; plus size: 38-44, 46, 48 regular; 38-42 short; 40-44, 46, 48 long.
L 54-2150W HART SCHAFFNER & MARX® SUIT. 100% wool worsted grey flannel in soft shoulder model. Features two button front with center vent. Specify size: 38-44, 46, 48 regular; 38-44 short; 40-44, 46, 48 long.
M 54-2169W HART SCHAFFNER & MARX® SUIT. Dacron® polyester and wool pin stripe on navy. Features soft shoulders, two button front with center vent. Specify size: 38-44, 46, 48 regular; 38-44 short; 40-44, 46, 48 long.
• 54-2170W HART SCHAFFNER & MARX® "LIGHTWEIGHT" SUIT. Dacron® polyester and wool. Wrinkle resistant. Same style as 54-2169W. Specify tan or navy; plus size: 38-44, 46, 48 regular; 38-44 short; 40-44, 46, 48 long.

N 50-885W CHRISTIAN DIOR COLLAR ACCESSORIES. Gold tone. 4-pc set consists of collar slide, collar pin and stays.

P 50-886W CHRISTIAN DIOR FOUR-IN-ONE BELT. Versatile set consists of two buckles, one for casual wear and one for dress. Reversible leather belt from brown to black. One size fits all. W-1¼".

See last page for warranty information.

70   71

TOTAL RELAXATION

43-856W MITSUBISHI GOLF SWING TRAINER. Microprocessor monitors: 1. head speed; 2. carry; 3. head angle; 4. direction; 5. duffing; 6. out of bounds. 14 club settings. Battery powered. 12" x 18" mat.

44-1080W MARCY RECUMBENT EXERCISE MODULE. More comfortable and efficient than upright pedaling. LCD readouts: time, speed, calories per minute and total calories. Weighted flywheel.

64-550W PUCH 15-SPEED MOUNTAIN BIKE. Strong chromemoly lightweight frame in two men's all-terrain frame sizes. Quick Release® alloy wheels and 26", 2.125 knobby gum wall tires. Sun Tour wide ratio derailleur, cantilever brakes with motorcycle levers and water bottle fittings (bottle not incl.) Specify frame size 19½" or 21½".

GROSFILLEX "BOUTIQUE" FURNITURE. Designed in France and made from synthetic resin, coated with polyurethane lacquer for protection. Removable cushions are covered in weather resistant Dralon® in a distinctive gray and rose stripe. **22-1024W HOLLANDER DELUXE BEACH UMBRELLA.** Polyester fabric, six ribs, 5½' dia., 1¾" pole. **22-1023W PAIR OF 5-POSITION ADJUSTABLE CHAIRS.** Adjust from dining height down to reclining height. W-26", H-40", D-24". **22-1022W PAIR OF 4-POSITION ADJUSTABLE OTTOMANS.** Can be used as table without cushion. D-17". **22-1021W LUXURY CHAISE LOUNGE.** Adjustable back and seat adjust simultaneously, foot adjusts independently. W-28", H-36", L-80".

118

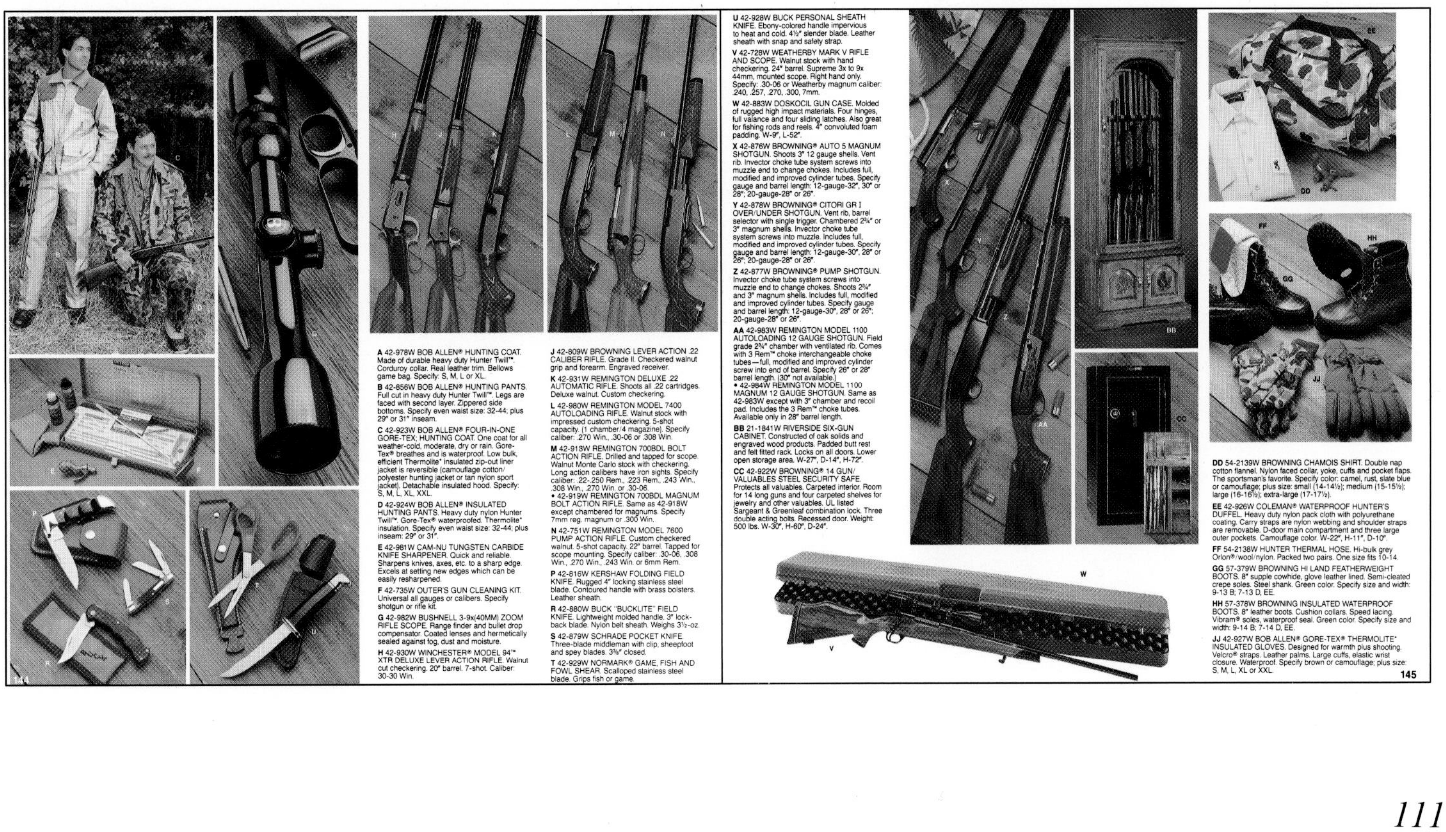

Photographed at the beautiful El San Juan Hotel, Isla Verde, Puerto Rico.

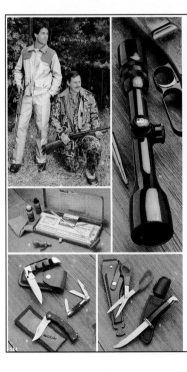

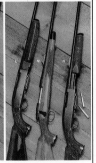

A 42-978W BOB ALLEN® HUNTING COAT. Made of durable heavy duty Hunter Twill™. Corduroy collar. Real leather trim. Bellows game bag. Specify S, M, L, or XL.

B 42-856W BOB ALLEN® HUNTING PANTS. Full cut in heavy duty Hunter Twill™. Legs are faced with second layer. Zippered side bottoms. Specify even waist size: 32-44; plus 29" or 31" inseam.

C 42-923W BOB ALLEN® FOUR-IN-ONE GORE-TEX® HUNTING COAT. One coat for all weather—cold, moderate, dry or rain. Gore-Tex® breathes and is waterproof. Low bulk, efficient Thermolite® insulated zip-out liner jacket is reversible (camouflage cotton/polyester hunting jacket or tan nylon sport jacket). Detachable insulated hood. Specify: S, M, L, XL, XXL.

D 42-924W BOB ALLEN® INSULATED HUNTING PANTS. Heavy duty Hunter Twill™. Gore-Tex® waterproofed. Thermolite® insulation. Specify even waist size: 32-44; plus inseam: 29" or 31".

E 42-981W CAM-NU TUNGSTEN CARBIDE KNIFE SHARPENER. Quick and reliable. Sharpens knives, axes, etc. to a sharp edge. Excels at setting new edges which can be easily resharpened.

F 42-735W OUTER'S GUN CLEANING KIT. Universal all gauges or calibers. Specify shotgun or rifle kit.

G 42-982W BUSHNELL 3-9x(40MM) ZOOM RIFLE SCOPE. Range finder and bullet drop compensator. Coated lenses and hermetically sealed against fog, dust and moisture.

H 42-930W WINCHESTER® MODEL 94™ XTR DELUXE LEVER ACTION RIFLE. Walnut cut checkering. 20" barrel, 7-shot. Caliber: 30-30 Win.

J 42-809W BROWNING LEVER ACTION .22 CALIBER RIFLE. Grade II. Checkered walnut grip and forearm. Engraved receiver.

K 42-931W REMINGTON DELUXE .22 AUTOMATIC RIFLE. Shoots all .22 cartridges. Deluxe walnut. Custom checkering.

L 42-980W REMINGTON MODEL 7400 AUTOLOADING RIFLE. Walnut stock with impressed custom checkering. 5-shot capacity. (1 chamber 4 magazine). Specify caliber: .270 Win., -30-06 or 308 Win.

M 42-910W REMINGTON 700BDL BOLT ACTION RIFLE. Drilled and tapped for scope. Walnut Monte Carlo stock with checkering. Long action calibers have iron sights. Specify caliber: .22-.250 Rem., .223 Rem., .243 Win., .308 Win., .270 Win. or 30-06.

N 42-919W REMINGTON 700BDL MAGNUM BOLT ACTION RIFLE. Same as 42-919W except chambered for magnums. Specify 7mm reg. magnum or 300 Win.

P 42-751W REMINGTON MODEL 7600 PUMP ACTION RIFLE. Custom checkered walnut. 5-shot capacity. 22" barrel. Tapped for scope mounting. Specify caliber: .30-06, .308 Win., .270 Win., .243 Win. or 6mm Rem.

Q 42-816W KERSHAW FOLDING FIELD KNIFE. Rugged 4" locking stainless steel blade. Contoured handle with brass bolsters. Leather sheath.

R 42-880W BUCK "BUCKLITE" FIELD KNIFE. Lightweight molded handle. 3" lockback blade. Nylon belt sheath. Weighs 3½-oz.

S 42-879W SCHRADE POCKET KNIFE. Three-blade middleman with clip, sheepfoot and spey blades. 3¾" closed.

T 42-929W NORMARK® GAME, FISH AND FOWL SHEAR. Scalloped stainless steel blade. Grips fish or game.

U 42-928W BUCK PERSONAL SHEATH KNIFE. Ebony-colored handle impervious to heat and cold. 4½" slender blade. Leather sheath with snap and safety strap.

V 42-728W WEATHERBY MARK V RIFLE AND SCOPE. Walnut stock with hand checkering. 24" barrel. Supreme 3x to 9x 44mm. mounted scope. Right hand only. Specify: 30-06 or Weatherby magnum caliber: .240, .257, .270, .300, 7mm.

W 42-883W DOSKOCIL GUN CASE. Molded of rugged high impact materials. Four hinges, full valance and four sliding latches. Also great for fishing rods and reels. 4" convoluted foam padding. W-8", L-52".

X 42-876W BROWNING® AUTO 5 MAGNUM SHOTGUN. Shoots 3" 12 gauge shells. Vent rib. Invector choke tube system screws into muzzle and to change chokes. Includes full, modified and improved cylinder tubes. Specify gauge and barrel length: 12-gauge-32", 30" or 28"; 20-gauge-28" or 26".

Y 42-878W BROWNING® CITORI GR I OVER/UNDER SHOTGUN. Vent rib, barrel selector with single trigger. Chambered 2¾" or 3" magnum shells. Invector choke tube system screws into muzzle. Includes full, modified and improved cylinder tubes. Specify gauge and barrel length: 12-gauge-30", 28" or 26"; 20-gauge-28" or 26".

Z 42-877W BROWNING® PUMP SHOTGUN. Invector choke tube system screws into muzzle and to change chokes. Shoots 2¾" and 3" magnum shells. Includes full, modified and improved cylinder tubes. Specify gauge and barrel length: 12-gauge-30", 28" or 26"; 20-gauge-28" or 26".

AA 42-983W REMINGTON MODEL 1100 AUTOLOADING 12 GAUGE SHOTGUN. Field grade 2¾" chamber with ventilated rib. Comes with 3 Rem™ choke interchangeable choke tubes—full, modified and improved cylinder screw into end of barrel. Specify 26" or 28" barrel length. (30" not available.)

AA 42-922W REMINGTON MODEL 1100 MAGNUM 12 GAUGE SHOTGUN. Same as 42-983W except with 3" chamber and recoil pad. Includes the 3 Rem™ choke tubes. Available only in 28" barrel length.

BB 21-1841W RIVERSIDE SIX-GUN CABINET. Constructed of oak solids and engraved wood products. Padded butt rest and felt fitted rack. Locks on all doors. Lower open storage area. W-27", D-14", H-72".

DD 54-2139W BROWNING CHAMOIS SHIRT. Double nap cotton flannel. Nylon faced collar, yoke, cuffs and pocket flaps. The sportsman's favorite. Specify color: camel, rust, slate blue or camouflage; plus size: small (14-14½); medium (15-15½); large (16-16½); extra-large (17-17½).

CC 42-922W BROWNING® 14 GUN VALUABLES STEEL SECURITY SAFE. Protects all valuables. Carpeted interior. Room for 14 long guns and four carpeted shelves for jewelry and other valuables. UL listed Sargeant & Greenleaf combination lock. Three double acting bolts. Recessed door. Weight: 500 lbs. W-30", H-60", D-24".

EE 42-926W COLEMAN® WATERPROOF HUNTER'S DUFFEL. Heavy duty nylon pack cloth with polyurethane coating. Carry straps are nylon webbing and shoulder straps are removable. D-door main compartment and three large outer pockets. Camouflage color. W-22", H-11", D-10".

FF 54-2136W HUNTER THERMAL HOSE. Hi-bulk grey Orlon®/wool nylon. Specify size and width: 9-13 B; 7-13 D, EE.

GG 57-379W BROWNING HI LAND FEATHERWEIGHT BOOTS. 8" supple cowhide, glove leather lined. Semi-cleated crepe soles. Steel shank. Green color. Specify size and width: 9-13 B; 7-13 D, EE.

HH 57-378W BROWNING INSULATED WATERPROOF BOOTS. 8" leather boots. Cushion collars. Speed lacing Vibram® soles, waterproof seal. Green color. Specify size and width: 9-14 B; 7-14 D, EE.

JJ 42-927W BOB ALLEN® GORE-TEX® THERMOLITE® INSULATED GLOVES. Designed for warmth plus shooting Velcro® straps. Leather palms. Large cuffs, elastic wrist closure. Waterproof. Specify brown or camouflage; plus size: S, M, L, XL or XXL.

145

111

On-the-job posters, ticklers and double-bonus promotional events are woven into the tapestry of most incentive programs — and for good reason. While the prizes, plaques and travel packages are important, peer group approbation is just as meaningful. Meetings that become pep rallies and reminders posted on the bulletin board or mailed to the home, serve to keep everyone's competitive spirit honed to a fine edge.

Beautiful catalogs and exciting ceremonies, prizes boasting recognizable brand names, travel to exotic places in the company of other winners—these are all symbols. To the winners, they say:

> *"You're the Best."*
> *"We love you."*
> *"We count on you."*
> *"You're at the top of your profession."*
> *"We appreciate you more than money can say."*

Losers can indulge in one of three mental attitudes:

> *"I'll do better next time."*
> *"The contest was unfair."*
> *"Who cares!"*

The first (and usually the largest) group will at least try to do better. They will look to their superior or their peers for some help. They may get more serious about homework and time allocation. Perhaps, if they are salesmen, they might even learn to listen to, instead of talking at, their customers.
The second ("unfair") group divides into two segments. The first sub-segment really has one or more legitimate gripes, e.g.:

- *The goals were wrong for his assigned customers.*
- *The territory was truncated before or during the contest.*

- *The plant failed to deliver or delivered inferior merchandise.*

Real problems such as these should lead to a negotiated retro-fix.

The second sub-segment of the "unfair" criers are the perpetual paranoids, always blameless, no matter what their failings. This bunch and the "Who cares" phalanx of losers fall on the wrong side of the 80% equation (80% of profitable sales are made by 20% of the salesmen). They should probably change either their job description or their affiliation. Perhaps that's the next Carlson enterprise—Outplacement Counseling.

S&H MOTIVATION

The 25-year old S&H Motivation, Inc. (SHM) was once a division of The Sperry & Hutchinson Company of Green Stamps fame. Today they are a Chicago-based, autonomous subsidiary of PHLCORP, Inc. In a field where only four heavy hitters control almost all of the volume, they are ranked number three. (Maritz, Carlson Marketing Group and Business Incentives, Inc. are numbers one, two and four, respectively.)

S&H Motivation has three primary levels of product-related incentive programs. This graduated concept is called their "Performance Merchandise Awards System" (PMAS). This system is built on three Award Book choices.

The First Level is keynoted by the 168-page "Luxury Book of Awards". A 10-⅞" X 11-⅞" jumbo catalog featuring 2,583 executive-level gifts with retail values ranging from $10.00 to $10,000.00 (with a yacht thrown in for good measure at $31,215.00).

AWARDS

S&H MOTIVATION
Frank Pirri, *President*
Steve Erickson, *Vice President of Marketing*
Agency: *In-house*

LUXURIOUS LIVING

1 Stiffel Lamp. Column-styled maple lamp with antique brass finished accents is a classic light fixture for any room. Space-pleated shade is cream colored. Three-way lamp measures 54½"H. Fruitwood finish. **DQ2290**

2 Waterford Executive Bar Set. Handmade mahogany case holds two Lismore spirit decanters and four Lismore double old-fashioned glasses. Portable case is accented with solid brass fittings, and includes storage area for cigars or bar accessories. **DQ2260**

3 EMI Bronze Lion. Lost wax bronze casting of a Jet. Henri Vidal sculpture. Large 12½"H x 24½"W casting provides a distinctive focal point in any living room, study or office. **DQ2270**

4 Teli Crystal and Wood Phone. Crystal by Orrefors of Sweden joins hand-polished mahogany to create a distinctive phone. Features modern conveniences, such as nine one-button direct call keys, 31-number speed dial memory, and tone/pulse dialing. Also with last number redial, temporary memory (for numbers recently dialed) and mute. **DQ2280**

5 Lladro Luggage Set. Inspired by the Spanish-American traditional art of saddlery and belt making, Lladro has created this distinctively styled California series. The two-tone effect of long grain leather combined with smooth leather are fine examples of this superb Spanish craftsmanship and styling. Chestnut colored.
Passport case **DQ2241**
Large travel bag **DQ2242**
Club bag **DQ2243**

6 Lynx Coat. Fully let-out 50" Canadian lynx coat with shawl collar and silk-bemberg lining. Made in USA. Sizes 6-18. **DQ2300**

7 Hekman Entertainment Center. This maple entertainment center is a handsome and innovative place to store your TV, video cassette recorder and more. Inside the top sliding doors are two adjustable shelves, swivel TV shelf and four outlets. The bottom drawers are actually doors that hide two fixed shelves, one pull-out shelf, record, disc and video tape dividers. 43½" x 24⅜" x 81"H. **DQ3190**

From preceding page: Lladro "Born Free" Porcelain Figurine. With the character and charm of a handmade work of art, this figurine of European porcelain is appreciated by collectors everywhere. Handpainted by artists who ensure that the original colors are perfectly reproduced, it is truly a work of art worthy of prominent display. 15½"H. Base included. **DQ2250**

‡See Value Index for warranty information.

C2

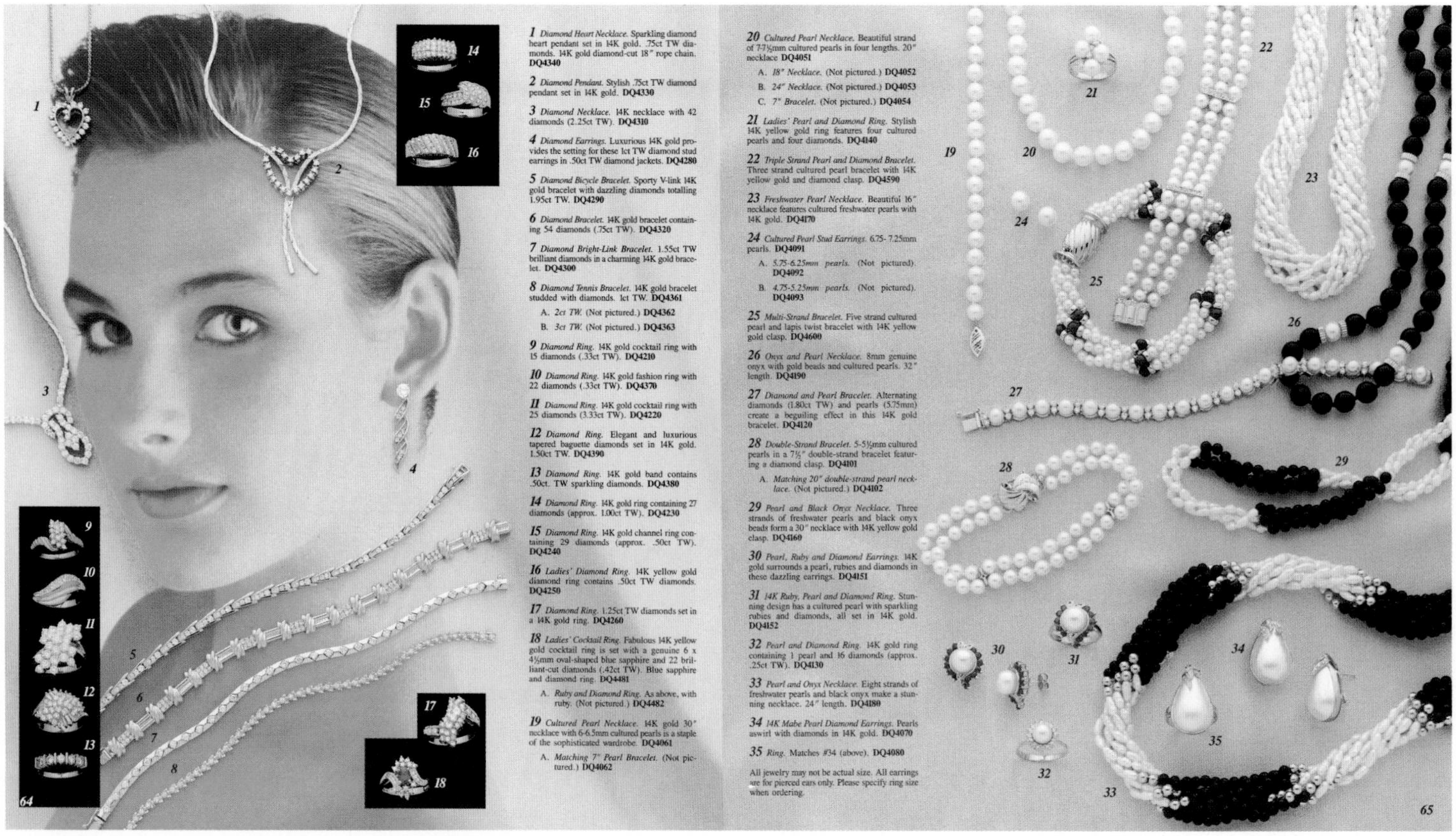

1 Diamond Heart Necklace. Sparkling diamond heart pendant set in 14K gold. .75ct TW diamonds. 14K gold diamond-cut 18" rope chain. **DQ4340**

2 Diamond Pendant. Stylish .75ct TW diamond pendant set in 14K gold. **DQ4330**

3 Diamond Necklace. 14K necklace with 42 diamonds (2.25ct TW). **DQ4310**

4 Diamond Earrings. Luxurious 14K gold provides the setting for these 1ct TW diamond stud earrings in .50ct TW diamond jackets. **DQ4280**

5 Diamond Bicycle Bracelet. Sporty V-link 14K gold bracelet with dazzling diamonds totalling 1.95ct TW. **DQ4290**

6 Diamond Bracelet. 14K gold bracelet containing 54 diamonds (.75ct TW). **DQ4320**

7 Diamond Bright-Link Bracelet. 1.55ct TW brilliant diamonds in a charming 14K gold bracelet. **DQ4300**

8 Diamond Tennis Bracelet. 14K gold bracelet studded with diamonds. 1ct TW. **DQ4361**

A. *2ct TW.* (Not pictured.) **DQ4362**

B. *3ct TW.* (Not pictured.) **DQ4363**

9 Diamond Ring. 14K gold cocktail ring with 15 diamonds (.33ct TW). **DQ4210**

10 Diamond Ring. 14K gold fashion ring with 22 diamonds (.33ct TW). **DQ4370**

11 Diamond Ring. 14K gold cocktail ring with 25 diamonds (3.33ct TW). **DQ4220**

12 Diamond Ring. Elegant and luxurious tapered baguette diamonds set in 14K gold. 1.50ct TW. **DQ4390**

13 Diamond Ring. 14K gold band contains .50ct. TW sparkling diamonds. **DQ4380**

14 Diamond Ring. 14K gold ring containing 27 diamonds (approx. 1.00ct TW). **DQ4230**

15 Diamond Ring. 14K gold channel ring containing 29 diamonds (approx. .50ct TW). **DQ4240**

16 Ladies' Diamond Ring. 14K yellow gold diamond ring contains .50ct TW diamonds. **DQ4250**

17 Diamond Ring. 1.25ct TW diamonds set in a 14K gold ring. **DQ4260**

18 Ladies' Cocktail Ring. Fabulous 14K yellow gold cocktail ring is set with a genuine 6 x 4½mm oval-shaped blue sapphire and 22 brilliant-cut diamonds (.42ct TW). Blue sapphire and diamond ring. **DQ4481**

A. *Ruby and Diamond Ring.* As above, with ruby. (Not pictured.) **DQ4482**

19 Cultured Pearl Necklace. 14K gold 30" necklace with 6-6.5mm cultured pearls is a staple of the sophisticated wardrobe. **DQ4061**

A. *Matching 7" Pearl Bracelet.* (Not pictured.) **DQ4062**

20 Cultured Pearl Necklace. Beautiful strand of 7-7½mm cultured pearls in four lengths. 20" necklace **DQ4051**

A. *18" Necklace.* (Not pictured.) **DQ4052**

B. *24" Necklace.* (Not pictured.) **DQ4053**

C. *7" Bracelet.* (Not pictured.) **DQ4054**

21 Ladies' Pearl and Diamond Ring. Stylish 14K yellow gold ring features four cultured pearls and four diamonds. **DQ4140**

22 Triple Strand Pearl and Diamond Bracelet. Three strand cultured pearl bracelet with 14K yellow gold and diamond clasp. **DQ4590**

23 Freshwater Pearl Necklace. Beautiful 16" necklace features cultured freshwater pearls with 14K gold. **DQ4170**

24 Cultured Pearl Stud Earrings. 6.75-7.25mm pearls. **DQ4091**

A. *5.75-6.25mm pearls.* (Not pictured). **DQ4092**

B. *4.75-5.25mm pearls.* (Not pictured). **DQ4093**

25 Multi-Strand Bracelet. Five strand cultured pearl and lapis twist bracelet with 14K yellow gold clasp. **DQ4600**

26 Onyx and Pearl Necklace. 8mm genuine onyx with gold beads and cultured pearls. 32" length. **DQ4190**

27 Diamond and Pearl Bracelet. Alternating diamonds (1.80ct TW) and pearls (5.75mm) create a beguiling effect in this 14K gold bracelet. **DQ4120**

28 Double-Strand Bracelet. 5-5½mm cultured pearls in a 7½" double-strand bracelet featuring a diamond clasp. **DQ4101**

A. *Matching 20" double-strand pearl necklace.* (Not pictured.) **DQ4102**

29 Pearl and Black Onyx Necklace. Three strands of freshwater pearls and black onyx beads form a 30" necklace with 14K yellow gold clasp. **DQ4160**

30 Pearl, Ruby and Diamond Earrings. 14K gold surrounds a pearl, rubies and diamonds in these dazzling earrings. **DQ4151**

31 14K Ruby, Pearl and Diamond Ring. Stunning design has a cultured pearl with sparkling rubies and diamonds, all set in 14K gold. **DQ4152**

32 Pearl and Diamond Ring. 14K gold ring containing 1 pearl and 16 diamonds (approx. .25ct TW). **DQ4130**

33 Pearl and Onyx Necklace. Eight strands of freshwater pearls and black onyx make a stunning necklace. 24" length. **DQ4180**

34 14K Mabe Pearl Diamond Earrings. Pearls aswirl with diamonds in 14K gold. **DQ4070**

35 Ring. Matches #34 (above). **DQ4080**

All jewelry may not be actual size. All earrings are for pierced ears only. Please specify ring size when ordering.

64 65

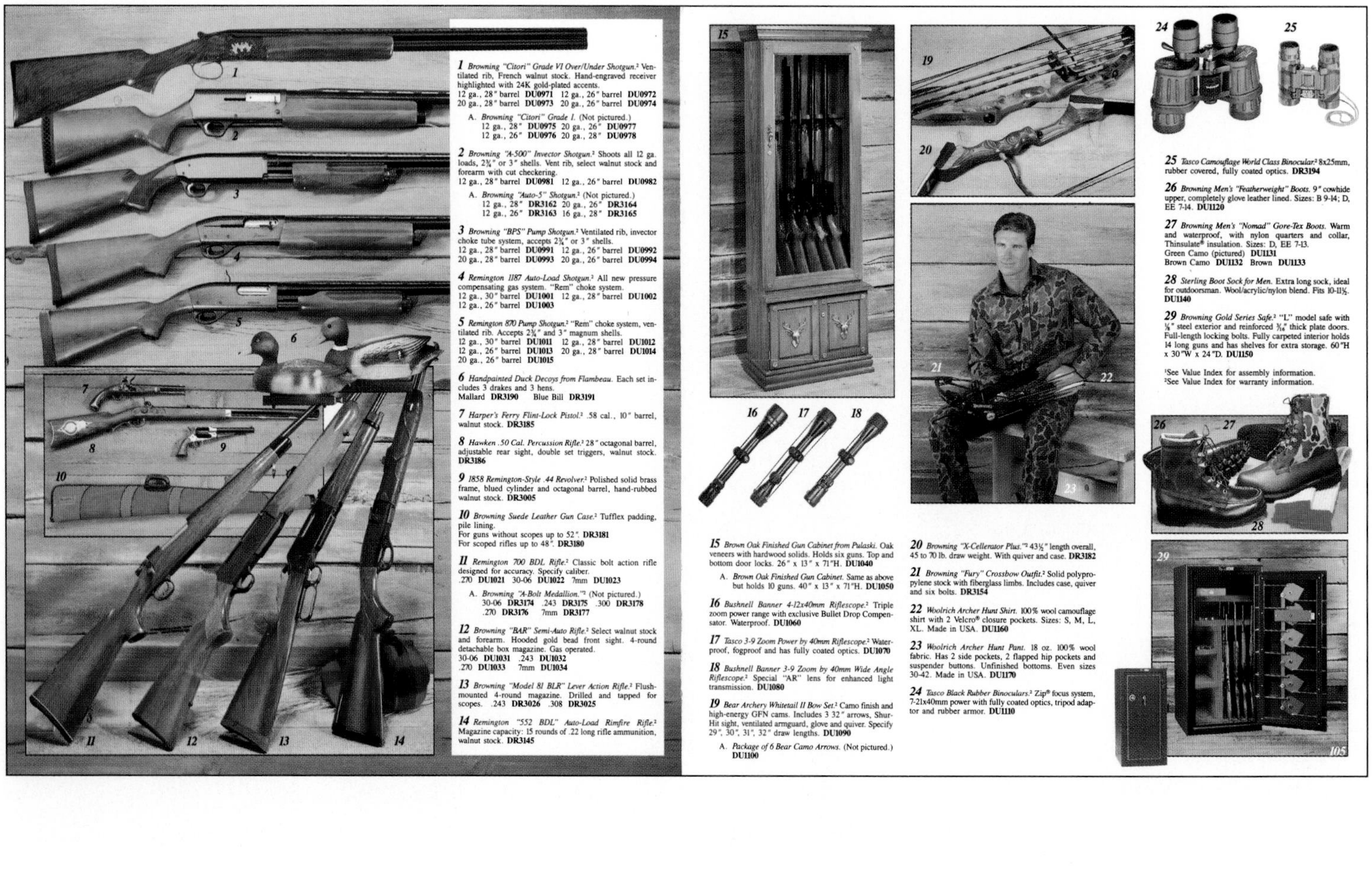

1 Browning "Citori" Grade VI Over/Under Shotgun.[2] Ventilated rib, French walnut stock. Hand-engraved receiver highlighted with 24K gold-plated accents.
12 ga., 28" barrel **DU0971** 12 ga., 26" barrel **DU0972**
20 ga., 28" barrel **DU0973** 20 ga., 26" barrel **DU0974**

A. *Browning "Citori" Grade I.* (Not pictured.)
12 ga., 28" **DU0975** 20 ga., 26" **DU0977**
12 ga., 26" **DU0976** 20 ga., 28" **DU0978**

2 Browning "A-500" Invector Shotgun.[2] Shoots all 12 ga. loads, 2¾" or 3" shells. Vent rib, select walnut stock and forearm with cut checkering.
12 ga., 28" barrel **DU0981** 12 ga., 26" barrel **DU0982**

A. *Browning "Auto-5" Shotgun.*[2] (Not pictured.)
12 ga., 28" **DR3162** 20 ga., 26" **DR3164**
12 ga., 26" **DR3163** 16 ga., 28" **DR3165**

3 Browning "BPS" Pump Shotgun.[2] Ventilated rib, invector choke tube system, accepts 2¾" or 3" shells.
12 ga., 28" barrel **DU0991** 12 ga., 26" barrel **DU0992**
20 ga., 28" barrel **DU0993** 20 ga., 26" barrel **DU0994**

4 Remington 1187 Auto-Load Shotgun.[2] All new pressure compensating gas system. "Rem" choke system.
12 ga., 30" barrel **DU1001** 12 ga., 28" barrel **DU1002**
12 ga., 26" barrel **DU1003**

5 Remington 870 Pump Shotgun.[2] "Rem" choke system, ventilated rib. Accepts 2¾" and 3" magnum shells.
12 ga., 30" barrel **DU1011** 12 ga., 28" barrel **DU1012**
12 ga., 26" barrel **DU1013** 20 ga., 28" barrel **DU1014**
20 ga., 26" barrel **DU1015**

6 Handpainted Duck Decoys from Flambeau. Each set includes 3 drakes and 3 hens.
Mallard **DR3190** Blue Bill **DR3191**

7 Harper's Ferry Flint-Lock Pistol.[2] .58 cal., 10" barrel, walnut stock. **DR3185**

8 Hawken .50 Cal. Percussion Rifle.[2] 28" octagonal barrel, adjustable rear sight, double set triggers, walnut stock. **DR3186**

9 1858 Remington-Style .44 Revolver.[2] Polished solid brass frame, blued cylinder and octagonal barrel, hand-rubbed walnut stock. **DR3005**

10 Browning Suede Leather Gun Case.[2] Tufflex padding, pile lining.
For guns without scopes up to 52". **DR3181**
For scoped rifles up to 48". **DR3180**

11 Remington 700 BDL Rifle.[2] Classic bolt action rifle designed for accuracy. Specify caliber.
.270 **DU1021** 30-06 **DU1022** 7mm **DU1023**

A. *Browning "A-Bolt Medallion."*[2] (Not pictured.)
30-06 **DR3174** .243 **DR3175** .300 **DR3178**
.270 **DR3176** 7mm **DR3177**

12 Browning "BAR" Semi-Auto Rifle.[2] Select walnut stock and forearm. Hooded gold bead front sight. 4-round detachable box magazine. Gas operated.
30-06 **DU1031** .243 **DU1032**
.270 **DU1033** 7mm **DU1034**

13 Browning "Model 81 BLR" Lever Action Rifle.[2] Flush-mounted 4-round magazine. Drilled and tapped for scopes. .243 **DR3026** .308 **DR3025**

14 Remington "552 BDL" Auto-Load Rimfire Rifle.[2] Magazine capacity: 15 rounds of .22 long rifle ammunition, walnut stock. **DR3145**

15 Brown Oak Finished Gun Cabinet from Pulaski. Oak veneers with hardwood solids. Holds six guns. Top and bottom door locks. 26" x 13" x 71"H. **DU1040**

A. *Brown Oak Finished Gun Cabinet.* Same as above but holds 10 guns. 40" x 13" x 71"H. **DU1050**

16 Bushnell Banner 4-12x40mm Riflescope.[2] Triple zoom power range with exclusive Bullet Drop Compensator. Waterproof. **DU1060**

17 Tasco 3-9 Zoom Power by 40mm Riflescope.[2] Waterproof, fogproof and has fully coated optics. **DU1070**

18 Bushnell Banner 3-9 Zoom by 40mm Wide Angle Riflescope.[2] Special "AR" lens for enhanced light transmission. **DU1080**

19 Bear Archery Whitetail II Bow Set.[2] Camo finish and high-energy GFN cams. Includes 3 32" arrows, Shur-Hit sight, ventilated armguard, glove and quiver. Specify 29", 30", 31", 32" draw lengths. **DU1090**

A. *Package of 6 Bear Camo Arrows.* (Not pictured.) **DU1100**

20 Browning "X-Cellerator Plus."[2] 43½" length overall, 45 to 70 lb. draw weight. With quiver and case. **DR3182**

21 Browning "Fury" Crossbow Outfit.[2] Solid polypropylene stock with fiberglass limbs. Includes case, quiver and six bolts. **DR3154**

22 Woolrich Archer Hunt Shirt. 100% wool camouflage shirt with 2 Velcro® closure pockets. Sizes: S, M, L, XL. Made in USA. **DU1160**

23 Woolrich Archer Hunt Pant. 18 oz. 100% wool fabric. Has 2 side pockets, 2 flapped hip pockets and suspender buttons. Unfinished bottoms. Even sizes 30-42. Made in USA. **DU1170**

24 Tasco Black Rubber Binoculars.[2] Zip® focus system, 7-21x40mm power with fully coated optics, tripod adaptor and rubber armor. **DU1110**

25 Tasco Camouflage World Class Binocular.[2] 8x25mm, rubber covered, fully coated optics. **DR3194**

26 Browning Men's "Featherweight" Boots. 9" cowhide upper, completely glove leather lined. Sizes: B 9-14; D, EE 7-14. **DU1120**

27 Browning Men's "Nomad" Gore-Tex Boots. Warm and waterproof, with nylon quarters and collar, Thinsulate® insulation. Sizes: D, EE 7-13.
Green Camo (pictured) **DU1131**
Brown Camo **DU1132** Brown **DU1133**

28 Sterling Boot Sock for Men. Extra long sock, ideal for outdoorsman. Wool/acrylic/nylon blend. Fits 10-11½. **DU1140**

29 Browning Gold Series Safe.[2] "L" model safe with ⅛" steel exterior and reinforced 3/16" thick plate doors. Full-length locking bolts. Fully carpeted interior holds 14 long guns and has shelves for extra storage. 60"H x 30"W x 24"D. **DU1150**

[1]See Value Index for assembly information.
[2]See Value Index for warranty information.

105

Level Two is aimed at middle management and distributors. To reach this market, SHM's 48-page "Achievement Book of Awards" (another jumbo catalog) presents 841 incentive products with retail values ranging from $6.00 to $3,685.00.

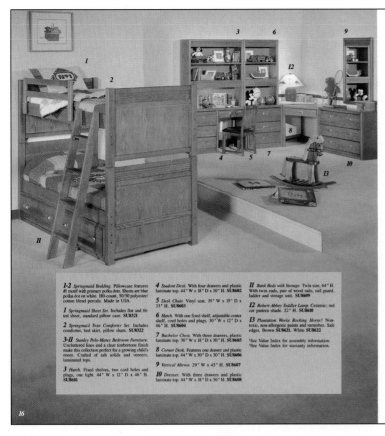

BEDROOM, PLAYROOM, FUN ROOM

14 *Little Tykes Partyware.[2]* Ages 2-6. Your child will enjoy playing house with this realistic table setting for two. Set includes two each: plates, bowls, cups, forks, knives, spoons, and placemats. Also with frying pan and lid, spatula, serving spoon and bud vase. **SQ2960**

15 *Little Tykes Big Table and Chairs Set.[2]* Table features 1-pc. molded top, two seamless drawers. Measures 20" H x 26" W x 26" D. Set includes two Kindergarten Chairs (11½" seat height, 19" H x 12" W x 13" L.). **SQ2940**

16 *Grand Basket Wicker Buggy.[2]* Beautiful natural-varnish doll buggy with moving wheels, mattress and pillow. Assembly required. **SU8640**

17 *Goldberger Baby Softina Doll.[2]* Adorable doll features moving eyes; twin-tail hair-do; pink, ruffled dress. With comb, brush, bottle and towel. 16", washable all-vinyl foam. **SU8590**

18 *Little Tykes Party Kitchen.[3]* This kitchen for kids includes a three-burner range, a "tinted glass" oven. Sink has swivel faucet with storage cabinet underneath. Drop-leaf table for dining. Chalkboard message center. Partyware and kitchenware sold separately. **SQ2950**

19 *Little Tykes Kitchenware.[2]* Features this 13-piece set includes: apron, quilted hot mitt, two double-sided cookie cutters, rolling pin, spoon, ladle, muffin pan, 1-cup measuring cup, salt and pepper shakers and a casserole dish. Top rack dishwasher-safe. For ages 2-6. **SQ2970**

20 *Binney & Smith Crayola Draw 'n Do® Desk.[2]* Designed to encourage unsupervised creative art activities. Sturdy, portable storage unit contains special two-sided, wipe-clean work surface, wipe-off cloth, 16 Crayola crayons, 8 Easy-Off® crayons, drawing bar with 3 doodle discs and holder, pencil, drawing paper, Draw 'n Do® and You Book. **SU8630**

21 *Casio Keyboard.[3]* Features four familiar Disney tunes, five preset tones and six auto-rhythms. Built-in speaker. **SU8690**

1-2 *Springmaid Bedding.* Pillowcase features #1 motif with primary polka dots. Sheets are blue polka dot on white. 180-count, 50/50 polyester/cotton blend percale. Made in USA.

1 *Springmaid Sheet Set.* Includes flat and fitted sheet, standard pillow case. **SU8321**

2 *Springmaid Twin Comforter Set.* Includes comforter, bed skirt, pillow sham. **SU8322**

3-11 *Stanley Polo-Mates Bedroom Furniture.* Uncluttered lines and a clear timbertone finish make this collection perfect for a growing child's room. Crafted of ash solids and veneers; laminated tops.

3 *Hutch.* Fixed shelves, two cord holes and plugs, one light. 44" W x 12" D x 46" H. **SU8601**

4 *Student Desk.* With four drawers and plastic laminate top. 44" W x 18" D x 30" H. **SU8602**

5 *Desk Chair.* Vinyl seat. 19" W x 19" D x 33" H. **SU8603**

6 *Hutch.* With one fixed shelf, adjustable center shelf, cord holes and plugs. 30" W x 12" D x 46" H. **SU8604**

7 *Bachelor Chest.* With three drawers, plastic laminate top. 30" W x 18" D x 30" H. **SU8605**

8 *Corner Desk.* Features one drawer and plastic laminate top. 44" W x 30" D x 30" H. **SU8606**

9 *Vertical Mirror.* 29" W x 45" H. **SU8607**

10 *Dresser.* With three drawers and plastic laminate top. 44" W x 18" D x 30" H. **SU8608**

11 *Bunk Beds with Storage.* Twin size, 64" H. With twin ends, pair of wood rails, rail guard, ladder and storage unit. **SU8609**

12 *Robert Abbey Toddler Lamp.* Ceramic; red cat pattern shade. 22" H. **SU8610**

13 *Plantation Works Rocking Horse.[5]* Non-toxic, non-allergenic paints and varnishes. Safe edges. Brown **SU8621**. White **SU8622**

[2]See Value Index for assembly information.
[3]See Value Index for warranty information.

16

THE POLISHED GENTLEMAN

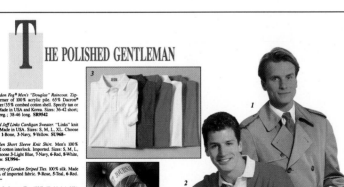

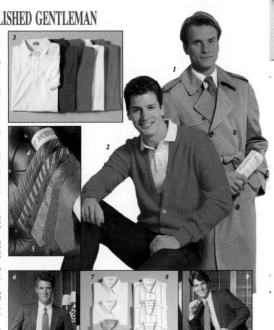

1 *London Fog® Men's "Douglas" Raincoat.* Zip-out warmer of 100% acrylic pile. 65% Dacron® polyester/35% combed cotton shell. Specify tan or navy. Made in USA and Korea. Sizes: 36-42 short; 36-46 reg.; 38-46 long. **SR9542**

2 *Lord Jeff Links Cardigan Sweater.* "Links" knit orlon. Made in USA. Sizes: S, M, L, XL. Choose 6-Red, 1-Bone, 3-Navy, 9-Yellow. **SU968–**

3 *Larlen Short Sleeve Knit Shirt.* Men's 100% combed cotton interlock. Imported. Sizes: S, M, L, XL. Choose 3-Light Blue, 7-Navy, 6-Red, 8-White, 9-Yellow. **SU994–**

4 *Liberty of London Striped Ties.* 100% silk. Made in USA of imported fabric. 9-Rose, 5-Teal, 6-Red. **SU938–**

5 *Yves St. Laurent Ties.* 100% silk. Made in USA of imported fabric. Red Paisley **SU9000**. Teal Paisley **SU9276**. Blue Foulard **SU9273**.

6 *Stanley Blacker Pressless Suit.* 55% polyester/45% worsted wool blend. Two-button front jacket. Made in USA. Available in pinstripe or solid. Sizes: Regular 38-44, 46. Long 40-44, 46, 48. Short 38-44. Gray Pinstripe **SU9174**. Navy Pinstripe **SU9173**. Gray Solid **SU9184**. Navy Solid **SU9183**.

7 *Hathaway Men's Button-Down Oxford Shirt.* 60% cotton and 40% polyester. Long sleeves. Sizes: 14½-16 x 32; 14½-17½ x 33/34; 15-17½ x 35. Made in USA. Blue **SU9283**. White **SU9288**. Cream **SU9281**. Blue/white stripe **SU9293**. Brown/white stripe **SU9291**.

8 *Perry Ellis Portfolio Men's Dress Shirt.* Long sleeve, 100% cotton. Package of two shirts per size and color. Imported. Sizes:14½-16½ x 32/33; 15-17½ x 34-35. White/black stripe **SU9257**. White/blue stripe **SU9253**.

A. *Perry Ellis Solid Dress Shirt.* (Not pictured.) Sizes: 14½-16½ x 32/33; 15-17½ x 34-35. White **SU9268**. Blue **SU9263**. Pink **SU9266**. Gray **SU9264**.

9 *Jack Nicklaus Golden Bear® Blazer by Hart Schaffner & Marx.* Miniature hopsack weave of Dacron® polyester and worsted wool. Made in USA. Sizes: Reg 38-50; short 38-44; Long, 39-50; X-Long 42-48. Choose: 3-Navy, 1-Wheat, 4-Gray, 9-Medium Blue. **SU937–**

10 *Telux® Depth Gauge Dive Watch.[3]* Analog thermometer gives accurate temperature ±2°. Luminous dial. Uni-directional timing bezel deeply notched for ease in setting. French quartz movements. Black case, yellow bezel **SU9599**. Blue case, black bezel **SU9593**. Red case, black bezel **SU9596**.

11 *Seiko LaSalle Men's Watch.[3]* Distinctive men's watch in a 22K gold finish. Day, date and 24-hour subdials. Moon phase indicator, water resistant. **SQ5340**

12 *Woolrich Crew Jacket.* Fleece-lined jacket with Thinsulate® insulated sleeves. Suplex® nylon shell. Inside zippered pocket. Ribknit cuffs and high-wind collar. Made in USA. Sizes: Reg, S, M, L, XL. Long M, L, XL. Emerald/navy **SU9905**. Red/charcoal **SU9906**. Royal/navy **SU9903**. Charcoal/gray **SU9904**.

13 *Chalkline Satin NFL Jackets.[3]* Nylon quilt-lined jacket. Welt pockets, snap front. Knit collar, cuffs and bottom band. Specify team.

A. *Adult Jacket.* "Pro Twill" satin. Sizes: S, M, L, XL, XXL. **SQ1821**

B. *Youth Jacket.* "Athletic" satin. Sizes: 6/8, 10/12, 14/16, 18/20. **SQ1822**

14 *Sebago Beefroll Loafer.* Classic handsewn loafer. Made in USA. Sizes: A, B, C, D, E, EE, EEE, 6½-13. Cordovan (pictured) **SU9471**. Brown **SU9472**. Black **SU9473**.

15 *Sebago "Docksides" Boat Shoe.* Handcrafted of specially tanned cowhide. Non-slip white rubber sole. Made in USA. Sizes: N, 8-12, 13; M&W, 6-12, 13. Tan (pictured) **SU9481**. Brown **SU9482**. Sandsuede **SU9483**. Bone **SU9484**.

16 *Johnston & Murphy Shoes.* "The Deerfield" is a classic moc toe tasseled slip on. Sizes: A 9½-12, 13; B 9-12, 13; C 8-12, 13; D 7½-12, 13; E 8-11. 1-Black, 2-Burgundy, 3-Walnut. **SU915–**

17 *Johnston & Murphy Shoes.* The "Greenich" wing tip bal oxford. Sizes: A 9-12, 13; B 9-12, 13; C 8-12, 13; D 7½-12, 13; E 8-11, 12. Colors: 2-Black, 3-Brown, 3-Burgundy. **SU922–**

18 *Heyman "Thames" Designer Argyle Hose.* Traditional argyle pattern. One-size stretch fits sizes 10-13. Machine washable; cotton/nylon. Set of 3 pairs. Made in USA. Dark assortment. **SU9512** Light assortment. **SU9511**. Light assortment.

19 *Heyman "Wales" Argyle Hose.* Knit of acrylic/nylon. Machine wash. Size 10-13. In 3 pairs of asst. dark tones. **SU9521**. Light assortment **SU9522**.

20 *Christian Dior Socks.* Over-the-calf. Three to a set. Navy, black, brown. One size fits 10-13. Made in USA. **SI8785**

21 *Jockey Crewneck T-Shirts.* 100% Power-knit® combed cotton. Set of 6. Made in USA. Sizes: S(34-36), M(38-40), L(42-44), XL(46-48). White. **SR9628**

A. *V-Neck T-Shirts.* (Not pictured.) Same as above, with v-neck. **SR9627**

22 *Jockey Classic Briefs.* 1 x 1 ribbed cotton. Set of 6. White. Made in USA. Sizes 30-42. **SR9629**

23 *Trylon Striped Terry Velour Robe.* 48" kimono style has loop terry interior, velour exterior. Tie belt. 100% Brazilian cotton. One size fits both men and women. Imported. White/blue. **SR9630**

A. *Trylon Solid Terry Velour Robe.* (Not pictured.) Same as above. White **SU9648**. Royal **SU9643**. Red **SU9646**.

24

The Level Three program features incentives for salesmen and production workers. These gifts are presented in 9 different Step-up Plateau Books. SHM calls this series their "Classics Collection". Pricing for the items in these books starts at $20.00 in Book Number 1 and goes as high as $500.00 in Book Number 9. As we see in this example, all 9 "Classics Collection" plateau books can be gathered and bound as a single 52-page, 8-3/8" X 10-7/8" catalog, with either standard or customized covers.

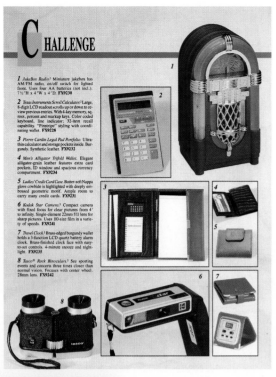

SHM believes each module of the Performance Merchandise Awards System must complement the other two. In their eyes, any incentive awards program should be vertical in structure so as to involve as many individuals within a client company as possible. To keep all three catalogs separate from one another, yet working together as a cohesive whole, two procedures are followed:

1. *Virtually all the items in any one catalog are exclusive to that catalog. There is no merchandise crossover between catalogs; ergo, there is no pickup of photographs from one book to another.*
2. *To make the three PMAS catalogs a coherent whole, all of the books are produced by the same creative and production teams.*

Steve Erickson, Vice President of Marketing, feels that local, autonomous control is the only way to maintain their present high standards and client-sensitive, highly customized merchandise and travel presentations. He has good reason for his opinion. In 1988, SHM published 27 custom catalogs, 19 million books in all. The name of that game is Control & Coordination.

The incentive industry is a dynamic, creative field. New ideas abound. New products and services are constantly being tested. New media choices are coming on-line, which means totally new forms of presentation are just around the corner.

For the foreseeable future, however, catalogs will continue to play a dominant role in this field. Somehow, the customer has to see the merchandise. Electronic media for the shop-at-home or incentive market cannot yet deliver an inexpensive 4-color merchandise presentation that one may peruse at leisure. That day may come, but until then, at least as far as SHM is concerned, the catalog is still king.

SPERRY & HUTCHINSON, INC. (GREEN STAMPS)

A quiet explosion is about to take place in the catalog industry. Surprisingly, the unlikely locus of this blast will be Main-street, USA. The sleepy Consumer Incentives Industry is about to burst onto the marketing scene after years of hiatus. Retailers, grocers and service vendors of all persuasions will soon be caught up in a round of high-tech sales promotion programs, and incentive/premium catalogs will abound.

Remember when it seemed the whole world was running around with their tongues stuck to their teeth as a result of licking trading stamps? What in the world happened? Where did all those little green and blue stamps go?

For a long time, and excepting some truck stop and small regional programs, the stamp redemption business has been in a state of limbo. It's in that promotional pasture-in-the-sky along with Burma Shave signs, nickel beers, free lunches, Tom Mix rings and the chicken feed bags Ma used to make into blouses. But technology is about to change all that.

In 1916, the upstart trading stamp industry was bubbling along at a 40 million dollar per year pace—a very large sum for those days. Came The Great Depression, and sales were sent plummeting to a low of around 10 million in 1934. At their peak in 1968-69, trading stamps were redeemed for over $830 million worth of merchandise. In those days, stamps were available to 84% of the American public at one or more stores or filling stations in their neighborhoods.

Today, trading stamp industry sales figures are less than half what they were in 1968-69—inflation notwithstanding. As of 1988, only 9% of our grocery stores were offering trading stamps. In spite of these negative statistics, optimistic contrarians have announced that the downswing of the pendulum has just about reached its nadir.

Whenever a market becomes saturated with one type of incentive program, it is time for a change. And there did come a time when just about every grocery store and gas station in town was giving away trading stamps or dinner plates. At that point, the competitive edge premium promotions once offered ceased to exist. The cycle had run its course.

Does this mean that the consumer incentive industry is dead? Hardly. Consider it from this point of view:

When you're the only grocer in the neighborhood offering incentives, and you get your buddy with the filling station on the corner to offer the same incentive program to his customers, the two of you have a real competitive advantage over all the other guys on the block.

That's about where the industry is right now. There was a glut of trading stamps in the late 60s. Consumer burnout was the result. Mrs. Jones got tired of chasing the best trading stamp deals all over town. But, the pendulum may be about to start its backswing.

Will traditional trading stamps be the new premium vehicle? Quite unlikely. Will the industry change? It's already happening.

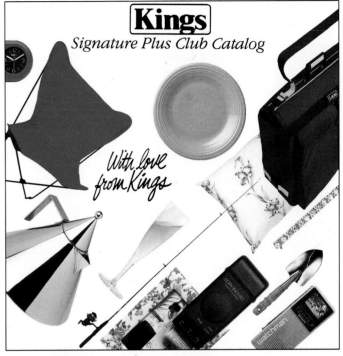

Kings
Signature Plus Club Catalog

With love from Kings

SPERRY & HUTCHINSON, INC.
George Simpson, *Director, Marketing Services*
Agency: *CGI*
David Christenson, *President*
Dean Alexander, *Designer*

Computer hardware, electronic communications links and advanced database technology are the keys to this renaissance. One exciting example is Sperry & Hutchinson's new ''Smart Card''. Here's how it works:

At your favorite store, or through the mail, you will be offered a gold-colored, plastic convenience card with a built-in magnetic strip. It looks exactly like any of your bank credit cards.

This ''S&H Gold Card'' becomes, in effect, your stamp-saver book or savings account. It can also be used to gain check cashing privileges. As you make your purchases, a POS terminal at the checkout counter will credit your account with the correct number of points. These points are recorded on the magnetic strip on your card. They are also batch-fed to S&H's master computer as a backup and more permanent record. When you redeem your points for either merchandise, services, travel or cash, your card and account will be debited.

Gone is the muss and fuss of gluing stamps into little books. S&H is able to deliver a leaner, more accurate and efficient incentive program to its clients. And the stores are not burdened with the theft, security and labor problems associated with the old stamp-saver books.

The Fast Track

"As a young couple, my husband and I are just getting our first glimpse of the Good Life. We just moved to the city and each have a new job—so it will be awhile before we have a 'designer showplace' to call home. But when we do get something, we go for both quality and style.

After all, just because an item is used everyday, it doesn't have to be *ordinary*. In seeking out classic design, we choose things that will please the eye this year, next year, ten years from now. Because great design never goes out of style—whether it's a tea kettle, a flower vase, or a crystal decanter.

We're working on achieving our dreams, but we never lose sight of living in the present. We will make sacrifices along the way, but style isn't one of them. Neither is quality. In having fine things to use...this is the good life for us."

...*Betty & Ken Berke*, PINE HALL, NY

A **NEW** Ultra-contemporary water kettle. Designed by Aldo Rossi in 1986 of polished 18/10 stainless steel. Manufactured in Italy by Alessi. 2½-qt. capacity. **J9630**

B **NEW** The elegance of the Orient. Graceful crystal vase in Oriental "Shansi" style to enhance any arrangement. Handcrafted in Europe. 14" high. **K4129**

C **NEW** A work of art. The "Maya" bowl designed by Giulio Confalonieri. Gleaming 18/10 polished stainless steel, manufactured in Italy by Alessi. 10" diameter at top. **K4126**

D **NEW** A shining example of fine design. Silverplated brass "Rosenschale" bowl designed by Josef Hoffmann. Manufactured by Alessi in Italy. 9" diameter. **A4647**

E **NEW** Simply exquisite. Atlantis full lead crystal decanter in the classic, understated, Wimbledon pattern. Faceted crystal top. 9½" high. **K4127**

F **NEW** A lesson in good taste. Silver Palate Good Times Live™ VHS video tape. 40 minute video features ideas for entertaining complete with special recipes included in a 32 page recipe book. From Simon & Schuster. **H9190**

G **NEW** Set design. Ettore Sottsass, Jr. designed this timeless salt, pepper and toothpick set in 24% lead crystal with 18/10 polished stainless steel caps and stand. Manufactured in Italy by Alessi. **J9632**

H **NEW** Picture perfect. Silverplated 5" × 7" oval frame, the ultimate way to display cherished photos. **A4646**

Also available: 3½" × 5" size. **A4645**

A **NEW** Copy-Jack™ 40 hand-held copy machine. Produces 1.6" wide copies by just sliding the scanner over material to be copied. Portable, rechargeable battery. Includes recharger, roll of paper, carry case. 2.5 × 6.7 × 1.8".[2] **A1603**

B **NEW** Write on LAMY. Safari™ ball point pen with rubber push button plunger, spring clip, contoured, easy to hold shape. Charcoal. **A1739**

C **NEW** Factory"—9 desk essentials in a Swiss Army Knife design. Incorporates stainless steel scissors, hole punch, stapler, tape measure, knife, staple remover, magnifying lens, tape dispenser and storage compartment. Red case. **A1604**

D **NEW** Sharp wallet-size electronic calculator/telephone directory/schedule book. Stores up to 50 entries and sorts them for easy recall. Long-life lithium battery. 12-digit, 2-line LCD display.[2] **A1607**

E **NEW** Timely. Paul Peugeot moon phase watch. Accurate quartz movement. Goldplated case and leather strap.[2] **A0492**

F **NEW** Colorful sport watch. Quartz movement, moveable deeply knurled bezel. Adjustable wristband may be cut to fit any size wrist. Second hand, water resistant up to 56 meters. Luminous easily readable dial. **A0490**

G **NEW** World time quartz travel clock by Lorus. Key city rotating bezel. Hinged cover/stand. 5-minute snooze alarm. Luminous markers, hands. Battery included. 2½ × 3 × ⅝".[2] **G5287**

H **NEW** Bright idea. Micro-Max™ miniature penlight by Brinkmann, is up to 50 times brighter than ordinary penlights! Built-in ring for keychain use. Made of waterproof/shock proof anodized aluminum. Beam adjusts

2-Warranty information. See page 59.

from spot to flood. Uses one AAA battery, included. Only 3¼" long.[2] **M9380**

I **NEW** Becker's built a better stapler. Contemporary design enhances any desk or office. Only 5¾" long. **A1606**

J **NEW** Thin Air™ by Tekna®. Ultra-thin 2-speed, 5-position desk fan of ABS high impact design. 5 position folding base directs air flow. 4 × 5 × ¾".[2] **H7041**

K **NEW** Walk 'n talk. Panasonic miniature cordless phone. Flip open handset fits easily in pocket. Two-way paging, digital security codes and speaker phone. Includes 2 rechargeable batteries, with built-in recharger in base. 10 number memory.[2] **A1608**

L **NEW** Talk about style. Contemporary telephone designed by Ettore Sottsass of Milan. Tone/pulse switchable. Last number redial. 10 number

memory. Tri-color, shown.[2] **A1610**

M **NEW** Panasonic Easa-Phone™. Integrated telephone system with remote beeperless answering system, 15 number memory dialer, 2-way/memo, Auto-Logic™, recordable OGM chip, monitor speaker. Desk/wall mount.[2] **A1609**

P **NEW** The Complete Organizer® from Buxton. Rich leather agenda book with 20 month calendar, telephone and address section, slots for business and credit cards, expenses section, note pad and pen. Burgundy leather. **A0292**

Q **NEW** Canon palm-size printing calculator with easy-to-use slant key design. 8-digit memory. 1½" thermal printing. Auto off. Operates on optional AC4 adaptor or 4 AA batteries, included.[2] **A1605**

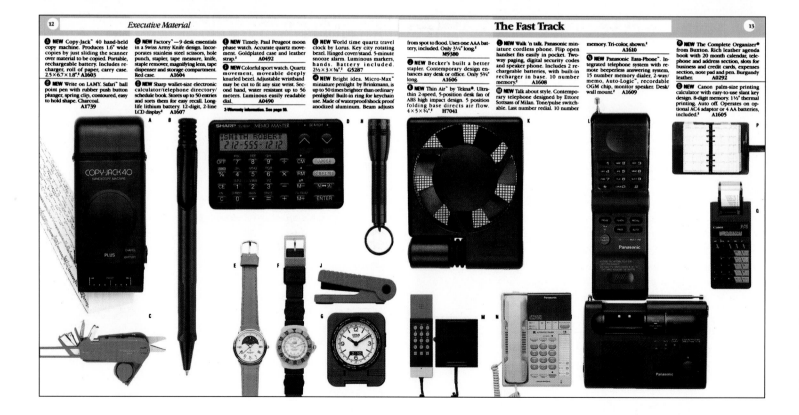

As the new systems mature, each customer record will be expanded to track purchases by SKU. At that point, the marketing implications become awesome. S&H and their clients will be able to track customer preferences on a scale heretofore impossible. This input will be used to guide purchasing, target advertising efforts, and to expand markets via both enhanced site selection and increased market penetration.

Of equal import, customers and vendor corporations alike will benefit from in-depth, more sharply defined market segmentation. Households will receive only those promotions that are of real interest to the residents. Large-scale list regression means megadollar savings for the stores and their sources. Consumers will benefit as the retailers learn more about customer preferences and then stock their shelves and plan their promotions accordingly.

28 — Child's World

"I love being a father. I had no idea how much fun it would be—or how much responsibility. The busy life my wife and I lead is now *really busy*. Fortunately, there are a lot of things to help us manage our industrious new arrival.

When we go out, Amy rides in a roomy and safe stroller—which folds up like an umbrella when not in use. Very convenient. At home, as we move around the house, Amy goes with us—in a playard that rolls from room to room without having to be disassembled.

For more longer trips, getting the right car seat was important to us. Our Century car seat not only offers safety and security for our precious cargo—but may be put in place or removed with one hand. And once we've arrived it converts into a carrier—or an ingenious portable rocker. And to feed our on-the-go baby we have a travelling bottle warmer that goes wherever she does.

We want the time we spend with Amy to be the best—and safest. After all, she is the one who makes our Good Life that much sweeter."

...Bill Hatcher & Amy, LINCOLN, NE

A At right: Ever popular baby carrier. Your baby feels safe and secure riding close to your heart, your hands are free. Polyester/cotton. Imported. **P0952**

B NEW A born traveller. Graco "Travel-Rite"™ umbrella stroller folds in a snap. Front swivel wheels, posi-lock rear wheel brake. **P0672**

C Pack up and go. Gerry "Double Take"™ expandable diaper bag zips open for more than double the take-along space. Vinyl lined with separate diaper pocket and bottle loop. Adjustable shoulder strap.[2] **P0958**

D NEW Lunch on the run. Snugli™ portable bottle warmer heats baby's bottle in 10-15 minutes. No batteries or electricity needed—just snap the disc. Later boil the non-toxic heat pad for 15 minutes to re-charge. Nylon bag.[2] **P0960**

E Safe journey. Century safety infant car seat. A 2-pc. safety system with "stay-in-car" molded base plus removable deluxe carrier with four position carry handle and built-in rocker. 3-point shoulder harness. **P0839**

F NEW Portable playard from Century. Convenient thru-the-door size and fast fold design lets you move it from room to room with ease. Rugged steel frame, padded top rail and sides. Removable vinyl pad. 27 x 41 x 30"H. **P0533**

2-Warranty information. See page 98.

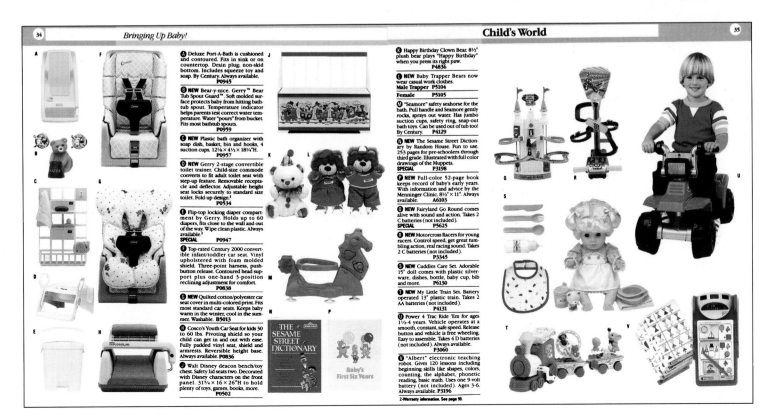

34 — Bringing Up Baby!

A Deluxe Port-A-Bath is cushioned and contoured. Fits in sink or on countertop. Drain plug; non-skid bottom. Includes squeeze toy and soap. By Century. Always available. **P0945**

B NEW Bear-y-nice. Gerry™ Bear Tub Spout Guard™. Soft molded surface protects baby from hitting bathtub spout. Temperature indicator helps parents test correct water temperature. Water "pours" from bucket. Fits most bathtub spouts. **P0959**

C NEW Plastic bath organizer with soap dish, basket, bin and hooks, 4 suction cups. 12⅛ x 4½ x 18¼"H. **P0957**

D NEW Gerry 2-stage convertible toilet trainer. Child-size commode converts to fit adult toilet seat with step-up feature. Removable receptacle and deflector. Adjustable height seat locks securely to standard size toilet. Fold-up design.[2] **P0534**

E Flip-top locking diaper compartment by Gerry. Holds up to 60 diapers, fits close to the wall and out of the way. Wipe clean plastic. Always available. SPECIAL **P0947**

F Top-rated Century 2000 convertible infant/toddler car seat. Vinyl upholstered with foam molded shield. Three-point harness, push-button release. Contoured head support plus one-hand 3-position reclining adjustment for comfort. **P0838**

G NEW Quilted cotton/polyester car seat cover in multi-colored print. Fits most standard car seats. Keeps baby warm in the winter, cool in the summer. Washable. **B5013**

H Cosco's Youth Car Seat for kids 30 to 60 lbs. Pivoting shield so your child can get in and out with ease. Fully padded vinyl seat, shield and armrests. Reversible height base. Always available. **P0836**

I Walt Disney deacon bench/toy chest. Safety lid seats two. Decorated with Disney characters on the front panel. 31¾ x 16 x 26"H to hold plenty of toys, games, books, more. **P0502**

THE SESAME STREET DICTIONARY

Baby's First Six Years

Child's World — 35

K Happy Birthday Clown Bear. 8½" plush bear plays "Happy Birthday" when you press its right paw. **P4836**

L NEW Baby Trapper Bears now wear casual work clothes. Male Trapper **P5104** Female **P5105**

M "Seamore" safety seahorse for the bath. Pull handle and Seamore gently rocks, sprays out water. Has jumbo suction cups, safety ring, snap-out bath toys. Can be used out of tub too! By Century. **P4129**

N NEW The Sesame Street Dictionary by Random House. Fun to use. 253 pages for pre-schoolers through third grade. Illustrated with full color drawings of the Muppets. SPECIAL **P3198**

O NEW Full-color 52-page book keeps record of baby's early years. With information and advice by the Menninger Clinic. 8½" x 11". Always available. **A6103**

P NEW Fairyland Go Round comes alive with sound and action. Takes 2 C batteries (not included). SPECIAL **P5625**

Q NEW Motorcross Racers for young racers. Control speed, get great tumbling action, real racing sound. Takes 2 C batteries (not included). **P3345**

R NEW Cuddles Care Set. Adorable 15" doll comes with plastic silverware, dishes, bottle, baby cup, bib and more. **P6130**

S NEW My Little Train Set. Battery operated 13" plastic train. Takes 2 AA batteries (not included). **P3060**

T Power 4 Trac Ride 'Em for ages 1½-4 years. Vehicle operates at a smooth, constant, safe speed. Release button and vehicle is free wheeling. Easy to assemble. Takes 4 D batteries (not included). Always available. **P4131**

U "Albert" electronic teaching robot. Gives 120 lessons including beginning skills like shapes, colors, counting, the alphabet, phonetic reading, basic math. Uses one 9-volt battery (not included). Ages 3-6. Always available. **P3196**

2-Warranty information. See page 98.

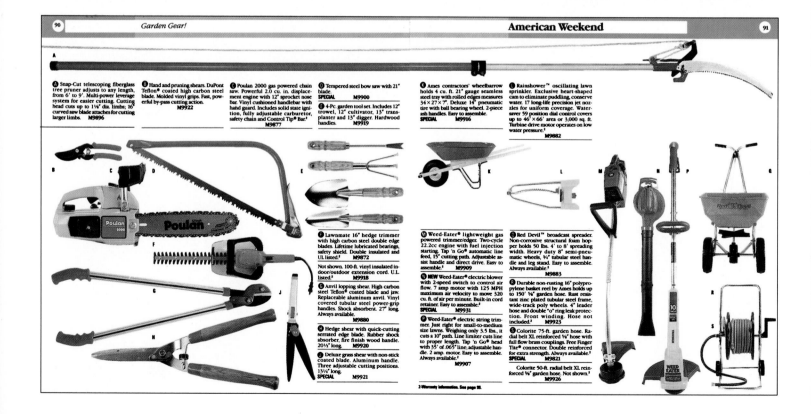

Today's consumer premium and incentive catalogs are merchandised with products aimed at the same markets as the original stamp plan books. There's one major difference: no licking and saving. It's all done by computers. In this case, a magnetically coded Gold Card tracks a customer's purchases, credits her account with one point for every ten cents spent, and provides her with instant check cashing approval.

IV
DEALER CATALOGS

There's one breed of super-catalogs consumers rarely get a chance to see. These are the books published by manufacturers and distributors and mailed to store buyers and dealers.

Rich looking, opulent, interesting catalogs they are, with print runs often so small they're produced on sheetfed presses. Paper stock is usually much heavier and of a better grade than is seen in a typical consumer catalog. Separations are the best available. And the creative team can pull out all the stops because special effect techniques, expensive as they may be, do not add up to unaffordable dollars when quantities are low.

The purpose behind all this creativity and high cost production is not to send an art director or president on an ego trip. Impact is the intent. In order to do their job, these little jewels have to sell positive corporate image, individual products and most of all, themselves.

Why must these catalogs peddle their own paper? Because they must be deemed worthy of saving. The store buyer is inundated with catalogs and direct mail pieces from hundreds of competing vendors. They are all mailed in ''the season'' and the theory is that they'll produce immediate orders. But sometimes buyers have their own internal clocks, and they may choose to ignore normal trade-related timing. Then there's the matter of rebuying and/or special ordering. If the catalog isn't in the file, the sale may be lost. And if the catalog wasn't interesting enough to make it into the file in the first place, the chances of making the sale are zilch.

These dealer catalogs have another very valuable function. It works like this. Many of the photographs in these books are expensive four-color shots involving complicated setups, expensive models, costly props and first rate photographers. In most cases, stores cannot afford to spend this kind of heavy duty money for their print ads and POP displays.

Here's where the dealer catalog provides the solution. Duplicate transparencies, or in some cases, duplicate separations are made available to the customers of these manufacturers. Now, the stores have copies of the same photos that appear in the dealer catalog—at little or no cost to the retailer.

The store wins because their ads look more professional, prestigious and attractive. The manufacturer is way ahead of the game on two counts: 1). His product is shown exactly as he thinks it should be presented, and 2). There's a good chance the buyer will commit more deeply to that manufacturer's line; providing, of course that the ads work, and/or the store wants continuity in a series of ads and displays.

Particularly in the larger stores, buyers and assistants tend to move from department to department fairly frequently. It's all a part of navigating the rocks and shoals of a burgeoning retail career. They no sooner learn all the ins and outs of one category, when they're transferred to another. Sometimes, ''in the interests of broadening their experience'', these moves can be as extreme as a leap from children's outerwear to the luggage department.

Where will they gain the necessary insight into their new field? Trade shows and trade publications? To be sure. Friends and peers? Very valuable. Training programs? Yes, in the better stores, but not always. Dealer and manufacturer catalogs? You bet!

Most of these insider's catalogs devote a good bit of space to backgrounding the reader while selling the publisher's company. It's a marvelous opportunity to walk through a complete process, from raw material to finished product. Again, everybody benefits. Buyers add to their reservoir of knowledge, and the vendor has the opportunity to develop a thesis in his own words and with his own spin on the story.

We started out by lamenting the fact that these gorgeous catalogs are rarely if ever seen by the consumer. There are exceptions. Some of these books can be ordered directly from the publisher. Occasionally, retailers will have a few available for their better prospects. In most cases, these alternate forms of catalog distribution are only available when the product being sold carries a fairly high price tag.

Catalog buffs will be well rewarded if they watch their print media ads for offers of this kind. It may cost a dollar or two to have a look at each of these catalogs, but in almost every case, it will be money well spent.

BROWNING

Dealer catalogs can be, and frequently are, more attractive and interesting than most consumer catalogs. These catalogs focus on a relatively narrow range of interests. They also tend to target people with specific hobbies, interests and life-styles. As a result, they speak the language, inform in detail, present with clarity and offer sales help at all levels.

Hobbyists and aficionados can add new buzz-words to their vocabulary, while cognoscenti are addressed in their accustomed vernacular. Lovers of the genre avidly read every word about their hobby. And, since there's no need to sell the concept, the best presentations are without clutter or mood-evoking props and lighting. And if a store buyer or salesperson needs more information than the catalog offers, there's always someone at the home office or plant who has all the answers.

Browning's catalog is a prime example. From the conveniently three-hole-punched spine to the very last toll-free customer service telephone number, this book is a gem. The entire catalog connotes dedication to the outdoors, to hunting and competitive shooting, and to the people who enjoy those sports.

Browning's expository copy—written under the supervision of Copy Chief, Roger Stitt—is quite different from the ordinary. The sales message is clear and descriptions are full — even for shoes and outerwear. But, after telling us the facts, Browning's copy answers our "whys". For example, the BPS pump shotgun has bottom ejection. Spent shells don't arc out the side of the gun, they eject straight down. Now, why should that make any difference to the gun's owner? It sounds like a production engineering modification. So what's in it for me? Here is Browning's answer:

THE HUNTING ADVANTAGE OF BOTTOM EJECTION

Unlike most other shotguns, the BPS ejects spent shells straight down, out the bottom of the receiver.

Ejected shells never fly across your line of sight, distracting you from your target. Empties are always at your feet for easy collecting. Bottom ejection makes the BPS equally suitable for right or left-handed shooting. Also, it is much more difficult for brush, seeds or other foreign matter to get into the action.

One, two, three, four solid reasons for you to buy the BPS. No fluff in that copy. Every point is an important consideration to a thoughtful customer (and a darn good script for the dealer's salesman).

Yes, Browning's publication is a dealer catalog, but with a difference. The 21,000 stores that sell the Browning line hand out thousands of Browning catalogs each year to their favorite customers. Another group of enthusiasts write directly to Browning requesting catalogs. In all, over 100,000 of these "dealer" catalogs find their way into consumers' hands every year. That is serious Public Relations!

Recent surveys have demonstrated the high esteem Browning's customers have for the publication. The average shelf-life of this catalog is an astonishing 8 months! Shelf-life in this case equates to time kept on the coffee or bedside table (or as Art Director Brent Evans said, "perhaps even in the outhouse"). That is truly extraordinary life-span. Most consumer catalogs are round-filed within 2 to 3 weeks.

BROWNING—1988 Catalog
Don Gobel, *President*
Ron Mosier, *Vice President, Sales*
T. David Ziegler, *Sales Promotion Manager/ Catalog Director*
Brent Evans, *Creative Director/Art Director*
Roger Stitt, *Copy Chief*
Bonnie Snedden, *Production Manager*
Robert Casey and George Gruber, *Photographers/Illustrators*
Chris Oswald (Non-hunting) and Ron Mosier (Hunting), *Division Managers*
Wolfer Printing [Los Angeles], *Printer, on 100# Capistrano Gloss for cover and 50# Somerset Gloss for text*
Blanks Engraving [Dallas], *Color Separator*

Doom-and-gloomers who are prophesying the death of multi-line catalogs might want to take a closer look at catalogs like Browning's. This catalog offers much more than shotguns, rifles and handguns. In pagination sequence, the breakdown is:

Shotguns.. *24 pages*
Rifles .... *14 pages*
Handguns .... *4 pages*
Knives & Hunt Accessories .... *6 pages*
Archery .... *2 pages*
Gun Safes .... *7 pages*
Clothing & Accessories................................ *22 pages*
Footwear .... *12 pages*

Generic pages and covers make up the balance of the 96 pages in this book. But, look here, 37% of the merchandise pages in this firearms catalog are softgoods and footwear! We're talking shirts, slickers, underwear, pants, boots and socks. What this product-mix points out is: if you have a fine reputation with your readers, and if you offer them items they need or want (when they want them), and if you are perceived as an expert in the field—your customers will buy these related, but out-of-line items, from you.

Browning relies heavily on their once-a-year catalog to do a multifaceted marketing job. It is their primary dealer communications device. It strokes and informs their ultimate customers. But on top of that, Brent Evans, Art Director of the Browning catalog, has another responsibility. He is entrusted with maintaining the image of superior quality that Browning has earned over its 110 years of business.

In the light of that responsibility, Brent was kind enough to outline some of his thoughts in a recent letter. Regarding the broader aims of the catalog, he said:

Browning has one of the most solidly corroborated traditions of quality merchandise in the market. These facts are the guiding forces behind all of our advertising efforts, especially our catalogs. From conceptualization and design to color control and printing, our staff concentrates on delivering and enhancing the message that Browning is still as it has always been known throughout its history, 'The Best There Is'.

Over the years, Browning has used various themes and graphic devices to convey this aura of distinction to their audience. Easier to do if your name is Brooks Brothers, and your customers include a preponderance of old family investment bankers — most of whom graduated from an Ivy League college.

Browning does serve customers of the upper social strata. But they must also touch the hearts and minds of ranchers, farmers, large and small game hunters, and a diverse assortment of marksmen. The folks who walk through the doors of Browning's 21,000 dealers truly represent a broad cross-section of the United States population. A difficult and moving target for Browning's marketing team to hit.

How is this solved? By being tuned-in. Back to Brent Evans' comments. He recognized, from his own experience, a point of common ground that all his customers might share. His inspiration for this award winning catalog came about. . .

. . . as I left my elk camp 4:00 a.m., I viewed the panorama of stars in the clear mountain air. It occurred to me that as the ancients governed their entire existence by the movements of the stars in the heavens, so the hunter's pursuits revolve around yearly cycles begun millennia ago. All I did was alter the familiar constellations to depict images to which those in our market relate. We then repeated vignettes of those new constellations on each spread of the book as a graphic tie with our products, and a reminder of that theme.

The construction of a fine gun is an artform as much as it is a manufacturing process. Skilled members of the Engravers Cooperative of Liege and gunsmiths in Herstal, Belgium, do most of the engraving and final assembly work for Browning's top line guns. Here's how Copy Chief Roger Stitt describes the uncompromising standards established for the guns of Browning [underlines added]:

A gun must possess the clean, poised lines that draw the eye initially to rate the adornment that treats the eye. Artistic expression, cut in steel and carved in walnut, achieves a permanence that must be matched equally by a permanence in the gun's functional reliability. <u>Only guns that promise generations of shooting pleasure, rather than mere decades of utility, deserve such a compliment.</u> In short, the longevity, the durability, the sureness of function and the aesthetic design of Browning guns, have made them especially desirable subjects for the consummate skill of Herstal, Belgium's master engravers.

There follows words and pictures describing the many steps and skills involved in producing this complex work of art. To those involved in the sport, or craftsmen of any persuasion, the following excerpt connotes a quality-level that is itself a work of art.

Fitting the barrels to the receiver is critical. To do this, <u>the gunsmiths use a lamp to blacken the parts with smoke. The parts are assembled and operated to find the 'high' points, where the lamp black rubs off. Since the smoke is only one thousandth of a millimeter thick,</u> handworking these high, bearing points achieves the precise fit that prevents the metal from galling and the gun from 'shooting loose.' [underlines added]

It will be a long time before robots replace these talented gunsmiths and artists. And, robots will never replace the likes of the creative team that originated this hard-working, informative, and very appealing publication.

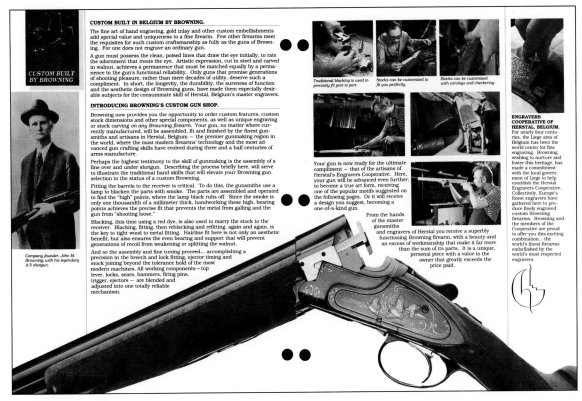

GOLD SERIES SAFES

Four top-of-the-line, maximum security safe models are offered to meet your dimension, capacity and price requirements: Deluxe, "L", "E" and Trimline models. All Browning Gold Series safes now have a new, rich brown metallic enamel paint.

New Special Edition Presentation Series Safes. These beautiful safes are the best in Browning detailing and fine finish ... the ultimate safe for the collector of Browning guns. The door face features a gold Browning signature along with a full color reproduction of a painting featuring a bald eagle defending her nest from an aggressive bobcat. The scene is permanently affixed to the safe using a special acrylic transfer process that reproduces the scene true to the original oil painting. The exterior of each safe is finished in an exceptionally rich, black metallic, gold metal fleck paint. Interior carpet is a deep burgundy. The Presentation Series Safe option is available on two Gold Series models: the Deluxe models RD6324 and RD8324. Lockup features of these Deluxe models are outlined below. The Presentation option also includes a clear, plexiglass interior door panel to show-off the finest locking system in the industry. See page 54 for photograph.

Deluxe Models. The finest in Browning security. They have classic Browning superior finish plus they incorporate all the advanced features detailed previously. A main component of their strength is the full length locking bolts that lock through the square door reinforcing, into the heavy steel channel, reinforcing the doorway. The exterior is finished with Browning's new, rich, brown metallic enamel with gold pin striping. Charcoal gray painted models are also available for a slight, extra charge.

"L" Model Safes. These versatile, value-packed safes are lighter and more economical than Deluxe models. They have rugged 1/8" steel exteriors and reinforced 3/16" plate doors. Full-length locking bolts lock behind the heavy steel reinforcing along the door frame. Available in two models and five interiors including the General Purpose for jewelry, pistols or other valuables.

"E" Model E1946 Safe. This exceptionally affordable safe has a secure 1/8" exterior steel plate body, and a 3/16" thick steel reinforced door. Features a sturdy, reinforced door frame. The interior door panel is pegboard for additional utility.

The space-saving Trimline. There just isn't any house or apartment too small for a Trimline safe — it easily fits into a closet. The 1/8" steel plate shell offers a sturdy barrier against break-in. The door is recessed and the door frame is steel reinforced on all sides. Lockup is tight with four 5/8" independent, active locking bolts. Shelves and floor are carpeted.

Sargent & Greenleaf Group II heavy duty combination locks.

Custom ball and needle bearing hinges. (Cutaway view)

RD6324 RD8324 E1946 "E" Trimline RL2436 "L" with metallic charcoal gray color paint option

56 · 57

WASATCH GOOSE DOWN PARKA

The Wasatch is ready for whatever brings you outdoors during the coldest days of winter: hunting, trapping, snowmobiling, ice fishing or an outside job. From its premium quality goose down insulation to its Legacy™ Cloth exterior it has all the Presentation Series Down features and top quality components throughout (see page 63). Browning 550 Fill Power goose down insulates you against the cold. The luxurious Legacy™ Cloth exterior is protected from moisture by a superior Hydro-Pel™ finish that repels water and stains. The removable wire-rimmed dual adjust hood provides protection from the elements without impairing your vision. The Wasatch has a REACTAR™ pocket sewn inside the right shoulder for the optional REACTAR™ recoil reduction pad. The Wasatch features eight oversize pockets, enough for all your gear. *Models: Tan (57500), Granite (57508). Sizes: S, M, L, XL, XXL.*

• Rugged Legacy™ Cloth exterior fabric with Hydro-Pel™ rain/stain repellent finish • High count nylon taffeta lining • 550 Fill Power goose down • Wire-rimmed dual adjust hood with drawcord and barrel locks • YKK Delrin 2-way freeze resistant zipper • Front zipper storm flap • Fleece-lined, handwarmer pockets • Knit inner wrist cuffs • Genuine leather trim on sleeves and pockets • Mesh interior pocket for REACTAR™ pad • Two roomy inside pockets • Elastic waist drawcord with cord locks.

PRESENTATION GOOSE DOWN

NEW GOOSE DOWN GORE-TEX® TROOPER CAPS
Browning Trooper Caps are the quality alternative to the lesser offerings available elsewhere. New Browning Troopers are insulated with 30 grams of 550 Fill Power Browning goose down. For 1988, all Troopers protect you from the weather with a new, 100% waterproof, breathable Gore-Tex® insert for unparalleled wind and rain protection. Legacy™ Cloth and Matrix™ Cloth make up the rugged exteriors. Soft, deep pile, Mouton plush ear flaps fold down for the ultimate in warmth. An adjustable drawcord lets you cinch your Trooper Cap down on blustery days. Colors match Browning Jackets, including the new Cattail™ Camo pattern. *Models: Autumn Tan (82551), Blaze (82556), Granite (82558), Cattail Camo (82559). Sizes: M, L, XL.*

* Gore-Tex® is a registered Trade mark of W. L. Gore, Inc.

Autumn Tan Wasatch Parka (Shown without detachable hood)

Granite Silvertip II

SILVERTIP II GOOSE DOWN COAT
It wasn't easy making the famous Silvertip better, but we did — the new Presentation Series Silvertip II. We started with 550 Fill Power premium Browning goose down. The outer shell is luxurious Legacy™ Cloth, with a finish of Hydro-Pel™ rain and stain repellent to keep it looking good. It's built to last: pockets and cuffs are trimmed with genuine leather. A snap closure storm flap and internal knit cuffs keep out drafts. A Browning REACTAR™ pad pocket is sewn into the right shoulder for the optional REACTAR™ recoil pad. *Models: Autumn Tan (15500), Granite (15508). Sizes: S, M, L, XL, XXL.*

• Rugged Legacy™ Cloth exterior fabric with Hydro-Pel™ rain/stain repellent finish • High count nylon taffeta lining • 550 Fill Power goose down • Internal elastic waist drawstring • YKK Delrin freeze resistant 2-way zipper • Mouton plush collar • Snap-secured storm flap • Mesh interior pocket for REACTAR™ recoil pad.

SORTIE II GOOSE DOWN JACKET
Browning's new Sortie II Jacket is an all-around weather friend — the kind you'll find yourself taking just about anywhere. It has all the Presentation Series Down features that make it the best there is. We have increased the overall length of the Sortie II by about 3" over the old Sortie model. We've also added an internal elastic drawstring and a snap closure storm flap over the front zipper to keep out the elements. 550 Fill Power Browning goose down fills out the classic quilt-through styling. The shell fabric is new Endura™ Cloth, a three-ply 100% nylon Supplex® fabric with super durability and the feel of cotton poplin. Hydro-Pel™ finish repels rain and stains. The 29" back length is versatile for driving, sitting . . . just the right length for everyday winter wear. A down-filled stand-up collar cuts the chill at your neck. *Models: Autumn Tan (14509), Blue (14507), Green (14505), Tan Camo (14503). Size: S, M, L, XL, XXL.*

• 550 Fill Power goose down • Endura™ Cloth 100% nylon Supplex® shell treated with Hydro-Pel™ • High count nylon taffeta lining • Internal adjustable waist drawcord • Two-way front zipper with storm flap • Hidden handwarmer pockets • Knit, nylon sleeve cuffs • 29" back length.

Autumn Tan Silvertip II. Left; Granite Wasatch. Right.

Tan Camo Sortie II Jacket

Blue Sortie II Jacket *Gold Sortie II Jacket*

SORTIE II GOOSE DOWN VEST
The Browning Sortie II Goose Down vest is ideal for cutting the chill on frosty fall days or any time the temperature drops. It has all the great features of the new Sortie II Jacket. The tunnel quilts are filled with Browning's high loft, 550 Fill Power Goose down. For 1988 we have added a snap closure storm flap over the front zipper for added warmth and versatility. A kidney flap ensures extra warmth for your lower back. *Models: Camo (36503), Green (36505), Tan (36509), Blue (36507). Sizes: S, M, L, XL, XXL.*

• 550 Fill Power goose down • Endura™ Cloth 100% nylon Supplex® shell treated with Hydro-Pel™ • High count nylon taffeta lining • Two-way front zipper with storm flap • Hidden handwarmer pockets • Down-filled, stand-up collar • Kidney flap.

Sortie II Vest

GOOSE DOWN STUFF VEST
The new Browning Goose Down Stuff Vest is so light and compact when stuffed in its own carry bag that you can carry it anywhere. The Stuff Vest is filled with warm Browning 550 Fill Power goose down. A unique arm gaiter at sleeve openings blocks the wind. The new Quantum™ Cloth shell is stormproof by construction: The extremely high thread count polyester shell fabric is so tightly woven that it blocks out wind and resists rain without fabric coating. This means that the Quantum™ fabric remains soft and quiet, yet highly water repellent and windproof, without having to use any type of coating which would destroy its softness and compactibility. *Models: Forest Green (39505), Red (39504), Taupe (39502). Sizes: S, M, L, XL, XXL.*

Goose Down Stuff Vest

• Rugged Quantum™ Cloth lightweight high density shell • High count nylon taffeta lining • 550 Fill Power goose down • Arm gaiter at sleeve openings • Stuffs into carrying pouch (included) • Two zippered pockets • Differentially cut longer in back.

Goose Down Stuff Vest in Carry Bag.

64 · 65

ERTL REPLICAS

Combining form and function is not always easy, but here's a catalog that's found the way. The company is Ertl. They manufacture toys and model kits. But these toys don't look like toys, they are miniature versions of the real thing. They carry the John Deere, Ford, Case and Navistar International logos, among others. Actually, the replicas are so exact that Ertl has to obtain permission and licenses before they can market these marvelous miniatures.

Ertl, the company, had its beginnings in the Ertl family basement in 1945 in Dyersville, Iowa. Today, the modern Ertl plant is a model itself. A model of efficiency, cleanliness and of mid-American quality standards and values. In this one plant they produce over 5 million units per year of more than 600 toy SKU's. They use 100,000 pounds of wire for axles and shafts and 26,000 gallons of paint per year. 14,500 pounds of little steel balls in vibrating machines remove sharp edges from steel parts to keep the kiddies from harm. And it takes 21 forklifts and 100 licensed forklift operators just to move materials and inventory around the plant. These folks have come a long way from the original ''factory'' in the Ertl family basement!

Replicas '87 is the exceptionally well-conceived catalog that underpins Ertl's marketing program. It is ACA's Gold Award winner in the Wholesale, Multiple Product category. The judges were understandably impressed with Replica's ''clean and thorough presentation from cover to cover''. Here's why.

LAYOUT AND DESIGN

It almost seems that Replicas' art directors spend a part of their time on the road with Ertl salesmen. This book is as user-friendly as a catalog can be. As one ACA judge remarked, ''It's a very simple ordering vehicle. . . which is what a wholesale catalog should be. I would want to order over and over again with it, just because it's so easy to use.''

PAPERSTOCK AND PRESSWORK

The cover paperstock is heavy in weight and soft of finish. It has been die-cut to produce a fold-up flap on the back cover. The resulting pocket carries price sheets, order forms and late-breaking product news. Varnished, 4-color images are surrounded by an overall matte gray tint that covers the rest of the surfaces. As a result, the photos and solid tints in type areas literally shine. They seem to pop right off the cover.

First-rate paperstock and presswork in the body of the book maintain the high standards set by the covers. The feel is that of a slightly semi-gloss finish, combined with top quality inks that are loaded with varnish. Again, the weight of the stock is

Just like the real thing. Only smaller.

ERTL Replicas '87

ERTL COMPANY—Ertl Replicas '87
Fred Ertl, Jr., *President*
Gary Roop, *Vice President, Marketing*
John Dunkel, *Marketing Director*
John Skul, *Catalog Director/Creative
    Director/Production Manager*
Jack McCullough, *Art Director*
McCullough Graphics, *Copy/Agency*
French Studios, *Photographer*
Wagner Printers [Davenport, IA], *Printer,
    on 100# Consoweb Brilliant for cover
    and 80# Consoweb Brilliant for text*
Tech Graphics [Davenport, IA], *Color Separator*

substantial. These covers and interior pages will stand up to a lot of handling and wear.

In the binding process, the catalog has been 3-hole punched. The folks at Ertl know their customers: it is a common practice for store buyers to keep their favorite catalogs in massive 3-ring binders. In the words of one ACA judge: ''This tells toy retailers that this is definitely a catalog that they should not be without. . . .'' (And one doesn't want to be left out, does one?)

Ertl offers their customers a rare combination. Well thought-out, attractive presentations and a really fine line of children's products. What a thrill it must be for a child to own a modern loader, just like the one Dad is driving at work. . . . or the same Farmall Model 350 tractor that Grandpa still uses every day. One can imagine that most buyers and their young customers look forward to this catalog every year.

Open to the inside front cover: BOOM! An INDEX, and in living color. One of two indices in the catalog, this one leads the reader to major product categories: Farm, Construction, Steel/Action Vehicles, Mini Die-Cast, Radio Control, Children's Sounds, Features, Riding, and (lo and behold) Index.

The second index—referred to in the first index—is sorted by product number. This, of course, serves the interests of the re-buyer who knows the line and doesn't want to waste time hunting for an item.

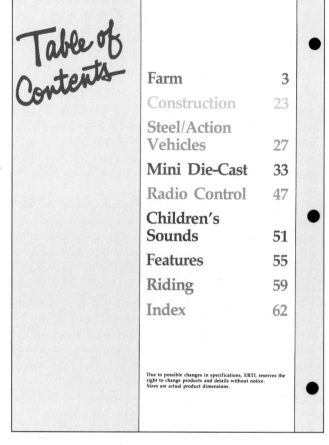

Table of Contents

Due to possible changes in specifications, ERTL reserves the right to change products and details without notice. Sizes are actual product dimensions.

Ertl is a heavy user of modular layout and pickup art, but with enough spin on the ball to obfuscate the fact. By substituting swashes for holding lines and by overlapping process color elements, a completely new phoenix is created from last season's look. It's good, it's creative, it works and it's cost efficient.

Dilemma: how to integrate new products into an existing category within a catalog; and how to flag the new items to store buyers. Simplest solution in the world! In the Ertl catalog, new items appear in their logical category (where the interested buyer will find them). But, they are labeled with a graphic device that says "NEW" in white type reversed out of solid tints. KISS wins again!

PANDE CAMERON & LAURA ASHLEY

Pande Cameron and Laura Ashley publish prime examples of slick, expensive-looking home furnishings dealer catalogs. One, Laura Ashley, assumes that the reader is completely familiar with the Laura Ashley name and line. Pande Cameron makes no such assumption. The two in apposition present the extremes of presentation within the same upscale context.

Pande Cameron has been manufacturing and importing oriental rugs for more than 65 years. They should be, and indeed they are, very well known in the trade. Nevertheless, they still find their catalogs work best when they instruct and inform. In this issue, the lessons start on the inside front cover and continue for another 19 pages.

First, we are given a synoptic history of the company, and then a full page, in-depth discussion of the term "oriental", as it is defined by Pande Cameron. Pages 2 and 3 set the stage for the series of room scenes that follow, each designed by a different, well-known decorator. On these pages, store buyers and their customers are treated to a collection of 20 exquisite rooms covering a wide range of periods and styles. There's ample proof here that a Pande Cameron is at home in any decor.

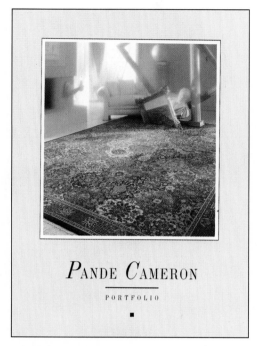

PANDE CAMERON—Portfolio
Daniel R. Hodges, *President*
Sally James, *Advertising Director*

Everyone knows an oriental's legendary ability to make the simplest of rooms look like a million rupees. But what you may not realize is how versatile they can be. So we asked a group of interior design visionaries to help you visualize a Pande Cameron oriental's remarkable flexibility and decorating impact.

These design professionals were each given a room—four bare walls and a few basic pieces of furniture. And each designed three decors that were made elegantly, charmingly or dramatically different—just by changing wall color, adding some key accessories and, of course, a different Pande Cameron.

Consider, for example, the room opposite. If you turn the page, you will see how a beautifully cultivated Pande Cameron, well-placed plants and gauzy draperies (page 5) turn our basic room into a light, airy oasis.

By contrast, East is the inspiration, modern is the mood as our room is transformed by the addition of a stunning chinese-design Pande Cameron and dramatic black-and-white accessories (page 4, bottom).

Lastly, for lovers of Victoriana (page 4, top) we substituted a delicate pastel Pande Cameron, flowers, ruffles and touches of lace—the heart of a room that's pure romance.

These and the pages that follow are but a small sample of the enormous changes you can make—without changing the furniture you already have.

You don't even have to be a professional to get this professional look. Just borrow some of the tricks of the trade.

Start by selecting a key piece (it could be your Pande Cameron oriental or your Great-Grandmother's grandfather clock) and build a room around it. For example, an abstract painting's crayon colors (page 10) demanded upholstery, pillows and a Pande Cameron that were primarily bright and bold. The curliqued antique rattan (page 13) however, called for the charming companionship of an intricately woven oriental and turn-of-the-century collectibles.

Next, size up the dimensions of the room and the placement of furniture when selecting the size of your carpet. It can be used to pull a room together—or divide it. A large, evenly patterned rug (page 6) unifies elegantly—without adding clutter. A smaller rug (page 14) can separate living, dining or study areas—without walls. In fact, don't hesitate to mix orientals of different designs or colors. Many Pande Camerons are designed to co-exist in perfect harmony.

Do consider using your oriental over a broad range of floor types—marble, wood, tile, even broadloom. Let your imagination travel to high-traffic areas like hallways and stairs. Or let our durable orientals drench a bathroom or kitchen in warm, rich color. Wherever there's room for improvement, there's room for a Pande Cameron.

So let your surroundings and our carpets inspire you. You'll find the decorating solution you've been looking for is right under your feet.

2   3

On pages 18-19, a serious student/buyer/salesman will find a masterfully synoptic treatise on oriental rug manufacturing the Pande Cameron way. All is here that's necessary to create an informed Pande Cameron customer. (There are public libraries for those foolish enough to be interested in any other brand.)

You may custom-order any carpet in any size or color combination at a nominal additional charge.

■ AGRIPPA 9786 (Beige/Apricot) Caucasian design. 11′ × 18′; 12′ × 15′; 10′ × 16′; 10′ × 14′; 9′ × 12′; 8′ × 10′; 6′ × 9′; 4′ × 6′; 3′ × 5′; 2′6″ × 4′ Runners: 2′9″ × 24′; 21′; 18′; 15′; 12′; 10′; 7′

■ AGRIPPA 9791 (Red) Keshan design. Also available in Ivory/Apricot 11′ × 18′; 12′ × 15′; 10′ × 16′; 10′ × 14′; 9′ × 12′; 8′ × 10′; 6′ × 9′; 4′ × 6′; 3′ × 5′; 2′6″ × 4′ Runners: 2′9″ × 24′; 21′; 18′; 15′; 12′; 10′; 7′

■ AGRIPPA 9817 (Ivory/Blue) Meshed design. 11′ × 18′; 12′ × 15′; 10′ × 16′; 10′ × 14′; 9′ × 12′; 8′ × 10′; 6′ × 9′; 4′ × 6′; 3′ × 5′; 2′6″ × 4′

■ AGRIPPA 9791 (Ivory/Apricot) Keshan design. Also available in Red 11′ × 18′; 12′ × 15′; 10′ × 16′; 10′ × 14′; 9′ × 12′; 8′ × 10′; 6′ × 9′; 4′ × 6′; 3′ × 5′; 2′6″ × 4′ Runners: 2′9″ × 24′; 21′; 18′; 15′; 12′; 10′; 7′

■ AGRIPPA 9812 (Blue/Red) Isphahan design. Also available in Champagne. 11′ × 18′; 12′ × 15′; 10′ × 16′; 10′ × 14′; 9′ × 12′; 8′ × 10′; 6′ × 9′; 4′ × 6′; 3′ × 5′; 2′6″ × 4′ Runners: 2′9″ × 24′; 21′; 18′; 15′; 12′; 10′; 7′

■ AGRIPPA 9869 (Beige) Polonaise design. 11′ × 18′; 12′ × 15′; 10′ × 16′; 10′ × 14′; 9′ × 12′; 6′ × 10′; 6′ × 9′; 4′ × 6′; 3′ × 5′; 2′6″ × 4′

■ AGRIPPA 9820 (Red) Keshan design. 11′ × 18′; 12′ × 15′; 10′ × 16′; 10′ × 14′; 9′ × 12′; 8′ × 10′; 6′ × 9′; 4′ × 6′; 3′ × 5′; 2′6″ × 4′

On the product sell pages of their book, Pande Cameron continues to use a presentation format designed 20 years ago in conjunction with David Mann. At the time, David was President of Jamian Advertising Agency in New York. The agency has since been sold, and now David is consulting with home furnishings clients from his home/office in Bedford, New York. The point here is not so much David's age, but rather the incredible staying power of a really good advertising design (or copy approach, for that matter).

Do they still work? According to store buyers, the answer is a resounding ''Yes''. And, if imitation is the sincerest form of flattery, these ads are still the best. As proof, next time you have a chance, look at what Pande Cameron's competition is doing.

There are occasions when a vendor is so well established that their name alone connotes all the necessary images. The mere mention of firms such as Tiffany, Neiman-Marcus, Steuben and Laura Ashley is enough to evoke the concept of quality.

When an art director is given the opportunity to design a catalog for one of these famous clients, he's like a kid in a cookie factory. No copywriters with their yards of type to worry about. No need for insert photos, callouts, banners or keys. He can give free rein to his imagination, with but a singular command from on high: Make it memorable.

When Pluzynski/Associates was commissioned by Laura Ashley to produce the Spring 1989 catalog, there must have been a celebration amongst the talented inhabitants of Pluzynski's bull pen. And just look at what this team came up with.

Paper stock: The cover is of 20 point Carolina C1S which has been printed and embossed with a three dimensional lizard texture.

LAURA ASHLEY—Spring 1989
Pluzynski/Associates, *Agency*

The body stock is Vintage Gloss of 80 lb. cover weight. The tissue flyleaves are 14 lb. Vellum with an overall pattern printed using translucent UV inks to increase opacity.

Bindery: Scored, perfect bound, two-hole punched and then hand tied using black laid line complete with tassels.

Presswork: 2-color matte black backgrounds with 4-color halftones using top quality, high varnish inks.

Sweet Pea

Available in sheets, pillowcases, comforter, pillow sham,
bedskirt, draperies, duvet cover and decorative pillows
(neckroll, square, breakfast)
50% Kodel® polyester/50% combed cotton
color: multi

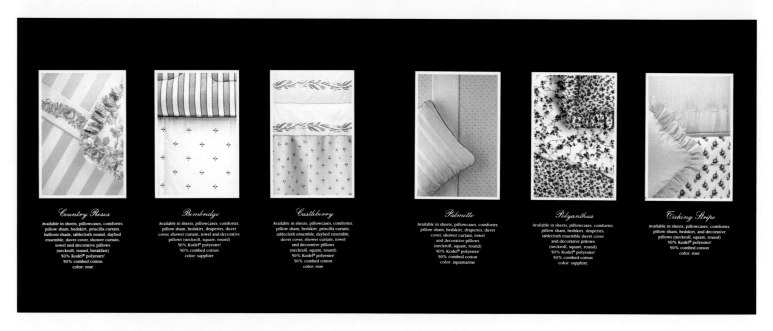

Country Roses

Available in sheets, pillowcases, comforter,
pillow sham, bedskirt, priscilla curtain,
balloon shade, tablecloth round, daybed
ensemble, duvet cover, shower curtain,
towel and decorative pillows
(neckroll, round, breakfast)
50% Kodel® polyester/
50% combed cotton
color: rose

Bembridge

Available in sheets, pillowcases, comforter,
pillow sham, bedskirt, draperies, duvet
cover, shower curtain, towel and decorative
pillows (neckroll, square, round)
50% Kodel® polyester/
50% combed cotton
color: sapphire

Castleberry

Available in sheets, pillowcases, comforter,
pillow sham, bedskirt, priscilla curtain,
tablecloth ensemble, daybed ensemble,
duvet cover, shower curtain, towel
and decorative pillows
(neckroll, square, round)
50% Kodel® polyester/
50% combed cotton
color: rose

Palmetto

Available in sheets, pillowcases, comforter,
pillow sham, bedskirt, draperies, duvet
cover, shower curtain, towel
and decorative pillows
(neckroll, square, round)
50% Kodel® polyester/
50% combed cotton
color: aquamarine

Polyanthus

Available in sheets, pillowcases, comforter,
pillow sham, bedskirt, draperies,
tablecloth ensemble duvet cover
and decorative pillows
(neckroll, square, round)
50% Kodel® polyester/
50% combed cotton
color: sapphire

Ticking Stripe

Available in sheets, pillowcases, comforter,
pillow sham, bedskirt, and decorative
pillows (neckroll, square, round)
50% Kodel® polyester/
50% combed cotton
color: rose

Laura Ashley doesn't have to shout. Books have been published telling her story. The patterns of the House of Laura Ashley are famous for their originality and livability. The LA story has been told and retold in other essays and articles authored by their own firm and by others.

The folks at Laura Ashley still believe in use of the written word to remind old customers and to inform the new. But more often than not, their customers are treated to a catalog such as this: a masterpiece of understated, virtually wordless elegance. What a remarkable alternative this is to the traditional catalog. Unfortunately, it's an option reserved for the enviable few who have earned the privilege that comes with fame.

WINN POSTERS

Larry Winn, founder of Winn Corporation, is a natural born promoter. Anyone who can make the leap from a small out-of-the-way poster shop in a poor location (in Seattle, Washington) to a nationally known publisher and printer of fine art and poster reproductions in 10 years—is a promoter.

Publishing and distributing art reproductions is a difficult, competitive, slow-pay, problem-ridden business. On the other hand, the markups (gross margins) are other-worldly. And therein lies the incentive! *If* you can winnow out the chaff and build a loyal group of reasonably affluent (and ethical) customers among art retailers and decorators, the rewards are extraordinary.

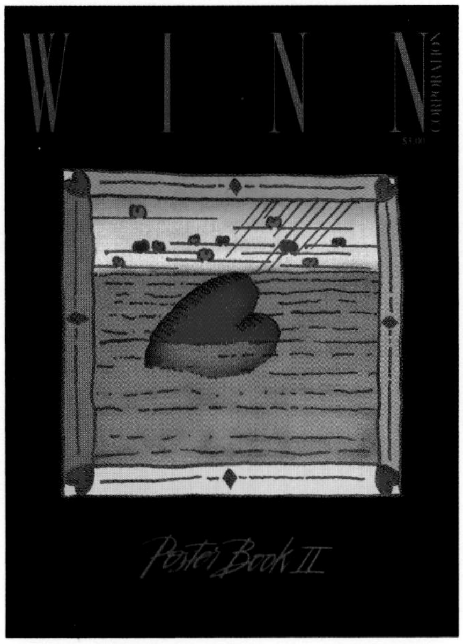

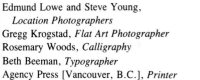

WINN POSTERS—Poster Book II
Larry Winn, *President*
Pamela Palnick, *Vice President, Marketing/ Creative Director and Copy Chief*
Dwight McCabe, *Direct Marketing Manager*
Patrick Howe, *Art Director*
Ellen Bollard, *Assistant Art Director*
Ned Levensohn, *Copywriter*
Edmund Lowe and Steve Young, *Location Photographers*
Gregg Krogstad, *Flat Art Photographer*
Rosemary Woods, *Calligraphy*
Beth Beeman, *Typographer*
Agency Press [Vancouver, B.C.], *Printer*
Graphic Color [Eugene, OR], *Color Separator*

A number of clues in Winn's Poster Book II catalog help us to understand how Larry Winn has succeeded where fainter hearts have floundered. Most of his special touches are centered around an obvious consideration for his customers.

The inside front cover and pages 46-48 demonstrate a user-friendly approach to indices. Calligraphy by Rosemary Woods graces the primary index, which is arranged, quite logically, by category. There is a second, three-page index set in (prox.) 5-½ point type in the center of the catalog. This detailed listing of about 650 images is conveniently contiguous to the order form. Here, sortation is by artist, and includes titles, sizes and cross-references to pages and sections where the images may be seen. In combination, these two indices serve all of Winn's customers very well.

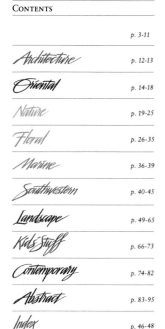

Dear Customer,

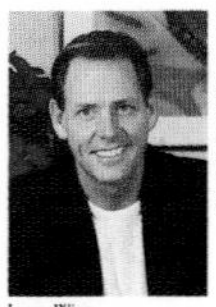
Gregg Krogstad Photography
Larry Winn

Ten years ago I started in this business with a tiny poster shop in a terrible location. At the time I had no idea Winn would grow to become the national leader in fine art publishing. I just wanted to sell some posters.

Despite the drawbacks, that small shop became a success. My customers knew they could trust me to steer them clear of passing fads with a solid, no-nonsense selection of quality images for both home and commercial display. They appreciated the excellent framing we offered, the way I stood behind everything we sold. And they told their friends.

To this day posters remain my first love. That's why I'm pleased to introduce this exciting new 1986 Winn Poster Book. Thanks to you—your orders, comments, and suggestions—we've put together what I feel is an even stronger collection than our first poster catalog.

All of us here put in long, thoughtful, truly enjoyable hours sorting through thousands of posters in search of the best. The result is a broad, carefully chosen collection that reflects the solid aesthetic sensibility you've come to expect from Winn; a thorough understanding of design; and a commitment to imagery that will stand the test of time.

The important lessons I learned in that small poster shop continue to guide us today. We know you appreciate fast, full delivery of your orders. And you like the way our customer service people gladly go the extra mile to meet the special needs of your business.

The table of contents at right will help you find specific areas of interest, but I encourage you to look carefully through the entire collection. I think you'll have as much fun as we did discovering new creative possibilities.

We're committed to being the best in the poster business. Keep your eyes open for special new Winn poster releases in the upcoming year: new artists, new imagery, diptychs, triptychs, oversized posters. If you'd like to be part of this, I'd welcome your comments and suggestions on the enclosed card.

Thanks again for your support.

Sincerely,

Larry Winn

Larry Winn

P.S. We make a special effort to keep a full inventory so we can fill your complete order promptly. In fact, most orders of unframed pieces are on their way to you within 24 hours. Be sure to see the order form for information on overnight delivery, expert framing, and other Winn catalogs.

2

CONTENTS

Our thanks to The Four Seasons Olympic Hotel (p. 3), Bank and Office Interiors (p. 49 and p. 83), the Design Concern (accessories, p. 83), and Masins Furniture and Interiors (p. 11, 19 and 26), for access to their beautiful interiors used in our location photography.

Dimensions for framed and unframed posters are given in this catalog in inches, to the nearest inch, width before height.

Flat art photography by Gregg Krogstad, location photography by Edmund Lowe and Steve Young (p. 14, 40 and 66).

Prices subject to change without notice.

Printed in Canada.

On the Front Cover: D.G. Smith, **Winn Heart**, Original lithograph poster. For more information, see page 74.

Index

Artist	Code	Title	Section	** Frame Size	Page
A					
Adams, Mark	AMP-200-2200	Garden Rose	Floral	A3, A4*	29
Adams, Mark	AMP-202-2200	Green Footed Tumbler	Contemporary	A3	80
Adams, Mark	AMP-201-2200	Inlet	Marine	A4, A5*	36
Alvarez, Elba	AEP-100-2200	Atlas Galleries	Abstract	A4	88
Alvarez, Elba	AEP-103ABC-2200	Aurora ABC (Triptych)	Abstract	A4 ea.	89
Alvarez, Elba	AEP-104ABC-2200	Paradiso ABC (Triptych)	Abstract	A4 ea.	87
Alvarez, Elba	AEP-101-2200	Platform Action	Abstract	A4	89
Alvarez, Elba	AEP-102ABC-2200	Refraction ABC (Triptych)	Abstract	A4 ea.	88
Arai, A.K.	AAP-303-2200	Arcade	Architecture	A4	13
Arai, A.K.	AAP-302-2200	Department Store	Architecture	A4	13
Arai, A.K.	AAP-300-2200	Masonic Temple	Architecture	A6	13
Arai, A.K.	AAP-304-2200	Romanesque Cloister	Architecture	A4	13
Arai, A.K.	AAP-301-2200	Villa For A Painter	Architecture	A5	12
Audubon, J. J.	AJP-100-2200	Carolina Parakeet	Nature	A4	25
Avery, Milton	AMP-101-2200	The Conversation	Contemporary	A6	82
B					
Barton, Dawna	BDP-101-2200	Dinner Call	Nature	A4	23
Barton, Dawna	BDP-102-2200	Geraniums	Floral	A4	29
Barton, Dawna	BDP-100-2200	Teddy Bear Parade	Kids Stuff	A4	72
Beck, Kimberly	BKP-300-2200	Birds	Nature	A3	23
Billout, Guy	BGP-201-2200	Bell Street Terminal	Marine	A3	39
Buffett, William	BWP-301-2200	Bayview	Tropical	A4	11
Buffett, William	BWP-302-2200	California Foothills	Tropical, Landscape	A2	10& 57
Buffett, William	BWP-303-2200	California Orange Grove	Tropical, Landscape	A2	10& 57
Buffett, William	BWP-300-2200	Sunset	Tropical	A4	11
Bukovnik, Gary	BGP-108-2200	California Still Life I	Floral	A5	35
Bukovnik, Gary	BGP-109-2200	Japanese Magnolia	Floral	A6	35
Bukovnik, Gary	BGP-100-2200	Tiger Lilies	Floral	A4	34
Bullas, Will	BWP-200-2200	Recruit	Kids' Stuff	A4	71
Burke, Jane M.	BJP-102-2200	Bearly Ballet	Kids' Stuff	A3	73
Burke, Jane M.	BJP-103-2200	Bunny Hop	Kids' Stuff	A3	71
Burke, Jane M.	BJP-100-2200	Out For A Waddle	Kids' Stuff	A3	73
Burke, Jane M.	BJP-101-2200	The Forebears	Kids' Stuff	A3	73
Byrd, Eddie	BEP-101-2200	Fruit	Contemporary	A3	80
Byrd, Eddie	BEP-100-2200	Spice Poster	Contemporary	A3	80
Byrd, James	BJP-503-2200	ADI Gallery	Abstract	A4	95
Byrd, James	BJP-501-2200	Pink Wedge	Abstract	A4	95
Byrd, James	BJP-502-2200	Plum Punch	Abstract	A4	95
Byrd, James	BJP-500-2200	Ruby Blue	Abstract	A5	95
C					
Camp, Robin E.	CRP-201-2200	All Wound Up	Kids' Stuff	A4	70
Carlson, Nancy	CNP-104-2200	Each Day Take Time To Relax	Kids' Stuff	A2	68
Carlson, Nancy	CNP-106-2200	Exercise	Kids' Stuff	A2	68
Carlson, Nancy	CNP-107-2200	Fat Cat	Kids' Stuff	A2	68
Carlson, Nancy	CNP-100-2200	Good Morning	Kids' Stuff	A3	69
Carlson, Nancy	CNP-101-2200	Good Night	Kids' Stuff	A3	69
Carlson, Nancy	CNP-105-2200	Gymboree	Kids' Stuff	A3	69
Carlson, Nancy	CNP-102-2200	It's OK To Be You	Kids' Stuff	A2	69
Carlson, Nancy	CNP-103-2200	The Real Food Co.	Kids' Stuff	A2	69
Champlong, G.	CGP-200-2200	Bon Voyage	Marine	A3	39
Chatham, Russell	CRP-102-2200	Cokedale Ridge	Landscape	A3	50
Chatham, Russell	CRP-103-2200	Evening Marsh	Landscape	A3	50
Chatham, Russell	CRP-159-2200	Maxwell Gallery	Landscape	A3	49
Chatham, Russell	CRP-105-2200	Ranch At Three Forks	Landscape	A3	50
Chatham, Russell	CRP-100-2200	Stone Press Gallery	Landscape	A4	50
Chatham, Russell	CRP-104-2200	Valley Of The Moon	Landscape	A3	50
Chihuly, Dale	CDP-207-2200	Charles Cowles Gallery	Contemporary	A4	78
Chihuly, Dale	CDP-209-2200	Decade Of Glass	Contemporary	A4	77
Chihuly, Dale	CDP-205-2200	Institute Of American Indian Art	Contemporary	A4	78
Chihuly, Dale	CDP-204-2200	Philadelphia Museum Of Art	Contemporary	A4	77
Chihuly, Dale	CDP-203-2200	Renwick Gallery	Contemporary	A4	78
Chihuly, Dale	CDP-200-2200	St. Louis Art Museum	Contemporary	A4	77
Chihuly, Dale	CDP-201-2200	Tucson Museum Of Art	Contemporary	A4	78

46

Artist	Code	Title	Section	** Frame Size	Page
Chihuly, Dale	CDP-202-2200	Umelecko/ Prumyslove Museum	Contemporary	A4	78
Comess, Herb	CHP-200-2200	Music Box	Contemporary	A4	74
Crane, Jean	CJP-506-2200	Art Expo '85	Floral	A4	27
Crane, Jean	CJP-508-2200	Art Expo II	Floral	A3	26
Crane, Jean	CJP-509-2200	Bouquet	Floral	A3	27
Crane, Jean	CJP-500-2200	Channel 10	Floral	A4	27
Crane, Jean	CJP-507-2200	Cyclamen	Floral	A4	26
Crane, Jean	CJP-501-2200	Golden Lilies	Floral	A4	26
Crane, Jean	CJP-502-2200	Magnolia	Floral	A4	26
Crane, Jean	CJP-505-2200	Tulips In Round Vase	Floral	A4	27
Crane, Jean	CJP-503-2200	White Lilies	Floral	A4	27
Crane, Jean	CJP-504-2200	Yellow Peonies	Floral	A4	26
Currier, M. A.	CMP-100-2200	Plums	Contemporary	A5	81
D					
Davis, Susan	DSP-400-2200	Wolf Trap	Kids' Stuff	A5	68
DeWit, Deborah	DDP-200-2200	Autumn At Balbithan	Contemporary	A4	81
DeWit, Deborah	DDP-203-2200	Kirsty's Drive	Landscape	A4	54
DeWit, Deborah	DDP-205-2200	Lake Albert	Landscape	A4	54
DeWit, Deborah	DDP-202-2200	Luna	Landscape	A4	54
DeWit, Deborah	DDP-204-2200	Palace Of Fine Arts	Landscape	A4	54
DeWit, Deborah	DDP-201-2200	Wave	Marine	A4	38
Dine, Jim	DJP-400-2200	Cardinal	Contemporary	A5	76
Dixon, Maynard	DMP-100-2200	Earth Knower	Southwest	A4	43
Dunwell, Steve	DSP-300-2200	Mystic	Marine	A4	38
E					
Elias, Sheila	ESP-100-2200	Pompidou Trois	Abstract	A4	94
Ellis, Ray	ERP-200-2200	Reflections	Marine	A3	39
Elmer, Margaret	EM-101-2200	Chicken	Kids' Stuff	A2	67
Elmer, Margaret	EM-105-2200	Circus I	Kids' Stuff	A3	66
Elmer, Margaret	EM-106-2200	Circus II	Kids' Stuff	A3, A4*	67
Elmer, Margaret	EM-107-2200	Circus III	Kids' Stuff	A3, A4*	67
Elmer, Margaret	EM-108-2200	Circus IV	Kids' Stuff	A3, A4*	67
Elmer, Margaret	EM-109-2200	Circus V	Kids' Stuff	A3	66
Elmer, Margaret	EM-104-2200	Goat	Kids' Stuff	A2	67
Elmer, Margaret	EM-112-2200	Roll	Kids' Stuff	A2	67
Elmer, Margaret	EM-100-2200	Sheep	Kids' Stuff	A2	67
F					
Feddersen, Joe	FJP-109-2200	N.Y. Art Expo '85	Abstract	A4	92
Fong, Alex	FAP-202-2200	Fantasy Flight I	Nature	A4	22
Fong, Alex	FAP-203-2200	Fantasy Flight II	Nature	A4	22
Fong, Alex	FAP-200-2200	Restful Moment	Nature	A3	22
Fong, Alex	FAP-201-2200	Wings Of Love	Nature	A4	22
Foott, Jeff	FJP-400-2200	Sea Otter	Kids' Stuff	A3	70
G					
Gilbert, Dan	GDP-300-2200	African Hall	Kids' Stuff	A4	70
Girvin, Tim	GJP-100-2200	Gelato	Contemporary	A2	80
Goad, Dan	GZP-102-2200	American Egrets	Nature	A3	21
Goad, Dan	GZP-100-2200	Blue Heron	Nature	A3	20
Goad, Dan	GZP-104-2200	Gray Herons	Nature	A3	21
Goad, Dan	GZP-133-2200	L.A. Art Expo 1985	Nature	A4	20
Goad, Dan	GZP-107-2200	Louisiana Herons	Nature	A3	20
Goad, Dan	GZP-180-2200	N.Y. Art Expo '86	Nature	A4	21
Goad, Dan	GZP-108-2200	Reddish Egrets	Nature	A3	21
Goad, Dan	GZP-106-2200	Snowy Egrets	Nature	A3	21
Goad, Dan	GZP-111-2200	Texas Art Expo '84	Nature	A4	20
Goad, Dan	GZP-103-2200	White Pelican	Nature	A3	21
Goad, Dan	GZP-178-2200	Winn Blue Heron	Nature	A4, A3*	19
Goad, Dan	GZP-177-2200	Winn Snowy Egret	Nature	A4	20
Goad, Dan	GZP-179-2200	Winn Two Blue Herons	Nature	A4, A3*	19
Goad, Dan	GZP-176-2200	Winn Two Reddish Egrets	Nature	A4	20
Goode, Frederick	GFP-100-2200	Japanese Suite	Oriental	A3, A4*	14
Gray, Larry	GLP-100-2200	California Sunset	Landscape	A4	58
Grigg, Carol	GCP-105-2200	Daughters Of The Moon	Southwest	A4	44
Grigg, Carol	GCP-106-2200	Earth Healer	Southwest	A4	44
Grigg, Carol	GCP-104ABC-2200	Heron Dance ABC (Triptych)	Southwest	A3 ea.	45
Grigg, Carol	GCP-101AB-2200	Heronry AB (Diptych)	Southwest	A4 ea.	45
Grigg, Carol	GCP-103-2200	Out Of The White Road	Southwest	A4	44

*Deluxe framing
**See "Acrylic Costs" on Order Form (pg. OF2) for explanation of A codes.

Space is necessarily limited in this catalog by the desire to display as many images as possible. Nevertheless, the promoter in Mr. Winn knows the value of making a sales point. Room sets are used to delineate chapters and for graphics that require props and sets to establish scale and mood. Sidebars are used extensively: in this case to discuss the Japanese Suite on one page, and on the right, to promote overnight delivery.

Eleven images might a crowd make, if Art Director Patrick Howe were less talented. Grey (not black) hairline rules contain the posters and prints with white borders. Airy white space on every page gives a spacious, uncluttered sensation, where other AD's might have dollied in on the merchandise to get more detail. The tiny type would be unacceptable in most consumer catalogs, but we're selling art here—to artists. Clunky, 9-point Times Roman would do nothing but get in the way.

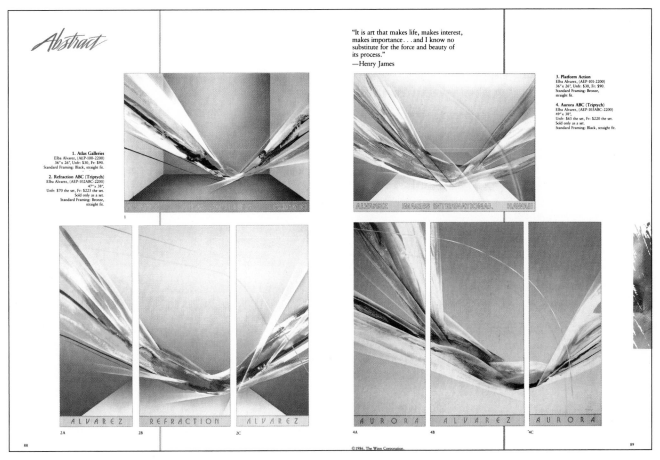

Abstract

"It is art that makes life, makes interest, makes importance . . . and I know no substitute for the force and beauty of its process."
—Henry James

1. Atlas Galleries
Elba Alvarez, (AEP-100-2200)
36" x 26", Unfr: $30, Fr: $90.
Standard Framing: Black, straight fit.

2. Refraction ABC (Triptych)
Elba Alvarez, (AEP-102ABC-2200)
47" x 38".
Unfr: $70 the set, Fr: $225 the set.
Sold only as a set.
Standard Framing: Bronze, straight fit.

3. Platform Action
Elba Alvarez, (AEP-101-2200)
36" x 26", Unfr: $30, Fr: $90.
Standard Framing: Bronze, straight fit.

4. Aurora ABC (Triptych)
Elba Alvarez, (AEP-103ABC-2200)
49" x 38".
Unfr: $65 the set, Fr: $220 the set.
Sold only as a set.
Standard Framing: Black, straight fit.

©1986, The Winn Corporation.

Big city decorators and art lovers have enjoyed the drama and scale of the triptych artform for years. In many circumstances, these three-panel, screen-inspired works of art can establish the mood of a room or entire apartment. They also make a definitive statement about the artistic taste of the owner. Winn has not been unaware of this trend, and some outstanding examples are seen in all their catalogs.

The Winn catalog we've just seen is the 96-page master catalog. It won the ACA Gold Award, top honors, in the Wholesale — Single Product Line category. The Poster Book II Supplement is an off-season catalog of 24 pages. It started life with modest expectations, but blossomed into a roaring success, including the prestigious Gold Echo Award for Order Generation from the Direct Marketing Association.

The marketing results were truly outstanding. Compare, if you will, the reasonable assumptions established as objectives and the final results.

Objectives: New product introduction, increase poster sales by 50% over successful control (Poster Book I Supplement). Penetrate house non-buyer list by a minimum of 5%. Increase average unit of sale through push on framing. Lift sales through slow summer season with enclosed monthly savings coupons.

Results:

Increase over successful control book:

Sales	*Up 209%*
Units sold	*Up 159%*
Average unit sale	*Up 19%*
Sales per page	*65% Increase*
Penetration of house non-buyers	*6% of sales*
New customers	*7% of sales*
Profitability (including G&A)	*40% Net Profit*
Seasonal effect	*20% Incremental*

Was this spectacular performance a result of the coupons? The layouts? The copy? The right product? Perhaps, but my guess is that it came from a combination of all of the above, PLUS a reputation for extraordinary fulfillment. All of Larry Winn's catalogs carry occasional sidebars quoting letters he has received from customers attesting to his fine customer service. An example:

Even though I am a small account, I feel I am your most important one. At least that's the way I was treated by your local representative.

Thanks to his time and efforts I was awarded a contract that was very important to me. Not only is your artwork of consistent high quality—so is your service.

These are the reasons I turn to Winn first.

Paula Shaffer
Art Consultant
Metairie, LA

Other *signed* letters mention the selection, the service and the well thought-out organization of the catalog. Customer loyalty is earned, not sold.

Poster Book II Supplement

Pamela Palnick, *Vice President, Marketing Director, Direct Marketing Manager and Copywriter*

Ellen Bollard, *Art Director*

Rachel Ruud, *Marketing Assistant*

Terry Pagos, *Studio Photographer*

Cary Cartmill, *Flat Art Photographer*

Rosemary Woods, *Calligraphy*

Beth Beeman and Wizywig, *Typographers*

Agency Press, *Printing*

Zenith Graphics [Vancouver, B.C.], *Color Separator*

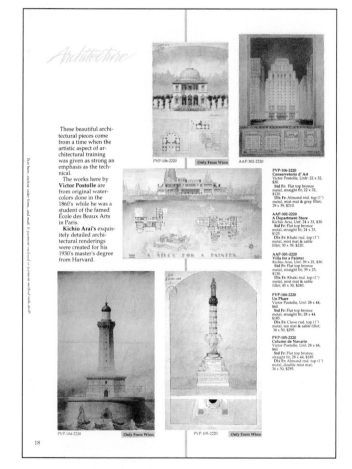

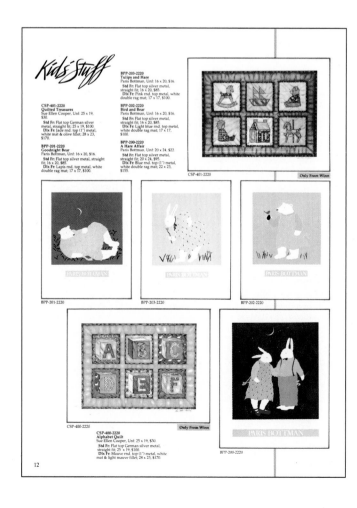

Winn's offerings are as variegated as his customers. Gentle landscapes are followed by thought-evoking abstract art. ''Kids' Stuff'' mingles with architectural posters. Commercial decorators find images for skyscraper lobbies. Mom and Pop shops in country villages order for their local constituents.

Winn now owns its own atelier and commissions reproductions from other fine printers. Posters are still their volume product. But, in other catalogs, they now present limited editions and unique works by famous artists. Larry Winn has indeed proven he is a promoter—in the sense of graduating from one plateau to another, and higher, level. Congratulations to Larry Winn for his double award win.

V
NICHE MARKETING

"Niche Marketing" is one of the newer buzzwords in salons frequented by the advertising fraternity. Niche is defined as: *a place or position suitable or appropriate for a person or thing: 'to find one's niche in the business world.'* Direct marketers have another manner of expressing the same concept. In their own circles they use the term 'rifle' (as opposed to 'buckshot')—direct mail (versus mass media).

Specialist merchants and manufacturers have their own way of expressing the idea. "Stick to your own knitting" (STYOK), or "Doing what one does best" (DWODB) ring a little more true to the entrepreneur and the product engineer than does the latest Madison Avenue jargon. No matter the terms used, niche catalogs are hot. Yes, there's still plenty of room for larger catalogs with broad-ranging merchandise selections; but it's tough out there for the big guys. Many catalog dinosaurs are already history, others are perilously close to the edge of extinction.

MBA's and PHD's at the large, multi-line catalog houses and retail store chains are constantly tweaking databases to find sub-segments around which to build new store divisions and catalog programs. They're using all the latest computer technology to max out their merchandise mix and flow. Compelled by immutable market forces and changing buying habits, the big merchantile organizations are finally taking a hard look at niche markets. Meanwhile, the existing STYOK's and DWODB's are ahead of the game and enjoying exponential sales gains.

How come? What is the secret that makes these narrow-focus catalogs such viable marketing tools? There is, of course, no single factor, no magic elixir, but there are a few macro ingredients that seem to apply universally to the group.

- *Many STYOK and DWODB catalogs have a fairly limited assortment of goods to offer. This would not do in a traditional retail store, where old merchandise rapidly becomes stale. OTC retail inventory must be refreshed frequently, lest customers become bored, and stop dropping by. Catalogers can live with customers who buy only or twice a year.*
- *Neighborhoods change, sometimes in just a matter of a few years. It's not easy for a store owner to pick up and move. But catalogs can easily follow customers to their new homes.*

- *Many of today's older, larger catalog houses carry a heavy burden of bureaucracy and an OTC (Over-The-Counter) mentality. 'Movement' and 'change' are treated as pejorative words in such a climate.*
- *Big catalogs require long merchandising and production schedules. Some merchandise buying lead-times can be out 9 to 12 months or more. Smaller, more focused catalogs can be out of the starting blocks in a fraction of the time.*
- *Specialized products are sometimes very hard to find. STOYK'S are product specialists, and what's more, their sales/service staff should be able to answer your questions.*
- *At retail, low-traffic merchandise needs high-density populations. In mail order, the world is your neighborhood. It costs no more to mail a catalog to Alaska than it does to mail one to your buddy on the next block.*
- *STYOK's and DWODB's carry more inventory depth and breadth in their particular category than is viable for a store. It is almost impossible for any multi-departmental retailer to stock all the styles and all the SKU's for all classifications in the store. True, inventory turns are just as important to a mail order merchant as they are to the retailer. But with the whole wide mail order world as your oyster, a large and multifaceted customer-base can absorb a broad spectrum of styles and SKU's.*

In the following pages, we're going to enjoy a look at a few STYOK's and DWODB's and their catalogs. Their successes are based on: their reputations, their presentations, and their ability to locate prospects and customers who need and want what they have to offer. Respectability, responsibility, knowledge, fairness, pride and the desire to serve one's customers well—these are the images and elements common to all the catalogs gathered in this select group of niche marketers.

These exemplary publications tell stories and provide information—they don't just sell items. A rapport is established with the reader. Finer points are explained in depth. A little history here, an informal picture of the craftsmen there. Nice touches that provide the customer with a sense of security. What's more, they form the intellectual basis, the logical excuse, to pay just a little bit more to deal with an expert—and get the best there is.

ALMOND PLAZA

Food catalogs are even more fun to produce than they are to read. Everybody loves the stuff, and that emotion is usually reflected in the final printed product. You can just imagine, for instance, the scene in the photographer's studio—after the shooting is done. . .

The Almond Plaza Holiday Celebration catalog lets us in on the fun. Nuts, cookies and candy fall all over each other. Starting with the cornucopia-like Front Cover, and continuing without letup throughout the whole catalog, there's a feeling of organized, gormandized bedlam. No Mondrian layouts or grid patterns here. Instead, the shape and flow of the merchandise seems to have directed the layout. Slices of cake and carefully broken cookies subtly demonstrate texture and content. All the while, waterfalls of candies, and cans overflowing with nuts imply quantities beyond our wildest dreams. The relatively short copy maintains the same upbeat dynamic. Here's a sample of their absolutely irresistible copy:

LINN'S EXTRAORDINARY FRUIT PRESERVES

Great gifts for anyone who lives outside the Sunshine state. Our Raspberry-Rhubarb, Kiwifruit and Olallieberry jams are made in California—practically next door to the fields in which the fruits are grown. The fruits are gathered, cooked in small batches with only natural sugar flavoring and no preservatives, watched carefully and protected to preserve the large fruit chunks. Voila! A jam that tastes amazingly like the fruit fresh from the vine!

ALMOND PLAZA—Holiday Celebration 1987
Dann Bryant, *Catalog Director*
Dave Williamson, *Creative Director*
Chris Babcock, *Art Director*
Alan Greene, *Merchandiser*
Diane Dirkx, *Copywriter*
Kay Riley, *Production Manager*
Dave Williamson & Associates, *Agency*
Karl Parry, *Photographer*
Alden Press [Elk Grove Village, IL], *Printer, on 60# Somerset for cover and text*
Tru Color [W. Hollywood, FL], *Color Separator*

The California Almond Growers Exchange (an agricultural cooperative) founded Almond Plaza in 1949. The catalog, as one might expect, features almonds; not exclusively, but almost. We could find only 2 spreads out of 24 in this catalog that did not proffer almonds in one form or another. The assortment of nut-based candies on this spread is just for starters. . .

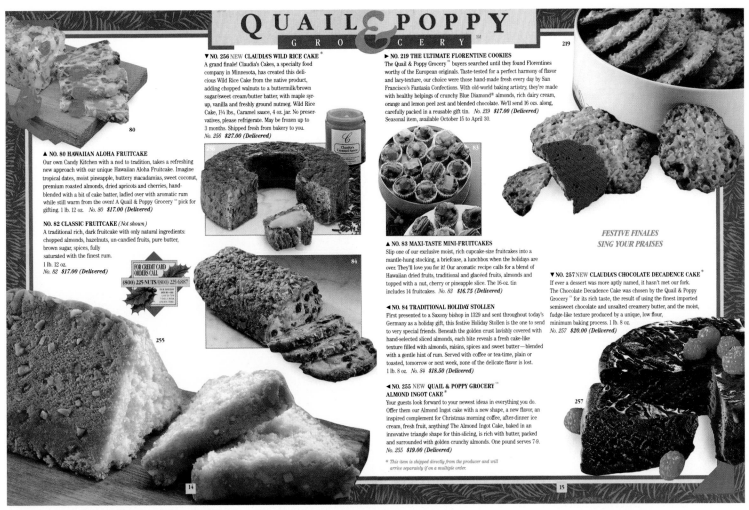

QUAIL & POPPY
G R O C E R Y

▼ NO. 256 NEW CLAUDIA'S WILD RICE CAKE *
A grand finale! Claudia's Cakes, a specialty food company in Minnesota, has created this delicious Wild Rice Cake from the native product, adding chopped walnuts to a buttermilk/brown sugar/sweet cream/butter batter, with maple syrup, vanilla and freshly ground nutmeg. Wild Rice Cake, 1¼ lbs., Caramel sauce, 4 oz. jar. No preservatives, please refrigerate. May be frozen up to 3 months. Shipped fresh from bakery to you.
No. 256 *$27.00 (Delivered)*

► NO. 219 THE ULTIMATE FLORENTINE COOKIES
The Quail & Poppy Grocery ™ buyers searched until they found Florentines worthy of the European originals. Taste-tested for a perfect harmony of flavor and lacy-texture, our choice were those hand-made fresh every day by San Francisco's Fantasia Confections. With old-world baking artistry, they're made with healthy helpings of crunchy Blue Diamond® almonds, rich dairy cream, orange and lemon peel zest and blended chocolate. We'll send 16 ozs. along, carefully packed in a reusable gift tin. No. 219 *$17.00 (Delivered)* Seasonal item, available October 15 to April 30.

▲ NO. 80 HAWAIIAN ALOHA FRUITCAKE
Our own Candy Kitchen with a nod to tradition, takes a refreshing new approach with our unique Hawaiian Aloha Fruitcake. Imagine tropical dates, moist pineapple, buttery macadamias, sweet coconut, premium roasted almonds, dried apricots and cherries, hand-blended with a bit of cake batter, ladled over with aromatic rum while still warm from the oven! A Quail & Poppy Grocery ™ pick for gifting. 1 lb. 12 oz. No. 80 *$17.00 (Delivered)*

NO. 82 CLASSIC FRUITCAKE *(Not shown)*
A traditional rich, dark fruitcake with only natural ingredients: chopped almonds, hazelnuts, un-candied fruits, pure butter, brown sugar, spices, fully saturated with the finest rum.
1 lb. 12 oz.
No. 82 *$17.00 (Delivered)*

FOR CREDIT CARD
ORDERS CALL
(800) 225-NUTS/(800) 225-6887

▲ NO. 83 MAXI-TASTE MINI-FRUITCAKES
Slip one of our exclusive moist, rich cupcake-size fruitcakes into a mantle-hung stocking, a briefcase, a lunchbox when the holidays are over. They'll love you for it! Our aromatic recipe calls for a blend of Hawaiian dried fruits, traditional and glacéed fruits, almonds and topped with a nut, cherry or pineapple slice. The 16-oz. tin includes 14 fruitcakes. No. 83 *$16.75 (Delivered)*

◄ NO. 84 TRADITIONAL HOLIDAY STOLLEN
First presented to a Saxony bishop in 1329 and sent throughout today's Germany as a holiday gift, this festive Holiday Stollen is the one to send to very special friends. Beneath the golden crust lavishly covered with hand-selected sliced almonds, each bite reveals a fresh cake-like texture filled with almonds, raisins, spices and sweet butter—blended with a gentle hint of rum. Served with coffee or tea-time, plain or toasted, tomorrow or next week, none of the delicate flavor is lost.
1 lb. 8 oz. No. 84 *$18.50 (Delivered)*

◄ NO. 255 NEW QUAIL & POPPY GROCERY ™ ALMOND INGOT CAKE *
Your guests look forward to your newest ideas in everything you do. Offer them our Almond Ingot cake with a new shape, a new flavor, an inspired complement for Christmas morning coffee, after-dinner ice cream, fresh fruit, anything! The Almond Ingot Cake, baked in an innovative triangle shape for thin-slicing, is rich with butter, packed and surrounded with golden crunchy almonds. One pound serves 7-9.
No. 255 *$19.00 (Delivered)*

FESTIVE FINALES
SING YOUR PRAISES

▼ NO. 257 NEW CLAUDIA'S CHOCOLATE DECADENCE CAKE *
If ever a dessert was more aptly named, it hasn't met our fork. The Chocolate Decadence Cake was chosen by the Quail & Poppy Grocery ™ for its rich taste, the result of using the finest imported semisweet chocolate and unsalted creamery butter, and the moist, fudge-like texture produced by a unique, low flour, minimum baking process. 1 lb. 8 oz.
No. 257 *$20.00 (Delivered)*

* This item is shipped directly from the producer and will arrive separately if on a multiple order.

No less than eight different baked products tempt almond lovers on this lively spread. Almost behind the scenes, a small credit-card-cum-telephone bug is decked with holly to deliver the sales/service message. Little marketing touches such as these prove that this bunch of almond farmers hasn't been in the mail order business for 40 years without learning a few tricks of the trade. Here again, the copy does an outstanding selling job in just a few, well chosen words.

One of the few spreads-without-nuts presents smoked turkey, a glazed and smoked ham, and an apple-smoked beef tenderloin. These photos and the resulting ink-on-paper are just about the best we have ever seen—even in the catalogs of full-time meat purveyors. [At $32 a pound, we will, regretfully, have to make do with this purely visual enjoyment of the smoked tenderloin!]

QUAIL & POPPY
G R O C E R Y

▼ NO. 320 & 321 HONEY CURED SMOKED TURKEY *
We've chosen the juiciest, most succulent smoked turkeys from Cavanaugh Lakeview Farms for you to serve your family and friends. Only young tender birds are treated with a special honey cured smoking process that uses natural juices to keep them extra-moist. Expect it to arrive fully-cooked and ready to enjoy as is or heated.
No. 320 9-10 lbs. *$48.00 (Delivered)*
No. 321 11-12 lbs. *$54.00 (Delivered)*

► NO. 322 SMOKED TURKEY BREAST *
Only the finest broad-breasted birds are chosen and shipped because they retain their own special natural-juice during the smoking process. You can be assured of moist, tender honey-cured white meat ready to slice thin for elegant serving or thick for sandwiches.
No. 322 5-6 lbs. *$43.00 (Delivered)*

FOR CREDIT CARD
ORDERS CALL
(800) 225-NUTS/(800) 225-6887

▼ NO. 323 & 324 GLAZED SMOKED WHOLE HAM *
The Quail & Poppy ™ grocers know that ease and entertaining go hand-in-hand. Our fully cooked ham arrives with a shimmering glaze of honey and maple sugar, spiral-cut around and down the center bone. Two easy cuts and you're ready to serve the most juicy, moist and flavorful ham we've found!
No. 323 6-7 lbs. (½ ham) *$47.00 (Delivered)*
No. 324 10-12 lbs. *$70.00 (Delivered)*

► NO. 337 & 338 APPLE-SMOKED BEEF TENDERLOIN *
The subtle tang of apples, natural herbs and spices mingles with the vigorous taste of beef for an unforgettable flavor worthy of any celebration. With this Beef Tenderloin there is no waste, and unfortunately, probably no leftovers! Simply reheat or serve cold.
No. 337 Serves 3-5, 20 oz. *$40.00 (Delivered)*
No. 338 Serves 6-8, 2 lbs. *$55.00 (Delivered)*

* This item is shipped directly from the producer and will arrive separately if on a multiple order.

additional shipping charge during warmer months. Allow 2 to 4 weeks for delivery. All meats are shipped frozen, via ground UPS. Available as a mail order item only. Additional charge for air shipment to Alaska and Hawaii. Please call for more information.

These spreads are outstanding examples of designers Dave Williamson and Chris Babcock's ability to indulge the reader's continuing interest—even while presenting these spreads of very similar merchandise. All the food is appetizing, but the eye never stalls out on any one photograph. The more a reader looks at a page, the more he is aware of other products, other copy points and other subliminal messages. That's Layout!

The artist's trick of highlighting areas of greatest note and allowing less important elements (e.g., the cans, on page 26) to remain more or less in shadow, works especially well in this book. With apologies to the package designer, a can is a can is a can. Except, as in this case, where they are cleverly used, almost as labels, to identify the various items in variety packs. The story here is nuts, not cans. The message comes across, loud and clear.

BIOBOTTOMS

FRESH AIR WEAR FOR KIDS

Chasing the children's market in the mailorder catalog world is no mean task. There are two built-in problems. The lesser of the two evils has to do with Moms. A fair percentage of new mothers are too young to be trained mailorder buyers. What's more, they may be fresh out of school (a terrible direct response market) or citified retail shoppers. The second problem is a real tough nut. It goes like this: "A basic truth of the mailorder catalog business is that one must build and *keep* an active customer list."

How can that be done when kids grow up so quickly? The answer is, "It ain't easy, and many have failed in the attempt."

Biobottoms Fresh Air Wear For Kids catalog may have the answer. They started out in 1984 with a truly unique product—another basic requisite of the mail order industry. In this case, the product is a diaper cover made of real-from-the-lamb wool. From this unique launching pad, Biobottoms has extrapolated a product line that includes Diaper Ducks!, A Step Up Potty, all kinds of toddlers' toys, a Baby Jogger, sleep wear, slipper socks and long johns. Thence Biobottoms follows their up-growing customers all the way to size 12 with fifteen pages of clothing and accessories that range from the unique—Dr. Bailen's Bicycle Helmet—to a carefully selected assortment of RTW necessities.

An eye for the unusual, an understanding of children's turn-ons and some very creative buying elevates even the RTW sections of the Biobottoms catalog far above the ordinary store-bought stuff.

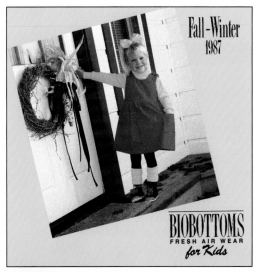

BIOBOTTOMS FRESH AIR WEAR FOR KIDS—Fall-Winter 1987
Anita Dimondstein, *Catalog Director*
Donjia Hughes, *Consultant*
Lee Romero, *Designer*
Joan Cooper and Anita Dimondstein, *Merchandisers*
Joan Cooper, *Copywriter*
Matt Farruggio, *Photographer/Illustrator*
Laserscan [Phoenix, AZ], *Color Separator*

The spread on pages 5 & 6 tells the story of the Biobottoms diaper cover. As this company expands its product lines to cover a wider age range, it may be that the catalog should acquire a new title to keep pace. The story is all here, but what will most certainly catch a young parent's eye is the subhead: "Pinless 10 Second Diapering". The secret, we discover, is a full-front, velcro-like panel. That's a *real* customer benefit!

The children's photography, as we mentioned before, is absolutely outstanding. On the Front Cover, the cutest little blonde in the world is standing exactly as any kid her age would. Just look at that right foot!

Presenting Ultra-soft, Breathable, Natural Diaper Covers

Biobottoms are diaper covers. They go where plastic pants used to, but they do what plastics can't! *Biobottoms* let fresh air in next to the skin while they keep moisture out of everything else. *Biobottoms* also let you use cloth diapers conveniently. Let you diaper without pins, painlessly. They're cool in summer, warm in winter, easily machine washable and they eliminate the biggest cause of diaper rash. It sounds like another miracle fiber at work, but *Biobottoms* are pure, virgin wool.

They're Wool, They Work

Wool, you see, is the most absorbent fiber in nature. And *Biobottoms* are a very special wool. A fully-felted woven wool, it packs thousands of thirsty fibers together to create an astonishingly effective wetness barrier. But while *Biobottoms* soak up moisture, they don't get soggy. Just one *Biobottom* keeps clothes and bedding dry through four or five diaper changes. You change them as often as you would plastic pants. But the change is definitely for the better.

With Love From Lambs Instead of Laboratories

Before *Biobottoms*, there were cloth diapers with plastic pants or disposables with plastic built-in. Both stay dry outside by keeping babies wet. Plastics also trap warmth as well as wetness, raising temperatures as high as 104 degrees . . . hot and sticky for a baby, but perfect for bacteria. Natural, breathable *Biobottoms* let air in to cool and dry skin. They help stop diaper rash because they don't let it start.

Pinless 10 Second Diapering

Top to bottom, inside and out, *Biobottoms* are designed to make diapering easy. All edges are bound with triple stitching, smooth and very durable. Leg bands fit snugly, without leaving red rings. A full-front velcro-like panel lets the fit adjust as the baby grows. *Biobottoms* hold cloth diapers in place without pins; eliminating pricked fingers. Double layer construction provides super absorbency. Extra snaps (sizes C, D, & E) baby proof the fastening. *Biobottoms* stand up to vigorous washing. In fact, they thrive on it. You want to be sure to remove all traces of urine & detergent, so machine washing & line drying are recommended.

Help Make the World a Cleaner Place

Evidence linking disposables and skin rashes is growing. So is evidence of disposables. Dirty throwaways don't go away. They pile up in the nation's trash. In fact, they already amount to nearly a third of it. And it's all stubbornly non-biodegradable. That growing heap of untreated human waste is a health and ecological disaster.

The Diapering Hotline

For the first two and a half years, diapers are the most important thing your baby wears. But almost no one wants to talk about it. Except us. We invite your questions on Biobottoms. And baby bottoms in general. Just write or call. We'll either have the answer. Or we'll help you get it. Write for information on diaper rash, our handbook on diapering and reprints about disposable diapers.

Comfortable, Breathable, Super Absorbent, Pin Free

BIOBOTTOMS

If babies had their way they'd wear nothing but fresh air. Biobottoms are the next best thing!

The Classic Biobottom
Creamy white wool, full cut for most coverage. Velcro-like tabs eliminate pins, making fitting easy. All edges bound for smoothness. Soft cuffs hug legs without leaving rings.
CLASSIC STYLE #1082. Price $13.50

The Rainbow Classic
Same full cut, same lamb soft wool, same features as the Classic. With edges trimmed in rainbow stitching.
RAINBOW CLASSIC STYLE #1083. Price $13.50

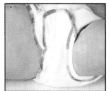
The Rainbow Bikini
Fashioned higher on the legs for extra freedom, cooler comfort and just for fun. Creamy wool with rainbow stitching.
RAINBOW BIKINI STYLE #1183. Price $13.50

How to Biobottom

Here's how to turn a diaper into one beautiful BIOBOTTOM, with no pins & in almost no time. It makes changing diapers quite a change.

■ Fold cloth diaper in thirds. Or completely line BIOBOTTOM with diaper.
■ Place diaper on BIOBOTTOM, keep all edges inside.
■ Fold BIOBOTTOM around baby and adjust velcro to fit.
■ Change cover just when it begins to feel damp, about every four or five diaper changes.
■ Use with your own standard diaper, diapers from diaper service or our terry diaper made especially for US.

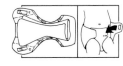

How many, how big?

You'll need some for wearing, some for washing. Six is a minimum. Eight to ten makes it convenient. For sizes, just follow the chart. Note: babies with very chubby legs may need one size larger, and if your baby is within a pound or two of the next size, get the next size.

Choose Sizes by Weight

A—Up to 14 lbs.	C—18 to 22 lbs.
B—14 to 18 lbs.	D—22 to 27 lbs.
	E—27 to 32 lbs.

The Bottom Line.

Biobottoms and cloth can save you $500 to $800 over disposables, even with a diaper service. True, Biobottoms cost a little more than cloth and plastic pants. About $1.75 a week. But what's the cost of comfort for your baby?

Order by Phone
Use your VISA / M/C.
Call 707-778-7945

Sneakers featuring jungle scenes, turtlenecks adorned with dinosaurs, a foul weather playsuit and a terry robe for tots all make these sometimes unexciting merchandise categories absolutely irresistible.

Order forms are the most important pages in a catalog. That's where the sale is consummated, where the final go/no-go decision is made. Biobottoms makes excellent use of their well designed order form with a number of sales-hyping devices, e.g.:

SIZE MYSTERY SOLVED

Children's sizing can be confusing. We've solved it by a simple code after each item. Look for:
   S: runs almost one size smaller than usual.
   S/A: runs slightly smaller than usual.
   A: true to size.
   A/L: slightly larger than usual.
   L: almost one size larger than usual.

CUSTOMER AWARDS

Send us your best! We're looking for your favorite diapering or Biobottoms Fresh Air Wear tip, anecdote or photo. If we use them in a future catalog, we'll send you a $50.00 Biobottoms Gift Certificate.

AT YOUR SERVICE

We're here to make shopping at Biobottoms a pleasure. Our staff (mostly moms), can help you with outfitting, diapering, even toilet training! Call with your questions.

NETWORKING

"Here are some catalogs and magazines that we enjoy. We'd like to share them with you. . . ." [There follows a full order form page of ads for these pubs and catalogs, complete with an ordering coupon.]

The Biobottoms order form does all the other righteous things that a good order form should, such as: providing Federal Express shipping service, featuring their unconditional guarantee, offering gift wrap and in general, making the sales-close a pleasant experience. It is a busy order form, but one in which the customer will not get lost or off-put while ordering.

There are three areas that Biobottoms might consider to improve their already excellent presentation.

The first has to do with telephone ordering. They have made the decision not to offer free 800 telephone ordering to their customers. There are mixed opinions on this subject, but it is certainly worth a split-run test to find out the real answer.

In any event, 800 or not, it would be a good idea to display the telephone number (phone bug) on many of the interior catalog pages. In "Selling 101", a basic lesson is taught: "Ask for the order, not once, but often." What's more, many consumer catalogers find that the *majority* of their orders are telephone orders. Too large a market segment to treat lightly. I could only find Biobottoms' ordering phone number displayed in two positions, one on the back cover and another in small type at the top of one order form page. In fact, the phone number does not even appear in the paragraph on the order form that gives telephone ordering information!

HOW TO ORDER

PHONE IN YOUR ORDER
We're here to help you personally with your order Monday-Friday 8AM-6PM (PST), and Saturdays 9AM-4PM. SPECIAL HOLIDAY SHOPPING HOURS! 8AM-9PM beginning Nov. 1st.

SEND IT BY MAIL
Use our convenient order form. Please print clearly. Use your personal check, money order, Mastercharge, or Visa.

AT YOUR SERVICE
We're here to make shopping at Biobottoms a pleasure. Our staff (mostly moms), can help you with outfitting, diapering, even toilet training! Call with your questions.

NO RISK ORDERING
If you need to return or exchange an item, simply follow the directions you receive with your order. Let us know when we make a mistake. We're small but spunky and won't stop until all our customers are satisfied.

SIZE MYSTERY SOLVED
Children's sizing can be confusing. We've solved it by a simple code after each item. Look for:
   S: runs almost one size smaller than usual.
   S/A: runs slightly smaller than usual.
   A: true to size.
   A/L: slightly larger than usual.
   L: almost one size larger than usual.

BIO-DOLLARS
$50
GIFT CERTIFICATE

CUSTOMER AWARDS
Send us your best! We're looking for your favorite diapering or Biobottoms Fresh Air Wear tip, anecdote or photo. If we use them in a future catalog, we'll send you a $50.00 BIOBOTTOMS GIFT CERTIFICATE.

SHARE OUR CATALOG WITH FRIENDS

We're small, but growing quickly. You can help us by sharing names of friends and relatives who might like our catalog too. They won't be disappointed! Also, if you are not ordering now, but want to receive our next catalog, attach your label here.

Name _____
Street _____
City _____ State _____ Zip _____

Name _____
Street _____
City _____ State _____ Zip _____

Name _____
Street _____
City _____ State _____ Zip _____

Name _____
Street _____
City _____ State _____ Zip _____

Name _____
Street _____
City _____ State _____ Zip _____

Parent Tested . . . Child Approved
All our products are parent tested, child approved, practical, durable and fun. And best of all, kids like to wear our clothes . . . all day long . . . day after day.

SATISFACTION GUARANTEED
It's simple! Your purchase is risk free. If you are not satisfied with your purchase, please return it for a refund or exchange. No questions asked.

We appreciate your comments and your suggestions for new products.
_____
_____
_____
_____
_____

NETWORKING

A 124-page quarterly magazine covering Breastfeeding, Homebirth, Cotton Diapers, Alternative Health Care, Midwifery, Education, Fathers, and Parents Talking to Parents. $15.00 for one year Subscription. Sample Issue $2.00.

Dear Parents and Friends,
Here are some catalogs and magazines that we enjoy. We'd like to share them with you. Just fill out the coupon! If you're ordering from our catalog, tag on the "networking" total to the order blank in the space provided. If you are only ordering catalogs, simply fill out the coupon below and enclose it with your check made payable to Biobottoms. We'll take care of the rest.

SEND YOUR REQUESTS TO:

BIOBOTTOMS
FRESH AIR WEAR
P.O. Box 1060
3820 Bodega Avenue
Petaluma, CA 94953

The Company Store
Our Store is 84 Pages of Natural Products:
Give your child the highest quality natural products: The Company Store's down-filled jackets and comforters, wool crib pads and much more. For a free catalog, call toll free, 1-800-356-9367, ext. 14J.

J.CREW
LIVING WELL—If you take your weekends and leisure-wear seriously, you appreciate apparel designed with contemporary but enduring style under uncompromising quality standards.
Simply make a request, and we'll provide you with this season's subscription for $1.

We will be happy to send you a copy of our latest catalog.

The Diapering Hotline
For the first two and a half years, diapers are the most important thing your baby wears. But almost no one wants to talk about it. Except us. We invite your questions on Biobottoms. And baby bottoms in general. Just write or call. We'll either have the answer. Or we'll help you get it. Write for information on diaper rash, our handbook on diapering and reprints about disposable diapers.

All issues will be sent directly to you from the companies you select.
☐ Mothering $2.00
☐ Company Store .... FREE
☐ J. Crew $1.00
☐ Biobottoms .... FREE

HANDLING CHARGE ... $1.00
TOTAL [   ]

Name _____
Address _____
City _____ State _____ Zip _____

These comments about the phone bug apply—in spades—to the guarantee. Biobottoms displays their fine, unconditional guarantee only once, and that is on the order form. Absolutely *one* of the right places. But, before I decide to order, I have to be convinced—about the product *and the company selling the product*. It's a darned good guarantee! Shout it often, don't whisper. You won't wake up the baby.

Photographing babies and toddlers has to be a labor of love. The normal earthchild at those ages spends most of his or her time wearing a grimace or an absolutely blank look. We choose not to remember them that way, but next time you have the opportunity, put a stop watch on little Willy's changes of expression. Cute doesn't last long.

Some of the shots of wee 'uns in Biobottoms catalogs are the best we've seen. These kids are for real. They're kids doing kids' things and looking very pleased with themselves about the whole situation. And still, the merchandise can be seen — clearly. Our compliments to the director, stylist, photographer and off-camera person making funny faces!

Here again, great kids looking and acting like real kids. In our opinion, these spreads illustrate a disparity that exists in the design of this book. The merchandise and photographs are dead on target, but the cropping and harsh, industrial-strength layouts and typefaces are not in keeping with either a child's world or a woman's sensibilities. Stores are filled with merchandise for children. Therefore, there has to be an emotional appeal wrapped around this delightful merchandise in order to give the customer a reason to buy through the mail.

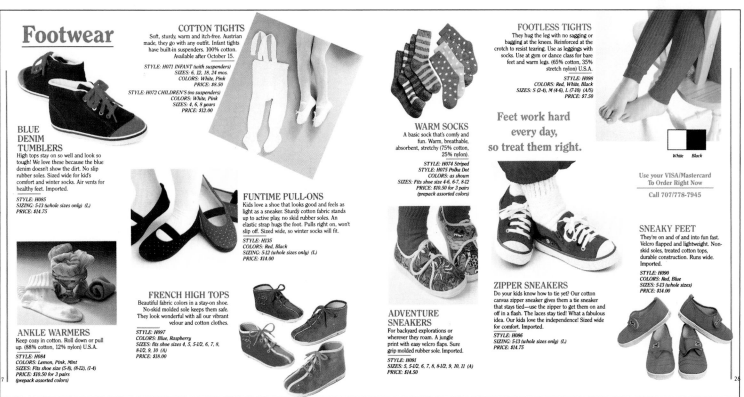

Dress Me In Comfortable Cotton

COZY TERRY TOPS
Comfy super terry tops for all day wear. Fits like a stretchy, warm baby sweatshirt. Cozy cotton rib trim. Custom dyed. Machine wash and dry. (86% cotton, 14% poly)

STYLE: H050
COLORS: Purple, Blue, Yellow, Pink
SIZES: 6, 12, 18, 24 mos., 3T (A/L)
PRICE: $10.00

SUPER TERRY PANTS
Keep those tootsies covered with our mostly cotton terry knit pants/tights. Gentle non-twist elastic in waist and plenty of room for diapers. Our popular basic in 4 custom-dyed colors. Machine wash/dry. (86% cotton, 14% poly)

STYLE: H051
COLORS: Purple, Blue, Yellow, Pink
SIZES: 6, 12, 18, 24 mos., 3T (A/L)
PRICE: $10.00

Red   Purple

VELOUR ZIP JACKET
Our most popular zip-up jacket! Velour keeps kids warm without any itch! Always first choice for our kids on a chilly day. Easy pull zipper and roomy hood. U.S.A.

STYLE: H049
COLORS: Blue, Red, Purple
SIZES: 6,12,18 mos., 2,4,6,8 (A)
PRICE: $15.50

BABY ANIMAL SHIRTS
An adorable indispensable baby basic. 100% cotton T-shirt with colorful silk-screened barnyard animals. Machine wash/dry. U.S.A.

STYLE: H146
COLORS: Pigs, Chicks
SIZES: 12, 18, 24 mos. (A)
PRICE: $7.00

WOODEN RATTLE & TEETHING RING
Let your baby grab onto this pure wood rattle and chew, chew, chew! Nontoxic, smooth, just the right size for tiny fingers and mouths. Absolutely safe. Swedish design.

STYLE: H003
PRICE: $14.50

10

The ACA judges seem to have agreed with our conclusions. They use the terms ''blocky'' and ''cluttered'' when describing the layouts, but they are also very generous with their comments about the merchandising and copywriting in this catalog.

One judge's final comment is indeed fitting: ''After reading this catalog. . . you feel like you know the owners, and you want to buy something from them''.

142

BRECK'S FLOWERS

Breck's catalogs are perennial winners. And why not? Who can hate mom's apple pies or flowers? But let's face it. From issue to issue—and even from year to year—the Breck's catalogs pick up many of the same photographs, use very similar layouts and print essentially the same expository copy.

Why then all the excitement and all the awards? I suspect it has to do with the judges who sit on the award panels. Virtually all these judges are professionals—they recognize the work of other professionals. And, Breck's is a workhorse of a catalog that reeks of professionalism. Indeed, the "Catalog Age" headline introducing this Gold Award winner boldly declares: "Breck's exudes confidence and authority. Judges hail catalog as an exemplary mail-order vehicle."

Many of the direct response industry's top guns have, at one time or another, been paid to make their creative contributions to Breck's marketing efforts. The results speak for themselves—70 successful years in the mailorder business is quite a laudable performance for any catalog program. As a result of all this valuable input (and, no doubt, a lot of testing and tracking), Breck's observes most of the well documented tenets of mail-order selling. But, in addition, from the pages of the Breck's catalog, two messages blast through loud and clear. They are, "Have we got a deal for you!" and "Buy now!".

For instance, just look at the selling job that the front cover does. First, there's the tip-on medal that says, "SALE EX-TENDED until Aug. 31, 1987." Tip-on's are expensive, but wait. . . . . . it also means that they can mail the same catalog to the same customer without any 4-color changes—and still get a strong response. That's a good investment! Here are some of the other high-powered hypes on the same front cover:

SEND NO MONEY
1987 ADVANCE SALE
SAVE AS MUCH AS 50%
FREE BONUS for Ordering Now
Sale ends July 31, 1987

and then the more subliminal:

Serving American Gardeners Since 1818
    $2.00 (cover price)

Open the catalog and POW!

"FREE BONUS Just for ordering now! 5 Apricot Beauty Tulips. We have a very special gift for you. . . ."
    "FREE Dutch Bulb Plant Guide. Breck's experts in Holland. . . ."

Followed by a powerful personalized letter that says in part:

"Holland's late spring means Mrs. John E. Koopman has 31 more days to save 50% on bulbs to plant this fall in Gaffney [her home town]. . . ." The letter goes on, *". . . . . FREE Bonus offer—five of these gorgeous Tulips to plant this fall in the Koopman Garden—free with. . . ."* and finally, *"Send No Money! . . . ."* and, *"No Risk! Satisfaction fully guaranteed. . . ."*

BRECK'S—1987 Sale Catalog
Leo Vandervlugt, *Catalog Director*
Sargeant House, *Consultant & Designer/Copywriter*
Rob Van Reisen, *Merchandiser*
Photographer/Illustrator: *Various*
Meredith Burda [Lynchburg, VA], *Printer, on 60# Coated Stock for cover and 38# Coated for text*
Meredith Burda, *Color Separator*

Holland's Late Spring Means Mrs. John E. Koopman Has 31 More Days to Save 50% on Bulbs to Plant This Fall in Gaffney

1987 Advance Sale Deadline Extended to August 31 for Breck's Preferred Customers

Cold, stormy weather hit Europe with unusual fury last winter causing the late arrival of Holland's blooming season. But that's good news for you, Mrs. John E. Koopman.

Because Breck's can reserve bulbs later than usual, we can accept a limited number of additional orders for Dutch Bulbs we'll ship direct to America this fall.

Best of all, we've obtained an additional quantity of Apricot Beauty Tulips so we can also extend our FREE Bonus offer -- five of these gorgeous Tulips to plant this fall in The Koopman Garden -- free with any order for $25 or more sent before your extended Advance Sale deadline expires on August 31, 1987.

Send No Money! Pay after you inspect your bulbs when they arrive at proper fall planting time for Cherokee County, South Carolina.

No Risk! Satisfaction fully guaranteed. Use the special Preferred Customer order form in the back of this catalog to take advantage of your extended savings privileges.

Breck's catalog readers aren't interested in a bunch of persiflage. They know their flowers and they want to see, in as much detail as possible, how these flowers will look when they bloom. These punchy pages do an almost perfect job of satisfying their readers' desires. In some cases, as on pages 4 & 5, there is generic copy that describes the history and appropriateness of a genre of flowers. After that lead-in, minimal copy suffices to differentiate between the sub-species. On other pages, for instance 8-9, each flower has its own copy block, and its own story to tell.

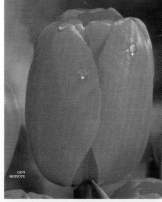

Long-Lasting Mid-Season Tulips

Nobody does it better! Skilled Dutch hybridizers crossed early and late-blooming Tulips to create spectacular Mid-Season Tulips. These Dutch beauties have super-sturdy stems to carry their dramatic 5″ flowers. Long-lasting in both garden and bouquets. We recommend planting multiple bulbs of each variety in garden groupings plus combination groupings of your favorite varieties in special beds where you'll be able to enjoy their classic beauty spring after spring. Breck's Dutch bulb experts have specially selected the six outstanding varieties shown here for coordinated growth and blooming in gardens throughout America long after earlier Tulips are finished. Enjoy the world's finest Tulip blooms direct to you from Holland.

C57588 Bing Crosby . . These traditional neon-red Tulips for your mid-season garden are real showmen. Handsome 5″ blossoms hold their color exceptionally well in the garden and exciting in bouquets. Sturdy 21″ stems.

C56085 Attila. Violet-blue goblets held proudly on tall 20″ stems make a dramatic statement. Big 5″ flowers mix well with other Tulips setting off bright colors to advantage. Blooms late April to early May.

C57604 Golden Melody . . What a lovely song of spring this buttercup-yellow Tulip will sing in your garden. Enjoy long-lasting 5″ blooms on 20-22″ stems in late April and early May. A great choice for creating cheerful cut bouquets.

8 Bulbs (any one variety)	
After 7/31/87 $6.50	Sale **4.49**
16 Bulbs (any one variety)	
After 7/31/87 $13.00	Sale **8.49**
32 Bulbs (any one variety)	
After 7/31/87 $26.00	Sale **14.99**

BRIGHT STAR TULIP COLLECTION
SAVE 39% on 8 bulbs each mid-season Tulip this page.
C58867 Bright Star Tulip Collection (24 bulbs, 8 ea. color)
After 7/31/87 $19.50 . . . . Sale **11.99**

C57646 Kansas . . There is no finer white mid-season Tulip available anywhere. Big, 5″ snow-white blooms are distinctively accented with a yellow base hidden inside. Strong 20″ stems hold these gems in garden and lovely bouquets late April-early May.

C56887 Black Pearl . . It's unusual to find a black bloom in the spring garden, and this is the blackest Tulip yet. Distinctive, long-lasting 5″ blooms on sturdy 24-26″ stems early- to mid-May. Dramatic in garden and bouquets. Uniquely sets off other Tulips.

C57620 Don Quixote . . No spring planting or bouquet is quite complete without a splash of pink. This heartfelt beauty boasts long-lasting 5″ blooms on 20-22″ stems late April to early May. One of the versatile Triumph Tulips, a Dutch favorite.

8 Bulbs (any one variety)	
After 7/31/87 $6.50	Sale **4.49**
16 Bulbs (any one variety)	
After 7/31/87 $13.00	Sale **8.49**
32 Bulbs (any one variety)	
After 7/31/87 $26.00	Sale **14.99**

GARDEN GEM TULIP COLLECTION
Money-saving collection includes 8 each Tulip this page.
C58883 Garden Gem Tulip Collection (24 bulbs, 8 ea. color)
After 7/31/87 $19.50 . . . . Sale **11.99**

Complete Mid-Season Tulip Collection
Best-buy collection includes eight top quality bulbs 12 cm. or larger of each outstanding Mid-Season Tulip shown on these two pages. Individually packaged for color-coordinated planting. Each bulb fully guaranteed.
C57661 Complete Mid-Season Tulip Collection SAVE 44%!
48 Bulbs (8 bulbs each of all 6 varieties)
After 7/31/87 $39.00 . . . . Sale **21.99**

BING CROSBY · ATTILA · GOLDEN MELODY · KANSAS · DON QUIXOTE · BLACK PEARL

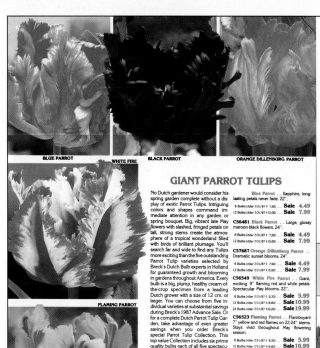

BLUE PARROT · WHITE FIRE · BLACK PARROT · ORANGE DILLENBURG PARROT · FLAMING PARROT

GIANT PARROT TULIPS

No Dutch gardener would consider his spring garden complete without a display of exotic Parrot Tulips. Intriguing colors and shapes command immediate attention in any garden or spring bouquet. Big, vibrant late May flowers with slashed, fringed petals on tall, strong stems create the atmosphere of a tropical wonderland filled with birds of brilliant plumage. You'll search far and wide to find any Tulips more exciting than the five outstanding Parrot Tulip varieties selected by Breck's Dutch Bulb experts in Holland for guaranteed growth and blooming in gardens throughout America. Every bulb is a big, plump, healthy cream-of-the-crop specimen from a leading Dutch grower with a size of 12 cm. or larger. You can choose from five individual varieties at substantial savings during Breck's 1987 Advance Sale. Or for a complete Dutch Parrot Tulip Garden, take advantage of even greater savings when you order Breck's special Parrot Tulip Collection. This top-value Collection includes six prime quality bulbs each of all five spectacular varieties shown on this page.

Blue Parrot . . Sapphire, long-lasting petals never fade. 22″.

6 Bulbs (After 7/31/87 $ 7.50)	Sale **4.49**
12 Bulbs (After 7/31/87 $15.00)	Sale **7.99**

C56481 Black Parrot . . Large, glossy maroon-black flowers. 24″.

6 Bulbs (After 7/31/87 $ 7.50)	Sale **4.49**
12 Bulbs (After 7/31/87 $15.00)	Sale **7.99**

C57687 Orange Dillenburg Parrot . . Dramatic sunset blooms. 24″.

6 Bulbs (After 7/31/87 $ 7.50)	Sale **4.49**
12 Bulbs (After 7/31/87 $15.00)	Sale **7.99**

C56549 White Fire Parrot . . Giant, exciting 9″ flaming red and white petals. Spectacular May blooms. 22″.

6 Bulbs (After 7/31/87 $ 8.30)	Sale **5.99**
12 Bulbs (After 7/31/87 $16.60)	Sale **10.99**
24 Bulbs (After 7/31/87 $33.20)	Sale **19.99**

C56523 Flaming Parrot . . Flamboyant 7″ yellow and red flames on 22-24″ stems. Stays vivid throughout May flowering season.

6 Bulbs (After 7/31/87 $ 8.30)	Sale **5.99**
12 Bulbs (After 7/31/87 $16.60)	Sale **10.99**
24 Bulbs (After 7/31/87 $33.20)	Sale **19.99**

PARROT TULIP COLLECTION
Top-savings collection includes 6 each all five tropical-looking Parrot Tulips this page.
C58248 Parrot Tulip Collection SAVE 49%!
1 Collection (30 bulbs, 6 each variety)
After 7/31/87 $39.10 . . . . Sale **19.99**

Lovely Ladies Tulips
Exceptional Beauty — Great Savings

GREENLAND
Perhaps Holland's most beautiful Tulip is this lovely lady. Artistic warm/cool combination of rosy-pink May blooms embraced by emerald "arms." Fascinating pearl sheen inside. 24″.

C57067 Greenland Tulip SAVE 50%!

8 Bulbs (After 7/31/87 $ 8.70)	Sale **4.99**
16 Bulbs (After 7/31/87 $17.40)	Sale **8.99**
24 Bulbs (After 7/31/87 $26.10)	Sale **12.99**

SPRING GREEN
NEW FOR 1987! Unique and different. Frilled, reflexing petals with distinctive emerald and sea green feathering on white. May blooms held high on strong 20″ stems. Long-lasting in bouquets. Cream-of-the-crop bulbs from leading Dutch growers.

C57349 Spring Green Tulip SAVE 31%!

6 Bulbs (After 7/31/87 $ 6.40)	Sale **4.99**
12 Bulbs (After 7/31/87 $12.80)	Sale **8.99**
24 Bulbs (After 7/31/87 $25.60)	Sale **15.99**

ARTIST TULIP
Festively colored, exquisitely shaped flowers – as if they came right off a Van Gogh canvas. Big salmon, rose and emerald blooms in May on strong 12″ stems. A Dutch favorite.

C56424 Artist Tulip SAVE 48%!

6 Bulbs (After 7/31/87 $ 7.70)	Sale **4.99**
12 Bulbs (After 7/31/87 $15.40)	Sale **8.99**
24 Bulbs (After 7/31/87 $30.80)	Sale **15.99**

LOVELY LADIES TULIP COLLECTION
SAVE 43%! Top savings on three of Holland's most exquisite floral creations. Includes 8 Greenland, 6 Spring Green and 6 Artist Tulips. Cream-of-the-crop bulbs direct from Holland.
C57455 Lovely Ladies Tulip Collection
1 Collection (20 bulbs) After 7/31/87 $22.80 . . . . Sale **12.99**

Then, by gosh, the rest of the Breck's catalog proceeds to live up to all those promises! On almost every page there's a deal, a combination price, a special sale or another incentive to buy. On top of that, "A Breck's Exclusive" and "Direct from HOLLAND" bugs are used wherever possible.

Breck's doesn't take any chances with their copy keying either. There's no confusion about which copy goes with which illustration in this catalog: each block is headed with the name of the flower, and each photo is clearly labeled as well.

In the words of one ACA judge: "The catalog's excellent design and execution make it almost impossible to resist, even if you swore you'd never plant another bulb!"

The spatial relationship between Breck's copy and artwork is honed to a fine edge. Where introduction, romance or exposition are needed, the writers have been allowed the room to do the job; and they have used that space to good advantage. Where a picture alone can do the selling job, close-up photographs illustrate not only color, but texture and shape. On these spreads, copy is little more than price and a catalog number.

Breck's mails over 5 million catalogs per year, and most of those catalogs go to a list of households generated from their own database, not from rented lists. As any cataloger will tell you, a house list should respond three to six times as well as any group of rented names. Brings to mind the question asked of an English groundskeeper by an American visitor: "How do you grow such beautiful lawns?", and the response: "Well, when we started the lawn, in the year 1515. . . ." Some good things—a 5-million name customer file included—take time.

The theme is: "Zing! went the strings of my purse." Mixed metaphor? Perhaps, but here are all these beautiful flowers serving as a background for one of the hardest sells in the mailorder business today. The copy on the right hand side of the insert between pages 2 and 3 pushes just about every 'buy' button identified in "Copywriting 101", including (please note) reference to the county and state of the recipient. (See the paragraph that begins, "Send No Money!")

BUTTERFLY DAFFODILS

Exclusive! When Breck's first saw the results of Dutch hybridizers' breakthroughs in improving exotic, fragrant Split Corona Daffodils, we reserved Holland's entire crop for our customers in America. That was several years ago when the supply was so limited we could offer them only in a mixture. At long last, Holland's production is large enough so you can order your favorite Butterfly Daffodils individually. Brand-new varieties with ruffled centers are long lasting in the garden and bouquets. Mid-spring 4″ blooms on strong 18-20″ stems. Available in America only from Breck's! **Order now and SAVE 30%!**

C64808 Aloha . A welcome, brand-new addition. Ruffled yellow cups surrounded by white perianth. Deliciously fragrant mid-spring blooms flutter atop sturdy 18-20″ stems.

C64766 Malia . . Like a lovely, lacy petticoat. Solid gold on gold blooms are a special treat in the April-May garden.

C64881 Leilani . Dazzling white perianth and tropical orange cup. Multiplies annually for increased beauty each year.

C64782 Kapalua . . Fragrant, exotic beauty for garden and bouquets. White-on-white petticoat frills atop 18-20″ stem.

5 Bulbs (any one variety) After 7/31/87 $ 9.30	**Sale 6.99**
10 Bulbs (any one variety) After 7/31/87 $18.60	**Sale 12.99**

BUTTERFLY DAFFODIL COLLECTION
SAVE 38%! Collection includes 5 each of the lovely Butterfly Daffodils on this page – 20 in all.
C66985 *Butterfly Daffodil Collection*
20 Bulbs (1 collection) After 7/31/87 $37.20 .... **Sale** 22.99

DELUXE DAFFODIL MIXTURE

Enjoy Holland's finest Daffodils next spring at an amazingly low price! Breck's bulb experts have made a super buy on a mixed group of prime quality Daffodils from leading growers throughout Holland – including a number of rare varieties unavailable in sufficient quantities to offer individually. Professionally color-coordinated for a long season of spectacular blooms. Top quality, top size, top value. Each bulb fully guaranteed to grow and bloom in your garden next spring.

C65003 Deluxe Daffodil Mixture

12 Bulbs (mixed varieties) After 7/31/87 $ 14.70	**Sale 8.99**
24 Bulbs (mixed varieties) After 7/31/87 $ 29.40	**Sale 16.99**
48 Bulbs (mixed varieties) After 7/31/87 $ 58.80	**Sale 29.99**
96 Bulbs (mixed varieties) After 7/31/87 $117.60	**Sale 56.99**

Special 52% Savings!

In a departure from the standard layout of this catalog, the Breck's "Sampler Sale" offers "34 opportunities to sample Holland's finest bulbs". From this spread, if you ordered one from each offer, you would own 196 bulbs at a cost of $89.86, an average of less than $0.46 per bulb! OR, you can buy two complete 120-Day Flowering Sampler collections for only $46.99, less than $0.20 per bulb. Be still my heart!

The *piece de resistance* of the "order now" sales pitch is on the back of the Breck's order form. Again, it is a personalized letter, this time referring to the cold winter in Hillegom (Holland) that has worked to the specific benefit of Mrs. John E. Koopman. In the third paragraph is the promise of "the biggest, hardiest bulbs [Breck's has] ever been able to ship for planting in [Mrs. Koopman's] South Carolina garden".

And then, BANG: "Send No Money—Because you are one of Breck's Preferred Customers, Mrs. John E. Koopman, your credit is already established. . .". Wasn't it nice of Hans Van Amstel, Director of Breck Holland B.V., to send Mrs. Kloopman that wonderful personal note! Too bad, postal regs require a return address; in this case: Peoria, Illinois.

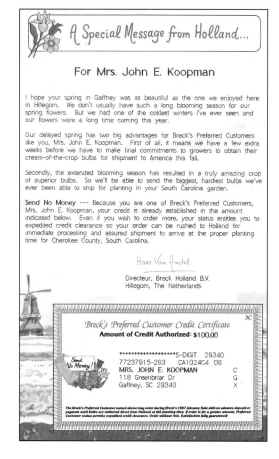

CLASSICS IN THE MAKING

Mason & Sullivan's Classics In The Making is a 2-year old catalog directed to the model-building hobbyist. Its market is those individuals who enjoy making new little things that look like old big things. Subheads on the cover of this 36-page book accurately describe the contents: "Reproduction Kits You Can Build" and "Projects For Every Skill Level".

Model builders of all proficiency levels will love this collection. Whether you have only an hour or two to spend in the building or days of available time. As one ACA judge commented: "The pictures are so compelling, even if you're not that interested in model-building, you still want to try it."

Virtually every conceivable area of interest is represented. Here is a partial list of the kits available in the 1988 catalog:

Firearms and Cannon
Musical Instruments
Classic Cars, Fire Vehicles & Trucks
Antique Toys
Desktop & Floor Globes
Optical Instruments
Railroad Engines & Cars
Working Steam Engines
Boats—Power & Sail of all sizes and shapes
Commercial, Military & Private Aircraft
Farm Vehicles
Rockets & The Space Shuttle
Clocks & Barometers
Furniture Reproductions
Miniature Furniture
Wind Mill, Printing Press & a 1815 Ship's Combat Station
Machines by Leonardo Da Vinci
Chess Sets, including lead casting kits
Celestial, Weather & Timekeeping Instruments
Embroidery Kits for Antique Reproductions
Knives, Scales & A Culpeper Kaleidoscope and (of course),
A Walking Stick with Compass & Flask

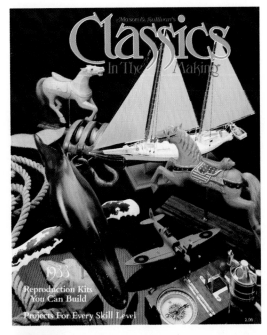

CLASSICS IN THE MAKING—1988 Catalog
John Hanson, *President*
Mark Leach, *Catalog Director/Merchandiser*
Swanson Advertising, *Designer*
Jeff Pozgay, *Copywriter*
Picone Photo Illustrators, *Photographer*
W.A. Krueger [Jonesboro, AR], *Printer on 70#
    Escanaba cover and text*
Spectragraphics New England [Boston, MA], *Color
    Separator*

Model-makers with specific areas of interest will, no doubt, look to catalogs more centered on their particular specialty. But even the most expert model ship or aircraft builder can find relaxation and a change of pace with these less demanding kits.

Classics' copywriters do not attempt to delve into an in-depth historical background of, or offer dissertations on, a genre or particular model.

Classics' present market is weighted towards the forty-plus age

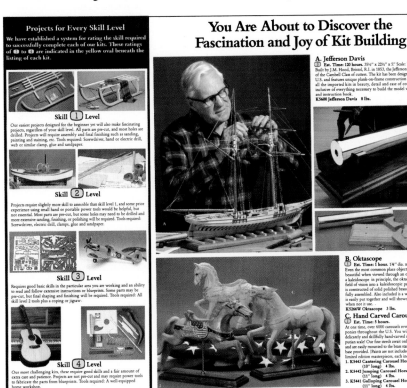

Ah, the power of a store front window display. The story is clearly told: "We have something here for every hobbyist." The gatefold on the left IFC tells us immediately that we don't have to be skilled model builders to play. Classics has devised a 4-level rating system that describes the skills necessary to succesfully complete a kit. This unthreatening gatefold gives chapter and verse, and pictures and words that enable us to best rank ourselves. These skill level 'bugs' then appear in the copy for each item throughout the entire catalog.

group, the same market served by the parent company's successful Mason & Sullivan Clock Kit catalogs. While the customer list of this new catalog program is relatively small (6,900, 9-month buyers), the quality of both the catalog and the products bodes well for the future.

As additional new customer acquisition programs are tested, one cannot help but wonder if additional customers will not be found. Younger audiences and/or special interest groups other than model hobbyists are good possibilities. It's true that lists of pre-teen, male, active mailorder buyers are somewhere between rare and non-existant. But they do exist. And most of these kids do have parents and grandparents who are largely at a loss for appropriate gifts. Classics In The Making offers a grand solution to their dilemma.

Eclectic is where it's at. From a miniature Chippendale dining set to binnacles and printing presses. From a flying machine of Leonardo da Vinci and a miniature 'cello to whales, lighthouses, weather instruments, aircraft, fire engines and choo-choo trains.

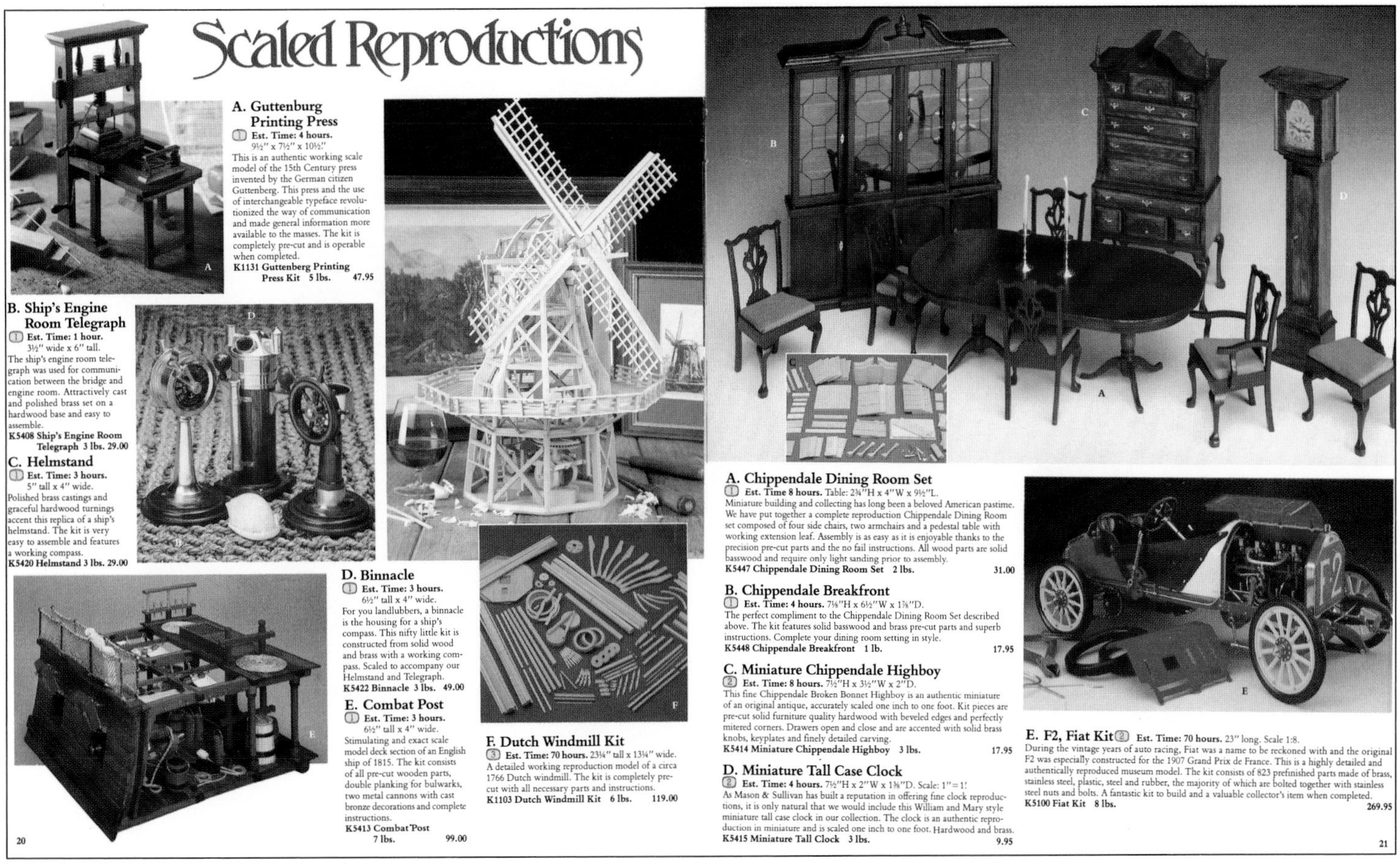
Scaled Reproductions
A. Guttenburg Printing Press
Est. Time: 4 hours. 9½" x 7½" x 10½."
This is an authentic working scale model of the 15th Century press invented by the German citizen Guttenberg. This press and the use of interchangeable typeface revolutionized the way of communication and made general information more available to the masses. The kit is completely pre-cut and is operable when completed.
K1131 Guttenberg Printing Press Kit 5 lbs. 47.95
B. Ship's Engine Room Telegraph
Est. Time: 1 hour. 3½" wide x 6" tall.
The ship's engine room telegraph was used for communication between the bridge and engine room. Attractively cast and polished brass set on a hardwood base and easy to assemble.
K5408 Ship's Engine Room Telegraph 3 lbs. 29.00
C. Helmstand
Est. Time: 3 hours. 5" tall x 4" wide.
Polished brass castings and graceful hardwood turnings accent this replica of a ship's helmstand. The kit is very easy to assemble and features a working compass.
K5420 Helmstand 3 lbs. 29.00
D. Binnacle
Est. Time: 3 hours. 6½" tall x 4" wide.
For you landlubbers, a binnacle is the housing for a ship's compass. This nifty little kit is constructed from solid wood and brass with a working compass. Scaled to accompany our Helmstand and Telegraph.
K5422 Binnacle 3 lbs. 49.00
E. Combat Post
Est. Time: 3 hours. 6½" tall x 4" wide.
Stimulating and exact scale model deck section of an English ship of 1815. The kit consists of all pre-cut wooden parts, double planking for bulwarks, two metal cannons with cast bronze decorations and complete instructions.
K5413 Combat Post 7 lbs. 99.00
F. Dutch Windmill Kit
Est. Time: 70 hours. 23¼" tall x 13¼" wide.
A detailed working reproduction model of a circa 1766 Dutch windmill. The kit is completely pre-cut with all necessary parts and instructions.
K1103 Dutch Windmill Kit 6 lbs. 119.00
20
A. Chippendale Dining Room Set
Est. Time 8 hours. Table: 2¾"H x 4"W x 9½"L.
Miniature building and collecting has long been a beloved American pastime. We have put together a complete reproduction Chippendale Dining Room set composed of four side chairs, two armchairs and a pedestal table with working extension leaf. Assembly is as easy as it is enjoyable thanks to the precision pre-cut parts and the no fail instructions. All wood parts are solid basswood and require only light sanding prior to assembly.
K5447 Chippendale Dining Room Set 2 lbs. 31.00
B. Chippendale Breakfront
Est. Time: 4 hours. 7⅛"H x 6½"W x 1⅞"D.
The perfect compliment to the Chippendale Dining Room Set described above. The kit features solid basswood and brass pre-cut parts and superb instructions. Complete your dining room setting in style.
K5448 Chippendale Breakfront 1 lb. 17.95
C. Miniature Chippendale Highboy
Est. Time: 8 hours. 7½"H x 3½"W x 2"D.
This fine Chippendale Broken Bonnet Highboy is an authentic miniature of an original antique, accurately scaled one inch to one foot. Kit pieces are pre-cut solid furniture quality hardwood with beveled edges and perfectly mitered corners. Drawers open and close and are accented with solid brass knobs, keyplates and finely detailed carving.
K5414 Miniature Chippendale Highboy 3 lbs. 17.95
D. Miniature Tall Case Clock
Est. Time: 4 hours. 7½"H x 2"W x 1⅜"D. Scale: 1"=1'
As Mason & Sullivan has built a reputation in offering fine clock reproductions, it is only natural that we would include this William and Mary style miniature tall case clock in our collection. The clock is an authentic reproduction in miniature and is scaled one inch to one foot. Hardwood and brass.
K5415 Miniature Tall Clock 3 lbs. 9.95
E. F2, Fiat Kit Est. Time: 70 hours. 23" long. Scale 1:8.
During the vintage years of auto racing, Fiat was a name to be reckoned with and the original F2 was especially constructed for the 1907 Grand Prix de France. This is a highly detailed and authentically reproduced museum model. The kit consists of 823 prefinished parts made of brass, stainless steel, plastic, steel and rubber, the majority of which are bolted together with stainless steel nuts and bolts. A fantastic kit to build and a valuable collector's item when completed.
K5100 Fiat Kit 8 lbs. 269.95
21

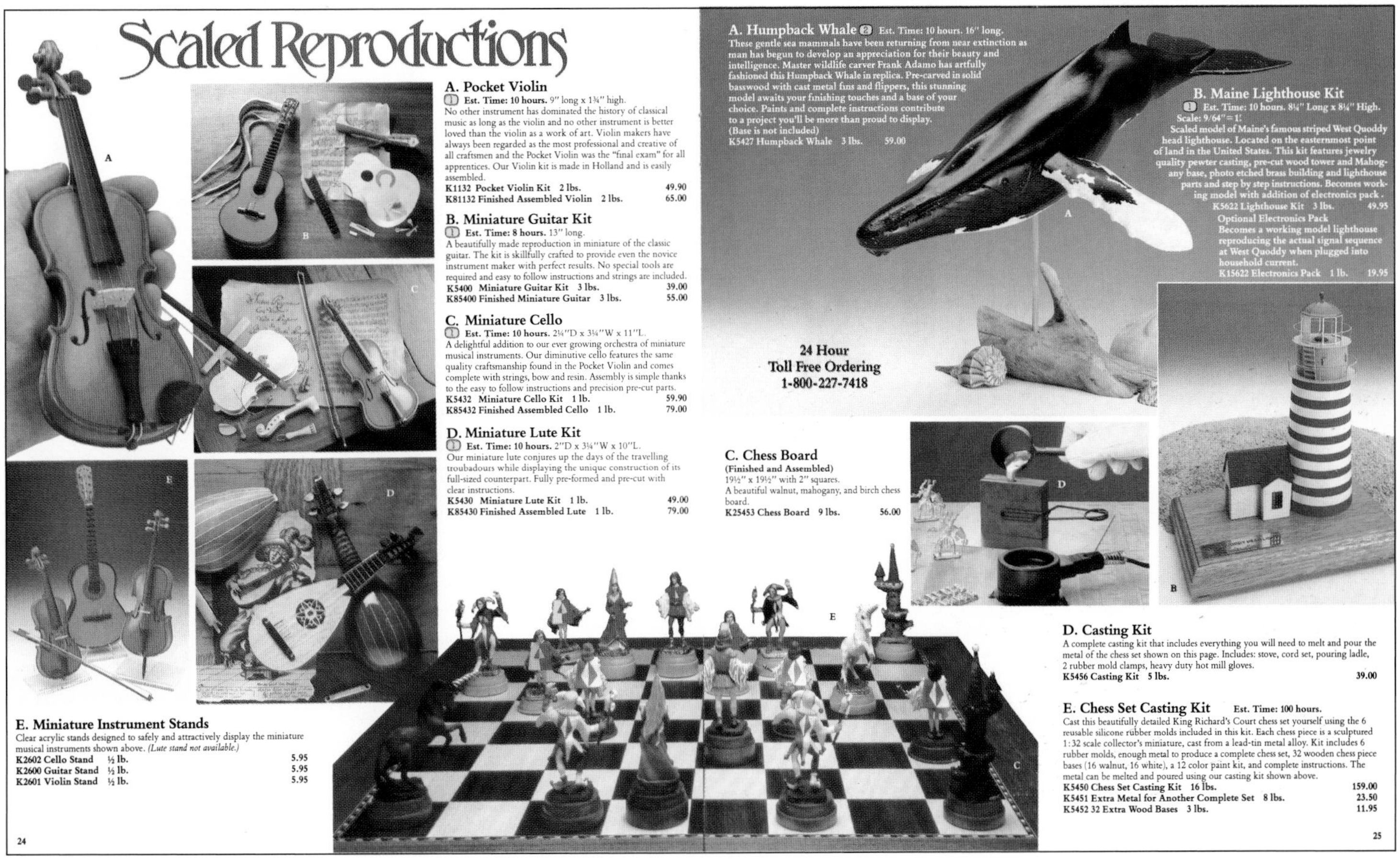
Scaled Reproductions
A. Pocket Violin
Est. Time: 10 hours. 9" long x 1¾" high.
No other instrument has dominated the history of classical music as long as the violin and no other instrument is better loved than the violin as a work of art. Violin makers have always been regarded as the most professional and creative of all craftsmen and the Pocket Violin was the "final exam" for all apprentices. Our Violin kit is made in Holland and is easily assembled.
K1132 Pocket Violin Kit 2 lbs. 49.90
K81132 Finished Assembled Violin 2 lbs. 65.00
B. Miniature Guitar Kit
Est. Time: 8 hours. 13" long.
A beautifully made reproduction in miniature of the classic guitar. The kit is skillfully crafted to provide even the novice instrument maker with perfect results. No special tools are required and easy to follow instructions and strings are included.
K5400 Miniature Guitar Kit 3 lbs. 39.00
K85400 Finished Miniature Guitar 3 lbs. 55.00
C. Miniature Cello
Est. Time: 10 hours. 2¼"D x 3¼"W x 11"L.
A delightful addition to our ever growing orchestra of miniature musical instruments. Our diminutive cello features the same quality craftsmanship found in the Pocket Violin and comes complete with strings, bow and resin. Assembly is simple thanks to the easy to follow instructions and precision pre-cut parts.
K5432 Miniature Cello Kit 1 lb. 59.90
K85432 Finished Assembled Cello 1 lb. 79.00
D. Miniature Lute Kit
Est. Time: 10 hours. 2"D x 3¼"W x 10"L.
Our miniature lute conjures up the days of the travelling troubadours while displaying the unique construction of its full-sized counterpart. Fully pre-formed and pre-cut with clear instructions.
K5430 Miniature Lute Kit 1 lb. 49.00
K85430 Finished Assembled Lute 1 lb. 79.00
E. Miniature Instrument Stands
Clear acrylic stands designed to safely and attractively display the miniature musical instruments shown above. (Lute stand not available.)
K2602 Cello Stand ½ lb. 5.95
K2600 Guitar Stand ½ lb. 5.95
K2601 Violin Stand ½ lb. 5.95
24
A. Humpback Whale Est. Time: 10 hours. 16" long.
These gentle sea mammals have been returning from near extinction as man has begun to develop an appreciation for their beauty and intelligence. Master wildlife carver Frank Adamo has artfully fashioned this Humpback Whale in replica. Pre-carved in solid basswood with cast metal fins and flippers, this stunning model awaits your finishing touches and a base of your choice. Paints and complete instructions contribute to a project you'll be more than proud to display.
(Base is not included)
K5427 Humpback Whale 3 lbs. 59.00
B. Maine Lighthouse Kit
Est. Time: 10 hours. 8¼" Long x 8¼" High. Scale: 9/64"=1'
Scaled model of Maine's famous striped West Quoddy head lighthouse. Located on the easternmost point of land in the United States. This kit features jewelry quality pewter casting, pre-cut wood tower and Mahogany base, photo etched brass building and lighthouse parts and step by step instructions. Becomes working model with addition of electronics pack.
K5622 Lighthouse Kit 3 lbs. 49.95
Optional Electronics Pack
Becomes a working model lighthouse reproducing the actual signal sequence at West Quoddy when plugged into household current.
K15622 Electronics Pack 1 lb. 19.95
24 Hour
Toll Free Ordering
1-800-227-7418
C. Chess Board
(Finished and Assembled)
19½" x 19½" with 2" squares.
A beautiful walnut, mahogany, and birch chess board.
K25453 Chess Board 9 lbs. 56.00
D. Casting Kit
A complete casting kit that includes everything you will need to melt and pour the metal of the chess set shown on this page. Includes: stove, cord set, pouring ladle, 2 rubber mold clamps, heavy duty hot mill gloves.
K5456 Casting Kit 5 lbs. 39.00
E. Chess Set Casting Kit Est. Time: 100 hours.
Cast this beautifully detailed King Richard's Court chess set yourself using the 6 reusable silicone rubber molds included in this kit. Each chess piece is a sculptured 1:32 scale collector's miniature, cast from a lead-tin metal alloy. Kit includes 6 rubber molds, enough metal to produce a complete chess set, 32 wooden chess piece bases (16 walnut, 16 white), a 12 color paint kit, and complete instructions. The metal can be melted and poured using our casting kit shown above.
K5450 Chess Set Casting Kit 16 lbs. 159.00
K5451 Extra Metal for Another Complete Set 8 lbs. 23.50
K5452 32 Extra Wood Bases 3 lbs. 11.95
25

Delight in the easily-read typeface. Enjoy some of the cleanest, carefully thought-out and technically refined photography one could wish for in a book of this type. President John Hanson has done his groundwork: the products and the presentation are absolutely top drawer. From here on out, it's just a question of finding those patient people who love model-making.

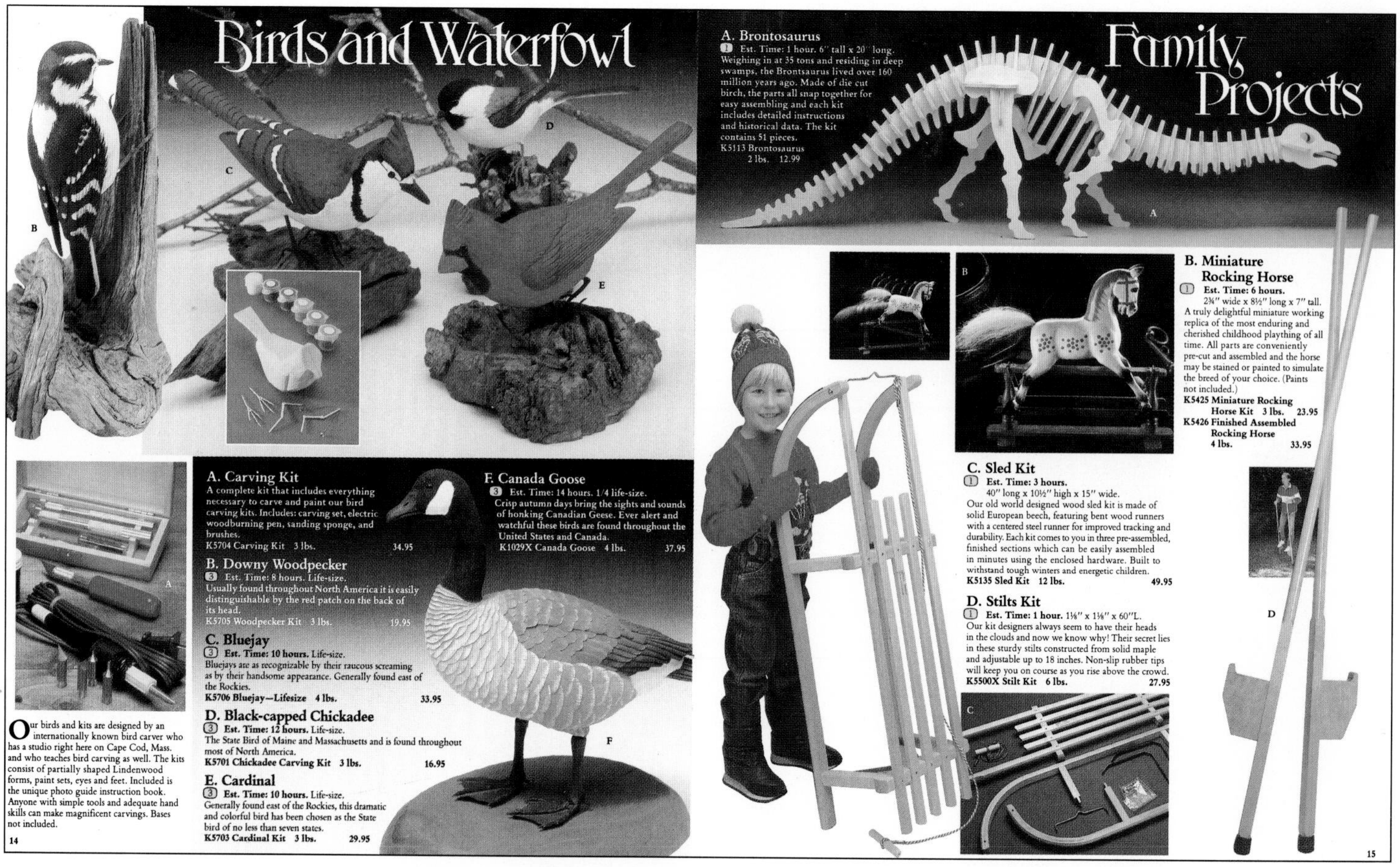
Birds and Waterfowl
A. Carving Kit
A complete kit that includes everything necessary to carve and paint our bird carving kits. Includes: carving set, electric woodburning pen, sanding sponge, and brushes.
K5704 Carving Kit 3 lbs. 34.95
B. Downy Woodpecker
3 Est. Time: 8 hours. Life-size.
Usually found throughout North America it is easily distinguishable by the red patch on the back of its head.
K5705 Woodpecker Kit 3 lbs. 19.95
C. Bluejay
3 Est. Time: 10 hours. Life-size.
Bluejays are as recognizable by their raucous screaming as by their handsome appearance. Generally found east of the Rockies.
K5706 Bluejay—Lifesize 4 lbs. 33.95
D. Black-capped Chickadee
3 Est. Time: 12 hours. Life-size.
The State Bird of Maine and Massachusetts and is found throughout most of North America.
K5701 Chickadee Carving Kit 3 lbs. 16.95
E. Cardinal
3 Est. Time: 10 hours. Life-size.
Generally found east of the Rockies, this dramatic and colorful bird has been chosen as the State bird of no less than seven states.
K5703 Cardinal Kit 3 lbs. 29.95
F. Canada Goose
3 Est. Time: 14 hours. 1/4 life-size.
Crisp autumn days bring the sights and sounds of honking Canadian Geese. Ever alert and watchful these birds are found throughout the United States and Canada.
K1029X Canada Goose 4 lbs. 37.95
Our birds and kits are designed by an internationally known bird carver who has a studio right here on Cape Cod, Mass. and who teaches bird carving as well. The kits consist of partially shaped Lindenwood forms, paint sets, eyes and feet. Included is the unique photo guide instruction book. Anyone with simple tools and adequate hand skills can make magnificent carvings. Bases not included.
14
Family Projects
A. Brontosaurus
1 Est. Time: 1 hour. 6" tall x 20" long.
Weighing in at 35 tons and residing in deep swamps, the Brontsaurus lived over 160 million years ago. Made of die cut birch, the parts all snap together for easy assembling and each kit includes detailed instructions and historical data. The kit contains 51 pieces.
K5113 Brontosaurus 2 lbs. 12.99
B. Miniature Rocking Horse
1 Est. Time: 6 hours.
2¾" wide x 8½" long x 7" tall.
A truly delightful miniature working replica of the most enduring and cherished childhood plaything of all time. All parts are conveniently pre-cut and assembled and the horse may be stained or painted to simulate the breed of your choice. (Paints not included.)
K5425 Miniature Rocking Horse Kit 3 lbs. 23.95
K5426 Finished Assembled Rocking Horse 4 lbs. 33.95
C. Sled Kit
1 Est. Time: 3 hours.
40" long x 10½" high x 15" wide.
Our old world designed wood sled kit is made of solid European beech, featuring bent wood runners with a centered steel runner for improved tracking and durability. Each kit comes to you in three pre-assembled, finished sections which can be easily assembled in minutes using the enclosed hardware. Built to withstand tough winters and energetic children.
K5135 Sled Kit 12 lbs. 49.95
D. Stilts Kit
1 Est. Time: 1 hour. 1⅛" x 1⅛" x 60"L.
Our kit designers always seem to have their heads in the clouds and now we know why! Their secret lies in these sturdy stilts constructed from solid maple and adjustable up to 18 inches. Non-slip rubber tips will keep you on course as you rise above the crowd.
K5500X Stilt Kit 6 lbs. 27.95
15

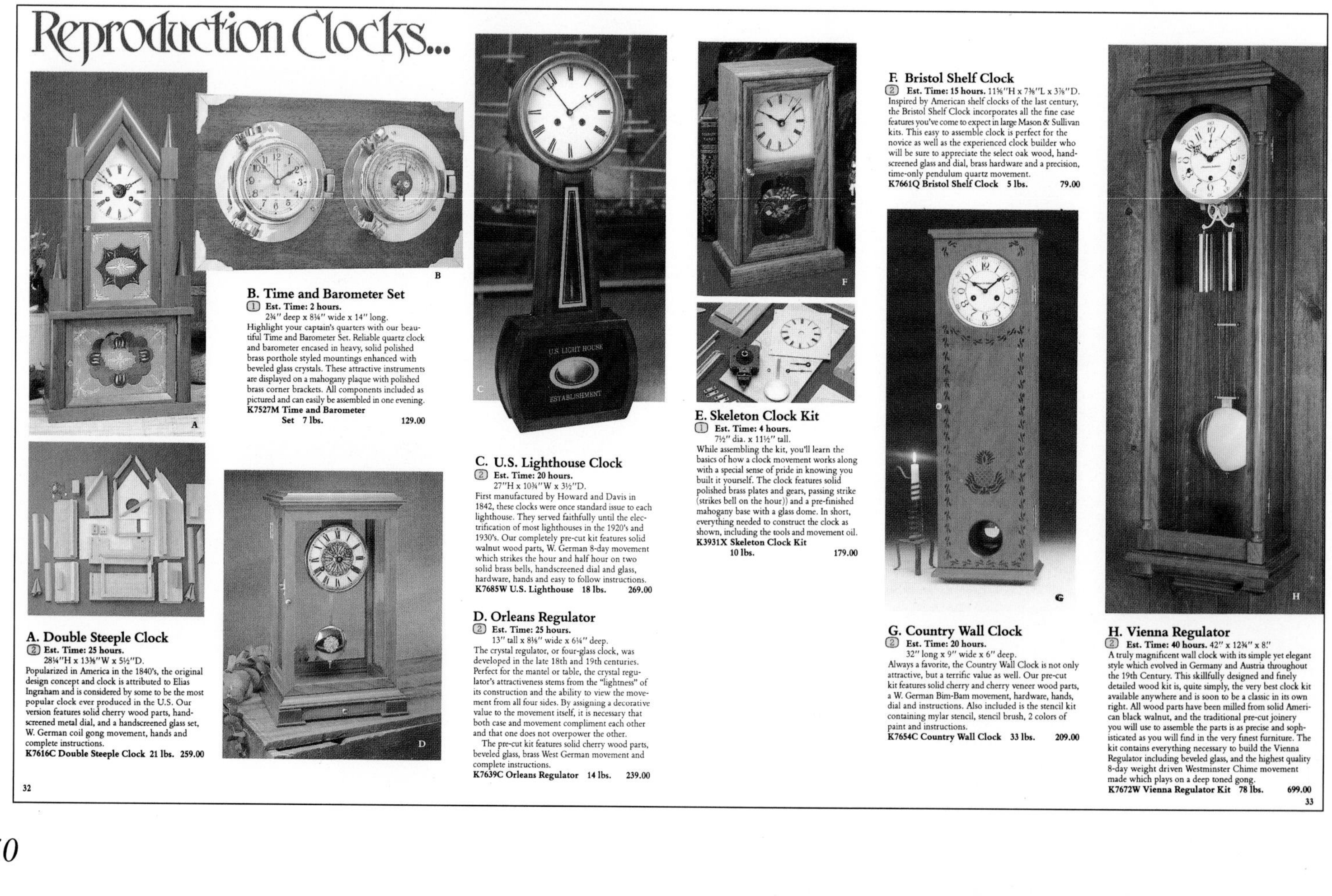
Reproduction Clocks...
A. Double Steeple Clock
2 Est. Time: 25 hours.
28¼"H x 13⅜"W x 5½"D.
Popularized in America in the 1840's, the original design concept and clock is attributed to Elias Ingraham and is considered by some to be the most popular clock ever produced in the U.S. Our version features solid cherry wood parts, hand-screened metal dial, and a handscreened glass set, W. German coil gong movement, hands and complete instructions.
K7616C Double Steeple Clock 21 lbs. 259.00
B. Time and Barometer Set
1 Est. Time: 2 hours.
2¾" deep x 8¼" wide x 14" long.
Highlight your captain's quarters with our beautiful Time and Barometer Set. Reliable quartz clock and barometer encased in heavy, solid polished brass porthole styled mountings enhanced with beveled glass crystals. These attractive instruments are displayed on a mahogany plaque with polished brass corner brackets. All components included as pictured and can easily be assembled in one evening.
K7527M Time and Barometer Set 7 lbs. 129.00
C. U.S. Lighthouse Clock
2 Est. Time: 20 hours.
27"H x 10¾"W x 3½"D.
First manufactured by Howard and Davis in 1842, these clocks were once standard issue to each lighthouse. They served faithfully until the electrification of most lighthouses in the 1920's and 1930's. Our completely pre-cut kit features solid walnut wood parts, W. German 8-day movement which strikes the hour and half hour on two solid brass bells, handscreened dial and glass, hardware, hands and easy to follow instructions.
K7685W U.S. Lighthouse 18 lbs. 269.00
D. Orleans Regulator
2 Est. Time: 25 hours.
13" tall x 8⅛" wide x 6¼" deep.
The crystal regulator, or four-glass clock, was developed in the late 18th and 19th centuries. Perfect for the mantel or table, the crystal regulator's attractiveness stems from the "lightness" of its construction and the ability to view the movement from all four sides. By assigning a decorative value to the movement itself, it is necessary that both case and movement compliment each other and that one does not overpower the other.
The pre-cut kit features solid cherry wood parts, beveled glass, brass West German movement and complete instructions.
K7639C Orleans Regulator 14 lbs. 239.00
E. Skeleton Clock Kit
1 Est. Time: 4 hours.
7½" dia. x 11½" tall.
While assembling the kit, you'll learn the basics of how a clock movement works along with a special sense of pride in knowing you built it yourself. The clock features solid polished brass plates and gears, passing strike (strikes bell on the hour)) and a pre-finished mahogany base with a glass dome. In short, everything needed to construct the clock as shown, including the tools and movement oil.
K3931X Skeleton Clock Kit 10 lbs. 179.00
F. Bristol Shelf Clock
2 Est. Time: 15 hours. 11⅝"H x 7⅜"L x 3⅞"D.
Inspired by American shelf clocks of the last century, the Bristol Shelf Clock incorporates all the fine case features you've come to expect in large Mason & Sullivan kits. This easy to assemble clock is perfect for the novice as well as the experienced clock builder who will be sure to appreciate the select oak wood, hand-screened glass and dial, brass hardware and a precision, time-only pendulum quartz movement.
K7661Q Bristol Shelf Clock 5 lbs. 79.00
G. Country Wall Clock
2 Est. Time: 20 hours.
32" long x 9" wide x 6" deep.
Always a favorite, the Country Wall Clock is not only attractive, but a terrific value as well. Our pre-cut kit features solid cherry and cherry veneer wood parts, a W. German Bim-Bam movement, hardware, hands, dial and instructions. Also included is the stencil kit containing mylar stencil, stencil brush, 2 colors of paint and instructions.
K7654C Country Wall Clock 33 lbs. 209.00
H. Vienna Regulator
2 Est. Time: 40 hours. 42" x 12¾" x 8."
A truly magnificent wall clock with its simple yet elegant style which evolved in Germany and Austria throughout the 19th Century. This skillfully designed and finely detailed wood kit is, quite simply, the very best clock kit available anywhere and is soon to be a classic in its own right. All wood parts have been milled from solid American black walnut, and the traditional pre-cut joinery you will use to assemble the parts is as precise and sophisticated as you will find in the very finest furniture. The kit contains everything necessary to build the Vienna Regulator including beveled glass, and the highest quality 8-day weight driven Westminster Chime movement made which plays on a deep toned gong.
K7672W Vienna Regulator Kit 78 lbs. 699.00
32
33

COLLECTORS' PAPERWEIGHTS

Collectors' Paperweights is high on my list of the Great Catalogs of the 20th Century. Not because the paperweights are beautiful or because I collect paperweights. They are, and I don't. Not because it is thick (180 pages), or that it is exceptionally well printed, or even because it is opulent in presentation and rich with merchandise.

It's tops in my eyes because it is AUTHORITATIVE!

L. H. Selman Ltd. has been active in the paperweight field for more than twenty years. They have been publishing since 1975. And, their extensive knowledge of the field is readily apparent in this catalog. As a matter of fact, to call this award winning publication a catalog is almost a misnomer. It is a price guide, a reference book, a Who's Who of today's artists. It contains a glossary of trade terms as well as a discussion of restoration and authentication techniques. There's a bibliography, and even a treatise on the history of the paperweight as an art form, tracing its beginnings to 18th century France.

As one ACA judge commented, "Forget the coffee table. . . This catalog belongs in your library."

The power that emanates from this catalog is derived from Collectors' Paperweights' position of absolute authority. With this masterful tour de force of a catalog, Lawrence H. Selman has given us lesser mortals a target that will endure for a very long time.

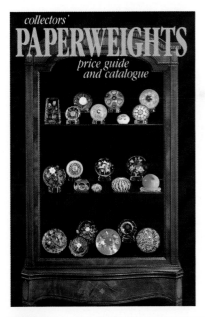

COLLECTORS' PAPERWEIGHTS—1987 Price Guide and Catalogue
Lynn Walker-Lightfoot, *Catalog Director*
Genevieve Heth, *Designer*
Nikki Silva, *Copywriter*
Jon Covello and Paul Schraub, *Photographers*
Stephen Pollard, *Typographer*
Publishers Press [Salt Lake City, UT], *Printer, on 10 pt. C1S for cover and 80# Shasta Gloss for text*

TABLE OF CONTENTS

Over 50 pages are devoted to antique paperweights from Baccarat, Clichy, Saint Louis, early American, Bacchus, Whitefriars, Val St. Lambert, Pinchbeck and various Bohemian sources. Prices for these antiques extend from $350 to $20,000, with the majority in the high three- to low four-figure range. Prices, even for contemporary paperweights, vary from $100 to $3,000. Not too surprising, considering the amount of time involved and the quality of the workmanship. Without doubt, they are certain to increase in value over time. Most assuredly worth another look into Grandma's trunk up in the attic!

New or more contemporary paperweights are illustrated in chapters delineated by artist and/or manufacturer. Each of these chapters—25 in all—begins with a photograph and biography of the artist, a description of his work and a replica of his "signature cane" (hallmark).

Lawrence H. Selman and the Paperweight Press are to be congratulated on a fine publication-cum-catalog. They have earned a preeminent position and leadership status in their chosen niche. In the catalog world, that is the ultimate in market positioning.

A HISTORY OF PAPERWEIGHT MAKING

THE EARLIEST GLASS paperweights, sulphides, were sculpted ceramic cameos completely encased in crystal. First developed during the 1750s in France, sulphides were later refined and perfected in England by Apsley Pellatt, who took out a patent on the technique in 1819. Glass encrustations, which often commemorated important individuals and historic events, were extremely popular throughout the nineteenth century. In addition to paperweights, they were used to ornament a variety of glass objects including decanters, perfume bottles, seals, candlesticks, buttons, and jewelry.

There is little definitive information available as to when French glass factories first produced millefiori paperweights, but it is believed that the major inspiration came from the Exhibition of Austrian Industry held in Vienna in 1845. It was there that a Muranese glassworker, Pietro Bigaglia of Venice, displayed his "round shaped millefiori paperweights of transparent glass in which were inserted quantities of small tubes of all colors and forms assembled so as to look like a multitude of florets." Although some paperweights may have been produced in France prior to Bigaglia's display, it is generally accepted that this was the beginning of France's interest in producing paperweights as saleable objects.

During the classic period of millefiori and lampwork paperweight making (1840–1860), three outstanding glass factories in France set the pace in style and production of fine quality pieces: Compagnie des Cristalleries de Baccarat, Cristalleries de Saint Louis, and Clichy-la-Garenne. In a surprisingly short period of time, these French factories perfected the millefiori technique, introducing and developing the lampwork style as well. The high quality and the range of styles and design motifs created in France during this time have never been surpassed.

English glass factories were quick to imitate the French, and soon millefiori paperweights were being produced by factories in London and Birmingham. Prominent English makers in the nineteenth century were Bacchus, Whitefriars, and Islington.

2

In the United States, the production of paperweights in large numbers did not begin until after the New York Exhibition of the Industry of All Nations, held in New York City in 1853. Many of the early American weights were imitative of the French style: scrambled, close packed millefiori, and concentrics in clear glass or on latticinio grounds. However, the American makers were quick to contribute their own distinctive styles and techniques to paperweight making, particularly in the area of lampworking.

After about 1860 interest in paperweights tapered off in France, Britain and other European countries. It continued to flourish in America, with some production continuing intermittently into the early part of this century. The best-known American makers were the New England Glass Company, the Boston and Sandwich Glass Company, Gillinder, Mount Washington, and Millville.

Paperweight making was on the verge of becoming a lost art in the 1950s when Paul Jokelson, an importer and avid paperweight collector, approached the glass factories of Baccarat and Saint Louis with the idea of reviving the classic art. This was a difficult and challenging proposition, since paperweights had not been produced in significant numbers for more than eighty years. Artists and craftsmen spent nearly twenty years in research and experimentation rediscovering the techniques used in making sulphide, millefiori and lampwork paperweights. Once they succeeded, interest in contemporary paperweights blossomed.

Since that time several other glass factories, such as Perthshire in Scotland, have joined Baccarat and Saint Louis in producing fine quality modern paperweights. At the same time, individual glass artists are also producing paperweights. These contemporary factories and studio artists are responsible for the paperweight renaissance of the last thirty-five years. Their work has produced an exciting new generation of paperweights.

3

HOW PAPERWEIGHTS ARE MADE

The encasing process

Certain aspects of the paperweight making process, such as encasing a design in crystal, faceting, and finishing a piece, are the same for both millefiori and lampwork style weights. Once the millefiori canes or lampwork figures have been made they are arranged on a metal template and heated to just below the melting point. A metal collar is placed around the arrangement. The glassworker gathers a ball of molten glass on the end of a long iron pontil rod and rolls and works it into shape on a metal plate or "marver." He then lowers the red-hot glass into the collar and picks up the preheated design. This first gather of molten glass makes up the ground of the weight.

After the design is picked up, the piece is reheated in the "glory hole," the opening of the heating oven. Another gather of clear molten glass is added to form the dome of the weight. The worker rolls the pontil rod back and forth across the arms of his glassworking chair so that the still-soft glass will not sag or become misshapen. During this process the dome of the weight is shaped and smoothed with a wet wooden block or contoured pad of tissue or newspaper. While the glass is still pliable, tongs are used to form a slender neck at the base of the weight. When the piece has cooled sufficiently the worker gives a sharp tap to the pontil rod. The weight breaks off and falls into a bed of sand.

The next step is to gradually and evenly cool the weight in an annealing oven. This process is extremely critical. Sometimes the gathers of glass and design elements within a weight cool at different rates causing the piece to crack or shatter.

The final stage of the process is grinding and polishing. During this stage the "pontil mark" or scar that was made when the weight was separated from the pontil rod is ground down. Then, if desired, the dome of the weight is faceted or cut with a grinding wheel.

A paperweight is hand crafted during each step of its creation. Even if many weights of the same design are made by a glass factory, each has its own individual character.

Picking up the bouquet

Shaping the dome

Millefiori

The Italian word *millefiori* means "thousand flowers" and is used to describe the decorative elements which make up some of the most popular paperweight designs. The first step in making a millefiori paperweight is to produce a variety of glass rods or canes. The glassworker gathers molten glass from the furnace and works it into shape on a marver. If color is desired, the gather is rolled in colored glass powder, or colored glass is coated over the molten glass. It is then pressed into an iron mold and allowed to cool. Once the glass has hardened another gather of molten glass is added. The piece is again worked on the marver and pressed into a mold of a different shape. This process can be repeated several times to build layers of colors and designs within a rod.

At this stage the rod is about three inches in diameter and six inches long. The piece is reheated and another glassworker attaches a second pontil rod to the cane. The two workers quickly move apart, stretching the heated cane until it is pencil thin and sometimes over thirty feet long. The most uniformly stretched portions of the rod are

Attaching the second pontil rod

Stretching the cane

Complex millefiori canes

Lampworking

7

From the scratch-board art depicting "A History of Paperwight Making" to full-color photographs showing "How Paperweights Are Made", the uninitiated among us are given more than enough information to tantalize.

Merchandise from the great houses of paperweight manufacture soon follow: Baccarat, Clichy, Val St. Lambert and many other famous names in the tabletop world fill these pages.

ANTIQUE AMERICAN

PAPERWEIGHT MAKING arrived in the United States in the 1850s almost a decade after its appearance in Europe. It is believed that American glass factories first became interested in paperweight production after viewing the European weights on display at the Great Exhibition in London in 1851. It is likely, however, that Americans traveling abroad in the 1840s had also seen examples of paperweight making.

Many early American weights were imitative of the French-style scrambled, close millefiori, and concentric patterns set on clear glass or on latticinio grounds. In general, the American weights contained canes which were less complex in structure than the French. However, the American makers quickly infused their own style into their work and branched off into a variety of creative lampwork subjects.

Three American glass factories stand out as principal paperweight producers in these early years: the New England Glass Company of East Cambridge, Massachusetts (NEGC); the Boston and Sandwich Glass Company at Sandwich on Cape Cod, Massachusetts; and the Mount Washington Glass Works of South Boston and New Bedford, Massachusetts. All three factories were founded by Deming Jarves, an enterprising Boston merchant. The three factories often drew from the same group of skilled craftsmen, many of whom came from European apprenticeships. Occasionally, these craftsmen swapped millefiori rods. It is therefore often difficult to distinguish between the paperweights made at each factory, though each glasshouse had a distinct history and reputation.

Another American factory which was well known for its paperweights is Whitall Tatum and Company, in Millville, New Jersey. As early as the 1860s, workers at Millville were experimenting with paperweight making during their off hours. Over the years a variety of distinctly American styles and design motifs were developed at Millville including the factory's most famous design, the Millville rose.

Paperweight making was practiced longer in the United States than in Europe, with some production continuing intermittently into the early part of the twentieth century.

10

1 Concentric rings of pastel millefiori canes set over a clear ground surround a bold geometric cane. $325

2 Two ripe red apples on a stem with four serrated leaves are set over a clear ground. $650

3 Arranged on a stem with four leaves, two brightly striped apples are set over a clear ground. $950

11

ANTIQUE BACCARAT

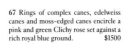

THE GLASS FACTORY that is today called Compagnie des Cristalleries de Baccarat was founded in 1764 under the name Verrerie de Sainte Anne. Located in the Alsace-Lorraine region of France within fifty miles of Cristalleries de Saint Louis, Verrerie de Sainte Anne specialized in plate glass, mirrors, and a wide range of utilitarian glassware. During the 1820s the factory, which had by then started producing fine lead glass, was sold and renamed Cristalleries de Baccarat.

In 1846, under the management of Emile Godard, the craftsmen at Baccarat perfected the production of millefiori paperweights. By 1848 exquisite lampwork flowers, bouquets, butterflies and other motifs were also being produced. Paperweight manufacture at Baccarat was a small but significant part of the company's production for almost twenty years.

Baccarat excelled in the making of silhouette canes, which were frequently used in carpet grounds, trefoils, mushrooms, overlays and close packed weights. Eighteen of the best-known Baccarat silhouettes, called the Gridel series, were based on the paper cutout designs created in 1847 by Joseph Emile Gridel, the nine-year-old nephew of Jean-Baptiste Toussaint, Baccarat's manager at the time.

Less than a quarter of the antique paperweights produced by Baccarat contain date or signature canes. When a signature cane is present it is always accompanied by a date cane; some date canes appear alone. Date canes are comprised of four distinct rods fused together, with a single numeral in each rod.

67 Rings of complex canes, edelweiss canes and moss-edged canes encircle a pink and green Clichy rose set against a rich royal blue ground. $1500

68 Concentric rings of vividly colored Clichy canes are set over a tomato-red ground in this jewel-like miniature weight. $800

69 An interesting array of classic Clichy canes, including a perfectly formed pink and green rose and a superb white and green rose, is arranged in a spaced millefiori design against a midnight blue ground. $2600

35

The good news is that the art form is alive and well. Twenty-five contemporary artists are represented on the pages of this catalog, and a brief biography establishes the verities of the individual artist.

Within each of these chapters, examples of modern work are displayed with exactly the same respect as is shown to the antique, and considerably more valuable, items in the front of the catalog.

RICK AYOTTE

RICK AYOTTE is the only contemporary glass artist specializing in lampwork bird paperweights. A paperweight artist since 1976, Ayotte's colorful and finely detailed birds are often set in naturalistic surroundings which include intricate foliage, blossoms, berries, butterflies, and nests.

A native of Nashua, New Hampshire, Ayotte studied at Lowell Technological Institute and later took a job as a scientific glassblower. In 1970 he started his own business, Ayotte's Artistry in Glass, which specialized in novelty glassware and gifts. While working in the scientific glassblowing industry, Ayotte became acquainted with glass artist Paul Stankard, who first introduced him to the idea of making paperweights. Ayotte found paperweight making a creative challenge as well as an opportunity to combine his skill and expertise in glass with a longtime interest in ornithology.

Ayotte's fascination with birds began when he was in high school. During that time he charted migratory bird groups and studied their food and eating habits. He also began carving life-size birds from wood.

Ayotte's glass paperweights reflect his knowledge and love of ornithology as well as his mastery of the art of glassmaking. His colors are vibrant and alive, and his birds and environments are accurate and realistic. He has also developed a compound layering technique, which involves creating two separate encased layers within a weight. This technique has given him the ability to achieve unusual depth and dimension in his work.

Ayotte produces paperweights in editions of twenty-five to seventy-five pieces, and signs his work with an engraved "Ayotte" on the base.

145 A golden-fronted leafbird is perched in a tropical golden shower tree with blossoms and seed pods in this colorful compound weight. $550

146 An orange and yellow flowering quince surrounds a finely crafted winter wren set over a clear ground. $475

147 A male and female screech owl resting on a pine branch with cones and delicate green needles are set over a clear ground. $450

MICHAEL O'KEEFE

WORKING IN A CONVERTED storefront in Seattle's south end, glass artist Michael O'Keefe is creating a new and exciting look in paperweights. O'Keefe's distinctive weights feature three-dimensional translucent forms in a range of soft colors. The exterior shape of each piece is specially designed to complement the interior motif.

O'Keefe began learning about glass while studying at the Center for Creative Studies in Detroit, where he received his BFA in photography. After graduating in 1976 he worked at the Poultry Glassworks in downtown Detroit, where he first became familiar with paperweight making.

At Poultry Glassworks O'Keefe learned the silver veiling technique which he uses in creating his paperweights. Silver veiling involves the melting together of silver and glass. By reheating the glass the silver is drawn to the surface where the design is developed. Then additional glass encases the design and the outside is fire polished.

The unusually subtle and delicate colors in O'Keefe's weights are due to the ingredients he uses in his glass mixture. Certain elements in the formula cause the silver to react in specific ways. When the glass is pulled and twisted, the silver causes the glass to change color—sometimes from brown to yellow, or from yellow to blue. Another factor which controls the color is the rate at which the glass is reheated and cooled.

Although his pieces involve sophisticated technology and a high degree of craftsmanship, O'Keefe manages to maintain an overall feeling of simplicity and elegance in his work. Each piece is engraved on the bottom with the artist's name and the date.

214 This spiral design, reminiscent of the inside swirl of a seashell, is formed in pale blue glass by the process of silver veiling. $100

215 In this weight the same silver veiled design as above is executed in amber glass. $100

216 Blue glass and silver veiling are combined in this fan-shaped spiral design, which is also available in amber glass. $100

361 Concentric rings of millefiori set on a translucent color ground form the base of this Perthshire perfume bottle with encased glass thread stopper. Signed in the center of the base with a P cane. Colors vary. $110

362 Close packed millefiori on a dark blue ground make up this elegant Perthshire doorknob with brass fittings. $90

363 This miniature perfume bottle by David Salazar, which matches one of his paperweight designs (see number 291), sets the moon and stars against a dramatic night sky. $120

157

The back of the Collectors' Paperweights catalog is as powerful as the front. It is, in effect, a series of appendices that includes Related Objects (e.g. cuff links), Suggested Reading, a Glossary, an article on Paperweight Restoration, and offerings of Contemporary Sulphides (e.g. cameos) and Gridel Animals from the houses of Baccarat, Cristal d'Albret and Saint Louis.

367 Gold foil insects, birds and shamrocks are encased in clear glass over a color ground in these distinctive pieces of jewelry by John Gooderham.

Pierced earrings (bee, bird or butterfly):
Regular: $60
Single white overlay: $80
Double blue over white overlay: $100

Lapel pin or tie tack (swan, shamrock, horse or elephant): $50

368 Handsome millefiori cufflinks, pendant, and lapel pin or tie tack by Saint Louis are available in red, green or blue.

Lapel pin or tie tack: $90
Pendant: $100
Cufflinks: $150

369 This elegant pendant by David Lotton is made of web thread iridescent glass with gold wire fittings. $40

159

Lovers of esoterica will delight in the Glossary, wherein are found such entries as:

> *Cane: a molded or bundled glass rod that has been pulled out to miniaturize the interior design.*
> *Cinquefoil: a garland of canes having five loops.*
> *Flash: a thin coating of transparent glass applied to the base of a paperweight. . . .*
> *Jasper ground: paperweight background formed by a mixture of two colors of finely ground glass.*
> *Latticinio: a lacy backdrop created from white and clear glass.*
> *Torsade: an opaque glass thread loosely wound around a filigree core, usually found near the base of a mushroom weight.*

This is, indeed, a book for one's permanent library. A delightful delectation for the dilettante, but heavy-duty datum for the cognoscenti.

COMFORTABLY YOURS

"**W**e ain't gettin' any younger!'' You've heard that old bromide a hundred times. But that doesn't make it a bit more palatable nor one whit less true. The fact is, America is ageing, but the ageing process is not the same downhill slide we used to know. Nobody knows that better than Richard Balkite, President of Mature Marketing Network of Greenwich, CT, formerly Director of Senior Marketing at Donnelley Marketing. Hear now these statistics from the man who is responsible for selling millions to this market:

Americans 55 and over own nearly three quarters *of the nation's personal financial assets,*

80% of the money in Savings & Loans is theirs,

they generate one-third of all personal income—866 billion dollars (that's billion, with a ''B''),

more than 30% of this group (the same as in the 25-49 age group) are considering the purchase of a new car!

Marketers of every product from insurance to ice cream, boots to bras, and toasters to treadmills have fielded special teams to go after this rapidly growing and very affluent market segment. Some have found the mother lode, others have backed off, shaking their heads trying to figure out what went wrong.

Many of the first stabs at selling to senior citizens came a cropper for a darned good reason. Marketing gurus started to hang labels on these potential customers that said, ''You are an old person''. During the 1950s, '60s and right up until the late '70s, terms like Golden Age, Senior Citizen and Gray Power were indiscriminately hitched onto sales slogans and travel packages. Consumers from age 49 to 100 were all tagged with the same epithet, and they stayed away from the offending stores and ticket counters in droves.

COMFORTABLY YOURS
Elaine Adler, *President*
Agency: *In-house*

That's Comfortably Yours President Elaine Adler in the upper left hand corner. . . and there she is again, wearing a white wig (in a fruitless attempt to look older) on the right hand spread, with model Bonnie Trompeter, her good friend. Comfortably Yours gets right down to business from the Outside Front Cover to the fully merchandised Outside Back Cover. Absolutely no frills here. Just a good hardworking mailorder catalog with all the copy necessary to do a good, strong selling job.

Pegging a segment of our population by age makes about as much sense as choosing a group of prospects based upon the color of their eyes. Ask any reasonably healthy adult with five, six or seven decades under his belt if he feels old. The response you get may include a litany of aches and pains, but that is not the point. The people inside those creaking bodies have the same interests, speak the same vernacular, and indulge in the same cultural pursuits as they did when they were younger.

Older citizens tend to buy fewer *things* and more *services*. They have a better eye for value. Gradual dis-accumulation quite happily relieves the unnecessary clutter from their lives. But how many good-ol'-boy bourbon drinkers do you know who made the switch to Amaretto on their 50th birthday? And who do you think are buying all those golf course condos in Florida, Colorado, Arizona and the Carolinas?

The Comfortably Yours catalog was launched in 1982 to address the wants and needs of the not-so-young body such as: comfort, convenience, warmth, safety, personal appearance and health.

Arthritis, bulges, bad feet and weak knees aren't fun, but for most people of age, they are an immutable fact of life. For these folk, with their bodily creaks and squeaks, there are products available to help make life more bearable. Before Comfortably Yours came along, these specialized products were extremely difficult to find. In fact, most of us did not know of their existence. A few large drug stores have a limited stock of this type of item—frequently at very high margins. Department stores do little to serve the ageing or disabled markets.

The Comfortably Yours catalog, on the other hand, has 52 pages chock-full of the most imaginative and thoughtfully chosen essentials ever assembled between two covers. Every item in this assortment has been carefully selected to make life easier and more comfortable for this group of consumers. A sample:

Safety Boots—*'Angled tread' sole is embedded with gritty, sandpaper-like substance that grips wet, slippery or icy surfaces. . . .*

Special Moisturizer—*Replenishing lost moisture is essential to nourish and protect your skin for maintaining a healthy, youthful look! Daily use of my Special Moisturizer with collagen leaves your face feeling soft, supple, non-greasy and as radiant as ever!*

5-Power Mirror—*It's difficult applying eye makeup when you need glasses to see. So frustrating that a lot of women who wear glasses have given up trying. . . .*

Princess and the Pea Cushion—*. . . you won't feel anything but comfort. This marvelous seating aid is designed to reduce the jolts and bumps of driving, and for anyone who must sit for long periods of time.*

Ventilated Socks—*The cuffed anklets have cushioned soles that are uniquely ventilated to keep your feet warm in winter and cool in summer. . . .*

There are Hand-Held Infrared units, Zoned Electric Mattress Pads, Heated Footstools, Lecturaid (an amplifier that looks like a Walkman), and dozens of convenience and safety products for the bath and bedrooms. There's a selection of prosthetic devices and a spread labeled ''Healthful Gourmet'' for those on restricted diets. Special purpose underwear is a major category and super-comfort footwear is featured throughout the catalog—over 300 items in all.

Comfortably Yours is, in many respects, an outstanding example of mailorder at its best.

- *In the first place, the catalog reaches out to a customer who finds it difficult to travel, even to a local store. A very real and much needed service.*
- *The majority of the items found in this catalog are very difficult to find in any one community, much less from any single source, be it store or catalog.*
- *Elaine Adler, President of the mailorder firm, is in constant and close touch with her customers. She's made aware of calls and requests from customers that are even slightly out of the ordinary. Her eighty-plus year old mother was part of the original inspiration for Comfortably Yours, and Elaine is an active director of The Home & Hospital of the Daughters of Jacob, in Bronx, New York. This firm's owner is in contact with the real world in which her customers live.*
- *A large circle of the Adler's friends and relatives serve as a mega-size test panel for every one of the items in the catalog. Their instructions are: ''Don't be nice. If there are any flaws, dysfunctions or fit problems, tell me!''—and they do.*
- *Comfortably Yours buys U.S. Patriotic? Very! (As a matter of fact, Elaine has always driven automobiles made in this country, even when it was not easy to buy a quality machine here.) For the Comfortably Yours customer, buying American has another very positive connotation. It means that most items are in stock all the time. Even when an item is on backorder, it is realistic to anticipate quick delivery. In the most recent catalog, only one RTW item came from overseas.*
- *The Comfortably Yours catalog is sensitive to the physical limitations of some of its customers. The typeface is the very legible Century Old Style, well leaded, and with plenty of boldface and italic font shifts for emphasis and legibility.*
- *There's a total lack of glitz. This is a working catalog. The emphasis is clearly on product quality and function; and on the comfort and well-being of the Comfortably Yours customer.*

In 1987, there were 55 million residents of the United States age fifty-five or older. That group is forecast to expand 62 percent by the year 2015, while the general population will increase by only 19 percent. The number of women over forty will grow by more than 50 percent within the next 25 years! This ageing population will not have the same characteristics as in generations past. God willing, they will never have lived through the gut-wrenching terror of a full scale depression. Their corporate and personal pension plans differ vastly from the pittances of the past. And, for at least the next 20 years, the Social Security Fund seems sufficient (if we can keep the politicians' paws out of the barrel).

Some demographers and economists feel the implications for our country are far-reaching and exciting. Others have said the portents suggest major disruptions in the fabric of the United States economy. Who can know which group of pundits is correct? But, at least for Comfortably Yours, the future seems obvious and bright.

Support garments and lingerie are major categories with Comfortably Yours. So much so, that a new catalog called "Shapely Figures" was mailed early this year. In the original Comfortably Yours book, these categories continue to grow, but so too do areas like exercise machines, jump suits and skin moisturizers. To relieve the miseries of arthritis, bursitis and the associated neuralgias and aches, Comfortably Yours offers a selection of gels, balms and braces. Sufferers will be happy to hear that modern technology (and Comfortably Yours) has made it possible to buy hand-held infrared heating units that have the same salutary effect as high-priced units in high-priced doctors' offices.

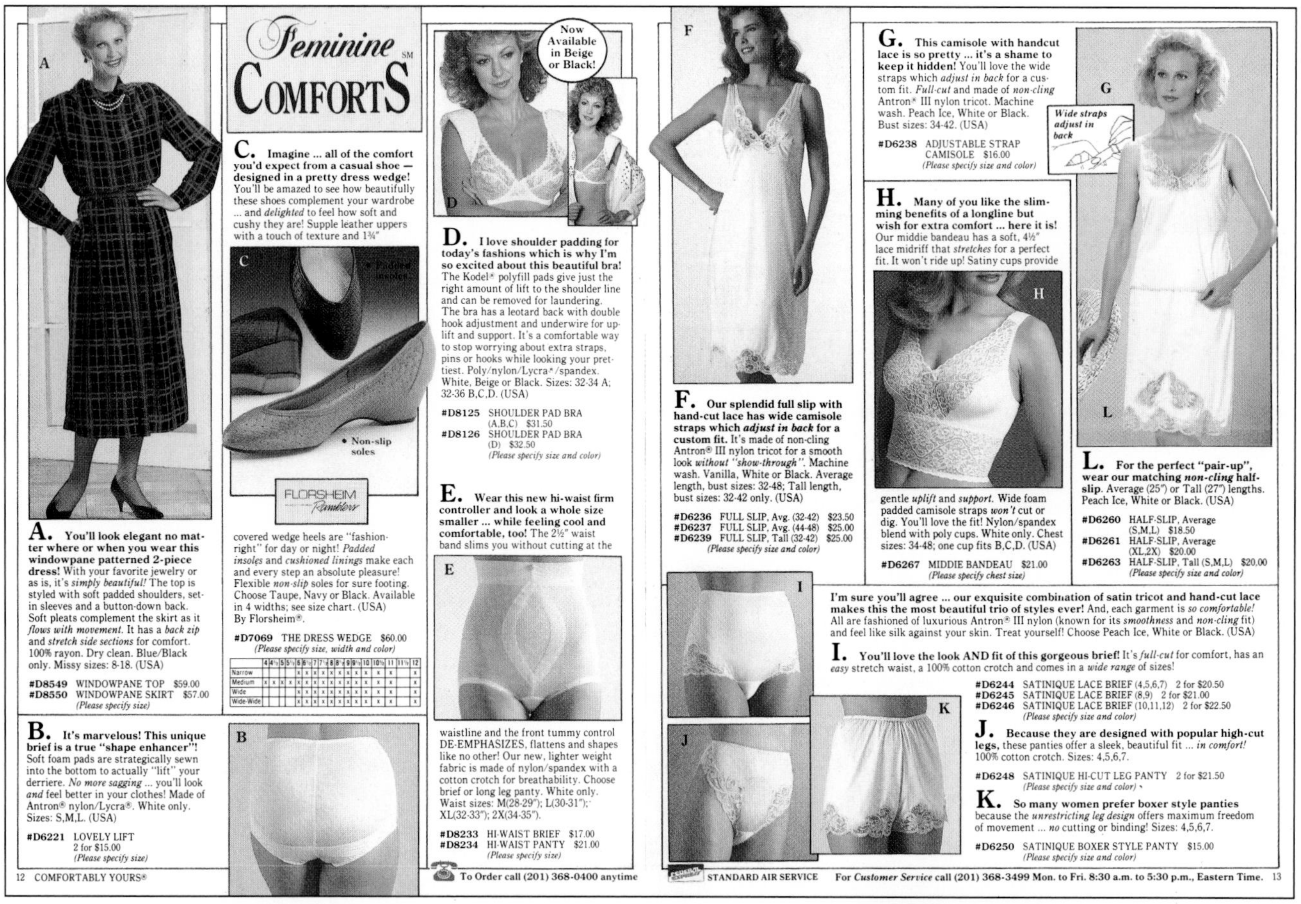

Feminine COMFORTS

A. You'll look elegant no matter where or when you wear this windowpane patterned 2-piece dress! With your favorite jewelry or as is, it's simply beautiful! The top is styled with soft padded shoulders, set-in sleeves and a button-down back. Soft pleats complement the skirt as it flows with movement. It has a back zip and stretch side sections for comfort. 100% rayon. Dry clean. Blue/Black only. Missy sizes: 8-18. (USA)

#D8549 WINDOWPANE TOP $59.00
#D8550 WINDOWPANE SKIRT $57.00
(Please specify size)

B. It's marvelous! This unique brief is a true "shape enhancer"! Soft foam pads are strategically sewn into the bottom to actually "lift" your derriere. No more sagging ... you'll look and feel better in your clothes! Made of Antron® nylon/Lycra®. White only. Sizes: S,M,L. (USA)

#D6221 LOVELY LIFT
2 for $15.00
(Please specify size)

C. Imagine ... all of the comfort you'd expect from a casual shoe — designed in a pretty dress wedge! You'll be amazed to see how beautifully these shoes complement your wardrobe ... and delighted to feel how soft and cushy they are! Supple leather uppers with a touch of texture and 1¾"

• Padded insoles
• Non-slip soles

FLORSHEIM *Femelace*

covered wedge heels are "fashion-right" for day or night! Padded insoles and cushioned linings make each and every step an absolute pleasure! Flexible non-slip soles for sure footing. Choose Taupe, Navy or Black. Available in 4 widths; see size chart. (USA) By Florsheim®.

#D7069 THE DRESS WEDGE $60.00
(Please specify size, width and color)

	4¼	5	5½	6	6½	7	7½	8	8½	9	9½	10	10½	11	11½	12
Narrow		x	x	x	x	x	x	x	x	x	x	x	x	x		
Medium		x	x	x	x	x	x	x	x	x	x	x	x	x	x	x
Wide			x	x	x	x	x	x	x	x	x	x	x	x		
Wide-Wide			x	x	x	x	x	x	x	x	x	x	x			

Now Available in Beige or Black!

D. I love shoulder padding for today's fashions which is why I'm so excited about this beautiful bra! The Kodel® polyfill pads give just the right amount of lift to the shoulder line and can be removed for laundering. The bra has a leotard back with double hook adjustment and underwire for up-lift and support. It's a comfortable way to stop worrying about extra straps, pins or hooks while looking your prettiest. Poly/nylon/Lycra®/spandex. White, Beige or Black. Sizes: 32-34 A; 32-36 B,C,D. (USA)

#D8125 SHOULDER PAD BRA (A,B,C) $31.50
#D8126 SHOULDER PAD BRA (D) $32.50
(Please specify size and color)

E. Wear this new hi-waist firm controller and look a whole size smaller ... while feeling cool and comfortable, too! The 2½" waist band slims you without cutting at the

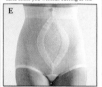

waistline and the front tummy control DE-EMPHASIZES, flattens and shapes like no other! Our new, lighter weight fabric is made of nylon/spandex with a cotton crotch for breathability. Choose brief or long leg panty. White only. Waist sizes: M(28-29"); L(30-31"); XL(32-33"); 2X(34-35"). (USA)

#D8233 HI-WAIST BRIEF $17.00
#D8234 HI-WAIST PANTY $21.00
(Please specify size and color)

F. Our splendid full slip with hand-cut lace has wide camisole straps which adjust in back for a custom fit. It's made of non-cling Antron® III nylon tricot for a smooth look without "show-through". Machine wash. Vanilla, White or Black. Average length, bust sizes: 32-48; Tall length, bust sizes 32-42 only. (USA)

#D6236 FULL SLIP, Avg. (32-42) $23.50
#D6238 FULL SLIP, Avg. (44-48) $25.00
#D6239 FULL SLIP, Tall (32-42) $25.00
(Please specify size and color)

G. This camisole with handcut lace is so pretty ... it's a shame to keep it hidden! You'll love the wide straps which adjust in back for a custom fit. Full-cut and made of non-cling Antron® III nylon tricot. Machine wash. Peach Ice, White or Black. Bust sizes: 34-42. (USA)

Wide straps adjust in back

#D6238 ADJUSTABLE STRAP CAMISOLE $16.00
(Please specify size and color)

H. Many of you like the slimming benefits of a longline but wish for extra comfort ... here it is! Our middie bandeau has a soft, 4½" lace midriff that stretches for a perfect fit. It won't ride up! Satiny cups provide gentle uplift and support. Wide foam padded camisole straps won't cut or dig. You'll love the fit! Nylon/spandex blend with poly cups. White only. Chest sizes: 34-48; one cup fits B,C,D. (USA)

#D6267 MIDDIE BANDEAU $21.00
(Please specify chest size)

I. You'll love the look AND fit of this gorgeous brief! It's full-cut for comfort, has an easy stretch waist, a 100% cotton crotch and comes in a wide range of sizes!

#D6244 SATINIQUE LACE BRIEF (4,5,6,7) 2 for $20.50
#D6245 SATINIQUE LACE BRIEF (8,9) 2 for $21.00
#D6246 SATINIQUE LACE BRIEF (10,11,12) 2 for $22.50
(Please specify size and color)

L. For the perfect "pair-up", wear our matching non-cling half-slip. Average (25") or Tall (27") lengths. Peach Ice, White or Black. (USA)

#D6260 HALF-SLIP, Average (S,M,L) $18.50
#D6261 HALF-SLIP, Average (XL,2X) $20.00
#D6263 HALF-SLIP, Tall (S,M,L) $20.00
(Please specify size and color)

I'm sure you'll agree ... our exquisite combination of satin tricot and hand-cut lace makes this the most beautiful trio of styles ever! And, each garment is so comfortable! All are fashioned of luxurious Antron® III nylon (known for its smoothness and non-cling fit) and feel like silk against your skin. Treat yourself! Choose Peach Ice, White or Black. (USA)

J. Because they are designed with popular high-cut legs, these panties offer a sleek, beautiful fit ... in comfort! 100% cotton crotch. Sizes: 4,5,6,7.

#D6248 SATINIQUE HI-CUT LEG PANTY 2 for $21.50
(Please specify size and color)

K. So many women prefer boxer style panties because the unrestricting leg design offers maximum freedom of movement ... no cutting or binding! Sizes: 4,5,6,7.

#D6250 SATINIQUE BOXER STYLE PANTY $15.00
(Please specify size and color)

Soothing COMFORTS

A. I could barely read the signature on the last birthday card Aunt Pauline sent me. The pain that writing caused her arthritic hands was obvious. When this pen came to my attention, I immediately sent it to her. The difference in handwriting on her hand was none was miraculous. The special design of this pen takes pressure off the wrist and fingers. The suede finish is non-slip and makes the pen easy to hold onto — virtually eliminates writing discomfort.

#D3773 BIOCURVE™ PENS (Pack of 4) $14.50

B. This slipper has been made the same wonderful way for over 30 years! The process molds the top of the slipper INTO the foot — the results are superb comfort and footwear that lasts and lasts! And, because there are no nails, stitching, or gluing to come apart, it's machine washable! Made of 100% rubber sole and cotton/polyester uppers with side bands for stretch comfort. Black only. Medium and wide widths. See size chart. Imported.

#D7008 CLASSIC SLIPPER $27.50
(Please specify size and color)

	5	5½	6	6½	7	7½	8	8½	9	9½	10	10½	11	11½	12
Medium	x	x	x	x	x	x	x	x	x	x	x				
Wide			x	x	x	x	x	x	x	x	x	x		x	

C. There's usually someone in every family who suffers from allergies, asthma or other respiratory problems ... in mine, it is Bill who has allergies. He tested this year-round, 4-in-1 air treatment center and wouldn't give it up! It's so versatile ... as a humidifier it helps relieve dry, sore throats and itchy skin, prevent brittleness in furniture and reduces static electricity. As an air cleaner, it has a special urethane/nylon filter that traps dust, pollen and smoke particles. If humidity is high, simply run the unit dry — it works as an energy-saving air circulator to keep the room more comfortable! Simply attach the rear guard and you've got a lightweight 8" portable fan! The compact size (10¾" x 13" x 10½"d) makes it easy to place anywhere! Weighs just 7 lbs., 15 oz. UL listed.

#D3855 AIR TREATMENT CENTER $125.00

"4-IN-1 AIR TREATMENT CENTER"

Distributes cool/warm air evenly

Treated Air
• Side handles for portability
• Filter for trapping dust, smoke, etc.
• Water reservoir for humidifier

Treated Air — Fan unit for circulation — Air Treatment Center — Raw Air

D. There was certainly no shortage of people who wanted to "test" this wonderful new pain relieving gel — from my mother to many people in the office. Whether they suffer from arthritis, bursitis, joint inflammation or muscle spasm, they all reported the same soothing relief. Cool-Hot Gel is a therapeutic analgesic that's applied to the surface of the skin and penetrates deep down giving your aches and pains welcomed relief for hours! It's greaseless, colorless, and has a subtle refreshing fragrance. 16 oz.

#D3755 COOL-HOT GEL (16 oz.) $12.00
#D3827 COOL-HOT GEL (32 oz.) $21.00

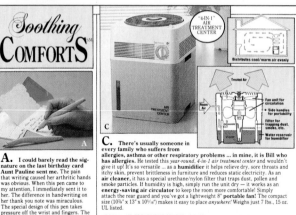

E. As my mother began to show the effects of osteoporosis, her shoulders rounded. Ever since she wears this amazing posture brace, she stands taller. Worn under clothing, it fastens in front, gently returning shoulders to a more natural, normal position. Made of soft cotton, tricot and foam. Machine washable. Men, as well as women, may be helped by this fabulous posture brace. (Men measure chest; S(28-32"); M(34-36"); ML(38-40"); L(42-44". (USA)

#D2109 POSTURE BRACE $15.00

Relieves the pain of arthritis, bursitis, neuralgia, backaches, muscular soreness, more ...

F. In as little as 5 minutes, you can have soothing relief from aches and pains — without medication! This hand-held unit emits infrared heat that penetrates deep into the body and actually soothes nerve endings and blood vessels below the surface, where pain originates. It's safe, very effective and easy to use! Just place the unit wherever it hurts and in moments you'll feel the difference! Even works through clothes. High/low heat settings. 8"L, 3¼" dia. Weighs 8 oz. Carrying case included. 110V. UL listed.

#D3877 HAND-HELD INFRARED HEAT $40.00

G. A footstool is a wonderful treat ... add heat and it's a downright luxury! Put your feet up and enjoy the soothing warmth of this heated footstool. The lovely floral tapestry on the hinged, foam-padded lid conceals a powerful heater, with three settings: low, medium and high. Sturdy hardwood frame and legs have a polished walnut finish. And, a built-in 2"D storage compartment holds your favorite magazines! Measures: 12"H x 16½"W x 12"D. Has a 6' cord; operates on 60 watts. AC, UL listed.

#D7758 HEATED FOOTSTOOL $62.00

ALSO AVAILABLE! Our heated footstool with 1 heat setting. Measures: 8"H x 14"W x 9"D. Operates on 45 watts. AC, UL listed.

#D5112 HEATED FOOTSTOOL (1 Setting) $44.00

H. Anyone who suffers from cold hands, Raynaud's syndrome, arthritis or poor circulation will appreciate these soothing Thermocure gloves. They provide comfort and maximum warmth to the joints of your hands while protecting you from dampness, cold and the elements. Made of dense wool with a touch of nylon for washability. Choose White (80% wool/20% nylon) or Grey (70% wool/30% nylon). Unisex Sizes: S, M, L. P.S. They're a favorite with skiers. Made in Canada.

#D3787 THERMOCURE GLOVES $14.00 (Please specify size and color)

NEW! The same wonderful Thermocure benefits offering warmth insulation and perspiration absorption are now available in women's and men's socks! Women's socks, choose White with Blue trim or White with Pink trim in sizes: S(6-8); M(8-10); L(10½+). Men's socks (100% wool), Grey only, in sizes: S(7-8); M(8-10); L(10½+).

#D7097 WOMEN'S THERMOCURE SOCKS $13.50
#D7098 MEN'S THERMOCURE SOCKS $13.50
(Please specify size and color)

I. For arthritis, bursitis, or an aching back, an electric mattress pad is better than an electric blanket. I'll tell you why. With a pad, the heat comes up from below. It rises toward your body and warms your back for soothing comfort. It's trapped inside the covers by the top blanket, so when you get into bed on a chilly night — Ahhhh! Now I'll tell you why this electric pad is special. It's zoned to keep your feet the warmest, then your mid-section, then your chest. Its automatic thermostat adjusts the pad as the room temperature changes. No more waking up sweating or shivering. Completely machine washable and dryable 100% polyester. UL listed. (USA)

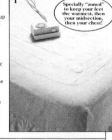

Specially "zoned" to keep your feet the warmest, then your midsection, then your chest!

#D3001 TWIN SINGLE CONTROL $47.00
#D3079 FULL SINGLE CONTROL $54.00
#D3002 FULL DUAL CONTROL $59.50
#D3003 QUEEN DUAL CONTROL $67.00
#D3004 KING DUAL CONTROL $93.00

J. When I felt how lightweight and comfortable these smart looking casual shoes are, I knew at once that they are perfect for everyday walking and wear! With 2 straps that easily adjust with Velcro®, they fit securely and there are no laces to tie! These "leather look" shoes are really made of easy-care vinyl. They are a must for cushiony comfort! Black, Taupe or White (ideal for those wearing uniforms). See size chart (shoe runs narrow). (USA)

#D7090 CASUAL SHOES $28.00
(Please specify size and color)

	5	5½	6	6½	7	7½	8	8½	9	9½	10	10½	11
Medium	x	x	x	x	x	x	x	x	x	x	x		
Wide		x	x	x	x	x	x	x	x	x	x	x	
Wide-Wide			x	x	x	x	x	x	x	x	x		

2 Velcro® adjustable straps

the Healthful Gourmet

Epicurean delights that every palate will appreciate!

A. Entice your tastebuds with the *garden-fresh goodness* of our *all-natural* "vegetable paté"...Cowboy Caviar® is reminiscent of ratatouille yet so versatile! A wholesome blend of fresh eggplant, aromatic onion, plump tomato and savory bell pepper is simmered with *just a touch* of garlic and spice! *NO* preservatives or cholesterol! Makes a delectable dip for veggies, mouth-watering hors d'oeuvres, and, for a memorable meal, heat and toss with pasta! (We passed a jar around with whole wheat bread and decided to stay in for lunch!) The 16.5 oz. glass mug is yours for the tasting...a great gift!

#D3927 COWBOY CAVIAR®
(Two 16.5 oz. Mugs) $20.00
#D3947 COWBOY CAVIAR®
(One 32 oz. Jar) $18.00

B. Quick and delicious Quinoa ("keen-wa") is the newest, most exciting alternative to rice! This light whole grain is high in protein, calcium-rich and *remarkably easy to prepare*...ready in 15 minutes! It's subtle nutty flavor blends beautifully with seasonings and sauces—perfect in soups, salads, stuffings, pilaf, casseroles, even desserts! Rich in essential fiber, vitamins and minerals, low-sodium and NO cholesterol! Net wt.: 12 oz. (each box). **Taste the difference Quinoa makes in our new pasta shapes, too!** (You'll never go back to plain noodles again!) Rotini, flats and *wheat-free* elbows perk up every pasta dish! Cooks in just 4–5 minutes! Net wt.: 8 oz. (each box).

#D3933 QUINOA WHOLE GRAIN
(4 Boxes) $15.00
#D3934 QUINOA ROTINI PASTA
(4 Boxes) $12.00
#D3936 QUINOA FLAT PASTA
(4 Boxes) $12.00
#D3935 QUINOA ELBOW PASTA
(4 Boxes) $12.00
#D3932 QUINOA ASSORTMENT
1 Grain & 3 Pasta Shapes
(4-Box Assortment) $12.50

C. Don't let a restricted diet leave *your* cupboard bare! Our Pantry Package offers full-flavor goodness and nutritional benefits...for everyone. (Low-sodium, no added sugar, fat-free, low-calorie, etc.) Includes: 8 oz. each of French, Russian and Italian dressings; two 4 oz. jars each of mayonnaise and ketchup; 4 oz. each of grape, strawberry and black raspberry jelly; 30 single-serving packets of bouillon (10 each of chicken, beef and onion); two 4 oz. jars of gelatin dessert (1 strawberry, 1 raspberry).

#D3937 PANTRY PACKAGE
$27.50

Also Available! Our dietetic gelatin dessert 6-pack! Handy 4 oz. jars let you make one serving at a time or a delightful mold...with Strawberry, Cherry, Lime, Orange, Strawberry-Banana and Raspberry! Each jar makes 32–4 oz. servings!

#D3938 GELATIN DESSERT 6-PACK $15.00

D. Only the natural goodness of specially concentrated fruit juices provides the sweetness in our scrumptious toppings! *No refined sugar!* We held a meeting of our most confirmed chocoholics and all agree—velvety "Fudge Sweet" is heavenly and guilt-free! No cream or butter, less than 1% fat and *only 16 calories per teaspoon!* Delicious for dipping or topping! Our "All Fruit" syrups got a 4-star rating, too! No pectins, gums or starches and *only 9.5 calories per teaspoon!* Perfect on pancakes, in sauces and for the most splendid spritzers! Our pack of 4 includes two 10 oz. jars of "Fudge Sweet" and two 12 oz. bottles of "All-Fruit" syrup (1 Strawberry and 1 Raspberry).
P.S. No preservatives or artificial ingredients!

#D3925 TOPPINGS (Pack of 4) $20.00

E. From the original recipes of a gourmet candymaker come our *decadent* chocolate confections—freshly made to satisfy *every* sweet tooth...even if you can't eat sugar! They're made from the *finest* ingredients including cocoa, dairy cream, pure vanilla and NO SUGAR! Choose "Nuts 'N Chewies" (clusters and caramels), "Select Assortment" (favorites with fruits, nuts and other delicacies) or "Sweet Shop Duet"—a box of each! Net wt.: 7.5 oz. (each box). **Brittle Lovers Beware: Our Pecan Brittle is the *absolute best* we've ever tasted**...and *it's* SUGAR-FREE, *too!* We left it out for all to taste and it disappeared—lickety split! Net wt.: 12 oz.

#D3928 "NUTS 'N CHEWIES" (2 Boxes) $20.00
#D3929 "SELECT ASSORTMENT" (2 Boxes) $20.00
#D3930 "SWEET SHOP DUET" (2 Boxes) $20.00
#D3939 "BEST PECAN BRITTLE"
(1 Box) $15.00

National Gourmet Foods Association Award for "Best American Candy"

G. Our luscious all-fruit preserves are just that—ALL FRUIT! No pectin, starches or gums to mask the true fruit flavor, no artificial ingredients, no preservatives and NO ADDED SUGAR! They're called *Fancifuls™* because you'll enjoy them any way that suits your *fancy:* on toast, muffins, ice cream, pound cake...you name it! Our pack of 4 includes one 10 oz. jar each: Strawberry, Blueberry, Raspberry and Orange-Pineapple.

The ideal accompaniment to our Conserves, Apple Butters and Fancifuls™—outstandingly delicious Sugar-Free Oatcakes! These traditional biscuits *from Scotland* are rich in protein, calcium, iron and B-complex vitamins and have bran for fiber as well as unique flavor and texture. *You'll love them!* Net wt.: 10.5 oz. (each box).

#D3944 FANCIFULS (Pack of 4) $19.00
#D3924 FANCIFULS (Pack of 4) WITH 1 BOX OF OATCAKES $22.00
#D3926 OATCAKES (4 Boxes) $12.00

F. When you spread our all-fruit conserves and apple butters on rolls, muffins, toast or croissants, you'll soon realize the remaining possibilities are *endless!* Each conserve is a zesty blend of 3 fruits and Oregon walnuts—wondrous atop desserts, as fillings, even mixed with plain yogurt! Our apple butters are not only the perfect "breadfellows" but warmed on ham or glazed on duck, create a taste to please any palate! Both have *no* preservatives or artificial ingredients! Our pack of 4 includes two 10 oz. jars of conserves (Apricot-Pineapple and Orangeberry-Nut) and two 10 oz. jars of apple butter (Apple-Apple and Strawberry-Apple).

#D3943 CONSERVES & APPLE BUTTERS
(Pack of 4) $18.00
#D3923 CONSERVES & APPLE BUTTERS
(Pack of 4)
WITH 1 BOX OF OATCAKES $21.00

Prosthetic devices, hearing aids, canes and wheelchairs are mingled with items from "The Healthful Gourmet". Subtitle: "Epicurean delights that every palate will appreciate!" The Comfortably Yours catalog is, in a word, eclectic.

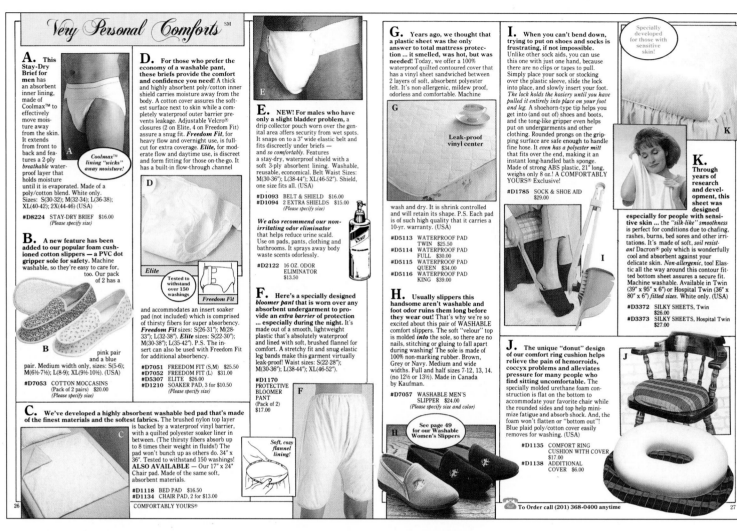

Very Personal Comforts℠

A. This Stay-Dry Brief for men has an absorbent inner lining, made of Coolmax™ to effectively move moisture away from the skin. It extends from front to back and features a 2-ply *breathable* waterproof layer that holds moisture until it is evaporated. Made of a poly/cotton blend. White only. Sizes: S(30-32); M(32-34); L(36-38); XL(40-42); 2X(44-46) (USA)

Coolmax™ lining "wicks" away moisture!

#D8224 STAY-DRY BRIEF $16.00
(Please specify size)

B. A new feature has been added to our popular foam cushioned cotton slippers — a PVC dot gripper sole for safety. Machine washable, so they're easy to care for, too. Our pack of 2 has a pink pair and a blue pair. Medium width only, sizes: S(5-6); M(6½-7½); L(8-9); XL(9½-10½). (USA)

#D7053 COTTON MOCCASINS (Pack of 2 pairs) $20.00
(Please specify size)

C. We've developed a highly absorbent washable bed pad that's made of the finest materials and the softest fabrics. The brushed nylon top layer is backed by a waterproof vinyl barrier, with a quilted polyester soaker liner in between. (The thirsty fibers absorb up to 8 times their weight in fluids!) The pad won't bunch up as others do. 34" x 36". Tested to withstand 150 washings! **ALSO AVAILABLE** — Our 17" x 24" Chair pad. Made of the same soft, absorbent materials.

#D1118 BED PAD $16.50
#D1134 CHAIR PAD, 2 for $13.00

D. For those who prefer the economy of a washable pant, these briefs provide the comfort and confidence you need! A thick and highly absorbent poly/cotton inner shield carries moisture away from the body. A cotton cover assures the softest surface next to skin while a completely waterproof outer barrier prevents leakage. Adjustable Velcro® closures (2 on Elite, 4 on Freedom Fit) assure a snug fit. *Freedom Fit*, for heavy flow and overnight use, is full-cut for extra coverage. *Elite*, for moderate flow and daytime use, is discreet and form fitting for those on-the-go. It has a built-in flow-through channel and accommodates an insert soaker pad (not included) which is comprised of thirsty fibers for super absorbency. *Freedom Fit* sizes: S(26-31"); M(28-33"); L(32-38"). *Elite* sizes: S(22-30"); M(30-38"); L(35-42"). P.S. The insert can also be used with Freedom Fit for additional absorbency.

Tested to withstand over 150 washings

#D7051 FREEDOM FIT (S,M) $25.50
#D7052 FREEDOM FIT (L) $31.00
#D5307 ELITE $26.00
#D1210 SOAKER PAD, 3 for $10.50
(Please specify size)

E. **NEW! For males who have only a slight bladder problem,** a drip collector pouch worn over the genital area offers security from wet spots. It snaps on to a 3" wide elastic belt and fits discreetly under briefs — and *so comfortably.* Features a stay-dry, waterproof shield with a soft 3-ply absorbent lining. Washable, reusable, economical. Belt Waist Sizes: M(30-36"); L(38-44"); XL(46-52"). Shield, one size fits all. (USA)

#D1093 BELT & SHIELD $16.00
#D1094 2 EXTRA SHIELDS $15.00
(Please specify size)

We also recommend our non-irritating odor eliminator that helps reduce urine scald. Use on pads, pants, clothing and bathrooms. It sprays away body waste scents odorlessly.

#D2122 16 OZ. ODOR ELIMINATOR $13.50

F. Here's a specially designed *bloomer pant* that is worn over any absorbent undergarment to provide an *extra barrier* of protection ... especially during the night. It's made out of a smooth, lightweight plastic that's absolutely waterproof and lined with soft, brushed flannel for comfort. A stretchy fit and snug elastic leg bands make this garment virtually leak-proof! Waist sizes: S(22-28"); M(30-36"); L(38-44"); XL(46-52").

#D1170 PROTECTIVE BLOOMER PANT (Pack of 2) $17.00

Soft, cozy flannel lining!

G. Years ago, we thought that a plastic sheet was the only answer to total mattress protection ... it smelled, was hot, but was needed! Today, we offer a 100% waterproof quilted contoured cover that has a vinyl sheet sandwiched between 2 layers of soft, absorbent polyester felt. It's non-allergenic, mildew proof, odorless and comfortable. Machine

Leak-proof vinyl center

wash and dry. It is shrink controlled and will retain its shape. P.S. Each pad is of such high quality that it carries a 10-yr. warranty. (USA)

#D5113 WATERPROOF PAD TWIN $25.50
#D5114 WATERPROOF PAD FULL $30.00
#D5115 WATERPROOF PAD QUEEN $34.00
#D5116 WATERPROOF PAD KING $39.00

H. Usually slippers this handsome aren't washable and foot odor ruins them long before they wear out! That's why we're so excited about this pair of WASHABLE comfort slippers. The soft "velour" top is molded *into* the sole, so there are no nails, stitching or gluing to fall apart during washing! The sole is made of 100% non-marking rubber. Brown, Grey or Navy. Medium and wide widths. Full and half sizes 7-12, 13, 14. (no 12½ or 13½). Made in Canada by Kaufman.

#D7057 WASHABLE MEN'S SLIPPER $24.00
(Please specify size and color)

See page 49 for our Washable Women's Slippers

I. When you can't bend down, trying to put on shoes and socks is frustrating, if not impossible. Unlike other sock aids, you can use this one with just one hand, because there are no clips or tapes to pull. Simply place your sock or stocking over the plastic sleeve, slide the lock into place, and slowly insert your foot. *The lock holds the hosiery until you have pulled it entirely into place on your foot and leg.* A shoehorn-type tip helps you get into (and out of) shoes and boots, and the tong-like gripper even helps put on undergarments and other clothing. Rounded prongs on the gripping surface are safe enough to handle fine hose. It *even has a polyester mitt* that fits over the end, making it an instant long-handled bath sponge. Made of strong ABS plastic, 21" long, weighs only 8 oz.! A COMFORTABLY YOURS® Exclusive!

#D1785 SOCK & SHOE AID $29.00

Specially developed for those with sensitive skin!

K. Through years of research and development, this sheet was designed especially for people with sensitive skin ... the *"silk-like" smoothness* is perfect for conditions due to chafing, rashes, burns, bed sores and other irritations. It's made of soft, *soil resistant* Dacron® poly which is wonderfully cool and absorbent against your delicate skin. *Non-allergenic,* too! Elastic all the way around this contour fitted bottom sheet assures a secure fit. Machine washable. Available in Twin (39" x 95" x 6") or Hospital Twin (36" x 80" x 6") *fitted* sizes. White only. (USA)

#D3372 SILKY SHEETS, Twin $26.00
#D3373 SILKY SHEETS, Hospital Twin $27.00

J. The unique "donut" design of our comfort ring cushion helps relieve the pain of hemorrhoids, coccyx problems and alleviates pressure for many people who find sitting uncomfortable. The specially molded urethane foam construction is flat on the bottom to accommodate your favorite chair while the rounded sides and top help minimize fatigue and absorb shock. And, the foam won't flatten or "bottom out"! Blue plaid poly/cotton cover easily removes for washing. (USA)

#D1135 COMFORT RING CUSHION WITH COVER $17.00
#D1138 ADDITIONAL COVER $6.00

26 COMFORTABLY YOURS®

To Order call (201) 368-0400 anytime 27

A little bit of comfort or a little less pain often looms larger than life in the long days of housebound individuals. The Comfortably Yours catalog is a direct response to their needs. The active elderly, too, will find a treasure chest of garments and devices that make it just a little easier to get through a busy day.

Given today's demographics, there is a core business here that has nowhere to go but up. As Comfortably Yours itself matures into a multifaceted, multi-market business, Mike and Elaine Adler, and their son Jim, will have their hands full, keeping pace with the forecast growth in their marketing niche.

CONSOLIDATED DUTCHWEST STOVES

If you were a homeowner back in the pre-OPEC '60s, you may remember 15 cents-a-gallon home heating oil. Hardly seems possible. Today, $1.00 oil is hard to come by. What's more, it has been higher, and it soon will be again. That's just terrific in the eyes of President Bruce McKinney of Consolidated Dutchwest. He sells wood and coal burning stoves.

Mention woodstove, and most of us will conjure up an image of the simple old potbellied railroad stove or grandma's black iron, chrome-trimmed cookstove. These stoves were nothing but an open combustion chamber with a hole at the top, a damper at the bottom and a couple of grates in between; and it was a constant job to keep the dampers adjusted so that some of the heat stayed in the house instead of going up the chimney

The modern child-of-OPEC stoves are a far cry from the old-timers. They still burn wood and coal, and the black castiron exterior looks about the same, but there the similarities cease. The new stoves are complex, highly efficient, fully automatic mechanisms. The best incorporate high-tech components, such as platinum-based catalytic combustion units and internal temperature probes. They use far less fuel and exhaust infinitely less smoke and pollution. And most importantly, they are healthier because no smoke is released inside the home.

 CONSOLIDATED DUTCHWEST—Stove and Accessory Catalog
John Meddaugh, *Catalog Director*
Kay Kopper, *Designer*
Jenny McKinney, *Merchandiser*
Michael Stillman, *Copywriter*
Ross Chapple, *Photographer/Illustrator*
Quad/Graphics [Pewaukee, WI], *Printer, on 80# Freedom Gloss for cover and 45# Somerset text*
Ultra Scan [Hudson, NH], *Color Separator*

The magazine-like front cover is followed by 4 pages of almost solid type describing the services of Dutchwest and the basic *raison d'etre* for the modern catalytic stove. No less than 5 different phone numbers are listed, each dedicated to a specific area of customer service. Pages 6 & 7 are typical of the opening spreads used to introduce each of the seven families of stoves offered in the catalog.

STOVES

THE Federal Convection Heaters

The Federal Convection Heaters from Consolidated Dutchwest offer a combination of engineering achievements, elegant styling, and useful features unique among stoves today.

Our top-of-the-line models, these exceptional stoves possess more of the features people want in a stove than any others you will find. They are easy to use, classically beautiful, and highly efficient. Now, each one has been carefully re-engineered to meet current and future environmental standards. The Federal Convections meet the EPA (federal) standards for 1988 and 1990, as well as current and 1988 Oregon and Colorado standards.

What sets these stoves apart from others is the concern for the details of wood and coal burning that has gone into

their design. Starting with the elegant cabinet, patterned after fine furniture of the federal period, each of the stove owner's concerns has been carefully addressed. Advanced combustion engineering provides for exceptionally high fuel efficiencies. Clean-burning catalytic technology substantially reduces creosote for a safer chimney. Side doors, grates and ashbins make these models easy to load, start and clean. These, and the many other features you will read about in the following pages, make the Federal Convection Heaters the number one choice of experienced wood and coal burners throughout the country.

The Federal Convection Heaters are available in three sizes. The Small Federal Convection is well-suited for heating several rooms or most of a smaller house. The Large Federal Convection, our most popular model, is sized to serve as a primary heat source in many typical American homes. The Extra-large Federal Convection is designed for heating extra-large areas, or for use in particularly cold climates. One of these models is likely to be perfect for your needs. Specifications and further details to help you choose the correct one appear on page 14.

6   7

stove can actually become too hot, while other parts of your house, or even the same room, stay cool. The air flow developed within the Federal Convection helps to circulate the heat more evenly around your house. Areas farther from the stove receive more heat, while the immediate location of the stove does not become overly hot. The result is your stove can effectively heat a larger area, while all parts of your house remain at a more moderate temperature. It is a more comfortable type of heating.

The second advantage of a convection stove is that it aims its heat in the proper direction. A radiant heater aims its heat equally in all directions. Unfortunately, not all directions are equally beneficial. Most stoves are installed a few feet in front of a wall or fireplace. Heat radiated from the front warms your house, but heat radiated from the back will be absorbed into that wall. That heat is lost. The advantage of a Federal Convection Heater is that it picks up heat from the back of the firebox and redirects it to the front. Heat which is radiated from the back of a typical stove flows from the front portals of a Federal Convection. This enables the convection stove to provide more usable heat than a radiant stove, even one of comparable efficiency or power output.

An Optional Fan to Increase Circulation

While the rising of hot air creates a natural airflow within the convection system, there is also an optional blower (standard with fireplace inserts) available to increase its speed. The fan increases

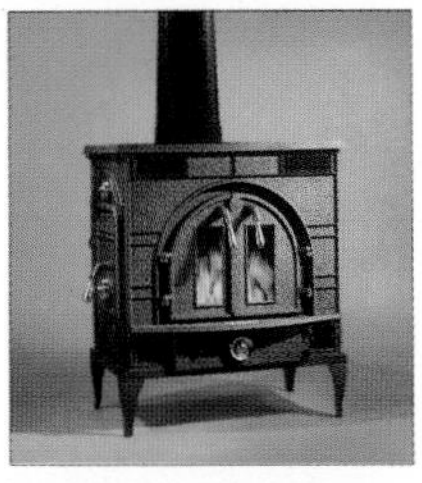

the flow fivefold, and is highly recommended if you want to get the maximum heating power possible from the convection design. The blower can be mounted on the side or back of freestanding stoves (side of inserts) and is thermally protected so it will not be harmed if the stove is operated with the fan off. This means you can use your stove on milder days without running the blower, and continue to use your stove during power failures—all without fear of damaging the fan. There is even an optional thermostatic on/off control available. Please see page 67 for details.

"We have been so pleased and spoken so highly of our stove that two of our friends have purchased Consolidated Dutchwest stoves."

J. Ludwig/Unadilla, N.Y.

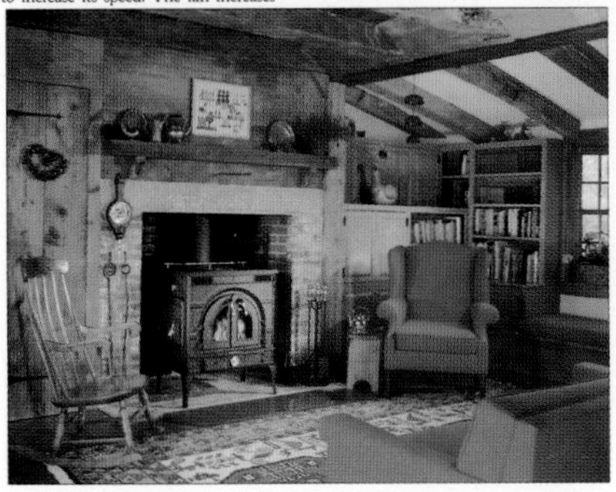

Section 3. Safe and Durable Construction

Safety Tested

Nothing is more important with any appliance than safety. Each model of convection heater has been tested by the Arnold Greene Testing Laboratories/CONAM in accordance with applicable UL, NFPA, and other standards, and carries the laboratory's certification plate. They come with detailed instructions on properly installing and operating a stove, and maintaining safe clearances from combustible materials. Basic information on installations and safe clearances can also be found in the "Installation Planner" enclosed with this catalogue. As noted previously, the Federal Convection Heaters employ catalytic combustion to burn off creosote and other gasses, thereby keeping your chimney safer too.

Durable Cast-Iron Construction

The Federal Convection Heaters (with the natural exception of items like glass windows and brass trim) are built entirely of cast iron. Cast iron is an ideal medium for building stoves, both for its durability and heat transferring properties. It has the ability to withstand the high temperatures generated within a stove without the warping and burn out typical of sheet steel. Like the century-old cast-iron stoves still in operation today, a Federal Convection is built for a long and useful life.

Cast iron provides another important benefit. It has the ability to store heat during the hottest part of the fire, and transfer it to your home after the fire has died down. This effectively increases the heating time of a load of fuel, plus provides heat at a more constant, steady pace. These properties of durability and even heat transfer, which have made cast-iron cookware the choice of homemakers for generations, also make it the perfect material for building stoves.

Castings range from 3/8" to 1/2" thick, making Consolidated Dutchwest stoves heavier than most other cast-iron brands. While this makes them a little harder to lift, it also provides greater durability for the stove, plus increases its ability to store heat.

To place your order call toll-free
1-800-225-8277

9

Following the room scenes, extensive copy in each chapter of the catalog delves into the primary advantages of a specific stove. The variations are not cosmetic. Every stove is designed to suit a different set of circumstances, from fireplace inserts for the larger home, to freestanding units, and even stoves engineered for use in mobile homes.

For the technically or ecologically minded customer, Dutchwest provides a formidable amount of emission-related facts and figures demonstrating conformity to the standards of certain state authorities—Colorado and Oregon are especially stringent in theirs. Dutchwest is prepared to meet and exceed these regulations, and those of any other regulatory body.

Three Sizes of Federal Convections

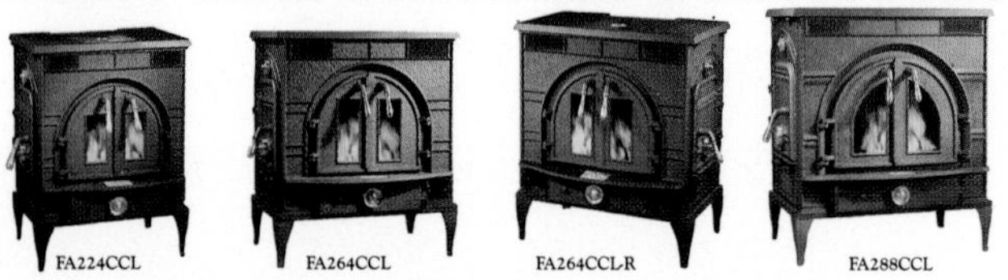

FA224CCL FA264CCL FA264CCL-R FA288CCL

The Federal Convection Heaters come in three sizes: small, large, and extra-large. The Small Federal Convection is sized to heat a few rooms, or most of a smaller house. Its compact size makes it ideal for installations in smaller rooms. The Large Federal Convection, our most popular stove, is well-suited to handle most of the heating needs of a typical home. There is also a second version of this model which has its side door on the right (side doors are on the left of all other models). The Extra-large Federal Convection is our largest stove, and it is meant for heating extra-large areas, or for use in very cold climates. Each model is also available as a fireplace insert (see pages 16-19).

The Federal Convection Heaters are our top-of-the-line, and best-selling stoves. They reflect our commitment to fully understanding all of the needs of the wood or coal burner, and building a stove which meets every one of them. Not just issues of efficiency or appearance are addressed. These stoves take into consideration the many other issues of wood and coal burning, such as direction of heat, quality of materials and construction, convenience, flexibility, safety, and impact on our environment. We believe the Federal Convection Heaters to be the best stoves built anywhere, at any price, and we are confident that, the more you compare them to others, the more clear it will be why we make this statement.

Small Federal Convection

The most compact in terms of size of the Federal Convection series, the Small Convection Heater is ideal for heating several rooms, or most of a smaller house. Typical heating capacities are 7,000-9,500 cu. ft.* Dimensions are 22" wide x 29½" high x 17" deep. Weight is 380 lbs. The Small Convection holds logs up to 19" long or 40 lbs. of coal. It can hold a wood fire up to 8 hours, or longer with hard coal. Comes with a 6" internal diameter oval flue, reversible for top or back venting. Oregon overall average efficiency rating: 78.9%.

Model FA224CCL $799.95 (delivered)
Monthly Payment Plan (See pg. 66) **$27.00**
After May 25, 1988 $849.95 (delivered)

Large Federal Convection

Our best-selling stove model, the Large Convection Heater is designed for heating larger areas, typically 9,000-13,000 cu. ft.* Dimensions are 26" wide x 29½" high x 17" deep. Weight is 436 lbs. The Large Convection holds logs up to 22" in length or 48 lbs. of coal. It can hold a wood fire up to 11 hours, or longer with hard coal. Includes a reversible 6" oval flue, to vent top or back. Oregon overall average efficiency rating: 78.8%.

Model FA264CCL $999.95 (delivered)
Monthly Payment Plan (See pg. 66) **$33.00**
After May 25, 1988 $1079.95 (delivered)

Right Side Loading Large Federal Convection

The Right Side Loading Large Convection Heater is identical to the regular Large Convection Heater except that its side door is on the right. Side doors on all other convection heaters and other Consolidated Dutchwest stoves are on the left. This model is meant for installations where an obstruction will make it difficult to use a left side door.

Model FA264CCL-R $1,049.95 (delivered)
Monthly Payment Plan (See pg. 66) **$35.00**
After May 25, 1988 $1129.95 (delivered)

Extra-large Federal Convection

This is the largest and most powerful stove we make. It is meant primarily for people living in larger homes, colder climates, or anyone who wants to derive the maximum amount of heat possible from a stove. Typical heating capacities are 12,000-16,500 cu. ft.* Dimensions are 28" wide x 32½" high x 19" deep. The weight is 634 lbs. The Extra-large Convection holds logs up to 25" long or 80 lbs. of coal. It can hold a wood fire as long as 15 hours, or longer with hard coal. Comes with an 8" diameter oval flue, reversible for top or back venting. Oregon overall average efficiency rating: 75.5%.

Model FA288CCL $1,179.95 (delivered)
Monthly Payment Plan (See pg. 66) **$39.00**
After May 25, 1988 $1259.95 (delivered)

Stove Model #		FA264CCL	FA224CCL	FA288CCL	FA264CCL-R
Fuel Capacity	Wood	55 lbs.	40 lbs.	80 lbs.	55 lbs.
	Coal	48 lbs.	40 lbs.	80 lbs.	48 lbs.
Burn Time*	Wood	11 hours	8 hours	15 hours	11 hours
	Coal	21 hours	18 hours	30 hours	21 hours
Maximum Log Length		22 inches	19 inches	25 inches	22 inches
Maximum BTU Output*		67,000	49,000	85,000	67,000
Heating Capacity (cubic feet)*		9,000-13,000	7,000-9,500	12,000-16,500	9,000-13,000
Height x Width x Depth		29½" x 26" x 17"	29½" x 22" x 17"	32½" x 28" x 19"	29½" x 26" x 17"
Flue Height	6" legs (standard)	30"	30"	32½"	30"
	4" legs (see pg. 47)	28"	28"	30½"	28"
	2" legs (see pg. 47)	26"	26"	28½"	26"
Flue Opening Diameter		6" oval	6" oval	8" oval	6" oval
Stove Weight		436 lbs.	380 lbs.	634 lbs.	436 lbs.
Price through May 25, 1988		**$999.95**	**$799.95**	**$1,179.95**	**$1,049.95**
Monthly Payment (See pg. 66)		**$33.00**	**$27.00**	**$39.00**	**$35.00**
After May 25, 1988		$1079.95	$849.95	$1259.95	$1129.95

14

Plus free accessories package now through May 25, 1988. See page 66.
*See page 35 for explanation of how readings were determined.

Efficiency, Emissions, Power Output & Burn Times

Large Convection Heater*
Model #FA264CCL

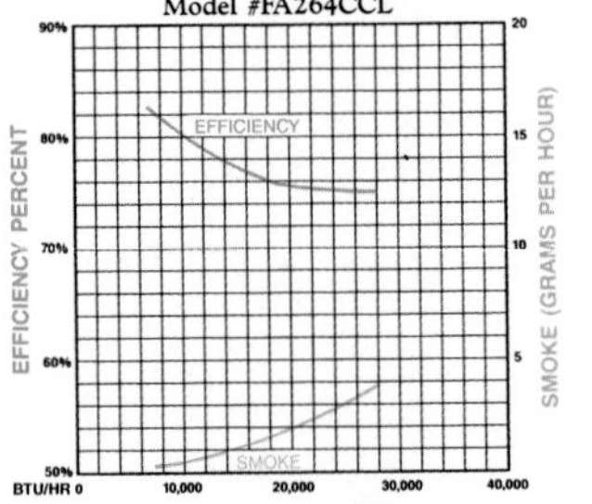

Oregon Procedure
Average Efficiency — 78.8%
Average Emissions — 1.2 grams/hour

Colorado Procedure
Particulate Emissions — 1.3 grams/hour
Carbon Monoxide — 42.1 grams/hour

Extra-Large Convection Heater*
Model #FA288CCL

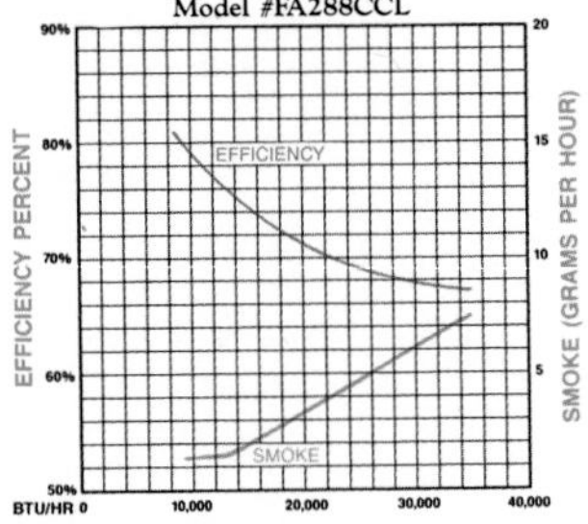

Oregon Procedure
Average Efficiency — 75.5%
Average Emissions — 2.2 grams/hour

Colorado Procedure
Particulate Emissions — 2.7 grams/hour
Carbon Monoxide — 98 grams/hour

Small Convection Heater*
Model #FA224CCL

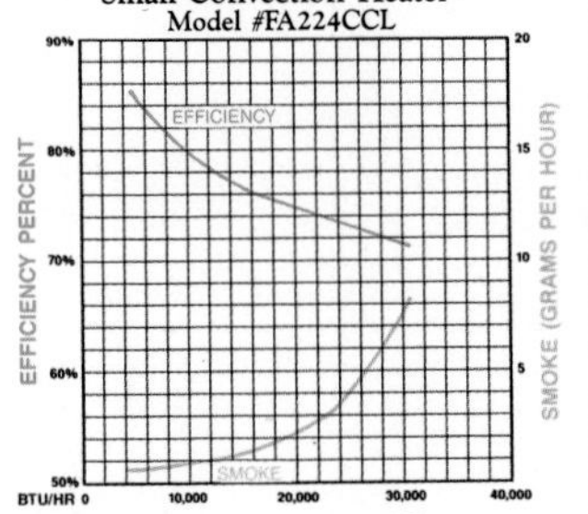

Oregon Procedure
Average Efficiency — 78.9%
Average Emissions — 2.0 grams/hour

Colorado Procedure
Particulate Emissions—2.6 grams/hour
Carbon Monoxide — 50 grams/hour

*For an explanation of the meaning of these charts, please see page 5. Each of these models is certified for sale in Colorado and Oregon, both under current and 1988 standards. All testing was performed with a blower (model FA905 or FA906) in place, so residents of Colorado and Oregon must order one of these with each convection stove (see page 67).

Graphs show efficiency and emissions readings at various output levels (using Oregon procedure testing). Tables show average emissions and efficiency readings under both Oregon and Colorado procedures. To compare emissions readings with maximum permissible amounts under these and federal standards, please see the tables on page 5.

To Place Your Order Call Toll-free at
1-800-225-8277
All prices include delivery to your home.

Visit Our Stores—See page 65 and the back cover for details.

15

STOVES

THE Federal Box Heaters

The Federal Box Heaters are scaled-down versions of the Rocky Mountain Heater. Built for heating from one to several rooms, they are compact yet very effective stoves.

The Small Federal Box Heater is sized to heat one or two rooms, while the large Federal Box Heater can heat two to three rooms, or a larger open area. For the homeowner with heating needs in this range, the Federal Box Heaters are an excellent choice.

A Compact Design
The Federal Box Heaters are built to fit in tight installations. Their narrow width—only 13 inches—allows them to fit in small fireplaces, corners, and other tight areas where nothing else will fit. In many cases, people who would otherwise not be able to enjoy the benefits of wood and coal heating are able to do so using one of these stoves.

Even if you do have room for a larger stove, a Federal Box Heater may best suit your needs. Owners have used them to heat a couple of rooms, an addition, a cabin, a small home or condominium, or have used them as a supplemental or back-up heat source for larger areas. Any home calling for less than a typical house-heater is a prime candidate for one of these fine stoves.

Effective Performance
The Federal Box Heaters have borrowed the same design employed by the Rocky Mountain Heater. The Rocky Mountain's design has proven to be very effective at producing substantial volumes of heat from a limited amount of space. This ability is particularly important with smaller stoves, since they cannot be cranked up to higher levels by simply using large loads of fuel.

The "box heater" design rests fuel directly against the stoves' side walls, their largest surfaces, to assure maximum transfer of the intense heat at the point of combustion. An enormous amount of heat will be radiated from these two surfaces. Next, we have employed the double-chambered baffling system and catalytic combustion used in our larger stoves to further boost output. Fuel burns in the main chamber (the firebox), while the gasses it gives off rise to the upper chamber. Further combustion of these gasses, plus the transfer of their heat to your home, are encouraged by the secondary chamber. When wood is burned, a catalytic combustor is placed within the connector between chambers. The combustor burns the wood smoke, increasing efficiency as much as 50%, while substantially reducing creosote and wood smoke pollution.

Wood and Coal Burning
The Federal Box Heaters will burn either wood or coal. Conversion between fuels takes only a few seconds, and everything needed to burn each fuel is included. A series of rocker grates is provided for "shaking" a bed of coal, while the large front door makes loading both fuels easy.

An Ashbin, Cook Top, Glass Window, Firescreen & Other Features
The Federal Box Heaters have many more features you wouldn't expect from a stove their size. Each has an ashbin with slide-out drawer for easy, neat ash removal. Since smaller stoves usually need to be cleaned out more often than larger ones, this is a particularly useful feature. Three air sources give you complete control over burning rates. You can run hot fires for quick heating, or slow-burning fires for longer burn times. An air source beneath the grate makes it very easy to start a fire. Each air source is controlled by a solid brass spin dial.

A polished cook top is provided for heating a pot or kettle. There is a glass window for watching the fire, plus a firescreen for safe open-door (fireplace-style) burning. There is even a probe thermometer to let you monitor combustion temperatures.

The Federal Box Heaters combine the traditional European "box heater" design with American Federal-period styling. The European "box heater" is a stove that is deeper than it is wide, with logs aimed front to back, rather than side to side. To this design, we have added the raised lines and graceful arches typical of American Federal-period styling, a fluted top, and solid brass trim (dial dampers and door handle). The result is an elegant, aesthetically balanced stove which will fit well with any decor.

Small Federal Box Heater
Our smallest stove, the Small Federal Box Heater, is meant to heat one or two rooms. It will fit in tight installations. Typical heating capacities range from 3,000-5,000 cu. ft.* Dimensions are 13" wide x 29½" high x 16" deep. Weight is 255 lbs. The Small Box Heater will hold logs up to 13" or 30 lbs. of coal. It has a 6" reversible round flue collar for top or back venting. Oregon overall average efficiency rating: 76.2%.

FA207CL	$489.95 (delivered)
Monthly Payment Plan (See pg. 66)	$20.00
After May 25, 1988	$499.95 (delivered)

Large Federal Box Heater
The Large Federal Box Heater is suitable for heating a few rooms, a small cabin, an addition, or similar areas. It too will fit in tight installations, but has greater fuel and heating capacity than the smaller model. Typical heating capacities are 5,000-7,500 cu. ft.* Dimensions are 13" wide x 29½" high x 21" deep. The weight is 299 lbs. It holds logs up to 18" long or 45 lbs. of coal. Vents from the top or back through a 6" round reversible flue collar. Oregon overall average efficiency rating: 74.0%.

FA209CL	$599.95 (delivered)
Monthly Payment Plan (See pg. 66)	$20.00
After May 25, 1988	$639.95 (delivered)

The Box Heater Specifications

Stove Model #		FA207CL	FA209CL
Fuel Capacity	Wood	20 lbs.	30 lbs.
	Coal	30 lbs.	45 lbs.
Maximum Burn Time*	Wood	5 hrs.	7 hrs.
	Coal	14 hrs.	19 hrs.
Maximum Log Length		13"	18"
Maximum BTU Output*		27,000	42,000
Heating Capacity* cu. ft.		3,000-5,000	5,000-7,500
Stove H x W x D		29½"x13"x16"	29½"x13"x21"
Flue Height 6" legs (standard)		30½"	30½"
4" legs (see pg. 47)		28½"	28½"
2" legs (see pg. 47)		26½"	26½"
Flue Opening Diameter		6" round	6" round
Stove Weight		255 lbs.	299 lbs.
Price through May 25, 1988		$489.95	$599.95
Monthly Payment (See pg. 66)		$20.00	$20.00
After May 25, 1988		$499.95	$639.95

Plus free accessories package now thru May 25, 1988. See pg. 66.
*See page 35 for explanation of how readings were determined.

The Large Box Heater pictured here holds logs up to 18 inches or 45 pounds of coal.

Efficiency and Emissions Ratings

Small Box Heater Model#FA207CL†

Large Box Heater Model#FA209CL†

Oregon Procedure	FA209CL	FA207CL
Average Efficiency	74.0%	76.2%
Average Emissions	3.7 grams/hr.	3.7 grams/hr.

Colorado Procedure	FA209CL	FA207CL
Particulate Emissions	5.1 grams/hr.	4.9 grams/hr.
Carbon Monoxide	84. grams/hr.	86. grams/hr.

†For an explanation of these charts and figures, please see pg. 5. These stoves are certified in Oregon and Colorado under both current and 1988 standards, and meet federal standards for 1988. Graphs show efficiency and emissions (Oregon procedure) at various burning levels.

All prices include delivery to your home.

32   33

These little freestanding units deliver BTU's at an incredible rate for the amount of fuel they consume. This 26″ X 28″ x 30″(H) tyke delivers 42,000 BTU's loaded with either wood or coal. The wood will burn for 7 hours, the coal for 19! The attractive photographs set in modern homes refute the impression that stoves are only for fishing camps and farm houses.

Consolidated Dutchwest products are now available in nine showrooms on the East Coast and in the Midwest. Once more, we find a manufacturer/merchant capturing customers from both the OTC retail market and the mailorder contingent. This is a winning combination more and more retailers are adopting to gain market share and enhance profitability.

Stoves are a once-in-a-lifetime purchase; ergo, a less than effective traffic builder. Dutchwest has solved this problem by manufacturing and selling a complete line of fireplace accessories, stove controls and embellishments, water heaters and wood chopper's tools—all designed to keep the stores and catalogs exciting. The prices for these items are very competitive, and the products are work-tested, reliable standards of the trade—no gimmicks here. Add-on items such as these allow Dutchwest to stay

in touch with their customers, to sell them additional merchandise and to foster word-of-mouth recommendations.

Consolidated Dutchwest has turned back the clock to find their own special market niche. They've also reached back in time to an era when the customer came first, and the price had to be right. With this catalog in hand, it would be difficult for a serious stove buyer to consider any other source.

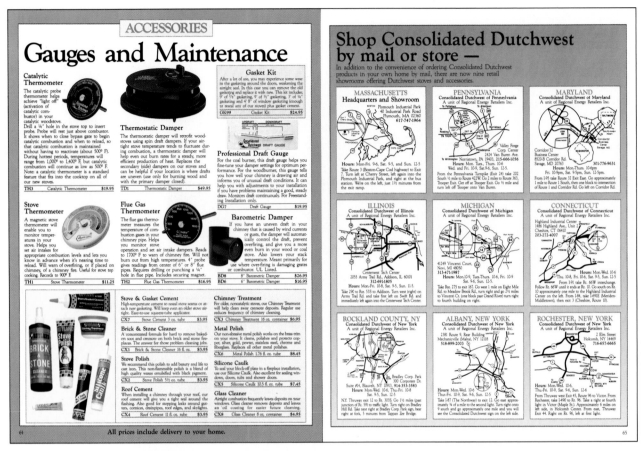

The

Stove Buyer's Guide

Recently, the Secretary of the U.S. Department of the Interior warned that we could see energy shortages more serious than those of the devastating energy crisis of the 1970's. He cautioned that the "low" oil prices of the past two years have shut down most domestic oil exploration, making us more dependent on OPEC and other foreign sources than ever before. He warned it is just a matter of time before those nations once again turn our dependence against us, as they did in 1973. Within the next five years, he predicted, will come a more serious oil shortage than ever before. He is not alone in these concerns. Many economists, energy experts, and others share the same fears that our falling domestic oil production is setting us up for shortages more serious than the last time.

Will America be driven to its knees again the next time OPEC pulls the plug? We don't think so. Since that last crisis, Americans have done much to reduce our demand for foreign oil. Most of us have tightened up and insulated our homes to reduce heat loss. We drive more fuel efficient cars. Our new appliances require less electricity than older models. Right now, you are reading about wood and coal burning stoves. Like millions of other Americans, you are either currently heating or seriously considering heating your home with renewable wood or plentiful coal. This is something people were not doing in 1973. No one was paying much attention to how much oil or gas we burned, or how quickly our electric meters were spinning. Energy was cheap then, and none of us thought the supply would ever end.

Today we know supplies are limited, and the price of these fuels will never be cheap again. As a result, we are doing something about the energy "crisis" every day. You are doing something about it right now. So yes, the Interior Secretary is right. Oil and gasoline prices may climb back over a dollar, and perhaps there will again be some shortages at the pump. However, as long as we remain vigilant about the need for conservation and our own self-sufficiency, we will not be driven into the cold by OPEC or anyone else. The fact that you are as interested in renewable energy today as the last generation was not in its day, is a sign that America can win "the moral equivalent of war."

The Advantages of Owning a Stove

Why Are Stoves So Popular Today?

The primary reason stoves are popular today is still good, sound economics. A stove can save a typical homeowner an enormous amount on his or her heating bills. While fuel prices may have flattened out, they are still historically very high. Not only are we unlikely to see the $3 per barrel oil prices of the early 1970's again; we are unlikely to see even the $8 prices that drove millions of people to stove stores in the middle 70's. Energy simply is not cheap. A stove is still an effective way of holding heating bills down to pre-crisis levels.

As a matter of fact, savings may well be greater today than at any other time. Today's high-efficiency stoves require substantially less fuel to heat your home than the best available only a few years ago. The potential for savings is even greater, since these stoves are less expensive to operate. The economic reasons for purchasing a stove are as great, if not greater, today than they were at any other time.

Of course, fuel economy is just one of the reasons why people buy stoves today. Reliability is another important reason. Most heating systems (including gas and oil) are dependent on electrical power to function. If that power goes out for a day,...or two,...or three, your house will get very cold, and there won't be much you can do about it. A stove offers the one source of heat you can depend upon regardless

Inside

The Advantages of Owning a Stove
Page 2

Catalytic Combustion
Page 3

Choosing Your Stove
Page 4

The Installation Planner 1987-88

In planning for your new stove, the first item on your agenda should be its installation. The type of installation is very important for many reasons, including the obvious ones of safety and aesthetics, and the less obvious one of stove performance. While most everyone recognizes the relationship between a proper installation and stove safety, many people do not realize that the quality of the installation has a major impact on the performance of a stove. Particularly with today's high-efficiency stoves, designed to perform on a level unheard of a few years ago, it is important to provide them with a setting that will allow them to perform as they should. In this regard, you should pay particular notice to the section on providing an adequate chimney draft if you are purchasing a state or federal environmentally certified or other high-efficiency stove. With a little extra care, you will be able to provide your stove with an installation that is not only safe and attractive, but one that enables your stove to reach its full potential.

This planner has been broken down into the two basic areas you need to consider when installing a stove. The first has to do with its placement within your house. Where will a stove heat best? Where will it look best? Additionally, you will need to plan for the safety of the installation. The primary considerations for safety have to do with clearances. You will need to keep the stove a safe distance from walls and other combustible materials, protect combustible floors, and provide other protections where necessary. It is extremely important to do this right as nothing is more important than having a safe installation.

The second area you need to consider is the chimney. Are you going to use a masonry chimney or a metal one? Where will that chimney be located? How will your stove be connected to it? A good chimney, combined with a tight connection to your stove, can make an enormous difference in the way your stove performs.

The first part of this installation planner will deal with the location of your stove within your home. The second part will deal with your chimney. Specific figures such as clearances and sizes of protectors given in this planner pertain to stoves offered by Consolidated Dutchwest. The general guidelines, and types of clearances which must be observed, will apply to most other stoves as well, but if you purchase another brand, you will need to use the specific figures provided by that manufacturer instead.

Note: this booklet is intended as a guide only. When installing a Consolidated Dutchwest or other stove, refer to the instructions provided with the stove. You should also contact your local building inspector or fire marshal about restrictions and inspection requirements in your area.

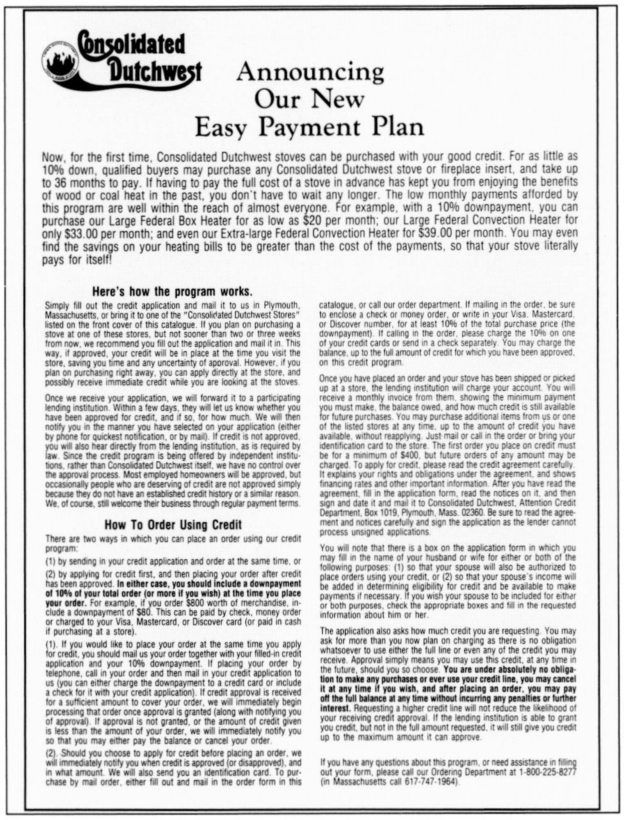

Consolidated Dutchwest

Announcing Our New Easy Payment Plan

Now, for the first time, Consolidated Dutchwest stoves can be purchased with your good credit. For as little as 10% down, qualified buyers may purchase any Consolidated Dutchwest stove or fireplace insert, and take up to 36 months to pay. If having to pay the full cost of a stove in advance has kept you from enjoying the benefits of wood or coal heat in the past, you don't have to wait any longer. The low monthly payments afforded by this program are well within the reach of almost everyone. For example, with a 10% downpayment, you can purchase our Large Federal Box Heater for as low as $20 per month; our Large Federal Convection Heater for only $33.00 per month; and even our Extra-large Federal Convection Heater for $39.00 per month. You may even find the savings on your heating bills to be greater than the cost of the payments, so that your stove literally pays for itself!

Here's how the program works.

Simply fill out the credit application and mail it to us in Plymouth, Massachusetts, or bring it to one of the "Consolidated Dutchwest Stores" listed on the front cover of this catalogue. If you plan on purchasing a stove at one of these stores, but not sooner than two or three weeks from now, we recommend you fill out the application and mail it in. This way, if approved, your credit will be in place at the time you visit the store, saving you time and any uncertainty of approval. However, if you plan on purchasing right away, you can apply directly at the store, and possibly receive immediate credit while you are looking at the stoves.

Once we receive your application, we will forward it to a participating lending institution. Within a few days, they will let us know whether you have been approved for credit, and if so, for how much. We will then notify you in the manner you have selected on your application (either by phone for quickest notification, or by mail). If credit is not approved, you will also hear directly from the lending institution, as is required by law. Since the credit program is being offered by independent institutions, rather than Consolidated Dutchwest itself, we have no control over the approval process. Most employed homeowners will be approved, but occasionally people who are deserving of credit are not approved simply because they do not have an established credit history or a similar reason. We, of course, still welcome their business through regular payment terms.

How To Order Using Credit

There are two ways in which you can place an order using our credit program:

(1) by sending in your credit application and order at the same time, or

(2) by applying for credit first, and then placing your order after credit has been approved. **In either case, you should include a downpayment of 10% of your total order (or more if you wish) at the time you place your order.** For example, if you order $800 worth of merchandise, include a downpayment of $80. This can be paid by check, money order or charged to your Visa, Mastercard, or Discover card (or paid in cash if purchasing at a store).

(1). If you would like to place your order at the same time you apply for credit, you should mail us your order together with your filled-in credit application and your 10% downpayment. If placing your order by telephone, call in your order and then mail in your credit application to us (you can either charge the downpayment to a credit card or include a check for it with your credit application). If credit approval is received for a sufficient amount to cover your order, we will immediately begin processing that order once approval is granted (along with notifying you of approval). If approval is not granted, or the amount of credit given is less than the amount of your order, we will immediately notify you so that you may either pay the balance or cancel your order.

(2). Should you choose to apply for credit before placing an order, we will immediately notify you when credit is approved (or disapproved), and in what amount. We will also send you an identification card. To purchase by mail order, either fill out and mail in the order form in this catalogue, or call our order department. If mailing in the order, be sure to enclose a check or money order, or write in your Visa, Mastercard, or Discover number, for at least 10% of the total purchase price (the downpayment). If calling in the order, please charge the 10% on one of your credit cards or send in a check separately. You may charge the balance, up to the full amount of credit for which you have been approved, on this credit program.

Once you have placed an order and your stove has been shipped or picked up at a store, the lending institution will charge your account. You will receive a monthly invoice from them, showing the minimum payment you must make, the balance owed, and how much credit is still available for future purchases. You may purchase additional items from us or one of the listed stores at any time, up to the amount of credit you have available, without reapplying. Just mail or call in the order or bring your identification card to the store. The first order you place on credit must be for a minimum of $400, but future orders of any amount may be charged. To apply for credit, please read the credit agreement carefully. It explains your rights and obligations under the agreement, and shows financing rates and other important information. After you have read the agreement, fill in the application form, read the notices on it, and then sign and date it and mail it to Consolidated Dutchwest, Attention Credit Department, Box 1019, Plymouth, Mass. 02360. Be sure to read the agreement and notices carefully and sign the application as the lender cannot process unsigned applications.

You will note that there is a box on the application form in which you may fill in the name of your husband or wife for either or both of the following purposes: (1) so that your spouse will also be authorized to place orders using your credit, or (2) so that your spouse's income will be added in determining eligibility for credit and be available to make payments if necessary. If you wish your spouse to be included for either or both purposes, check the appropriate boxes and fill in the requested information about him or her.

The application also asks how much credit you are requesting. You may ask for more than you now plan on charging as there is no obligation whatsoever to use either the full line or even any of the credit you may receive. Approval simply means you may use this credit, at any time in the future, should you so choose. **You are under absolutely no obligation to make any purchases or ever use your credit line, you may cancel it at any time if you wish, and after placing an order, you may pay off the full balance at any time without incurring any penalties or further interest.** Requesting a higher credit line will not reduce the likelihood of your receiving credit approval. If the lending institution is able to grant you credit, but not in the full amount requested, it will still give you credit up to the maximum amount it can approve.

If you have any questions about this program, or need assistance in filling out your form, please call our Ordering Department at 1-800-225-8277 (in Massachusetts call 617-747-1964).

Consolidated Dutchwest publishes an annual, perfect bound catalog-cum-textbook for their retail store and mailorder customers and inquirers. It is, without question, the bible of the wood-burning stove industry. Now in its eighth edition, the 1987-88 version is a delight to read and a veritable treasure trove of information for the potential stove buyer.

In addition to the basic 68-page publication, there are two bound-in, 8-page, full-size inserts printed on offset stock. These separate sections are the "Stove Buyer's Guide" and "The Installation Planner". Both are chock-full of explanations, diagrams, illustrations and useful tables presented in easily understood text and drawings. A third, 4-page insert announces Consolidated Dutchwest's new Easy Payment Plan, and provides the necessary fill-in forms for buyers who wish to take advantage of this 36-month payment option. The installed cost of a stove, chimney, floor and wall protectors and various other accessories can easily reach $2,000. Certainly an amount worthy of an extended payment schedule in many households.

FAHRNEY'S PENS

Large circulation catalogs get most of the publicity, particularly in these days of mega-mergers and billion dollar corporations. But, there are other ways to go. Small, comfortable, easy-to-manage catalog programs do exist, and some are doing quite nicely. The secret lies in specialization.

Fahrney's Pens, Inc. is an outstanding example of a small business catalog program. As the name implies, writing instruments is their line—their only line. You'll not find M. Bich's Bic throwaways at Fahrney's, at least not in their catalog. This is an establishment for those who appreciate fine writing instruments. Waterman, Mont Blanc, Parker, Porsche, Ferrari, Cross, Lamy, and Cartier are some of the names, and $8,000 is the top ticket.

The foundation for the Fahrney's catalog is the retail store opened in 1929 by Mr. Earl Fahrney, and located only two blocks from 1600 Pennsylvania Avenue. Today they provide office supplies to commercial and government offices, including the White House, both Houses of Congress and a number of embassies. The 60-year old retail business and the 13-year old catalog business have expanded largely by word of mouth. In recent years, however, Fahrney's advertising manager, Christel Bolgiano has generated a steady stream of new mailorder customers through small-space print ads in various publications.

Over the years, Fahrney's house list has grown steadily. As of now, there are 55,000 customers, many of whom are repeat buyers. It's surprising how many people are absolutely addicted to pens and pencils—happily a victimless crime. Although true aficionados may have one or two favorite pens, they often own literally hundreds of different sized and shaped writing instruments. Perhaps that's why pens have, for years, been a favorite gift, to give or to receive.

FAHRNEY'S PENS—Fine Writing Instruments
1987-88
Jon J. Sullivan, *President*
Christel Bolgiano, *Marketing Manager/Catalog Director/Art Director/Copywriter*
David Sharpe, *Photographer*
United Litho/Graphic, *Typographer*
Peake Printers [Cheverly, MD], *Printer, on 80# Cameo Gloss for cover and 70# Sterling for text*
Peake Printers, *Color Separator*

Dramatic lighting and props, suggestive of better things in better days, are used to showcase pens and pencils in the moderate ($30-$240) price range. Short shrift is given to the technical aspects of these instruments; rather, style and antecedents take precedence in the copy. One almost wishes some performance pros and cons were discussed, and some "when to use which" advice offered.

The rich settings, large variety of pens, and range of price points make this a catalog with wide appeal to audiences of all kinds.

The rich, elegant Gentlemen Series from Waterman

Ladies and gentlemen prefer the Gentlemen Series instruments for their exquisite craftsmanship in luxuriant lacquers and precious gold and sterling silver. Almost jewel-like in appearance and worth, the Gentlemen Series includes fountain pen with 18K gold nib and matching ball pen, .7mm pencil and roller ball pen. All four pieces are now available in sterling silver trimmed with gold or in glowing bordeaux, dark blue or black lacquer. All are shipped in Waterman gift box with international guarantee card.

STERLING SILVER GENTLEMEN INSTRUMENTS

Sterling Silver Fountain Pen
With your choice of extra-fine, fine, medium or broad nib.
#16071 $240.00

Sterling Silver Ball Pen
#26062 $120.00

Sterling Silver Roller Ball
Shipped with roller refill, but may be interchanged with Waterman micro-marker refill. #46029 $200.00

Sterling Silver .7mm Pencil
#36020 $120.00

LACQUER GENTLEMEN INSTRUMENTS
Please specify bordeaux, blue or black lacquer when ordering.

Lacquer Fountain Pen
With Waterman's trademark 18K gold nib in your choice of extra-fine, fine, medium or broad. #160 $190.00

Lacquer Ball Pen
#260 $90.00

Lacquer Roller Ball Pen
Shipped with roller refill, but can also use Waterman micro-marker refill.
#460 $100.00

Lacquer Pencil
Twist-action design with .7mm lead.
#360 $90.00

Yes, we have Gift Certificates!
If you would like to order a Fahrney's Gift Certificate, please contact our catalog department at 1-800-336-4775. In Maryland, call collect (301) 568-6551. We will forward the certificate and a catalog promptly.

Get Your Order Overnight!
For fast, convenient delivery, send your orders UPS Next Day Air or Second Day Air. Please see order form for details.

5   6

A study in color—the new Montblanc SL Series

Montblanc's Brand New Bottle!

Above:
A unique design with Montblanc's famous logo on cap. Ink is suitable for all fountain pens. Available in black, blue/black, blue, turquoise, red, green or burgundy. Two oz.
#391 $5.50 each.

Special Note:
Due to the international scope of many of the items presented throughout this catalog and the fluctuations in foreign exchange rates, prices and availability are subject to change without notice.

Montblanc's fundamental SL Series features vibrant colored matte and metallic finishes for an entirely new, contemporary look! Fahrney's is especially pleased to offer our customers a mid-priced range of writing instruments of this caliber of performance.

The SL line consists of Montblanc's latest Quickpen design with roller refill, fountain pen with gold-plated nib, plus 5mm pencil and ball pen (both with push-top mechanism). With colors like Viridian Green, Ruby Red, Navy Blue, Matte Black and Smoky Chrome, you're sure to find a style to satisfy any taste, and any writing style! Each has a contrasting clip adorned with the unmistakable Montblanc star.

COLORED MATTE SL LINE

Matte SL Fountain Pen.
Choose extra-fine, fine, medium or broad gold-plated nib.
#2118 $69.50

Matte SL Ball Pen.
#2918 $35.00

Matte SL .5mm Pencil.
#2518 $35.00

Matte SL Quickpen.
Includes black roller refill.
#2318 $49.50

Please specify green, red, blue or black when ordering.

SMOKY CHROME SL LINE

Chrome SL Fountain Pen with chrome-plated steel nib.
Choose extra-fine, fine, medium or broad nib.
#9120 $49.00

Chrome SL Ball Pen.
#9220 $30.00

Chrome SL .5mm pencil.
#9420 $30.00

Chrome SL Quickpen.
Includes black roller refill.
#9320 $33.00

13   14

167

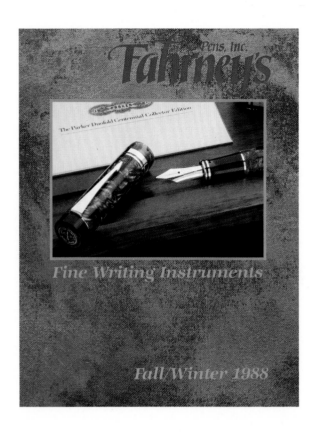

The new Fall/Winter 1988 catalog marks a dramatic departure for Fahrney's. The new, larger size permits almost life-size reproduction of the pens, greatly enhancing detail and color rendition. Unfortunately, the rather jumpy type and grainy backgrounds detract some from the pens themselves. I would suspect that future issues in this new format will work out these, and a few other minor problems.

168

In the greater order of things, order forms are not generally seen as a matter for passionate acclaim. But there can be exceptions. In this unusually extensive order form, Fahrney's has seen fit to provide a mini-monograph on fountain pens. Advice is given on How To Select a Fountain Pen, Care & Feeding, and even First Aid. What's more, and of perhaps even greater note, is the following:

When ordering a pen, send us a sample of your handwriting. It will help us to select the proper point width for you.

Custom-built fountain pens! Tack fittings, too, one presumes. How very civilized. And the copy goes on to say:

Also remember that like any fine mechanism, a pen must go through a two-to-four-week breaking-in period. Treat a pen properly and it will last a lifetime, paying the dividend with enjoyable writing.

Fine paper and a good pen! Ah yes, enjoyable writing it is, unlike scribbling with the ubiquitous ballpoint, which, as George F. Will says "... is like pushing a primitive plow through soggy loam."

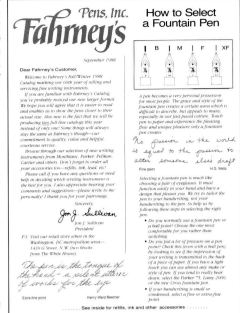

Pelikan pens from Germany offer an example of the broad price range the Fahrney's catalog brings to their customers. On this one spread, Pelikans can be purchased for as little as $33 and as much as $495 (for the Pelikan Toledo). This, by the way, is a fine example of coattail merchandising: fairly ordinary pens shown with a high-ticket pen—preferably from the same manufacturer—adding implied value to the lesser pens.

Fahrney's is doing a number of things right in their new catalog, not the least of which is the introduction of personalization. As of this issue, an in-house facility will engrave initials on pens and pencils within 48 hours. One of the worst kept secrets of successful mail order houses is that personalization sells and sells. It's a pretty safe guess that Fahrney's catalog response rate will get a big lift as a result of this new service, and from the recent resurgence of interest in traditional writing instruments.

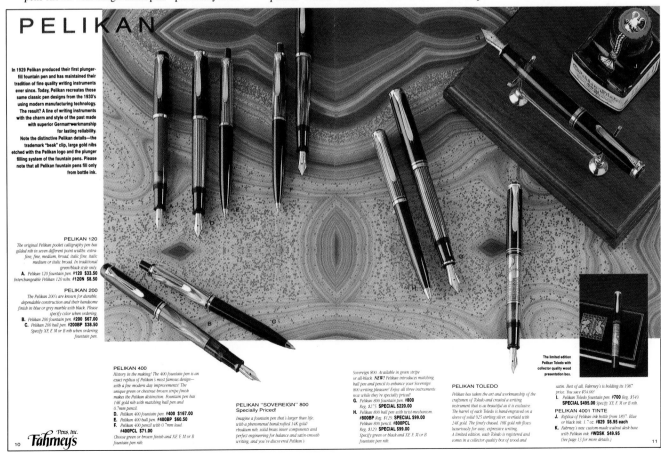

HEARTHSONG

A CATALOG FOR FAMILIES

Barbara Kane, founder of HearthSong, has more than a unique marketing proposition, she has a sincere and powerful message for parents.

I want to encourage parents to allow their children time to be children. I feel that too often, in our culture, children are pushed to grow up too fast.

The issue of war toys and violence also concerns many parents. I want my children to play with toys that express our love and reverence for one another as human beings, and a concern for our environment, the earth. And like many other parents, I prefer high quality toys made of natural, non-toxic materials—the smooth texture of wood, the soft warmth of real wool, cotton and silk.

Most of all, children need time for creative, imaginative play. In fact, it is through play that children learn most readily.

Our company was founded with the goal of providing access to an idea as well as to products. This idea, expressed through our merchandise and its presentation, is that childhood is an important and unique time which we as adults can recognize, nourish and protect. Through our catalog we would like to join with you in honoring the innocence and joy of childhood and support you in your efforts to create a wholesome environment for today's children.

HearthSong, a company dedicated to childhood, is also dedicated to preserving the spirit of play. . . .

For those who might consider these words out of style, old hat or non-relevant, let it be known that Barbara Kane's first catalog, published in 1983, pulled an incredible 14% response.

Presently, HearthSong employs only 35 full-time people. (A blessing shared by many midsize mailorder businesses is a small staff.) Nevertheless, this tiny group will merchandise, create, produce, mail and fulfill orders from over 2 million catalogs in 1988. That number implies a whole lot of very happy kids.

Fashion catalogs work best when they are designed around an upright format. The space utilization works better where standing models are involved. HearthSong is not concerned with the realities of dealing with 6′ tall models. This is a Kids catalog; ergo, it is an oblong book measuring 10-⅞″ X 8-⅜″. The oblong shape works well for this kind of merchandise. Many of the HearthSong items (and models) lend themselves to horizontal and rectangle-shaped photographs, and layouts become more graphic and compelling.

Of equal importance, the oblong page allows for "caption copy". That is, the copy in most instances is contiguous to the item being described. Caption copy may be above, below, beside or wrapped around the product, but it's always very close. Readers love this type of layout because the words are linked much more powerfully to the item. Interested buyers do not have

HEARTHSONG, A CATALOG FOR FAMILIES—Holiday 1988
Barbara Kane, *Founder and Merchandise Manager, Creative Director/Copy Chief*
Lynn Ostling, *Director of Marketing Communications/Art Director*
Tim Hicks, *Catalog Director*
Bernadette Wulf, *Production Manager*
Matt Farruggio, *Photographer*
Lori Almeida, *Illustrator*
Arandel Schmidt, *Printer*
Summerfield Graphics, *Color Separator*

to chase from key numbers to copy blocks to find product information.

Art Director Lynn Ostling has made very effective use of delicate one- and two-color overall pin-dot structures to tie her spreads together. These barely suggested tints set off the process color nicely, and give a soft "feel" to the pages. Subtle background colors also offer an opportunity to soften the vignettes and holding shadows that tie many of the silhouetted photographs down onto the page.

One has to envy President Barbara Kane's fun. Imagine earning a living by searching the world over for unique toys! And they are unique. Giant colored pencils, with color cores ¼ of an inch thick. Two and three story dollhouses, complete with little people—and the kitchen sink. A Snail's Pace Race, a cherry wood Tic-Tac-Toe set, a loom, a lyre and a handwoven Chinese lunch basket. Books and games, village blocks from Germany and the famous hardwood Flying Machine. And, of course, a kit called "Juggling for the Complete Klutz".

It's difficult to survive in the world of children's catalogs.

Mailorder businesses are largely dependent upon repeat buying by the same customers. And, prospecting for new customers is an expensive proposition.

But my bets are on HearthSong. They have their stores, and they have a real-world and very significant statement to make. Many of the products they sell will become family heirlooms. They obviously know where to find their customers (as witnessed by their 14% response to that first, hand-drawn, black & white catalog). And, the pass-a-long readership and recommendations must be outstanding.

The HearthSong catalog does its job extremely well on all counts. The challenge, then, is to discover enough new merchandise to refresh the book, and their two stores, at least three times a year. What a heck of a lot of fun meeting that challenge will be!

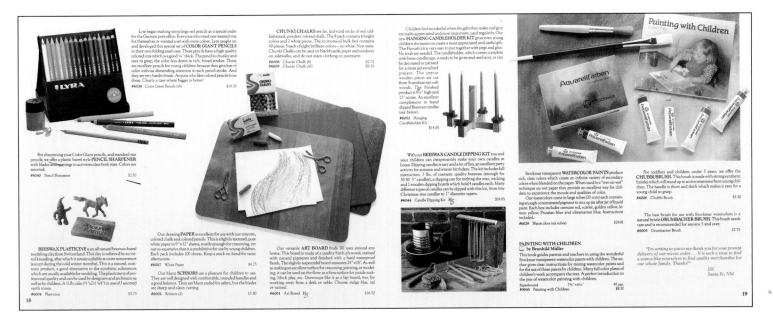

MUSEUM OF MODERN ART

We cannot divulge much in the way of marketing information when it comes to any of the philanthropically supported organizations. The dollar figures are always closely held secrets — and for a very good reason. Membership fees, smaller gifts and fund raising activities contribute only a limited portion of their financial requirements. These societies and organizations are supported largely by important endowments and personal gifts from wealthy individuals, estates, trusts and foundations. Wealthy donors (known as ''Fat Cats'' in the development industry) have an aversion to having their favorite charities perceived as a bunch of grubby merchants. This, in spite of the fact that catalog programs, greeting cards, bird feeders, magazines, and many other forms of fund-raising efforts quietly contribute significant amounts to the cause.

But these fund-raising operations do more than just sell merchandise. They are valuable public relations tools. They help to encourage new or renewed memberships. They create good will, and promote the name and reputation of the sponsoring organization to new audiences. If they can do all that, and make a few dollars along the way, it would seem they are worthwhile endeavors, and should be given the recognition they have earned.

Louise Chinn and her staff at the Museum of Modern Art have been doing a splendid job for years. They were kind enough to provide the DMA with some non-sensitive information about their Christmas catalog. And the news this year is all good! Sales up 33%. Orders generated up 42%, although the quantity mailed was only up 24%. And here's a big number: the response rate was up 14%! All that on top of their previous year's outstanding response and sales increases.

A look through this catalog explains, at least in part, how these sales records were achieved. In this year's collection of merchandise—some new, some repeated from past years—there's something for almost everyone on your shopping list. And, whichever items you may choose, MOMA's impeccable good taste virtually guarantees the success of your gift.

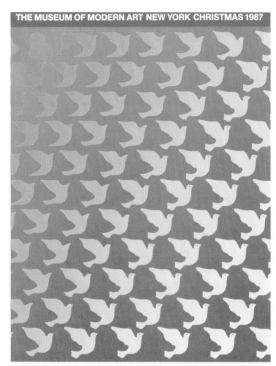

THE MUSEUM OF MODERN ART NEW YORK CHRISTMAS 1987

MUSEUM OF MODERN ART—Christmas 1987
Louise Chinn, *Director of Retail Operations*
Agency: *In-house*

Here we see functional modernism at its best. The roots are in Art Deco and the Dynasties of China, Bauhaus and Brancusi, with a little bit of Silicon Valley thrown in for good measure.

MOMA makes it so easy to make the right choice. The reader has only to settle upon the *kind* of gift to give. The Museum staff has already selected the best in each category. All that's left for the donee to do is decide what to say on the card.

Table Lamp
Designed by K. J. Jucker and Wilhelm Wagenfeld in 1924 and manufactured in West Germany by Tecnolumen. The balanced proportions of this lamp closely adhere to the original Bauhaus design. Handcrafted of clear and opaque glass and nickel-plated metal, each lamp is numbered and bears the Bauhaus logo. Museum Design Collection, 1953. 14H", 7"diam. **#3099.** $690.00, members $621.00.

Desk Blotter
This matte-black desk pad presents a firm, smooth writing surface. Stain-resistant, heavy-gauge linoleum is easy to clean. 15L × 21½W". **#3017.** $19.50, members and nonmembers.

Alarm Clock
Clock face designed exclusively for the Museum. A desktop or bedside alarm clock with a handsome black leather frame, just the accessory for the executive. Quartz movement, repeat alarm. Battery included. **#3742.** $50.00, members $45.00.

Volcano
An exciting sand puzzle from Switzerland, by Kurt Nael. A turn of this water-and-sand whimsy displays the liquid forces of nature. Watch as black sand interacts with water to form gullies and mountains and finally erupts in volcanic spouts. **#3049.** $50.00, members $45.00.

Suprematist Porcelain Demitasse Cup and Saucer, see page 14.

3

Brass Bookmarks
Designed by Michael Kalil exclusively for the Museum. Each gift-packaged set includes three distinctive designs in satin-finished brass. 2"diam. **#1798.** $20.00, members $15.00.

Twin Pen
Designed in 1982 by Gerd Müller for Lamy. An innovative ballpoint pen and gravity-feed mechanical pencil in one: simply turn the brushed stainless-steel barrel to switch functions. Tungsten-point pen and .5mm lead. 6L". **#3032.** $50.00, members $45.00.

Helicoidal Letter Opener
Designed by Enzo Mari and manufactured in Italy by Danese. The symmetry of this elegant letter opener of satin-finished stainless steel is derived from a flattened spiral design. 8½L". **#1645.** $15.00, members $11.25.

ET 55 LCD Calculator
Designed by Dieter Rams in 1980 and manufactured by Braun. Often copied, the original Braun calculator features all the standard functions, plus eight-digit display and four-key memory. Travel case included. Museum Design Collection, 1982. 5½L × 3W × ⅜D". **#3071.** $85.00, members $76.50.

Reumatikerpenna (Pen)
Designed by Hans Tollin in 1978 and manufactured in Sweden by RFSU Rehab. A ball-point pen unmatched for writing comfort, originally designed for people suffering from arthritis or rheumatism. Museum Design Collection, 1983. **#3267.** $8.50, members and nonmembers.

Screwdrivers
Designed by Shohei Mihara and manufactured in Japan. These unobtrusive desktop screwdrivers with anti-rust steel shanks have solid rubber handles and casings. **#3026.** Small Flat Head. **#3029.** Small Phillips Head. Each $10.00, members and nonmembers. **#3028.** Large Flat Head. **#3030.** Large Phillips Head. Each $12.00, members and nonmembers.

Slide Album
Covered in charcoal Navaleather, an unusually soft, fine-grained surface, this slide album contains ten easily removable plastic slide envelopes. Each envelope holds 15 35mm slides and has a metal edge for the unique magnetic binding system. Includes slide register for identification. Ideal for professional presentations. 8W × 13L". **#3025.** $150.00, members $135.00.

Leather Boxes
Designed by Claudia Serafini and Oscar Maschera and handmade in Italy by Arte Cuoio. These unusually simple leather boxes are as functional as they are intrinsically beautiful. Made from the finest French leather, aniline-dyed a rich cognac and stitched with contrasting thread, they make exquisite caches for jewelry, change, or small desk accessories. Gift-boxed. **#3663.** Round. **#3751.** Square. **#3752.** Rectangle. $40.00, members $36.00.

Leather Graphics Tube
Designed by Bruno Morassutti and made in Italy. A distinctive telescoping graphics tube from the artisans of Arte Cuoio. Hand-shaped from the finest aniline-dyed leather, this tube expands from 28¾ to 50 inches to carry and professionally present blueprints, drawings, or important documents. Lined with acid-free paper, with an adjustable strap for perfect balance. **#3753.** Cognac Leather. **#3670.** Black Leather. $250.00, members $225.00.

Bauhaus Chess Set
Designed by Josef Hartwig in 1923 and manufactured in Switzerland by Kurt Naef. The shapes of these chess pieces symbolize their movement on the board rather than literally represent their names (as in conventional chess sets). Handsome wood storage box. Chess pieces represented in the Museum Design Collection, 1953. **#1926.** Chess Pieces. $125.00, members $112.50. **#3082.** Chess Board. 14" square. $50.00, members $45.00.

For information about our **Executive Gift Service,** please call 1-212-708-9760, 10:00–5:00, EST.

To place credit card orders call toll-free 1-800-553-5464, ext. 116. In Ohio, call 1-800-282-0746, ext. 116. For information or customer service, please call 1-212-708-9888, 9:30–5:30, EST.

8

9

Eames Lounge Chair and Ottoman
Designed in 1956 by Charles Eames and manufactured by Herman Miller. Unlike imitations, the original Eames lounge chair is universally recognized as a modern classic. Assembled entirely by hand, the shell is covered with a solid veneer of Brazilian rosewood; seat back and arm cushions are carefully tailored and individually upholstered in top-grain black or brown leather. Museum Design Collection, 1960. Chair, 33H × 32½W × 33D"; 15" seat height. Ottoman, 15H × 26W × 21D". **#V5410.** $2,250.00, members $2,025.00. *Please add $75.00 for shipping (contiguous U.S.) and allow 13 weeks for delivery.*

Noguchi Table
Designed by Isamu Noguchi. An acclaimed sculptor, Noguchi began creating furniture and lamps in the 1940s. Working with the manufacturer Herman Miller, he designed this organic, curvilinear coffee table, which quickly became a collector's item. Recently reissued by Herman Miller, the Noguchi table remains an impeccable accent piece. Ebony-finished poplar with a thick glass top. Museum Design Collection, 1980. 15¾H × 50W × 36D". **#V5413.** $1,210.00, members $1,089.00. *Please add $75.00 for shipping (contiguous U.S.) and allow 13 weeks for delivery.*

Marble Platter
Designed by Mark Gillen and handcrafted in the Philippines. The unusual undulating surface of this exquisite centerpiece is derived from a native shell pattern. Carved from solid, indigenous white marble. **#3080.** $200.00, members $180.00.

Join us now and receive discounts of **10% to 25%** on most merchandise in this catalog, while sharing in the richly varied life of one of the world's great museums. As a Museum Member, you will enjoy a wide range of privileges.

To join, use our order form or call our toll-free number. If you join now, you may take advantage of Member discounts immediately. For further information on membership categories and privileges, call 1-212-708-9696, 9:30–5:30, EST.

Villa Steiner Lamp
Designed by the renowned Austrian architect Adolf Loos in 1910 for the Villa Steiner in Vienna. Straightforward in style, this lamp clarifies Loos's fresh and lucid approach. Solid-cast base with nickel finish. Shade of opaline-flashed glass. 17¾"H, 10¼"diam. **#V5599.** $1,150.00, members $1,035.00.

Russian Suprematist Porcelain
Designed by Nikolai Suetin and originally manufactured by the Petrograd Porcelain Factory. Currently reproduced in Portugal by Mottahedeh exclusively for the Museum. Museum Design Collection, 1985. **#1494.** Demitasse Cup and Saucer. Cup, 2½"H". $30.00, members $22.50. **#1541.** Large Plate. 11¼"diam. $42.00, members $31.50.

Chambord Coffee Set
Designed by Carsten Jorgensen and Tassilo von Grolman and manufactured in France. Return to streamlined styling with this push-down coffee maker and service. Brews coffee quickly to ensure optimal flavor. High-quality glass with metallic handcrafted finish. **#3092.** Eight-Cup Coffee Maker. $67.50, members $60.75. **#3093.** Sugar Bowl and Creamer. $27.00, members $24.30.

14

15

Direct-Angle Reading Level
Manufactured in West Germany by BMI. A level with a vial set in a rotating sleeve for direct slope readings. Made of black impact-resistant plastic with highly visible green markings, it has an "open back" so 60° and 45° lines can be marked directly through indicated slots. Museum Design Collection, 1982. 10L × 2W". **#3089.** $17.00, members and nonmembers.

Hobby- and Multi-Halogen Flashlights
Designed by Udo Geissler and manufactured by Osram. Our popular Multi-Halogen has inspired a variation just right for bookish campers in the wild or at home. The new Hobby-Halogen has many of the features of the mighty Multi—an extra-wide searchlight beam, a pencil beam for pinpointing distant objects, and a magnetized base—but is equipped with a reading lantern instead of the Multi's hazard-warning flasher. Both are black plastic with tungsten-halogen lamps and require four AA batteries (not included). Multi-Halogen represented in the Museum Design Collection, 1985. **#3072.** Hobby-Halogen (with reading lantern) $27.00, members $24.30. **#3452.** Multi-Halogen (with hazard-warning flasher). Not shown. $35.00, members $31.50.

Hand Drill
An easy-to-use hand drill from Fiskars. The handle fits securely into the hand for maximum drilling pressure, while metal gears provide smooth operation. Four high-speed drill bits store in the strong ABS plastic housing. **#3785.** $12.50, members and nonmembers.

Italicus Scissors
Designed by Antonia Campi in 1964. These polished-steel desk scissors serve their purpose with uncommon grace. Museum Design Collection, 1965. 10½L". **#7334.** $26.00, members $23.40.

Ski Goggles
Designed by Jan Matthias in 1979 and manufactured by Carrera in Austria. A streamlined ski goggle with a web-formed frame that flexes to fit every head, and draft-free, foam-covered vents that prevent lens fogging. An extra-wide, fully elasticized headband secures with Velcro for maximum comfort and fit. Headband wraps around the goggle frame to protect tinted lens. Museum Design Collection, 1982. **#3132.** Black. **#3055.** White. $80.00, members $72.00.

For information about our **Executive Gift Service,** please call 1-212-708-9760, 10:00–5:00, EST.

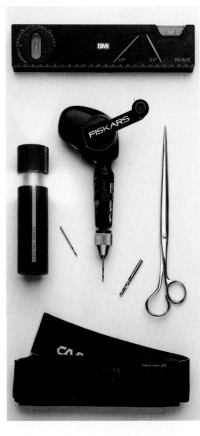

Ice Cream Scoop and Spade
Designed by Sherman Kelly and manufactured by Zeroll. Represented in the Museum Design Collection. The ice cream scoop is a classic example of good design. Both implements are cast aluminum and have cores filled with defrosting liquid for clean scoops. **#5467.** Scoop. **#3362.** Spade. Not shown. Each $12.00, members and nonmembers.

Magnastrip
Designed and manufactured by Magnaform exclusively for the Museum. Affix notes with magnets to Magnastrip's vinyl-coated steel plate. Its adhesive back attaches to almost any surface at home or in the office. Four magnets—three black, one red for "hot" items—complement the pinstripe design. **#1492.** $12.00, members $9.00.

Screwpulls
Designed by Herbert Allen and manufactured by the Hallen Company. Pull corks with ease with these teflon-coated corkscrews. Frames fit on the lip of the bottle and center the screw for precise removal of any cork. **#3234.** Pocket Screwpull (with metal flip-out knife). **#3038.** Table Screwpull (with stand and plastic cover). Not shown. $15.00, members and nonmembers.

Screwdriver
An exceptional multipurpose screwdriver from Fiskars. The ergonomically designed, PVC vinyl handle conforms to the grip for more turning power. Includes five interchangeable bits, three slotted and two Phillips, which conveniently store in the handle. **#3069.** $9.50, members and nonmembers.

Mini-Mag Flashlight
Designed by Anthony Maglica and manufactured in the U.S. Lightweight and compact, the Mini-Mag is a superior AA-battery flashlight. Water-resistant, it has a beam that adjusts from flood to narrow. Constructed of aircraft-grade aluminum with a gunmetal finish. Batteries not included. Gift-boxed. **#3602.** $15.00, members and nonmembers.

Bend-A-Light
A unique concept in battery-operated flashlights. The nine-inch flexible shaft with a high-intensity beam can be bent into almost any configuration, enabling the user to light small, hard-to-see areas. Batteries included. **#3133.** $16.50, members and nonmembers.

To place credit card orders call toll-free 1-800-553-5464, ext. 116. In Ohio, call 1-800-282-0746, ext. 116. For information or customer service, please call 1-212-708-9888, 9:30–5:30, EST.

The artists at MOMA have wisely eschewed flamboyant layouts and cluttered photographs. Each item, each of these functional artforms has so much to say. It would be a criminal offense to drown out their individual messages with a mindless barrage of background noise. Once again, MOMA, well done!

Lest MOMA be accused of catering only to the esthetics of their members, these pages from the kitchen and the nursery departments belie the thought.

Cooking can be fun, but it can also be very dull. If one always prepares the *same* food, in the *same* way, using the *same* utensils, it can be a real drag. But if instead, a kitchen is full of grown-up toys the likes of these—they can hardly be called pots and pans—what a kick cooking can be!

MOMA's toy department is small, but exclusive. It excludes all the juvenile mind-molesters, the Killer Kops and Waldo the Warrior types, and instead offers the Balloon Mobile, a Paper Zoo, and the delightful Ark-I-Pets. God rest ye merry MOMA folks, let nothing change your way. Our children's dreams are filled with love, not nightmares from their play.

Cookware
Designed by Richard Sapper and manufactured in Italy by Alessi. Seven years in the making, this Alessi cookware sets a new standard for fine cooking utensils. The design of each piece reflects a special concern for function, material, structural unity, and physical beauty. No serious cook should be without these first-class utensils. Chef consultants, Pierre and Michel Troisgros: **#3137.** Small Frying Pan (black steel). 7"diam. $60.00, members $54.00. **#3131.** Large Frying Pan (black steel). 10¼"diam. $75.00, members $67.50. **#3150.** Small Saucepan with Lid (heavy-gauge copper with 18/10 stainless-steel lining). 2½"H", 4¼"diam. $140.00, members $126.00. Chef consultants, Raymond Thuilier and Jean-André Charial: **#3151.** Dutch Oven (black-enameled cast iron). $175.00, members $157.50.

Margrethe Bowls
Designed by Sigvard Bernadotte and Acton Bjørn in 1950. Named after the queen of Denmark, these plastic bowls stack inside one another for easy storage. Rubber-rimmed bases will not slide. Dishwasher-safe. Set of three: 1½, 2, and 3 quart. **#3091.** $24.00, members $21.60.

Vivace Vase, see page 27.

Wine Coaster/Bottle Tray
Designed by Jørgen Møller and manufactured by Georg Jensen Silversmiths. This multipurpose stainless-steel tray can be used as a wine coaster or small serving plate. 6"diam. **#3522.** $18.00, members and nonmembers.

Porcelli Kettle
Designed by Lorenzo Porcelli and manufactured by Dansk. A clean and sleek stainless-steel kettle, as functional as it is decorative. The spout, inspired by waterflow drawings by Leonardo da Vinci, produces a beautiful arched ribbon of water. Two-quart capacity. 8½"H". **#3311.** $59.00, members $53.10.

Groovy Trivets
Manufactured in the U.S. by Copco. These heat-resistant trivets are perfect for hot or cold use in the kitchen or on the table. 7½"diam. Red (set of 2) **#3789.** $6.00. White (set of 2) **#3790.** $6.00, members and nonmembers.

Chopping Bowl and Chopper
Masterfully mince vegetables, nuts, meats, or fresh herbs in seconds with this chopping bowl and chopper. Polyethylene plastic is washable, sanitary, and will not absorb odors. Stainless-steel blade has a round handle for comfort. Bowl, 9¾"diam. **#3081.** $12.00, members and nonmembers.

22

23

S. Point Toys
Half the fun of these colorful toys is putting them together. Brightly contrasting plastic pieces fit snugly together with hinges and connecting pins. Doors and engine compartment open, flat bed dumps, flaps lift, and wheels turn. All parts, spare hinges, pins, wheel pincers for disassembly, and a convenient storage/gift box are included. As an assembly toy, recommended for ages three and over; as a play toy, suitable for ages six and over. *Not recommended for children under three.* **#3723.** Truck. $50.00, members $45.00. **#3724.** Plane. $35.00, members $31.50.

Children's Place Setting
Bright, nearly indestructible Munching™ Ware is as much fun for messy kids as it is for the adults who clean up after them. Designed to minimize mess with such thoughtful features as attached saucers that catch spills, wide bases for stability, and rubber feet that grip table surfaces. The thick handles of the fork and spoon are easy for tiny hands to grip and control. Recommended for ages six months and older. **#3058.** Three-Piece Dish Set. $15.00, members and nonmembers. **#3060.** Fork and Spoon. $4.50, members and nonmembers.

Balloon Mobile
Made in Denmark by Flensted Mobiles. In this whimsical mobile, five paper balloons float in a gentle breeze. **#3718.** $14.00, members and nonmembers.

Elephant Party Mobile
Made in Denmark by Flensted Mobiles. These colorful plastic elephants frolic in midair. Includes three baby elephants for use as bookmarks or favors. **#3313.** $10.00, members and nonmembers.

Paper Zoo
Designed by Ernst Roch and manufactured exclusively for the Museum. An entertaining and educational device to develop manual skills and stimulate the imagination. This paper-folding kit contains a 12-page booklet and 36 sheets of colorful paper that form a variety of exotic and domestic animals. **#1939.** $12.00, members $9.00.

Ark-I-Pets®
Designed by Jack Stone and produced exclusively for the Museum. Arrange these paper animals in natural settings or line them up in twos to board the ark. Each colorful set contains an ark, assorted landscapes, and two each of 12 animals to cut, fold, and play with. **#1563.** Ark-I-Pets®. **#1564.** Jungle Ark-I-Pets®. $14.50, members $10.87.

Shufflebook and Animal Shufflebook
Written and illustrated by Richard Hefter and Martin Stephen Moskof. Bold and bright pictures are printed on both sides of sturdy cards, with a noun phrase on one side and action words on the reverse. These cards tell a new and amusing story each time they are shuffled and laid out side by side. Each book has 52 cards; use books together or separately. **#6794.** Shufflebook. **#3923.** Animal Shufflebook. Each $9.00, members $6.75.

Magic Rings Puzzle
A colorful, mind-boggling puzzle involving rotating rings and simple mathematics. The beginner's challenge is to arrange five rings so that all the equations, i.e., $1 + 3 = 4$, are correct. For a more difficult task click on two additional rings, and for a real brain teaser add two more. The resulting nine-piece puzzle has over 45 million possible combinations, with only a few solutions. **#3717.** $10.00, members and nonmembers.

Count One to Ten
Designed by Robin Page. This book creatively teaches children to count using a curious flip-over and accordion-action design. Numbers one through ten are shown in digits, words, and symbols for added learning. The two-foot-long, expandable format will provide hours of fun and play. For ages 18 months and over. **#20629.** $9.00, members and nonmembers.

To place credit card orders call toll-free 1-800-553-5464, ext. 116. In Ohio, call 1-800-282-0746, ext. 116. For information or customer service, please call 1-212-708-9888, 9:30–5:30, EST.

28

29

175

PATAGONIA/PATAGONIA KIDS

The press is replete with bad news about mailorder sales. Sounds of gnashing teeth, woeful wailings and rending garments abound. Is Chicken Little right at last? Not very darned likely! Business cycles aside, the mailorder business is in great shape. Some of the practitioners are not.

A damning assortment of poor mailorder practices has been brought to light in recent surveys. In these studies, nondelivery, wrong merchandise, and poor communications top the list of customer turnoffs. As a double-check, firms and publishers from the direct response industry placed actual telephone orders with the worst offenders to verify these consumer complaints. Unfortunately, the results were the same.

The problems extant in the mailorder community cannot be blamed on catalog glut or consumer indifference. If that were the case, then all catalogers would be in trouble. The stumbling block, in most cases, is a question of attitude, particularly as it relates to customer service and satisfaction. As proof, I submit the enviable track record of one (of the many) companies that is doing it right.

Patagonia is not one of the doom-and-gloomers predicting the demise of the mailorder business. Not hardly. Two mailings per year of 250,000 each, plus store distribution of 100,000 catalogs powers this very successful 70-million dollar outerwear business. Founder and President Yvon Chouinard has even expressed some desire to slow down the growth of the mailorder segment of his business, un-American as that may seem. He is concerned that hyper-expansion might infringe upon his time with the "Fun Hogs" and take him away from his favorite challenge, the constant field testing and upgrading of Patagonia products.

Corporate growth has been 35% for the past 3 years. Catalog sales during the same period have been compounding at 50% annually. Sales increases on this scale—far above population expansion—have to come from somewhere. They are accomplished, in this case, by carving a chunk of market share out of the hides of merchants who are not doing as good a job—with their people, with their products or with their customers. Patagonia products are relatively high ticket, high margin goods, the combination every store buyer tries to put together. It's small wonder managements on the other side of this market share equation are singing the blues.

"Catalog Business" reports that Patagonia's response rate from their house list is a very healthy 15%, with an average order of $100 from the adult catalog and $70-$80 from the new children's book. Let's take a look at how they do it.

- *Bold and beautiful layouts and photography, including some stunning shots of Patagonia apparel in action, most reproduced from photographs sent to Patagonia by customers.*
- *Two toll-free 800 ordering numbers, one of which is "Voice/TDD". Voice/TDD translates as "Telecommunications Device for the Deaf".*
- *An editorial approach to copywriting that makes every catalog worthwhile reading for active sports aficionados and armchair athletes alike.*
- *Very helpful cross references near editorial copy directing readers to the pages on which the merchandise is sold.*

PATAGONIA—Fall 1988
Yvon and Malinda Chouinard, *Owners*
Mary Palzet, *Vice President, Mail Order Division*
Shirley Aitchison, *Marketing Manager*
Tricia Grossi, *Catalog Director*
Kris McDivitt, *Creative Director*
Hal Arenson and Su Clayson, *Art Directors*
Nora Gallagher, *Copy Chief*
Jennifer Ridgeway, *Photo Editor*
Lynn Blanche, *Production Manager*
Glen Cormier, *Photographer*
Graphic Arts Center [Portland, OR], *Printer*

PATAGONIA KIDS—Fall 1988
Tricia Grossi, *Senior Buyer*
Jennifer Ellsworth, *Kids' Line Director and Catalog Director*
Hal Arenson and Kris McDivitt, *Creative Directors*
Kathy Metcalf, *Art Director*
Photos: *from customers*
Graphics Arts Center, *Printer*

- *Founder Yvon Chouinard refers to items in the Patagonia line as "technical products". And indeed they are. The copy for the Patagonia Fishing Vest lists 17 special-purpose pockets, D-rings and features in addition to a 290-word copy block describing the vest. The use of the word technical also relates to the fabrics and layered construction used to achieve the desired level of protection from the elements under widely varying circumstances.*
- *The individuals answering the telephones are thoroughly familiar with the items they are selling. They are recruited because they have been there. They've climbed the mountains, schussed the slopes, waded the streams and ridden the ranges. They are prepared to discuss your needs, not just accept your order.*
- *A national network of dealers and Patagonia-owned stores is in place to derive synergistic impact from the catalog.*
- *The Patagonia image, from top to bottom, projects an aura of quality and authority.*

A typical catalog spread features a real ski lift operator on a high tower wearing Patagonia insulated trousers and Synchilla Vest. On the left hand page, one pair of the trousers was photographed inside-out to show the lining.

George Rossman maintaining the Palmer lift at Timberline Lodge ski area, Mt. Hood. RILEY CATON

The trousers are tailored, lined and finished with a heavy duty zipper and closures.

The insulation in the trousers will keep you warm without bulk.

This pair of trousers is inside out to show the lining.

INSULATED TROUSERS
It is difficult to combine the qualities of complete function with complete good looks. In the Insulated Trousers, however, we believe we've accomplished that goal. The trousers are tailored with lean back pockets that button down. They look like well-made trousers. But their fabric is a combination of Cordura® and Supplex®. Cordura has been used to make luggage. Supplex nylon looks and feels like cotton. (We use Supplex for our Alpine Gear.) This combination fabric looks remarkably like cotton twill. We found a 60 gr. insulation that will keep you warm below freezing, but is thin enough to keep the trousers slim. Thus the trousers are made for those who must work or play in extreme cold. The Insulated Trousers may be the most perfect product we've ever made: true function, true form. Machine wash and dry. Imported.
Insulated Trousers #55851 $135.00
Colors: Khaki (041), Indigo (025), Charcoal (154) (shown)
Waist: 30 31 32 33 34 35 36 38 40
Inseam: 32½" 33¾" 34½" 34½"
September Delivery

MEN'S CORD SHIRT
Most of us can remember a favorite cord shirt, one that made us loathe to relinquish it to the trash can after it had become threadbare. This shirt is a classic cord; from the twice-stitched buttons, the double-needle finished seams, and the paired buttons at the cuffs, it's got old integrity. The corduroy is so fine it will lie like smoke against your skin. Garment washed, shrinkage is 4%. Imported.
Cord Shirt #54501 $45.00
Colors: (top to bottom) Oxblood (099), Eggplant (074), Spruce (057), Cobalt (020)
Sizes: S-XL

Here, one of the many editorial spreads in this catalog deals in great detail with the range of weather conditions encountered by skiers. Recommendations for the appropriate ski wear and equipment are laced with instructions on their use and rationale for their selection. On the far left you'll see the reference table that sends the reader to the page on which each item discussed in the editorial can be found.

If this vest were a car, the hyperbolic salesman would tell you "it's loaded". And yet, when you read down the list of seventeen features, they all make sense. On the left side of the spread is the "Sawed-off Raincoat"—a real eye-catcher of a name for what others might call a waterproof jacket. Disrespectful? Perhaps. But the name is a stopper, and that's all a catalog subhead can hope to do.

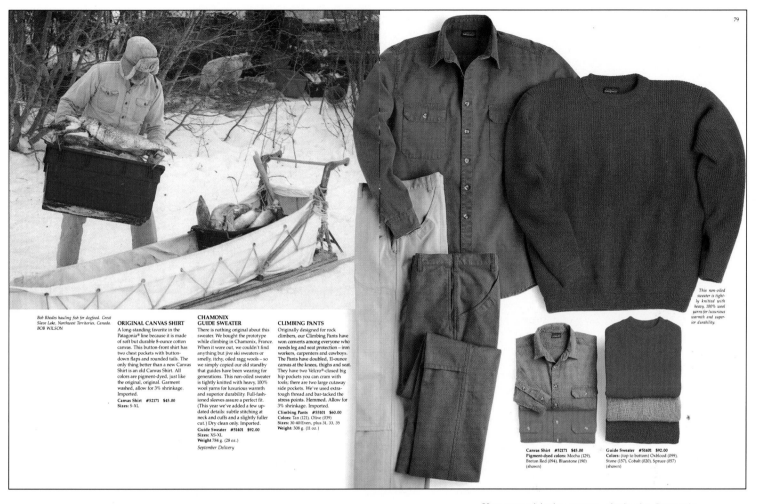

Bob Rhodes hauling fish for dogfood. Great Slave Lake, Northwest Territories, Canada.
BOB WILSON

ORIGINAL CANVAS SHIRT

A long-standing favorite in the Patagonia® line because it is made of soft but durable 8-ounce cotton canvas. This button-front shirt has two chest pockets with button-down flaps and rounded tails. The only thing better than a new Canvas Shirt is an old Canvas Shirt. All colors are pigment-dyed, just like the original, original. Garment washed, allow for 3% shrinkage. Imported.

Canvas Shirt   #52171 $45.00
Sizes: S-XL.

CHAMONIX
GUIDE SWEATER

There is nothing original about this sweater. We bought the prototype while climbing in Chamonix, France. When it wore out, we couldn't find anything but jive ski sweaters or smelly, itchy, oiled ragg wools – so we simply copied our old standby that guides have been wearing for generations. This non-oiled sweater is tightly knitted with heavy, 100% wool yarns for luxurious warmth and superior durability. Full-fashioned sleeves assure a perfect fit. (This year we've added a few updated details: subtle stitching at neck and cuffs and a slightly fuller cut.) Dry clean only. Imported.

Guide Sweater   #51401 $92.00
Sizes: XS-XL.
Weight 784 g. (28 oz.)

September Delivery

CLIMBING PANTS

Originally designed for rock climbers, our Climbing Pants have won converts among everyone who needs leg and seat protection – iron workers, carpenters and cowboys. The Pants have doubled, 11-ounce canvas at the knees, thighs and seat. They have two Velcro®-closed big hip pockets you can cram with tools; there are two large cutaway side pockets. We've used extra-tough thread and bar-tacked the stress points. Hemmed. Allow for 3% shrinkage. Imported.

Climbing Pants   #55101 $60.00
Colors: Tan (121), Olive (039)
Sizes: 30-40/Even, plus 31, 33, 35
Weight: 308 g. (11 oz.)

This non-oiled sweater is tightly knitted with heavy, 100% wool yarns for luxurious warmth and superior durability.

Canvas Shirt   #52171 $45.00
Pigment-dyed colors: Mocha (129), Breton Red (094), Bluestone (190) (shown)

Guide Sweater   #51401 $92.00
Colors: (top to bottom) Oxblood (099), Stone (157), Cobalt (020), Spruce (057) (shown)

Uncompromisingly country, that's the Patagonia look. A big block of customers live in the largest cities, but Vice President Mary Palzet is having none of the city in her catalog.

No doubt Patagonia Kids' editors are inundated with photos of dear little Johnnie or Sue. But, here's one that will be hard to top. The caption reads "Adventures in babysitting". Obviously Hunter is having a ball. Sister Lucia is in a flat-out chase.

Illustrations in the Kids catalog are not quite as sensational as some found in the adult version, but outdoors action and function are still the themes. On the left hand page, the copy tells of the Patagonia Child Care center where "paint, sandbox and spaghetti wash-and-wear tests" are conducted. The copy goes on to describe the nationwide, all-season prototype program designed to push all the garments to their limits.

Patagonia Kids starts them young. The bunting outfit worn by the bundle being lugged around by his mother starts at a size described as "Small (10-15 lbs)". The mini-schussboomer outfits run to size 14.

In both Patagonia Kids and the seniors' book, the merchandise is shown off-figure. Difficult to style for the camera, but a wise choice. Construction, not fashion, is the Patagonia story. Linings, collar and cuff designs and detailing can be seen much more clearly than if the garments were full of people.

PHELAN'S

This year, the American Catalog Awards judges conferred prizes in 34 distinct areas of catalog merchandising. One of the categories was entitled, "New Consumer Catalog". Under that heading, two Gold (First) prizes were awarded. The honorees are as different as night and day.

Pottery Barn is one of the co-golds. (An article discussing that ultra-slick production starts on page 53.) The new owners at Williams-Sonoma teamed up with the Pottery Barn bunch to engineer a guaranteed winner.

Sharing the Gold Award this year is a newcomer from California: Phelan's Catalog—High Performance Horse Gear And Riding Apparel. We wish them the best of luck in their new enterprise.

Right off the top, the Phelan's copy is as good, or better, than any catalog copy to be found—anywhere. It is so concerned, so authoritative and so detailed, that any equestrian will immediately become involved. The copy is long, but not overblown. It is informal, but not cute or slangy. And it is logical! For example:

NEWMARKET BOOT

Why trash your nice leather riding boots in winter riding conditions? Our canvas and rubber boot, named after the famed wet racing town of Newmarket, is made to ride in—comfortable, washable (scrubbable), and colorful. The corrugated rubber sole is less likely to slip in a wet stable yard or wet stirrup. We find them a great complement to our riding jeans.

Any rider who's ever cursed a muddy boot that won't come off will appreciate the handy heel step and heel loop that make removing this boot almost as easy as putting it on.

Available in olive green, tan, burgundy, or blue. Made by Lady Northhampton of England in full sizes for women.

 PHELAN'S—High Performance Horse Gear And Riding Apparel 1987/1988
Patricia Phelan, *Catalog Director*
Bonnie Phippin, *Designer*
Maryann Truitt, *Merchandiser*
Stewart Brand, Patricia Phelan and Maryann Truitt, *Copywriters*
Gerry Bybee [Bybee Studios], *Photographer*
Frye & Smith [Costa Mesa, CA], *Printer, on 60# Royal Roto for cover and text*
Frye & Smith, *Color Separator*

Not a question left unanswered, including the "why?" (as in: why should I buy it?)

For a retail catalog or newspaper ad, perhaps OK; for mailorder, these are no-no's.

The type setter had an easy time of it when he set all copy to the same column width. Saved a few dollars, no doubt. But as a result, the photos had to be worked around the copy instead of using the copy to enhance, and direct attention to the products. To make matters even worse, the items being sold are frequently lost in shadows or buried in complex situations. In other areas, densely colored subjects were silhouetted against white backgrounds. This technique will invariably give a muddy rendition of softgoods (and leather) totally lacking in acceptable detail definition.

Putting pencil to paper—or more accurately, plugging this catalog into our computer model—reveals an even more ominous set of (typical) start-up symptoms. The first has to do with the fact that the catalog is under-merchandised. Given that this is in all likelihood a test, there does not seem to be a chance in hell that Patty will get much of her bait back. Question: Will there be enough funding to try at least twice again with more fully merchandised books? That's what it's going to take. But I think Patty Phelan already knows that. Her wonderful introductory letter (unfortunately located on the OBC) sets the stage for an evolutionary, customer-sensitive growth:

"I set out to do three things with this company: find or create innovative equestrian products taking advantage of new materials and design ideas; find beautiful, quality-made traditional goods, and import from overseas outstanding items that express the passion for horses that exists worldwide.

Our goal is to serve the athleticism of horse and rider, the safety of horse and rider, and the high aesthetic and adventuresomeness of the sport.

This catalog is only a start in that direction. As a customer, you are now a part of the process of making our service become as good as it can be. Please comment on the catalog, the products in it, and how you're treated as a customer. Let us know how your purchases work out for you.

Most important: Tell us about things you would like to see carried in the catalog—*great items that you've seen or that you can imagine. And tell us about yourself—what kind of riding you do, with what kind of horse, and what kind of gear and apparel you're looking for.*

We want to print exciting (or soulful) color photography of horses and riders. If you have some, send it along—if a Phelan's product is

in the shot, so much the better. We'll pay $50 for every photo used in the catalog....."

4

"To finish is to win"
Endurance, long distance riding, and ride-and-tie races make awesome demands on horse and rider — and on equipment. Matching the high level of athleticism in these sports is a high degree of design imagination and equipment innovation; the cutting edge of equestrian gear design these days. We've been talking to the top riders to find out what kind of gear they're buying, making for themselves, or fantasizing. We figure if something's good enough for a 100 mile race, most trail riders would like it too. All of our trail products have to perform superbly in competition before we'll carry them.

Maryann Truitt, in charge of Customer Service for Phelan's, riding in the Big Creek Ride and Tie with her partner, accomplished endurance athlete, Mary Ann Buxton.

I felt great after riding 100 miles in this saddle. Usually my back kills me after a long ride..."

Sandy Shuler, D.V.M.
World Champion, 1986,
FEI 100-Mile Endurance
Race, Italy.

EPIC Endurance Saddle
What's most conspicuous about this saddle is the high quality of craftsmanship, but what's most important about it is the extraordinary comfort it provides for both horse and rider. The impeccable design by England's top saddler, Frank Baines, accommodates not only the competitive rider but anyone who spends extended time in the saddle. The horse's perspective: the Epic Endurance Saddle's spring tree has panels which extend beyond the cantle, reminiscent of the 19th Century Cape Fan military saddles designed to handle the rigors of wartime use, maximizing the distribution of the rider's weight on the horse's back. The saddle's cut-back head avoids impact on the withers, and a deeper than normal gullet increases airflow along the horse's spinal column, reducing overheating and fatigue.

The rider's perspective: the saddle is built with a deep, comfortable seat. The extended flaps allow the rider to remain long in the leg with close horse contact, staying balanced and upright even while traveling over rough ground. The knee pads have been molded of extremely durable compressed foam, and all stitching is done with special German plaited thread to prevent eventual rotting. Two front folding rings, six D-rings and a crupper ring, all solid brass, are firmly integrated into the saddle's structure to secure attachments.

The black leather saddle weighs 14 pounds and is available in medium width in sizes 16, 17, and 18 inch. (To determine size see order form.) Narrow and wide tree widths and custom fitting or color options can be arranged by special order for an extra charge.
■ *EPIC Saddle #101* **$900**

The Endurance Stirrup
These stirrups are to ordinary stirrups what running shoes are to street shoes — vastly more comfortable and practical, if stranger looking. This stirrup was developed for competitive riders who may spend hours in the forward or standing position, who sometimes are forced to dismount to massage circulation back into their lower extremities to ease the pain brought on by narrow unyielding stirrups.

The solution is a wide step (4-1/2 inches front to rear) and serious padding under the foot — a 1/2-inch thick neoprene pad with a high-traction surface. Having the rider's weight more evenly dispersed than in a conventional stirrup greatly reduces rider fatigue. The sides of the stirrup are attractively padded with leather to prevent scuffing on your boot. The metal is a corrosion resistant polished magnesium alloy, so although the Endurance Stirrup is much bigger than a standard English iron, it's only a few ounces heavier — each alloy stirrup weighs 30 ounces.
■ *Metal stirrup #160* **$87**

The Lite Stirrup
Riders who want a lighter (and lower priced) Endurance Stirrup may prefer the one made of ivory-colored injection-molded nylon with a narrower (3 inch) step. It weighs only 14 ounces per stirrup. Either stirrup can be used with leathers from 1 to 2 -1/4 inches wide.
■ *Lite Stirrup #175* **$52**

What Is This Madness?
A history of Ride & Tie by Bud Johns.
■ *Book #10* **$8**

Endurance and Competitive Trail Riding
Linda Tellington-Jones' classic on the sport.
■ *Book #11* **$13**

ENDURANCE & TRAIL RIDING

Cantle Bag
This full size bag has an extra large two-way zipper that gives easy access from either side of the horse, and the leather pulls make it easy for cold or gloved fingers to use. There's plenty of space inside to store extra clothing, halter and lead, or a picnic lunch. The small outside pocket keeps trail maps, keys, or money readily accessible. Two lash points are handy for tying down a large jacket or blanket. Suitable for either an English or Western saddle (as long as there are D-rings or straps to attach to). In red, blue, or black cordura nylon.
■ *Cantle bag #910* **$34**

Pommel Bag
This smaller cordura bag designed to fit the pommel provides quick front access while riding. It's the perfect spot for a sandwich or binoculars. In red, blue, or black.
■ *Pommel bag #915* **$22**

Grommeted Sea Sponge
This natural sponge holds six times as much water as a synthetic sponge and looks better to boot. It's wonderful on long hot rides to cool down your horse (or yourself!) at a creek or vet check. Comes with a leather tie.
■ *Sea Sponge #930* **$15**

Canteen of the '80s
These plastic one pint containers are lightweight, easy to fill and won't spill either when closed or while drinking. In red, white, blue, yellow or clear.
■ *Water Bottle #920* **$3.50**

The cordura nylon web holder has a velcro closure flap, two grommets and leather ties for extra security against jarring loose. In red, blue or black.
■ *Bottle Holder #925* **$10**

Our second mega-concern is somewhat related to the first. This catalog has only 16 pages. The public at large tends to perceive anything less than 32 pages as a brochure or direct mail piece, not a catalog. Special interest groups—and certainly, Phelan's audience qualifies here—will be satisfied with 24 pages. More pages mean more merchandise, which in turn offers customers more opportunities to buy. Another mailorder rule of thumb: a customer is not your customer until s/he has bought from you more than twice.

In this typical Phelan's spread one can see clearly the predominant weight of copy versus photography. Every slug of copy gives the reader a good reason to continue reading, to become more involved. For instance: a saddle arouses serious interest on the part of two animals, the horse and the rider. Here, Patty Phelan has taken both into consideration. An introductory paragraph is followed by two leads: ''*The horse's perspective*'', and ''*The rider's perspective*''. The text then approaches the saddle from both top and bottom points of view.

Western Bridle
With its traditional cowboy knotted browband, this bridle looks handsome on every horse we've put it on. It's made of fine beveled domestic leather in chestnut brown with solid brass fittings. Split reins with conway buckles are included. Full or cob size.
■ *Western Bridle #201* **$85**

EPIC Multi-Bridle
The most convenient, versatile, and sporty-looking leather bridle around, made in England by EPIC. Great for hunting or picnicking with your horse — you can tie your horse securely and drop the bit easily for feeding and watering.

Sizes/Color: Bridles are made in fine black English leather with solid brass fittings. Cheek pieces are approximately 1/2 inch wide (although partially rounded on style #215). On both styles the noseband is flat and tapered with 3/4 inch width at the center, and the browband is 1/2 inch. Available in full or cob sizes. If not sure of size, measure your horse's head from the corner of the mouth across the poll to the opposite side of the mouth.
■ *Multi-Bridle/Flat Leather #210* **$75**
■ *Matching Flat Reins #211* **$40**
■ *Multi-Bridle/Rounded Leather #215* **$115**
■ *Matching Rounded Reins #216* **$50**

Arabs wearing the Multi-Bridle, flat leather on the left, rounded leather on the right.

EPIC Saddle with Thiedemann Pad

Engraved Snaffle
This fine stainless steel 5-inch bit is made in California by Sleister and hand engraved on the rings with a delicate pattern.
■ *Snaffle #222* **$52**

Hackamore
A high quality, well balanced, lightweight aluminum hackamore with leather noseband. Like our snaffle, it's made by Sleister in the U.S.
■ *Hackamore, for standard horses, 9-1/4 inch shanks #219* **$40**
■ *For Arabs, with smaller noseband #220* **$40**

Contoured Saddle Pads
These pads with billet and girth straps are made to fit our EPIC saddles. (Not shown in photo)
■ *Quilted Cotton on underside with wool-like fleece on top #330* **$30**
■ *All Virgin Wool #331* **$65**

Thiedemann Saddle Pad
This German quilted pad has a durable 100% cotton fabric on the outside, and a dual fiber lining to absorb the horse's sweat. In lovely bright colors, with slotted billet straps, approx. 19 by 22 inches. This pad will hold its shape wash after wash. Colors: kelly green with navy trim; grey, burgundy; navy with white trim; black with yellow trim.
■ *Thiedemann #300* **$58**

Navajo Pad
These 100% virgin wool pads are beautifully woven in Navajo-style patterns. The 30x30 inch size can be used with either Western or English saddles. Machine washable. In multi-colors with either primary color in pink, purple, green, red, or grey. Specify color choice and second preference.
■ *Navajo Pad #310* **$24**

EPIC All-Purpose Saddle
Made to the same demanding standards as our Endurance saddle, the All-Purpose Saddle is designed for the rider who wants the benefits of EPIC workmanship but prefers a conventional-looking saddle for jumping, eventing, or flatwork. It's built with the same deep seat, only on a standard spring tree without the extended panels of the Endurance saddle. It is preferable for a short-backed horse, because the saddle does not cover as much surface area on the horse's back. We've kept most of the Endurance design features cut-back head, D-rings on both sides, wide gullet, and firm knee pads.

Sizes/Color: In fine black English leather, in medium widths, sizes 16 inch, 17 inch, and 18 inch. (A 17-medium will fit most horses and riders.) Other sizes and widths can be specially ordered but do require additional charges and shipping time.
■ *All-Purpose #115* **$850**

Cord Girth
A 14-strand English-style girth (4-3/4 inches wide), it prevents chafing and sweating. Best girth for long distance riding, and easily washed. Split ends on both sides, with "never-rust" solid nickel roller buckles and tongues. In black or white, sizes 46, 48, 50.
■ *Cord girth #140* **$22**

Leather Girth
Durable and supple German overlay leather padded girth, slightly tapered behind the elbow to prevent chafing. Triple elastic at one end makes for easier saddling. Reinforced buckles are sewn in by hand. Black leather in sizes 48-54.
■ *Leather girth #145* **$68**

Stirrup Leathers
Top quality rawhide leathers from Germany. Each pair of leathers is cut from the same hide to ensure that they will wear evenly. The rough side of the leather faces out so the smooth side is in contact with the stirrup iron (it can take more friction than the rough side). With beveled edges, triple stitches, and stainless steel buckles for utmost strength. In black, regular length 52 inches, 1-1/8 inch width.
■ *Stirrup leathers #150* **$50**

Navajo Pads
Hackamore
Snaffle
Leather Girth
Cord Girth

6 | 7

TOOLS FOR THE STABLE

For telephone orders call 415-332-6001

Lead Ropes
The strongest, most durable, easiest to handle, and incidentally the most visually interesting rope in the world is made for mountain climbing. Our 11-mm rope from Chouinard is tested at 8,000 lbs. It should do for holding your horse. We offer several lengths of lead rope, each with appropriate solid brass and bronze hardware. Color combinations in each rope vary. Tell us your favorite colors and we'll match one to suit.
■ *Lead Rope #970* **$20**

Lead with Quick Release
For maximum dependability in an emergency situation, or for everyday use at a hitch rail and for grooming, we recommend our 10 foot length with solid brass panic-release snap.
■ *Lead Rope #970* **$23**

Neoprene Splint Boots
Non-slip leg protectors are easy to rinse clean. In red, blue and black with velcro.
■ *Front boots #981* **$30**
■ *Rear boots #982* **$33**

Combination Lead & Rein
The 8 foot length has a swivel-eye bolt snap at each end—appropriate for trail riding, competition, or casual grooming. Makes tying up easy out on the trail.
■ *Combination #971* **$17**

Tie Down
Trailer tie-down is 2 ft. in length with brass panic release snap on one end and swivel-eye bolt on the other.
■ *Tie Down #972* **$15**

Super Stable Fork
Designed for wood chip bedding, this fork has 16-tines spaced less than an inch apart—manure is easy to pick up and it won't fall through the tines. Made of black space age plastic with anodized metal handle, it's extremely lightweight, rustproof, virtually unbreakable.
■ *Super Fork #960* **$35**

Stable Tote
We designed this tote to carry a flake of hay, but it's so versatile you may find yourself carrying everything from laundry to firewood in it. You can snap the sides up to keep hay from falling out, but the tote also opens out completely flat (you can feed the horse with it lying on the ground and easily pick up scraps). Cotton canvas duck in red, black, or blue with suede trim.
■ *Stable Tote #945* **$32**

Over-the-Shoulder Grooming Tote
Have you ever needed to lead your horse and carry your grooming supplies, saddle, and bridle, at the same time? This canvas grooming tote fits comfortably over your shoulder and neatly holds brushes, clippers, and ointments. Inside pockets with full velcro closures for keys and money or sharp items like scissors. In sturdy cotton canvas, red, black or blue with suede trim.
■ *Grooming Tote #950* **$45**

The Endless Scarf
For an elegant look, cozy warmth, and a lightweight feel on the neck, nothing matches this tube scarf. You can also pull it up over your head balaclava-style, and it's great for keeping wind or rain from getting down the neck of your foul-weather gear.

The Polar Plus Fleece material will not pill up or lose shape. It's the perfect item to pack on a trail ride for those brisk rides back to the barn in the evening. One size fits all for both men and women in red, navy, grey, black or white.
■ *Scarf #530* **$13**

For helmet size, measure circumference at widest part of head.

Western Hat-Helmet
Ever wonder why Western riders aren't wearing hard hats? Turns out some of them are. This traditional-looking cowboy hat has a strong fiberglass shell and an adjustable chin strap. It's approved by the US Pony Club and is excellent for kids and adults alike. In brown felt, sizes XS, S, M, and L.
■ *Western Helmet #715* **$50**

Leather Halter
Made by hand of 1-inch-wide extra strong black German leather with solid brass hardware. Double cheekpieces are triple stitched, with adjustable chin strap. Snap at throat latch makes grooming easier.
■ *Leather Halter #240* **$65**

Jockey Helmet
This is the British racing helmet—far superior to any US Caliente-style helmet. Heavy duty construction with adjustable straps. Product-tester, Jan Borromeo, was competing in Nevada when another rider careened into her. Jan's horse went down so hard its breath was knocked out, while Jan's head smacked a boulder. Her report: 'I hit right on my temple. If it weren't for that helmet I'd be drooling into my shoes. The helmet wasn't even cracked.' In standard helmet sizes.
■ *Jockey Helmet #725* **$75**

Jockey Helmet Cover
Racey, brightly colored helmet covers of satin acetate that used to be seen strictly on jockeys are now brightening up event and trail riding. Tie string allows a sure fit on most helmets. Comes in a variety of solid colors and two-color triangle patterns. Tell us your favorite colors and your helmet brand and size.
■ *Helmet Cover #700* **$19**

The Riding Bra
Attractive enough to be worn with or without a shirt, this soft lycra bra provides excellent support without binding or irritating. The wide back and sides hold breasts close to body. Give us your rib cage measurement (measure just below breasts and send cup size). Terrific colors: black, red, blue, turquoise, hot pink, white or silver.
■ *Riding Bra #540* **$24**

Endless Scarf
Riding Bra
Helmet Covers
Super Fork
Stable Tote
Lead Rope
Combination Lead
Grooming Tote
Neoprene Boots
Leather Halter

8 | 9

There are some beautiful photos of horses and horse scenes in this catalog. Unfortunately, the product graphics do not keep pace, for a number of reasons. The layouts are not mailorder catalog layouts. The merchandise is scrinched into corners in some cases and stuffed down at the bottom of pages in others.

Traditional styles last because they work

The Trail Bomber
We've given the WWII leather flight jacket a new look and refined it a bit for the equestrian. Made of supple yet durable cowhide, the Trail Bomber isn't one of those leather items so overloaded with superfluous zippers and straps or so heavy you regret lugging it around. Whether you're bombing along on the trail, out for a breezy afternoon hack, or still working at the stable when the sunset chill sets in, this solid jacket in bittersweet chocolate color is comfy armour.

Most important to the rider, the jacket is cut with (ventilated) gussets under the arm and stylish by-swing pleats in the back so there is no impairment to arm movement. Its knitted cuffs and waistband keep the wind out, and so does the solid brass zipper. The modest natural mouton collar looks good down and feels good up. The roomy front pockets with snap flaps have hand warmer pockets behind them, and there's another pocket inside the jacket in the light brown cotton lining.

The sign of a great leather jacket: The longer you use it, the better it feels and the better it looks.
Women's sizes: S (6-8) M (10-12) L (14-16)
■ *Womens' Bomber #630* **$280**
Men's sizes: S (38) M (40) L (42-44) XL (46)
■ *Mens' Bomber #635* **$290**

The Irresistable Bat
A tiny hand with a big swat. This 19-inch wrapped stick bat with a flexible rubber grip is unique in the equestrian world. Even novice riders and phlegmatic horses know exactly what it means: "Git!"
■ *Bat #940* **$18**

Bomber Jacket

Bat

Equestrian Theme Shirt
Ruff-Hewn is justifiably famous for the quality of its good-looking, hard-working clothes. The company claims that Teddy Roosevelt's Rough Riders charged up San Juan Hill in Ruff-Hewn cavalry uniforms. This 100% cotton riding shirt with traditional hunt motif in a quiet kaleidoscope of colors goes nicely with our jodhpurs and breeches.

This shirt looks well hacking, hunting, or relaxing after hours. Background colors: golden yellow for women, taupe for men.
Women's Sizes (S, M, L)
■ *Golden shirt #510* **$55**
Men's Sizes (S, M, L, XL)
■ *Taupe Shirt #515* **$55**

FOR STYLISH COMFORT
ASTRIDE OR AFOOT

Classic Corduroy Breeches and Jodhpurs
Cut in the flattering turn-of-the-century flared military style, our breeches and jodhpurs are manufactured near Dusseldorf, Germany, by Kentucky with the finest precision textile technology and materials. Both jodhpurs and breeches are made of wide wale cotton corduroy with enough lycra to stretch easily for added comfort and movement.

They are machine washable, cool dry, and get softer and cozier with wear. Both styles are available in jet black or olive green with fine matching leather patches.

The Breeches have the traditional hip-flare from hip to knee for complete freedom of movement, with creamy leather patches that grip snugly at the knee. Cotton-lined side pockets, no back pocket. Tapered velcro closures at mid-calf ensure smooth fitting into any boot.
Sizes: In even waist measurements only. For men sizes 32 to 38. Women's sizes 26 to 32. Specify color, olive green or black.
■ *Kentucky Breeches #420* **$145**

The Jodhpurs are pegged above the knee for comfortable movement, then reinforced with leather panels along the full inside length of the leg and around the cuff. An elastic stirrup keeps the pant leg from riding up when you're wearing paddock boots. The jodhpurs come with cotton-lined side pockets and a zippered rear wallet pocket. Sizes: In even waist measurements only. For men sizes 32 to 38. Women's sizes 26 to 32. Specify color, olive green or black.
■ *Kentucky Jodhpurs #422* **$175**

Breeches

Jodhpurs

There are some older, bigger catalogs aimed at Phelan's market. Miller, for instance, has been around for years, and is considered by some to be the bible of the industry. This is not to say that there isn't room for another horseman's merchandiser. It only means that any newcomer to the stable has to project a different and/or more attractive persona. There's more than enough love of the sport in this catalog to fill that bill. All that's needed now is someone who loves direct marketing.

PINNACLE ORCHARDS

The American Catalog Awards (ACA) judges gave Pinnacle Orchards' Holiday Gifts '87 Catalog their Gold Award in the Food category. It was an interesting choice at a time when there are a number of far more extravagant, slickly produced catalogs in the industry. Clearly, the choice was made because this catalog is a "back to basics" book.

Nut farms, orchards, and meat growers in the direct marketing business have discovered that their customers like all foods, or like to give a selection of food gifts—not just nuts, apples or ham. Pinnacle Orchards has made use of this knowledge in merchandising their catalog. In their 51 years of existence, they've migrated from the original horse-drawn shipments of Comice "Christmas Pears" to a broad selection of farm related gifts. Christmas decorations, cakes, candies, smoked meats and fish, cheeses, dried fruits and live flowers fill out the basic Pinnacle product line, which consists primarily of Oregon orchard-grown fruit.

Holiday gifts '87

PINNACLE ORCHARDS

Simple, grid-pattern layouts with large, easily-read type make it a pleasure to shop from this catalog. The copy is both close to and keyed to the photographs. Frequent and prominent display of the Pinnacle Orchards Guarantee reinforces the company's longevity and unconditional return policy. The latter is essential to mailorder in general, but has a very special implication when selling perishables.

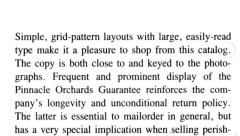

PINNACLE ORCHARDS—Holiday Gifts '87
Ted Fraedrick and Steven Spatz, *Catalog Directors*
Mary Dugan, *Designer/Copywriter*
Jack Allen, *Photographer/Illustrator*
Craftsman Press [Seattle, WA], *Printer, on 60#*
  Allegheny for cover and text
Trade Litho [Portland, OR], *Color Separator*

Your favorite fruit chest full of good things to eat for clients and friends. You've told us this is one of our very nicest gifts, sure to please the most discriminating friend. Or business associate. Guaranteed to make a positive statement about your quality and care. Contains a rich assortment of plump Comice Pears, Delicious Apples, roasted Almonds, Datenut Cupcakes, Coffee Chews, Hard Candies and decadently delicious Chocolate Truffles. Net wt. approx. 10½ lbs.
Order Gift 27   **$29.95**
Available November 1 through January 15.

OUR GUARANTEE
If you or your friends are not absolutely delighted with every gift you receive, we will replace the gift or refund your purchase price, providing the address supplied was correct. Since 1937, we've fully and unconditionally guaranteed your complete satisfaction with every gift we send.

"I received a fruit shipment of Apples and Pears for my 82nd Birthday on December 25. Pears are my favorite fruit. And to be honest, those Pears were the best I've eaten in my 82 years."
—Gus Permann
Glen Allin, North Dakota

Snack Pack Three-in-One Quantity Savings. Because we wrap and pack our gift boxes so carefully, speed them on their way by refrigerated truck, then UPS them to your door, we can offer you a quantity discount on three gifts to a single address. Order one of these and get Snack Pack Gifts 21, 22 and 23, deliver them yourself and save $8.00. Net wt. approx. 10½ lbs.
Order Gift 3243   **$45.95**
Available November 1 through January 15.

Send a Pear 'n' Cheese Snack Pack with Chocolate Truffles. Just right for a midnight snack. Or for that special someone you'd like to remember. Four elegant Comice Pears surround a hearty wheel of Cheddar, 8 oz. of Sharp and 8 oz. of Mild. A handy Pear Slicer comes with this delightful gift. And six elegant individually wrapped Truffles of dark, rich Chocolate. Heavenly! Net wt. approx. 3½ lbs.
Order Gift 21   **$18.95**

Quantity Savings. Save $7.35 with 3 boxes to the same address.
Order Gift 3021   **$49.50**

Or try a juicy Pears 'n' Apple, Cheese 'n' Sausage Snack Pack with Truffles. Delightful to give. Delightful to receive. All the good things you could ask for in one handy Snack Pack box. A wonderful variety of good eating in a single economical gift. Sure to make you someone's favorite gift giver this year. Net wt. approx. 3½ lbs.
Order Gift 22   **$18.50**
Available November 1 through January 15.

Quantity Savings. Save $7.55 with 3 boxes to the same address.
Order Gift 3022   **$47.95**

Comice, Almond 'n' Cheddar Snack Pack. Here's a super gift for college students burning the midnight oil. Sweet, juicy Comice Pears, accented by crunchy Almonds and a bar of delicious Cheddar. Great snacking and superb gifting. Or a special remembrance to tell someone you care. Net wt. approx. 3½ lbs.
Order Gift 23   **$16.50**
Available November 1 through January 15.

Quantity Savings. Save $7.55 with 3 boxes to the same address.
Order Gift 3023   **$41.95**

Comice in a Basket. Our very favorite basket...found after a long and diligent search...and piled high with a heavy load of our very finest Comice Pears. Altogether over eleven pounds of life's juicy luxuries. The basket is guaranteed to be useful afterwards in a dozen different ways from sewing basket to planter. Net wt. approx. 11 lbs.
Order Gift 30   **$28.50**
Available November 1 through January 15.

Planter Basket Combo. Now here's your chance to try it all. Sweet Comice and tender buttery Bosc Pears and crisp Red and Golden Delicious Apples. One of the most impressive gifts of all! Net wt. approx. 11 lbs.
Order Gift 33   **$27.95**
Available November 1 through January 15.

A Basket of Comice and Red Delicious Apples. A tisket, a tasket, what a fantastic basket! Dark and handmade, filled to the brim with beautiful Red Delicious Apples and blushing Comice Pears. Lovely holiday eating for everyone. Net wt. approx. 11 lbs.
Order Gift 32   **$27.95**
Available November 1 through January 15.

Comice and Bosc in a handy Basket. Here's something you'll like! Our distinctive Comice and buttery Bosc Pears...half 'n' half. The unique flavor of Bosc gives special character to recipes like the one below. And halves brightened with lemon, sugar, nutmeg and a sprinkling of orange juice bake tender in minutes. Net wt. approx. 11 lbs.
Order Gift 31   **$27.95**
Available November 1 through January 15.

Pear Praline Pie
5 fresh Bosc Pears   ½ t. gr. ginger
⅓ c. sugar   dash salt
¼ c. flour   1 unbaked pie shell
½ t. grated   Pecan Praline
lemon peel   topping
Peel and slice pears. Toss gently with sugar, flour, lemon peel, ginger and salt. Sprinkle ¼ of pecan topping in pastry-lined pie plate. Add pear mixture. Sprinkle top with remaining topping. Bake 400° 40 mins. Serve warm or cold. Top with ice cream or whipped cream, if desired. **Pecan Praline Topping:** Combine ½ cup brown sugar, ½ cup chopped pecans, ⅓ cup flour. Cut in ¼ cup butter.

Beautiful buttery Bosc Pears. Here's a sumptuous western pear you may not have met. While it provides delicious out-of-hand eating, it is especially noted for its excellent flavor when cooked. A baked Bosc Pear heightened with cinnamon provides a very special treat. Twelve lovely russet-colored Pears. Net wt. approx. 6½ lbs.
Order Gift 8   **$16.75**
Available November through January.

"I received a box of your delicious pears as a gift. They're the best in the world."
—*Robert Starnes*
Monroe, North Carolina

A combination of golden brown Bosc and blushing green Comice. Now you can try some of each. Six spectacular Comice and nine fresh winter Bosc. A low calorie treat you're sure to love. Because sweet, juicy Comice and tender buttery Bosc have less than 100 calories per pear. Plus a whole host of nutrients and fiber your body needs. Not only are they good for you, they're the sweetest thing going. And a favorite for holiday giving. Net wt. approx. 11½ lbs.
Order Gift 9   **$19.50**
Available November 1 through January 15.

Complimentary letters from satisfied customers alternate with recipes such as this one for Praline Pie, a sandwich of sugared and seasoned pears between layers of Pecan Praline topping, served with either whipped or ice cream. Not on my diet, but I wish they had shown a photograph of the finished product for us to salivate over.

Pinnacle gets down to some serious business gift-giving with their Select-A-Club Plan. Recipients are mailed a Personal Membership Certificate extolling the goodies they will soon receive. The famous Harry and David's "Fruit-of-the-Month Club" pioneered this very successful business gift plan many years ago. Those on the receiving end of this gift format are almost universally grateful for the opportunity to enjoy healthful, fine tasting natural foods of a quality rarely found in local supermarkets.

While business gifts account for a large percentage of these Club package sales, in-laws, grandparents and favorite aunts and uncles are often on either the receiving and giving end of these plans. What could be more appropriate as a gift to those dearly loved, but seldom seen, relatives and friends?

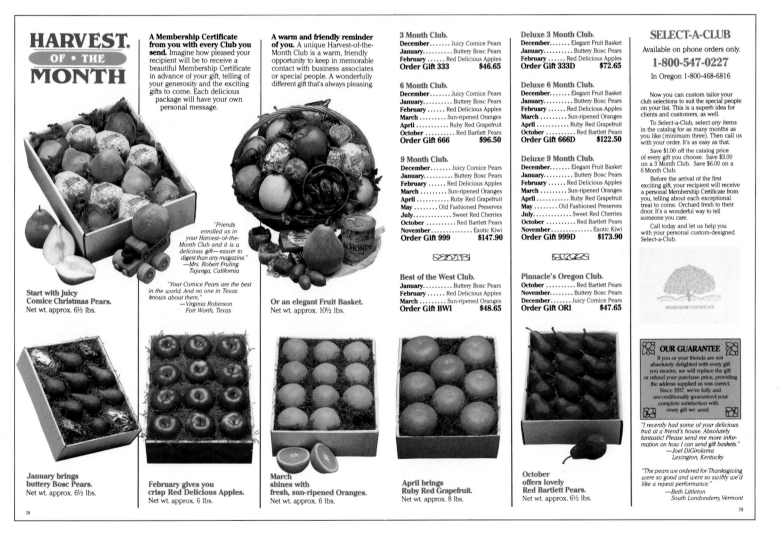

HARVEST OF THE MONTH

A Membership Certificate from you with every Club you send. Imagine how pleased your recipient will be to receive a beautiful Membership Certificate in advance of your gift, telling of your generosity and the exciting gifts to come. Each delicious package will have your own personal message.

"Friends enrolled us in your Harvest-of-the-Month Club and it is a delicious gift— easier to digest than any magazine."
—Mrs. Robert Fruling
Tujunga, California

"Your Comice Pears are the best in the world. And no one in Texas knows about them."
—Virginia Robinson
Fort Worth, Texas

A warm and friendly reminder of you. A unique Harvest-of-the-Month Club is a warm, friendly opportunity to keep in memorable contact with business associates or special people. A wonderfully different gift that's always pleasing.

Start with juicy Comice Christmas Pears. Net wt. approx. 6½ lbs.

Or an elegant Fruit Basket. Net wt. approx. 10½ lbs.

January brings buttery Bosc Pears. Net wt. approx. 6½ lbs.

February gives you crisp Red Delicious Apples. Net wt. approx. 6 lbs.

March shines with fresh, sun-ripened Oranges. Net wt. approx. 6 lbs.

April brings Ruby Red Grapefruit. Net wt. approx. 8 lbs.

October offers lovely Red Bartlett Pears. Net wt. approx. 6½ lbs.

3 Month Club.
December....... Juicy Comice Pears
January......... Buttery Bosc Pears
February ...... Red Delicious Apples
Order Gift 333 $46.65

6 Month Club.
December....... Juicy Comice Pears
January......... Buttery Bosc Pears
February ...... Red Delicious Apples
March .... Sun-ripened Oranges
April .... Ruby Red Grapefruit
October .... Red Bartlett Pears
Order Gift 666 $96.50

9 Month Club.
December....... Juicy Comice Pears
January......... Buttery Bosc Pears
February ...... Red Delicious Apples
March .... Sun-ripened Oranges
April .... Ruby Red Grapefruit
May .... Old Fashioned Preserves
July............. Sweet Red Cherries
October .... Red Bartlett Pears
November............. Exotic Kiwi
Order Gift 999 $147.90

Best of the West Club.
January......... Buttery Bosc Pears
February ...... Red Delicious Apples
March .... Sun-ripened Oranges
Order Gift BW1 $48.65

Deluxe 3 Month Club.
December....... Elegant Fruit Basket
January......... Buttery Bosc Pears
February ...... Red Delicious Apples
Order Gift 333D $72.65

Deluxe 6 Month Club.
December....... Elegant Fruit Basket
January......... Buttery Bosc Pears
February ...... Red Delicious Apples
March .... Sun-ripened Oranges
April .... Ruby Red Grapefruit
October .... Red Bartlett Pears
Order Gift 666D $122.50

Deluxe 9 Month Club.
December....... Elegant Fruit Basket
January......... Buttery Bosc Pears
February ...... Red Delicious Apples
March .... Sun-ripened Oranges
April .... Ruby Red Grapefruit
May .... Old Fashioned Preserves
July............. Sweet Red Cherries
October .... Red Bartlett Pears
November............. Exotic Kiwi
Order Gift 999D $173.90

Pinnacle's Oregon Club.
October .... Red Bartlett Pears
November....... Buttery Bosc Pears
December....... Juicy Comice Pears
Order Gift OR1 $47.65

SELECT-A-CLUB
Available on phone orders only.
1-800-547-0227
In Oregon 1-800-468-6816

Now you can custom tailor your club selections to suit the special people on your list. This is a superb idea for clients and customers, as well.

To Select-a-Club, select *any* items in the catalog for as many months as you like (minimum three). Then call us with your order. It's as easy as that.

Save $1.00 off the catalog price of every gift you choose. Save $3.00 on a 3 Month Club. Save $6.00 on a 6 Month Club.

Before the arrival of the first exciting gift, your recipient will receive a personal Membership Certificate from you, telling about each exceptional treat to come. Orchard fresh to their door. It's a wonderful way to tell someone you care.

Call today and let us help you with your personal custom-designed Select-a-Club.

MEMBERSHIP CERTIFICATE

OUR GUARANTEE
If you or your friends are not absolutely delighted with every gift you receive, we will replace the gift or refund your purchase price, providing the address supplied us was correct. Since 1937, we've fully and unconditionally guaranteed your complete satisfaction with every gift we send.

"I recently had some of your delicious fruit at a friend's house. Absolutely fantastic! Please send me more information on how I can send gift baskets."
—Joel DiGirolama
Lexington, Kentucky

"The pears we ordered for Thanksgiving were so good and went so swiftly we'd like a repeat performance."
—Beth Littleton
South Londonderry, Vermont

18   19

Here is another example of how the same simple grid pattern allows the reader to easily find the excellent photos and informative copy for each item. Telephone ordering information is loud and clear, as is the Rush Delivery Service information seen on other spreads. A few of the pages show signs of oversaturated color—not a good idea when reproducing either food or cosmetic photographs. The whiteness of the free-sheet paper stock and the excellent inks employed could have done with a little less ink-on-paper to present an accurate picture of these delicious-looking gourmet delights.

The finest Smoked Salmon Fillet from the Pacific Northwest. Centuries ago, the Indians of the Pacific Northwest discovered a unique method of preserving their salmon by smoking it slowly over native alderwood fires. You wouldn't believe how good it tastes. Fully cooked to be moist, tender and flaky, its mouth-watering flavor is smooth and mellow. Although no preservatives are added, refrigeration isn't needed until after opening...and then it will last six weeks in your refrigerator. Fully cooked. Ready to enjoy. Net wt. 1 lb. 2 oz.
Order Gift 95   **$37.95**
Available Year 'round.

OUR GUARANTEE
If you or your friends are not absolutely delighted with every gift you receive, we will replace the gift or refund your purchase price, providing the address supplied us was correct. Since 1937, we've fully and unconditionally guaranteed your complete satisfaction with every gift we send.

"Thanks to you, I am through with this year's Christmas presents. What a painless and pleasant way to shop."
—Marian Kobayaski

Smaller Fillet. Net wt. 6 oz.
Order Gift 896   **$16.95**
Available Year 'round.

ORDER TOLL FREE
with Visa, MasterCard or American Express

1-800-547-0227

24 hours a day 7 days a week

In Oregon 1-800-468-6816
8:00 to 5:00 weekdays

Try our Two Box Smoked Salmon/Smoked Oyster Combo. This is the first time we've offered this unique gift for Christmas. But if you like the delicate flavor of smoked salmon and smoked oysters, you'll love the opportunity to give or receive this gourmet gift. No refrigeration is necessary until the air-tight pouch is opened, allowing you to experience the subtle smokehouse taste of this Northwest delicacy. Net wt. 11 oz.
Order Gift 891   **$26.50**
Available Year 'round.

Pacific Seafood Chest. Because you fell in love with our fine smoked salmon, we've put together this wooden chest chock full of the abundance of the Pacific Ocean, much of it smoked. 7¾ oz. Red Sockeye Salmon, 7 oz. Hard Smoked Salmon, 7½ oz. Smoked Kippered Salmon, 5¾ oz. Smoked Sturgeon, 4½ oz. Tiny Pacific Shrimp, 3¼ oz. Smoked Salmon Pâté, 7 oz. English Biscuits and a 12 oz. bottle of Norman Bishop's Unique Dressing in a solid wooden box with cover. A definitely out-of-the-ordinary offering that's guaranteed to please the most discriminating.
Order Gift 96   **$53.95**
Available Year 'round.

Smoked Salmon and Cheese. A prize catch for your holiday table...or any table throughout the year. Prized smoked salmon prepared over a slow alderwood fire. Still one of the finest ways of preparing fish, smoked salmon is one of the greatest delicacies you'll ever taste. Handwoven willow basket contains 7½ oz. of Kippered Smoked Salmon, 7¾ oz. of Red Sockeye Salmon, 3½ oz. Smoked Salmon Pâté, 3¼ oz. Hard Smoked Salmon, 8 oz. of Sharp Cheddar Cheese, 8 oz. of Monterey Jack and a 7 oz. package of imported English Biscuits. Superb! Net wt. 38 oz.
Order Gift 90   **$36.95**
Available Year 'round.

23

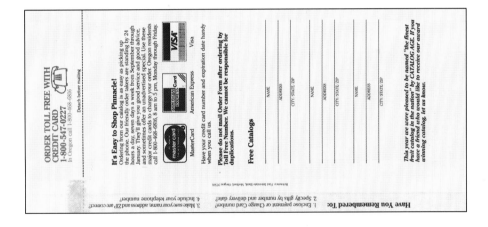

A key element in any back-to-basics catalog is the order form. Pinnacle has raised theirs to new heights of clarity and ease of use. *All* the ordering information, both mail and phone, is on the front cover of the form. The inside form allows for twelve separate orders, with ample space, both horizontally and vertically, for normal human handwriting or even 10 pitch typing—unlike the squeezed-down-squinched-up penmanship ordained by many, less generous order forms.

The back of the order form offers moderately priced tidbits from the Pinnacle Pantry (perhaps for the "one for you and two for me" gift giver?!). Years of tracking by hundreds of mailorder houses have proven the order form to be one of the best selling positions in the book. Here again, Pinnacle has shown that they are true professionals by doing a solid job of merchandising the order form.

Another word of thanks to the folks at Pinnacle for their large size BRE (Business Reply Envelope). Most of us hate to fold our personal or business checks. Banks are unhappy because these checks are hard to scan, and many individuals just plain resent having to crease their personal checks in order to fit them into mickey-mouse envelopes.

This large envelope format has three additional advantages:

- *It allows Pinnacle to promote the Toll-Free telephone number one last time.*

- *There is ample space to display good sized replicas of the three major credit cards they accept.*

- *Room is available to make reference to their Corporate Sales Department and business gift program discounts.*

Finally, on the envelope flap, a unique touch. A simple statement inspired, no doubt, by corporate procedures in some client companies, but of great reassurance value to all Pinnacle customers. It reads: "Reference: First Interstate Bank, Medford, Oregon 97501". Between the hardwood trees and the rock-bound banks, you get the feeling that these folks are going to be around for awhile.

RELIABLE MOTORING ACCESSORIES

Western Europeans and Americans share at least one great love, the ultimate gadget—the automobile. The Reliable Motoring Accessories catalog celebrates this preoccupation with a blatantly upscale catalog of aftermarket whistles and bells for high-end cars.

Beretta, Ferrari, Porsche, BMW and Jaguar are just a few of the famous names dropped redundantly in the Reliable Motoring copy. The products hitched to these names encompass almost every accessory made for these extravagant vehicles, except those that require a great deal of technical support.

The list of Reliable Motoring's accessory items would boggle the mind of a civilian, who simply uses his car for transportation. Alarm systems and even fuel line locks to foil the bad guys. Bras of all colors—including transparent versions — to prevent the pits. Lights, smoked lenses and light-up signs to advertise the make of your car. Wood kits to trim a Mercedes interior, steel kits for fenders and retrofit kits to make your car look like the model you couldn't afford.

Sixty pages of beautifully presented, expensive, high quality items that will keep any status-car-buff in dreamland for hours. As the editors of "Catalog Age" commented: ". . . the copy reflects Reliable Motoring's automotive expertise and its ability to address both the needs and the fantasies of its market." Under closer scrutiny, it becomes clear that the operative word here is "fantasies". Hundreds of SKUs are available for more mundane vehicles. (How else to keep the response rates up?)

THE FINEST AUTOMOTIVE ACCESSORIES CATALOG. WITH 49 YEARS OF RELIABLE SERVICE

FOR MERCEDES, PORSCHE, CORVETTE, JAGUAR... AND MORE! ULTIMATE COVER UPS— CAR COVERS IN COLORS GIFTS FOR THE AUTO ENTHUSIAST

RELIABLE MOTORING ACCESSORIES— Style '88
Jack Rosen and Valerie Stokes, *Catalog Directors*
Tom Marx [Marx Advertising], *Consultant*
Marcia Mack, *Designer*
Jack Rosen, *Merchandiser*
Valerie Stokes, *Copywriter*
Miad Photography, *Photographer*
Robert Moroz, *Production Manager*
Anderson Lithograph [Los Angeles, CA], *Printer, on 100# Sonoma Gloss for cover and 70# Capistrano Web Gloss Book for text*
Orbis Graphic Art [Anaheim, CA], *Color Separator*

From the barcoded, magazine-like front cover to the inkjet printed, editorial/promotional back cover, Reliable Motoring's catalog tracks their readers' life-styles with a dream book of automotive accessories presented in a simple, yet *simpatico* format.

The flow of this catalog is different than most. Gadgets, models, desk accessories, toys and sweat-shirts (with car manufacturers names emblazoned thereupon), sun glasses and signs occupy the first 12 pages—before the scene has been set by the HiTech, high-priced merchandise. Interesting juxtaposition!

Prices in these peripheral categories are on a scale with the cars they relate to. A child's car seat lists at $129.95, and if you choose to add the Superwool™ cover, the price will be $279.90. Or perhaps the little guy needs a pillow in the shape of a Porsche for only $119 (plus $13.00 freight and handling). Sun-glasses, by the way, are offered at up to $279—by Ferdinand Porsche out of Carrera, of course.

The lingerie section of Reliable's catalog lists bras and covers for virtually every performance car on the road today. The typefaces are necessarily small, but one presumes the young eyes of the readers will be capable of finding their model's protective attire. If a right-off-the-shelf style is not available, custom bras can be created to fit any possible aberration or variation.

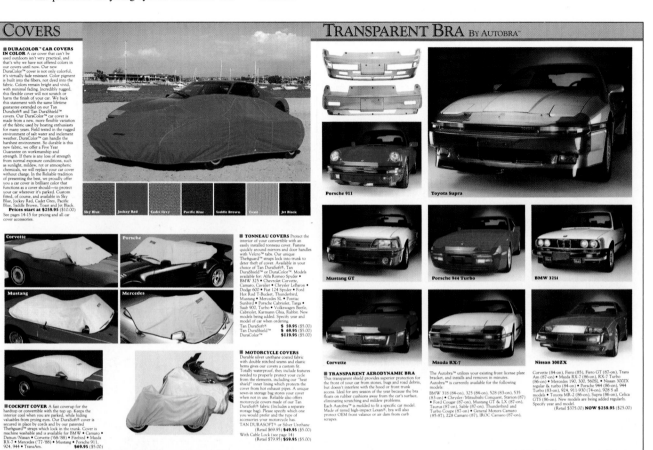

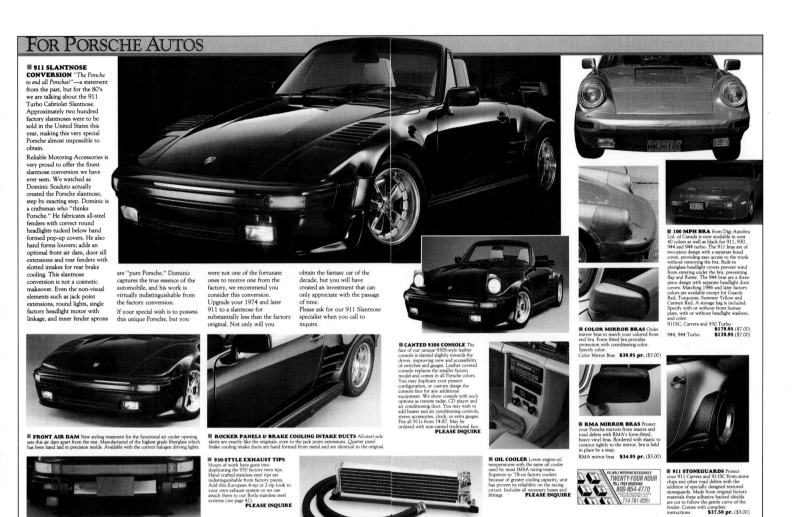

FOR PORSCHE AUTOS

■ 911 SLANTNOSE CONVERSION *"The Porsche to end all Porsches!"*—a statement from the past, but for the 80's we are talking about the 911 Turbo Cabriolet Slantnose. Approximately two hundred factory slantnoses were to be sold in the United States this year, making this very special Porsche almost impossible to obtain.

Reliable Motoring Accessories is very proud to offer the finest slantnose conversion we have ever seen. We watched as Dominic Scaduto actually created the Porsche slantnose, step by exacting step. Dominic is a craftsman who "thinks Porsche." He fabricates all-steel fenders with correct round headlights tucked below hand formed pop-up covers. He also hand forms louvers; adds an optional front air dam, door sill extensions and rear fenders with slotted intakes for rear brake cooling. This slantnose conversion is not a cosmetic makeover. Even the non-visual elements such as jack point extensions, round lights, single factory headlight motor with linkage, and inner fender aprons

are "pure Porsche." Dominic captures the true essence of the automobile, and his work is virtually indistinguishable from the factory conversion.

If your special wish is to possess this unique Porsche, but you were not one of the fortunate ones to receive one from the factory, we recommend you consider this conversion. Upgrade your 1974 and later 911 to a slantnose for substantially less than the factory original. Not only will you

obtain the fantasy car of the decade, but you will have created an investment that can only appreciate with the passage of time.

Please ask for our 911 Slantnose specialist when you call to inquire.

■ FRONT AIR DAM New styling treatment for the functional air cooler opening sets this air dam apart from the rest. Manufactured of the highest grade fiberglass which has been hand laid in precision molds. Available with the correct halogen driving lights.

■ 930-STYLE EXHAUST TIPS Hours of work have gone into duplicating the 930 factory twin tips. Hand crafted stainless steel tips are indistinguishable from factory pieces. Add this European 4-tip or 2-tip look to your own exhaust system or we can attach them to our Borla stainless steel systems (see page 42). **PLEASE INQUIRE**

■ ROCKER PANELS & BRAKE COOLING INTAKE DUCTS All-steel side skirts are exactly like the originals, even to the jack point extensions. Quarter panel brake cooling intake ducts are hand formed from metal and are identical to the original.

■ CANTED 930S CONSOLE The face of our unique 930S-style leather console is slanted slightly towards the driver, improving view and accessibility of switches and gauges. Leather covered console replaces the smaller factory model and comes in all Porsche colors. You may duplicate your present configuration, or custom design the console face for any additional equipment. We show console with such options as remote radar, CD player and air conditioning duct. You may wish to add heater and air conditioning controls, stereo accessories, clock, or extra gauges. Fits all 911s from 74-87. May be ordered with non-canted traditional face. **PLEASE INQUIRE**

■ OIL COOLER Lower engine-oil temperatures with the same oil cooler used by most IMSA racing teams. Superior to '78-on factory coolers because of greater cooling capacity, unit has proven its reliability on the racing circuit. Includes all necessary hoses and fittings. **PLEASE INQUIRE**

■ 100 MPH BRA from Digi Autobra Ltd. of Canada is now available in over 40 colors as well as black for 911, 930, 944 and 944 turbo. The 911 bras are of two-piece design with a separate hood cover, providing easy access to the trunk without removing the bra. Built-in plexiglass headlight covers prevent wind from entering under the bra, preventing flap and flutter. The 944 bras are a three-piece design with separate headlight door covers. Matching 1986 and later factory colors are available except for Guards Red, Turquoise, Summer Yellow and Carmen Red. A storage bag is included. Specify with or without front license plate, with or without headlight washers, and color.
911SC, Carrera and 930 Turbo **$179.95** ($7.00)
944, 944 Turbo **$129.95** ($7.00)

■ COLOR MIRROR BRAS Order mirror bras to match your colored front end bra. Form fitted bra provides protection with coordinating color. Specify color.
Color Mirror Bras **$39.95 pr.** ($3.00)

■ RMA MIRROR BRAS Protect your Porsche mirrors from insects and road debris with RMA's form-fitted, heavy vinyl bras. Bordered with elastic to contour tightly to the mirror, bra is held in place by a snap.
RMA mirror bras **$34.95 pr.** ($3.00)

■ 911 STONEGUARDS Protect your 911 Carrera and 911SC from stone chips and other road debris with the addition of specially designed textured stoneguards. Made from original factory materials these adhesive backed shields are cut to follow the gentle curve of the fender. Comes with complete instructions. **$37.50 pr.** ($3.00)

52

53

Reliable Motoring zeros in on a few of the top name automobile makers by combining a number of brand-specific items into specialized, manufacturer-related chapters. Here, in the opening spread of a six-page Porsche section, the famous Porsche 911 Cabriolet Slantnose custom modification is offered to the reader. The price? The familiar, but ominous, "Please Inquire".

This is a man's catalog. As befits the genre, the layouts are staccato in form and make use of sharp-cornered halftones and rigidly delineated copy blocks. The photography is crisp and feature driven without artistic compromise. There are no softening props or even illustrative backgrounds. In keeping with contemporary, masculine catalog art, most of the products appear against either dramatic backgrounds or white silhouettes.

RUE DE FRANCE

Russian Roulette with a six-shooter is a safe sport compared to starting a kitchen-table mailorder business. The odds are five to one in your favor with the former. The odds on the latter these days are about one hundred and twenty to one—the wrong way. However, every once in a while, we hear of someone who has beaten the odds (on kitchen-table mailorder, not Russian Roulette). Almost without exception, these extraordinary folks all have two things in common. They have intimate, in-depth product knowledge, and they have something to sell that is unique and/or not readily available.

This ACA Silver Award winner is a delightful case in point. Rue de France presents ''The Traditional Country Lace of France'' in a simple, straightforward 32-page catalog. No frills, no exaggerated claims, even the photography is austere. There's almost a sense of French frugality in the look of the book, if not in the prices.

These roomsets look as though Rue de France's President, Pamela Kelley, rented a starving artist's Paris atelier for location shots (perhaps, with the thought of convincing the IRS that this was a business trip). Not so! These photographs were all done in a studio. The sets and props were all very carefully conceived to dissemble.

RUE DE FRANCE—Spring 1987
Pamela F. Kelley, *President/Copywriter*
Kimberly Jacot, *Catalog Director and Production Manager*
Kathryn Wooley, *Art Director*
Brendan P. Kelley, *Consultant*
Al Fisher, *Photographer*
Judy Sclednick, *Stylist*
R.R. Donnelley [Old Saybrook, CT], *Printer, on 60# Sterling cover and text*
R.R. Donnelley [Lancaster, PA], *Color Separator*

A claw-foot tub, a be-spattered wall and a pedestal sink in one photo bring back memories of a misspent youth on the Left Bank. Other room settings used in staging the French lace evoke the bygone era of seldom-used front parlors.

POINT D'ESPRIT

Serene and simple, Point d'Esprit adds a soft texture statement without overpowering your room. For a richer look, use additional widths, shirred more lavishly on your windows. We recommend using one sheer panel (94" wide) for each 30" to 40" of window width. Available in natural. Machine wash.

Point d'Esprit By The Yard

CODE	WIDTH		PER YARD
720GYD	94"	. . . .	$35.00
COLOR: NATURAL			

Grand Galon Trim

CODE			
7YYD	1"	. . . .	$2.50
COLOR: NATURAL			

We've hung the Point d'Esprit over the blinds and it softens the look of the windows. Your quality is excellent and we have a unique and wonderful look in our rooms.

MAUREEN ROMANI, SAN JOSE, CALIFORNIA

▲ **Point d'Esprit Sheer Panels**

CODE	LENGTH		94" WIDE
720GSP	63"	. . . . (EA)	$ 83.75
720GSP	72"	. . . . (EA)	96.50
720GSP	84"	. . . . (EA)	109.75
720GSP	90"	. . . . (EA)	117.75
720GSP	Ties	. . . . (PR)	6.00

◀ **Point d'Esprit Tiebacks**

CODE	LENGTH		94" WIDE PAIR
720GTB	63"	. . . . (PR)	$ 94.50
720GTB	72"	. . . . (PR)	108.00
720GTB	84"	. . . . (PR)	121.50
720GTB	90"	. . . . (PR)	130.50
COLOR: NATURAL			

SNOW PETALS

Snow petals is an heirloom pattern, passed down through the generations of lacemakers, to softly drape your windows in the French country look. We have used a pair of 63" tiebacks to create the pedestal sink cover. Available in natural. Machine wash, iron lightly.

Snow Petals By The Yard

CODE	WIDTH		PER YARD
721CYD	23"	. . . .	$23.50
721CYD	35"	. . . .	33.00
COLOR: NATURAL APPROX. 11" REPEAT			

Petit Galon Trim

CODE			
7XYD	½"	. . . .	$2.25
COLOR: NATURAL			

I can hardly wait to place my next order. Your curtains have added so much to my home!

INGRID CORY, HACKETTSTOWN, NEW JERSEY

▲ **Snow Petals Flat Panels**

CODE	LENGTH		23" WIDE	35" WIDE
721CFP	36" or 40"	. . . . (EA)	$39.00	$61.00
721CFP	45" or 54"	. . . . (EA)	44.50	69.00
721CFP	63" or 72"	. . . . (EA)	55.50	83.00
721CFP	84" or 90"	. . . . (EA)	63.00	95.50

► **Snow Petals Tiebacks**

CODE	LENGTH		35" WIDE PAIR
721CTB	63"	. . . . (PR)	$166.00
721CTB	72"	. . . . (PR)	181.50
721CTB	84"	. . . . (PR)	193.00
721CTB	90"	. . . . (PR)	205.00
COLOR: NATURAL			

A lighter heart and a more cheerful hand styled another group of photographs in the same catalog. Visions of sun dappled rooms, tea on the table, and a beautiful young mother just out of sight come to mind. *Surely, the sounds of horse and carriage will soon announce Mama's arrival for l'heure du the.*

The proof of that pudding's conscious purpose is to be found in Ms. Kelley's letter to her customers on the inside Front Cover of her catalog:

Bonjour! . . . Lace from France summons up a quieter past . . . an antique joy reserved for the few who care. To sit in a quiet room on a spring day and see delicate lace curtains sway to and fro in a gentle breeze, I find to be one of life's delights!

The product this catalog sells is "Traditional Country Lace of France". In many OTC retail stores, this merchandise would be found in the store's basement, buried somewhere in the C&D (curtains and draperies) department. Since they can be displayed on less costly wall space, lace curtains can usually be located. But, considerations of turns per year and sales per square foot preclude extensive inventory or shelf space—particularly in the case of high ticket imports.

Pamela Kelley and her husband Brendan spotted this marketing niche, and decided to do something about it. At the time, they were living in the Marais quarter of Paris, where many of the district's antique windows framed graceful curtains made of the beautiful country lace. It was upon that historic inspiration that the house of Rue de France was built.

Starting with only 3,000 catalogs mailed in all of 1982, the Kelleys have built their catalog program to mailings totaling 850,000 catalogs per year. The original catalogs were done in black and white, and featured actual swatches of the laces. The new Rue de France catalogs are 24–to 32-page, four-color, professionally produced books that obviously have found a broad acceptance by mail order buyers. Swatches are still available in two separate sample books. One book features laces and the other, the French Provencal fabrics offered in the current Rue de France catalog. Each swatch book costs $3.00, and on average, 200 customer requests are received every month.

Drawing from our own experience with clients in the same product category (high-end domestics), we know there is a limitation on the size of this market—particularly with respect to the mailorder segment. To many women, linens, sheets and towels and yes, curtains and draperies, are touchie-feelie items. Unless they know the brand and the style from firsthand experience in a store or a friend's home, they are reluctant to buy from a mailorder house.

Frequency of purchase is another limitation on the upside potential for this product area. Ask yourself: "How many times in the past decade have I bought more than one or two curtains or bed sheets or blankets, and how much did I spend?" If you've recently started a new household, the answer is: "Last month or last year, and a lot." But, the majority of those who are in what is euphemistically described as "the middle years" rarely spend large sums for linens. Perhaps on average, Ms. Middle America Age 45 will purchase $600-$800 worth of curtains every five years. Less than $200 per year! Hardly enough to support a mail order business when NCA (new customer acquisition) can cost up to $50 per customer.

What's more, a mailorder business, in order to be successful, must maintain at least a small, full-time, year-round cadre of highly trained employees. Redecorating (and especially, C&D) is a seasonal market. And surely, one store or catalog cannot change the buying habits of a nation, nor can it make citizens shop 12 months every year for something they normally buy twice a year. Horchow, Hanover, Hammacher and a host of other catalog houses have worked out the answer to these seasonal peaks and valleys. It lies in product diversification. This can be implemented as either: 1) a broader range of products merchandised in the same catalog, or 2) a totally separate catalog program mailed to the same customers and/or to a new group of prospects.

The reward for running a good mailorder business is customer loyalty. If your catalog can be trusted, your customer can be trusted to come back to you—*if* you have something to sell that she wants or needs, now. In Rue de France, Ms. Kelley has a marvelous platform for growth. She has convincingly demonstrated that she is expert in "The Traditional Country Lace of France" (which is also the subtitle of the catalog).

In her most recent catalogs, Paula Kelley makes it quite clear that her experience is firsthand. "My husband and I began Rue de France when we were living in Paris several years ago," states her opening letter. It concludes, "We continue to provide you with French products that must meet Rue de France's exacting standards for '*qualite*'. Of course, all our products come with the Rue de France unconditional guarantee!" With those two statements, Ms. Kelley has positioned Rue de France as an experienced resource with local knowledge of French merchandise suppliers; *and* with the clout to insist upon timely and first rate quality performance from a sometimes erratic *fabricant*.

The Rue de France team has done a marvelous job of transiting from the kitchen table to the big time. With perhaps just a few new marketing directions, their core business has the potential to grow at least fourfold without testing the upper limits of their mailorder franchise.

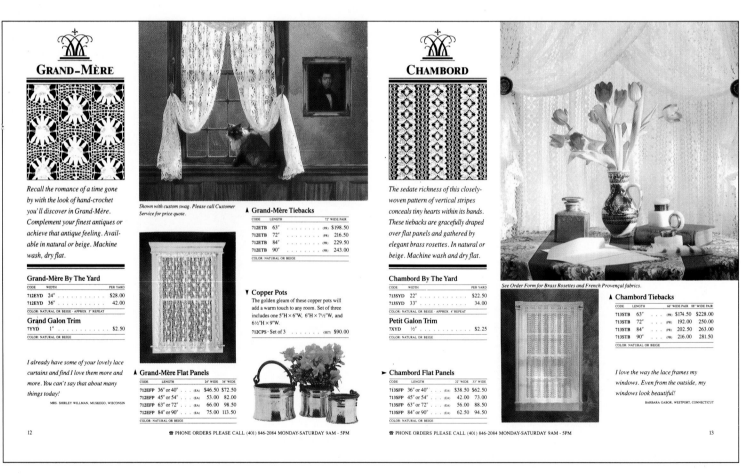

Details of the major lace patterns are highlighted with black and white, high contrast renditions that amplify the overall design. In the same column, usually on the left side of the spread, lace by the yard and lace trim are sold.

Perhaps the copy is sufficient for those knowledgeable about lace, but to me, it seems sparse indeed. There's so much history to tell, so many uses to suggest, and so many helpful hints and product tips to relate. Why make the copy seem like the grunts of misogynistic Parisian waiter serving a table of American church ladies? Moreover, when selling the non-lace items that appear in the catalog, an entirely new set of 'verites' must be established, and *that* takes copy!

LA VIE EN FRANCE

The view through your window could hardly be as charming as these village scenes from life in France. They're sure to capture your fancy! Available in natural. Machine wash, dry flat.

◄ **Cloud Valance**
716NVC · Valance . . . . (EA) 24.00
13"L × 72"W
716NYD · By The Yard . . . . (PER YD) $ 7.00
13" WIDE
COLOR: NATURAL

◄ **Petit Village**
716HCC · Café Curtains . . . . . (PR) 49.00
35"L × 72"W
716HYD · By The Yard . . . . (PER YD) $18.00
35" WIDE
COLOR: NATURAL

Brittany Coast Panels

CODE	LENGTH		23" WIDE
716HFP	45" or 54"	(EA)	$30.00
716HFP	63" or 72"	(EA)	33.00

COLOR: NATURAL

My Petit Village café curtains delight my customers and never fail to elicit compliments.

MURIEL'S RESTAURANT, NEWPORT, RHODE ISLAND

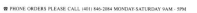

▲ **Ballon Flat Panel**

CODE	LENGTH		23" WIDE
717OFP	36" or 40"	(EA)	$26.50
717OFP	45" or 54"	(EA)	30.00
717OFP	63" or 72"	(EA)	33.00

COLOR: NATURAL

▲ **Ballon Baby Quilt & Pillow Set**
Sweet dreams for the little one in your life. This cheerful comforter & pillow set is the perfect baby present. Cotton/poly appliquéd with our Ballon lace, 100% cotton batting (41" × 43"). Machine wash, dry flat. Available in blue (05) or primrose (12).
717OCS · Quilt & Pillow . . . . (SET) $80.00

LA TABLE

Rue de France creates the perfect setting for your entertaining. Capture the true essence of European dining with our so very French "faïence", glassware and bistroware.

▼ **Biot French Glassware**
In the finest French tradition from Provence. Available in set of 6 glasses in either size in green (13), clear (00), or blue (05).
717BGWM · 6¼"H glasses . (SET OF 6) $132.00
717BGWL · 7"H glasses . . (SET OF 6) 144.00
717BGP · 8"H pitcher . . . . . (EA) 45.00

► **Bistroware**
Set the tone for pleasant dining with "Guy De Grenne" Bistroware. The plastic-handled, stainless 24 piece set, packaged in an attractive wooden box, provides service for six. In white (01) or navy (04). Dishwasher safe.
717GDS · Bistroware . . . . . . (SET) $70.00

▲ **Lavandin Pottery**
The refined simplicity of this delicate motif – the lavender for which the South of France is famous – is elegant and understated.
717LPS · 5-pc. placesetting . . (SET) $116.00
717LSV · Small Vase . . . . . . (EA) 27.00
717LPT · Pitcher . . . . (EA) 70.00
717LCS · Candlestick . . . . . (EA) 33.00
For pitcher and candlesticks see page 8.

▼ **Tablelinens by "Le Jacquard"**
The beautiful pastel, 100% cotton damask is subtly embellished with a delicate motif of swans to grace your table. In petal pink (12), champagne (02), and white (01).
717JSPM · Placemat · 15" × 20" . . (EA) $ 7.00
717JSNK · Napkin · 24" × 24" . . . (EA) 9.00
717JSTS · Tablecloth · 69" × 69" . (EA) 66.00
717JSTL · Tablecloth · 69" × 102" . (EA) 110.00

☎ PHONE ORDERS PLEASE CALL (401) 846-2084 MONDAY-SATURDAY 9AM - 5PM

▲ **Rue de France Pillows**
Rue de France originals add a lavish decorator's note to any room. We use our favorite lace patterns with a cotton/poly broadcloth backing in colors to match your decor. Specify backing of white (01), natural (02), beige (03), navy (04), copen blue (05), pewter grey (06), peach (10), primrose (12), seafoam (15), teal (20), or lilac (21). Poly-filled.

724FPW · Les Chats · Natural · 12" × 16" . . . . (EACH) $28.50
724RPW · Roses · Natural · 12" × 16" . . . . (EACH) 28.50
724BPW · Doves · Natural · 12" × 16" . . . . (EACH) 28.50
724APW · Belle Fleur · Natural · 12" × 16" . . . . (EACH) 28.50
724DPW · Old Calais · White or Beige · 12" Square . . . . . (EACH) 31.00
724HPW · Petit Village · Natural · 12" × 16" . . . . (EACH) 28.50
724MPW · Marguerite · White or Beige · 12" × 16" . . . . . (EACH) 31.00

▲ **Exclusive Dove Note Cards**
Our elegant Dove logo has been embossed on these informal note cards especially for Rue de France. An envelope of blue quilted French Provençal cotton completes this charming gift idea.
724BNC . . . . (SET OF 10) $16.50

© 1987 RUE DE FRANCE, INC.

Rue de France
78 Thames Street
Newport, Rhode Island 02840

Deliver to current resident.

BULK RATE
U.S. POSTAGE
PAID
RUE DE FRANCE

The Rue de France pillows on the Outside Back Cover should be a winner. Not only is a selection from 5 well-known lace patterns offered, but 11 backing colors are also available. This kind of customization almost always pays off, particularly if a knowledgeable Customer Service representative on the Rue de France end of the telephone is able to offer intelligent decorating advice.

SHOPSMITH

O ne of the greatest mistakes a marketer can make is to become so preoccupied with his medium that he forgets his basic business premise (i.e. to make money on what he is selling). Broadcast television is a case in point. An increasing number of packaged goods marketers seem to have run out of logical reasons for consumers to purchase their viands and emoluments. (Note: they call us consumers, not customers.) As a result, many of these sciolistic showmen have become pseudo Broadway producers. They seem totally preoccupied with their stage-bits, computer graphics and audience psychodynamics—instead of concentrating on moving the merch. The apparent attitude is, "If the toothpaste bombs, it's the product manager's fault, not ours. We put on a helluva a show". The other version of that cop-out is: "Ratings are up. What do you want from me, entertainment *and* profit?"

The same trap exists in the catalog world. The dinosaurs are dying because they are stuck in the quicksand of catalog production bureaucracies. (Dinosaurs, in this case, are what used to be generically called "the majors", e.g. Montgomery Ward, Sears Roebuck, J.C. Penney and the rest of that retail-cum-mailorder ilk.) All too often, middle management focuses on getting the catalog out. How sad, when the real job is to sell merchandise.

Oddly enough, the inspiration for this diatribe is an evolutionary marketing system that is apparently focused very sharply on the guts, not the glory.

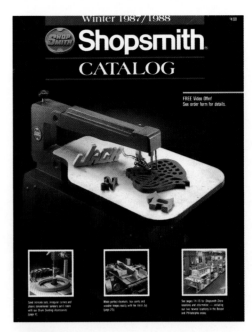

SHOPSMITH—Winter 1987/88
David Drake, *Catalog Manager*
Cindy Lash, Jan Hafner and Sue Hafle, *Designers*
Mark Bremer and Al Schneider, *Copywriters*
Biel's Photographic Studios, *Photographer*
Jeffrey Raco, *Managing Editor*
Maxwell Communications [St. Paul, MN], *Printer,*
    on 40# Lithoblade for cover and text
Printing Preparations [Dayton, OH],
    Color Separator

Right up front, Shopsmith presents their newest product, the Scroll Saw, a much upgraded version of the jigsaw. It can be purchased as a stand-alone tool or as an add-on attachment to the Mark V. As with all Shopsmith catalog covers, insert photos highlight other featured products and store locations.

The reader is 42 pages into this 64-page catalog

before the basic Mark V systems are found. One can reach two conclusions from this unusual positioning: (1). The mailing list is primarily derived from a database of Mark V owners, and/or (2). The Shopsmith executives have read Gene Flack and Red Motley's sales manuals, and have decided to let the sizzle sell the steak.

Shopsmith has been around for about sixteen years. You may remember their small space, and later, full page black and white ads in magazines such as "Popular Mechanics", "Popular Science", and various tabloid newsprint vehicles. In those days, Shopsmith was a one-product company. They offered the at-home woodworking hobbyist a multi-purpose lathe-type tool.

These tools are similar in operation and function to the machines that many of their (sometimes blue-collar) customers operated in plants across the United States every day. They require a certain degree of tool setup knowledge to operate, plus the leisure time and mindset of a dedicated hobbyist.

You've heard this before, but it cannot be repeated too often: A direct response marketer must build a loyal and happy customer base. If he does, he can go back to those same individuals and sell them other, related products. If he does not, the cost of constantly buying new customers (with media dollars) will eat up any profit, if the resulting orders turn out to be one-time only events.

It's a thrill to see the extent to which Shopsmith's executives have recognized the truth of this adage and have expanded their company's product line in these short, sixteen years. This award-winning, fully merchandised catalog is just one mark of a well-run company. There are many others. They have orchestrated a masterful job of an engineered corporate evolution, and they're not through yet.

The basic "Shopsmith" has now grown up to Mark V Model 510. And the catalog program is no longer a solo act. An accompanying magazine called "Hands On, The Home Workshop Magazine", tackles a variety of woodworking projects in each issue, and incidentally recommends a Shopsmith product here and there. And, to top all that, as of last count, there were 18 Shopsmith stores covering the United States from coast to coast.

All this could not have happened except for the fact that the product line has been filled out in an extraordinary manner.

The Mark V, Model 510, with standard accessories for sawing, drilling, sanding, boring and turning sells for $1,729. A very nice ticket indeed for any single mailorder product.

But this is a one-time, lifetime sale. What can Shopsmith do for an encore? The answer: their latest catalog carries 584 SKU's in addition to the basic Mark V. If you bought one of each, the cost would be $24,903.07.

From $1,729 to $24,900! That is line extrapolation raised to exponential dimensions.

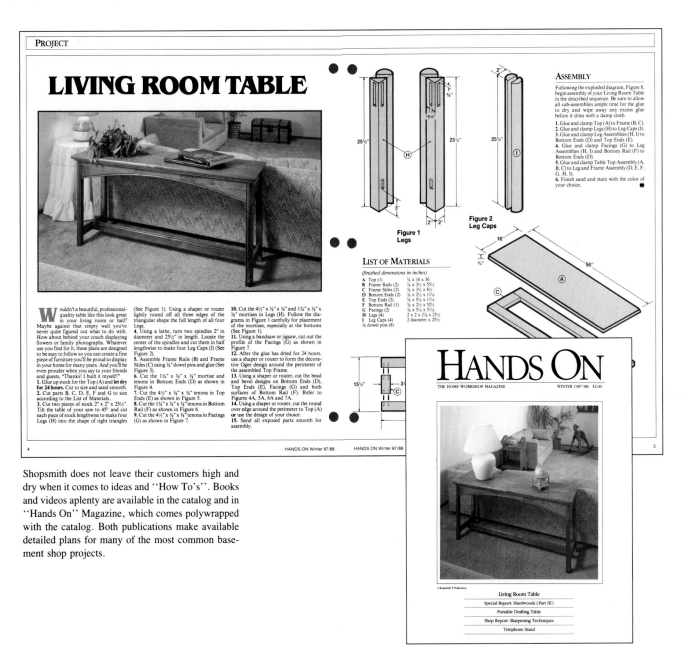

Shopsmith does not leave their customers high and dry when it comes to ideas and "How To's". Books and videos aplenty are available in the catalog and in "Hands On" Magazine, which comes polywrapped with the catalog. Both publications make available detailed plans for many of the most common basement shop projects.

Sanding Doesn't Have to be Tedious!

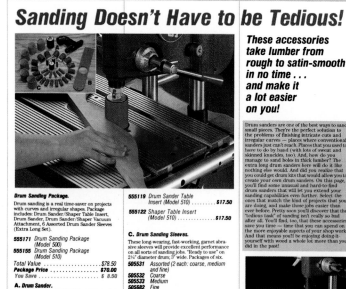

These accessories take lumber from rough to satin-smooth in no time ... and make it a lot easier on you!

Drum sanders are one of the best ways to sand small pieces. They're the perfect solution to the problems of finishing intricate cuts and irregular curves — places where conventional sanders just can't reach. Places that you used to have to do by hand (with lots of sweat and skinned knuckles, too). And, how do you manage to sand holes in thick lumber? The extra long drum sanders here will do it like nothing else would. And did you realize that you could get drum bits that would allow you to create your own drum sanders. On this page, you'll find some unusual and hard-to-find drum sanders that will let you extend your sanding capabilities even further. Select the ones that match the kind of projects that you are doing, and make those jobs easier than ever before. Pretty soon you'll discover that the "tedious task" of sanding isn't really so bad after all. You'll find, too, that these accessories save you time — time that you can spend on the more enjoyable aspects of your shop work. And that means you'll be enjoying doing-it-yourself with wood a whole lot more than you did in the past!

Drum Sanding Package.
Drum sanding is a real time-saver on projects with curves and irregular shapes. Package includes: Drum Sander/Shaper Insert, Drum Sander, Drum Sander/Shaper Vacuum Attachment, 6 Assorted Drum Sander Sleeves (Extra Long Set).

555171 Drum Sanding Package (Model 500)
555155 Drum Sanding Package (Model 510)
Total Value $78.50
Package Price **$70.00**
You Save .... $ 8.50

A. Drum Sander.
2¼" diameter is perfect for fast contour sanding all sorts of shapes. Can be used in vertical or horizontal position. Abrasive sleeves lock firmly in place by rubber expansion cylinder. Fits on main, auxiliary and Belt Sander spindles. 3" high.
505552 Drum Sander **$22.00**
Note: If you purchase the Drum Sander and Fence it is recommended you also purchase the Table Insert.

B. Drum Sander/Shaper Table Insert.
Circular cutout in center of table permits drum to drop below the table surface to sand edges completely and equally.
505509 Drum Sander/Shaper Table Insert (Model 500) **$17.50**

D. Sanding Drums.
These special drums have soft sponge rubber backing and unique slots that let you easily replace sleeves using flat paper. Simply cut standard sheets of sanding paper to size and wrap around the drum. Squeeze out slack and tuck both ends into the slot. Then insert the locking tube and turn the key. Fast and easy. two size kits available. Each includes a precut sheet of sandpaper to use as a pattern. Fits ⅛" chuck.
DA-4150 1" x 3" Sanding Drum .. **$15.00**
DA-4151 2" x 3" Sanding Drum .. **$16.00**

555119 Drum Sander Table Insert (Model 510) **$17.50**
555122 Shaper Table Insert (Model 510) **$17.50**

C. Drum Sanding Sleeves.
These long-wearing, fast-working, garnet abrasive sleeves will provide excellent performance on all sorts of sanding jobs. "Ready to use" on 2¼" diameter drum; 3" wide. Packages of six.
505531 Assorted (2 each: coarse, medium and fine)
505532 Coarse
505533 Medium
505682 Fine
Each **$9.00**

Drum Sander/Shaper Fence
When used with the Shopsmith Drum Sander, this fence is extremely useful in accurately controlling depth-of-cut in edging operations. Exclusive in-feed fence screw can be adjusted to produce a depth-of-cut as slight as ¹⁄₆₄".
555144 Drum Sander/Shaper Fence (Model 500) **$75.00**
555113 Drum Sander/Shaper Fence (Model 510) **$75.00**

E. Extra Long Drum Sanding Set.
The sanders you've been looking for to do extra long sanding.
These hard-to-find extra long drum sanders are ideal for use in your drill press when sanding holes in thick lumber. Now a greater assortment of sleeves — 3 fine, 2 medium and 1 coarse for each of four drums: 1½" x 2"; 1" x 2"; ¾" x 2"; ½" x 2".
DA-0148 Extra Long Drum Sanding Set **$24.00**

Replacement Sleeves.
DA-0195 (24) Assorted Sleeves **$6.50**
DA-0196 (12) Coarse Sleeves **$3.50**
DA-0197 (12) Medium Sleeves **$3.50**
DA-0198 (12) Fine Sleeves **$3.50**

Place an order TODAY! Call 1-800-543-7586, In Dayton 898-6070.

Eliminate long hours of laborious hand sanding with a Shopsmith 6" Belt Sander ...

... now with dust collection ability.

No one likes to hand sand.
A belt sander is a labor saving accessory that lets you forget about that tedious job. Its straight line cutting action removes stock quicker and easier than any other sanding method. And no other sander is quite so versatile.
The Shopsmith Belt Sander can be operated in either the horizontal or vertical position. This gives you accurate, convenient sanding of both narrow edges and wider surfaces.
Depending on dimensions, you can contour sand curves and other shapes over the idler drum.

Free-running belt on back side.
The Shopsmith Belt Sander gives you two sanding capabilities on the front and back of the belt. A heavy steel plate provides the front support you need for even, smoothly sanded surfaces.
The back side of the belt runs free of support, so you can give a smooth finish to any odd-shaped pieces you're working on.

Multi-position table.
The Belt Sander table is one of the best you'll find anywhere. It measures a full 6" x 9" (unlike the small ledges found on many machines). You can use it across the belt, parallel to it on either side, or at any angle.
The table can also be used as a "rip fence" to improve precision when sanding edges. Used in conjunction with your MARK V Miter Gauge, the table can even be mounted over the belt for greater accuracy and control when sanding mitered edges, bevels and chamfers.
An auxiliary spindle is provided for attaching a drum sander, which is perfect for sanding deep holes in thick stock.

Automatic tensioning knob.
Tension adjustments are automatic on the Shopsmith Belt Sander. It takes all the guesswork out of the job. An exclusive tensioning knob releases quickly for easy belt removal and, when the new belt is in place, returns to the proper tension setting immediately.

New dust collection feature.
To increase your comfort and safety level, the Shopsmith Belt Sander has a new dust collection feature that hooks to the Shopsmith DC3300 (see pages 34-35) for virtually dust-free sanding. You'll enjoy a cleaner shop with less work on your part!
No other belt sander on the market today can match the unique features of the Shopsmith 6" Belt Sander. No other Major Accessory can save you more time and hard labor. Order your Shopsmith Belt Sander right away and put it to work for you in your home shop!

505642 The Shopsmith 6" Belt Sander **$299.00**
Owner's Manual included.

Accessories:
Major Accessory Power Stand
505993 Belt Sander Power Stand ... **$159.00**
See page 7 for details.
Power Stands not available in Canada.

DC3300 Belt Sander Dust Chute.
Adapt your Shopsmith Belt Sander for use with the DC3300 Dust Collection System. Some filing required.
300002 DC3300 Belt Sander Dust Chute **$12.00**

Mounting Base
Included with Power Stand.
505655 Mounting Base **$17.50**

Retractable Casters
Attach to stand-mounted Major Accessories.
555076 Retractable Casters **$59.00**

Coupling Kit
Required to mount the Belt Sander on the MARK V.
555124 Coupling Kit **$9.00**
Components of the Coupling Kit are included with the MARK V and Major Accessories. Call our Customer Services Department if you are unsure as to whether or not you need to purchase a Coupling Kit.

Belt Sander Eccentric Tube.
(Two required) Included with the Belt Sander.
513777 Belt Sander Eccentric Tube ... **$8.00**

Sanding Belts.
Shopsmith sanding belts are 6" x 48" and come in garnet and aluminum oxide. Garnet belts are sharper and will sand faster. Aluminum oxide belts are of a finer grit and tougher ... ideal for tool sharpening and fine finish sanding.

Garnet Belts.
555005 120-grit/Very Fine (1)		**$7.50**
555024 120-grit/Very Fine		**$25.00**
(Pkg. of 4) **Reg. $30.00**		
Save		$5.00
555534 100-grit/Fine (1)		**$7.50**
505520 100-grit/Fine		**$25.00**
(Pkg. of 4) **Reg. $30.00**		
Save		$5.00
505535 80-grit/Medium (1)		**$7.50**
(One included with Belt Sander.)		
505521 80-grit/Medium		**$25.00**
(Pkg. of 4) **Reg. $30.00**		
Save		$5.00
505536 60-grit/Coarse (1)		**$7.50**
505522 60-grit/Coarse		**$25.00**
(Pkg. of 4) **Reg. $30.00**		
Save		$5.00
555004 40-grit/Coarse (1)		**$7.50**
555023 40-grit/Coarse		**$25.00**
(Pkg. of 4) **Reg. $30.00**		
Save		$5.00

Aluminum Oxide Belts.
555000 150-grit/Ultra Fine (1)		**$7.50**
555025 150-grit/Ultra Fine		**$25.00**
(Pkg. of 4) **Reg. $30.00**		
Save		$5.00

Remember, all products are backed by Shopsmith's 30-Day Money-Back Guarantee.

Most housewives would find this sort of catalog spread somewhat less than enthralling. On the other hand, a dedicated hobbyist of either sex might easily spend ten or fifteen minutes totally immersed in almost every spread of this catalog.

When an experienced woodworker peruses these pages, he doesn't just look at an item and make a buy/no-buy decision. In his mind's eye, he will visualize the dozens of objects he would be able to make—if only he owned this new tool. The merchant would only cloud the issue if he were to illustrate too many finished products. In the same vein, there are well-meaning but misguided catalogers who use too many props and busy backgrounds in their photographs. The effect is to lock the reader into what the *merchant* thinks is the right use or ambience for his product. If the customer dances to a different drumbeat, the sale is unnecessarily and irretrievably lost.

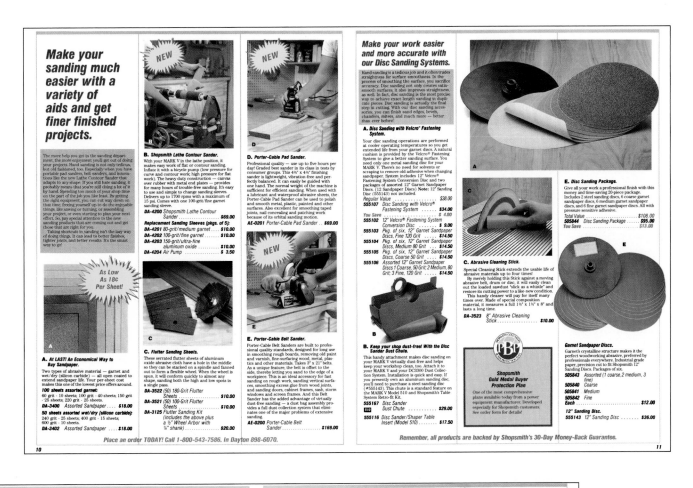

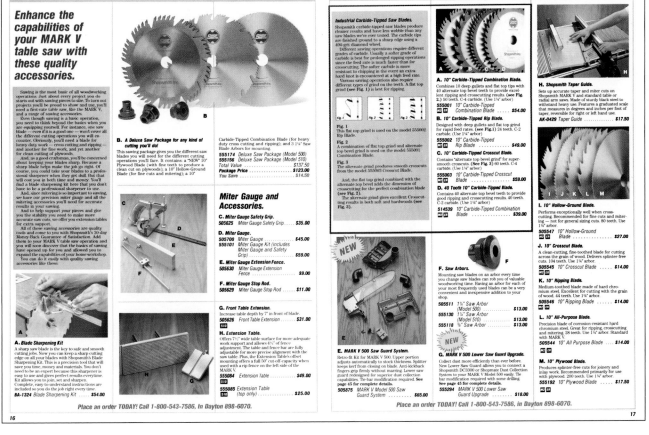

"Give 'em the damn razors as long as we can sell them the blades." Though the phrasing may be indelicate, the lesson is sound. And it is not lost on the stewards of Shopsmith. Bits, blades and abrasives wear out, and where better to go for replacements than to the man who sold the original tool. He knows what's right. Right?

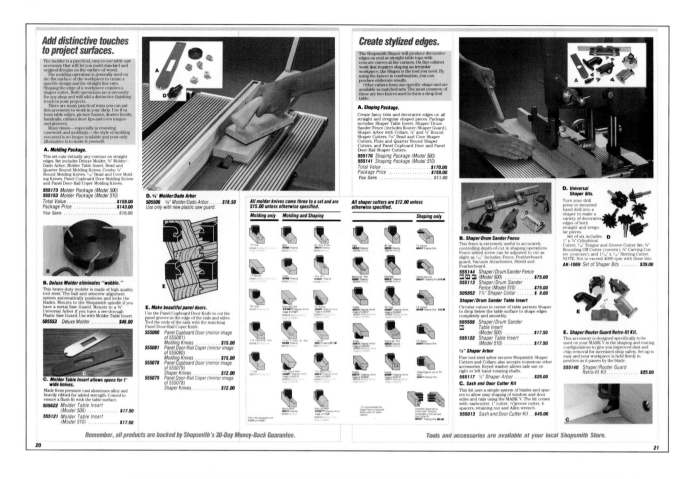

In the world of woodworking, shapers, molders and routers are the tools of demarcation between the ranks of amateur hobbyists and the advanced practitioner. Jigs, calipers, chisels, reamers and files are used by both. And all of the above are sold in this catalog. But this is really a book for serious hobbyists. Shopsmith's sophisticated inventory strongly favors the more skilled joiner/cabinet maker, as opposed to the stairs-and-studding carpenter.

Find everything you need for working with wood at your nearby Shopsmith Store!

If you're a do-it-yourselfer who loves to work with wood, you owe it to yourself to come browse, learn or buy at the store built just to meet your needs! Whether you're interested in home improvements, arts and crafts, fine furniture or a rewarding, satisfying way to relax — your Shopsmith Store is **the** place to go for all your woodworking needs **plus** all the professional advice you'll ever want.

" Mr. Folkerth, I can't tell you how pleased I was with the *attitude* and *friendly service* and complete satisfaction I received from your staff at a Shopsmith Store. From the moment I arrived I was treated with the utmost in courtesy. Their sincere attitude and helpful information are surely an asset to your company and should be recognized for the fine image they put forth on behalf of 'Shopsmith'. There is no doubt in my mind that you stand behind what you sell... I feel as though I am a real part of the 'Shopsmith Family'.
Jim Sanders
Huntsville, Alabama "

Continuing Education.
As with every store in the Shopsmith System, we're not just a place where you can buy woodworking equipment and supplies — we're a teaching center too! Our specially trained Shopsmith experts will provide you with one-on-one guidance and solutions to just about any woodworking problem.

At Shopsmith, we believe the best way to learn is by doing. That's why all of our 3-day courses feature hands-on training by expertly qualified instructors.

Choose from:
• Three-Day Fundamentals of Woodworking Course
• Three-Day Cabinetmaking Course
• 90-Minute "Sawdust Sessions"

So choose the courses that interest you and make your reservations today! It's a decision you'll never regret.

" I know, through personal experience at your Shopsmith school, how personally involved your people get. This type of concern for the customer combined with a fine product will keep the Shopsmith family growing.
Daniel J. Polzien
Fraser, Michigan "

Expanding the Shopsmith Store Network!
Shopsmith is continually moving forward to serve you better. We are always on the alert to answer your woodworking needs with new products and also have plans to open several new stores in the near future throughout the country. Occasionally we'll even relocate a store to a more convenient location for our customers — as was the case recently in the Minneapolis/St. Paul area.

Two of our newest store locations — in the Boston and Philadelphia areas — have been received with overwhelming response.

Be sure to check on the next page for a store near you and stop in. You'll see all the latest Shopsmith innovations and get a first-hand look and demonstration of any and all Shopsmith products. You'll be glad you did!

Tools and accessories are available at your local Shopsmith Store.

14

The growing network of Shopsmith stores offers more than just Shopsmith merchandise. Face-to-face consultation and a variety of training seminars are available at all locations. For the truly dedicated, two, 3-day instruction programs are conducted, one for beginners, and one for budding cabinet makers. For mailorder customers, the catalog offers toll-free telephone assistance and advice. And, when breakdowns occur, as can happen, even with a Shopsmith product—no problem. Simply return your power tool to Shopsmith. They'll fix it. And by gosh, they'll give you a loaner to use in the interim.

Shopsmith isn't out to win Art Directors Club awards. Their objective is to do business. And they've found the best way to do business is to listen to their customers, to become a friend. Based on that philosophy, I would look for Shopsmith to expand their product line into other related areas some time in the not too distant future. They have the formula, the real estate and the direct marketing know-how. When and if the move is made, this company will be well on the road to greatness.

SMITH & HAWKEN

CATALOG FOR GARDENERS

The fundamental question in the catalog world is, "Does it work?" Usually that question means "Does it make money?"

Paul Hawken of Smith & Hawken has been publishing his Catalog for Gardeners since 1979. He has authored books and appears regularly on television. His books and TV series deal with subjects centered around growing and running businesses. It seems safe to assume his catalog is a financial success. It works.

Perhaps the primary reason for Smith & Hawken's success has to do with the structure of the business itself. But, for the moment, we should take a close look at one of the most attractive catalogs to be found on anyone's coffee table.

To set the scene, S&H's covers are always as appealing and as commanding as a magnificently designed store window display. And, these covers do their job. They make you want to come inside. They tell you that you will be missing something beautiful and important if you pass by without looking.

Once inside the Smith & Hawken catalog, the promise of the cover is made good. White space, copy and photographs are delicately balanced. The reader's eyes are surprised and delighted as they move from area to area and from item to item. That is good layout! The excellent choice of Palladium typeface, weight of type and the use of italics for the editorial comments and practical advice all add to the visual pleasure of a Smith & Hawken catalog. What's even more important, this beautifully balanced typeface is easy to read.

The photography does what all good catalog photography should do. It tells you (as much as any illustration can) all you need to know about a product to make a buying decision. But in this case, the process of taking the picture presents much more than the usual artistic challenge. Flowers delight the eye, but they can be a brute to photograph. To the camera, most gardens are messy and cluttered (it's a function of the one-eyed, two dimensional camera lens). S&H's photography transcends these problems by virtue of careful planning and first-rate execution.

Smith & Hawken catalog copy is absolutely top drawer. Catalog Director Alice Rogers works with a team of product specialists to produce copy that flows and informs. One hopes that someday she will teach a graduate-level course in Direct Response Copywriting at some famous university. Our industry needs to train many more people in the art and science of communications.

All the correct expository points are made in the S&H copy: sizes, colors, correct use, materials, prices and styles. But, these prerequisite elements are just the landing field for the Rogers team's flights of prose. Smith & Hawken's copy works because it is well researched, has tremendous creative flair, and it is professional. It involves and intrigues the reader. It informs. It creates a want, then a need, and finally supplies left-brain logic and information that permits the reader to make an intelligent decision (or create a logical excuse) to buy. And aside from all that, it's a fun read!

The Smith & Hawken Catalog for Gardeners is directed to ladies and gentlemen of distinction. The graphics, copy and merchandise selection all make that point very clearly. Since they

SMITH & HAWKEN CATALOG FOR GARDENERS—Holiday 1987
Paul Hawken, *Owner and Chairman*
Bill Scranton, *President*
Alice Rogers, *Catalog Director/Creative Director, Art Director/Copy Chief/Production Manager*
Mercedes Fuller, *Senior Buyer*
Pentagram [San Francisco, CA], *General Format Design*
Shawn Sullivan, *Photographer*
ProType Graphics [San Rafael, CA], *Typography*
Foote & Davies, *Printer, on Champion Panaprint for Cover and Mead Northcote for text*

have positioned themselves to appeal to a cultured, refined market, S&H can well afford to eschew the brass-knuckled, competition-bashing turmoil of the off-price arena. Not for Smith & Hawken the three-ring retail circus wherein everyone carries the same merchandise, offers the same poor service and sends you to the manufacturer if you have a problem.

Planned obsolescence is an anathematic concept at Smith & Hawken. When Paul Hawken started his new business, the first items sold were a line of English garden tools made to last forever. These tools were built to a better design, used stronger materials and had the form and balance to do their job with less effort on the part of the gardener. The tradition of quality is firmly in place. In today's S&H catalogs, we're treated to a panorama of beautifully made direct imports and private label products. Some are truly unique items from all over the world. Others provide the means to do a gardening job more efficiently. Another group is comprised of those just plain hard-to-find items local stores never seem to stock. Every item appears to be the best available in its category. Not exactly the sort of merchandise mix to be easily found on the shelves of your mall-based mass merchant.

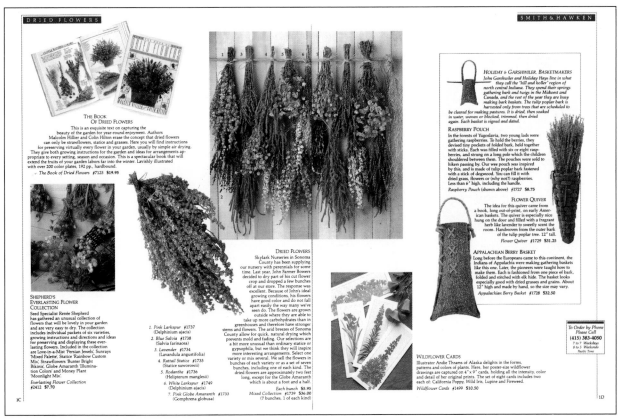

Few catalogs can be honestly called irresistible, but this one certainly can. Perhaps the only 'turnoff' is the name of the book, which is the ''Smith & Hawken Catalog for Gardeners''. In fact, this might just as well be a catalog for someone who has never set foot on sod in his life. It's a book for lovers of fine tools. It's a book for cliff-dwellers, and a book for plantation owners. It's difficult to conceive of a home that would not welcome this catalog.

It's a book kept lively by frequent layout change, although the merchandise is relatively static from year to year. On these two spreads, one from the 1987 Holiday catalog and one from the 1988 Holiday book, a dramatic layout change revitalizes a category that might become stale if only pickup art and layouts were used.

Catalog merchants learned long ago that—excluding merchandise—the single most important element of their marketing mix is *Customer Service*. Customer Service is a marketing function and a merchandising function. It must transcend the usual intra-corporate departmental boundaries. It should be the core concern in every nook and cranny of a mailorder business: from the front office to the green eyeshade department; and from the buyer's desk to the loading dock. This customer-oriented mindset carries over to, and is clearly spelled out in the Smith & Hawken guarantee:

Every item in our catalog comes with our full recommendation. Should any dissatisfaction arise, your problem will be promptly and cheerfully corrected or your money refunded. If a particular item does not meet with your complete approval, for any reason or no reason [underline added], simply return it to us and we will promptly refund your money or replace the item, as you wish. You take absolutely no risk. We want you to be completely satisfied with our products from the moment you receive them, for as long as you use them. If you have a problem or question about your order, please call our direct Customer Service line, (415) 383-6292, and we will be happy to help you.

Fortunately, many of today's successful catalogers have comparable guarantees and a similar attitude towards Customer Service. *Could this be the reason that mailorder sales are growing at almost double the rate of OTC retail store sales?*

To conceive the goals, to achieve objectives, to implement the ideals—all this takes people. Paul Hawken and President, Bill Scranton, have strong opinions about the ''people'' part of their business. They believe in contrapuntal partnerships where partners have different skills, but similar philosophies. They do not believe in rigid structure—it stifles both creativity and productivity. In his latest book, *Growing A Business* (published by Simon & Schuster), Paul writes of the concept called ''hybrid vigor'':

When different strains of plants or animals are crossbred, 'hybrid vigor' is sometimes the result. The best traits of each species combine in a new species that is superior to either parent. Plant and animal breeders are always seeking hybrid vigor. The smart employer does the same thing.

Smith & Hawken mails a total of 15 million catalogs per year in four flights. A very large universe, especially considering the relatively narrow focus of their market. Clearly, the combination of superb customer service, truly extraordinary products and an enlightened approach to intra-company human relations is growing a very healthy business.

A successful creative effort must have a point of view, as well as some fairly precise merchandising guidelines. Catalog Director Alice Rogers has been kind enough to express her basic design philosophy as it applies to the Smith & Hawken Catalog for Gardeners:

Our catalogs are designed to clearly convey as much information on the process and resulting pleasures of gardening as is possible in a catalog format.

Layouts are organized in spreads rather than by individual pages to create a more expansive, less confusing, viewing area: the relative sizing of photographs, the increased availability of white space flowing throughout the spread, and the use of sidebars to organize blocks of information all combine to allow the reader's eye to move across the spread in a natural progression without having images or information compete for attention. The outer rules on either edge of every spread both define a plane and help stop the eye from moving randomly off the page. Our photography strives to show products clearly, in even light, and with great detail, combining whenever possible location and editorial shots illustrating gardens that are mature, timeless and yet intimate.

The shameless plug for Paul Hawken's new book and PBS television series, ''Growing a Business'', does not detract one whit from the merchandise on this page or from the impact of the catalog as a whole. Quite the reverse! You know you're going to be well treated by someone whose business philosophy is expressed in these words:

How do you grow a business so that it works for the customers, the employees, the community and the founders? In this day of mega-mergers, hostile takeovers, ''Greenmail'' and deteriorating service, the book attempts to show what common sense never forgot: taking care of people, whether they be customers or fellow workers, is darn good business.

The story of the garden tools manufactured for Smith & Hawken in England is the story of the genesis of the Smith & Hawken business: establish that there is a need. Then, respond to that need with the best there is.

Generic copy, such as this, is mixed with extra-long item copy in a combination that makes for fascinating reading, as it simultaneously establishes an authoritative position for the publisher.

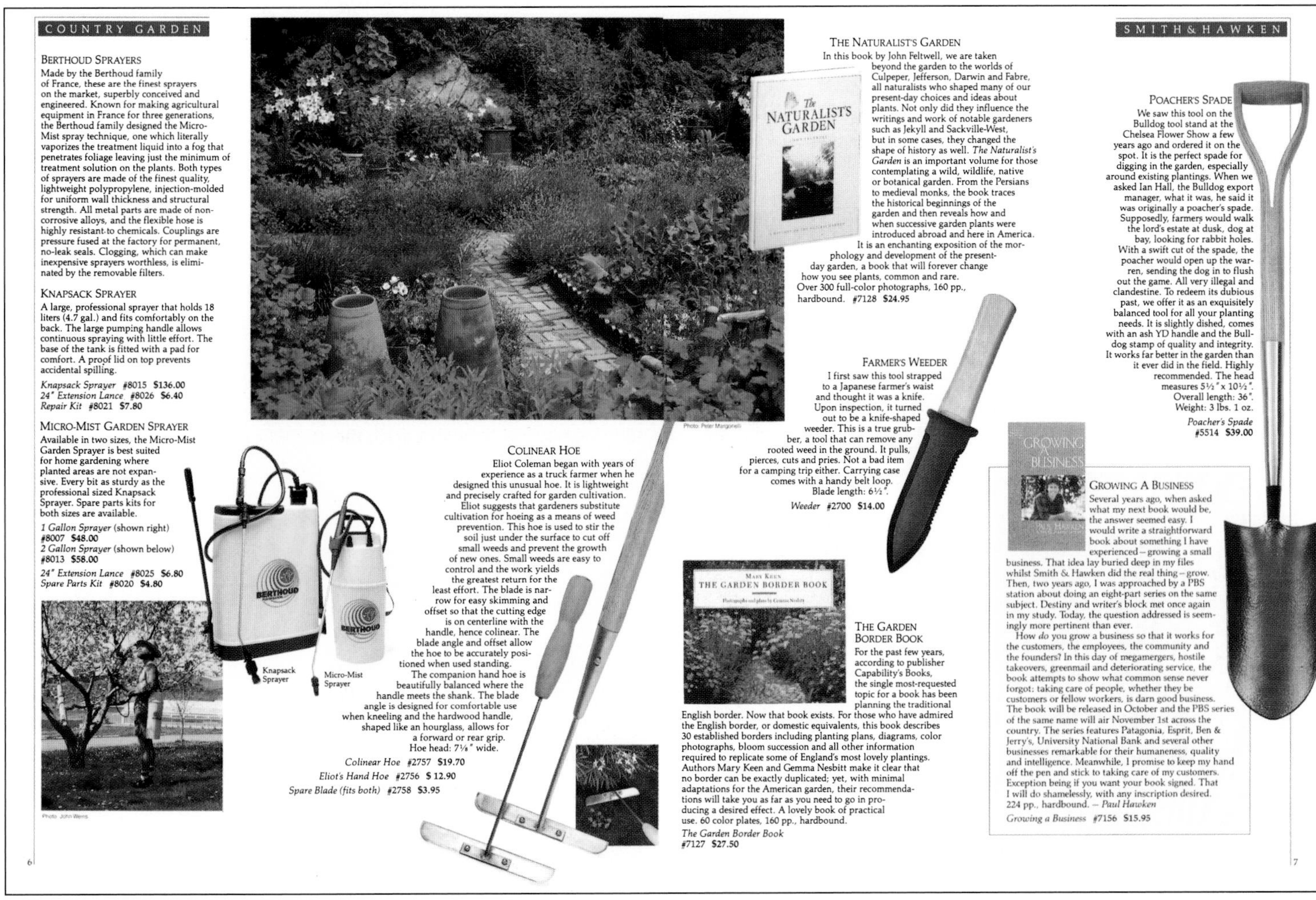

COUNTRY GARDEN

SMITH & HAWKEN

BERTHOUD SPRAYERS

Made by the Berthoud family of France, these are the finest sprayers on the market, superbly conceived and engineered. Known for making agricultural equipment in France for three generations, the Berthoud family designed the Micro-Mist spray technique, one which literally vaporizes the treatment liquid into a fog that penetrates foliage leaving just the minimum of treatment solution on the plants. Both types of sprayers are made of the finest quality, lightweight polypropylene, injection-molded for uniform wall thickness and structural strength. All metal parts are made of non-corrosive alloys, and the flexible hose is highly resistant to chemicals. Couplings are pressure fused at the factory for permanent, no-leak seals. Clogging, which can make inexpensive sprayers worthless, is eliminated by the removable filters.

KNAPSACK SPRAYER

A large, professional sprayer that holds 18 liters (4.7 gal.) and fits comfortably on the back. The large pumping handle allows continuous spraying with little effort. The base of the tank is fitted with a pad for comfort. A proof lid on top prevents accidental spilling.

Knapsack Sprayer #8015 **$136.00**
24" Extension Lance #8026 **$6.40**
Repair Kit #8021 **$7.80**

MICRO-MIST GARDEN SPRAYER

Available in two sizes, the Micro-Mist Garden Sprayer is best suited for home gardening where planted areas are not expansive. Every bit as sturdy as the professional sized Knapsack Sprayer. Spare parts kits for both sizes are available.

1 Gallon Sprayer (shown right) #8007 **$48.00**
2 Gallon Sprayer (shown below) #8013 **$58.00**

24" Extension Lance #8025 **$6.80**
Spare Parts Kit #8020 **$4.80**

Photo: John Wiens

Photo: Peter Margonelli

Knapsack Sprayer

Micro-Mist Sprayer

THE NATURALIST'S GARDEN

In this book by John Feltwell, we are taken beyond the garden to the worlds of Culpeper, Jefferson, Darwin and Fabre, all naturalists who shaped many of our present-day choices and ideas about plants. Not only did they influence the writings and work of notable gardeners such as Jekyll and Sackville-West, but in some cases, they changed the shape of history as well. *The Naturalist's Garden* is an important volume for those contemplating a wild, wildlife, native or botanical garden. From the Persians to medieval monks, the book traces the historical beginnings of the garden and then reveals how and when successive garden plants were introduced abroad and here in America. It is an enchanting exposition of the morphology and development of the present-day garden, a book that will forever change how you see plants, common and rare. Over 300 full-color photographs, 160 pp., hardbound. #7128 **$24.95**

COLINEAR HOE

Eliot Coleman began with years of experience as a truck farmer when he designed this unusual hoe. It is lightweight and precisely crafted for garden cultivation.

Eliot suggests that gardeners substitute cultivation for hoeing as a means of weed prevention. This hoe is used to stir the soil just under the surface to cut off small weeds and prevent the growth of new ones. Small weeds are easy to control and the work yields the greatest return for the least effort. The blade is narrow for easy skimming and offset so that the cutting edge is on centerline with the handle, hence colinear. The blade angle and offset allow the hoe to be accurately positioned when used standing.

The companion hand hoe is beautifully balanced where the handle meets the shank. The blade angle is designed for comfortable use when kneeling and the hardwood handle, shaped like an hourglass, allows for a forward or rear grip. Hoe head: 7⅛" wide.

Colinear Hoe #2757 **$19.70**
Eliot's Hand Hoe #2756 **$ 12.90**
Spare Blade (fits both) #2758 **$3.95**

FARMER'S WEEDER

I first saw this tool strapped to a Japanese farmer's waist and thought it was a knife. Upon inspection, it turned out to be a knife-shaped weeder. This is a true grubber, a tool that can remove any rooted weed in the ground. It pulls, pierces, cuts and pries. Not a bad item for a camping trip either. Carrying case comes with a handy belt loop. Blade length: 6½".

Weeder #2700 **$14.00**

THE GARDEN BORDER BOOK

For the past few years, according to publisher Capability's Books, the single most-requested topic for a book has been planning the traditional English border. Now that book exists. For those who have admired the English border, or domestic equivalents, this book describes 30 established borders including planting plans, diagrams, color photographs, bloom succession and all other information required to replicate some of England's most lovely plantings. Authors Mary Keen and Gemma Nesbitt make it clear that no border can be exactly duplicated; yet, with minimal adaptations for the American garden, their recommendations will take you as far as you need to go in producing a desired effect. A lovely book of practical use. 60 color plates, 160 pp., hardbound.

The Garden Border Book
#7127 **$27.50**

POACHER'S SPADE

We saw this tool on the Bulldog tool stand at the Chelsea Flower Show a few years ago and ordered it on the spot. It is the perfect spade for digging in the garden, especially around existing plantings. When we asked Ian Hall, the Bulldog export manager, what it was, he said it was originally a poacher's spade. Supposedly, farmers would walk the lord's estate at dusk, dog at bay, looking for rabbit holes. With a swift cut of the spade, the poacher would open up the warren, sending the dog in to flush out the game. All very illegal and clandestine. To redeem its dubious past, we offer it as an exquisitely balanced tool for all your planting needs. It is slightly dished, comes with an ash YD handle and the Bulldog stamp of quality and integrity. It works far better in the garden than it ever did in the field. Highly recommended. The head measures 5½" x 10½". Overall length: 36". Weight: 3 lbs. 1 oz.

Poacher's Spade
#5514 **$39.00**

GROWING A BUSINESS

Several years ago, when asked what my next book would be, the answer seemed easy. I would write a straightforward book about something I have experienced – growing a small business. That idea lay buried deep in my files whilst Smith & Hawken did the real thing – grow. Then, two years ago, I was approached by a PBS station about doing an eight-part series on the same subject. Destiny and writer's block met once again in my study. Today, the question addressed is seemingly more pertinent than ever.

How *do* you grow a business so that it works for the customers, the employees, the community and the founders? In this day of megamergers, hostile takeovers, greenmail and deteriorating service, the book attempts to show what common sense never forgot: taking care of people, whether they be customers or fellow workers, is darn good business. The book will be released in October and the PBS series of the same name will air November 1st across the country. The series features Patagonia, Esprit, Ben & Jerry's, University National Bank and several other businesses remarkable for their humaneness, quality and intelligence. Meanwhile, I promise to keep my hand off the pen and stick to taking care of my customers. Exception being if you want your book signed. That I will do shamelessly, with any inscription desired. 224 pp., hardbound. – *Paul Hawken*

Growing a Business #7156 **$15.95**

6

7

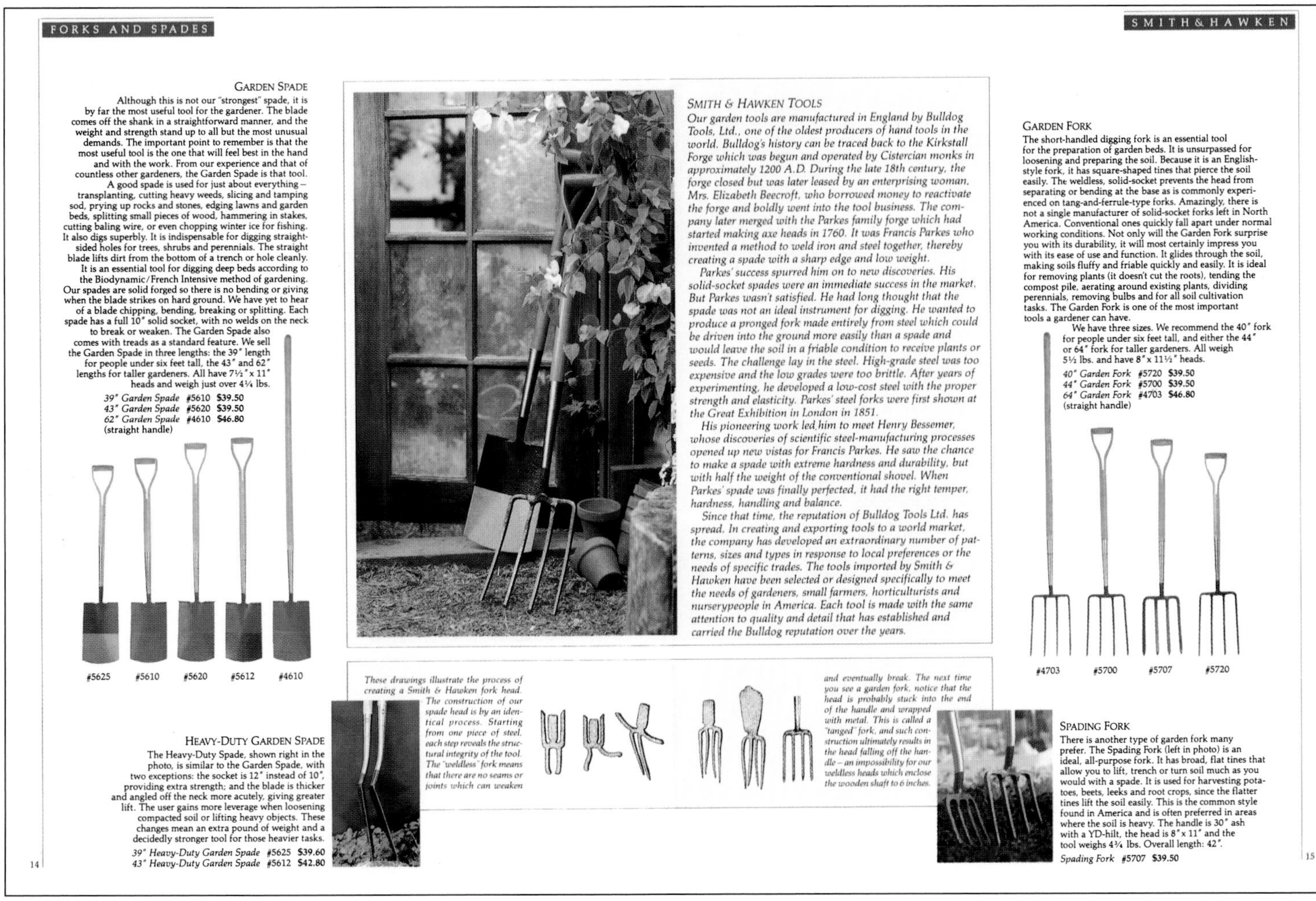

FORKS AND SPADES

SMITH & HAWKEN

GARDEN SPADE

Although this is not our "strongest" spade, it is by far the most useful tool for the gardener. The blade comes off the shank in a straightforward manner, and the weight and strength stand up to all but the most unusual demands. The important point to remember is that the most useful tool is the one that will feel best in the hand and with the work. From our experience and that of countless other gardeners, the Garden Spade is that tool.

A good spade is used for just about everything – transplanting, cutting heavy weeds, slicing and tamping sod, prying up rocks and stones, edging lawns and garden beds, splitting small pieces of wood, hammering in stakes, cutting baling wire, or even chopping winter ice for fishing. It also digs superbly. It is indispensable for digging straight-sided holes for trees, shrubs and perennials. The straight blade lifts dirt from the bottom of a trench or hole cleanly. It is an essential tool for digging deep beds according to the Biodynamic/French Intensive method of gardening. Our spades are solid forged so there is no bending or giving when the blade strikes on hard ground. We have yet to hear of a blade chipping, bending, breaking or splitting. Each spade has a full 10" solid socket, with no welds on the neck to break or weaken. The Garden Spade also comes with treads as a standard feature. We sell the Garden Spade in three lengths: the 39" length for people under six feet tall, the 43" and 62" lengths for taller gardeners. All have 7½" x 11" heads and weigh just over 4¼ lbs.

39" Garden Spade #5610 **$39.50**
43" Garden Spade #5620 **$39.50**
62" Garden Spade #4610 **$46.80**
(straight handle)

#5625 #5610 #5620 #5612 #4610

SMITH & HAWKEN TOOLS

Our garden tools are manufactured in England by Bulldog Tools, Ltd., one of the oldest producers of hand tools in the world. Bulldog's history can be traced back to the Kirkstall Forge which was begun and operated by Cistercian monks in approximately 1200 A.D. During the late 18th century, the forge closed but was later leased by an enterprising woman, Mrs. Elizabeth Beecroft, who borrowed money to reactivate the forge and boldly went into the tool business. The company later merged with the Parkes family forge which had started making axe heads in 1760. It was Francis Parkes who invented a method to weld iron and steel together, thereby creating a spade with a sharp edge and low weight.

Parkes' success spurred him on to new discoveries. His solid-socket spades were an immediate success in the market. But Parkes wasn't satisfied. He had long thought that the spade was not an ideal instrument for digging. He wanted to produce a pronged fork made entirely from steel which could be driven into the ground more easily than a spade and would leave the soil in a friable condition to receive plants or seeds. The challenge lay in the steel. High-grade steel was too expensive and the low grades were too brittle. After years of experimenting, he developed a low-cost steel with the proper strength and elasticity. Parkes' steel forks were first shown at the Great Exhibition in London in 1851.

His pioneering work led him to meet Henry Bessemer, whose discoveries of scientific steel-manufacturing processes opened up new vistas for Francis Parkes. He saw the chance to make a spade with extreme hardness and durability, but with half the weight of the conventional shovel. When Parkes' spade was finally perfected, it had the right temper, hardness, handling and balance.

Since that time, the reputation of Bulldog Tools Ltd. has spread. In creating and exporting tools to a world market, the company has developed an extraordinary number of patterns, sizes and types in response to local preferences or the needs of specific trades. The tools imported by Smith & Hawken have been selected or designed specifically to meet the needs of gardeners, small farmers, horticulturists and nurserypeople in America. Each tool is made with the same attention to quality and detail that has established and carried the Bulldog reputation over the years.

These drawings illustrate the process of creating a Smith & Hawken fork head. The construction of our spade head is by an identical process. Starting from one piece of steel, each step reveals the structural integrity of the tool. The "weldless" fork means that there are no seams or joints which can weaken and eventually break. The next time you see a garden fork, notice that the head is probably stuck into the end of the handle and wrapped with metal. This is called a "tanged" fork, and such construction ultimately results in the head falling off the handle – an impossibility for our weldless heads which enclose the wooden shaft to 6 inches.

GARDEN FORK

The short-handled digging fork is an essential tool for the preparation of garden beds. It is unsurpassed for loosening and preparing the soil. Because it is an English-style fork, it has square-shaped tines that pierce the soil easily. The weldless, solid-socket prevents the head from separating or bending at the base as is commonly experienced on tang-and-ferrule-type forks. Amazingly, there is not a single manufacturer of solid-socket forks left in North America. Conventional ones quickly fall apart under normal working conditions. Not only will the Garden Fork surprise you with its durability, it will most certainly impress you with its ease of use and function. It glides through the soil, making soils fluffy and friable quickly and easily. It is ideal for removing plants (it doesn't cut the roots), tending the compost pile, aerating around existing plants, dividing perennials, removing bulbs and for all soil cultivation tasks. The Garden Fork is one of the most important tools a gardener can have.

We have three sizes. We recommend the 40" fork for people under six feet tall, and either the 44" or 64" fork for taller gardeners. All weigh 5½ lbs. and have 8" x 11½" heads.

40" Garden Fork #5720 **$39.50**
44" Garden Fork #5700 **$39.50**
64" Garden Fork #4703 **$46.80**
(straight handle)

#4703 #5700 #5707 #5720

HEAVY-DUTY GARDEN SPADE

The Heavy-Duty Spade, shown right in the photo, is similar to the Garden Spade, with two exceptions: the socket is 12" instead of 10", providing extra strength; and the blade is thicker and angled off the neck more acutely, giving greater lift. The user gains more leverage when loosening compacted soil or lifting heavy objects. These changes mean an extra pound of weight and a decidedly stronger tool for those heavier tasks.

39" Heavy-Duty Garden Spade #5625 **$39.60**
43" Heavy-Duty Garden Spade #5612 **$42.80**

SPADING FORK

There is another type of garden fork many prefer. The Spading Fork (left in photo) is an ideal, all-purpose fork. It has broad, flat tines that allow you to lift, trench or turn soil much as you would with a spade. It is used for harvesting potatoes, beets, leeks and root crops, since the flatter tines lift the soil easily. This is the common style found in America and is often preferred in areas where the soil is heavy. The handle is 30" ash with a YD-hilt, the head is 8" x 11" and the tool weighs 4¾ lbs. Overall length: 42".

Spading Fork #5707 **$39.50**

14

15

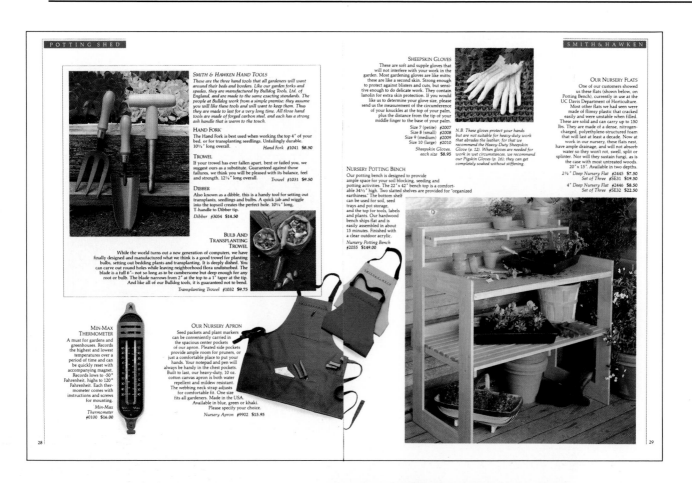

The range of merchandise offered in a Smith & Hawken catalog will satisfy the serious indoor and outdoor gardener, just as it will please the ''patio potato''. Where technical information is important, Smith & Hawken supplies a surfeit. Where mood is as important as manufacturing specifics, Smith & Hawken takes the opportunity to lighten up the copy, as in this example for a Courting Swing:

Did you ever sit in a wooden swing on a summer's eve under an elm and watch the fireflies? I never did either, but it sounds wonderful, and I think this is the swing to do it in. . . .

Or another example, on page 45, describing Wind Chimes:

They are tuned to a pentatonic scale with the precise harmonic intervals characteristic of the music of ancient Greece and China. According to Greek mythology, Orpheus raised stones with the song of his lyre. As useful as that would be in the garden, we can only say that the sound of these chimes is the most soothing you will ever hear. . . .

There is a vast distance between glib copywriting and the kind of wordsmithing that has grace, style *and* a powerful sales impact. The former is written by the dilettante who writes copiously, sees all the right plays and has great facility with words. The latter may or may not have all those attributes, but, as exemplified by the S&H copy, the writer has, without question, total knowledge of his product. Smith & Hawken offers us the opportunity to "pleasure our eyes" with beautiful layouts and photographs, inform ourselves by reading erudite, well-presented copy, and to buy products with the absolute assurance that we're buying the best available.

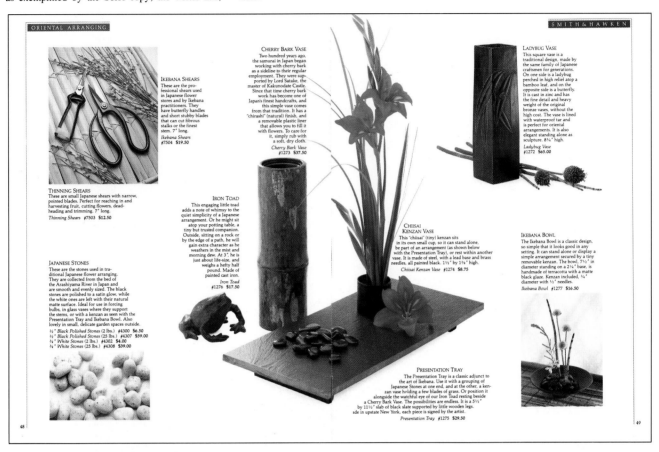

SPIEGEL

Today, Spiegel is the #1 mailorder house in the United States. And, quite deservedly, Spiegel has received more publicity and direct marketing accolades in the last 22 years than almost any other direct marketer. But these guys have been in the catalog business for a long time, why all the fuss now?

To find the answer, we have to spend a moment tracing Spiegel's history. The first store—Spiegel & Company, Fine and Durable Furniture—was opened by Joseph Spiegel in Chicago on April 30, 1865. The booming, roaring, meat-packing Midwest proved to be fertile ground for the rapidly expanding Spiegel business and family until 1893. Suddenly, the bitter sting of the United States' first modern depression reached Chicago, and for the next four years, expensive furniture was not high on the buy list of most households.

The Spiegel family business was forced to convert its inventory and style of operation from an absolute top-of-the-line furniture retailer to a company selling low priced, production-line borax. Wild and wooly days they were, when whore house madams were among the wealthiest customers, and switches and turnovers became the standard tools of the Spiegel salesmen's trade (poor Joe had absolute fits). Simultaneously, son Modie Spiegel convinced his father, and a number of other investors, that the new Spiegel's would have to sell everything on credit (more fits). The motto that would drive the growth of Spiegel for generations was born in those hard days: "We Trust The People".

Their time-payment customers were primarily working-class families with little or no credit history. But Modie Spiegel had an infallible instinct for separating the deadbeats from the good guys, and the family business prospered.

In 1905, Arthur Spiegel (Joseph's youngest son) bootstrapped his way into the mailorder business. We are told the family had no faith whatsoever in the prospects for this new enterprise. Nevertheless, as means of keeping this rather undisciplined, but energetic youngest son busy, they went along with his project. Arthur turned out to be a promotional genius. Although the family had restricted his early mailings and newspaper ads to a 100-mile radius in order to limit the damage they anticipated, Arthur's business boomed.

The secret to his runaway success was the slogan: "We Trust The People Everywhere". Arthur had extended the by-now standard Spiegel credit terms to his new mailorder customers. Spiegel historian, James Cornell, chronicled the precise offering:

Terms were clearly defined for each item: 15 percent down and 10 months to pay for the most expensive, a "genuine leather sofa bed" at $82.50; and 13 percent down and 10 months to pay for the least expensive, a "solid oak library case" at only $5.25. Customers could pay monthly installments of from 50 cents to $7.00 depending on the terms. . . . The outstanding bargain was the five-piece "Spiegel Special Parlor Suite," 2,180 pounds of parlor furniture for only $28.50.

Then the Roller Coaster ride began in earnest. By 1912, wearing apparel was introduced in the catalog, and Spiegel rapidly became a full line mailorder operation, with almost completely different inventory from the old furniture business.

SPIEGEL—1987 In Home
Richard Rosen, *Senior Divisional Advertising Manager*
Agency: *In-house*
Patt Parker, *Art Director*
Luta Ltd., *Designer*
Jan Donaldson, Sylvia Box and Elaine Kiner, *Copywriters*
Moebius Printing [Milwaukee, WI], *Printer*
Martinez & Rutter [Dallas, TX], *Color Separator*

—1987 Fall Collection
Richard Rosen, *Senior Divisional Advertising Manager*
Agency: *In-house*
David Brown, *Art Director*
Sleepeck Printing [Bellwood, IL], *Cover Printer*
Mels Litho Service, *Cover Color Separator*
R.R. Donnelley, Krueger Ringier, Inc. and Meredith Burda, *Body Printers and Color Separators*

Tragically, Arthur died of overwork and pneumonia at age 32. In spite of this loss, mailorder sales were soon dwarfing the old furniture business, and the direct response division was split off into a separate company. Not too incidentally, this separation also had the salutary effect of insulating the small family business from potential disaster. The Spiegel family wanted some form of legal insulation from the rapidly growing, heavily leveraged non-retail end of the business.

Out of the blue came another crash. World War I shortages and credit restrictions sent sales plunging, and the business shrunk to one-quarter of its former size. But after the War, the Roller Coaster zoomed upwards, and by 1929, shares of Spiegel stock were selling at an incredible $118. The onslaught of the Great Depression sent the stock crashing to a pitiful seven cents by 1932. Another rapid series of structural changes ensued, and 1937 saw the shares back to $120.

Once again, sales plunged as World War II cut revenues by half, from $42 million to $20 million, and net losses exceeded $2.4 million in a single year. (To put things in focus, National Bellas Hess, the third largest mailorder company in the land, went bankrupt during the same period.)

Several Spiegel stores were opened and rapidly closed. Chain store acquisitions were made in the 1940s; but by the '50s they too were gone. At its peak, the original business had mailorder sales of $300 million. But the 1960s saw the bloom disappear from the high credit, low-end RTW and home furnishings mailorder

Forerunner of Spiegel catalogs,
a brochure published by Joseph Spiegel

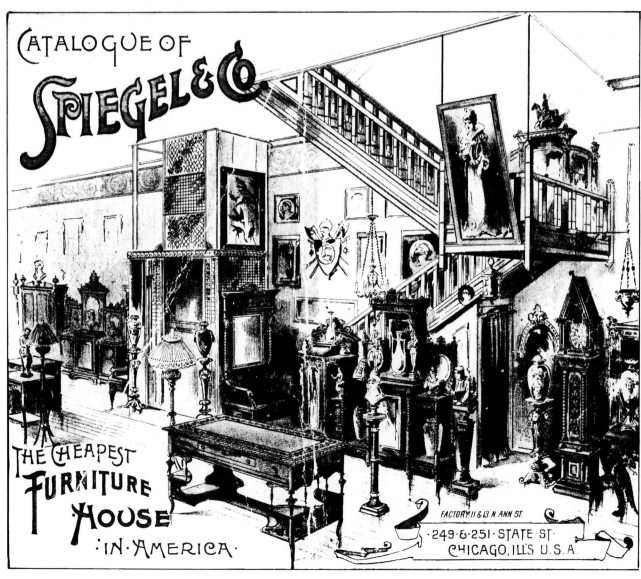

market. Profits started to slump. In 1965, the Spiegel family sold the business to Beneficial Life. At first glance this seemed an odd acquisition for an insurance giant, until one realized that interest income from charge accounts was the top (and sometimes the only) profit center in the company.

Unfortunately, under the new regime, profitability continued to slide—badly. By the mid 1970s, Spiegel was not very far from closing its doors forever. Just in the nick of time, a knight in shining armor by the name of Henry A. (Hank) Johnson appeared on the scene. Before coming to Spiegel, Hank Johnson had paid his dues in the mailorder game—in full! Right after World War II, he did a stint under the formidable Sewell Avery of Montgomery Ward. In 1949, Hank left Wards to start a 25-year career at the now defunct Aldens (known until 1946 as The Chicago Mail Order Company). During his tenure at Aldens, Hank completed his college undergraduate work, and went on to acquire his MBA from the prestigious University of Chicago—after he had seen the wrong side of age 40. Two years and two swift career changes saw Hank leaving his post as Executive Vice President, and second in command at Aldens, to join the new Avon Fashions by

Mail as CEO. A final move in 1976 found Hank Johnson ensconced as the new top gun at Spiegel. And that's when all the fun and excitement really got started.

Mr. Johnson and his associates faced the problem of restructuring a sick company; doing an annual volume of $300-million, selling a wide range of products, and losing their shirts. In one of the most daring moves ever made in the world of major corporations, Hank Johnson walked away from 500,000 of Spiegel's low income customers. He simply stopped mailing to them. He also got rid of all the budget merchandise they had been purchasing. As a part of the same drastic revolution, the stores were all closed, and today, with the exception of 10 outlet stores in Chicago (and 3 "For You" Large Size stores), Spiegel is a 100% mailorder operation.

With new buyers, new resources and new merchandise in place, the final challenge was the rebuilding and the restructuring of Spiegel's customer base. This gargantuan NCA effort was accomplished largely through the use of direct mail packages (the now-famous "Discover Spiegel" series), a targeted group of mini catalogs, and some ultra-sophisticated mailing list machinations.

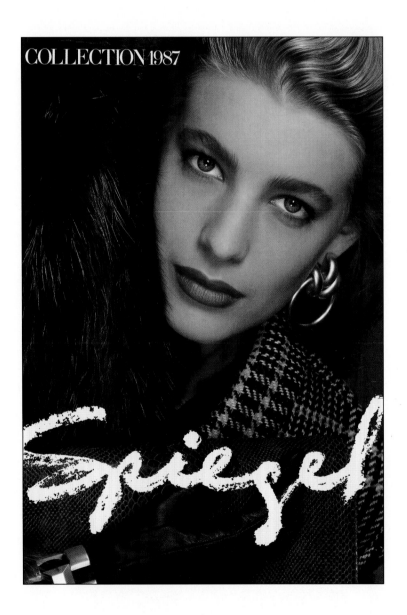

Spiegel's ECHO award winning "Fall Collection 1987" catalog is a big book in many ways. It measures 9″ X 13″, consists of 550 pages and weighs about 3 pounds. That's BIG! And it is a broadly merchandised book. It's exactly the kind of catalog a lot of direct response pundits refer to as dinosaurs. Why, then, is this Leviathan surviving and thriving? Certainly *not* because it has two front covers, and half the book is printed upside down. Perhaps a clue can be found in Spiegel's own words, as quoted in their ECHO Award Portfolio:

Program Objective: *To be Spiegel's single most important sales generating catalog in the 1987 Fall season. To strengthen the image of Spiegel as an upscale fashion authority.*
    Major Benefits: *This catalog serves as a window to the store, making assortments of merchandise available to a broad circulation so that specialty catalogs with in-depth, focused assortments can be circulated to an economically sufficient base. . . .*

Ah ha! "*. . . so that specialty catalogs with in-depth, focused assortments can be circulated. . .*". Why, for goodness sakes, Spiegel is prospecting with their monster master catalog! Aside from all its wonderful image-building qualities (and a whole lot of nice fat orders), this multi-line, multi-page mega-book functions as database fuel, an NCA tool!

The Spiegel woman is eclectic. She is half a dozen different kinds of city kids, and just as many grande dames. She runs a ranch in Colorado, an orchard in Washington, a restaurant in Reno, and a marina in Del Ray Beach. She has no kids, or a bunch. She may be 25 years wild or leaning on 60. She is not poor! (Her household income is around $50,000.) But she appreciates value. She is not an advance-fashion freak. She knows a designer name when she sees it, but is not impressed *unless* the quality is there and the look is for her.

Although designer names appear regularly on these pages, Spiegel's theme is, "Here's a look you'll love", *not* "If you don't dig this, drop dead." A glance at the following (and only partial) list of Spiegel vendors corroborates the depth of their interest in offering appropriate designer labels and upscale products.

Housewares and Home Furnishings

Liberty of London	Le Creuset
Laura Ashley	Mikasa
Bill Blass	Technics
Sheridan of Australia	Pioneer
Ralph Lauren	Fisher

Ready-To-Wear

Anne Klein	Alexander Julian
Willi Smith	Stanley Blacker
Calvin Klein	Bill Blass
Ralph Lauren	Burberry
Liz Claiborne	Pierre Cardin

There's RTW here for the world. Big or small, young or old, man or woman, city or country, East or West, you're covered!

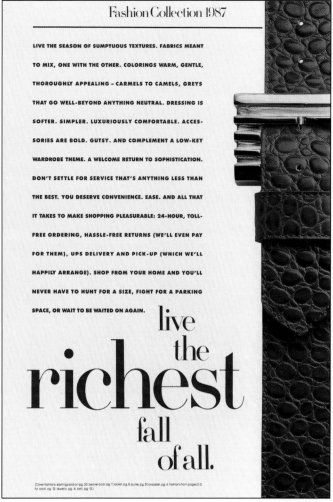

A. The American-type pheasants take flight across a red and green field of plaid. From Ralph Lauren. Cotton knit with a henley neck. Imported. (Also shown under "C.")
Misses: S(4-6); M(8-10); L(12-14).
A0450 0926—State size letter.
(1 lb. 10 oz.) 79.00

THE ROLL BAG. Rugged craftsmanship in Karatsu leather, naturally tanned (captain). From Polo Ralph Lauren Luggage Co. Front flap has brass hardware. Shoulder strap, one inside pocket. In Havana 3½"Wx11"Dx5¼"H.
N2650 5889—(1 lb. 4 oz.) 200.00
(Belt and boot sold at right.)

A. Continued
BRAIDED BELT, in Havana brown leather. From Polo Ralph Lauren Leather Goods. 1½" wide. (8 oz.)
Waists: 30", 32", 34". State size.
A2650 6226 .... 90.00

RIDING BOOT from Ralph Lauren. All leather with leather lining; strap-and-buckle detail at top and ankle. 1" heel. Saddle Brown.
B(Med.): 6, 6½, 7, 7½, 8, 8½, 9, 10.
T2050 3630—State size and 8.
(3 lbs. 8 oz.) 540.00

B. The plaid shirt. Recognizably Ralph Lauren, in a wine-multi print with one patch pocket. Brushed cotton, machine wash. Imported.
Misses: 4, 6, 8, 10, 12, 14.
A0450 0916—State size.
(1 lb. 14 oz.) 79.00

THE HUNTING SKIRT is encircled with a pheasant border print in rich, wine-colored wool challis. It's full, shirred, with side pockets, side button closure. From Ralph Lauren. Dry clean. Imported and made in USA. (Belt sold under A.)
Misses: 4, 6, 8, 10, 12, 14.
A0450 0917—State size.
(1 lb. 12 oz.) 259.00

C. The hunting influence redefines Ralph Lauren's denim dress. With a gun patch at shoulder and a long, straight shape. Pure cotton, in indigo or black. Machine wash. Made in USA. (Belt and T-shirt sold under A.)
Misses: 4, 6, 8, 10, 12, 14.
B0450 0924—Indigo blue
B0450 0925—Black
State color and size.
(2 lbs. 15 oz.) 99.00

D. Ralph Lauren's pheasant sweater. Earthy jewel tones in pure wool. Dropped shoulder. Navy/royal/purple plaid with pheasant print on front. Dry clean. Imported.
Misses: S(4-6); M(8-10); L(12-14).
A0450 0918—State size letter.
(1 lb. 13 oz.) 258.00

CHAMBRAY WORKSHIRT from Ralph Lauren. Long sleeves; chest pockets. Machine wash. Blue. Made in USA.
Misses sizes: 4, 6, 8, 10, 12, 14.
A0450 0919—State size.
(2 lbs.) 59.00

THE SKIRT in stone-colored "Roughout" (light nap) suede. Long and slim with a button front, side pockets. Leather clean. Imported. (Boots sold under A.)
Misses: 4, 6, 8, 10, 12, 14.
A0450 0920—State size.
(3 lbs. 5 oz.) 198.00

An American Autumn. Expressed with elegance and grace.

Ralph Lauren

AMERICAN weekend

Through all the fads, you found the American classics that stand the test of time.

A-B. GREAT VALUES ON LEVI'S® DENIMS! Longtime American favorites, a new whitewash finishing process makes them as faded and comfortable as those you've washed 100 times. Imagine how comfortable they'll be in a few months! Cotton denim, machine wash.

[A] LEVI'S JEAN JACKET is slightly oversized with dropped shoulders, 2 side slash pockets. Unlined. Button front with 2 flap chest pockets. Navy. Made in USA.
Chests: S(36-38); M(40-42); L(44-46); XL(48-50). State size letter.
A4750 6660—(2 lbs. 10 oz.) 49.90

[B] LEVI'S JEANS have 5-pocket, straight leg styling. Made in USA and imported.
Waists: 28, 29, 30, 31, 32, 33, 34, 35, 36
Inseams: 30, 32, 34.
State color, waist, and inseam; specify waist.
W4750 6643—Navy (on model).
W4750 6492—Gray.
W4750 6588—Black.
W4750 6493—Black. (2 lbs. 2 oz.) ... 32.90

BRAIDED BELT. 1" wide leather with solid brass buckle. Made in USA.
Waists: 30, 32, 34, 36, 38, 40
B4250 1197—Tan
B4250 1199—Black
B4250 1199—Brown (13 oz.)
State color, size. 22.00

C. Oakbrook® shaker sweaters, at a stock-up price. Colorful ramie/cotton with raglan sleeves, ribbed cuffs, neck and waist. Hand wash. Imported.
Chests: S(34-36); M(38-40); L(42-44); XL(46).
B4250 3037—Red. B4250 3032—Natural.
B4250 3033—Blue. B4250 3034—Gold.
B4250 3035—Teal Green.
B4250 3036—Black (not shown).
State color, size letter. (2 lbs.) 29.90

SAVE 25% ON 3 PAIRS. Oakbrook crew socks in sporting colors. Cotton/nylon. Made in USA. Fits sizes 10-13.
C4050 1900—Bright Yellow.
C4050 1901—Royal Blue. C4050 1902—Red.
C4050 1903—Black.
C4050 1904—White (not shown).
State color. (12 oz. each) Pr. 6.00 ... 3 Pr. for 13.50

D. Oakbrook striped cotton twill shirts are overdyed and garment washed for extra softness and even deeper color. Slightly oversized. Machine wash. Imported.
Necks: S(14-14½); M(15-15½); L(16-16½); XL(17-17½).
B4750 6421—Natural. B4750 6423—Green.
B4750 6419—Red. B4750 6422—Blue.
B4750 6420—Gold.
State color, size letter. (1 lb. 4 oz.) 30.00

E. ANY TWO HENLEYS, $15 OFF. Try all these great colors on their own or under your shirt. From Oakbrook, with dropped shoulders and front placket. Ribbed cuffs. Cotton knit. Machine wash. Made in USA or imported.
Chests: S(34-36); M(38-40); L(42-44); XL(46).
B4250 3018—Gray. B4250 3015—Med. Blue.
B4250 3016—Yellow. B4250 3017—Red.
B4250 3014—Plum.
State color, size letter.
(1 lb. 5 oz.) Each 30.00 .... Any 2 for 45.00

F. The "Cambridge" boot by Frye. All leather with plain toe and 14" shaft. Pull rings inside shaft. 1¼" stacked leather heel with rubber lift. Delivered from mfr.; allow 28 days plus transit.
D(Med.): 7, 7½, 8, 8½, 9, 9½, 10, 10½, 11, 11½, 12, 13.
W4950 3572T—Burnt Cherry.
W4950 3576T—Black (not shown).
State color, size. D. (4 lbs. 6 oz.) 150.00

On the flip side of Spiegel's ''Big Book'' is the 252-page Home Collection, with its definite torque towards the traditional. But, designs for more modern life-styles are not neglected. In this issue, they are well served in an inspired 20-page section on the themes ''Absolute White'', ''Absolute White Plus Pastels'', ''Absolute White Plus Black'', and a series of pages headlined ''Absolute Options'' (lamps and accessories). This book-within-a-book moves the reader through a series of very attractive contemporary and eclectic decorating schemes. The muse of mod is truly awakened when we arrive at the kitchen. Here, we find merchandise and interiors reminiscent of designs all the way from the Museum of Modern Art's Bauhaus collection to Impressionistic paintings of the Montana mesas.

The Spiegel catalog sells more than 70 major merchandise classifications (Department Codes). For marketing purposes, these 70 categories have been simplified to 20 discrete, product-related clusters. In addition, buying patterns, payment history and method of payment (bank, T/E card, Spiegel charge or cash) are retained on each customer record. Using this information, and a number of proprietary filters, Spiegel can manipulate their 5-million name list of active buyers with pinpoint accuracy.

Home Collection 1987

LIVE THE NEW STANDARD OF LUXURY. WALK WITH US ON OUR ''HOUSE TOUR'' – THE FIRST IN ANY CATALOG – WHERE FALL IS A LOVE AFFAIR WITH QUALITY. FROM THE WARMTH OF TRADITIONAL TO THE COMFORT OF COUNTRY TO A NEW ANGLE ON CONTEMPORARY ''WHITES'', OURS IS A BELIEF IN STYLE THAT ENDURES. DON'T SETTLE FOR SERVICE THAT'S ANYTHING LESS THAN THE BEST. YOU DESERVE CONVENIENCE. AND EASE. AND ALL THAT IT TAKES TO MAKE SHOPPING PLEASURABLE: 24-HOUR, TOLL-FREE ORDERING, HASSLE–FREE RETURNS (WE'LL EVEN PAY FOR THEM), UPS DELIVERY AND PICK-UP (WHICH WE'LL HAPPILY ARRANGE). SHOP FOR YOUR HOME IN YOUR HOME. YOU'LL NEVER HAVE TO WALK FROM SHOWROOM TO SHOWROOM, BEG FOR PRODUCT INFORMATION, OR WAIT TO BE WAITED ON AGAIN.

live the richest fall of all.

A. VALUE: LEATHER SOFA. Our luxurious furniture brings you the supple comfort of the finest grain leather at an affordable price. Imagine, a leather sofa under $1,000. All pieces have durable kiln dried hardwood frames that have urethane padding covered with Dacron® polyester. Bone color leather is given a glove soft finish. Brass nailhead trim. Chair and ottoman have exposed cherry-stained legs. Freight delivered from mfr: add 30 days to standard transit.
CHESTERFIELD SOFA is 28"Wx32"Dx29"H.
N6050 9100F —Plus $100 delivery†. 999.00
WING CHAIR is 34"Wx33"Dx41"H.
N6050 9101F—Plus $55 delivery.† 799.00
OTTOMAN is 26"Wx23"Dx16"H.
N6050 9102F—Plus $35 delivery † 399.00
CHAISE LONGUE (not shown) is 70"Wx32"Dx29"H.
N6050 9103F—Plus $100 delivery † 999.00

SEND FOR SWATCHES: This leather furniture is available in additional colors. For free swatches, write Spiegel Swatching Service, P.O. Box 1369, 1739 Kiwett Drive, High Pt NC 27261. State catalog number for item(s) for which you want swatches.

B. Heirman's executive desk offers 18th century design that has been recalled for contemporary aesthetics. Mahogany solids and veneers are accented with inlays of swirl mahogany and burl. The warm mahogany finish gives it an antiqued patina. Features carved cabriole legs with ball and claw feet and crotch mahogany drawer fronts. Dark brown leather top has gold-color tooling. Four drawers, (one a file drawer): center drawer has lock and key. Freight delivered from mfr: add 30 days to standard transit. 58"Wx29"Dx30"H.
N6150 8475F —Plus $100 delivery † 999.00

C. Our carved bookcases have arched pediments that are a strong neo-classic element. Yet the breakfront 2-piece design is traditionally of 18th century origin. One case affords you distinctive display: two (as we show) or more build an impressive library. Northern white pine solids and veneers wear a dark pine finish. Base has 2 adjustable wood shelves (20½"Wx12½"D). Upper deck has 6 adjustable wood shelves. Intricate wood carvings accent the top of each fluted post. Doweled, glued and mortised/tenoned joints. Freight delivered from mfr: in 2 cartons, some assembly required. Add 45 days to standard transit. 60"Wx17"Dx85"H.
N6150 8399F —Plus $150 delivery † . . . . . System 1199.00

D. This classic Kermanshah-style rug brings palatial richness to your room. Plush ½" deep pile of worsted wool ensures lasting resilience. Sizes include handknotted fringe. Dry clean. Woven of multi colors. Imported. Delivered from importer: allow 30 days plus transit. State size when ordering.
A6750 3688T—47x72". (12 lbs.) 249.00
A6750 3691T—26x108". (14 lbs.) 249.00
A6750 3689T—5'7"x8'4". (21 lbs.) 449.00
8'1"x11'4"L. Freight delivered
A6750 3690F—Plus $70 delivery † 599.00

E. What better companion in the study than a faithful dog? For this exclusive design, we've brought 3 together to form an unusual table base. Each dog is cast of brass, using the lost wax mold method for exact detailing. Black finish is hand-applied. 30" round glass top is ½"-thick, with clear polished edge. Base is 19"Wx19"Dx16"H. Freight delivered.
N6650 2641T—(25 lbs.) 399.00

F. SAVE 20%. Form is just as important as function in this striking solid brass lamp from Frederick Cooper. Each lamp is expertly handcrafted. The tent shade notches, counterweight arm offers easy adjustment of height. (35½" to 62"). On/off dimmer switch, uses 60W max. bulb (not included). 110-120V. AC. UL listed.
N6650 2541T—(25 lbs.) . . . . Reg. $299 239.00

†Allow 2–3 weeks transit. For delivery to Alaska or Hawaii, see page 564.

A Leather furniture
B Desk
C Bookcases
D Rug
E Accent table
F Floor lamp

RICH IN TRADITION: GENTLEMEN'S STUDY

Rush hour is over. You crave a little comfort...the kind you'd find in a gentlemen's club. Even if you can't devote a whole room to this look, our creamy leather sofa is an oasis in itself—and a wonderfully contemporary side of tradition.

308 •

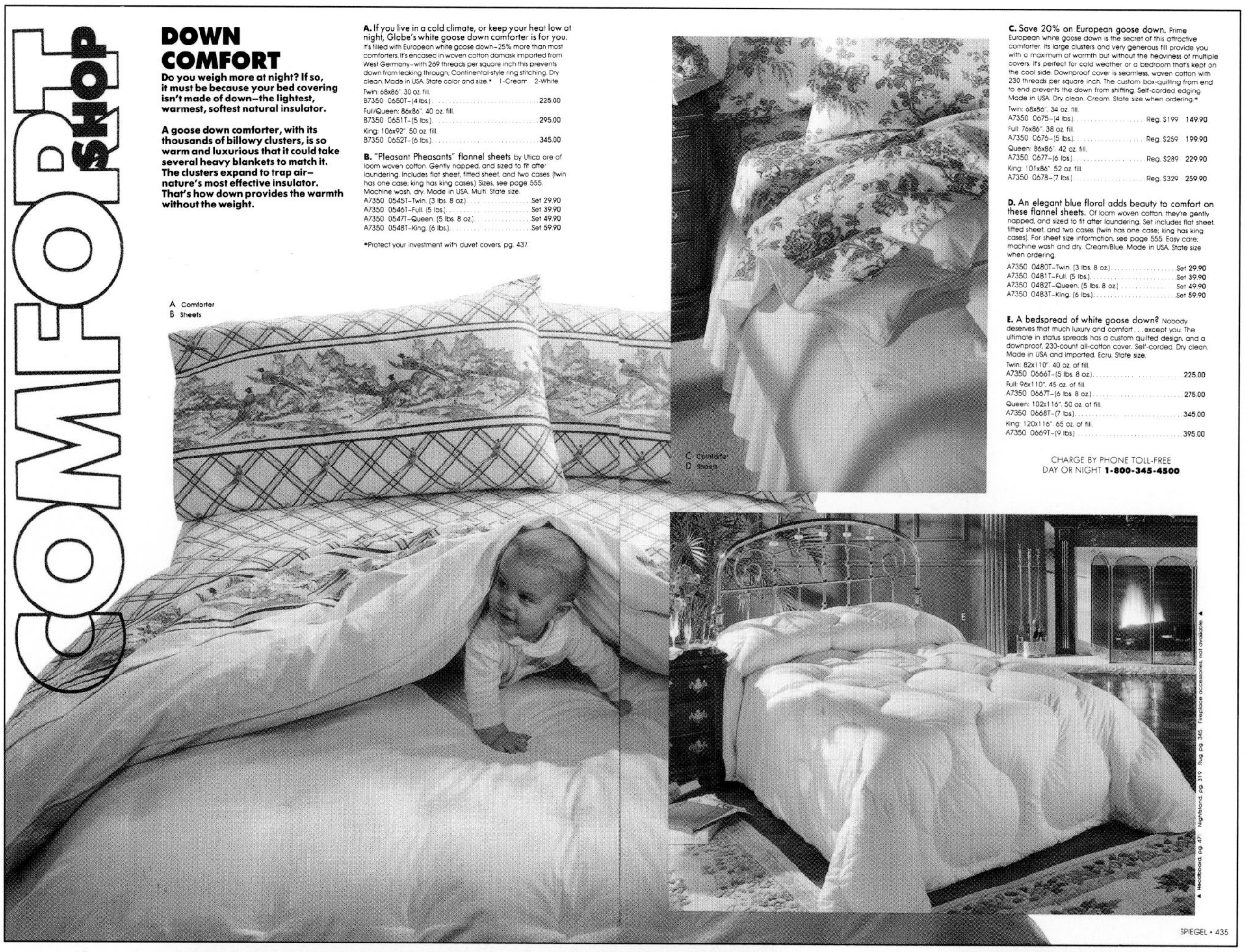

COMFORT SHOP

DOWN COMFORT

Do you weigh more at night? If so, it must be because your bed covering isn't made of down—the lightest, warmest, softest natural insulator.

A goose down comforter, with its thousands of billowy clusters, is so warm and luxurious that it could take several heavy blankets to match it. The clusters expand to trap air—nature's most effective insulator. That's how down provides the warmth without the weight.

A. If you live in a cold climate, or keep your heat low at night, Globe's white goose down comforter is for you. It's filled with European white goose down—25% more than most comforters. It's encased in woven cotton damask imported from West Germany—with 269 threads per square inch this prevents down from leaking through; Continental-style ring stitching. Dry clean. Made in USA. State color and size.* 1-Cream 2-White

Twin: 68x86". 30 oz. fill.
B7350 0650T–(4 lbs.) 225.00
Full/Queen: 86x86". 40 oz. fill.
B7350 0651T–(5 lbs.) 295.00
King: 106x92". 50 oz. fill.
B7350 0652T–(6 lbs.) 345.00

B. "Pleasant Pheasants" flannel sheets by Utica are of loom woven cotton. Gently napped, and sized to fit after laundering. Includes flat sheet, fitted sheet, and two cases (twin has one case; king has king cases.) Sizes, see page 555. Machine wash, dry. Made in USA. Multi. State size.
A7350 0545T–Twin. (3 lbs. 8 oz.) .... Set 29.90
A7350 0546T–Full. (5 lbs.) .... Set 39.90
A7350 0547T–Queen. (5 lbs. 8 oz.) .... Set 49.90
A7350 0548T–King. (6 lbs.) .... Set 59.90

*Protect your investment with duvet covers, pg. 437.

A Comforter
B Sheets

C Comforter
D Sheets

C. Save 20% on European goose down. Prime European white goose down is the secret of this attractive comforter. Its large clusters and very generous fill provide you with a maximum of warmth but without the heaviness of multiple covers. It's perfect for cold weather or a bedroom that's kept on the cool side. Downproof cover is seamless, woven cotton with 230 threads per square inch. The custom box-quilting from end to end prevents the down from shifting. Self-corded edging. Made in USA. Dry clean. Cream. State size when ordering.*

Twin: 68x86". 34 oz. fill.
A7350 0675–(4 lbs.) .... Reg. $199 149.90
Full: 76x86". 38 oz. fill.
A7350 0676–(5 lbs.) .... Reg. $259 199.90
Queen: 86x86". 42 oz. fill.
A7350 0677–(6 lbs.) .... Reg. $289 229.90
King: 101x86". 52 oz. fill.
A7350 0678–(7 lbs.) .... Reg. $329 259.90

D. An elegant blue floral adds beauty to comfort on these flannel sheets. Of loom woven cotton, they're gently napped, and sized to fit after laundering. Set includes flat sheet, fitted sheet, and two cases (twin has one case; king has king cases). For sheet size information, see page 555. Easy care; machine wash and dry. Cream/Blue. Made in USA. State size when ordering.

A7350 0480T–Twin. (3 lbs. 8 oz.) .... Set 29.90
A7350 0481T–Full. (5 lbs.) .... Set 39.90
A7350 0482T–Queen. (5 lbs. 8 oz.) .... Set 49.90
A7350 0483T–King. (6 lbs.) .... Set 59.90

E. A bedspread of white goose down? Nobody deserves that much luxury and comfort . . . except you. The ultimate in status spreads has a custom quilted design, and a downproof, 230-count all-cotton cover. Self-corded. Dry clean. Made in USA and imported. Ecru. State size.

Twin: 82x110". 40 oz. of fill.
A7350 0666T–(5 lbs. 8 oz.) 225.00
Full: 96x110". 45 oz. of fill.
A7350 0667T–(6 lbs. 8 oz.) 275.00
Queen: 102x116". 50 oz. of fill.
A7350 0668T–(7 lbs.) 345.00
King: 120x116". 65 oz. of fill.
A7350 0669T–(9 lbs.) 395.00

CHARGE BY PHONE TOLL-FREE
DAY OR NIGHT **1-800-345-4500**

SPIEGEL • 435

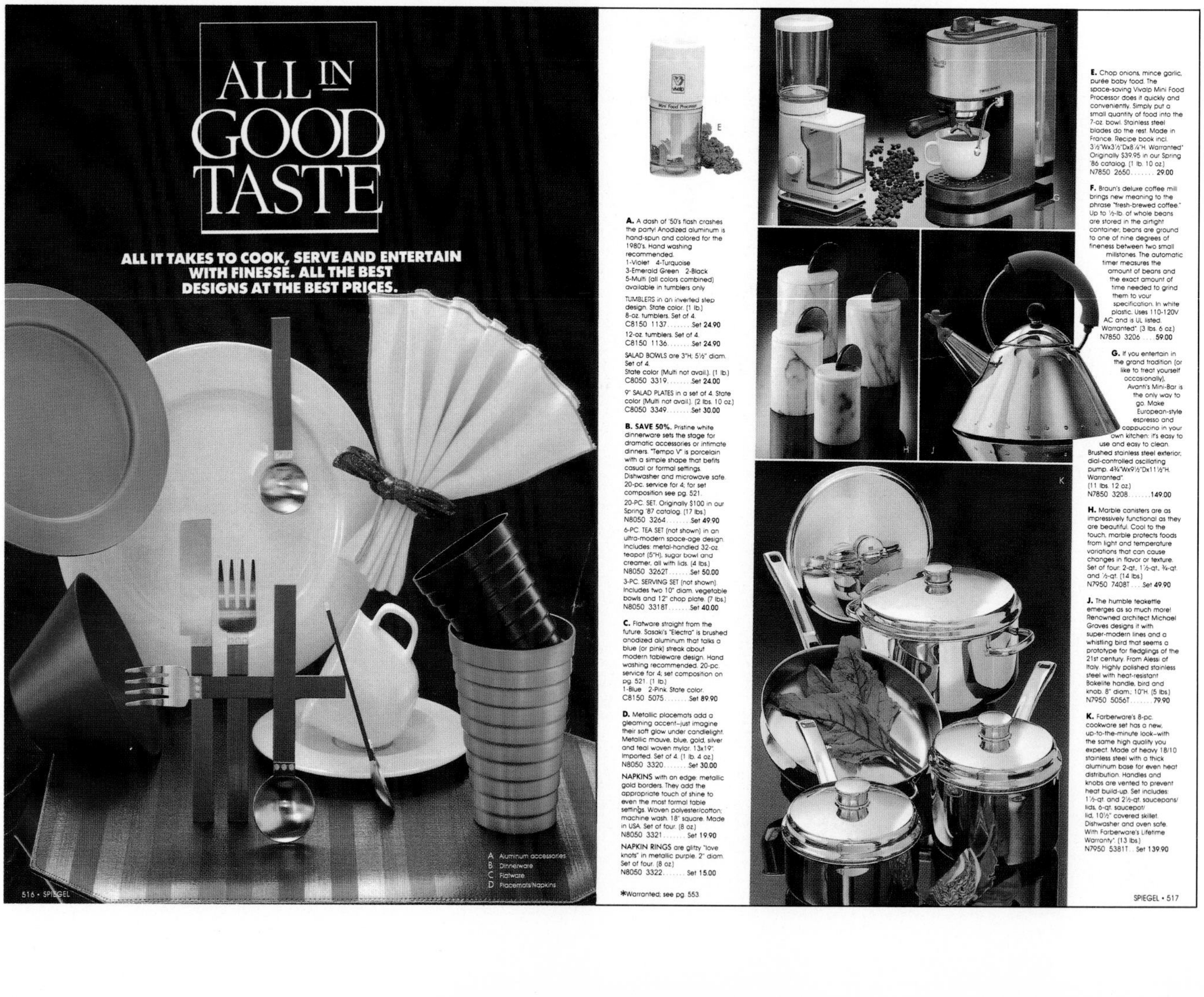

ALL IN GOOD TASTE

ALL IT TAKES TO COOK, SERVE AND ENTERTAIN WITH FINESSE. ALL THE BEST DESIGNS AT THE BEST PRICES.

A Aluminum accessories
B Dinnerware
C Flatware
D Placemats/Napkins

516 • SPIEGEL

A. A dash of '50's flash crashes the party! Anodized aluminum is hand-spun and colored for the 1980's. Hand washing recommended.
1-Violet 4-Turquoise
3-Emerald Green 2-Black
5-Multi (all colors combined) available in tumblers only

TUMBLERS in an inverted step design. State color. (1 lb.)
8-oz. tumblers. Set of 4.
C8150 1137 .... Set 24.90
12-oz. tumblers. Set of 4.
C8150 1136 .... Set 24.90

SALAD BOWLS are 3"H; 5½" diam. Set of 4.
State color (Multi not avail.). (1 lb.)
C8050 3319 .... Set 24.00

9" SALAD PLATES in a set of 4. State color (Multi not avail.). (2 lbs. 10 oz.)
C8050 3349 .... Set 30.00

B. SAVE 50%. Pristine white dinnerware sets the stage for dramatic accessories or intimate dinners. "Tempo V" is porcelain with a simple shape that befits casual or formal settings. Dishwasher and microwave safe. 20-pc. service for 4; for set composition see pg. 521.

20-PC. SET. Originally $100 in our Spring '87 catalog. (17 lbs.)
N8050 3264 .... Set 49.90

6-PC. TEA SET (not shown) in an ultra-modern space-age design. Includes: metal-handled 32-oz. teapot (5"H), sugar bowl and creamer, all with lids. (4 lbs.)
N8050 3262T .... Set 50.00

3-PC. SERVING SET (not shown). Includes two 10" diam. vegetable bowls and 12" chop plate. (7 lbs.)
N8050 3318T .... Set 40.00

C. Flatware straight from the future. Sasaki's "Electra" is brushed anodized aluminum that talks a blue (or pink) streak about modern tableware design. Hand washing recommended. 20-pc. service for 4; set composition on pg. 521. (1 lb.)
1-Blue 2-Pink. State color.
C8150 5075 .... Set 89.90

D. Metallic placemats add a gleaming accent—just imagine their soft glow under candlelight. Metallic mauve, blue, gold, silver and teal woven mylar. 13x19". Imported. Set of 4. (1 lb. 4 oz.)
N8050 3320 .... Set 30.00

NAPKINS with an edge: metallic gold borders. They add the appropriate touch of shine to even the most formal table settings. Woven polyester/cotton; machine wash. 18" square. Made in USA. Set of four. (8 oz.)
N8050 3321 .... Set 19.90

NAPKIN RINGS are glitzy "love knots" in metallic purple. 2" diam. Set of four. (8 oz.)
N8050 3322 .... Set 15.00

*Warranted; see pg. 553

E. Chop onions, mince garlic, purée baby food. The space-saving Vivalp Mini Food Processor does it quickly and conveniently. Simply put a small quantity of food into the 7-oz. bowl. Stainless steel blades do the rest. Made in France. Recipe book incl. 3½"Wx3½"Dx8¼"H. Warranted* Originally $39.95 in our Spring '86 catalog. (1 lb. 10 oz.)
N7850 2650 .... 29.00

F. Braun's deluxe coffee mill brings new meaning to the phrase "fresh-brewed coffee." Up to ½-lb. of whole beans are stored in the airtight container; beans are ground to one of nine degrees of fineness between two small millstones. The automatic timer measures the amount of beans and the exact amount of time needed to grind them to your specification. In white plastic. Uses 110-120V AC and is UL listed. Warranted*. (3 lbs. 6 oz.)
N7850 3206 .... 59.00

G. If you entertain in the grand tradition (or like to treat yourself occasionally), Avanti's Mini-Bar is the only way to go. Make European-style espresso and cappuccino in your own kitchen: it's easy to use and easy to clean. Brushed stainless steel exterior; dial-controlled oscillating pump. 4¾"Wx9½"Dx11½"H. Warranted*. (11 lbs. 12 oz.)
N7850 3208 .... 149.00

H. Marble canisters are as impressively functional as they are beautiful. Cool to the touch, marble protects foods from light and temperature variations that can cause changes in flavor or texture. Set of four: 2-qt., 1½-qt., ¾-qt. and ½-qt. (14 lbs.)
N7950 7408T .... Set 49.90

J. The humble teakettle emerges as so much more! Renowned architect Michael Graves designs it with super-modern lines and a whistling bird that seems a prototype for fledglings of the 21st century. From Alessi of Italy. Highly polished stainless steel with heat-resistant Bakelite handle, bird and knob. 8" diam.; 10"H. (5 lbs.)
N7950 5056T 79.90

K. Farberware's 8-pc. cookware set has a new, up-to-the-minute look—with the same high quality you expect. Made of heavy 18/10 stainless steel with a thick aluminum base for even heat distribution. Handles and knobs are vented to prevent heat build-up. Set includes: 1½-qt. and 2½-qt. saucepans/lids, 6-qt. saucepot/lid, 10½" covered skillet. Dishwasher and oven safe. With Farberware's Lifetime Warranty*. (13 lbs.)
N7950 5381T .... Set 139.90

SPIEGEL • 517

The Fall 1987 "In Home" Catalog is another of Spiegel's Echo Award winners. It had its genesis early in the reconstruction process. The launch came when Spiegel executives were able to identify a large enough group of home-oriented customers on the Spiegel data base to warrant publishing a targeted catalog. This 11″ x 12″ spectacular showcases an informal, eclectic assortment of household merchandise, with price tags ranging from the moderate to more than $1,000.

There's a consistent psychographic skew to this book. The target audience may be individuals living in a Greenwich Village garret, a New Orleans row house, a Wyoming ranch, a villa in Katmandu or a terraced duplex in Breckenridge. Yet, no matter how geographically dispersed they may be, and whichever decor or period is favored, these people all share a similar attitude as regards the motif of their home. The furniture and accessories are different, but the casual, almost cluttered manner in which they are arrayed around the room, is universal.

The Wizards of Spiegel react to the wants of various sectors of their market, as do all good catalogers. But, at the same time, they manage to portray just the right tilt towards an authoritative advance fashion image. This leadership, in both the home fashions and RTW areas, keeps their customers on their toes; and leaning just a little more forward than is their normal wont.

The Marcus family of Texas used these techniques. The Nordstrom family in Washington is currently using them. In these cases, however, one has the feeling that there was a good deal of instinctual marketing at work (based, as usual, upon decades of instruction and experience). At Spiegel, one suspects that, in addition to instinct, more sophisticated database-driven forces are at work.

Direct response marketers dance to a tune called by their customers. But it's difficult to dance on jello—particularly when the party is aboard ship in a gale. Here we have, on the one hand, a highly variable and varied customer base, rapidly changing tastes and styles, and ambient political and economic conditions that are increasingly difficult to forecast (particularly as relates to currency valuations, which have a mighty influence on heavy-duty importers such as Spiegel).

And, on the other hand, we have a customer data base that numbers over five million, a company selling over a *billion* dollars' worth of merchandise. (Imagine the commitments that have to be made months—even years—in advance.) So there you are, in a moving ballroom with a band that constantly changes tempo, trying to dance with five million partners at once on a floor that has the viscosity of warm gelatin!

Is this marketing dipsy-doodle, this corporate dance possible? And, if possible, is it working for Spiegel? Remember the "Program Objectives" and "Major Benefits" that were described on Spiegel's Echo entry? Well, the last question asked on that form is "Results". In that space, Spiegel tells us:

In its third season, the Spiegel In Home catalog is generating sales far beyond planned expectations. Orders [and] response rates are climbing as we continue to build our entire Home Store business. (Because of corporate policy, absolute numbers cannot be provided.)

Among the numbers that *have* been published by Spiegel are those concerning their average order:

* *Spiegel's overall average order is well over $100.*
* *In the Home Store business, the average order is a very enviable $200.*
* *90% of their customers pay with a credit card!*
* *65% are multi-buyers (i.e., regular customers)*

In addition to these exceptional results, Spiegel has recently acquired Eddie Bauer and Honeybee, two widely respected, yet completely different, catalog operations. Another 1988 acquisition was the Cara Corporation. Cara's business is writing computer software. With such in-house computer programming capability, one certainly gets the impression that canned, off-the-shelf marketing programs or static merchandising and fulfillment methods are not in the cards for the Spiegel team. Spiegel's current CEO, Jack Shea, is certainly to be congratulated for picking up Hank Johnson's baton and for his progressive orchestration of this leading edge corporation.

EPILOGUE

As you've seen, catalogs come in all kinds of shapes and sizes. Some are copy-heavy, some are artsy-craftsy. Some present an almost overwhelming amount of product, while others spend two or more pages describing a single item. Some catalog programs call for 40 or more books per year, others only mail once each year.

In other words, there are no set rules.

The form and content of a catalog depend upon its function. Retail store catalogs generate excitement and store traffic *now*. Incentive catalogs must have a long coffee table life. Business to business catalogs have cycles that reflect the buying patterns of their industries and contents that abets the sales mechanism of the publisher. And, of course, mailorder catalogs are virtually stand-alone salesmen.

The design, copy length and style, art treatments and marketing system behind a catalog will vary with the objectives and targeted markets of the catalog's sponsor. In each industry, there are some fairly stringent design elements that can be ignored only at great risk. On the other hand, a ''me too'' catalog can be the kiss of death. The righteous path is a highly individualistic catalog that follows the basic rules.

That's a tough challenge, but it is one that has been met and overcome by the long-term players in the field.

Is there any room left for another mailorder catalog? You bet! Granted, it's much simpler and generally less costly to open a store, but catalogs can do things that stores cannot.

- *Catalogs allow you to focus on a very limited number of products, or in a category in which you have great expertise.*
- *They permit you to grow a business without the management and real estate problems associated with operating a chain of stores.*
- *Catalogs can efficiently reach individual consumers spread over wide geographic areas (retail stores need concentrations of customers).*

How then does one decide which road to take, the store or the mailorder route? The answer may be both. If your market is thin, or if your product line is short, the catalog may be the better first step. If the reverse is true, then try the store first.

When you have both catalog and stores, the synergy commences. The catalog drives store traffic, and the stores give credence to the catalog while, at the same time providing outlets for overstocks. But be aware that while kitchen table mailorder start-ups may sound romantic, they are pretty much a thing of the past. Costs have risen astronomically, and running even a small time mailorder business is a full time job.

It takes a great deal of time and money to build a customer base large enough to reach profitable economies of scale. Once you've spent the time and money to build that foundation of good solid customers, you will need a constant flow of fresh and different items to keep the orders coming.

Not surprisingly, this is why existing businesses have significant advantages over start-ups when a mailorder catalog launch is contemplated. In addition, they have their G&A functions, professional level product knowledge, plus the all-important resources and remainders channels already in place.

But there are traps for these guys, too. Catalog marketing methods, customer service functions and inventory management systems are totally different from any other business. Mailorder (or more accurately, Direct Response) specialists have to be brought in, either on-staff or in the form of consultants, to keep newcomers from making old mistakes.

In this respect, general purpose advertising agencies are of little help. As a matter of fact, they can and do destroy many budding catalog programs. Most advertising generalists do not understand the medium, the long and short range marketing objectives or the very unique performance yardsticks associated with a well-rounded mailorder operation.

Lacking a true understanding of the business, a poorly planned program will inevitably produce a flop. Usually, the individuals involved, on both the client and agency side, mutually agree that ''mailorder is not for us''. The budding endeavor is cut off without ever having had a real chance of success. In some cases, the decision to quit may be correct on a personal basis, but wrong with respect to the client's best interests.

Direct Marketing agencies are in a far better position to understand at least the marketing objectives, but their overhead burden and markup schedules usually pump up the catalog production budget far beyond permissible cost per square inch.

A combination that has worked for many catalog merchants is a three-part team made up of a direct marketing consultant (or an in-house group of direct response pros), a direct marketing agency to handle media other than the catalog, and a catalog agency.

The direct marketing consultant brings breadth of experience to a project to which very few insiders are likely to have been exposed. What's more, his or her concerns are bottom line oriented, for instance:

- *What are our NCA costs and what is the future value of the newly acquired customer?*
- *What is the mailorder viability of each item we're selling, what are the margins, how many turns can we forecast— ergo, how much space and production cost can we afford to dedicate to that item?*
- *What overall creative approach is correct for this market and what corporate image do we wish to create? (Clients often want to look like ''Brooks Brothers'', when a ''Wallachs'' image would do a much better job.)*

- *He or she will be very concerned with the customer service module and the fulfillment systems. In some cases, s/he will be of great assistance in product line development and sourcing.*

Consultants come in many sizes and shapes, just like their clients. Some come from the artist's side of catalog production, others from the copy side. There are consultants with heavy merchandising experience and others with outstanding expertise in fulfillment. In the best of all possible worlds, you will find a consultant whose knowledge fills existing gaps in your own organization. In addition, you might try to find a consultant whose ego will permit him or her to recommend, and work with, other consultants in highly specialized fields such as fulfillment, telemarketing, legal and finance.

Full-fledged catalog agencies are rare birds. They all play in the big leagues, but their production engines are so efficient that they can also be invaluable to smaller catalog houses. They buy paper, printing and separations at prices well below those offered to the smaller catalog buyer. High-tech equipment and systems, prohibitively expensive to set up and man on an in-house basis, are standard equipment in some of these agencies.

Typically, a catalog agency staff is heavy on mechanical production and customer service, and light on highly creative (and expensive) personnel. Professional art, copy and photographic services are obtained from free-lance specialists who work under the direction of account coordinators and art directors from the catalog agency. Thus the agency is free to obtain for their client the best sportswear writer in New York, or the hottest children's photographer in San Francisco—on an as-needed basis.

Humbert Clark in San Francisco and Pluzynski/Associates in Manhattan are perfect examples of modern catalog agencies.

Pluzynski/Associates, for instance, has only 36 full-time employees, yet the company numbers among their clients such heavyweights as American Express, AT&T, Hoffritz, Coach Leatherware and Laura Ashley. Ed Pluzynski and his team also produce catalogs for many smaller clients such as Lady Godiva Chocolates and Community Kitchens. These accounts sometimes have printing runs small enough to run on sheetfed presses instead of the usual catalog tonnage produced on web equipment or rotogravure monsters.

The aforementioned high-tech equipment, skilled staffs and efficiencies of scale make catalog agencies a cost effective alternative for most catalog houses and retail chains. For example, today 4-color layouts and mechanicals are produced at Pluzynski/Associates on a *"lightspeed Color Layout System"* computer using Sun Microsystems or Apple Macintosh II workstations. This system can be integrated with *lightspeed's* Rapport telecommunications system for digitalized remote designer-to-designer or designer-to-client communications.

Lightspeed's new parent company is Crossfield, a well-known manufacturer of scanners for color separations. In the near future, direct computer-to-computer communications will link the *lightspeed* results to their Crossfield scanners. Original art and type (transparencies or flat copy) are digitalized and corrected in the scanner, and—look Ma, no hands—we arrive at the finished, plate-ready product without a drop of rubber cement, a bit of bleach or a single sheet of goldenrod.

A good catalog agency should function as if it were your own direct mail production department. This, of course, implies that the account executive (or customer service coordinator) at the agency must know a good deal about the internal systems and people in your company, as well as a whole lot about catalog production at his end of the game.

In turn, the account executive should be treated as a "client" by the creative departments of his employer, the catalog agency. He should be able to make all reasonable requests and demands on your behalf without fear of being blown out of the water by his own management. Important item: *he should not be overloaded with accounts.* Part of Pluzynski's success story is attributable to the fact that 11 of their 36 team members are on the account service staff.

This relationship is central to the success you both will derive from your association. In-house management teams involved with catalog operations are usually stretched fairly thin. As a rule, their time is better spent with merchandise, marketing, fulfillment and financial management than with proofreading and paper buying. Production headaches are best left to the folks—in-house or outside—who have the systems and the temperament to cope with all the variables, passions and nitty-gritties of catalog production.

On the other side of the coin, if a catalog agency is in the picture, they, too, have certain requirements. They need to have long-term relationships, smooth merchandise flow, timely and complete information, and reasonable schedules in order to earn a decent profit.

Responsibility for all of these sometimes adversative functions rests on the shoulders of the agency account executive. It is *not* part of his job description to be a marketing expert. As a matter of fact, the psyche of a good catalog agency account executive almost precludes his involvement in marketing abstractions. His function is to be the even-tempered, shock-absorbing communications link between two very difficult groups of people, the creatives from the agency and the merchants from the client side. That's enough of a burden for any one human being.

Catalog agencies differ in their areas of specialization. The oldest, and certainly one of the largest, is Allied Graphic Arts in New York. Bob Wyker, son of founder "Sollie" Wyker, and his uncle, Joseph, are carrying on AGA's king-of-the-mountain reputation in the arena of retail store traffic-generation catalogs. Over the years, AGA has produced store traffic catalogs for just about every major department and specialty chain in the U.S.

"Sollie", who started his career in graphic arts in the separation business, was the first to buy vast quantities of paper and hundreds of hours of press time *in advance* of his customers' commitments to AGA. It was a gamble that paid off—in better pricing for "Sollie's" clients and in customer loyalty to AGA.

AGA's commitment is not exclusively to department and specialty stores. They were on board when the William Beinecke cranked up the S&H Green Stamps promotions in the United States and Great Britain right after World War II. In terms of sheer numbers, Sperry & Hutchinson's was one of the largest catalog programs in the world. To put the icing on the cake, "Sollie" not only printed the S&H catalogs, he even printed the stamps and the stampsaver books!

One of the advantages of working with an AGA or one of its close competitors has to do with the flow of samples. This is especially true if one is an RTW store owner. A catalog agency with a large retail store client list in the RTW field has a special relationship with a wide range of manufacturers, designers and vendors. Over the years, Allied Graphic Arts has moved merchandise to and from just about every source known to merchant man. They are an integral part of the fashion world. They know where the bones are buried and where the good guys are. This intimate knowledge can be a tremendous "tips and traps" asset, especially to a younger catalog program.

If you want to consider building a relationship with a catalog agency rather than attempting an in-house organization, look *not* for a kindred spirit. Instead, seek out the agency and the account executive whose skills run contrapuntally to those found in your own organization and within your own expertise.

Fair warning, though: as an entrepreneur you'll find it difficult to let go and turn the production reins over to ''outsiders'' who might do things differently. Fear not: in the end, you'll come out the winner, especially if you've chosen the right agency team to hitch up to your company's objectives.

It certainly is possible to produce a catalog in-house, *if* a number of factors are present:

- If *you understand the difference between the various forms of catalogs, why they are designed as they are, and in which direction your catalog should be aimed in order to be most effective. Retail store traffic builders are completely different animals from mailorder catalogs. And, the Coach Leatherware layouts would be totally inappropriate to sell Hanover Shoes—even though they both sell leather goods through their catalogs. Look, for instance, at what happened to Esprit when they tried to use a blatantly store-traffic catalog as a mailorder vehicle. It was a very expensive bomb!*

- *And if you have someone on staff (or a consultant) who knows all the ins and outs of print and mailing production —not from the art director's perspective, but from the printer, separator and mailer side of the fence. Poor planning, bad judgment or just plain dumb mistakes at this end of the project can be disastrously expensive, in dollars, or even worse, in delivery timing.*

- If *you or your consultant know how to choose and use mailorder media. Mailing lists are, of course, one very important medium for catalogs. Here you should not—repeat, not—rely solely on list brokers when selecting your lists. The permutations of list selection are vast. In fact, they may soon be the basis of another book. For the moment, let it suffice to mention that most of the larger list brokers today are also list managers. If they rent a list that they manage, they collect double commissions. . . . 'nuff said?*

- *And finally, if there is a studio accessible to you that has had extensive experience in creating catalogs similar to the one you want to mail. Studios are made up of artists. Each of these artists has the ability to create commercial art within a fairly narrowly defined range. The designer or photographer who is an expert in doing IBM catalogs would be at a loss doing a lingerie presentation—in spite of what their salesman might say. You will also want to take a careful look at the studio's ability to store, ship and style your merchandise. These are major weak points in many otherwise very capable studio operations.*

Now the hard one, the question we hear most frequently: ''How much will it cost to start a mailorder catalog?''
The first cost is time.

1. *Time to learn the underlying business—from the seller's or manufacturer's side, not the consumer side: perhaps 5 to 10 years. You may have already fulfilled this obligation.*
2. *Next, the time necessary to study the direct response business—not to learn all the facts and techniques, just*

enough to handle the semantics and understand the basic propositions: 1 to 2 years (unless you can devote full-time to the project).
3. *Add another increment. of time to make the requisite change-over to mailorder sourcing (you may lose some of your old resources), plus the time to change your inventory systems and scheduling parameters.*
4. *Finally, time to train all hands before the first order hits the telephone or mail caging desk. This applies to buyers, credit managers, and general facta factotum, but most particularly to customer service and fulfillment personnel.*

Catalogs are expensive, much more expensive than most newcomers might ever anticipate. Top photographer's models are paid $2,000 and more per day. The base Third Class postage rate jumped 25% in 1988, to 16.7 cents for each piece. That's $167 per thousand, and you're only allowed 3.37 ounces per catalog, barely enough to mail a typical full-sized 48-page catalog with an order form and a cover. On top of that, paper costs are increasing at double digit rates, and creative costs seem to be paralleling today's increases in legal and medical fees.

These more obvious costs are easy to factor into a business plan. It's the less apparent but costly, insidious 'gotcha's' that clobber most start-ups. Let's look at just a few.

On the day your catalog arrives at the customer's home, you will need to have at least 85% of the first 30 days' worth of inventory usage on hand. In addition, the pipelines will need to be at least primed with the 15% balance—plus provision for backup orders— for high velocity, more successful items.

On the expiration date of the current catalog, you *will* have remainder (unsold) merchandise. Some of these items will be useful in the next issue of the catalog, but not all. The seasonal factor will eliminate some, and the dogs must go. If you do not own stores or have not arranged for other outlets, the remainder merchants will only offer you between 10% and 20% of the retail value of your leftover merchandise. This loss goes right to the bottom line, and can easily kill what, on the surface, looked like a successful mailing.

Catalog start-ups wither and perish for the same reason that wipes out many new businesses: lack of adequate capitalization. Most new catalog programs collapse somewhere around the third and the fifth mailing. The exact causative factors vary, but they usually involve the aforementioned inventory expense and loss, inadequate testing of product to find out what the customer wants, plus one element peculiar to the industry: rollout cost.

Moderate-sized catalog programs start with test mailings in the 150,000 range. This quantity is sufficient to permit split-run tests of lists, formats, items and offers. The second and third waves will be in the same or somewhat larger quantities. Their purpose is to validate initial test information and to test and refine new approaches and products. *One should not anticipate anything near breakeven, much less profitability, at these stages of the program.*

By now, outside investors are getting antsy. Additional capital investment is needed to fix all the fulfillment and customer service problems that have arisen. But the big nut is still around the corner. Having funded all this research, the time has come to start making some money. How? Rollouts, of course: big mailings to hundreds of thousands, even millions of prospects. All of which means a huge postage bill to be paid up front, printing, paper and list costs four or five times as great as the test costs. But the real killer is cost of inventory. Many of your suppliers have seen other start-ups, and they are going to be very cautious and very demanding.

At this point, even the slightest glitch can have profound effect on your program's viability. Some examples:

- *Poor performance by the USPS is one of today's serious problems—some "undelivereds" are running into double-digit percentages.*
- *Weather does have an effect upon mailorder sales, although the consequences are not usually as profound as is the case in over-the-counter sales.*
- *Missed printing and mailing dates: a frequent occurrence when a newcomer gets bumped by a magazine pressrun or in the event of a schedule conflict with a printer's old, high-volume customer.*
- *Poor performance by a major resource, resulting in a high percentage of returned merchandise or merchandise that was never delivered in the first instance.*
- *Major shifts in an economic trend can affect orders for nonessentials by as much as 50%, more than enough by far to totally invalidate all previous tests and finely drawn business plans.*

There are dozens of other macro factors weighing upon any new direct response operation, but to return to the question— "how much?"—think in mid six-digit terms. Anything else is unrealistic for even the smallest program.

To arrive at a reasonable financial forecast, a series of preliminary steps must be taken. First, select a direct response consultant, then work with your consultant to get estimates from appropriate catalog agencies, list brokers and outside fulfillment houses. The latter will give you a realistic fix on fulfillment costs, even if you are planning an in-house operation.

Establish figures for other promotional media including public relations. Consider the scale of your start-up and then calculate costs associated with the mail and phone customer service module. Finally, have a down-to-earth conversation with a responsible person at each of your major merchandise resources. Have them give you the real, unvarnished facts about delivery schedules, backup orders, payment terms and return policies.

At this point, and not a moment before, you and your consultant have enough information to put together a realistic set of projections. The scenario should include best-case/worst-case assumptions; and cover a period of at least three years. Any shorter time frame would fail to include the future value of a customer, and would therefore miss the whole point of a mail-order business.

If your situation warrants, the last step is a very open conversation with your major financial resource. Your bank or other primary investor(s) can now be shown your realistic cashflow projections. These charts and forecasts will indicate maximum negative cash position, anticipated schedule to break into the black, and when to expect recurrences of negative numbers to fund expansion (that last one will surprise and impress most loan officers).

With these financial points all buttoned-up, you'll be able to concentrate on merchandise and operations—the fun stuff—with a clear head and a good night's sleep. When all the contingencies are covered, the business should become a source of pleasure, an outlet for your creativity, and an annuity for your future.

Catalog marketing is fun, not easy, but fun. It can be likened to almost any sport. It requires a certain amount of courage, a solid knowledge of the fundamentals, attention to the little things, good coordination, the right instincts, lots of reserves and plenty of practice. As in any game, you try to limit your losses and make lots of points when the momentum is going your way.

The rewards go beyond the financial. There is a thrill in the air when the phones are ringing off the wall and the mail box is full. To search for and find a reliable source and a red-hot item of merchandise is a real high. The sense of accomplishment-cum-anxiety on the day you mail a million catalogs is akin to launching a state-of-the-art ship.

Catalog marketing is a business for people who love numbers, but it's also a business for the man or woman who has superb merchandising instincts. You will learn to use sophisticated communications media and techniques, and still be totally conversant with conveyors and packing materials.

It's a business where the back end is at least as important as the front end. Where the consumer is always—but always—right. It rewards creativity, but demands strict adherence to the rules of the game. To be sure, the trade is in a constant state of evolution, but skilled practitioners are rarely jolted with surprises.

Perhaps most of all, direct marketing is a field that puts a premium on product knowledge. If you know your product and your potential customers better than almost anyone else in your field, come on in, the water's fine.